Religion and Everyday Life and Culture

RELIGION AND EVERYDAY LIFE AND CULTURE

Religion in the Practice of Daily Life in World History
Volume 1

Richard D. Hecht and Vincent F. Biondo, Editors

PRAEGER

AN IMPRINT OF ABC-CLIO, LLC
Santa Barbara, California • Denver, Colorado • Oxford, England

Library of Congress Cataloging-in-Publication Data

Religion and everyday life and culture / Richard D. Hecht and Vincent F. Biondo, editors.
    p. cm.
  Includes bibliographical references and index.
    ISBN 978-0-313-34278-3 (set : alk. paper) — ISBN 978-0-313-34279-0 (set, ebook) — ISBN 978-0-313-34280-6 (volume 1 : alk. paper) — ISBN 978-0-313-34281-3 (volume 1, ebook) — ISBN 978-0-313-34282-0 (volume 2 : alk. paper) — ISBN 978-0-313-34283-7 (volume 2, ebook) — ISBN 978-0-313-34284-4 (volume 3 : alk. paper) — ISBN 978-0-313-34285-1 (volume 3, ebook)
    I. Hecht, Richard D. II. Biondo, Vincent F.

  BL74.R36 2010
  200.9—dc22   2010000893

ISBN: 978-0-313-34278-3
EISBN: 978-0-313-34279-0

14 13 12 11 10   1 2 3 4 5

This book is also available on the World Wide Web as an eBook.
Visit www.abc-clio.com for details.

Praeger
An Imprint of ABC-CLIO, LLC

ABC-CLIO, LLC
130 Cremona Drive, P.O. Box 1911
Santa Barbara, California 93116-1911

This book is printed on acid-free paper ∞
Manufactured in the United States of America

Contents

VOLUME 2: RELIGION IN THE PRACTICE OF PUBLIC LIFE

General Introduction: Religion in the Practice of Daily Life

World travelers throughout history have been fascinated by the cultural differences they encountered while abroad. Consider Herodotus, who is the earliest historian of classical Greek civilization. He was born around 484 BCE in Anatolia, which is today Turkey. He may have traveled from Mesopotamia, or what is today Iraq, to Italy and from there to Egypt and then to Russia before advising Pericles in Athens about the conflict between Greece and Persia. Or Ibn Battuta, one of the most famous world travelers of the Middle Ages, who was born in Morocco in 1304 and traveled along the Silk Road to China, India, and Southeast Asia and back over a 30-year period, recording his observations along the way.

Similarly, Bartolomé de las Casas was born in Seville, Spain, in 1484. He immigrated with his father to the Caribbean Island of Hispaniola in 1502. Las Casas traveled through parts of the Caribbean and Mexico and wrote a vivid description of life in the Americas. As a Dominican priest, he also became one of the most passionate defenders of the native population against European efforts to enslave them.

Herodotus, Ibn Battuta, las Casas, and countless other travelers distinguished as we do between the types of cultural differences that they observed. Some cultural differences are relatively small, such as whether to use a fork or chopsticks or whether to shake hands or bow when meeting someone for the first time. Some of these differences seem much more important and consequential for the people who perform them. After living with the Tarahumara in northern Mexico, one of the founders of the discipline of anthropology, E. B. Tylor, hypothesized in 1871 that people all over the world, regardless of their cultural traditions, require a procedure for handling the remains of a deceased family member. Similarly, the birth of a child is a significant event in many people's lives. Arnold van Gennep introduced the expression "rites of passage" to describe these universal human experiences, for which all religious traditions provide procedural guidelines and networks of meaning.

This three-volume daily-life project uses the lens of the everyday to clarify the reciprocal relationship between religion and culture. The historical influences of major ritual practices, such as the Catholic mass or Islamic pilgrimage to Mecca, are described in *Volume 1: Religion in the Practice of Daily Life in World History*. *Volume 2: Religion in the Practice of Daily Life in Public* and *Volume 3: Religion in the Practice of Daily Life in Private* explore in greater detail how less obvious practices of everyday life, such as paying taxes or teaching a child to read, are influenced by religion and culture while influencing them as well. Before discussing the interaction of religious practices and everyday life, it is first necessary to introduce the history of the academic study of religion to explain why religious practices are our focus in these volumes. What definition of religion will allow us to discuss the impact of both major and minor religious practices?

The major life-cycle rituals studied by such anthropologists as E. B. Tylor and Arnold van Gennep motivated theologians, sociologists, and historians to attempt to formulate universal definitions of religion. For example, Rudolf Otto in 1917 noted that the term, appearing in many religious traditions, that we translate, literally in the languages of these traditions, simply as "the holy" or "the sacred" means "that which is separate from the empirical world." The sacred or the holy could not be reduced to the immanent world. Expressions of that separate reality are always framed in power, which both attracts and repels us so that we are frightened and also curious about the sacred.

The very best example of these two simultaneous experiences—fear and fascination—could be seen, Otto believed, in the well-known narrative of Moses and the burning bush in the book of Exodus (3:1ff.). There we are told that Moses was herding the flock of his father-in-law Jethro when suddenly a divine messenger appeared to him in a flaming bush, which, importantly, was not consumed by the fire. As Moses approached the bush, God called to him, telling him to take off his sandals because the place upon which he stood was *admat kodesh*, which most English translations render as "holy ground." But what fascinated Otto in this text was the more fundamental meaning of a "separate ground" unlike everything around it. Otto's interpretation of the sacred remains an important marker for students of religion. The sacred could not be reduced to the world or anything in it: it is something fundamentally different from the immanent world. Yet it can be experienced only through the specificity and particularity of the world. Moses is in the desert; it is a specific bush and specific ground. Today, nearly a century after Otto's work, we still draw importance from his analysis. The sacred is never abstract, but always experienced, contained, and embodied in its particularity and specificity.

When attempting to define religion, theologians are more likely to debate important intellectual issues, or what the Protestant theologian Paul Tillich called questions of "ultimate concern." Traditionally, these central questions of human existence include the following: What happens when we die? Why are we here? Where do we come from? Why do good people suffer? Who are we? Religions seem to provide answers to these major questions of human existence. Theologians such as Karl Barth have emphasized how official church institutions and beliefs, creeds, or dogmas provide authoritative answers to these questions for religious followers. Tillich, however, sought to broaden the definition of religion so that a wider set of human activities and beliefs that were of ultimate concern to individuals could properly be called "religious." For Tillich, many aspects of culture could reflect this ultimate concern, including contemporary art.

Not only anthropologists and theologians have offered general definitions of religion, but sociologists and historians have as well. In 1912 Émile Durkheim and Sigmund Freud both published books attempting to define religion. In *The Elementary Forms of Religious Life*, Durkheim described how a symbol, or collective representation, can contain a sacred power able to unite a community. In *Totem and Taboo*, Freud agreed that religious symbols hold a great social power. As a clinical psychologist, his interviews with patients convinced him that religious symbols also help individuals to deal with powerful repressed emotions, such as those regarding parents, love, sex, and our deepest hopes and anxieties. It should be noted that in works such as *The Future of an Illusion* (1927) and *Civilization and Its Discontents* (1929), written after World War I and during the rise of Nazism, Freud became more critical of religion's ability to improve people's lives in a modern, industrial age. The destruction and violence he witnessed led Freud to reemphasize an older philosophical distinction between the blind faith of children and the more measured adult recognition of the importance of science and reason. However, his additional suggestion that psychoanalysis had the potential to help people more than religion offended many religious people.

After World War II, Mircea Eliade brought the European discipline of the history of religions to the United States, where he generalized comparatively across cultures and time periods. According to Eliade, human beings require order and orientation in a chaotic universe. Religion is made up of the myths and rituals that help us to orient ourselves in time and space. Creation myths, Eliade noted, are often narrated during rituals allowing the listeners or religious community to re-experience the events of creation and to renew the world as it was at creation. For example, during the weekly Eucharist, Catholics remind themselves and relive the foundational meal that stands at the origin of their community and that identifies the simple foods of wine and bread with the blood and body of the savior. Over the last half of the twentieth century, and up to the present day, the students of Eliade criticized his theory for being overly dependent upon generalities about complex religious traditions, while also overlooking the importance of particular historical and political contexts. For example, in an essay called "A Pearl of Great Price and a Cargo of Yams," Jonathan Z. Smith points out that religious practices such as those on the island of West Ceram may reenact eternal truths but they also may respond to recent sociopolitical traumas, or what he calls "situational incongruities." In this case, cargo cults, as many anthropologists who have studied the religious traditions and peoples of the South Pacific have called them, may reflect an ancient messianic hope and also be a response to recent encounters with vast disparities in wealth and technology.

Though each of the definitions of religion suggested by the social scientists and theologians mentioned above are useful and intriguing, religion remains elusive and difficult to define, because for most of us religion means more than a specific function or an answer to the meaning of life. Considering the variety of relationships with the sacred around the world, it becomes difficult to give religion a clear and brief definition.

One of the founders of the contemporary discipline of religious studies, Ninian Smart, brought together many of the definitions mentioned above into a flexible framework called a dimensional analysis. According to Professor Smart's definition, religion can contain several, but not necessarily all, of seven dimensions. Religious traditions have mythic, doctrinal, ritual, institutional, ethical, experiential, and aesthetic dimensions. Later on in his career, Smart would add political and economic dimensions to describe how secular ideologies such as communism or nationalism share striking resemblances with religion. Such a move is significant for our purposes because a discussion of both major and minor religious practices requires a broad definition of religion. Ninian Smart's dimensional analysis is ideally suited to help us understand how the sacred is experienced in the practices of men and women in their daily lives.

The efforts of the theologians, social theorists, and historians discussed thus far have led to important sea-changes in scholarship on religion over the past 30 years. Indeed, the topic of this three-volume set is a reflection of those changes. Perhaps one of the most important turns in scholarship on religion over the past 30 years has been the move to explore and to understand what is often referred to as "religion in daily life" or as "religion in lived experience." This represents a shift in emphasis since the United States Supreme Court gave its approval to the academic study of religion in the *Schempp v. Abington Township* case in 1963. The Court ruled that teaching about religion in public schools is important and does not violate the constitutional separation of church and state. Justice Thomas Clark, writing for the majority, stated the following:

> It might well be said that one's education is not complete without the study of comparative religion or the history of religion and its relationship to the advancement of civilization. It certainly may be said that the Bible is worthy of study for its literary and historic qualities. Nothing we have said here indicates that such a study of the Bible or of religion, when presented objectively as part of a secular program of education, may not be enacted consistently with the First Amendment.

The Court sought to deflect the charge that its ruling enshrined a "religion of secularism" by pointing out that the study of the Bible or religion when pursued objectively and within the context of a "secular program of education" is consistent with the First Amendment. This suggestion was underscored in the concurring opinions of Justices William Brennan and Arthur Goldberg. Justice Brennan wrote that "the holding of the Court . . . plainly does not foreclose teaching about the Holy Scriptures or about the differences between religious sects in classes in literature or history." Justice Goldberg wrote as follows:

> Government must inevitably take cognizance of the existence of religion and, indeed, under certain circumstances the First Amendment may require that it do so. And it seems clear to me from the opinions in the present and past cases that the Court would recognize the propriety of . . . the teaching *about* religion, as distinguished from the teaching *of* religion, in the public schools.

In 1963, and during the first decade of the expansion of the study of religion in public universities and colleges following the *Schempp* decision, the study of religion was oriented toward elite understandings of religious traditions and toward religious "ideas" disconnected from their historical, political, economic, cultural, and social contexts. Today, religion in daily life or religion in lived experience attempts to re-embed religion in the contexts of praxis, including increased attention to the role of ritual. In 1978 Ninian Smart spoke on the state of religious studies to the Wingspread Conference, sponsored by the Council on the Study of Religion. In his paper assessing the future directions of the study of religion, Smart called for attention to what he described as "religion on the ground," which became an important theoretical concern of his, alongside his dimensional analysis of religions and his efforts to expand religion to include worldviews. Smart may have been among the first scholars of religion who examined the problem of religion and politics, which today is considered so critical. This sea-change is also visible in other disciplines that have tried to re-contextualize their explorations of human phenomena. Anthropology, long a discipline of the human past, has become increasingly concerned with the contemporary; sociology, a discipline that has long understood its practice as limited to the contemporary, has become more and more interested in history. Indeed, the emergence of "cultural studies" or "cultural analysis" arose not simply as an expression of the dissolution of disciplinary boundaries, but also to return to context, to re-embed culture in its lived experiences. As Roland Barthes wrote in *Mythologies* in 1957, even something as profane as professional wrestling can perform and reveal larger, more sacred cultural and religious realities.

Volume 1 of this work introduces regional histories of the world's religions. What makes this collection unique is that it provides rich descriptions of how religions have influenced daily life. How have ritualistic and repetitive cultural traditions guided the lives of regular people from Buenos Aires to Taipei and from Nigeria to Montréal over the last 3,000 years? An emphasis on practice means that each of the chapters in Volume 1 of this project focuses upon the lives of everyday people. Since a presentation of the world religions on a grand scale requires the scholar to create monolithic, unchanging entities, a focus on practices in daily life allows for an improved understanding of the complexity and diversity of religions. The reader will find that each of the contributors has sought to describe as richly as possible the ways that religious practices inform our understanding of human cultures across the vast distances of history. We have asked the contributors to think boldly about how religion is interwoven with the practices of daily life and to construct their narratives around places, people, and events that illuminate the bond between religion and daily life.

The chapters in Volume 1 describe some geographic regions where a major world religion is dominant, such as the Muslim Middle East or Orthodox Eastern Europe, and others where religions come together to blend and compete, as in South Asia or Modern Europe. You will find that even where one tradition predominates, it often developed historically alongside other religions. This means that each of the contributors has paid attention to how religious traditions influence one another and how that influence may also extend to daily practice. For example, it is impossible to understand the growth of

Buddhism in India without understanding that the earliest strata of Buddhist tradition emerged from Hinduism. The prince who later changed his name from Siddhartha to the Buddha, or "Enlightened One," was born in northeastern India in the sixth century BCE. Scholars have pointed to early Buddhist practices as a rejection of the efficacious rituals of early forms of Hindu tradition. The sacrificial or ritual traditions of the Hindus were countered by the Buddha's insistence that meditation was the only way to overcome the suffering that was the universal human condition. Thus, without Hinduism there may never have been Buddhism. The Buddha may have been understood as a solitary renunciant of Hindu tradition; however, his intent was to end suffering for all sentient beings. Hindu tradition certainly had a great influence on the formation of significant components of early Buddhist life and thought. Ideas of *dharma* (law), *moksha* (salvation), and liberation from rebirth and suffering flowed between what we think of as distinct religious traditions. Buddhist tradition divided early in its history into two major schools. The Mahayana tradition interpreted the Buddha as a *bodhisattva*, a salvific figure who would not realize fully his own liberation until all sentient beings had been saved. The Theravadan tradition held onto a Hindu Buddha who had achieved salvation without the necessity of saving others. The color of a monk's robes often signals which tradition he follows.

Similarly, the mutual influences among Judaism, Christianity, and Islam are undeniable. We recognize that members of these religious communities may choose, or may have chosen in the past, to deny the mutual sharing of practices. In Islam the communal day of *juma* prayer was set for Friday afternoons so as to precede the Jewish Shabbat and the Christian Sabbath. Ramadan, the month-long fast that is one of the pillars of Islam, was a temporal extension of the Jewish fast on Yom Kippur. Jews and Muslims share many dietary restrictions (*kosher* and *halal*) concerning what can and cannot be eaten. Jesus was a Jew, and his religious vision can be situated in the context of first-century Judean piety. Christianity is a religion that began with the life of a young thirty-something Jewish man. It would have remained in Judea as perhaps another form of Jewish piety in later centuries had it not been for Paul, who made Christianity a religion about Jesus. Paul would not have been able to do that without the development of Jewish thought outside of Judea, in the Greco-Roman world. Much of what Paul reads into the life of Jesus and his teaching can be traced to the forms of Judaism that existed in Alexandria, Rome, Syria, and Anatolia. An astute reader will note interesting points of convergence, as well as important distinctions, throughout the chapters of Volume 1.

Volume 2 examines a series of themes that help us to understand how religions interact with the practices of public life. Volume 3 takes up other themes that are central to how religions are realized in the practices of private life. Although Volumes 2 and 3 are weighted toward living issues in the contemporary world, individual chapters explain the necessary historical contexts and are comparative beyond one religious tradition or geographic region. The chapters in Volumes 2 and 3 are devoted to providing rich descriptions of how religious practices influence our daily lives. These are divided into public and private for convenience rather than for theoretical reasons. Henri Lefebvre spent a considerable part of his scholarly career studying everyday life, and he argued that all our decisions, even the most private, have public implications. Lefebvre's observation is very appropriate for religious traditions that strive to maintain continuity between public and private spaces and times.

The relationship between public and private is a complex one and includes the relationship of religion and politics, or what in the United States is usually referred to as the church-state debate. Though many of us tend to think of religion as a largely individual matter, this is a relatively recent phenomenon that is no older than the Enlightenment tradition in Europe and the United States during the eighteenth and nineteenth centuries. Enlightenment thinkers sought to separate religion from the public sphere. In terms of legal protections from religious persecution, it may be possible for church not to influence state, but on a personal level we recognize that personal morality influences public morality. The separation of church and state as we have it in the United States is only one version of this separation. Finding the appropriate way to privatize one's most cherished social ideals, in a civil and yet honest manner, represents an obstacle to the unification of competing tribes. A diverse modern nation-state challenges religion's historical ability to organize both public and private, and one solution is for religion to become only a private, confessional matter. The citizen of the modern, enlightened world is defined by national in addition to ethno-linguistic identity.

This was not an easy transition for Christianity or Judaism in Europe and the Americas as it occurred over several centuries, and it involved much bloodshed. Today, the process of that separation continues to influence struggles between religion and state. Some might argue that a central problem of the new century will be whether that high wall of separation will be maintained. Indeed, there is a multi-front culture war going on over the place of religion in the modern state. But it is more than a struggle between science and faith, secularism and religion, or sacred and profane. It is a more complicated struggle involving liberal religious traditions that have normalized the separation and their position in the modern state as confession. Small religious minorities cling to the separation to protect themselves from the demands of a majoritarian religion. Jews and Catholics in the United States have traditionally been supporters of the separation so as to avoid greater conflicts over the definition of who really is a member of the state and the pressure to conform to the majority Protestant tradition.

The era of modern nation-states in the nineteenth and twentieth centuries led such sociologists as Émile Durkheim to recognize that secular nationalism competes with religious nationalism in providing unifying symbols. Following Durkheim, Robert Bellah analyzed this relationship in the use of religious language by U.S. presidents. In a famous essay published in 1967 and titled "Civil Religion in America," Bellah argued that the separation of church and state in the United States provided a social or religious space for the emergence of an elaborate and well-institutionalized civil religion, which was clearly differentiated from church and synagogue. The beginning point for his essay was John Fitzgerald Kennedy's inaugural address on January 20, 1961, in which he made reference to God three times:

> For I have sworn before you and Almighty God the same solemn oath our fore-bears prescribed nearly a century and three quarters ago . . . the belief that the rights of man come not from the generosity of the state but from the hand of God. . . .
>
> With a good conscience our only sure reward, with history the final judge of our deeds, let us go forth to lead the land we love, asking His blessing and His help, but knowing that here on earth God's work must truly be our own.

Bellah rejected understanding these references as an example of what every American president must do at the risk of losing support, nor did he consider these references ceremonial formalities. Rather, they told Bellah something important about the nature of religion in American life. Bellah noted that the references are more problematic and more illuminating because Kennedy was a Catholic and chose not to give his references a distinctively Catholic form. Bellah wrote that Kennedy did not present a doctrinal deity because this was a matter of his own private religious beliefs; they are not matters relevant in any direct way to the conduct of his public office. Others with different religious views and commitments to different churches or denominations are equally qualified participants in the political process.

The principle of separation of church and state guarantees the freedom of religious belief and association, but at the same time clearly segregates the religious sphere, which is considered to be essentially private, from the political one. Given this separation of church and state, Bellah asked, how could the president be justified in using the word "God"? He quickly answered that the separation of church and state does not deny the political realm a religious dimension. Instead, separating the state from particular private religious claims provides a social space for a public set of beliefs, symbols, and rituals that Bellah called "American civil religion."

Indeed, the force of this civil religion is demonstrated by the theological meanings of Kennedy's statements, especially the third reference, in which the young president reiterated that it is the nation's task on earth to work out the blessing of God or that God's work is our work. Bellah described this as an "activist and non-contemplative conception of the fundamental religious obligation," which he believed was associated with American Protestantism. The civil religion was so strong that it overruled any theology that the president as a Catholic might have wanted to give it. Thus, the importance of the references for Bellah is how deeply established civil religion is in the American outlook. Of course, the actual term "civil religion" was drawn from Jean-Jacques Rousseau's *The Social Contract*, in which Rousseau explained its central ingredients: the existence of a deity, a life to come, reward and punishment for virtue and vice, and the exclusion of religious intolerance. But Bellah quickly admitted that there is no necessary causal connection between Rousseau and the founders of the nation. Similar ideas were a part of the climate of the late eighteenth century, and thus Rousseau and the founders of the nation shared a similar worldview.

Bellah argued that American civil religion has its own myths, rituals, sacred places, and sacred objects. He commented on how national myths integrate traumatic events. The assassination of Abraham Lincoln in 1865 became understood as a sacrificial death that guaranteed the unity of the nation. The ritual calendar of American civil religion includes Thanksgiving and Independence Day, and in both celebrations, the myth of the nation is retold to new generations, just as any authoritative myth would be narrated again in a religious tradition.

Following the divisive Vietnam War and the Watergate scandal, Bellah wrote in the mid-1970s that American civil religion had become an "empty and broken shell." Civil religion provides an external covenant to ensure social continuity, but this covenant requires the love of a nation's citizens and not merely their obedience. The spiritual rhythms of the nation declined during the 1970s, according to Bellah, as the covenant had been betrayed by its most responsible servants. Bellah felt that not only had our political leaders betrayed the covenant, but they did not realize what it was or how that betrayal had affected the entire nation. Their betrayal was much worse, for these leaders knew that there would be no punishment for their breaking of the covenant. The covenant itself had lost any meaning. The church-state and civil religion debates are two examples of how private religion can influence public daily life on a national level.

The relationship of religion and politics is a complex one, and debates over the separation of church and state and the line separating the public and private spheres will not be settled once and for all in these volumes. We do, however, hope to provide the raw material that can support the various sides in these debates. The broad definitions of religion outlined above, the Supreme Court decision in the *Schempp* case, Ninian Smart's call for a study of religion on the ground, and growth in the field of cultural studies all attest to the continuing importance of religion and religious studies as we enter the twenty-first century.

According to the theory of everyday life articulated by Henri Lefebvre—and Hannah Arendt, his contemporary in political science, would agree—a vital public arena where these living debates are encouraged may be essential to preserving democracy and preventing future genocides. In fact, the scholarship on everyday life or daily life emerged after World War II in response to particular intellectual and historical factors. During the height of the Age of Empires, or what some scholars mean by "modernity," the initial European followers of the founders of the social sciences (Marx, Durkheim, Freud, and Weber) emphasized the aspects of their work that coincided with a secularization hypothesis influenced by social evolution. In short, it was tempting for Europeans to connect their military superiority with increased secularization. For many intellectuals, however, two wars between France and Germany, including the ethnic cleansing by Nazi Germany, were enough proof that modernity and progress were not the same. Instead modernity came to mean the other-worldly quest for homogeneity, a desire from which scholars of religion were not immune.

The spiritual vacuum, after secularization failed to create peace, has coincided with a new religious pluralism produced by postcolonial immigration since the 1960s. One of the great migrations in world history, which appears to be a permanent global transformation as a result of advances in transportation and communications, is considered by some a threat and by others an opportunity. After analyzing the causes of the rise of Nazism, Hannah Arendt concluded that only a diverse populace that actively participates in politics can prevent other episodes of genocide from occurring in the future.

While Arendt's political analysis of the rise of Nazism does not talk a great deal about the role of religion, her theory of the importance of democratic public spaces for face-to-face communication was seconded by Henri Lefebvre, who developed a theory of everyday life that includes traditional religious practices as well as the seemingly mundane repetitive details upon which we spend so much time and energy. According to Lefebvre's hypothesis, even decisions as simple as how to get to work or what to eat for breakfast have revolutionary

implications for religion and culture. To give only two examples, the importance of automobile transportation in American culture significantly raised the
value of oil discovered in Saudi Arabia. The Saudi Arabian government has
used some of the funds from American consumers to train religious leaders
and translate Islamic texts to be disseminated worldwide. As a result, one particular interpretation of Islamic doctrine has spread widely. Second, a desire to
eat bananas for breakfast resulted in the control of Guatemala by the United
Fruit Company during the first half of the twentieth century. This economic
and political arrangement contributed to the appeal of liberation theology,
which had a direct impact on the official doctrines of the Vatican. Thus, everyday decisions—such as whether to eat bananas or take the drive-thru lane—
have influenced the religious lives of half of humanity.

Throughout these three volumes our contributors explore the ways in
which religion is bound to the practice of daily life and also how daily life is
bound to religion. The implication of this definition is significant, and we have
alluded to it above. Religion cannot be separated or compartmentalized so that
it operates only within the wall of religious institutions and religious events
and dates within the calendar. All aspects of human life are shot through with
religion, and therefore the practice of daily life becomes a laboratory to observe
how deep the connection is between religion and how we practice our daily
lives.

Now you are much like the world travelers with whom we began our introduction to these three volumes of *Religion and Everyday Life and Culture*.
Whether you are a formal student of religion or history in high school or college, or you are a public librarian patron with a general interest in these topics,
the contributors to this work have made your travels much less arduous than
those of the past. All you need is the willingness to read about the differences
and similarities that emerge from the study of how religion shapes and structures our lived experience. At the end of each chapter you will find a brief
selection of widely available recommended information resources to assist with
further study, research, and discussion. Bon voyage!

Richard D. Hecht
Department of Religious Studies
University of California, Santa Barbara

Vincent F. Biondo
Department of Philosophy
California State University, Fresno

Introduction to Volume 1

Vincent F. Biondo

Man must be everyday, or he will not be at all.
—Henri Lefebvre, 1947

Everyday life begins before recorded history and occurs around the world in every language and culture. When we read the chapters in this historical volume of *Religion and Everyday Life and Culture* from the comfort of a modern library, we may have a tendency to imagine in the lives of pre-modern peoples in Africa or the Americas a less comfortable existence, yet one in which the sacred or supernatural forces played a greater role in day-to-day living. For peoples who do not have access to basic immunizations or antibiotics, for instance, the very real threat of a sudden life-threatening illness or accident beyond one's control means a more humble relationship with death and the afterlife, and therefore with life itself. In Chapter 7, on the Muslim Middle East, by Mashal Saif, for instance, we learn that when people say "I will meet you this evening for dinner," they often add "in'sha'allah" [if God so wills], a humble invocation that reminds individuals that plans and circumstances are beyond their immediate control.

For pre-modern and rural peoples, accidents, illness, hunting, and farming are key parts of everyday life in which religion is central. In the urban world of hospitals, supermarkets, and televisions, we are able to live from day to day without consciously thinking about mortality or the sacred. For modern city dwellers, daily life seems to be the least important part of human existence. It is what happens to us when we are not paying attention and what we do without thinking. Daily life is routine and quickly forgotten. It includes the most mundane activities, such as riding the bus to work, buying groceries, or doing the laundry. Daily life is how we actually live, even as we are imagining how we would want to live in a more perfect world. Though it takes up most of our time, daily life is so tedious and humdrum that it falls beyond the purview of elite ethicists, theologians, or politicians. Leaders, for instance, are appointed to respond to dramatic events with the appropriate ceremony. A serial killer on the loose, a devastating earthquake, and a G-8 summit are remarkable events that intrigue our imagination and demand responses from people in power. Yet the front page of the newspaper seldom captures the more subtle everyday decisions of the citizenry that become the cultural shifts that change world history. Imagine, for example, the first time a person in England added sugar to tea, or an American replaced his horse carriage with a Ford Model T, or her telephone with a broadband Internet connection. Within years, an unpredictable chain of events can alter world history dramatically, especially for workers in sugar-harvesting, oil-producing, or telephone operator–supplying regions.

Many academic disciplines aim to mold public opinion by providing elites with better tools for convincing others how to live their lives. Town planners control our mobility, and architects such as Le Corbusier in Paris control our living spaces. Our sanitation, food supply, health-care access, communications, media, and prisons are each constructed and controlled by experts who determine how we will live our daily lives. Of course, these experts save us time and worry in that a working sewer system, disease-free food, pharmacies, mobile phones, televisions, and jails (assuming we are not in them) add comfort to our lives when at home and help us to produce more when at work.

In contrast to the aspects of daily life that are managed by others, there are ways in which regular people influence world history. Consumers are free to support businesses that promote sustainable labor or environmentally friendly practices. The imagination is free to create public works of art or performance, to invent new words, or to influence the law. Yet it seems that specialized knowledge and superior motivation, combined with limitless financial resources, are aids in changing culture or law. Lacking specialized expertise or billions of dollars, the performance of religious values in daily life practices is an accessible way to influence culture, law, or history.

Because religious freedom in diverse urban centers has increased, religion is more accessible today than it was 100 years ago. In the nineteenth century, the support of powerful religious institutions in Europe for widespread slavery and poverty led Karl Marx and Sigmund Freud to clarify how institutions can be manipulated by educated men for personal profit. With a degree of cynicism they concluded that not every rich man who utters the word *God* necessarily has our best interests at heart. When Marx described religion as an opiate for the masses, he may have been referring to elite church donors who pay their priests to tell the poorer parishioners that private prayer is more effective than actively seeking a pay raise or proper medical treatment. Similarly, Freud disagreed with the corporal punishment of children by church authorities as the ideal method for instilling obedience. These secular criticisms have gained a high degree of acceptance in urban religious institutions since then, though skepticism remains in some rural regions. Following popular revolutions in France and America and the end of monarchies across Europe, Marx and Freud were optimistic that improved education could interrupt cycles of poverty and abuse.

In the secular academic disciplines of sociology and psychology, Marx and Freud are usually presented as opposing all religion. With great intellect, they did criticize blind faith, illiteracy, and unhealthy superstitions in modern European cities. Yet their criticisms were aimed at elites who use religious rhetoric to increase their own quality of life by lowering that of others. Despite humanistic goals, their methods and hope that rational science would replace religion seem misguided following the global resurgence of religion in politics since 1965. In the public sphere modern nation-states appear more secular; however, religious practices in daily life continue to hold revolutionary potential. (See chapter 15 in Volume 2, by Atalia Omer, for examples.) Because basic education in financial planning and child psychology remains reserved for University students, the widest access to education continues to be provided by religions.

For instance, Pentecostal Christianity was invented by a descendant of African American slaves, William Seymour, who moved to Los Angeles in 1906 to start a multiracial congregation of working-class people disappointed by large Catholic and Protestant institutions that were slow to modernize. Using music in worship, audience participation, and emotional testimonies, Pentecostal Christianity has become the most popular religion in the southern hemisphere in less than a century. Also growing rapidly in modern cities, Islam and Mormonism promote healthy lifestyles free from drugs and alcohol, and they provide social networks for dating and business.

Conversion to Pentecostalism, Islam, or Mormonism provides individuals with an instant community in a diverse and dizzying modern age, which has helped to make them three of the fastest-growing religions in the twenty-first century. In Volume 1, we also learn that older traditions such as Hinduism, Buddhism, Confucianism, Daoism, Judaism, Catholicism, and Protestantism continue to influence daily lives around the world. The chapters of Volumes 1, 2, and 3, however, are not organized by religion. Instead, we find in each geographic region in Volume 1, and daily life theme in Volumes 2 and 3, that world religions mix with one another and with local cultural traditions or popular practices. Scholars invented the terms *syncretism* and *folk religion* to describe the richness and diversity of religious practices that extend beyond the narrow coherence of religious orthodoxy formulated by elites or institutions.

In Chapter 3, on South Asia, for example, Kerry San Chirico describes one of the world's most complex religious environments. Whereas millions worship Siva and perform a pilgrimage to Kashi, a lone grandmother communes with Hanuman the monkey god at Asi for her granddaughter to excel in school. Elsewhere, saintly Muslim leaders known as Pirs are frowned upon by more orthodox Pakistani Muslims who do not recognize intermediaries between God and people. Though religious conflicts in South Asia garner more media attention, temples exist that are shared peacefully by Hindu and Muslim practitioners.

In Nigeria, Liz Graveling describes the coexistence of the Igbo summer yam harvest festival (*Iri ji*) with Sunni Islam and Pentecostal Christianity. In a meditative temple in Taiwan, Ryan Adams describes how a Buddhist temple can contain Daoist deities as well as a god of test taking who appeals to those studying for exams. On the island of Java, in Indonesia, Monika Arnez describes how Muslims have incorporated animistic ancestor worship, as when people visit cemeteries during the fasting month of Ramadan. Indonesian Catholics also may sacrifice an animal to ward off evil spirits.

Although modern European elites often speak of their nations as completely secular, Alberta Giorgi finds that religion still plays a role in baptisms, weddings, and funerals, and in the ways that scientific advances are adopted or rejected in daily life. As weekly participation in official Catholic or Orthodox Church institutions has declined, saints, icons, and home altars take on a greater importance in daily life. Chapters by Eloísa Martín, Joseph Williams, and Steve Lloyd-Moffett on Latin America, North America, and Eastern Europe, each contain rich descriptions of specific examples. Near Buenos Aires, for example, Martín describes a chapel devoted to a school teacher, popular singer, and folk saint named Gilda.

In addition to increased religious mixing, or syncretism, and private home spirituality, two themes that emerge from the chapters by Paul Hedges and Michael Guéno on China and Native America are the importance of ancestors and appeasing spirits. The cultural influence of Confucius has been particularly significant in China, where filial piety remains a noble ideal. In a dramatic legend, for instance, the Chinese princess Miaoshan cuts off her own hands to prove her love for her father. Tai Chi and Qigong are mind-body exercises of

Buddhists and Daoists with important impacts on daily life. Spirits are appeased in various folk traditions, including offering sticky buns to the Stove God on New Year's to assure prosperity.

As with folk religions in China, Native Americans may also have a sacrificial relationship with the gods so that one must give to receive. The chapter by Michael Gueno describes the importance of kinship and a sustainable relationship with nature for particular Native peoples. Traditional healers and spiritual leaders called shamans will use whatever technologies are available, whether chemical or psychological (such as in the Navajo Nightway ceremony), to maintain the health and harmony of a local community.

The concluding chapter of Volume 1 is a contemporary analysis of the mixing of traditional Catholic practices with new immigrant practices in the city of Montréal, Québec. Géraldine Mossière and Deirdre Meintel describe how Tamil Catholics are competing with French Catholics for church worship space. Additionally, Senegalese Muslim and Latino Pentecostal immigrants are reaching out to welcome and support new arrivals.

Often in the study of religion, the blending of folk with official practices and the mixing across traditions are overlooked by scholars because they do not fit into the clear world religions categories, or because they may not match the beliefs defined as orthodox. When scholars use the terms *folk religion* and *syncretism*, they often do so dismissively as if these concepts are beyond the realm of serious study, which should be directed toward understanding those in power. This is so partly because in the past the few people who encountered a religion different from their own were international diplomats whose job it was to compete for power. Whereas a century ago an English-language scholar needed to travel to India, Africa, or South America to study a religion different from their own, today as a result of immigration, air travel, and Internet technologies, every modern city is a human laboratory of diverse religious practices. Formerly, a cosmopolitan world traveler would sail between the continents to recognize the links between religion and culture. Today all citizens have the option to open their home to a neighbor, classmate, or co-worker to encounter a different perspective.

Interest in the study of daily life from a philosophical perspective goes beyond a catalogue of exotic beliefs and practices. Though readers of this volume might pretend that they are watching a television travel program, or reading *National Geographic*, scholarly interest in daily life actually has a specific origin in the 1920s, when Josef Stalin and Adolf Hitler rose to power through widespread popular support. That educated elites and the working class united to replace monarchies with fascist dictators contained a counterintuitive and mysterious impulse that Walter Benjamin and Henri Lefebvre thought we should study to prevent future genocides.

While avoiding the topic of religion explicitly, Benjamin and Lefebvre wanted to use critical tools invented by Karl Marx and Sigmund Freud to teach us how to avoid mass violence. Rather than criticizing self-serving politicians or journalists, Benjamin and Lefebvre saw the root of mass violence in some general contradictions of modern daily life at work and at home. For them, the modern world, with an emphasis on rational freedom, was actually isolating individuals from a nourishing sense of community. Self-contained farming villages were replaced by industrial cities that outsource the least desirable jobs. In addition to advances in convenience and comfort, such as plastic and electricity, science and technology were being used in advertising and town planning to make short-term profit more important than memorable social experiences. Scientists were building advanced chemical, biological, and nuclear weapons, which demanded a reevaluation of the Enlightenment claim that secular reason is more ethical than revealed law. Rapid urbanization and the growth of bureaucratized capitalism mean that extended family support networks and self-contained small businesses disappear, leaving fragmented human relationships. Living as isolated cogs in a friendless urban machine, we are barraged by spectacle and tedium, which paralyze our real human emotions and contribute to social anxiety and depression.

Whereas religious ethics continue to recommend limits on materialism and hedonism, the accumulation of capital is globally dominant and self-perpetuating. For instance, a peacekeeping military force is inclined toward violent acts to justify its budget. Public parks are built without any seating to discourage relaxation and promote consumption. Local convenience stores blast inaudible sound frequencies to physically nauseate local teenagers with less spending power. Supermarkets locate the most affordable and popular items, such as bread and milk, as far as possible from the entrance. New homes are built without sidewalks or bike lanes to discourage walking or biking. Each of these rational calculations increases profits by lowering our quality of life. Modern religions, however, provide a compelling antidote to increased loneliness and dehumanization by wealthy corporations and their representatives in government. Europeans in the twenty-first century enjoy increased individual freedom to pursue material comforts and entertainment options, but Benjamin and Lefebvre argued that happiness also requires real emotions, memorable social experiences, and a sense of belonging to a community.

Rather than trying to draw us into a depression about the great obstacles we will face in our lives, Benjamin and Lefebvre tried to use Marx and Freud in hopeful and positive ways. In modern democratic nation-states protected by the rule of law, they believed that ordinary citizens have more power to influence social life and public policy. On a personal level, they argued that we can add meaning to our lives through defensive collages (or *détournements*) that can help to break self-destructive habits by reappropriating commodity culture for our own ends. Turning from prosperous fashion photography, Robert Frank took documentary photographs in the American South during the 1950s in a style that draws our attention to race and class relations. Or more recently, San Diego skateboarder Shepard Fairey combined the face of retired pro wrestler Andre the Giant with a font from Mussolini-era propaganda posters and printed stickers to compete with international sportswear companies. In a turn of events in 2008, this former street vandal was featured on the cover of *Time* magazine and at Harvard's Art Museum after designing a popular poster in support of Barack Obama's presidential campaign.

Daily life practices, including religious rituals, change slowly because they maintain existing social relations and simultaneously contain a potential for revolutionary change. A Muslim woman such as Amina Wadud leading men in prayer may represent a revolutionary historical change and yet seem commonsensical in a particular place and time if her religious knowledge is superior in that moment. The impact of one timely photograph, or graphic artist, or Friday khutbah sermon on the human community is difficult to quantify, yet we sense that through small victories the terror of history can be beaten back and the allure of our inhumanity can be overcome if we string enough of these examples together or make them a part of our unconscious daily routine.

Volume 1 intends to provide snapshots of the role of religion in daily life from multiple places around the globe. Our goal here is to describe the ways in which diverse religious practices, even those that are heterodox or syncretistic, inform daily life in certain parts of the world. We encourage our readers to study further the daily life of any time or place that we have failed to include. Each chapter is followed by a useful bibliography for readers interested in further study.

If the goal of daily life studies is to improve people's lives by opposing cruel and inhuman industrialization and bureaucratization with real human emotions, memories, and relationships, then perhaps it is helpful to learn about the diverse practices with which peoples around the world try to accomplish this. Volumes 2 and 3 analyze particular issues in greater depth and provide insights into how the intersections of religion and culture, and private and public, in daily life transform history.

BIBLIOGRAPHY

Arendt, Hannah. *The Human Condition*. Chicago: University of Chicago Press, 1958.

Benjamin, Walter. *The Arcades Project*. Cambridge, MA: Harvard University Press, 1999.

Durkheim, Émile. *The Elementary Forms of Religious Life*. New York: Free Press, 1995.

Evans-Pritchard, Edward. *Witchcraft*. New York: Oxford University Press, 1937.

Fairey, Shepard. *Post No Bills*. Berkeley, CA: Gingko Press, 2002.

Frank, Robert. *The Americans*. New York: Grove Press, 1959.

Freud, Sigmund. *Psychopathology of Everyday Life*. New York: Macmillan, 1914.

Highmore, Ben. *Everyday Life and Cultural Theory*. London: Routledge, 2002.

Lefebvre, Henri. *Critique of Everyday Life*. London: Verso, 1991.

Marx, Karl. *Capital*. New York: Modern Library, 1906.

Smith, Jonathan Z. *Imagining Religion*. Chicago: Chicago University Press, 1982.

Wadud, Amina. *Qur'an and Woman*. New York: Oxford University Press, 1999.

Yang, Mayfair. *Chinese Religiosities*. Berkeley: University of California Press, 2008.

Chapter 1

Taiwan

Ryan Adams

ONE EVENING IN TAIPEI; EVERY MORNING IN TAIWAN

Walking down the crowded, neon-lit streets of Taipei, Taiwan, one evening, in the midst of hundreds of people jostling their way past one another, attempting to accomplish their myriad different tasks, I was suddenly stopped by a middle-aged man of unremarkable appearance. "Hey," he shouted at me over the din of various storefront loudspeakers hawking their latest sales items, "You sleep too much." I went from wary to wistful in an instant. Typically, when someone stops you on the street in Taipei, they are handing out some discount coupons for the latest in electronic gadgets, but perhaps I had been "recognized" by a well-disguised transcendent[1] Daoist sage, who had singled me out in the incalculable crowd to give me a piece of advice that could aid me in my quest toward "self-cultivation." I gave him my full attention.

"Yes, you; you sleep too much," he repeated. "You see, when you sleep too long, you remain inactive, and your body cannot circulate the blood and the qi—you know qi?" I nodded. "Well," he continued, "your body cannot circulate these adequately to all your organs. So, you must rise earlier in the day and get outside. It is good for you and your health. You will live longer and be happier. You will have more energy. It is your lucky day that you ran into me." With that parting assertion, he walked off into the night, leaving me to ponder over the strange encounter.

Indeed, there was much in the short conversation to ponder over. I had seen enough Chinese and Taiwanese films and read enough Chinese religious texts and stories to know that Daoist transcendents often appeared to worthy individuals to offer them some nugget of advice on how to better live and practice self-cultivation. Was I a worthy seeker? Moreover, I knew also of the Chinese cosmological concept of qi, the "underlying stuff of existence" that is "common to all schools of thought in China."[2] It is of qi that all things in the universe are composed, from gross matter to subtle energies to the very air we breathe, and many efforts in the practice of "biospiritual cultivation," to borrow Russell Kirkland's phrase, are centered, in some sense, upon the inhalation, circulation, and cultivation of qi within one's body. Finally, I was aware that each day is divided into two halves, from midnight until noon, and from noon until midnight, and that the morning hours are the time of the positive, the revivifying, or yang qi, the "swallowing" of which is beneficial to health and essential for practice, and that the afternoon and evening hours are the time of the negative, the "dead," or yin qi, when practice is not only no longer beneficial to one but can indeed be detrimental to one's health. Whether any of this indicated that the man I encountered was indeed a Daoist transcendent seemed to make little difference—for the wisdom that he imparted to me on my "lucky day" may just as easily have come from the average Taiwanese man in the street. Nevertheless, I made my way home and reset my alarm clock for an earlier wake-up time, just in case.

One wants to rise early in the morning in Taiwan at any rate, and the reason for this is related to the common wisdom described above. In these early hours, the mountains that ring the city of Taipei are typically shrouded in a mist that is the stuff of legends just as it is also something between the subtler and grosser manifestations of the stuff that is qi. Walking along the already bustling streets to one of the many parks found throughout the city, one finds there several small gatherings of people engaged in their various daily practices—practices meant to take advantage, in one way or another, of the ability to inhale and make personal use of the positive, life-giving morning qi.

In the parks, one sees individuals walking briskly, swinging their arms wildly, left and then right and so on, as they circle around the flowing man-made waterways, and always breathing in and out with a deep sense of purpose. Along the banks of a lotus pond one can find a group practicing the familiar art of taiji quan,[3] one of almost innumerable forms of qigong, a complex of practices that can be simply understood as "working with qi": "swallowing" it from without, generating it from within oneself, and circulating it throughout one's body.[4] In the midst of a small grove of trees, there are visible more individuals, practicing other methods of qigong, some vigorously moving their extremities as they breathe deeply, others moving slowly, almost imperceptibly. There are even large bands of couples engaged in ballroom dancing within cobblestone courtyards, as classical music blares over portable loudspeakers. The newest innovation that I have witnessed is a group practicing the type of country line dancing that one would more readily expect to find in a Texas honky-tonk than in a Taipei park, as a stereo piped out Hank Williams's tunes. A great many of these people will tell you, if you ask, that they are engaged in exercises that help them to imbibe the morning yang qi for the health of their bodies, minds, and spirits. They would probably not tell you that they are engaged in a religious practice or that they are seeking to become a Daoist transcendent (especially not those who, legend tells us, do so in secret), but they are all certain that the early morning hours are the best time for self-cultivation and that, furthermore, such activity is essential for maintaining good health, a strong body, and a clear and vibrant mind.

TIMELINE

1738: The first Longshan Temple in Taipei was founded and dedicated to Guanyin, the Buddhist Bodhisattva of Mercy and Compassion. The temple was rebuilt in 1919 and completed in 1924. Since then, further renovations have been undertaken, most notably following the bombing of the temple by American forces during World War II, when Taiwan was under Japanese governance.

1755: Construction began on the first Taipei Baoan Temple, dedicated to the Daoist deity Baosheng Dadi; it was completed in 1760.

1830: After relocating, the construction of the new Baoan Temple was completed. (The most recent restoration was commemorated in a ceremony held on May 24, 1995.)

1925: Reconstruction of the Confucius Temple in Taipei began, ending in 1939. The first Taipei Confucius Temple was built under the Qing Dynasty, in 1879, but it was later destroyed by the Japanese in 1907.

1949: Taiwan (governed as the Republic of China by the Nationalist Party) and mainland China (governed by the Chinese Communist Party as the People's Republic of China) began separate governance. In the same year, members of the Chinese Communist Party started the practice of *qigong*, basing it upon traditional body technologies in order to attempt to separate it from its "superstitious" underpinnings.

1966: Ciji, also known as the Buddhist Compassionate Relief Society, was founded by the Buddhist nun Dharma Master Zhengyan, in Taiwan.

1967: Foguangshan, or Buddha's Light Mountain, was founded by Buddhist monk Dharma Master Xingyun, in Taiwan.

1968: On January 25, the inauguration ceremony for the Xingtian Temple in Taipei was held. On January 18 of the following year, the temple was officially recognized as a nonprofit organization. Previous "incarnations" of the temple date back as early as 1943 in Taipei.

1989:   Fagushan, or Dharma Drum Mountain, was established by the Chan (Zen) Buddhist monk Dharma Master Shengyan, in Taiwan.

1992:   In mainland China, Li Hongzhi began teaching his Falun Dafa, also known as Falun Gong, in a series of public lectures. He claimed that the newly revealed practice had "ancient roots" in Chinese culture.

1999:   The Chinese Communist Party outlawed the practice and teaching of Falun Gong in mainland China. However, the movement continues in Taiwan as well as in many other countries around the world.

"RELIGION" IN TAIWAN?

Although this volume is meant to give descriptive accounts of the practice of religion in everyday life by everyday people, it behooves us to take a small detour into the land of theory. In doing so, it is hoped that our understanding of everyday religious practices will be significantly illuminated. In recent years, in scholarly circles concerned with religion in Taiwan and China,[5] there has been much debate over the very applicability of the term *religion*. One incredibly searching paper on this subject has been put forth by Robert Ford Campany, whose thoughts on the matter we should take the time to consider at some small length.

> So pervasive is the habit of reification that we do well to remind ourselves that "religions" do not exist as things in the world. The pertinent *res* include texts, images, and other artifacts; structures such as temples and tombs; and the people who made, used, or otherwise came into contact with these. Anything else is an idea. So, if "Daoism" or "Buddhism" are unitary, perduring things, they are so because we, possibly along with cultural others (though certainly not early medieval "Daoists" or "Buddhists," since the English language in which it is possible to form the word "Daoism" did not yet exist), imagine and construct them as such in the ways we speak, not because they are natural existents we find in the world alongside the *res* we characterize as "belonging" to them.
>
> Only slightly less abstract and more metaphorical are two nouns often attached to the adjective "religious" to form phrases naming the same purported entities named by the "isms," or else to the "ists" formed from these: "tradition" and "system."[6]

There has been in the scholarship of the last century a tendency to offer normative definitions of these "purported entities"—religions—and indeed to define hard-and-fast boundaries for what qualifies as religion and what should be exiled from this domain. We should remember that the concept of religion is itself as recently born as the nineteenth century in the West, and yet the term and the idea now can truly be said to have global currency and this is a fact that scholars must simply come to terms with. That being said, we should not feel confined by this or any other term. Rather, we should feel as exhilarated to discover new forms and species of religion as a biologist would be to discover a new species or variation of plant or animal life. In short, we should feel empowered to define and redefine our terms, using them to broaden our conceptualizations, rather than feel as though we are defined and confined by them.

In Taiwan, a Chinese society,[7] there is a long history of the blurring of lines between religions, sects, and traditions. In the modern period this trend continues unabated. However, since the appearance in China of Christian missionaries centuries ago, and especially during the nationalizing efforts of the twentieth century, there has been an effort to distinguish between religion and superstition. This and other important concerns have been forcefully confronted and analyzed in a new volume edited by Mayfair Yang, *Chinese Religiosities: Afflictions of Modernity and State Formation*. In her Introduction, Yang notes that "the problems of imposing the Western/Protestant category of 'religion' onto the unique features and organizational form of Chinese religious practices. . . . The term 'religiosity' takes the adjective 'religious' and makes it a noun. In adopting this term . . . , I wish to avoid two damaging distinctions that the old term 'religion' implies and activates: (1) the distinction between religion and superstition, and (2) the distinction between inner (individual) faith and collective religious institution."[8] Yang goes on to demonstrate the significance of this new understanding in relation to the Daoist tradition, where

> . . . this distinction [between religion and superstition] is especially inappropriate because of the intertwined histories of philosophical and textual Daoism, alchemical and body-cultivation technologies, the complex pantheon of gods, goddesses, and immortals, herbal and talismanic healing techniques, and a transcendental cosmology. Being at once magical technology, textual philosophy, self-cultivation, medical practice, and collective rituals, Daoism defies the distinction between magic/superstition and religion, and between religion and science.[9]

It is extremely important to consider these facts when venturing into the world of Taiwanese religiosities, and that is why I have allowed myself to quote from these insightful scholars at some length before returning once again to the realm of everyday practice. For although religious traditions in China and Taiwan have long allowed themselves to be adapted in the ongoing encounters and exchanges between traditions, certain practitioners have also long engaged in polemic attacks on one another in their attempts to distinguish their paths as superior ones in the effort toward self-cultivation. Robert Sharf, speaking of Buddhism in China, has noted of this trend, "In the final analysis, pure or unadulterated Buddhism is little more than an analytic abstraction posited by Buddhist polemicists, apologists, reformers, and now scholars."[10] We would benefit by considering at some length one final thought from Sharf, wherein he offers insight into how this perspective had once taken root in his own thinking:

> Following the lead of contemporary scholarship, I had unwittingly come to conceive of Chinese religion in general and Buddhism in particular in terms of a clearly delimited set of normative teachings—Confucianism, [D]aoism, Buddhism—each subdivided into various schools, sects, and lineages. (Such normative traditions are understood as definitive of "high religions," as opposed to "low" traditions, which were until recently, often ignored by sinologists and buddhologists alike. While the high traditions supposedly comprised clearly articulated and internally coherent doctrinal and ritual systems, the low traditions are frequently viewed as diluted, syncretic, diffuse, corrupt, or even degenerate transmutations of the elite norms.)[11]

In short, it is not for scholars to "take sides" wherein our subjects are concerned. Moreover, it is an offense both to our subjects and to our scholarship to take it upon ourselves to determine what is "religion" and what is not. It is our subjects who should inform us as to their understanding of religion and practice, and it is these widely variant perspectives that scholars must make account for. Again, this should be a source of exuberance and elation, to find that there are endless varieties of religious practice to study, rather than being a source of contention between us, as to who has a "correct" understanding and who does not. The most straightforward approach to this quandary in recent scholarship, to my thinking, has been offered by Russell Kirkland:

> When challenged to answer the question "Who is a [D]aoist?", I shall say that the correct answer must begin by determining how [D]aoists of past and present have answered that question. In deciding what we should acknowledge to be "[D]aoism," therefore, we do *not* get to choose an outcome that will result in the satisfaction of any of *our own* needs or desires. Instead, we have to recognize and acknowledge what the *[D]aoists* have understood to be [D]aoism, whether or not we happen to enjoy, or find benefit to ourselves in, their self-understanding.[12]

We must, in closing, note that the realm of the religious in China has never been easy to decipher, but that myriad traditions have existed alongside one another, at times both borrowing from and launching polemic attacks against each other. Today the situation is made perhaps even more complex by the twentieth-century discourses regarding religion, superstition, and tradition, as the discussion of Taiwanese religious practice below shall show. For our purposes, as scholars of religion, we should nevertheless feel justified in having set broad boundaries for what we may rightly consider to be "religion" in Taiwanese society and, having done so, we are "now free to move about the cabin," as it were, of Taiwan's multivocal and multifocal religiosities.

THE WAY OF TAIWANESE RELIGIOSITIES

There are, to be sure, both corporate entities and individuals who readily identify themselves, in English moreover, as Buddhist or Daoist in Taiwan, just as there are Christians and Muslims on the island, although the overall numbers of these latter groups remain relatively small.[13] This fact demonstrates once again that, whatever important insights academic scholars may teach us, such concepts are not merely concepts among everyday practitioners—that is, "things" that do not really exist "in the world." Rather, these terms, ideas, and entities have social currency among those Campany referred to as "cultural others," those who make up the practicing public. The varied traditions of Buddhism and Daoism in Taiwan have histories that stretch back millennia in the societies and cultures of Mainland China, and yet, like all religious traditions, the religiosities of Taiwan today are unique and must be understood in the context of their own time and place.

It has been noted many times that Taiwanese and Chinese practitioners "do" religion.[14] That is to say, religion in Taiwan is more about engaging in practice than it is a matter of belief.[15] Of course, implicit in any practice is a set of beliefs, most obviously the belief in the efficacy of the practice one is engaged in, and yet, it is often the case that practices are passed down through generations without explicit emphasis on their underlying cultural logics. Moreover, a large number of Taiwanese practitioners are less likely to consider themselves "members" of any one religious tradition or institution, but instead to *make use* of *what works* or what is called for in any given situation. Thus, for funeral rites to be performed, a family may employ the services of a Buddhist or a Daoist priest. We shall encounter again and again this common Taiwanese practice of using what works in religion and of employing what is necessary in various contexts.

This chapter shall therefore proceed through a discussion of religious practices found in a variety of temples located in Taiwan's capital, Taipei. In doing so, we shall encounter many similarities as well as important distinctions between popular religious practice in self-consciously Buddhist and Daoist temples. At the end of our tour of temple religion, we shall return to the self-cultivation practices of Taipei's parks by looking at the modern movement of Falun Gong.

TAIWANESE BUDDHISMS

In *Chinese Religiosities*, mentioned above, Richard Madsen provides an excellent examination of modern Taiwan's innovative approaches to both Daoism and Buddhism in the chapter "Religious Renaissance and Taiwan's Modern Middle Class."[16] Therein, Madsen explains the three most popular varieties of modern Buddhism on the island, namely, (1) Ciji, the Buddhist Compassionate Relief Society; (2) Foguangshan, Buddha's Light Mountain; and (3) Fagushan, Dharma Drum Mountain. Each of these movements started in Taiwan after the 1949 separation of the island from Mainland China. Whereas the latter two groups were founded by men who became monks in Mainland China before moving to Taiwan, Ciji was begun in the 1960s by a Buddhist nun, Zhengyan.[17]

The tale of Zhengyan's decision to become a nun and her ultimate founding of the Ciji Association are legendary in Taiwan and in studies of Taiwanese Buddhism.[18] As a young woman, Zhengyan decided to "leave the family" and "renounce the world" by shaving her own head and initiating herself into the monastic life—a most unorthodox procedure, if not an altogether unprecedented one—and she soon established a small community of nuns in the small town of Hualian, on Taiwan's remote east coast.[19] As the popular account has it, she once chanced to meet a group of Catholic nuns, who complained to Zhengyan that Buddhism, as opposed to Christianity, seemed to encourage its followers to withdraw from the world to seek personal enlightenment, all the while ignoring, according to their charge, people's suffering because of sickness and poverty.

Far from having the desired effect of converting Zhengyan to Catholicism, this encounter prompted the nun to show the world that Buddhism cared deeply about the sufferings of all, and moreover, could do something about it. Some forty years on, Ciji is one of the premier humanitarian relief groups in Taiwan, operating "four state-of-the-art hospitals, each with nine hundred beds; a television channel; and a secular four-year university with a standard medical school."[20] Moreover, the association has "over four million members, defined by their willingness to pledge a regular amount of money to the organization each month."[21] Buddha's Light Mountain and Dharma Drum Mountain also practice this type of "this-worldly Buddhism," wherein Buddhists are urged to engage the world in efforts to bring compassionate relief to suffering, rather than to take refuge from the world within the monastery walls.

However, Madsen also notes the following significant feature of these new approaches to Buddhist practice:

In all the groups, there is indeed much talk about "cultivating practice" (xiuxing), a term well known from books on Confucian philosophy, but one that I had never heard used much in ordinary conversation until I became engaged with these Taiwanese religious groups. The term refers to the process of spiritual development that enables one to understand how to apply them in the broadest possible contexts. The many multimedia publications of all the groups aim to facilitate this understanding.[22]

I have again allowed myself to cite Madsen at some length due to the invaluable insights his observations accord us. We will encounter the concept of *xiuxing*, or "cultivating practice," again and again as we consider the many religiosities and related practices available to the Taiwanese. Indeed, I would propose that one feature of Taiwanese and Chinese religion that all so-called traditions share—in some degree or another, and according to some definition or another—is the concept and the practice of *xiu*, "(self)-cultivation." It is hoped that the logic of this assertion will become more evident as we encounter more of Taiwan's myriad religious practices. For now, we can assert, along with Madsen, that such is indeed a common feature of the Buddhisms that have emerged in Taiwan over the last half-century. A final important aspect made evident by Madsen of these Buddhist groups is the move away from sectarianism and conflict between various traditions. He says, "The groups that I have described have encouraged the blending of different segments of the population and facilitated reconciliation between potentially warring factions."[23]

We can see then, that everyday practice among such Buddhists consists of more than mere morning and evening meditation, though of course, such practices are encouraged among and performed by many practitioners. Perhaps more important than this, however, is to move throughout one's day and one's life with a greater sense of compassion for those with whom one shares a society and a world. This extends to the regular giving of charity to those who are less fortunate than oneself in terms of health and wealth. Watching a "dharma lecture" on Ciji's television station or reading a magazine or book published by Dharma Drum Publications are also significant aspects comprised in the daily practice of Buddhism in Taiwan. Although all three groups discussed here maintain monasteries in Taiwan, many millions of practitioners associated with these groups have not become monks or nuns, and yet they aim to enact in their everyday lives to some small extent the compassion of a buddha or bodhisattva.

Although the three mentioned Taiwanese traditions of Buddhism account for millions of Taiwanese practitioners, they are not by any means the only types of Buddhism practiced. Another type of Buddhism can be found, for example, at the temple of Longshan, or Dragon Mountain, in Taipei. We will have occasion to discuss the many types of practice performed there in greater detail below, in a section devoted to this temple, though I will note here that such a temple is more likely to be relegated to the pool of what has been called Chinese "popular" religion by scholars, the name given to practices that typically take place in community temples. This distinction is unfortunate, considering that those who maintain and operate the temple, and those who practice there, clearly define both it and themselves as Buddhist.

As for other types of Buddhist practice, one is likely to encounter on any given day and in any given location, though most frequently on the outskirts of temples both Buddhist and Daoist, a Buddhist monk or nun on the street holding an alms box, chanting sutras, and engaging in that most timeless of Buddhist practices, collecting donations. One is just as likely, however, to encounter a Buddhist monk or nun engaged in less traditional practices in less obvious places, such as window-shopping at the mall at Taipei 101 or talking on cell phones. In my own experience, the most jarring encounter I have had occurred again while simply walking down the street one evening. I happened to pass by a gym with a picture window that opened onto the street. Through the window, onlookers could observe the range of exercise equipment available to them inside and the people making use of them. Making my way along the sidewalk I looked up to see facing the street, with shaved head and dressed in full robes, a Buddhist monk walking on a treadmill. Not being a member of the gym, I could not go in to inquire as to whether he was simply exercising or engaged in a new form of "walking meditation."

TAIWANESE DAOISMS

Daoism, as noted earlier in this chapter in a citation of Mayfair Yang's work, is even harder to define than is Buddhism, often either existing along-side so-called popular religion in Taiwan's thousands of local temples, or blending together with it entirely. There are, to be sure, "professional" Daoists, who offer their services in a variety of ways to everyday people in Taiwan, often performing liturgical services such as the *jiao* and *zhai* rituals for communities and their members.[24] Russell Kirkland identifies the *jiao* ceremony as being "a lengthy sequence of rituals that renew the local community by reintegrating it with the heavenly order," and the *zhai* as a ceremony with historically diverse goals: "One was designed to prevent disease by expiating moral transgressions through communal confession. Another labored for the salvation of deceased ancestors. A third was intended to forestall natural disasters and reintegrate the socio-political order with the cosmos." Through such liturgies, Kirkland concludes, "[D]aoism incorporated ritual frameworks derived from all segments of society, . . . and unified them through the activity of priests [daoshi]."[25] Kirkland is concerned in his formidable work with the history of Daoism in China, but these rituals are still performed by Daoist priests in Taiwan today. Nevertheless, these are the ritual practices of religious specialists who are employed by everyday actors, but not performed by these. More common practices of everyday Taiwanese are performed individually at temples that seem ubiquitous in any Taiwanese city or town. These temples are each dedicated to one or more Daoist gods or goddesses, though there can be found even at a small temple dozens of deities to which one may offer worship and from whom one may seek aid and comfort. Moreover, it is common to find "popular" deities alongside explicitly Daoist ones as well as various buddhas and bodhisattvas. To examine the practices of everyday Taiwanese that regularly go on at such temples each day, we will examine in turn one self-consciously Daoist temple, Xingtian Temple, followed by one self-consciously Buddhist temple, Longshan, coming at last briefly to discuss yet another type of Daoist temple, Baoan, and its neighboring Confucius Temple.

XINGTIAN TEMPLE

Xingtian Temple is located in northeastern Taipei and practices what Richard Madsen has described as a "reformed" version of Daoism.[26] As noted in note 16, although I have benefited from Madsen's recently published account of this temple in relation to the Buddhist groups discussed above, I have also had the opportunity to perform my own ethnographic work there over the past several years, having first been to Xingtian Temple during Chinese New Year in early 2005.

One enters the temple from either the left- or right-side doors, never through the center gate, which is reserved for the deities. In passing through the doors, one must step over the slightly raised stretch in the doorway, which is traditionally there to keep ghosts from entering the temple grounds. Stepping inside the temple proper, one finds oneself in the middle of a large, open courtyard where there are more often than not large, long tables for practitioners to place their offerings to the deities housed there. These gifts are conveniently available for purchase outside the temple either at close-by markets or from makeshift street vendors' stands. Common offerings include flowers (typically orchids), fruit of all kinds (which are abundantly available on this tropical island), and packaged food stuffs, including crackers, snack foods and canned sodas. Although many traditional Daoist temples include the practice of offering meat products, including some that on certain occasions display the disemboweled bodies of pigs out front, meat is not offered at Xingtian Temple, nor, of course, at any self-consciously Buddhist temple. It is just such an aspect of Xingtian Temple that led Richard Madsen to dub the temple one of "reformed" Daoism. Influenced by the twentieth-century debasement of "superstition" in contradistinction to true "religion," Xingtian Temple does not, according to its brochure, "burn spirit money, make offerings of gold, perform folk operas for gods, sanction traditional meat offerings, or maintain a donation box." At other typical Taiwanese temples, such as Baoan, which is discussed below, "spirit money" is offered on altars and tables along with food and flowers, and later, temple officiants burn the spirit money in furnaces located off to one side of the temple. One will also see, twice a month on specified days, homes and businesses set out such an offering table filled with burning incense, fruits, flowers, packaged foods and sometimes meats, as well as spirit money (burned in portable urns), to offer these to gods, ghosts, and ancestors to ensure continued blessing and to ward off harm. But again, one will find only certain of these common practices at Xingtian Temple.

First among these is the burning and offering of incense. When one enters any well-attended temple in Taiwan, one will most likely be overwhelmed by the smell of incense and the accompanying smoke. At Xingtian Temple there are two large bronze incense burners, one located between the main gate and the offering tables in the center courtyard, and the other between the courtyard tables and the row of gods housed in their sanctuaries along the back of the temple grounds. According to the temple literature—available in Chinese, Japanese, and English—five sacred deities are worshipped there: Guanyu (also known as Guangong or Enzhu Gong, to whom the temple is primarily dedicated), Yuefei, Lu Dongbin, Wangshan, and Zhangdan. The temple brochure also notes that other gods are worshipped there, including "revered figures from Confucianism, Buddhism, and [D]aoism." Practitioners are freely given sticks of incense to offer to the gods. These sticks are raised above the head, typically three times, in a practice called *baibai*, commonly translated as "worship," and then placed within the large incense burners, as is common temple practice. However, unlike at most temples, individual practitioners are not seen approaching the images of the gods themselves; rather, community volunteers and temple hands, dressed in robes of light blue, kneel before the gods and offer incense and prayers on behalf of the community of worshipers. Adherents of the temple can also be seen lining up every day to have one of these robed volunteers—usually, if not always, women—wave a burning stick

of incense around their bodies—up and down, side to side, front and back—
to purify the practitioner of negative energies in a ritual known as *shenjing*.

Beyond these acts of worship, offering, and purification, the temple, again
according to its brochure,

> . . . emphasizes its "Five Great Commitments" to society: Religion, Culture,
> Education, Medical Care, and Charity. . . . Purification of the heart and
> cultivation of a peaceful society are among the [Xingtian] Temple's most
> important obligations. . . . We believe the elimination of superstition will guide
> the community to the right path. We encourage others to respect the gods by
> personal improvement of virtue, rather than simply offering material
> enticements and indulgences. . . . Possession of good intentions and virtue will
> bring the assistance and protection of these gods.

Noted in these assertions is the central importance of both "Religion" and
"Culture" to the temple's self-proclaimed purpose. However, it is important to
cite the work of Richard Madsen one last time to note a particularly interesting aspect of religious practice in Taiwan. Madsen observes the following:

> . . . some of the members of these Taiwanese organizations describe their faith
> as "religionless." As a nun from Foguangshan put it, "This is our cultural
> tradition, it isn't a religion." A nun at the Ciji monastery spoke of her
> commitment as a "way to express the culture of my race." Members of Dharma
> Drum Mountain described their practice as more philosophy than religion, and
> . . . the leaders of Xingtian [Temple] talk of their deities as symbols of moral
> principles within their cultural tradition.[27]

This reminds us of the relative unimportance of deciding hard-and-fast
rules for what qualifies as religion in Taiwan and the importance of listening to
our cultural informants. Moreover, this notion of "religionless" religious
practice will be crucial to understanding another new religious movement in
Taiwan that also denies that it is a religion, but rather defines itself as a
cultivation practice: Falun Gong. However, before we come to this final
phenomenon of consideration, let us, as promised, visit the popular Buddhist
temple of Longshan in Taipei.

LONGSHAN BUDDHIST TEMPLE

Longshan is as good a representative of Taiwanese temple religion as any, and
indeed, it shares many features with the hundreds of temples one will find in
Taipei, and the thousands that are to be found across the entire island of Taiwan. In the first place, these temples share many common physical features,
although they vary in size from the minute—composed of a simple, singular

Longshan Temple courtyard between the Main Hall (to the left), which houses Guanyin, and the Front Hall (to the right), where practitioners burn incense, chant sutras, cast moon-blocks, pray, and leave offerings. Worshipers perform *baibai* and place a stick of incense into each of the large censors (c. 2008). (Photo by Ryan J. T. Adams.)

altar (usually housing a multitude of resident gods and goddesses despite its size)—to the extremely large. Longshan itself is one of the largest temples in Taipei, though there are temples in Taiwan that are significantly larger. It is strikingly beautiful, with scenes from legendary stories painted in vibrant colors, and stone and wooden engravings seemingly covering the entire structure.

When one enters the temple grounds through the outer gates and columns, one sees the ornate front of the temple proper and the three cascading man-made waterfalls emptying over stones into a small pond filled with colorful fish. This is the Waterfall of Cleaning Your Heart, and the temple's brochure advises that "[w]hen you come to the temple's Buddhist gate in the morning, you must clean, first, your heart with the spring water. So that you can clean your mind and dignify your body, that you are in a good position to worship the Buddha and learn the wisdom." I am unsure about the precise procedure for cleaning one's heart with the spring water, but simply standing in front of the falls and taking a few deep breaths seems to leave one in a more peaceful mood. As for cleaning your mind, I was once told by a practitioner at

Longshan, in English, the following: "While you Americans go to psychiatrists when you are feeling bad or having trouble in your lives, we Taiwanese come to temples to worship gods and goddesses, and then we feel better." Though certainly not every Taiwanese engages in temple practices, Longshan, like most temples in Taiwan, is usually bustling with the activity of practitioners.

The temple itself is structured in a rectangular form, housing a front hall and a rear hall, with an open courtyard in the center of which sits the temple's main hall. One is advised to enter through the right-hand door as one faces the temple, and exit through the left-hand door, the central main gate again being reserved for the deities. Between the entrance and exit, beneath the roof of the front hall, is the space reserved for practitioners engaged in prayer, sutra reading, chanting, and moon-block casting, a practice that will be discussed in detail below. One is advised—by signs in Chinese, Japanese, and English just inside the temple's entrance—as to how one should proceed in worshipping the many gods, goddesses, and Buddhist bodhisattvas of Longshan. I have recently had the experience of performing the worship "circuit" with a Taiwanese friend, who helped me to understand the temple practices through the eyes of a local who has frequented the temple since childhood. Her understanding of practice there nicely coincided with the advice given by the instructions provided by the temple, though she seemed unaware that these even existed. "My parents used to bring me here when I would have an important test, or some other significant event in life," she told me.

Starting out from the front hall, one takes seven incense sticks, which are freely available, and lights these using the one of the many candles that are also available. Turning to face the main hall in the center courtyard, one silently repeats one's name; the day, month, and year of one's birth; one's address; and a request for Guanyin's blessing, for it is to Guanyin pusa, the Buddhist Bodhisattva of Mercy,[28] that the main hall, and indeed the entire temple, is primarily dedicated. Housed in the central seat of the main hall sits a golden statue of Guanyin, which survived bombing from Allied aircraft during World War II, when Taiwan was under Japanese rule. As the temple's brochure proudly declares, "The whole main hall and a part of the right annex were burned out during the air raid, but the statue of [Guanyin] in the center of the main hall [was] left intact. This is the most famous manifestation of [the] efficacy of Longshan Temple." This last statement is highly significant because efficacy is perhaps the most important feature of Taiwanese and Chinese temple practices. It is the efficacious response of gods and goddesses to practitioners' needs and desires that accounts for the charismatic attraction of practitioners by gods and goddesses, and thus for the practitioners' devotion to various gods, goddesses, buddhas, and bodhisattvas.[29] And even at the

Buddhist temple of Longshan, it may very well be the case that one is worshipping or entreating a god, goddess, or Buddhist bodhisattva, for to cite the temple's brochure one final time, "Longshan Temple always keeps its nature as a Buddhist temple, but in the course of its development many deities of Daoism were also included. The variety of deities in this temple shows the tolerant mentality of the Chinese people in their religious life."

During our visit to Longshan Temple, as part of the worship circuit, my friend and I faced the main hall with our seven sticks of burning incense. To either side of Guanyin sit two other important bodhisattvas: Wenshu pusa[30] and Puxian pusa.[31] Along with these figures appear the 18 *arhans* as attendants, and two other figures as protectors or guardians, Weituo hufa and Qielan hufa. However, despite all these various attendants, my Taiwanese informant-friend told me that when praying at the main hall, one is both honoring them all, and yet primarily worshipping Guanyin. "Praying" and "worshiping" are terms used by locals to translate the Chinese *baibai*. This act entails the raising of the incense one holds in one's clasped hands while bowing one's head three times in the direction of the deity. When this is done, one takes one stick of incense and places it in that deity's censer, one of the large iron or bronze vessels, of which Longshan has seven. After placing one stick of incense in the censer, one once again performs *baibai* to the deity. The Guanyin censer sits on ground level in front of the main hall. From there one ascends three steps to the main hall platform itself, on which sits another censer, and here one repeats *baibai* before leaving these clearly Buddhist figures and moving to the rear hall, where the five remaining censers are placed.

Making one's way through the temple circuit can be a little like negotiating one of the subway stations, if you happen to be there at a busy time of day, or a special time of year, as I recently was in anticipation of the Chinese New Year. Nonetheless, people are careful not to interfere with one another's practice. Proceeding to the right side of the rear hall, one finds many more deities than the five remaining censers would seem to indicate, some of whom are shared by Buddhism and Daoism alike, and yet others who are traditionally simply Daoist or belong to the Chinese popular pantheon. Again, there is a profusion of attendants and additional gods that have been incorporated into the temple during its long history, such as Fude Zhengshen, the local Tudi gong, the god of any and every particular locality. However, I shall here limit my discussion to the temple's main deities, those most commonly sought out for specific reasons. In the right corner of the rear hall, the two main deities are Huatuo tianshi, who my friend informed me was a famous doctor in Chinese history and is thus sought out for those with problems of health, and Wenchang dijun, who is sought out by students for aid in taking tests, writing papers, and otherwise achieving high marks in academics. One thus performs *baibai* to these euhemeristic gods and places the third incense stick in the urn that is officially called the Wenchang censer. In front of the altar on which Wenchang sits, is what looks like a donation box, with a small slit in its top. My friend informed me that students make Xerox copies of their student ID cards to place in the box, to ensure that the blessings received in response to their prayers do not go astray. In front of each of the temple's deities there are also offering tables, on which are vast assortments of flowers, fruit, and packaged foods.

From Wenchang and Huatuo, one simply moves left to the censer for Shuixian, or "the god in the ocean," as my friend identified him. Next to this god, in the center and place of honor in the rear hall, is another goddess who is entreated for protection by and for seafarers, Mazu, "the goddess of the sea," a euhemeristic goddess who also has her own censer. Perhaps it is not surprising to find that on this island-nation, according to Mayfair Yang, "Mazu has the largest deity cult, her temples are the most numerous of all, and popular estimates are that 70–80 percent of Taiwanese worship her in some form."[32] To the left of Mazu are a series of goddesses (chief among them Zhusheng niangniang), all of whom, according to my source, are sought out by would-be parents, hoping either for a pregnancy or a healthy child. However, even if one is not in search of these, one still drops one's sixth stick of incense into the "fertility censer" that stands before these goddesses. Finally, one comes to the left corner of the rear hall, where Guansheng dijun—also known as Guangong, the god of war and another euhemeristic deity—is found.[33] My friend did not identify him as the god of war, although this is common knowledge, but instead suggested another role I knew the god to play, that of god of business people and police officers. It is common in Taiwan for businesses to have a shrine to Guangong. When one considers the popularity of Sun-tzu's *Art of War* in the West among business people, then the logic of this god's many roles becomes somewhat clearer. Indeed, my friend told me that she did not think that he was any longer sought out only by people hoping to succeed in business, but rather by anyone who is seeking any type of general success in any area of life. Thus, whatever one's motivations, one performs one's final *baibai* and places the last stick of incense in Guangong's censer.

Next to Guansheng dijun, however, is Yuelao shenjun, a final god of interest, and if one wishes, this last censer can just as easily be seen as a place of offering to him. He is sought out by singles in search of love. In front of Yuelao's altar is a bucket of moon-blocks, a common divinatory tool found at most Taiwanese temples. One casts these blocks to determine if Yuelao is willing to help one find one's life partner, and if he is, one takes from another box a small piece of red string. Symbolically, if not in practice, the string is meant to be tied on one end to the practitioner's wrist and on the other end to the wrist of their true love, surely to be found soon. I once encountered a group of high-school-aged students practicing at Longshan and asked why they had come. One responded quickly, "*Baibai*," while another, almost as fast, said, "We have a test!" Nonetheless, in my own experience, whenever I see teenagers at Longshan, who are clearly identifiable by their school uniforms, they seem to spend more time entreating Yuelao for love than they do Wenchang for success in school. Even so, both get a fair amount of attention from students.

Having completed the worship circuit and performed *baibai* to all of the temple's main deities, my friend and I returned once more to the front hall for a final practice of divination. Divination, as mentioned, is not the only practice going on here, although it is an extremely popular one. One will also find people kneeling in prayer; leaving offerings of flowers, fruits, and packaged foods; and reading silently or chanting Buddhist sutras. Although most practitioners are laypeople, one may spot the occasional monk or nun with shaved head and Buddhist robes. When I was there recently, prior to the trip with my friend, I saw a Buddhist monk meditating in lotus posture while listening to his iPod. I assumed he was listening to Buddhist chanting, although when I shared the episode with another Taiwanese friend, she jokingly said that it was more likely hip-hop music.

The temple practice commonly called divination is perhaps better under-stood as both my friend and the temple signs describe it, "communicating with the gods." Of course, because the images of the deities cannot speak, one needs to thus employ the moon-blocks. These small pieces of wood, roughly three inches long, always painted red and shaped liked crescent moons, are curved on one side and flat on the other. One simply takes two blocks from a bucket; announces to the deity one's name, birth date, address, and the names of one's parents; and then first asks if the deity is present to hear and to answer one's request. Then one casts the blocks to the ground. If the two flat sides face upward, then either you have not properly asked your question or you are seeking something that is not possible. Similarly, if the two curved sides face upward, then the answer is no. However, if one block lands with its curved side up and the other lands with its flat side up, then you have received a positive response. My friend suggested that I try it, and she was surprised when my first toss came up positive, indicating that my prayer was being heard. "That's good," she said, "obviously this can sometimes take a long time, since people like to do it until they get a 'yes' answer. Now, think carefully about what you want to ask." I did. In fact, I thought that I should probably inquire about the project of writing this very chapter on the everyday religious practices of Taiwan, in hopes that everything would go well. That was, after all, the whole reason that I was there. In the end, however, I chose instead to inquire about my health. Again I tossed the moon-blocks. Again they came up positive. "Wow," shouted my friend, "you are really lucky. Ok, now you pick a divination stick and then go and get a poem." I knew from having read the temple instructions that it was best to receive three positive responses in a row before moving on, but I was willing to follow my friend's lead, and scared that my good luck with positive answers could not continue for long. Heading back to the moon-block box, I pulled from the adjacent drum one of one hundred wooden sticks, each perhaps two or three feet long and each with its own number. I came up with 13, immediately worried because of my Western-based superstitions about the number. I placed the stick back in the drum and made my way over to the wall-mounted cabinet of poems, which supplied a wide variety of positive and negative responses from the deities. I opened drawer number 13 and showed my friend the small slip of paper with its poem. Again, she was surprised by my good fortune. "This is really good, but let's go ask the temple interpreter to see exactly what it means." We lined up at a small booth housing a few female interpreters and when we reached the front of the line, the woman seemed surprised to find a foreigner presenting her with a poem from the bodhisattva. Nevertheless, she asked me what I had inquired about and I told her, somewhat sheepishly, "My health." "Well," she immediately replied, "your health is fine; very good. You should instead spend your time thinking about your work or your studies." Little did she know that my studies were my work, but she was correct that I needed to be giving more thought and time to both. Had I instead inquired about the writing of this chapter instead of my health, however, who knows whether the results would have been the same.

My friend and I took one last look at the beautiful temple scene, and she told me about the offering tables of fruit, flowers, and food. "People bring these before they ask for blessing, and then bring more when they have received what they asked for." She even showed me that most of the flower arrangements included thank-you cards from practitioners, with their names clearly legible, so that the gods, goddesses, and bodhisattvas would know exactly who was repaying their kindness. Although Longshan and the practices that are performed there certainly do not account for the religious practices of all Taiwanese, and although, as mentioned earlier, both Daoists and Buddhists practice in places and in ways that are more exclusive to one tradition or the other than the side-by-side setting of Longshan, the temple does represent the practices and religiosities of a great many Taiwanese as well as the incredibly diverse nature of those practices and religiosities.

BAOAN DAOIST TEMPLE AND TAIPEI'S CONFUCIUS TEMPLE

If Xingtian Temple provides an example of a "reformed" Daoist temple, then Baoan may justifiably be called, for want of a better word, a traditional Taiwanese Daoist temple. The practices that are performed there are, for the most part, the same as those practiced at Longshan, although there are some notable differences. One is the offering—along with fruits, flowers, and packaged vegetarian foods—of meat products, which are usually cooked. There is also the practice, as noted above, of offering spirit money, later burned by temple officiants. You will not find people reading or chanting sutras, of course, or other religious texts. However, you will find the practice of casting moon-blocks, although there are only 60 poems through which the deities may communicate with you at Baoan, as opposed to Longshan's 100 poems.

Aside from these practices, the main activity remains the performance of the *baibai* circuit, counterclockwise around the temple, with incense offerings to the deities. Although the circuit procedure is much the same as it is at Longshan, many of the deities are different. Among the gods found at both temples, as they are indeed found at many Taiwanese temples, are the previously discussed Guangong, the god of war; Zhusheng niangniang, the Empress of Child-Bearing; Fude Zhengshen, the god of each particular locality, also known as Tudi gong; and Mazu, also known as Tianshang shengmu. But Baoan, being primarily Daoist (as opposed to Longshan, which is primarily Buddhist) is dedicated to Baosheng dadi, the Great Emperor Who Protects Life, yet another euhemeristic god who was in life a famous physician, and who sits in the center of the temple's main hall. Other deities worshipped at Baoan include Shennong, the god of agriculture, and Confucius.

It is perhaps striking to Westerners to find Confucius among the deities at a Daoist temple, but he is housed here in a role parallel to that of Wenchang at Longshan Temple, that of patron of students and scholars. Students even leave photocopies of their school ID cards on Confucius's offering table, just as they do with Wenchang at Longshan. All of these deities, and many, many more, have their places in the temple proper of Baoan, and yet, in the last 30 years, the temple has found it necessary to expand. According to their brochure, "Recent renovations to Baoan Temple include a rear building erected in 1981 for the worship of Daoism's most supreme deity, Yuhuang God [the Jade Emperor], in [the] Sky-High Treasure Hall on the fourth floor." In the winter of 1991, the Three-Jewel's Hall was opened on the building's third floor and "a new statue of

Sakyamuni [the historical Buddha] was enlightened and set in the room at the same time." The presence of Confucius, Sakyamuni Buddha, and the many Daoist gods and goddesses clearly represent some type of living tradition that incorporates the so-called Three Teachings of China, even if there is no such self-conscious "religion of the Three Teachings."[34]

Although it is important to once again note that there are today in Taiwan self-conscious practitioners of distinct Daoist and Buddhist religions or traditions, it is also true that there are many who make little distinction between these and are adept at making use of all the religiosities available to them, adopting teachings and practices, and adapting these to suit their own individual and public purposes. Of these, some may identify themselves as Buddhist and others as Daoist, yet many would reserve these words for religious professionals, monastics, and priests. As we have seen, such persons might even deny that they either have or belong to a religion, and yet they may be found practicing in Taiwan's temples as part of their culture.

With regard to Taiwanese culture, one final temple of interest is Taipei's Confucius Temple, located just across the street from Baoan. Unlike the often busy and sometimes hectic scenes of Longshan, Baoan, and Xingtian temples, the Confucius Temple is generally quiet and peaceful 364 days a year; the exception is September 28—Confucius's birthday and also Teacher's Day in Taiwan—when a large ceremony is performed in his honor at dawn. According to this temple's brochure, "The entire ceremony is comprised of 37 stages. In the main ritual, the attendants go to their appointed places, welcome the spirit of Confucius, perform three sacrificial rites, offer the sacrifices and wine, see off the spirit of the sage, and burn spirit money." On the other days of the year, however, the temple is more like a museum, with only a few souls wandering about, if any.

Even here, though, one will find, on a placard describing the life of Confucius, some merging of religious traditions. In describing the life of Confucius, the notice repeats the common belief that Confucius "studied ritual with Laozi," the purported founder of Daoism and supposed author of the *Daodejing*. Although it is incredibly important for scholars to note the lack of historical evidence for such a figure as Laozi, as well as to attempt, using historical evidence, to determine a likely date for the appearance of the book attributed to him, it is equally important for scholars of Chinese and Taiwanese religion and culture to note that many, if not most, Taiwanese and Chinese people believe that Laozi was a contemporary of Confucius and also that he wrote the *Daodejing*, which is also called the *Laozi*.[35] Beyond this, though this temple is explicitly Confucian, its layout and architecture are incredibly similar to those of Longshan and Baoan. Still, a clear distinction can be found in the fact that the Confucius Temple houses no gods or goddesses, but only the "spirit tablets" of Confucius—here found in the central seat of the central hall—and of many of his students, on which are inscribed each individual's name, and within which are housed their spirits.

One new feature of the temple since my last visit four years ago is the new Confucius Café, located on the temple grounds. One can of course buy coffee, tea, and trinkets there, but one will also find just outside the café a large board with dozens of pegs jutting out, on each of which hang dozens of inscribed wooden tablets. They are from students entreating Confucius for academic aid in both Chinese and English, such as one that I saw that read, "Dear Confucius, please help me to get into a good high school."

MEANWHILE, BACK AT THE PARK

Having seen how the temples of Taiwan incorporate similar practices while at the same time declaring their differences from one another, let us now investigate the practices occurring each morning at Taiwan's public parks. In doing so, we shall take as an example of such self-cultivation practices the new religious movement of Falun Gong, begun in China in 1992, outlawed there in 1999, and now practiced in many countries around the world, including Taiwan, the United States, Australia, and Western European countries. To be sure, Falun Gong has sought, almost from its inception, to distinguish itself from forms of *qigong*, as will be discussed below. Although making such careful distinctions between itself and the several hundred of *qigong* schools that flourished in Mainland China in the 1980s and 1990s, Falun Gong can be seen to have grown out of the *qigong* movement and, in its practice, to have much in common with it.[36]

Falun Gong emerged in China in 1992 and met with rapid popularity and growth, claiming tens of millions of practitioners worldwide by the end of the decade. The movement's founder, Li Hongzhi, introduced his teachings through a series of lectures that in 1994 were compiled into the "bible" of the movement, *Zhuan Falun*, "Turning the Law Wheel." In his writings, Li claims not only the ability to heal illness but presents himself as the universal savior of humanity. Li further asserts that Falun Gong is at once an ancient system of transformative practice that lies at the root of all such practices, and indeed of all religions throughout history, while also being uniquely superior to all such practices in that it represents an esoteric method that has never before been made public.

Li's rapid buildup of charismatic capital in China in the 1990s is no doubt in some measure owing to his constant proclamations to practitioners of all that he can and will do for them. Li asserts that through the body of his published works (books, video-, and audiotapes) he is capable of implanting within the bodies of practitioners a Law Wheel (Falun) and "energy mechanisms," over 10,000 of them, "like seeds being planted in your body," as well as to dispatch as a permanent guardian to each practitioner a Law Body (Fashen), which is identical with Li and which henceforth serves the precise function of representing Li as master and teacher to each disciple.

As enticing as these "gifts" of the master may be, they are, ultimately, according to Li and to the practitioners I have spoken with, not the reason for engaging in the practice of Falun Gong. Indeed, healing as well as the development of supernormal abilities are mere by-products of Falun Gong practice — and Li is explicit that one should not undertake cultivation to achieve these "low-level" goals. The telos of Falun Gong practice is the transformation of one's physical body or "human flesh-body" into an "immortal Buddha-body." Nevertheless, the healing of all illnesses remains a prominent selling point of Falun Gong. Almost without exception, the practitioners that I have spoken with claim perfect health since the time they took up the practice of Falun Gong. Moreover, I am constantly assured that it would be highly beneficial for me to practice Falun Gong as well, in that I would never experience sickness again nor have any need to waste money on doctors and hospitals.

Through his teaching, which appropriates and reinterprets such commonplace Chinese religious concepts as *qi, de, karma, gong,* and *xinxing,* Li is at once positioning himself and Falun Gong in the stream of the matrix of Chinese conceptual and practical frameworks, *and* is producing from a modern, global framework a teaching and practice that are heavily indebted to widespread popular understandings of Buddhism, Daoism, and *qigong.* His rapid buildup of millions of followers in Mainland China in the 1990s caused the Chinese Communist Party (CCP) and the China Buddhist Association to become suspicious of the movement, going so far as to denounce Falun Gong as a "heretical sect."[37] Over several years, beginning in 1995, the movement received increasingly negative publicity throughout areas of China, in response to which Falun Gong typically held massive though peaceful rallies, often attended by several thousand practitioners. These circumstances repeated themselves for at least one year, stretching from April 1998 to April 1999, with some news agency or other criticizing the movement and/or its founder, and "cultivators" mounting a massive protest in response. At the culmination of one such demonstration, some 10,000 Falun Gong practitioners staged a mostly silent protest on April 25, 1999, next to the CCP headquarters at Zhongnanhai in Beijing. By July 22 of that year, the CCP had moved to ban the practice of Falun Gong, calling the group an "evil cult" engaged in "illegal religious activities," and began a lengthy crackdown on practitioners. As a result, Li Hongzhi fled to the United States, where he continues to reside in exile.[38]

Today, the practice and the movement, claimed to have been eradicated in Mainland China by the CCP, continue around the world. Although the numbers of practitioners are hard to determine, as there are no such records maintained by the movement, practitioners I have spoken to in Taiwan place the number at anywhere between 300,000 and 3 million, with worldwide numbers at 100 million to "hundreds of millions."[39] If one is interested in meeting practitioners of Falun Gong in Taiwan, one need only rise early in the morning and make one's way to almost any of the public parks, although one may also find them distributing literature and doing their practice at any time of day at any number of tourist sites in Taiwan, such as the National Palace Museum in Taipei.

Falun Xiulian Dafa,[40] which is also known as Falun Gong,[41] is according to Li a system of cultivation practice with ancient roots that aims at the physical transformation of one's human flesh-body into an immortal Buddha-body. Throughout the course of Falun Gong practice, which includes the daily performance of five *qigong*-like physical exercises, cultivators accumulate *gong*, as opposed to the qi-cultivation of *qigong*. As Li writes, "We do not practice qi here. You do not need to practice such low-level things, and we will push you beyond it, making your body reach a state free of any illness."[42] However, this is not all that Master Li does for his followers. Continuing the above statement he says, "In the meantime, we will install in your body a system of ready-made mechanisms necessary for laying a foundation at the low level. This way, you will practice cultivation at a very high level."[43] The physical exercises serve to reinforce the operations of the mechanisms that Li installs in practitioners' bodies: "Otherwise, without giving anything, it is only for healing and fitness."[44]

Li's presentation of Falun Gong consistently references China's long history of practices aimed at transforming oneself through the cultivation of qi, but again, he distinguishes his Falun Dafa from these qi-based methods by asserting that his cultivation practice transforms the self/body through the accumulation of *gong* and the elimination of qi. "Think about it everyone: If your body has qi, it has illnesses."[45] Moreover, Li declares that "some people have blown qi all out of proportion: . . . qi does not have as much penetrative power as people have described. What really works is gong."[46] The Chinese word *gong* is traditionally used to translate the Buddhist notion of merit. Here and elsewhere, Li legitimates his teaching by drawing a connection with *qigong*, Buddhism, and Daoism while simultaneously establishing the inferiority of these previously taught methods of cultivation in relation to his Falun Dafa. According to Li, "the two upright schools of *qigong* cultivation practice, the Buddha School and the Dao School, have already made public many great cultivation methods previously taught in private. . . . Falun Gong is an advanced cultivation method of the Buddha School."[47] Li further notes that the

> . . . *qigong* that we refer to today was not, in fact, originally called *qigong*. . . . The two-character term, *qi gong*, is nowhere to be found in the texts *Scripture of Dan Cultivation*, the *Daoist Canon*, or the *Tripitaka*. . . . *Qigong's* original names were The Great Cultivation Way of Buddha, and The Great Cultivation Way of Dao. It had other names, such as Nine-fold Internal Alchemy, The Way of Arhat, The Dhyana of Vajra, etc.[48]

In 1995 Li edited and compiled his lecture series into *Zhuan Falun* (Turning the Law Wheel). The publication of *Zhuan Falun* served to mark the end of Li's appearances in public. It was no longer necessary to learn cultivation practice through a physical interaction with Li himself by attending one or more of his lectures. One could now learn and obtain all that is necessary in Li's cultivation practice through reading his publications. Indeed, possessing and reading the texts of Falun Gong, according to Li's teachings, serve practitioners as a substitute for being in the presence of Li himself. As Li wrote in 1995, "all of the *gong* and Fa lie in the book, and one will naturally obtain them by reading Dafa."[49] Elsewhere he writes that "genuine practitioners can obtain a Falun by reading my books, watching my lectures on video, listening to my lectures on audiocassette, or studying with Dafa students."[50] Thus, the body of Teacher Li became extended to the textual body of Li's publications, which in turn are utilized by practitioners to effect a transformation of their own bodies.

There are, of course, many other important aspects of Li's teaching. Nevertheless, because this chapter is primarily concerned with religious practice, what has been said provides an adequate introduction to move on to consideration of what followers of Falun Gong actually do to cultivate themselves. It is important, however, to note that Falun Gong, from at least the time of Li's earliest publications, has distinguished itself from the wide array of *qigong* methods, many of which do aim solely at healing and fitness, as well as from Buddhism and Daoism, by proclaiming itself "a genuine cultivation practice of both mind and body."[51] Moreover, Li has distinguished himself from other *shifu* (teachers or masters) as humanity's only savior: "Today we have made public to you this great practice. I have already delivered it to your doorstep. . . . Except for demons that will deceive you, nobody else will teach you, and in the future you will not be able to practice cultivation. If I cannot save you, nobody else can."[52]

FIVE DAILY EXERCISES

Having noted these important features of Li's teachings, let us consider the five Falun Gong exercises that practitioners are encouraged to perform each day.

Exercise 1: Buddha Showing a Thousand Hands

The first four exercises are performed by initially standing in the *ma*, [horse] stance familiar to practitioners of various methods of *qigong*. One is advised to keep one's lower jaw tucked in slightly, to press the tongue gently against the roof of the mouth, to gently close the eyes, and to maintain "a serene expression on the face."[53] Before beginning each exercise, practitioners are instructed to recite one of five verses in Chinese, composed of four lines of four characters each. "The verses are recited only once, in Chinese, right before each exercise. Each exercise has its own specific verse that you may recite out loud or just listen to on the exercise tape."[54] Having begun in this manner, one may proceed to perform the movements of the first exercise. This exercise entails moving the arms to eight various positions in a given order and stretching and relaxing the body. Its stated purpose is to open all the meridians of the body, a concept borrowed from Chinese medical traditions such as acupuncture. The benefits of opening all the meridians simultaneously through this exercise is declared by Li to be another of Falun Gong's unique characteristics, and this effect lies behind the logic of performing this exercise first.

One is told that upon the performance of Buddha Showing a Thousand Hands, one will feel a warmth within and around the body as well being made to "quickly enter the state of being surrounded by an energy field."[55] In this manner, using language that is again culled from popular understandings of *qigong* and acupuncture, Li Hongzhi says that any energy blockages in the body will be removed, allowing *qi* [energy] to freely flow through one's body. As a reminder of Li's role in a practitioner's physical practice, he declares in *Falun Gong*, "Of course, the movements would have no effect whatsoever if I didn't plant a set of mechanisms in your body."[56] Indeed, performing the physical movements of the Falun Gong exercises merely serves to reinforce the activities of the Falun and the *qiji* that Li has placed in practitioners' bodies.[57] Having opened the body's meridians, cleared blockages, and enclosed the body within an energy field, one is ready to progress to the second set of exercises.

Exercise 2: Falun Standing Stance

The Falun Standing Stance exercise consists of standing consecutively in four "energy-ball holding" positions, and it seems to be taken directly from various methods of *qigong*. One merely holds out one's arms as if one were holding an inflated beach ball made of energy, first with arms stretched out in front of one's chest, then in front of one's abdomen, then above the head; finally, one holds the hands out to the sides of one's head. One is encouraged to hold these positions in sequence for as long as one is able, though no set amount of time is given. The frequent performance of this exercise is said to "facilitate the complete opening of the entire body" as a "means of cultivation practice that enhances wisdom, increases strength, raises one's level, and strengthens divine powers."[58] Through prolonged performance of this exercise, Li teaches that one will come to feel a Falun [Law Wheel] rotating within the sphere of one's out-held arms.[59]

Exercise 3: Penetrating the Two Cosmic Extremes

Li teaches that performance of this third exercise "channels the cosmos energy and mixes it with the energy inside one's body."[60] Through this process the body is believed to intake and expel large amounts of energy, "enabling a practitioner to purify his or her body in a very short time."[61] Li teaches that this third exercise opens the meridians at the top of the head and below the feet, allowing energy to be taken in from and to be expelled into the upper and lower "cosmic extremes." In this exercise one moves one's arms up and down nine times, first alternating the left and right arms, and then moving them in unison. One is encouraged to increase the number of movements as one makes progress in one's practice, but is advised to always move the arms in multiples of nine. Nevertheless, one is instructed not to count the movements one makes, nor to practice with any intentions in mind. Rather, one is asked to trust in the regulating effects of the energy mechanisms Li has installed in the body. "We perform the exercises by following the mechanisms and gradually abandoning our intention-driven thinking, reaching a state free of mind-intent."[62] Furthermore, through this practice, the practitioner's "brain will be in constant communication with the vast universe."[63]

A final movement of this third exercise entails rotating the hands around the area of the abdomen four times to rotate the Falun that Master Li has placed there. But again, the activities of the Falun and the *qiji* are automatic, and the performance of the exercise is done merely to reinforce these. In a startling statement on this point Li writes, "There's no need for you to cultivate *gong* by yourself, for the mechanisms assume that role."[64] This statement would seem to contradict other of Li's statements regarding the means whereby one is encouraged to cultivate *gong* and *xinxing*, but at the same time, this admission would seem to be consistent with Li's declarations that he gives practitioners all that is needed for cultivation, and that apart from Li, human beings have no hope of salvation.

Exercise 4: Falun Heavenly Circuit

This exercise is designed to further allow the circulation of energy to all points of the body. It is accomplished by allowing the hands to glide over the entire body, without making contact with the body, moving the hands first down the front (the *yang* side of the body), down to the legs and feet by crouching, and then up the back, (the *yin* side of the body). Whereas the first exercise opened all of the body's meridians, this exercise is said to connect the meridians. "The most outstanding feature of this exercise," Li writes, "is its use of the Falun rotation to rectify all abnormal conditions in the human body. This enables the human body—a small universe—to return to its original state."[65]

This identification of the human body as a microcosm of the universe has a long and varied history in the teachings of Daoism and the methods and meditations involved with physical transformation of the body to achieve immortality or transcendence. Indeed, the Heavenly Circuit exercise is familiar to practitioners of various forms of *qigong*, as Li Hongzhi is aware: "This exercise used to be called Turning the Great Falun. This exercise slightly resembles the Dao School's Great Heavenly Circuit, but our requirements are different."[66] Such a declaration is typical of Li Hongzhi when he makes use of forms and concepts already familiar in the history of Chinese religious traditions. In one stroke he will legitimate his teaching by pointing out its connection to previous methods or notions, and at the same time he will dismiss the previous tradition as inferior to his pure, uncorrupted teaching.

Exercise 5: Strengthening Divine Powers

This final exercise of Falun Gong is performed by sitting in full lotus posture, with legs crossed and the soles of the feet resting face up on the thigh of the opposite leg, a posture taken from the traditional pose of Buddhist meditation. But unlike Buddhist meditation, one begins by moving one's arms through a progression of poses in this exercise "that strengthen divine powers (including supernormal abilities) and *gong* potency by turning the Falun using Buddha hand signs."[67] There is again no time limit set on the performance of this exercise, merely an admonition that the longer one performs it, the greater one's progress will be. When the hand movements have come to an end, it is advised that one should sit in meditation by allowing one's mind to "enter into *ding*," which is defined as "a meditative state in which the mind is completely empty, yet conscious."[68] Again we can see a correlation between this exercise and popular notions of Chan (or Zen) meditation "on emptiness." Of this state, Li writes: "When one does the exercise in this state, one's body undergoes full transformation. This is the optimum state, so we require that you achieve this state."[69] Moreover, this exercise, Li declares, "is something of high-level cultivation practice that I used to do by myself. I'm now making it public without any modifications. Because I no longer have time[,] . . . it will be very difficult for me to have another opportunity to teach you in person."[70]

A FINAL POINT OF PRACTICE IN FALUN GONG

"All cultivators of Falun Gong," writes Li, "must make cultivation of *xinxing* their top priority and regard *xinxing* as the key to developing *gong*. This is the principle for cultivating at high levels. Strictly speaking, the *gong* potency that determines one's level isn't developed through performing exercises but through *xinxing* cultivation."[71] Once again a passage of Li Hongzhi's teaching begs us to pause and consider just what are the implications of performing exercises in Falun Gong, as popular understandings of the movement are that the performance of the five exercises laid out by Master Li comprises the heart of Falun Gong practice. However, here we find that the moral and ethical dimension of Falun Dafa is truly the aspect whereby practitioners are able to raise their *xinxing*—that is, their moral quality or "heart nature"—and this in turn allows them to make rapid progress toward enlightenment, or what Li calls "Consummation."

> Why do I tell you to study, read, and memorize *Zhuan Falun?* To guide your cultivation! As to those who only do the exercises but don't study the Fa, they are not disciples of Dafa whatsoever. Only when you are studying the Fa and cultivating your heart and mind in addition to the means of reaching Consummation—the exercises, and truly changing yourself fundamentally while improving your *xinxing* and elevating your level—can it be called true cultivation practice.[72]

In closing, it must be said that Falun Gong is not, according to Li, a religion, but as we have seen, a "system of cultivation practice." As we have learned from our examination of religious practice in everyday life in Taiwan, the same has also been said by practitioners of a wide variety of Taiwanese religiosities. Moreover, all of these seem to share an emphasis, to some degree or another, on the practice of self-cultivation, which, in turn, relies as much on the effort to perfect oneself morally and ethically as on the performance of rituals, rites, and exercises.

LAST, A FIRST RELIGIOUS ENCOUNTER IN TAIWAN

On the first days of my current stay on the island for the purposes of study and research, I had another auspicious encounter that ended up revolving around religion. I was taking the subway to the immigration office to apply for my residence card and happened to find myself sitting opposite a woman in her thirties who was wearing both a Christian cross around her neck and Buddhist prayer beads on her wrist. Before I could strike up a conversation with her, however, she began asking me questions. I told her of my research into Taiwanese religions, and she immediately offered her help in finding the immigration office. Indeed, we ended up spending the better part of the day together, with her taking me to a place of Buddhist worship, giving me several copies of Buddhist sutras, and inviting me to her Christian church on the following Sunday. When I thanked her for her help, she merely said, "Well, today is when I normally volunteer for this Buddhist group, so I think it is just another way to do that." I replied that I thought her actions showed that she was both a good Christian and a good Buddhist. "You know," she responded, "Jesus said, 'Love is patient, love is kind,'" repeating the familiar passage from 1 Corinthians. I felt somehow guilty when I corrected her, saying, "Actually, that wasn't Jesus. That was Paul." She laughed and then paused to think for a moment. Then, she said, as if summing up a most common approach to religion in Taiwan, "But I think, whoever said it, that it is true. And anyway, what is important isn't the source, but that you put it into practice in your life."

NOTES

1. *Transcendent* is now the preferred translation in the field of Daoist studies of the Chinese term *xian*, which has typically been translated as *immortal* in the past. For more on the logic of this, see Stephen Bokenkamp's *Early Daoist Scriptures* (Berkeley: University of California Press, 1997) and Russell Kirkland's *Taoism: The Enduring Tradition* (New York: Routledge, 2004).
2. Bokenkamp, *Early Daoist Scriptures*, p. 15.
3. Popularly known in the West as T'ai-chi ch'uan, according to the antiquated romanization schema known as Wade-Giles. Throughout this chapter, I have

chosen to use the now (almost) standard Pinyin system. As some scholars continue to use the Wade-Giles system, I will note for my reader's those who do so.

4. For more on *qigong* and its rise (and fall) in China in the twentieth century, see David Palmer's *Qigong Fever: Body, Science and Utopia in China* (New York: Columbia University Press, 2007).

5. Taiwan was for centuries a province of China. In 1895, the island was ceded to Japan following the Sino-Japanese War. This period of Japanese rule continues to have significant cultural effects, although the island was returned to China in 1945, following the end of World War II. However, Mainland China and Taiwan have been ruled separately since 1949, when in the midst of a civil war—facing defeat by Mao Zedong's Communists, who founded the People's Republic of China on the Mainland—the Nationalist government of Chiang Kai-shek, or the Republic of China, retreated to the island of Taiwan. Chiang died in 1975 and in 1987 the Nationalist Party's rule by martial law was ended by his son, Chiang Chingkuo, and Taiwan became a functioning democracy. Mainland China (PRC) continues to claim that Taiwan (ROC) is a "renegade province" and seeks reunification. Taiwanese politics meanwhile continue to debate the merits of making a formal declaration of their independent-nation status, which might provoke China to respond violently, or of preserving the current status quo with the Mainland. Taiwan and China therefore share a common religious and cultural history, and yet these histories diverged sharply from one another at the midpoint of the twentieth century. One notable difference is that Taiwan did not experience any of the effects of the Mainland's Cultural Revolution and its religious suppression.

6. Robert Ford Campany, "On the Very Idea of Religions (in the Modern West and in Early Medieval China)," *History of Religions* 42.4 (2003), p. 293. I strongly recommend to readers that they consult the full article.

7. See note 5 above.

8. Mayfair Yang, "Introduction," in Mayfair Yang, ed., *Chinese Religiosities* (Berkeley: University of California Press, 2008), p. 18.

9. Ibid.

10. Robert Sharf, *Coming to Terms with Chinese Buddhism: A Reading of the* Treasure Store Treatise (Honolulu: University of Hawai'i Press, Kuroda Institute, 2002), p. 16.

11. Ibid., pp. 3–4.

12. Russell Kirkland, *Taoism: The Enduring Tradition*, p. 7 (emphasis is Kirkland's).

13. Richard Madsen has reported that Taiwan's Christian population, made up from various Christian traditions, both Catholic and Protestant, is less that 7 percent of Taiwan's total population (Madsen, "Religious Renaissance and Taiwan's Modern Middle Class," in *Chinese Religiosities*, p. 296). Nevertheless, on an island with more than 23 million inhabitants, 7 percent is no small number. I have no data concerning the number of Taiwan's Muslim population, although I have visited one of the two beautiful mosques in Taipei. Surely, Taiwan's Muslims are

far fewer than Taiwan's Christians. Because of constraints of space, I have chosen not to write about the practice of Christianity or Islam in Taiwan. I do not, in so doing, mean to suggest that these are not important and significant players in the religious landscape of the nation.

14. For a most salient argument regarding "religious models" in China, see Robert Hymes's Introduction in his *Way and Byway: Taoism, Local Religion, and Models of Divinity in Sung and Modern China* (Berkeley: University of California Press, 2002). Another recent notable study of "doing" religion in China may be found in Adam Yuet Chau's *Miraculous Response: Doing Popular Religion in Contemporary China* (Stanford, CA: Stanford University Press, 2006), which examines Chinese "popular" religious practice in Mainland China's Shaanbei Province.

15. Again, Robert Hymes's *Way and Byway* is of great help here in his discussion of the term *belief* on pages 12–13. My own opinion, based on my own experience doing ethnography in Taiwan, is that although terms and concepts such as *religion* and *belief* may have once carried Christian baggage, especially among Westerners, those bags were lost by the airline as the words traveled around the world. This, of course, is another common feature of modernity. Moreover, as Hymes points out, "one can certainly defend 'belief' as a category in the Sung Chinese world" (p. 12). However, the impact of Western categorizations of religion on China has been undoubtedly profound, especially during the twentieth century. For more on this, see again Mayfair Yang's Introduction to *Chinese Religiosities*, and indeed the entire volume.

16. I strongly recommend this chapter to those interested in religion in Taiwan, and indeed in the study of religion in general. I certainly refer to Madsen's discussion of three major Taiwanese Buddhist institutions, and I also discuss below the activities of religious practice at the one Daoist temple he discusses, Xingtian Temple. In this discussion I have cited his wonderfully insightful work, from which I have benefited, in regards to the temple; but because of my many experiences doing ethnography at this temple, my observations of practices there are my own.

17. Again, for more information on these groups and their founders, I direct my reader's to Madsen's work. Herein I limit my discussion to aspects that highlight the individual and innovative approaches to religious practice that these groups and their founders have encouraged.

18. For more on Zhengyan and Ciji, one should also consult C. Julia Huang's *Charisma and Compassion: Cheng Yen and the Buddhist Tzu Chi Movement* (Cambridge, MA: Harvard University Press, 2009), which is the first book to encompass an ethnographic account of the movement. (Note that Huang also uses the Wade-Giles romanization schema, rendering the Pinyin Zhengyan as Cheng Yen, and Ciji as Tzu Chi.)

19. Zhengyan did eventually receive official ordination and became the disciple of the Venerable Yinshun. Again, for more on the legend of Zhengyan, see C. Julia Huang, *Charisma and Compassion*, Chapter 1.

20. Huang, *Charisma and Compassion*, p. 1.

21. Madsen, "Religious Renaissance and Taiwan's Modern Middle Classes," in *Chinese Religiosities*, p. 299.
22. Ibid., p. 306.
23. Ibid., p. 316.
24. For an incredibly searching and insightful examination of the *jiao* [offering], see Robert Hymes's *Way and Byway*, Chapter 8, in which the author discusses the work of several scholars who have done ethnographic work on the *jiao* in various locales throughout Taiwan and China, across several decades. (Note that Hymes uses the Wade-Giles system, rendering *jiao* as *chiao*.)
25. Kirkland, *Taoism: The Enduring Tradition*, p. 89.
26. Madsen, "Religious Renaissance and Taiwan's Modern Middle Classes," in *Chinese Religiosities*, p. 298.
27. Ibid., p. 305.
28. Guanyin is known in Indian Buddhism as Avalokitesvara, or He Who Hears and Responds to the Sufferings of the World. The male bodhisattva from India became the female Guanyin in China. For more on Guanyin, I recommend *Kuan-yin* by Chun-fang Yu (her title uses Wade-Giles romanization). I shall not attempt to give detailed information regarding the gods and goddesses, Buddhas, and bodhisattvas of Longshan Temple or the other temples examined here, as these are available in many other scholarly works.
29. For more detailed analysis, I would again recommend Adam Yuet Chau's *Miraculous Response* as well as Robert Hymes's *Way and Byway*, though many other scholars also discuss the matters of efficacy and charisma in Taiwanese and Chinese religion.
30. Manjusri in Indian Buddhism.
31. Samantabhadra in Indian Buddhism.
32. Mayfair Yang, "Goddess across the Taiwan Strait," in *Chinese Religiosities*.
33. I remind my readers that it is to this god that the Daoist Xingtian temple was primarily dedicated.
34. The Three Teachings, or *sanjiao*, refer to Buddhism, Daoism, and Confucianism. Although it is again important to note that there is no "*sanjiao* religion," temple cults (dubbed "popular religion" by many scholars) often incorporate and pay homage to all three in some manner. Even temples that are self-consciously Buddhist or Daoist, as we have seen, may have aspects of both religions. Indeed, I have been to Buddhist monasteries in which buddhas and bodhisattvas are flanked on their altars by Guangong.
35. For scholarly insight into the disputed figure of Laozi and the probable dates of the *Daodejing*'s appearance, I recommend Victor Mair's *Tao Te Ching*, the title of which uses the Wade-Giles system. The question of Laozi's (Lao-tzu) existence is also comprehensively addressed by Russell Kirkland in *Taoism: The Enduring Tradition*.
36. For a detailed account of both the *qigong* movement in Mainland China in the twentieth century and the rise and fall there of Falun Gong in the 1990s, see David Palmer's *Qigong Fever*.

37. Palmer, *Qigong Fever*, p. 262.
38. For a more detailed account of these events, and indeed of the entire experience of Falun Gong in Mainland China in the 1990s, I again draw my readers' attention to David Palmer's *Qigong Fever*.
39. Such numbers are most certainly inflated, and in the parks in Taipei one is likely to see 50 or more people practicing forms of *qigong* or *taijiquan* for every five who practice Falun Gong. Nevertheless, this chapter means only to take Falun Gong as one example, although a distinctly notable one, of such "body cultivation technologies," which are incredibly numerous and diverse, but which can be seen to share certain common logics that are heavily indebted to both modernity and the history of such practices in China's culture and religions. David Palmer lays out a well-reasoned supposition of the number of Falun Gong practitioners in Mainland China in the 1990s on pages 256–261 of *Qigong Fever*, concluding that 10 million practitioners in China at that time appears a reasonable, and not insignificant, number of adherents.
40. Li Hongzhi writes on page 34 of *Falun Gong: Principles and Exercises for Perfect Health and Enlightenment* (Gloucester, MA: Fair Winds Press, 2001) that "Falun Gong originates from Falun Xiulian Dafa in the Buddha School." The *Oxford Concise English-Chinese Chinese-English Dictionary* defines *xiulian* in the following manner: "(of Taoists) practice austerities; practice asceticism." *Xiulian* may be translated simply as cultivation practice, and displays the importance, noted earlier, of *xiu* in Chinese religiosities.
41. For examinations of Falun Gong in the field of religious studies that deal with the political aspects of the movement in Mainland China, see David Palmer's *Qigong Fever*, Chapters 8 and 9, and Benjamin Penny's "Animal Spirits, Karmic Retribution, Falungong, and the State" in *Chinese Religiosities*. For a view of the movement from a political science perspective, see Maria Hsia Chang's *Falun Gong: The End of Days*.
42. Li Hongzhi, *Zhuan Falun*, 1st transl. ed. (Taipei, Taiwan, ROC: Yih Chyun Book Co., 2002), p. 6.
43. Ibid.
44. Ibid., p. 132.
45. Ibid., p. 308.
46. Ibid., p. 309.
47. Li Hongzhi, *Falun Gong*, p. 1, pp. 4–5.
48. Ibid., p. 2.
49. Li Hongzhi, *Falun Fo Fa: Essentials for Further Advancement*, 3rd transl. ed. (New York: The Universe Publishing Company, 2000), pp. 24–25.
50. Li Hongzhi, *Falun Gong*, p. 86.
51. Ibid., p. 89.
52. Li Hongzhi, *Zhuan Falun*, p. 323.
53. Li Hongzhi, *Falun Gong*, p. 94.
54. Ibid.

55. Ibid., p. 93.
56. Ibid., p. 141.
57. Ibid., p. 147.
58. Ibid., p. 107.
59. Ibid., p. 146.
60. Ibid., p. 113.
61. Ibid.
62. Ibid., p. 148.
63. Ibid., p. 149.
64. Ibid., p. 150.
65. Ibid., p. 120.
66. Ibid., p. 153.
67. Ibid., p. 129.
68. Ibid.
69. Ibid., p. 159.
70. Ibid., p. 155.
71. Ibid., p. 55.
72. Li Hongzhi, *Falun Fo Fa: Essentials for Further Advancement,* p. 79.

BIBLIOGRAPHY

Bokenkamp, Steven R. *Early Daoist Scriptures.* Berkeley: University of California Press, 1997.

Campany, Robert Ford. "On the Very Idea of Religions (in the Modern West and in Early Medieval China)." *History of Religions* 42.4 (2003): 297–319.

Chang, Maria Hsia. *Falun Gong: The End of Days.* New Haven, CT: Yale University Press, 2004.

Chau, Adam Yuet. *Miraculous Response: Doing Popular Religion in Contemporary China.* Stanford, CA: Stanford University Press, 2006.

Huang, C. Julia. *Charisma and Compassion: Cheng Yen and the Buddhist Tzu Chi Movement.* Cambridge, MA: Harvard University Press, 2009.

Hymes, Robert. *Way and Byway: Taoism, Local Religion, and Models of Divinity in Sung and Modern China.* Berkeley: University of California Press, 2002.

Kirkland, Russell. *Taoism: The Enduring Tradition.* New York: Routledge, 2004.

Li Hongzhi. *Falun Fo Fa: Essentials for Further Advancement.* 3rd translation ed. New York: The Universe Publishing Company, 2000.

———. *Falun Gong: Principles and Exercises for Perfect Health and Enlightenment.* Gloucester, MA: Fair Winds Press, 2001.

———. *Zhuan Falun.* 1st translation ed. Taipei, Taiwan, ROC: Yih Chyun Book Co., 2002.

Madsen, Richard. "Religious Renaissance and Taiwan's Modern Middle Classes." In Mayfair Yang, ed. *Chinese Religiosities: Afflictions of Modernity and State Formation.* Berkeley: University of California Press, 2008.

Mair, Victor H., trans. *Tao Te Ching: The Classic Book of Integrity and the Way*. New York: Bantam Books, 1990.

Palmer, David A. *Qigong Fever: Body, Science and Utopia in China*. New York: Columbia University Press, 2007.

Penny, Benjamin. "Animal Spirits, Karmic Retribution, Falungong, and the State." In Mayfair Yang, ed. *Chinese Religiosities: Afflictions of Modernity and State Formation*. Berkeley: University of California Press, 2008.

Sharf, Robert. *Coming to Terms with Chinese Buddhism: A Reading of the* Treasure Store Treatise. Honolulu: University of Hawai'i Press, Kuroda Institute, 2002.

Yang, Mayfair Mei-hui. "Goddess across the Taiwan Strait: Matrifocal Ritual Space, Nation-State, and Satellite Television Footprints." In Mayfair Yang, ed. *Chinese Religiosities: Afflictions of Modernity and State Formation*. Berkeley: University of California Press, 2008.

———, ed. *Chinese Religiosities: Afflictions of Modernity and State Formation*. Berkeley: University of California Press, 2008.

Chapter 2

China

Paul Hedges

INTRODUCTION

What do we think of when we speak of religion in China? Maybe images of Buddhist deities spring to mind—such as the graceful figure of the bod-hisattva/goddess Guanyin,[1] in her long flowing white robes and the fat, jolly Milofo—or figures of wise sages with flowing beards; or do we think of images of suppression, perhaps in reference to Christianity or Falun Gong? Whatever image comes to mind, it is likely that it cannot capture the diver-sity or full picture of religious life in China, especially in the daily life of the Chinese people. Indeed, before we try to picture it, we must address certain problems of our understanding. For a start, what we ordinarily understand by the term *religion* (assuming our basis is a modern, Western one) may be quite different from the way it is understood in China. For instance, one major strand of Chinese thinking is Confucianism, yet there is no unanimous agree-ment over whether this should be seen as a religious tradition. Moreover, the Chinese have no native word that directly relates to our modern Western usage of *religion*; the word used in modern Chinese (*zongjiao*) is inspired by a term coined in Japan to create an equivalent to our term *religion*. What this means is that when we approach "Chinese religion" we approach "alien terri-tory," and so we have to be careful not to impose our preconceptions of what religion is, or what religions do, on their traditions. Indeed, some things we may see as religious are not always seen by the Chinese as falling within the scope of religion; instead, they describe them with indigenous terms such as *mixin* (superstition) or *baishen* (worshipping the gods).[2] Nevertheless, it is possible to speak of the religious dimensions of their culture, but we must do so in terms meaningful to this context.[3]

Another problem is the vast size of China, for we are speaking of a single country that today holds around one-quarter of the world's population, and which historically may be considered an empire rather than a single nation. Therefore, we have to speak of an area the size of Europe that includes 55 ethnic minority groups and encompasses much diversity of belief and practice. Of the various ethnic groups, the majority are Han Chinese, on whom we concentrate; other ethnic groups are the Tibetans and Mongolians (who live along the borders of China), the Islamic Uighur people, the Manchu (who were the "barbarian" invaders who formed China's last imperial dynasty), and a host of small tribes in the Southwest. In recent years, Chinese religious practice has suffered from repression on mainland China. Consequently, the longest-surviving forms of practice are found outside the mainland, although the revival of traditional religion is a significant feature of contemporary life in the People's Republic of China.

The three major religious traditions in China are Daoism (Taoism), Confucianism, and Buddhism. Daoism and Confucianism are native traditions, whereas Buddhism was introduced from India around two thousand years ago. Alongside these, many other religions are practiced, including Islam, Christianity, Judaism, and a number of tribal or indigenous faiths. However, popular or folk religion is the mainstay of Chinese religious practice; this, especially in its interaction with the three main traditions, will be our focus.

TIMELINE

Selected Dynasties

c. 18th–12th centuries BCE:	Shang Dynasty
c. 12th century–221 BCE:	Zhou Dynasty
c. 6th century BCE:	Life of Confucius and legendary date for Laozi.
221–207 BCE:	Qin Dynasty
206 BCE–**220** CE:	Han Dynasty
c. 2nd century BCE:	Confucianism becomes state orthodoxy.
c. 1st century CE:	Buddhism enters China.
142 CE:	Celestial Masters tradition founded.
c. 2nd century CE:	Dao De Jing edited into standard version.
618–906:	Tang Dynasty
842–845:	Great Persecution of Buddhism.

1130–1200:	Life of Zhu Xi.
1279–1368:	Yuan (Mongol) Dynasty
1368–1644:	Ming Dynasty
1644–1911:	Qing (Manchu) Dynasty
1911:	End of Confucian educational and ritual system.
1911–1949:	Republican China (on mainland, continues in Taiwan)
1949–present:	People's Republic of China
1949:	Communist victory on mainland, many religious figures flee to Taiwan.
1966–1976:	Cultural Revolution in the People's Republic of China.
1980–present:	Liberalization of religious control and practice in the People's Republic of China.

THE CHINESE COSMOS

To understand Chinese religion, it is necessary to consider the traditional Chinese conception of the universe and its workings. We will therefore discuss a number of important concepts that belong to the elite traditions but which infuse the whole of Chinese culture and construct the world of everyday religion. Three important concepts are qi (chi), yin-yang, and the Five Agents. Many Chinese may see them not as religious, but as part of the way things are, that is to say, what the universe is like and how it operates. Nevertheless, they are ideas that are inherently spiritual, and they have explicitly religious connotations or sources.

Literally, qi can be translated into English as *air* or *breath*.[4] However, the term implies far more in traditional cosmological thought, where everything is composed of qi, and so it may be thought of as material energy, or spiritual matter, although neither of these concepts is adequate, for it is breath, spirit, matter, and more. It is therefore best not to translate the term. Indeed, because China has many different schools of thought, there are also many different interpretations of qi. For some, the physical world is a gross form of qi that has become hard or solid, whereas our minds are more subtle qi. It has also been interpreted in moral terms, with good behavior being seen as a pure form of qi, and immoral behavior as a less pure form. In mainstream Chinese cosmology, everything in the universe is composed of the same stuff, and it can be purified through certain practices. Probably the best known is *taiji* (tai chi), practiced daily by young and old in parks across China, especially early in the morning. *Taiji* is now practiced worldwide as well.

Yin and yang are terms now well-known in English, and they refer to the operation of qi, which can be in either mode. Yang is seen as light, male, active, heavenly, and hot. Yin is seen as dark, female, passive, earthly, and cold. How-ever, we should not read positive or negative, better or worse in these distinc-tions. In reality, neither can operate without the other, and so they are sides of the same thing. Although yang is seen as active and yin as passive, yin is in some ways more potent because yang may exhaust itself.

The Five Agents are also referred to as *five elements*, but the latter term is misleading. These Five Agents are fire, earth, metal, water, air, and so seem to relate to the Western notion of five elements; however, like yin-yang, they are more modes of being, always in dynamic movement. Everything moves through these different modes.[5] We will see below how these ideas feed into the everyday world of Chinese religious life.

Finally, we will discuss two common terms, *dao* and *tian*. Dao, which gives us the term *Daoism*, literally means "way" (although it has other connotations, too), and as a concept runs through much Chinese thinking. *Tian* literally means "sky," and it also means "heaven," which can be seen as a personified entity or as a general cosmic force. Some Daoists, Confucians, and practition-ers of folk traditions will refer to *dao* as the way to be followed, and to *tian* as the sense of the divine. However, various thinkers and traditions use these terms in different ways.

THE THREE TRADITIONS

Sanjiao (the Three Traditions) is a native Chinese term to refer to Confu-cianism, Daoism, and Buddhism. Sometimes they are seen as forming a con-nected whole, each having regard to a particular area of life. In this view, Confucianism is concerned with the public life and duties of man (I purposely say "man" because roles in the public sphere were traditionally performed by males). So a man would be a Confucian in public, whereas in personal life he would look to Ch'an Buddhism and Daoism for spiritual transformation—the former for meditation and awareness training, and the latter for methods of bodily cultivation.

The different nature of each religion is expressed picturesquely by Li Shiqian, a scholar of the sixth century CE, who said that Buddhism is like the sun, Dao-ism like the moon, and Confucianism like "the five planets."[6] Others have sug-gested that the three religions are all teaching the same thing in different ways. Whichever view one takes, it is certainly the case that popular practitioners rarely see a contradiction between following various traditions; indeed, it is quite prob-able that many people are unaware that their practices cross the boundaries quite as much as they do. However, at the same time, there were also movements in each tradition that saw themselves as exclusive, and there are clear differences between the three traditions. The blending of the three traditions, often unconsciously, while integrating local customs, is typical of folk religion, which exists separately and in relation to the three traditions.[7]

Confucianism

Confucianism has been for most of the last two thousand years the state ideology of China. It has provided a form of training for government and administration, and has also been seen as providing normative models for ethics, etiquette, and culture. In the Han Dynasty, it achieved the status of state orthodoxy, with Confucian classics providing the basis for both the examination system to appoint government officials and the rituals for state and imperial observance. The exams involved writing commentaries on the Confucian classics, based on the commentaries written by the great scholars of the past, following standard formats, for although "individual creativity was acceptable, it could only be added on top of the basic information about the texts."[8] Confucianism is thus involved with areas of thought and practice we would not normally see as religious. However, to make such a distinction of "religious" and "non-religious" ("secular") spheres is to impose our standards on China, as well as to misunderstand much of Confucian and Chinese thinking.

As a tradition, Confucianism is especially associated with one man, Kong Fuzi (Master Kong), known in the West as Confucius, who lived around the sixth century BCE.[9] We are misled, however, if we see his name as implying he is the founder of Confucianism. The Chinese term for Confucianism is *rujiao*—literally, "the tradition of the scholars," of which he is seen as a consolidating figure. Confucius never claimed to be an innovator, but merely someone who helped pass on ancient tradition, particularly the teachings of the then-declining imperial dynasty, the Zhou (Chou).

Distinctively, Confucianism is also a tradition of books and learning. Confucius is traditionally seen as the editor of the Five Classics, which were the mainstay of Confucian learning for a long time. According to the following passage from Sima Qian (Ssu-ma Ch'ien), a famous ancient historian of China, each text had a function:

> All Six Arts help to govern. The Book of Rites helps to regulate men, the Book of Music brings about harmony, the Book of History records incidents, the Book of Poetry expresses emotions, the Book of Changes reveals supernatural influence, and the Spring and Autumn Annals shows what is right.[10]

Although six texts are mentioned here, it was the Five Classics that became the norm in Confucian learning, because the Book of Music was said to be lost under the book burning instigated by Qinshi Huangdi, the man known as the First Emperor, who eliminated books by rival systems to his own preferred Legalist system.[11] As time went by, this collection grew to become the Thirteen Classics, but in the twelfth century they were replaced by a new collection of Confucian texts, the so-called Four Books, which are entitled as follows:

+ *The Analects*
+ *The Book of Mencius*
+ *The Doctrine of the Mean (Central Harmony)*
+ *The Great Learning*

The Analects is the best-known Confucian work today and is believed to contain the words of Confucius himself, being a collection of dialogues with his students; the earliest layers of this text are probably genuine. *The Book of Mencius* is the work of an early Confucian, whom we shall meet shortly; and the last two are chapters from the Book of Rites.

It may therefore seem that Confucianism is far removed from being a "religion" as we understand religions. The learning and study of Confucianism is related to ministerial or civil service advancement, not spirituality. Indeed, a number of scholars and Confucians believe that Confucius himself was an atheist, or had no interest in the spiritual world. Certainly, there are trends in Confucianism, represented by Xunzi (Hsun-tzu) (312–238 BCE), that go this way. According to him, belief in supernatural influence is simply primitive thinking, and he influenced a rationalist trend in Confucian thought:

> You pray for rain and it rains. Why? For no particular reason, I say. It is just as though you had not prayed for rain and it rained anyway.... You consult the arts of divination before making a decision on some important matter. But it is not as though you could not hope to accomplish anything by such ceremonies. They are done merely for ornament. Hence the gentleman regards them as ornaments, but the common people regard them as supernatural.[12]

We certainly know that many Confucians looked down on the religion of the people as superstition; however, Confucianism is bound up in overtly religious concerns, including a mystical strand associated with Mencius (c. 372–289 BCE), and highlighted in Neo-Confucianism. A recognition of this means most scholars now classify Confucianism as a religion, or at the very least, a tradition deeply imbued with spiritual and religious elements.[13] However, Xunzi's skepticism has undoubtedly influenced the elite/official disapproval or suppression of what is seen as the superstition of the masses.

Finally, we must note the core Confucian values. One is the Three Guiding Principles, which describe the relationships between an emperor and minister, a father and son, and a husband and wife, and to which two more relationships are often added—those between an older and younger brother, and an older and younger friend. These are held to mirror each other, with a comparable hierarchy of relationships existing from superior to inferior, but it also requires a reciprocal relationship of care and respect on each side. This Confucian value still infuses Chinese society deeply, so that, for instance, the oldest male in a class will often be seen as a guiding authority figure and referred to as *dage* (big brother) by his classmates. Confucianism also has Five Constant Regulations, which form a list of its main virtues: humaneness, righteousness, ritual/propriety, wisdom, and faithfulness.[14] Of these, humaneness and ritual/propriety are absolutely fundamental, as is another virtue, often seen as Confucian: filial piety, the duty owed by a child to a parent. Humaneness (*ren*) refers to the correct relationship of people, and it is summed up in Confucius's version of the Golden Rule: "never impose on others what you dislike yourself."[15] Ritual/propriety (*li*) is a much harder concept. It involves correct ritual behavior as well as personal conduct and manners. For this reason, Confucianism is often parodied as a tradition greatly concerned with formal and outward behavior. Although this is true of Confucianism in its worst forms, correctly understood *li* is about the inner cultivation of morality and relationship with *dao* or *tian*. One who has perfected these virtues becomes a "gentleman" or "person of virtue." These translations come from Confucius's terms for the perfected person, *junzi*, literally "a ruler's son," but he made it very clear that a true gentleman is not necessarily someone of good birth, but someone with good moral character.[16] Though all these virtues are generally seen as Confucian, in many respects they belong to Chinese culture in general. For instance, the formality associated with *li* can result in beautiful formalized ceremonies—such as the tea ceremonies found throughout the Far East, where the ritualized movements show social deference and are a way to harmonize with the cosmos— that go far beyond the bounds of Confucianism.[17]

Daoism

New scholarship of the last 30 years, which has only recently gained significant ground among an audience beyond specialists, has shown that our traditional picture of Daoism is wrong.[18] According to the old model, Daoism existed in two forms: "philosophical Daoism" (*daojia*), which consists of an otherworldly philosophy propounded in ancient texts—principally the *Daodejing* (*Tao Te Ching*), *Zhuangzi* (*Chuang Tzu*), and *Liezi* (*Lieh Tzu*)—of the sixth and fifth centuries BCE; and "religious Daoism" (*daojiao*), which consists of "corrupted" philosophical Daoism and "superstitious" beliefs and practices, such as exorcism and the writing of magical talismans to protect people from supernatural forces, that developed later. However, no such distinction exists: the early texts were written disparately and edited into their current forms only in the early centuries CE. The reality is both more interesting and compelling, showing that actual Daoist traditions incorporated a variety of practices stemming from philosophical texts, shamanic practices, and elsewhere. *Shaman* is a term used to describe the "priests" of many indigenous religions, who practice healing, possession by spirits, and communication with the spiritual world, and who, in the Chinese context, are ritual experts of early religion. These priests still exist among some ethnic groups, for instance the Manchu people of northeast China.[19] From these various strands of proto-Daoisms we find the first Daoist traditions emerging.[20]

DIVINE PEOPLE

One distinction between many Eastern and Western religions involves differing conceptions of the divine and the human. Whereas in the West we tend to see God as separate, in China (and elsewhere) it is possible for humans to become gods, either as immortals or as particular deities with a function in the heavenly pantheon. Whatever the case, it is important to note that the borderline between the human and divine worlds is thin and permeable, especially in folk religion. Confucius makes a good example here. Distinct views have arisen over whether Confucius should be worshipped. In 59 CE, an imperial edict made sacrifice to him compulsory in educational institutions, and over time, he came to be viewed as a deity, being given in 657 CE the title of "the perfect sage and ancient teacher," and from this time on until the sixteenth century he was treated as if he were a god. However, in response to questions raised by Christian missions at that time as to whether Chinese converts to Christianity could make sacrifices to Confucius, the emperor of the day, Kangxi, declared in 1530 CE that Confucius was not a god and that the sacrifices were simply done out of respect for him as a great human teacher and educator.

The *Daodejing* is attributed to a figure called Laozi (Lao Tzu), who supposedly was Confucius's elder. However, we know the text did not reach a finished form until centuries later, in the Han Dynasty.[21] Moreover, it seems it may originally have been intended as a text, like the Confucian Classics, to guide governors in ruling the state.[22] Nevertheless, the legend is important because Laozi is a symbolic founder who became a god in the later tradition. The

Daodejing has links with some other early texts, in particular the *Neiye*, which ties it to the Huang-Lao school of the Han Dynasty that sought to promote a united physical-spiritual well-being.[23]

Today, only two major schools of Daoism survive, the Celestial Masters and Complete Perfection. The Celestial Masters school is today based in Taiwan (the Celestial Masters fled from the Communists in 1949), and is often seen as a more popular form of Daoism: its priests are allowed to marry, and they are concerned mainly with performing exorcisms and writing amulets and other protective talismans for money. The practice of exorcism goes back to the earliest Daoist traditions, where the standard formula of words "swiftly, swiftly, in accordance with the statutes and ordinances" was formed as an integral part of the ritual, and is still used in all exorcisms today.[24] Various amulets with sacred symbols to ward off demons, along with wooden swords, incense, and bells, can be found in exorcism ceremonies. The Complete Perfection school is, by contrast, a monastic tradition, its priests being more highly trained and ascetic, with their focus being on spiritual transformation and development. Its headquarters, based at White Cloud Monastery, Beijing, is now the center of the Daoist Association of China.[25]

These traditions came to elaborate a vast pantheon of deities. Different traditions elaborate different versions, but the following provides a normative guide. The highest level of deities comprises the Three Pure Ones, including the deified Laozi, who are manifestations of the *dao*. However, because the Three Pure Ones are too exalted, the most significant deity, in popular thinking, has generally been the Jade Emperor, who rules the Daoist heaven. In this, there are many deities, including his wife, the Queen Mother of the West, and various deities who rule over particular areas of life. There is a god of culture, Wenchang, who can be seen as a deity for the Confucian tradition and to whom sacrifices could be made for success in the imperial exams. There are also gods of particular cities and towns, as well as gods of the earth, who exist in Daoism and folk tradition.[26] Reverence to these deities differs between popular and elite Daoist practices: in the former, each is interceded with for benefits, whereas, for initiates in the latter, the deities are envisaged as representing spiritual principles and devotion to them is concerned with internal purification.[27]

It is hard to say what characterizes Daoism, in that it has existed in many different forms at different times.[28] It has been described as China's countercultural tradition, although from the *Daodejing* onward it has also been associated with elite traditions and government. Nevertheless, because it has become subordinate to Confucianism, it has offered an alternative vision. Notably, principles such as nonaction (*wu-wei*) mean that one should act in accordance with *dao*, and not be concerned with human reputation or cunning, while withdrawal from public life to seek inner cultivation is often seen as Daoist. Certainly, in the forms in which they became most widely known, both the *Daodejing* and *Zhuangzi* mock Confucian virtues and concerns, and offer a vision of life free from stress and convention. Whereas Confucianism focuses on government service, Daoism focuses on inner spiritual cultivation (but both seek to align themselves with the *dao*) which may involve withdrawing from the world and living in a mountain hermitage, and practicing internal alchemy to ensure that one's inner spiritual life—which is closely tied to the body—is in harmony.

Finally, we must address a vexed question: the relationship between Daoism and popular religion. In the past, Western and Confucian scholars have equated popular religiosity to Daoism, whether this is belief in fox spirits or immortals, with most itinerant priests or local temples having been seen as Daoist. Contemporary scholarship, which has examined what was once dismissed as "superstitious religious Daoism," overturns this; most itinerant priests, probably descended from ancient shamans, are simply ritual experts, who may also practice exorcism and fortune telling to make a living, but who possess no connection to organized Daoist traditions, while the local temples would be constructed by the community as a place to hold shrines of deities that were significant to them. Established Daoist lineages are philosophically developed and spiritually refined, and distinct from folk religion and its priests, shamans, and mediums. However, issues remain: Celestial Master Daoism, as discussed above, is closer to popular religiosity than is Complete Perfection Daoism; traditions closer to folk religion, such as the Red Hat Sect and the associated Lushan ritual tradition, which emphasizes exorcism, possession by spirits, and other practices,[29] claim Daoist descent. Moreover, Daoism is associated with some deities of popular religiosity, such as the Three Star Gods, whose images are found in Daoist temples.[30] As with most traditions, there is no clear line between the officially approved religion of the elite hierarchy and the activities of devotees and popular expression. However, mainstream Daoism has always sought, officially, to distance and distinguish itself from superstition and popular religion.[31]

At this stage it is important to discuss immortality. The idea that human beings can attain physical immortality (or, at least, greatly expanded lifespans) is widespread in Chinese thought, as is the belief in immortal beings (*xian*) and in an elixir of immortality (often sought by alchemists). This idea has influenced elite religious thinkers, including emperors and Confucian scholars; for instance, we know the First Emperor sent envoys to find the lands of the immortals. The concept of immortals has also inspired popular deities, but is most commonly associated with Daoism. These traditions tell us that immortals lived to a great age and had magical powers. The following poem, for instance, tells us that:

In this world there is a Great Man, living in the middle continent.
His abode extends over ten thousand miles, yet is too small for a short sojourn.
Grieved at the world's unpleasant state, he easily rises and soars away.
He rides a pure rainbow streaming down, mounts cloudy ether and floats upward.[32]

However, Daoist traditions of personal cultivation have focused on "internal alchemy," rather than on the "external alchemy" of popular and elite belief in physical immortality. Daoists have sought to become "spiritual immortals" or "perfected people".[33]

Although both the popular and Daoist traditions may be linked through ancient shamanic figures, the *fangshi*,[34] they should be distinguished. However, confusion arises as traditional Daoists hid their teachings of internal alchemy in talk of external alchemy, and one popular group of deities, the Eight Immortals, is recognized by the Complete Perfection tradition. Therefore, it is hard to clearly distinguish between popular and Daoist beliefs.[35]

Buddhism

Three aspects of Chinese Buddhism deserve our particular attention: (1) it is Mahayana Buddhism; (2) indigenous schools developed in China; and (3) despite adaptation, it was sometimes identified as a foreign religion, resulting in persecution and hostility.

Buddhism has always perceived the Buddha as someone who went beyond the realms of normal human limitations; the Mahayana further developed this perception of the Buddha, seeing him as a deity or as a manifestation of universal Buddha-Nature. From this base, Chinese Buddhist schools developed, including Ch'an Buddhism, known as Zen, its Japanese name. Ch'an Buddhism is a meditation school according to which one can break down one's rational, everyday mind, which prevents one from seeing one's own inherent Buddha-Nature, by looking internally through quiet meditation and the use of nonsensical riddles (Chinese *gongan* and Japanese *koan*). It is also known for its iconoclasm, sometimes mocking traditional teachings, scriptures, and practices.[36]

The other major Chinese school is the Pure Land. This school is more devotional, believing that we live in a period of decline of the *dharma* (Buddha's teachings); as such, it is impossible to achieve enlightenment for ourselves. Instead, we have to rely on spiritual guides. The Mahayana tradition teaches that throughout millennia many buddhas have appeared, while other figures, bodhisattvas, having attained the qualifications for enlightenment, choose to help others on this path.

Of particular importance for the Pure Land is Amida Buddha, who created a paradise (Pure Land) in which people who call his name for help can be reborn and be assured of attaining enlightenment. The basic practice of this school is the reciting of the name of the Buddha (*namo omitofo*).[37] However, one of Amida's assistants, Guanyin (Kuanyin), became the most significant figure in Chinese devotion. Originally depicted as male, and believed to be capable of helping anyone who need assistance, Guanyin increasingly assumed a primarily female depiction, most commonly dressed in white. The Pure Land has become far and away the most popular form of Buddhism in China and beyond, being the world's largest Buddhist school, and Guanyin is among the most revered deities in the Far East.[38]

The Fourth Tradition: Folk Religion

Scholars are seldom interested in recording the history or enumerating the practice of the common people. Moreover, because such practice is unregulated, there are few or no guiding regulations or precepts, a fact further complicated by China's vast size, which means that many regional differences exist. Yet, it is related to the major traditions in terms, for instance, of deities. Guanyin is invoked by Chinese in all walks of life as a protecting goddess (debates abound over this term *goddess* because she is technically a bodhisattva; yet the term *goddess* seems to match her role and the understanding people have of her).

Likewise, many of Daoism's deities were once gods or goddesses of the people who became incorporated into the official pantheon, and who coexist with deities at the edges of official acknowledgement. The Stove God, for instance, who reports annually to the Jade Emperor, is best seen as not being a Daoist deity, yet he interacts, at the level of popular belief, with the supreme lord of the Daoist heaven. Very popular is a triad of deities named the Three Star Gods: Tianguan, Wenchang, and Shouxing. Tianguan bestows blessings and happiness; Wenchang, already mentioned, is also a god of wealth; and Shouxing bestows longevity. Another significant god of wealth is Guandi, who is commonly venerated in business centers.[39] It is also important to note that many of these deities were once human beings—many of whom are locatable historical characters—who through their particular virtues became deities after death.[40] The Eight Immortals, who became incorporated into the Daoist pantheon in the late imperial period, are also very popular. They appear in popular tales and stories as champions of justice, and the most important of them, Lü Dongbin, is frequently manifested in spirit writing sessions, in which divine figures reveal instructions or new scriptures to shamans in a state of trance.[41]

The common people also go to both Buddhist and Daoist temples, and seek out Buddhist or Daoist priests or Confucian scholar-officials for particular rites or practices, because all three traditions provide support for some popular practices. Simply put, there is no single or clear relation between Chinese folk religion and the "great traditions." Rather, there is a variety of interactions and interrelationships at various levels, and the boundaries of elite and popular tradition are not easy to determine. Indeed, many aspects of folk religion are found in all levels of the social spectrum, and others are more particular to the common people.[42]

What then marks out folk religion? Some have suggested that the concept of reciprocity (*shu*) is fundamental, whereby a duty is owed between humans and supernatural beings, and favors are returned.[43] Preserving harmony (*he*), both in relationships and within the natural order, is also central.[44] The concepts of salvation and good rebirth have also been suggested as being fundamental to folk religion.[45] However, all these factors can be found in more established traditions. The sociologist C. K. Yang therefore distinguishes between "institutional" and "diffused" religion—the former consisting of things that occur within established frameworks and temples, the latter occurring in areas that are not overtly religious, such as the home—and suggests this division is characteristic of folk religion.[46] For instance, one prime site for folk religion was the home shrine, an area set aside for devotion to a range of deities. However, folk religion has its temples, and this division maintains a divide between "secular" and "sacred" areas that makes little sense outside the modern Western (and Western-influenced) world. But if we use the terms with a notion of things that are institutional (belonging to established lineages and centrally defined traditions) and things that are diffused (either part of the general culture, meaning both the common people and the elites, or localized traditions without any centralized institution), it will help us to move toward an understanding of what folk religion is in the Chinese context, as well as helping us see what belongs to the religion of daily life. However, this definition is provisional and does not provide clear edges, in that many traditions, practices, and customs exist within, outside, and between the names we use to fix boundaries between the faith traditions. The folk and official religious systems are, however, distinct.[47]

HISTORY

China sees itself as having a five thousand-year record of unbroken cultural transmission, going back through the mists of ancient history and mythology to the three dynasties (Zhou, Shang, and Xia) and beyond. Ignoring the historical questions, which are not our concern, much of

Chinese religion looks back to golden eras. Indeed, many popular practices go back to this period, particularly shamanic traditions.[48] As we have seen, the Zhou Dynasty is important for Confucianism. Daoism also traces its roots, in Laozi, to this period. However, the most important period in the development of Chinese religion was the Han Dynasty, which saw the formation of Confucian and Daoist traditions, as well as the introduction of Buddhism.[49]

A scholar called Dong Zhongshu (179–104 BCE) is important to Confucianism, for he helped persuade the emperor to set up an imperial academy for studying the Confucian texts, as well as to award government positions to scholars trained in the Confucian tradition. This training lasted almost continually for over two thousand years, ending with the last imperial dynasty, in the twentieth century.[50]

Daoism's evolution is more complex. Various proto-Daoist schools and textual traditions existed in the early Han period. Among these, the Huang-Lao tradition is arguably the earliest Daoist tradition. But the tradition most commonly seen as the earliest form of Daoism is the that of the Celestial Masters. This tradition, which worshiped Laozi as a deity, formed in the area of present-day Sichuan Province. At that time, this province was outside the growing Chinese Empire, and as such, it existed as its own independent state. As China expanded, it eventually incorporated the province, and the Celestial Masters gave up their claims to rule and began disseminating their faith throughout the empire. Although this school appears to have died out, the present-day school called Celestial Masters claims direct descent from the first, with its present head being acclaimed as the sixty-fourth patriarch.[51]

The religion of Siddhartha Gautama, the Buddha, came to China in the early centuries CE. According to legend, emperor Mingdi dreamed of a golden giant from the West and asked his advisors who this was. They told him of a holy man who had lived and taught beyond the borders of the empire, which resulted in an invitation to Buddhist monks to come and preach. The actual facts of Buddhism's arrival are lost in time, although we know Buddhist monks often traveled on missionary journeys and may also have served communities of foreign traders in other lands, which probably accounted for the earliest Buddhist presence. Soon Buddhism became a noticeable presence in many parts of China.[52]

The following few hundred years—from the third to seventh centuries CE, a period of turbulence until stability was restored by the Tang Dynasty—saw various trends emerge: various Daoist traditions developed that helped build up a set of texts and practices that consolidated a Daoist identity; Buddhism grew to become the largest religion; and Confucianism consolidated its role, with Confucius himself becoming a deity. The period in which the Tang Dynasty ruled is often seen as the golden age of Daoism and Buddhism. There are several reasons for this: one is that Confucianism at this time was essentially a dry intellectual study for the civil service, and so those who wanted spiritual attainment looked for it in the other two faiths; another is that these two faiths enjoyed much imperial support and patronage. The Tang Dynasty thus changed the religious map of China.

Although Buddhism had outgrown Daoism as a popular form of religion, the hostility often came from Confucian scholars, not from Daoists. Complaints included the notions that reincarnation was absurd and that the Buddhist monastic life conflicted with Chinese values of filial piety, whereby a child's primary duty is to look after parents and continue the family line. However, most important, by the time of the Tang Dynasty, so many people were entering the monasteries that labor supplies were short, and so much gold and other precious metals were being used for statues that supplies for coinage were seen as threatened. The resulting suppression of Buddhism (842–845 CE) landed a blow from which the religion never fully recovered, with most schools of Chinese Buddhism disappearing. Although the persecution was reversed in 845 CE, government restrictions remained. These restricted numbers of monks and imposed a central ministry of religion that regulated religious institutions. Thereafter, imperial support was sporadic, and Buddhism became increasingly seen as unsophisticated.[53] Daoism also found itself bound by the same regulations and pressures. In part, this was due to the development of Neo-Confucianism, to which we now turn.

By the tenth century CE, a movement of scholars expressing dissatisfaction with the dry learning of Confucianism was gaining strength.[54] This movement became known as Neo-Confucianism, which found its greatest spokesperson in Zhu Xi (1130–1200). Zhu Xi changed the focus from the Five Classics to the Four Books, and his commentary on them became the basis of civil service exams from the twelfth until the twentieth century. Confucianism also started to discover its spiritual side, and it learned and incorporated methods of meditation and self-transformation from Daoism and Ch'an. It also looked back to Mencius, who became the second great sage of the tradition.[55]

Despite continued spiritual borrowing from Daoism and Buddhism, a normative pattern emerged of Confucian scholar-officials dismissing these traditions, in institutional forms, as suitable for uneducated people and composed of superstition. Possibly for the first time, people began to understand themselves as Confucians rather than Daoists when it came to alternative indigenous traditions.

THE MONKEY KING? THE STORY OF THE JOURNEY TO THE WEST

Xuan Zang, a Buddhist monk known to have been a historical figure, embarks on a journey to India to retrieve Buddhist scriptures, accompanied by three companions: Sun Wukong, the mischievous but powerful Monkey King; Pigsy, a pig spirit who had once been a general in the heavenly armies but who was punished for misdeeds by this rebirth; and Brother Sand, another celestial figure reborn as a water demon. He is also eventually accompanied by a horse who is actually a dragon. This unlikely party partakes in one of the best known and most loved stories of China, the Journey to the West. This story exists in many versions, but the basic form remains the same throughout and pokes fun at the established religious hierarchy of heaven and the human realms. In the story, Monkey mocks heaven but is brought under control by the Buddha, and is the real hero of the story. The story represents a lighter side to Chinese religion than is normally found, and shows an iconoclastic approach to religion.

Zhu Xi's thinking formed the dominant form of Confucian thought until the twentieth century, although some other interpretations of Neo-Confucianism existed, with a scholar called Wang Yang Ming (1472–1529 CE) offering a significant alternative stance.[56] Buddhism and Daoism survived in two main schools, though other forms existed. For instance, the Qing Dynasty sponsored an esoteric form of Mahayana Buddhism, the Vajrayana. However, things were far from static, with the Ming and Qing dynasties seeing new folk traditions developing, including established *sanjiao* (three traditions) schools, spirit writing of new scriptures—often on the borders of Daoism and folk religion—and the emergence of new deities.[57]

Once again, though, the religious landscape of China was to be rocked to its core. By the late nineteenth century, Confucianism had become associated with feudalism and had fallen into disfavor, so with the end of the last imperial dynasty, the Qing, Confucianism ended its reign as state ideology. As such, all Confucian religious and ritual practices ceased. The beginnings of Communist rule also saw official condemnation of Confucianism, but also of all religion, which was officially suppressed in the Cultural Revolution (1966–1976 CE). Many believed traditional Chinese religion had disappeared at this time; however, because of a relaxing of suppression and a new openness to religion, it has resurfaced with great force. Confucianism has also been revived as an indigenous philosophy and ideology by the Chinese government. Meanwhile, traditional religion in folk, Buddhist, and Daoist form continued in Taiwan, in Hong Kong, and in overseas Chinese communities.

Today, the People's Republic of China is officially an atheist state, but religion is thriving in various forms.[58] For instance, temples of Buddhism, Daoism, and folk religion are being rebuilt, and Christian churches are growing, with many people seeking out these or other forms of spiritual direction or inspiration in their lives. Many ethnic minorities still find their own traditions to be of great importance; for instance, the Uighur people of northwest China are deeply committed to their Islamic traditions, whereas the Tibetan ethnic minority's culture and traditions are deeply entwined with its Buddhist tradition.

DAILY LIFE

Filial Piety and Ancestor Veneration

We start our discussion of the daily practice of religion in China with filial piety, because this notion is foundational for Chinese culture. Indeed, filial piety is a Chinese cultural virtue rather than a Confucian one (to some extent, this is true of much that is said to be Confucian). Filial piety is the respect owed to one's parents, and it is related to wider duties to family and state. There are scriptural roots to ground filial piety in Confucianism in *The Classic of Filial Piety*, one of the Thirteen Classics, attributed to Confucius. (That this late work is attributed to him probably says more about how highly the virtue is regarded than it does about its Confucian basis.) On a popular level, the so-called Twenty-Four Paragons of Filial Piety were important inspirations.[59] These were stories of children who sacrificed or dedicated themselves to caring for their parents. In one story, a poor peasant barely earns enough money to buy medicine for his father, and when his father dies, he is unable to afford his funeral. This being the case, he sells himself into servitude to pay the costs. In another, a grown man continues to behave like a young child before his aged parents simply because it amuses them. Yet another tells of a son whose mother wants fresh fish in midwinter; to please her, he goes to the frozen river. There, he takes off his shirt and coat, lies down on the ice, and cries to melt the ice with his tears so he can find some fish. Enshrined in tradition, these tales exemplify ideals for all Chinese children. Although such a virtue may not seem to be a specifically religious affair, such a perception is to misinterpret the way that daily activities and religion intertwine in traditional Chinese thought. Moreover, the specifically religious endorsement of filial piety can be seen in the Chinese legends around Guanyin, which we discuss below.

Related to filial piety is a more overtly religious activity, ancestor veneration. In one form or another, this goes back to the Shang Dynasty. Traditionally, in mainland China, different clans had ancestral halls where spirit tablets, usually small wooden boards recording the name of the deceased, were kept. These were venerated in memory of the dead using food, incense, and other offerings. The "other offerings" are noteworthy. Anyone who frequents Chinese supermarkets may have noticed, often near the back, a stack of yellow paper and printed money (which may seem to be for a game at first sight) bearing the words "Hell Bank Notes," usually of various denominations, in millions of dollars or more. These will be burned at funerals, and at annual commemorations of the dead. The reason for this ritual relates to Chinese beliefs about the afterlife. Buddhist, Daoist, and folk traditions speak of a number of hells, typically 10, that must be traversed. These are overseen by judges, but like in human courts, they are open to bribery, hence the money. Also, many Chinese believe that in the afterlife, people live a similar life to the one lived here, so offerings of money come in handy. Also burned are other funerary items, typically paper models of horses that provide transport in the afterlife. Today, such items can include models of houses, cars, mobile phones, and washing machines. The offering should befit the status of the person in this life. The reader may here make connections to the famous terracotta warriors found near Xi'an, in China, where the emperor Qinshi Huangdi was buried alongside a whole army to provide him with suitable protection in the next world.[60]

Life-size terracotta warriors at the grand tomb of Emperor Qin Shi Huangdi (reigned 259–210 BCE), the founder of the Qin dynasty. Peasants discovered by chance the army of life-size terracotta warriors, with their horses and chariots, in 1974 about 25 miles east of Xian. There were more than 8,000 statues found in the emperor's tomb. The soldiers, all facing east, stand in 11 rows, their formation stretching more than 200 meters. (Corbis.)

It may be asked, however, whether Chinese people today really believe in the efficacy of such practices. Certainly, in mainland China oppression saw such practices driven underground. However, recent freedom of religion means that these practices are being revived; certainly in the countryside they are becoming increasingly prevalent. They can also be witnessed in many cities, too, and are practiced not just by the uneducated classes but also by educated people, including members of the Communist Party, all of whom are officially atheist. Here, a certain ambivalence enters the picture.[61] Some may do it simply as a cultural practice to show their respect for the dead, but others seem to think that perhaps their thoughts and prayers may reach their ancestors.

Government and Authority

Religion and government have always been closely linked in China. As we indicated earlier, both Confucianism and Daoism have their origins, at least partly, in texts written for rulers, while the early Daoist community, the Celestial Masters, combined in themselves a source both of spiritual authority and of temporal government. For all these groups, correct ruling relied on following cosmic principles, *dao* or *tian*. Meanwhile, the government of the country lay with the emperor as the Son of Heaven, holding his rulership by virtue of the Mandate of Heaven. Although such things are somewhat removed from daily life, they nevertheless lay out a pattern: the order of things is designed and run by higher principles; this being the case, government is not just a secular affair, but also a religious one. Moreover, pattern follows through: the nine kowtows (deep bowing, or literally, "head-knocking") that the emperor performed before the altar of heaven had the same ritual form as those performed by a peasant farmer at his father's funeral. Thus there was a sense of connectedness between all layers of religious life.

In terms of religious control, China never had an overarching religious hierarchy. In Confucianism, although some scholars are highly regarded, every individual is in large part responsible for his or her own spiritual life. Buddhist monasteries are also largely self-regulating, with each monastery having its own abbot. Some larger monasteries had offshoots, but these networks were never large enough to become dominant. One monastery, however, did have a precedence of respect: the Shaolin Temple, seen as the original Ch'an temple because of its association with the semilegendary founder, Bodhidharma. The Shaolin Temple was therefore declared by imperial decree to be "the first temple under heaven." However, this had little practical effect. Moreover, as Pure Land Buddhism was the larger school, such respect was not universal. Indeed, because of its association with *gong fu* and the fame this has generated, the

Shaolin Temple is today regarded with some contempt by other monks—many think monks train there only because they want to become famous—which makes it difficult for monks trained at Shaolin to transfer to other monasteries.

The organization of Daoism has more central control, but not dominance. At various periods, the heads of both the Complete Perfection and Celestial Masters schools have been declared supreme head of all Daoists by different emperors (some older texts even call the Celestial Master the "Daoist pope"). However, control over the whole tradition was never established in practice. At its turn, folk religion is largely practiced at the local level, and so has no hierarchy. In some places, authority resides with community elders, and some roles are held on the basis of powers, as is the case with healers and mediums.

The main form of religious control has therefore come from the imperial government, a practice firmly established in the Tang Dynasty. Besides controlling (or monitoring) numbers and regulations, government has traditionally decreed which traditions are "orthodox" (i.e., accepted religions) and which are "heretical" (i.e., unacceptable religions), a function still maintained today by the Communist government.[62] It is notable, therefore, that what many Westerners condemn as unwarranted political interference in matters of religion is actually a long-established part of Chinese culture. Certainly, the current government is not the first to employ its control mechanisms for reasons more "political" than "spiritual." This has seen a continuation of the condemnation of many folk traditions as superstition.

Rituals, Temple Devotion, and Festivals

Chinese religious life is marked by a variety of rituals and festivals. These relate to Confucianism, Daoism, Buddhism, and folk traditions. The Confucian rituals, of course, are no longer used, an operating Confucian ritual system today being found only in Korea. However, in the past, many of the theoretically most important festivals—including annual sacrifices to city gods and gods of the earth, the legendary protectors of particular localities—were enacted by Confucian officials, whose performances were nevertheless not closely linked to the activities of the ordinary people. For instance, every city had its own god, and the annual celebration was done by Confucian officials. However, such temples were often Daoist or part of the local/folk tradition, and people did not attend the dry Confucian ritual, but rather the more colorful ceremonies of the other priests.

Most of the key festivals in China included temple fairs.[63] Over a day or more of celebrations, vendors of all sorts and popular entertainers would set up tent outside the temple, and a general period of festivity would take place. With musicians and sideshows, these were loud and colorful events, and theatrical presentations of myths were often a center point. Today, such fairs are once again being revived in mainland China, and outside large temples, during major festivals, one can find all types of activities and sellers, as well as many worshippers, whose numbers appear to be increasing—although how much is "religious" and how much is "cultural tourism" is hard to assess.

Festivals entail both ritual activities enacted by the priesthood as well as the offering of individual devotions. In the latter, people go to various shrines within the temple complex and offer prayers before the images of particular deities. Primarily, this consists of the burning of incense. Sellers of incense can be found both inside and outside many temples. Devotees hold the lighted incense outside specific shrines with both hands, often held at the forehead, and typically make three bows before inserting the incense sticks into large containers—generally filled with sand—set up for this purpose. Generally, there are places to kneel at the shrine, and once here the most devout stand and kneel three times, touching their heads three times on each occasion—thereby making the ninefold "imperial" kowtow referred to above. Exact performances can differ depending on the devotee and other particulars. The personal devotions can be performed at any time, not just during festivals.

The main festivals and rituals, based on the lunar calendar, include the anniversaries of the Buddha's birthday (the fourth day of the eighth lunar month—usually around one to two months later than our solar calendar) and enlightenment (the eighth day of the twelfth lunar month); New Year (Spring Festival—the first fifteen days of the first lunar month); the birthday of Laozi (the fifteenth day of the second lunar month); the Qingming Festival (the third day of the third lunar month); the birthday of the Queen of Heaven (the twenty-third day of the third lunar month); the Dragon Boat Festival (the fifth day of the fifth lunar month); the Ghost Festival (the fifteenth day of the seventh lunar month); and Confucius's birthday (the twenty-seventh day of the eighth lunar month). These events may include elements specific to one major tradition but can also merge folk religion with mainstream tradition; furthermore, some are associated only with particular geographic regions.

Because it is impossible to discuss all rituals and festivals, we will just mention some aspects of the New Year celebration. Traditionally, the home shrine included the Stove God, who, on the eve of the New Year, reported to the Jade Emperor the conduct of the family. Thus, on this day, the family would eat sweet sticky buns and offer some to the Stove God, believing either that you could bribe the deity with this offering or that the sticky buns would plug his mouth, making him unable to report the misconduct of the family to the Jade

Emperor. These activities have been banned, but they are returning in the South and in the countryside. However, questions arise over whether various parts of the New Year celebrations are religious or cultural. Some actions that might be seen by some as having religious implications might not be read this way by others. For instance, one activity still widely practiced is attaching rhyming poetic couplets to the outside of the door, along with posters of the character *fu*, which means "good luck." These are traditionally seen as auspicious symbols that will bring good fortune in the coming year. However, for many educated people who do it today, it is done with an awareness of its meaning but without any sense that it is overtly religious, or even with a belief that good fortune will come from it. Is the continuity of such practices residual religion, simple superstition, or merely a yearning for cultural identity and continuity? Probably none of these hypotheses is adequate, because the terms we use carry a lot of presuppositions with them.

The New Year Festival ends with the Lantern Festival, on the fifteenth day of the first lunar month. Today largely a secular event, it has traditionally been associated with Daoism. Many legends associated with the day probably have roots before Daoism evolved, and are generally associated with the Jade Emperor and fire (the lighting of lanterns being a significant part of the popular celebration—during the rule of the Ming and Qing dynasties fireworks were employed). According to one legend, when once a celestial swan descended to the earthly realms and was shot by a hunter, the Jade Emperor, in his anger, vowed to burn the earth, so lanterns were placed outside people's houses to trick the heavens into thinking their houses were already on fire. In more established Daoist ritual, however, the day is associated with the elemental deity of Heaven.

Sacred Places

Chinese temples tend to have a similar pattern, which reflects imperial architecture. It may be fair to say, though, that both imperial and religious architecture share common features of traditional Chinese style, one being a series of courtyards and halls. Usually housing monastic communities, larger temples have living quarters for either monks or nuns, whereas smaller temples, especially those of the folk traditions, have just a single resident priest, or even no staff at all. In the past, itinerant priests were hired by the community as needed.[64] This practice is on the increase once more, especially in South China.

Temples usually are enclosed within high walls, and the main gateway is an elaborate affair, flanked on either side by a pair of lions—guardian figures common to many Chinese buildings. The size and importance of the building is reflected in the size of the lion guardians, some being only a couple of feet or less, others being towering figures set on large pedestals that dwarf the people who come to the temple. Traditionally seen as supernatural guardians, lions are still used today mainly for decorative purposes, and especially to give a building a traditional Chinese architectural style. Many animals—either real (such as the tiger and the bat) or mythical (such as the dragon, the phoenix, and the *qilin*, sometimes called Chinese unicorn)—have symbolic roles in Chinese popular thought. These creatures often symbolize protection, power, or good fortune.

The entry way of a temple leads into the first courtyard, at the end of which is a large hall with a shrine to one of the deities worshipped at the temple. Large temples have (at least) a second courtyard behind the first; major temples have multiple courtyards leading off to each side, and sometimes also other buildings (including monastic living quarters) and areas, such as a garden, or lily pools. Shrines also are found in many temples, around the outside of the courtyard. Larger monasteries tend to have a bell tower and a drum tower, and many temples, whether large or small, have inscribed stone plinths (called stelae) that often serve some commemorative function.[65] Inside the halls, which often have large doors, worshippers can get close to the images (but in general they are not allowed to approach them directly, and offerings are given to a monastic attendant, who may be a religious or lay person). It is not unusual for various smaller shrines to be found within the same hall, although one deity (or a row of deities, such as three buddhas) is normally given prominence.

In their general design, Buddhist and Daoist temples are not very different, but Daoist temples tend to have guardian deities represented as ferocious warriors at the gateways. Sometimes these are anonymous, fierce deities, but three notable guardian deities include the Divine General Wang, who has a red face, long beard, and three eyes and who wears gold armor and carries an iron whip; Guan Yu (or Guandi), a general of the third century CE, often depicted seated and with a long beard and red face, whose weapon is a Chinese halberd (his exploits are often portrayed in Chinese opera performances); and Zhen Wu, also called Xuan Wu (the Dark Warrior), Lord of the North, who is often depicted with a snake and turtle.[66] Many temples and other buildings carry images of two Door Gods, who are variously identified.[67] Another common feature is the alchemical burner, a large covered furnace that represents the pursuit of alchemy. Buddhist temples may have a *luohan* (Pali *arhant*) hall, a room with life-size statues of the Buddha's disciples—often 108 in number, though sometimes 500 are displayed—some of whom may be in grotesque or comical form, an influence of Ch'an's iconoclastic strand.

The layout of Confucian temples, traditionally known as *wenmiao* (literally, "temples of culture"), is similar to that of other temples. Their primary function is as a place for the education in the Confucian classics. However, they also hold a shrine to Confucius and, generally, to quite a few of his disciples who later became prominent scholars. The principal sacrifice enacted annually in all Confucian institutes has been the *tailao*, which involves sacrificing a pig, a cow, and a goat.

Mountains are also of the utmost significance in Chinese religion. China has five great mountains: Taishan (Mount Tai), Huashan, Songshan, Northern Hengshan, and Southern Hengshan. These are considered Daoist sacred mountains, but they are not exclusively Daoist—for instance, the renowned Buddhist Shaolin Temple is on Songshan, whereas Taishan was the site of sacrifices to heaven made by the emperor, according to the Confucian rites. Buddhism also has its own list of major sacred mountains—Wutaishan, Emeishan, Jiuhuashan, and Putuoshan—but, again, not being exclusively Buddhist, they also house Daoist temples. Many other sacred mountains exist, such as Wudangshan and Laoshan. Most mountains have housed temples or hermitages in the past, and are sites of popular devotional practice.

Women and Gender

Men and women have experienced religion differently in Chinese history. Barred from any role in Confucianism,[68] women have found more opportunities in Buddhism, Daoism, and folk religion. However, social customs and expectations have to some degree limited the religious roles available to women. Becoming a nun has been acceptable in Buddhism, but Confucian thought disapproves of this. A model of, and justification for, female celibacy was found, however, through the bodhisattva Guanyin. In becoming indigenized into Chinese culture, Guanyin became associated with the legend of a Chinese princess, Miaoshan. According to this legend, Miaoshan wishes to follow a celibate life and so flees from her father's palace to a local nunnery. But her father destroys this establishment, and Miaoshan has to go off into the wilderness to become an ascetic. Time passes, and her fame as a religious figure grows. But back home, her father has grown old and ill. Having tried everything to cure Mioshan's father, his servants set off to seek out a famed holy master who they believe can perform miracles; this master is, unknown to them, Miaoshan. Despite her powers, Mioshan can only cure her father if she cuts off her hands and gouges out her eyes to make the medicine, which she willingly does. The father is cured, Miaoshan returns home, and her deed is discovered. Because of her act, Miaoshan not only symbolizes filial piety, but she can also become a Buddha, having willingly sacrificed herself for another being.

Despite being gruesome, this story helped make female monasticism acceptable, suggesting that leaving society to pray and work for others could be an expression of filial piety.[69] A Chinese rationale for monasticism was thereby formed. In due course, it also established a pattern for women to leave their married life, either temporarily or permanently, to enter into lay religious orders. Therefore, as some scholars have argued, the story of Miaoshan and Guanyin helped establish the norms of Chinese culture, and it also offered an alternative route for women who did not wish to marry or who desired to leave their marriages.

KILLING OR PRAYING? MARTIAL ARTS AND RELIGION

Did you know that the traditional Chinese martial arts of *gong fu* (kung fu) and *taiji* (tai chi) have roots in Chinese religious practices? *Gong fu* is believed to have its origins at the famous Shaolin Temple, where the first patriarch of Ch'an (Zen) Buddhism is said to have taught. Whether this legend is true, Shaolin is famed for its *gong fu,* with Shaolin monks now regularly performing their amazing feats around the world. The origins of the relationship between this meditation school and martial practice is obscure; some suggest it may have originated in exercises designed to strengthen the body after long hours spent in seated meditation, whereas others speculate that fighting was a skill needed by monks on the dangerous paths that led from India to China. Yet, it is not Buddhism alone that has such associations between meditation and martial arts: *taiji* is thought to have been developed by a Daoist monk named Chang Sanfeng, and its spiritual home is on the famous mountain Wudangshan. The philosophy behind each martial art has a spiritual basis—something retained particularly by *taiji*, whose rhythmic movements are believed to harmonize mind, body, and spirit, and to help one become attuned to *dao*.

Daoism and folk religion offer the most opportunities for women; Daoism even allows them to reach the upper hierarchy of some Daoist lineages. However, on a day-to-day level, most Daoist priests would have been men, although the majority of devotees were probably, as today, women. Female deities exist in both Daoism and folk religion. In Daoism, the Queen Mother of the West, wife of the Jade Emperor, is an important figure. In folk tradition, Mazu, the Sea Goddess, plays an important role, and is sometimes associated with the Queen Mother or Guanyin. Prominent in coastal areas of Southeast China, she is particularly invoked by fishermen and all who live near the sea. The prominence given to yin in the Daoist tradition also helps support the significance of women and the feminine. In folk religion, there is a place for women as shamans, mediums, and living embodiments of goddesses, which gives them a degree of authority and social prestige, at least within local communities, that they could not have had otherwise.[70]

But there are ways in which religion oppress women. Confucianism certainly comes in for a lot of blame, in particular in the establishment of family hierarchies, where the husband is placed over the wife as the emperor is over the minister. (In fairness, though, such patriarchal assumptions have more to do with Chinese culture than with Confucianism itself.) This hierarchy, as we have seen, implies mutual respect and cooperation. The well-known practice of foot binding, although associated with Neo-Confucianism and having developed about the same time, has no evident connection with it. Important Confucian figures did make comments on the place of women, with Zhu Xi suggesting that women should be largely confined to the home, as no respectable woman would venture out into men's spheres. Indeed, women of respectable families should even be accompanied to the temple—only women of low class or unsure morals would be seen in such places on their own, although temple fairs were an exception.[71] However, whether this should be associated with the religious philosophy of Confucianism, or with the common social views of the day (as expressed by Zhu Xi), is a matter for debate. Whatever the case, women were generally disadvantaged in all aspects of Chinese culture. In many traditional tales, women are introduced with the words "She had the misfortune to be borne a woman." Notwithstanding, as we have seen, religion has provided women with opportunities beyond their roles as wives, mothers, and daughters, in which they have always been subordinated to males.

Physical and Spiritual Practice

The notion of body and spirit as separate and distinct that pervades modern Western thinking is not a part of the Chinese worldview. A holistic approach characterizes Chinese thinking, integrating the spiritual and the physical both in theory and practice; for instance, Chinese martial arts, the practice of qigong (chi gong)—slow and rhythmic bodily exercises akin to tai chi—and Traditional Chinese Medicine (TCM) all concern mind, body, and spirit.[72]

Arguably, TCM is the most widespread activity related to religion. I purposely use the phrase "related to religion," rather than "religious activity," because many Chinese do not see TCM as religious in nature. Such medicinal practices as acupuncture and Chinese herbalism are seen today as secular in mainland China and the West, and it is claimed that they have a scientific basis. However, as with most traditional cultures, healing and religion are closely bound up. In mainland China people are trained in TCM in secular universities in the same fashion in which people are trained in Western medicine, and the Chinese happily use the two forms of medicine as complements and see both as secular. Likewise, many will practice *qigong* simply for health. Nevertheless, many strands feed into TCM, *qigong*, and the worldview that surrounds them.

Physical practices for health and spirituality go back to ancient China, and physical-spiritual practices associated with the Huang-Lao tradition go back at least to the first centuries BCE, probably in relation to the cult of immortality that dominated thought during the rule of the Han Dynasty, and which we know existed before this period. As we have discussed, physical immortality has long been seen as a spiritual goal in popular Chinese thought, and has been taken seriously by the elite of Chinese society. We know that Han Dynasty emperors sent envoys to find the land of the immortals and bring back the elixir of immortality; and the first emperor, Qinshi Huangdi, was buried in a tomb surrounded by lakes of mercury encased in jade in the apparent belief that these physical substances would help him attain a life in the hereafter. Indeed, the experimentation of many early practitioners of this path with herbs and minerals helped lay the basis for Chinese herbalism. The paths of physical practice and the taking of concocted potions to attain immortality seem to have been combined by many followers, and so all of these developed together. As such, TCM's roots are in religious practices, and much of it manipulates qi and uses the theory of yin-yang and the Five Agents, thus tying in with the spiritual cosmology of Chinese thought. The boundaries between what is seen as religious and what is seen as secular are thus not always clear.

Many *qigong* traditions have stemmed from mainstream Daoism in the last few centuries, many claiming to be Daoist though possessing no actual Daoist lineage (the lines between official religion and popular practice being hard to define precisely).[73] Indeed, the boundary between *qigong* done for health and *qigong* practiced as religion is also porous. An excellent example is the well-known *qigong* group Falun Gong. At its height, it was one of the most popular forms of *qigong*, practiced on a daily basis by millions of Chinese around the world, especially in mainland China. Though many Falun Gong practiced simply for health, the philosophy behind the Falun Gong included ideas about morality and spirituality. Its leaders therefore wanted it to be officially recognized as a religion, and, in what appears to have been an extremely miscalculated move, called thousands of their followers to a mass demonstration in

Beijing in 1999. The government responded by outlawing the movement, fearful of its power to organize such a large mass protest under the government's very nose.[74] For its leaders and some followers, *qigong* should be seen as a religion, but for others it appears to be nothing more than a form of physical exercise—although one linked to the mind or spirit. As we have seen, the boundaries between the religious and secular are often blurred, especially in popular Chinese practice. Falun Gong, other forms of *qigong*, TCM, and martial arts can be practiced for religious reasons or simply for good health (no matter that the origins of these practices are religious).

Fortune-Telling, Exorcism, Fox Spirits, and Everyday Practices

Many Chinese, like members of many other cultures, are less concerned with what may be seen as elite religious concerns—heaven, spiritual enlightenment, etc.—than with the everyday concerns of life—for example, supporting the family, finding business opportunities, planning for the year to come, wondering how the crops will grow, and so forth. This being the case, they seek out religious professionals for help with their secular concerns—something that is as true of Protestant Christianity and Theravada Buddhism as it is of Chinese religion. It therefore seems appropriate to deal with a variety of these practices, and with other everyday matters.

All cultures have ways to try to predict the future, and perhaps the best known one in the Chinese context is the *Book of Changes*. Composed of cryptic passages that the trained reader may decipher, it employs a group of patterns, the 8 hexagrams that are conjoined into 64 hexagrams.[75] These patterns go back to Shang divination, involving cracks in bones and tortoise shells baked in fire. The favored method for producing the hexagram patterns (each of which had its own commentary) was to repeatedly toss and sort fifty yarrow sticks to produce the answer. However, unless one were a professional fortune-teller, more common practice used only two coins; this was faster and easier, but was considered less accurate.

Significantly, because the *Book of Changes* is one of the Five Classics of Confucian tradition, many fortune-tellers would have been Confucian scholar-officials. Indeed, in past times, scholars who did not pass official examinations could make a living by telling fortunes.[76] However, the *Book of Changes* is not the exclusive conserve of Confucianism, for both Daoist and Buddhist commentaries exist; moreover, priests of all traditions could be fortune-tellers. Yet, the *Book of Changes* is commonly associated with Daoism; for instance, the Wong Tai Sin Temple, a popular Daoist temple in Hong Kong, houses a separate host of practitioners who use a variety of methods, such as palm reading, face reading, or the random selection, and subsequent interpretation, of numbered bamboo sticks. Fortune-telling in China is often intended to enlighten people about likely future influences rather than to exactly predict events.

The Chinese horoscope is related to fortune-telling. The 12 animals that compose it are increasingly well known worldwide, with many people knowing both their Western and Chinese signs (this writer is a Gemini and a dog). Understanding one's sign in traditional China was important not just because it revealed aspects about one's personality, but also because it could help indicate who one's life partner should be. In pre-modern China, young people were not free to choose their husband or wife—this was left to the family, who would generally seek the services of a matchmaker. The matchmaker would consider such things as the social position of the couple and their zodiacal signs. This was a complicated matter, because the signs are related to both the Five Agents theory and the yin-yang theory, and the precise horoscope would need to be drawn up and interpreted. Thus, two dogs would never get along, but a dog and a pig might. However, a dog of the water element supporting a wood pig (water helps wood grow) would dominate a fire pig (for obvious reasons). Therefore, an exact match was needed. Because this involved an understanding of such things as the Five Agents theory, this area of life was bound up in the spiritual worldview of ancient China. Moreover, in traditional belief, the 12 animals had been appointed their roles by the Jade Emperor himself, and so the interpretation of the signs was bound up with an understanding of deities and cosmic hierarchy.

Other areas associated with popular religion but with crossovers into the major traditions are fox spirits and exorcism. Fox spirits are a distinctive aspect of Far Eastern folklore. These magical beings, who could take on human form, were seen as pranksters who tricked or harmed human beings. However, as supernatural entities, they could also provide blessings, so fox spirit shrines existed both to ward off harm and seek help. In the vast popular folklore on ghosts and the supernatural, many tales of fox spirits are found.[77] One widespread story involves a worthy and honorable (but poor) scholar who meets a beautiful young girl who is in fact a fox spirit. They fall in love, and through the magical powers of the fox spirit, various obstacles on their path are removed. Sometimes a twist in the tale prevents them from living happily ever after—in some versions, the girl is suspected of being a fox spirit or may need for some other reason to return to her people, leaving the human world. Often these tales display an ambivalence about the moral character of the fox spirit, who commits both kindly and mischievous, or even wicked, deeds—although the situations can be read in different ways.[78]

Although in some tales fox spirits can be seen as beneficial, they have been more likely to be seen as problematic, so professional exorcists have historically been called upon if it was believed that a fox spirit, or any other supernatural creature, was in residence nearby, or in possession of a person. Traditionally, Daoists, especially in the Celestial Master tradition, were seen as the best exorcists. However, other exorcists existed who did not belong to one of the major traditions, but who were simply ritual specialists of no tradition, drawing perhaps from aspects of ritual texts from Daoist, Buddhist, Confucian, and other sources.

Another aspect of popular religiosity is feng shui. Particularly as presented in the West, and as understood by some Chinese, this is a practice that is simply part of the Chinese cultural worldview, and not inherently religious. However, understood in the context of traditional Chinese cosmology, feng shui is not simply about arranging things to become "psychologically harmonious," but rather about determining the qi and "dragon vein" of a place that are involved in the physical-spiritual interplay that permeates much Chinese thought.[79] Feng shui traditionally involves harnessing supernatural forces in the environment to order the well-being of a place. However, that no real barrier exists between what we call the secular and religious spheres of life can be seen in the fact that the same principles can be used in arranging a house, a temple, or a grave. Today, many educated Chinese, at least on the mainland, are quite suspicious of feng shui and see it as superstitious nonsense; others, however, believe that it brings together a set of sound commonsense principles of natural planning; yet others see it as manipulating the qi force that permeates all things. Certainly, whether believed in or not, feng shui is still a vital part of much Chinese life outside the mainland—no major building in Hong Kong, for instance, would be planned without it. Feng shui is another sign that our usual ideas about religion are problematic in this cultural setting.

IMPACT OF DAILY LIFE ON HISTORY

As we have seen, there has often been no clear dividing line between popular practices and elite formulations, although many have wanted to maintain these distinctions. Certainly, influences from folk religion have affected established practice; however, exactly what is and is not established religion is hard to say. Belief in the possibility of personal immortality has impacted on established religion, or at least its perception, as we have seen (whether this belief arose among the people or the elite is hard to say). Popular practice also gave prominence to Guanyin—against the elite textual tradition, focused on Amida Buddha—making her cult the most widespread form of devotion. Likewise, many popular deities, such as the Eight Immortals and city gods, have infil-trated the official Daoist pantheon.

Popular religion has been very influential in religion-inspired rebellions that have characterized Chinese history. The Han Dynasty found itself much weak-ened by the Yellow Turban Rebellion (c. 2nd century CE), a popular uprising that employed Five Agents theory.[80] The Ming Dynasty also used religion to legitimize its overthrow of the foreign Yuan Dynasty, utilizing popular religious movements for this purpose. Meanwhile, the nineteenth century saw more popular religious uprisings. Perhaps the most notable is the Taiping (Great Peace) Rebellion, which lasted from 1850 to1871 CE and saw an independent religious state form in southern China. Although based on a form of Christianity, it was mixed with much native Chinese thought, and the central notion that gave it its name goes back at least 2,000 years, and influenced the Yellow Turban Rebellion. Popular religious uprisings inspired by popular religious belief have been frequent occur-rences in Chinese history. They have also been part of the reason why the govern-ment, from imperial to modern times, has watched and tried to regulate popular religions and legislate against what it sees as dangerous movements—whether the notorious White Lotus Societies of the late imperial period or the contemporary Falun Gong movement.[81]

Finally, we should conclude by mentioning one important aspect of folk reli-gion: the deification of historical figures and their establishment and worship in official pantheons (something that happened to both Laozi and Confucius), which has directly impacted the major traditions. In contemporary China, this process still seems to be in operation, with Mao Zedong (Mao Tse-tung) him-self, perhaps, approaching deification in the manner of many officials of the past. (This writer owns a luck charm, of the type hung from the internal mir-ror of many cars in the Far East, that instead of representing Guanyin or another deit,y holds a portrait of Chairman Mao himself.) Various scholars have noted this tendency to venerate Mao, which perhaps shows the strength and vitality of Chinese folk religion despite the turmoil and modernization of recent years.[82]

GLOSSARY

Ancestor Veneration: In Chinese culture, children owe a debt to those who brought them into this world, as well as to their ancestors. This debt is repaid partly by honor-ing the dead through veneration or worship. In much traditional Chinese thought, it is believed that this service is needed by the dead to be cared for in the afterlife, and that the ancestors grant blessings to those who performed the service—or curse those who neglect them. However, other currents see it simply as veneration and respect.

Dao (**Way**): This term carries many connotations in Chinese thought. Meaning "way" or "path," it can be the route to be followed, as in the *dao* of Confucius—or, more mundanely, a road. In cosmological terms, various Chinese traditions speak of the *dao* as the spiritual principle that underlies everything, often seen as ineffable and mysterious, yet directly known and seen through the operations of nature. It is not exclusively linked to the tradition of Daoism.

Filial Piety: As one of the central principles of Chinese culture, this notion underlies the relations that exist between people, especially family members. Filial piety means that a duty of obedience is owed by the inferior to the superior (i.e., son to father), but there is also a corresponding duty of care and guidance from superior to inferior (i.e., father to son). Its principles guide most relations in traditional Chinese society, including those between families, elder and younger friends, and emperor and minister and subjects.

Qi (**Chi**): Literally translated as "air" or "breath," the concept qi also means much more. In Chinese cosmology, it refers to the fundamental stuff of which the universe is composed. Thus everything—people and nature and gods—is made of qi. It can manifest itself in subtle and gross, pure and impure forms. Much traditional Chinese religious thought is concerned with purifying one's qi through ethical, spiritual, and physical practices, which are not traditionally distinguished in such ways, because all concern qi.

Sanjiao (**The Three Traditions**): In Chinese thought, the Three Traditions are Buddhism, Confucianism, and Daoism, and are often seen to be complementary practices. Combined with folk religion, these traditions form the basis of the cultural-religious matrix of Chinese society.

Tian (**Heaven**): Literally referring to the sky, this Chinese term can also refer to Heaven as an anonymous guiding principle or as personal deity. In this sense, it can be seen as another term for *dao* (Way), although some thinkers distinguish them, with Heaven being seen to accord with the *dao*. In this latter sense, it also forms part of the traditional cosmos of Heaven-Earth-Humanity, the three basic layers of the universe.

NOTES

1. In this article the Pinyin system for rendering Chinese into English will be used, as this is becoming the standard in Chinese studies; but where a term or name is commonly known in a different form, that will be given in parentheses.
2. Tik-sang Liu, "A Nameless But Active Religion: An Anthropologist's View of Local Religion in Hong Kong and Macau," in D. Overmyer, ed. *Religion in China Today* (Cambridge: Cambridge University Press, 2003), p. 67.
3. On the problems and possibility of using the term *religion*, see Paul Hedges, "Defining Religion: A Religious Orientation Typology," *Interreligious Insight*, 4.3–4.4 (2006), 9–15 and 34–42, and "Can We Still Teach "Religions"?: Towards an Understanding of Religion as Culture and Orientation in Contemporary Pedagogy and Metatheory," in G. Durka, L. Gearon, M. de Souza, and K.

Engebretson, eds., *International Handbook for Inter-Religious Education* (New York: Springer Academic Publishers, 2010).

4. For more information on qi, see James Miller, *Daoism: A Short Introduction* (Oxford: Oneworld, 2003), pp. 54–59.

5. For more information on yin and yang and the Five Agents, see Jeaneane Fowler and Merv Fowler, *Chinese Religions: Beliefs and Practices* (Brighton: Sussex Academic Press, 2008), pp. 47–64.

6. See "Sanjiao: The Three Teachings," http://afe.easia.columbia.edu/cosmos/ort/teachings.htm (accessed December 18, 2008).

7. Joseph Adler, *Chinese Religions* (London and New York: Routledge, 2002), pp. 12–13.

8. John H. and Evelyn Nagai Berthrong, *Confucianism,: A Short Introduction* (Oxford: Oneworld, 2000), p. 67.

9. Traditionally believed to be 551–479 BCE, Confucius's exact dates are uncertain—these dates are taken from records that suggest that a Chinese unicorn was seen in 551, which being an auspicious sign, was thought to signify the date of his birth.

10. *Shiji* (*Records of the Historian*, Sima Qian), quoted in Xinzhong Yao, *An Introduction to Confucianism* (Cambridge: Cambridge University Press, 2000), p. 51.

11. See David Burnett, *The Spirit of China: Roots of Faith in 21st Century China* (Oxford: Monarch Books, 2008), pp. 71–73. It should be noted, though, that some scholars see the term *legalism* as an anachronism later applied to a group of related thinkers; see Russell Kirkland, *Taoism: The Enduring Tradition* (London: Routledge, 2004), pp. 77–78.

12. Xunzi, *Hsun Tzu: The Basic Writings*, Burton Watson, trans. (New York: Columbia University Press, 1963), p. 85.

13. Yao, *An Introduction to Confucianism*, pp. 38–47.

14. Yao, *An Introduction to Confucianism*, pp. 34 and 217.

15. Confucius, *Analects of Confucius*, Xin Guanjie, trans. (Beijing: Huayujiaoxuechubanshe, 1994), p. 207 (A12:2).

16. Yao, *An Introduction to Confucianism*, pp. 214–215.

17. For a discussion on Confucian, Daoist, and Buddhist influences on Chinese tea culture, see Wang Ling, *Chinese Tea Culture* (Beijing: Foreign Languages Press, 2000), chapter 4.

18. Indeed, although the great twentieth-century scholar of religion Huston Smith once declared that Islam was the world's most misunderstood religion, I would suggest that he is wrong, and that this misfortune falls to Daoism. See Huston Smith, *The World's Religions: Our Great Wisdom Traditions* (San Francisco: Harper One, 1991), and Russell Kirkland, "The Taoism of the Western Imagination and the Taoism of China: De-Colonizing the Exotic Traditions of the East" (1997), http://kirkland.myweb.uga.edu/rk/pdf/pubs/pres/TENN97.pdf (accessed December 4, 2008).

19. The influence of shamanism on Daoism is disputed by the experts, with Kirkland arguing that there is no connection (Kirkland, *Taoism*, p. 44) and Kohn seeing it as one source; (Livia Kohn, *Introducing Daoism*) (London: Routledge, 2008), pp. 46–47.

20. For an overview of the development of Daoism, see James Miller, *Daoism: A Short Introduction*, 1ff. (This work has been republished as *Daoism: A Beginner's Guide*, 2008). It is worth noting that most introductions to Daoism and Chinese religion, including some cited herein, do not have a sophisticated view of Daoism relying on the old fashioned distinction.

21. Kohn, *Introducing Daoism*, p. 21; for a more critical and complex account, see Kirkland, *Taoism*, pp. 55–64.

22. See Kirkland, *Taoism*, pp. 55–64.

23. Adler, *Chinese Religions*, p. 27.

24. Kohn, *Introducing Daoism*, p. 120.

25. Ibid., pp. 190–191.

26. For more information on Daoist deities, see Yi'e Wang, *Daoism in China: An Introduction* (Warren, CT: Floating Worlds Editions, 2006), Chapter 4.

27. Kohn, *Introducing Daoism*, pp. 142–148, discusses Daoist transformative traditions.

28. Kirkland, *Taoism*, pp. 3ff.

29. Kohn, *Introducing Daoism*, pp. 156–157.

30. Ibid., pp. 164–169; we shall discuss some of these deities in due course.

31. See, for instance, Livia Kohn, *Daoism and Chinese Culture*, 2nd ed. (Cambridge, MA: Three Pines Press, 2004), pp. 64–65, where she notes two differences of Daoist and popular practice in early traditions, one of which is a different class of deities related to spiritual transformation, and another is the rejection of shamanic trances, blood sacrifices, and orgiastic fertility rites.

32. From Sima Xiangru, *Daren Fu (Rhapsody of the Great Man)*, quoted in Kohn, *Introducing Daoism*, p. 46.

33. Kirkland, *Taoism*, 182ff.

34. Kohn, *Daoism and Chinese Culture*, p. 50.

35. Scholars of Daoism disagree among themselves on how far the notion of immortals should be included in discussions of Daoism. For instance, the leading scholar Livia Kohn in her recent introductory work includes considerable discussion of them (e.g., *Introducing Daoism*, pp. 61–64 and 129), calling them an example of "the extreme dimension of Daoist body transformation" (p. 64), whereas Russell Kirkland, another much respected scholar, has said, it is not "specifically tied to practitioners of Taoism" (Kirkland, *Taoism*, p. 184). As a way to understand these disputes, James Miller, another scholar, usefully clarifies that the translation into English as *immortal* is problematic, noting that in Daoism a more sophisticated understanding of the self is sought (see Miller, *Daoism*, pp. 24–25 and 71–73), which is linked to discussion of immortals, but which differs from the popular understanding of this term. However, the understandings of elite Daoist initiates,

ordinary Daoist devotees, and ordinary people must be seen as linked, to some extent at least, to a common discourse around figures revered as immortals.

36. See Fowler and Fowler, *Chinese Religions*, Chapter 8, for more on Ch'an Buddhism.

37. See Fowler and Fowler, *Chinese Religions*, pp. 127–139 on the Pure Land School. For a sympathetic insider account from a Western practitioner, see Caroline Brazier, *The Other Buddhism: Amida Comes West* (Winchester, UK: O Books, 2007).

38. On Guanyin, see Fowler and Fowler, *Chinese Religions*, p. 231; Burnett, *The Spirit of China*, pp. 304–305; and Adler, *Chinese Religions*, pp. 102–103.

39. On popular Chinese deities, see Fowler and Fowler, *Chinese Religions*, pp. 227–238.

40. See C. K. Yang, *Religion in Chinese Society* (Berkeley: University of California Press, 1970), pp. 158–164. A good book, if it can be obtained, on the historical lives of many Chinese deities is Cheng Manchao, *The Origin of Chinese Deities*, D. Chen, Z. Fang, and H. Feng, trans. (Beijing: Foreign Language Press, 1995).

41. For more on the Eight Immortals, see Kohn, *Introducing Daoism*, pp. 167–169, and Fowler and Fowler, *Chinese Religions*, pp. 163–164.

42. See Fowler and Fowler, *Chinese Religions*, pp. 225–226, and Stephen F. Teiser, "Introduction," in Donald S. Lopez, Jr., ed., *Religions of China in Practice* (Princeton, NJ: Princeton University Press, 1996), pp. 21–25. Also available online at http://academic.brooklyn.cuny.edu/core9/phalsall/texts/lopez.html (accessed December 10 2008).

43. Adler, *Chinese Religions*, pp. 117–118.

44. Ibid., 120.

45. Fowler and Fowler, *Chinese Religions*, p. 225 mention this among Alvin Cohen's list of six factors, the first four of which are summed up by our first two factors of reciprocity and harmony.

46. Yang, *Religion in Chinese Society*.

47. Steven Sangren, *History and Magical Power in a Chinese Community* (Stanford, CA: Stanford University Press, 1987).

48. Indeed, one scholar even maintains about thought in the Han and Zhou Dynasties that "Every idea, every pattern of thought, has its genealogy, and . . . can be traced back . . . [to] the Shang" which would then feed into later Chinese tradition. David N. Keightly, "Late Shang Divination: The Magico-Religious Legacy," in *Explorations in Early Chinese Cosmology* (Journal of the American Academy of Religion Studies, vol. 50, no. 2), ed. Henry Rosemont, Jr. (Chicago: Scholars Press, 1984).

49. Adler, *Chinese Religions*, p. 58.

50. See Burnett, *The Spirit of China*, pp. 82–84.

51. Kohn, *Introducing Daoism*, pp. 86–87.

52. Burnett, *The Spirit of China*, pp. 101–103.

53. On the persecution and decline of Buddhism, see Donald W. Mitchell, *Buddhism: Introducing the Buddhist Experience*, 2nd ed. (Oxford: Oxford University Press, 2008), pp. 231–232.

54. On the emergence and development of Neo-Confucianism, see Yao, *An Introduction to Confucianism*, pp. 96–98.

55. For more on Zhu Xi and the Four Books, see Fowler and Fowler, *Chinese Religions*, pp. 177–180.

56. See Adler, *Chinese Religions*, 96–97.

57. For a good coverage of changes in Daoism in this period, but also crossing into folk religion, see Kohn, *Daoism and Chinese Culture*, pp. 171–85. On intermediaries between Daoism and folk religion, see Burnett, *The Spirit of China*, pp. 163–164, where he discusses spirit possession and the rise of the *fashi*, Ritual Masters, during the Song Dynasty.

58. On the situation in recent times, see Adler, *Chinese Religions*, Chapter 6; Fowler and Fowler, *Chinese Religions*, Chapter 10; Burnett, *The Spirit of China*, pp. 344–352; and Kohn, *Daoism and Chinese Culture*, Chapter 11.

59. See "The Twenty-four Paragons of Filial Respect: Their Stories & Verses In Praise," Dharma Master Heng Sure, trans., http://www2.kenyon.edu/ Depts/Religion/Fac/Adler/Reln270/24-filial2.htm#Preface (accessed December 10, 2008).

60. On the practice of ancestor veneration and the afterlife, see Adler, *Chinese Religions*, pp. 18–19 and 215–217.

61. It has been suggested that the religious revival happening at the moment is different in villages and cities. Lizhu Fan has suggested that the villages have a more communal notion of folk religion, and the cities a more privatized spirituality ("Popular Religion in Contemporary China," *Social Compass*, 50 (2003), pp. 449–457 and 456); therefore, we should not be surprised to see other differences.

62. The control and classification of religion in China today is still the object of much contention. See Fowler and Fowler, *Chinese Religions*, pp. 251–253; Burnett, *The Spirit of China*, pp. 290–291, 300–304, and 336–339; and Stephen Feuchtwang and Wang Ming-ming, "The Politics of Culture or a Contest of Histories: Representations of Chinese Popular Religion," *Dialectical Anthropology*, 16 (1991), pp. 251–272.

63. Yang, *Religion in Chinese Society*, pp. 82–86. For temple fairs in old Beijing, see http://www.chinaculture.org/gb/en_chinaway/2006-02/23/content _79634.htm (accessed January 20, 2009).

64. Kenneth Dean, "Local Communal Religion in Contemporary South-east China," in *Religion in China Today* (The China Quarterly Special Issues New Series, no. 3), ed. Daniel L. Overmyer (Cambridge: Cambridge University Press, 2003).

65. See Fowler and Fowler, *Chinese Religions*, p. 242. For a fuller description of Chinese temples, see Laurence Thompson, *Chinese Religion: An Introduction*, 4th ed. (Belmont, CA: Wadsworth, 1989), pp. 68–74.

66. For more on these deities, see Wang, *Daoism in China*, pp. 90–92 and Manchao, *The Origin of Chinese Deities*, pp. 53–58 and 148–155.

67. On various legends surrounding them, see http://www.chinaculture.org/gb/en _chinaway/2004-06/11/content_47393.htm (accessed January 20, 2009).

68. But see Berthrong and Berthrong, *Confucianism*, pp. 68–69 and 73–74 on the role of women.
69. Glen Dudbridge, *The Legend of Miaoshan*, rev. ed. (Oxford: Oxford University Press, 2004).
70. Lizhu Fan, "The Cult of the Silkworm Mother as a Core of Local Community Religion in a North China Village: Field Study in Zhiwuying, Baoding, Hebei," in Overmyer, ed., *Religion in China Today* (Cambridge: Cambridge University Press, 2003).
71. Yang, *Religion in Chinese Society*, pp. 84–85.
72. Kohn, *Daoism and Chinese Culture*, pp. 193–198, and Fowler and Fowler, *Chinese Religions*, pp. 63–64.
73. Kohn, *Daoism and Chinese Culture*, pp. 174–178 and 191–196.
74. Kohn, *Daoism and Chinese Culture*, pp. 196–198, and Burnett, *The Spirit of China*, pp. 306–312.
75. See "Yi Ching I Ching," available at http://acc6.its.brooklyn.cuny.edu/~phalsall/texts/iching.txt (accessed December 18, 2008).
76. Yang, *Religion in Chinese Society*, pp. 250–253.
77. These existed as stories and songs in the oral tradition, but many were written down, particularly in the Qing Dynasty.
78. One of the best known collections was put together by a man called Pu Songling (1640–1715); it is entitled *Strange Tales from Make-Do Studio*, Dennis C. Mair and Victor H. Mair, trans. (Beijing: Foreign Language Press, 1996).
79. Fowler and Fowler, *Chinese Religions*, pp. 260–265.
80. See Kohn, *Daoism and Chinese Culture*, pp. 68 and 101. As Kohn notes, and in contradistinction to many texts, the Yellow Turbans and nearly all later religious rebellions were not Daoist, a position erroneously held in such texts as Fowler and Fowler, *Chinese Religions*, and Burnett, *The Spirit of China*. The term Yellow Turban comes from the yellow headscarves worn by members of the rebellion, based on the Five Agents theory, whereby the Han Dynasty—seen as the fire phase and represented by the color red—was due to be superseded by the earth phase, represented by yellow, the color they wore as a sign of this cosmological-political change.
81. Burnett, *The Spirit of China*, pp. 227–232.
82. See Fowler and Fowler, *Chinese Religions*, p. 113, 253.

BIBLIOGRAPHY

These readings are provided as accessible sources of information; however, some are better or worse on particular aspects of Chinese thought. Both Fowler and Burnett provide outdated discussions on Daoism, using the discredited religious versus philosophical distinction, but they offer excellent general summaries of popular practices and other aspects of Chinese religion.

Adler, Joseph. *Chinese Religion*. London and New York: Routledge, 2002.

Berthrong, John H., and Evelyn Nagai Berthrong. *Confucianism: A Short Introduction*. Oxford: Oneworld, 2000.

Burnett, David. *The Spirit of China: Roots of Faith in 21st Century China*. Oxford: Monarch Books, 2008.

Cohen, Myron L., and Stephen F. Teiser. "Living in the Chinese Cosmos: Understanding Religion in Late Imperial China (1644–1911)." http://afe.easia.columbia.edu/cosmos/index.html (accessed December 10, 2008).

Fowler, Jeaneane, and Merv Fowler. *Chinese Religions: Beliefs and Practices*. Brighton: Sussex Academic Press, 2008.

Kohn, Livia. *Daoism and Chinese Culture*. 2nd ed. Cambridge, MA: Three Pines Press, 2004.

———. *Introducing Daoism*. London: Routledge, 2008.

Littlejohn, Ronnie L. *Daoism: An Introduction*. London and New York: I.B. Tauris, 2009.

Teiser, Stephen F. "The Spirits of Chinese Religion." http://academic.brooklyn.cuny.edu/core9/phalsall/texts/lopez.html (accessed December 18, 2008). This is an online version of a printed work: "Introduction," in Donald S. Lopez, Jr., ed. *Religions of China in Practice*. Princeton, NJ: Princeton University Press, 1996.

Yang, C. K. *Religion in Chinese Society*. Berkeley: University of California Press, 1970.

Yao, Xinzhong. *An Introduction to Confucianism*. Cambridge: Cambridge University Press, 2000.

Chapter 3

South Asia

Kerry San Chirico

INTRODUCTION

Writing about religion in practice in South Asia is an endeavor wrought with
peril. On the one hand, one runs the risk of oversimplification, turning untidy
phenomena into something inauthentically clear and circumscribable—and, as
we will see, religion in the practice of daily life in South Asia is anything but tidy.
On the other hand, one risks mystification, explicating beliefs and practices that
to the outsider may appear exotic, strange, even titillating, but to the neglect of
other aspects that are common and seemingly uninteresting—and religion is as
much about the mundane and pragmatic as it is about the transcendent. At the
heart of both dangers—oversimplification and mystification—is the issue of
representation. Conveying to the reader a sense of lived religions on the ground
in South Asia forces one to pick and choose—and this must be kept in mind by
the discriminating reader in the pages ahead. Discrimination (*viveka*) plays a significant role in Hindu philosophy; it is the means through which one determines
truth from falsehood, the impermanent from the eternal, and the very categories
for ordering and interpreting the world. Likewise, discrimination must be
employed while reading this essay. When a camera focuses on one image, or creates an image through its lens, it does so to the exclusion of a much broader field
of vision.

In the pages that follow, with a few exceptions, I will focus this study on
what I argue is a representative location: the area of the northern Indian state
of Uttar Pradesh that includes the ancient city of Varanasi, and that spans out
like so many spokes of a wheel to include hundreds of villages, temples,

mosques, and churches over the roughly 100 square kilometers that constitute the Banaras region. Almost halfway between New Delhi and Kolkata (Calcutta), the region is considered by many to be the center of Hindu civilization. This may be a bit of northern Indian hyperbole, because in fact there are many Hindu sacred centers throughout the Subcontinent. Nevertheless, the overstatement is not without some justification. As one of the most ancient cities in the world, it is referred to again and again in literature dating back to antiquity. Located on the western bank of the river *Ganga* (Ganges), the city rests on a plateau at the intersection of the Varuna river to the north, and the Assi river to the south. Ancient scriptures speak of Varanasi as Kāśī (the luminous), as the city of the iconoclastic god Śiva, as the place of the world's origin, as the world in microcosm, and as the pivot point between heaven and earth. As a *tīrtha*, a ford or crossing place between worlds, Varanasi has long been a destination for pilgrims seeking liberation or enlightenment. As the Sanskrit proverb famously proclaims, *Kashyam marnam mukti* [death in Kāśī is liberation]. Yet paeans to Kāśī make more than otherworldly claims; they also promise boons in this world, whether it be prosperity or the cleansing of heinous sins.

Through the centuries, numerous kings and saffron-clad renunciants, saints both male and female, and millions of unknown seekers have lived and died here. It is here in the fifth century BCE that Siddhartha Gautama, the Buddha, preached his first sermon. Like Jerusalem hundreds of miles west, the air is thick with piety and performance, with desire and longing for an encounter and transaction with the Divine and divinities and the Self. Like

People bathing in the Ganga (Ganges) River in Varanasi, India. The river is a holy place for all Hindus, as is the city born on its banks more than 2,500 years ago. (Photos.com.)

a geologist scanning the exposed layers of sediment at the Grand Canyon, the careful observer may spy the shifting layers of belief and practice as she moves between temples, mosques, and shrines while negotiating the city's narrow, cobbled alleyways. Here, a temple to Lord Ram and a priest interpreting the great epic *Rāmāyaṇa* on the banks of the holy river; there, the consecration of an aniconic statue (lingam) of Śiva; here, a procession of 10 men carrying a funeral bier, shouting slogans (*Rām nām satya hai*, "Ram's name is truth") as they approach one of many cremation grounds; there, a Muslim merchant sells Banarsi silk fabrics under the watchful gaze of a Sufi saint and a suspicious Hindu majority; here, a ubiquitous Bollywood film star proclaims the joys of Pepsi consumption above a tea stall; there, a cow blocks the path of an auto-rickshaw trying to take European tourists to their hotel; and now here, an unassuming middle-aged woman slowly makes her way down the steps to Assi Ghāṭ as the hazy eastern light begins to spread across the *Ganga*.

TIMELINE

2500 BCE:	Flourishing of the Indus Valley civilization.
1500 BCE:	Early Vedic hymns composed.
800 BCE:	Birth of Kāśī (also known as Varanasi and Banaras).
600 BCE:	Rise of ascetical alternatives to Vedism, such as what is now identified as Jainism.
c. 480–370 BCE:	Life of Siddhartha Gautama, the Buddha.
267–234 BCE:	Reign of Buddhist emperor Aśoka.
200 BCE:	Emergence of synthesis now designated Brahminical Hinduism.
50–52 CE:	St. Thomas arrives in Kodungallur, in Kerala.
300s:	Rise of tantra.
345:	Arrival of Thomas of Cana/Jerusalem and other Syrian Christians in Kerala.
500s:	Rise of Hindu bhakti or "devotionalism" in Tamil Nadu.
700s:	Arab-speaking Muslim traders arrive on the Malabar coast of Kerala.
c. 997:	Turko-Persian Mahmud of Ghazni (d. 1030) begins invasions of northwestern India, that is, Gujarat and Sindh.
1192:	Delhi Sultanate begins with Mamluk, or "Slave," Sultans.
1498:	First Portuguese *feitoria*, or "trading station," established on Malabar coast of Kerala. Goa founded.

1500s:	Kabīr and Tulsī Dās in Varanasi.
1526:	Mughal Empire begins with Babar's victory over the Delhi sultan at Panipat, northwest of Delhi.
1556–1605:	Reign of Mughal emperor Akbar.
1612:	British East India Company defeats the Portuguese, winning trading concessions from the Mughal emperor.
1706:	The first Protestant missionaries, the German Pietist Lutherans Heinrich Plutschau and Bartholomaeus Ziegenbalg, arrive in Tranquebar in Tamil Nadu for the Danish-Halle Mission.
1757:	British victory at the Battle of Plassey (Palashi, Bengal) against the nawab of Bengal—the commonly assigned beginning of British rule in India.
1857:	Indian Mutiny against the British East India Company. The British Crown takes full control of the Company. The last Mughal, Bahadur Shah II, is deposed by the British in Delhi.
1885:	Founding of the Indian National Congress in Bombay.
1906:	Creation of the All-India Muslim League in Dhaka.
1947:	Independence of both East and West Pakistan and India.
1948:	Independence of Sri Lanka.
1971:	After a nine-month "war of liberation" against West Pakistan, East Pakistan gains its independence as Bangladesh.

HINDU TRADITIONS

Sushila Devi is like so many Indian village women. She is semiliterate, having attended a government-funded Hindi medium school through class eight. Married at age 17, she bore her first child, a daughter, one year later. Her husband—Prem Kumar, a fellow member of a low-caste agriculturalist subcaste (or *jātī*)—was 25 when they married. Two more children followed, a boy, then a girl. Typhoid claimed the life of their second daughter in 1983. Thankfully, suitable spouses were found for the children less than two decades later. Sushila Devi was 39 years old when her first grandchild was born. Prem Kumar died four years later in a city health clinic. Now a widow, Sushila lives with her son's family in a village four miles west of the city. She may be in her late forties, but to Western eyes she looks more like 60 years old. Village life waxes and wanes for Sushila and her family. As farmers they depend on the annual monsoon for their livelihood, so to supplement their income they are involved in the famous Banarsi textile industry. Electricity was introduced in the village in 1973, but it comes and goes because demand exceeds supply. As Varanasi sees its first Western-style air-conditioned mall rise less than a mile from the river, nearby villagers still build houses made mostly of mud and thatch. And yet, perhaps surprisingly, many of these houses have television. The garble of serpentine wires running into the mostly mud village homes — not to mention the glossy, opulent images on the TV screen — evoke the contradictions of words such as *modern, poverty,* and *globalization,* and the unrealized promises of India's 1947 independence from the much compromised British Empire.

On this Tuesday, Sushila is eager to do *pūjā* (worship) at Assi Ghāṭ.[1] There are some 84 ghāṭs lining the western banks of the *Ganga* at Varanasi, aligned south to north like buttons on the placket of a dress shirt. Assi Ghāṭ is the southernmost one. It is certainly not as elaborate as the other ghāṭs, but for centuries it has been an important pilgrimage site. Steep stone steps lead down to a wide terrace. There, on a raised wooden platform, a *ghāṭiyā* (ritual priest) sits under a leaf umbrella, ready to mediate oblations — oblations that priest and adherent will prepare out of fruits, flowers, and sandalwood. Bathers stand in the water just a foot away, facing the rising eastern sun, methodically (and somewhat awkwardly) cleaning and cleansing themselves so as not to expose their nude bodies. Little children, who join their parents in the muddy bank, show less concern for propriety. Other men stand further out. With chai-colored water to their waists and hands cupped in front of their chests, they offer their morning prayers to the sun, undisturbed by the many wooden boats gliding along the river's banks and weighed down with a bounty of out-of-place tourists. Sushila has bathed in this goddess, *Ganga,* hundreds of times in her life. This morning, however, she is eager to make her way to the nearby *pīpal* tree, where other women have already begun their *pūjā.*

The leafy, green "holy fig" tree is no less than 200 years old and stands 30 feet tall. An elevated stone base, some 10 feet in diameter, creates a circular border around the *pīpal's* sinuous trunk. Around it are tied hundreds of red and white strings. At the base of the *pīpal* is a Śiva lingam, arguably the focal point of worship here at Assi Ghāṭ. Next to it is a five-foot tall rectangular shrine occupied by the divine monkey Hanumān, who is in orange bas-relief. Just to the right of Hanumān's shrine are four six-inch-high stones, dappled with red and orange vermilion. On the other side of the tree are no less than 13 more Śiva lingams, wet with *Ganga* water and spackled with vermilion. Finally, not to be left out, facing northwest is a microwave-oven–sized shrine to the goddess Durgā. With her multiple arms yet placid face, she sits astride a tiger armed with Śiva's *trīsul* (trident), ready to slay the evil buffalo-demon Mahiṣāsura — and those pitted against her devotees.

Sushila begins by removing her sandals, symbolically removing the dirt of the profane world as she moves into this sacred zone of the *pīpal* tree. With neither fanfare nor self-consciousness, she circumambulates the tree in the auspicious clockwise direction eight times, demarcating both space and time—pausing only to let young goats out of her way. Then one after another, she removes the implements of worship from her plastic bag—the red and orange vermilion for anointing the sacred images, the brass urn filled with *Ganga* water, incense, the fresh·flowers, and the sandalwood paste—like a doctor making a house call or a plumber removing tools from a toolbox. Each statue has its respective means of worship, and Sushila attends to them with care, as one would tend to a loved one. She first attends to Śiva, anointing the stone lingam with *camelī* flowers and holy water from the *Ganga*. The white flowers fall from her hands to rest on the cylindrical stone; the holy water douses the lingam, runs down into the *yonī*—the flat base representing the feminine divine principle—and into the ground. Then she attends to the other 13 smaller lingams. Next, she turns her attention to Hanumān-ji, devotee of Ram, protector of devotees, and healer of illness. She anoints those small stone images with vermilion before attending to Durgā, whom she also anoints. Most of these practices are done silently. Occasionally, one can see Sushila's lips moving, or perceive a look of longing. This entire ritual will take half an hour.

What is Sushila doing and why is she doing it? Having encountered a fairly typical scene in South Asia, we must now interpret it. To understand Sushila's activity and the context in which it occurs, some useful interpretive categories will be introduced. But first we must examine something even more basic, the meaning of *Hindu* and *Hinduism*.

Sushila is a Hindu, a word derived from the Indo-Aryan word for sea, *sindhu*, applied to the Indus river found in modern-day Pakistan. Persians borrowed and modified this designation, referring to *Hind* as the land of the Indus Valley. Greek and Latin speakers adapted the word further, employing it geographically to refer to all the unknown lands east of the Indus. *India* was thus born. When Islam came to the Subcontinent in the seventh century, *Hindu* was used to refer to the region's native peoples, and more specifically to those who did not convert to Islam. Thus we have the first use of the term to represent religious beliefs and practices. Note that this is a kind of negative definition. Still, *Hindu* as a self-designation would not be used until the nineteenth and twentieth centuries.

And what of Hindu-*ism*? One may be surprised to learn that the first use of the word in the English language did not occur until 1829.[2] Again, as with Muslims centuries earlier, the term was employed by the British to convey those beliefs and practices that appeared to be *not* Buddhism, Jainism, Islam, or Christianity. European philosophical, religious, and political trends played their part. By the post-Enlightenment colonial period, the term *religion* had come to be understood as a generic category; its many species were deemed "world religions."[3] By the end of the nineteenth century, Indians and non-Indians alike took for granted that Hinduism amounted to such a unified system. But is it? If we are to call Hinduism a religion, it is important that we understand how it is so. Richard H. Davis offers the following oft-mentioned observation:

> Hinduism does not share many of the integrating characteristics of other religious traditions we conventionally label "world religions." Hinduism has no founding figure such as the Buddha Śākyamuni, Jesus of Nazareth, or Muhammad. It has no single text that can serve as a doctrinal point of reference, such as the Bibles of the Judaic and Christian traditions, the Islamic Qur'ān, or the Ādi Granth of the Sikhs. Hinduism has no single overarching institutional or ecclesial hierarchy capable of deciding questions of religious boundary or formulating standards of doctrine and practice.[4]

Davis does not argue against Hinduism as a religion per se; his point is that the historical process by which Hinduism came to be understood as a unitary system is different from those of the aforementioned traditions.[5] Yet, questions remain. What exactly constitutes the system? What is essential to Hinduism? Who determines what is Hindu and what is not? Davis offers two helpful categories for understanding the answers to these questions. According to this scholar, there are two contrasting views, the "centralist" and "pluralist."[6]

> Centralists identify a single, pan-Indian, more or less hegemonic, orthodox tradition, transmitted primarily in Sanskrit language, chiefly by members of the brahmanic class. The traditions centers around a Vedic lineage of texts, in which are included not only the Vedas themselves, but also the Mīmamsā, Dharmaśās-tra, and Vedānta corpuses of texts and teachings. Vedic sacrifice is the privileged mode of ritual conduct, the template for all subsequent Indian ritualism. Various groups employing vernacular languages in preference to Sanskrit, questioning the caste order, and rejecting the authority of the Vedas, may periodically rebel against this center, but the orthodox, through an adept use of inclusion and repressive tolerance, manage to hold the high ground of religious authority.[7]

Up until very recently, this centralist view held sway and was reflected in most introductory Hinduism courses offered to undergraduates. It should be noted that such a view resembles, if not quite reduplicates, the self-understanding of the Brahminic class members mentioned above—that is, the priestly caste members who for centuries have understood themselves to be South Asia's religio-cultural brokers. These are the region's religious elites, and in the history of Western scholarship on South Asia, their views have long been taken as authoritative.

The pluralists are not so credulous, however. The vast array of different and often contradictory beliefs and practices compel them to argue that there is no normative Hinduism, but a collection of diverse ideas and practices existing both alongside and in interaction with one another in South Asia. This view is expressed by J. A. B. Van Buitenen as follows:

> In principle, Hinduism incorporates all forms of belief and worship without necessitating the selection or elimination of any. The Hindu is inclined to revere the divinity in every manifestation, whatever it may be, and is doctrinally tolerant. . . . Hinduism is, then, both a civilization and a conglomeration of religions, with neither a beginning, a founder, nor a central authority, hierarchy, or organization.[8]

Therefore, to return to our questions, the pluralist argues that Hinduism has no center, no authority, and certainly no essence. It is like a sponge that absorbs a multitude of practices, doctrines, and sects, or a banyan tree in which an original core is indistinguishable from later growth.[9] The pluralist view has led some to use the word *Hinduisms* to reflect religious diversity.

As is often the case, there is truth to both centralist and pluralist views. On the one hand, there does exist a strong Sanskritic, Brahminical, "classical" strand that understands the ancient Vedic scriptures to be (somehow) authoritative as the transcendent and super- or extra-human knowledge. On the other hand, contrary to the views of Brahmin elites, there are other forms that do not valorize the Veda, Sanskritic literature, or the "translocal" deities of Hinduism's upper castes. The sheer number of such traditions, as well as a secular scholar's a priori rejection of any tradition's exclusive claims to orthodoxy, prohibits one from dismissing them as mere aberrations from a norm. We are thus left with Van Buitenen's "conglomeration of religions," rather than a single tradition with a center and periphery.[10] In an essay dedicated to religion on the ground, however, it is more important to understand the religious phenomena we are encountering than to adopt one view over another. For our purposes, we need know that these issues exist, and more importantly, that the very word we use to describe the dominant religion of South Asia has a particular and contentious history.

If Hinduism (or Hinduism*s*) is a result of the ages, as Mohandas K. Gandhi once argued (and is the view of this chapter), then the categories of *popular* and *brahminical* Hinduism may be of some interpretive service for a field so vast. We shall see the interweaving of both strands in Sushila's practices at Assi

Ghāṭ. We may also find the terms *transcendental* and *pragmatic religion* helpful. Each shall be discussed in turn.

Popular Hinduism, a term used by David Gordon White, includes those Hindu traditions that are generally nontextual and whose data is transmitted orally, visually, and gesturally.[11] Orally, popular Hinduism is transmitted by way of songs, sayings, spells, and possession; visually, through various types of imagery; and gesturally, through ritual observances. Popular Hinduism's principal practices include venerating superhuman entities by attempting to communicate with and feeding such deities through "ritual divination techniques" and "controlled or uncontrolled possession."[12] Such entities have their locus in domestic space or in a particular *sthāna* (place), the site where said beings manifested themselves—for example, in a field, at a tree, or in the jungle. Every village has its own deity or *grāmadevata*.

> Every house, every street, all of the shops, the craft studios, the barns, the farms, the trees and bushes, the wells, the reservoirs and streams, the inhabitants (people, animals, and insects), the spirits of those who have lived and died there, and even the activities, thoughts, and emotions of everyone living there—all are part of one great spirit identified as a deity, a gramadevata. This deity is the community, just as the community is the deity. They are inseparable.[13]

Worship of such beings is generally minimalist: a shrine may consist of a slab and a simple stone or terra-cotta image beneath a tree, or the tree itself may be the object of worship.[14] With time, a multiplicity of deities may find their way to the *sthāna*, suggesting the familial nature of popular Hinduism. As White explains, "the deities of popular Hinduism are, before all else, multiple, veritable hordes of supernatural entities that often belong to families, clans, or lineages whose kinship structures are patterned after those of human society."[15] The *grāmadevatās* are themselves referred to in intimate, familiar terms such as *mām* (mom) or *bābā* (father) in the Banaras region. Likewise, each household has its own *kuladevatā*, the deity of the family, and each Hindu has his or her own *istadevatā*, the deity of personal choice. Sushila's chosen deity is Hanumān. There is then a "great chain of being" manifested by popular Hinduism, from the living to the dead, the auspicious to the ominous, and the divine to the demonic.[16]

One's relation to these beings varies, as would one's relationship to a mother or father, a crazy aunt, or a baby sister. Some may be shown genuine adoration, but many more are simply propitiated so as to avoid disturbances or harm. In the village, the *grāmadevatās* are daily venerated for protection, but they are also sought after for successful childbirth, good harvest, or at the laying of a cornerstone. Just as one would exchange goods to procure a specific end, such transactions between human and superhuman beings is a modus operandi of popular Hinduism. "The goal is rather one of manipulation, control, or coercion, and it is the ritual efficacy of the sacrificial offering with its attendant mantras—or simply the fact of satiating the hunger of the object of worship with a gift of often non-vegetarian food."[17]

All these activities may be placed under the "practical religion" rubric, concerned as they are with activities that revolve around a single motivation: the maintenance of life on the individual, familial, and village levels. But there is another, perhaps preeminent, concern of religion: reconciliation with death. Here our attention turns to Brahminical Hinduism and its transcendental function.

The designation *Brahminical Hinduism*[18] reflects a Hindu religious stream that has been, for thousands of years, developed, passed down, and mediated by the highest social category of priests and scholars in Hindu South Asia, the Brahmins. These are the ritual specialists hailing from hereditary endogamous groups accorded prestige for their station and vocation. Their technical language is Sanskrit, meaning refined or perfected; their scope is the entire Indian Subcontinent and now the world; and their domain is the temple. They live at the hierarchical apex in relation to the other major classes—in order of rank, *ksatryas* (warriors), *vaisyas* (merchants), *sudras* (laborers), and *dalits* (once called Untouchables)—as well as the thousands of *jātīs* (subcastes), often placed under these larger *varna* (class) groupings. Whereas popular Hinduism is described as oral, vernacular, polytheistic, local, and pragmatic, Brahminical Hinduism is largely textual, Sanskritic, theistic, translocal, and transcendental. The Brahminical worldview has been transmitted primarily through texts, usually Sanskrit texts, for thousands of years. The Vedas, understood to have been literally cognized by ancient seers and passed on to hereditary Brahmin clans, represents the authoritative core or charter for all subsequent authoritative scriptures. In history, these Vedic scriptures were then followed by high-caste expounders who conveyed their teachings orally and textually, leading to the development of Hindu philosophical and theological systems— and to heterodox teachers such as the sixth-century-BCE luminaries Buddha (Buddhism) and Mahavira (Jainism), who rejected the Brahminical worldview and its orthodoxies, which in turn led to further Brahminical development.

The gods of the Brahmins are high gods—such as Visnu, Śiva, and Devī, the Great Goddess—whose stories were enshrined by 700 CE in Sanskrit scripture, epic literature, and the genre of texts known as *Purānas* (ancient stories). They are worshipped in temples generally frequented by high- and low-status Hindus. Such deities are understood to be universal and translocal; other deities simply represent manifestations of the One.[19] Brahminical rites and ceremonies are conducted regularly and cyclically, and considered necessary to uphold both the cosmos and the social system. In all these respects, Brahminical Hinduism tends toward the universal and the universalizing. As such, it reflects the transcendental aspect of religion, whose purview is the concerns of humanity, including of course that which is arguably humanity's central concern: reconciliation with death. In the Brahminical Hindu context this means that great attention is paid to liberation from the cycle of rebirth; union with the divine; and the rites, practices, and meditative techniques that lead to various forms of *moksa* (liberation, salvation). Note the difference of location, scope, and practice of Brahminical Hinduism when it is compared to the more pragmatic popular Hinduism.

Both popular Hinduism and Brahminical Hinduism live in a complementary relationship, reinforcing each other in their differing spheres of influence. Despite the use of the term *Brahminical*, one should not think that the upper castes abstain from engagement in popular and pragmatic activities. Every Hindu will venerate a popular god of childbirth from preparturition until six days after childbirth; every Hindu will attend to the cult of the ancestors; and a high-caste Hindu will visit a local religious specialist in times of adversity to propitiate a hungry or angry supernatural being.[20]

Prior to returning to Assi Ghāṭ and Sushila Devi, there is one final topic to discuss, another element uniting not just high- and low-status Hindus, and popular and Brahminical Hinduism, but arguably all the religions of South Asia.[21] This is bhakti, commonly translated as devotion or intense sharing. Unfortunately, these terms fail to adequately evoke bhakti's full sense. The word itself is derived from the Sanskrit verbal root *bhaj*, meaning to divide and share, as one does a sacrificial offering. Bhaj can also denote enjoyment, as of food or music; waiting on someone, as a servant attends a king; making love, in a corporeal sense; or adoring, in a more spiritual manner.[22] All these meanings shade into what an Indian understands as bhakti, which can be identified by certain key characteristics: worship as a personal relationship with the divine in a communal setting; the supreme importance of a teacher or guru; the valorization of the regional and regional dialect over Sanskrit; and acts of asceticism, pilgrimage, drama, and recitation. This ubiquitous form of piety dates to at least sixth-century CE southern India. Over the centuries, bhakti slowly spread south to north, west to east, with peripatetic saints circumscribing and thereby hallowing South Asia anew. Speaking of the early bhakti saints, A. K. Ramanujan once explained that "they literally sang places into existence."[23] In those places already hallowed—places such as Varanasi—new devotional associations simply deepened the significance and singularity of the place. These saints also stressed the experience of God over slavish loyalty to Hindu practice or doctrine. As such, bhakti has long contained an element of social protest, even as different poet-saints and the sects they inspired have had different attitudes toward the relationship of the individual to society.

Arguably, the intent for most devotees throughout the centuries has *not* been total absorption into the Ultimate, Brahman, or the *ātman-brāhman* identification of nondualist *moksa* (liberation, salvation), but a unity-in-difference as of the lover-beloved, an eternal embrace between *devatā* and *bhakta* (devotee and deity), as these verses in Jayadeva's *Gītagovinda* exemplify: "Two lovers meeting in darkness . . ./And claw as desire rises to dizzying heights of love."[24] Evident here is the eroticism of much bhakti poetry, elaborated to an extent that makes the *Song of Solomon* appear tame by comparison. With rare exception, audiences have embraced the eroticism of such poetry. The relationship between Radha and Krishna has long been understood as an allegory of the human soul's love for God.

Varanasi was not immune from the radical raptures of bhakti. In fifteenth-century Varanasi, a time of antagonism between Muslim and Hindu, the iconoclastic weaver Kabīr rejected the organized religion and religiosity of Kāśī, his home. He taunted religious specialists for their inability to see past their particular theologies toward the God who is beyond all characterizations. A century later, the great Vaisnava (devotee of Visnu) poet Tulsī Dās rendered Vālmīki's Sanskrit tale of Lord Ram into Hindi, creating the *Rāmcaritmānas*, thereby drawing the unlettered masses into greater devotion to Lord Ram, the goddess Sītā, and the pantheon of other divine characters found in the epic. Devotion to Hanumān in northern India can be attributed to Tulsī's Hindi masterpiece. As it happens in this gods-saturated city, just a few yards from Assi Ghāt sits Tulsī's home. A Hanumān shrine, said to have been built by the poet, can be found in the house, along with Tulsī's wooden sandals. Hanumān (respectfully addressed as "Hanumān-ji") is one of the most popular deities in northern India; in Varanasi there may now be more temples to him than to Lord Ram. This makes sense, because Hanumān is a type of divine middleman, a go-between for those who may be intimidated by the perfection of Ram.

When we last left Sushila Devi she was standing before the divine monkey—or more accurately, the god in monkey form. But we did not know that when she awoke at 5 AM this Tuesday morning, she immediately went to her *pūjā ghar* (home shrine), performed *āratī*,[25] and began reciting the Hanumān *calīsa*, forty verses of praise to Lord Hanumān from Tulsī Dās's *Rāmāyana*:

> Oh Hanumān-ji, whoever is mindful of You is granted the fruit of eternal life . . . Oh Hanumān-ji, You hold the essence of Rama, always remaining his servant . . . Oh Hanumān-ji, You end the sufferings and remove all the pain from those who remember You. Hail-Hail-Hail Lord Hanumān-ji. I beseech you to grant me grace as my Divine Guru.

Tuesdays and Saturdays are generally dedicated to Hanumān on the Hindu calendar. In the *Rāmāyaṇa*, Hanumān is both Ram's military general and his most dedicated devotee, the one who leaps across the sea to Lanka to save Sītā from the evil demon king, Rāvana. On Tuesdays and Saturdays, Sushila makes a special effort to travel into Kāśī to render devotion to the monkey god, either here at Assi or, more often, at the nearby Sankat Mochan Temple.

In our discussion of popular Hinduism, we examined the reciprocity existing between Hindu and deity in daily life. The reader may recall the words *manipulation*, *control*, and *coercion* used to describe this relationship. Lest this description appear too cynical, we should perhaps now balance it. For indeed, it is often difficult to tell the difference between worship *with* devotion and worship *without* it, just as it is difficult to separate pragmatic and transcendental concerns from religious practice.[26] In fact, such a framing may betray the bias of those whose pragmatic concerns are generally fulfilled without recourse to divine beings. In the case of the poor, who can take nothing for granted, there is no such option. Suffice to say, when Sushila Devi worships Hanumān, she does so because of her love for him, *and* also because it is believed that his worship grants certain boons. Hence, both worldly and otherworldly concerns go hand in hand. And because in her life many boons have been granted, her love for Hanumān grows. This circular process draws her ever more deeply into a living relationship with her chosen god. When things do not go well—when prayers go unanswered, as when Sushila's young daughter died—an age-old opportunity for further reflection on the nature of the relationship between deity, universe, and devotee arises.

So today, as Sushila worships Hanumān at Assi, she also makes some requests. Her granddaughter is taking an exam, the type that will determine whether or not she will go to college. Mahavir, another name for Hanumān, is after all the patron deity not just of wrestlers but also of grammarians and students. Sushila makes this special request for academic success, reminding Hanumān, the divine middle-monkey, of her supreme devotion, while standing before his vermilion statue, then while daubing those small stones—also associated with Hanumān—with vermilion powder. As she stands before the large orange stone statue with hymns of the *calīsā* on her lips, something significant takes place—that is, *darśan*, the act of seeing and being seen by the deity. To gaze into the eyes of the divine is to absorb the divine light, to touch and be touched, resulting in nothing less than the brief union of human and divine and the reception of divine power and grace.

This en-graced power, or empowered grace, literally saturates Assi Ghāṭ. The Śiva linga, the stone aniconic symbol of the deity, is manifested in no less than 20 separate statues at the Assi *pīpal* tree, and is the putative center of worship in Assi and more broadly in Kāśī, "the luminous." Varanasi is Śiva's city, we must recall. This paradoxical deity is the Supreme Ascetic, but also the lord of erotic powers. He is the renouncer dwelling in cremation grounds, the transgressor of moral and social codes, and the fierce destroyer of the cosmos. But he is also a family man, husband to the goddess Pārvati and father to Ganeś and Skanda. Thanks to Tulsī Dās's synthetic vision of Śaivism and Vaisnavism, today in Varanasi Śiva is known as both the Father of the Universe *and* as Ram's archetypal devotee. In Tulsī's *Ramāyana*, we discover that Hanumān's true identity is . . . Śiva![27] Hence, to worship Hanumān as Sushila does, is to worship Śiva, Visnu, and the multiplicity of deities who are local manifestations of Hinduism's great celestial deities in a wholly approachable form. And because the Goddess is understood to be independent of both male deities and their divine partners, any worship of Śiva or Visnu redounds to the female partner. So when Sushila attends to that small shrine of Durgā under the *pīpal*, she does so with a sense of her fierce power not only as the demon slayer but also as *Śakti*, the divine principle animating the universe and giving all male deities their power. In the end, there is no place where the divine is not somehow present or cannot be made present. Ultimately, in Varanasi all stones and pebbles are said to be Śiva. We are brought finally to an understanding of why, amid the oft-purported existence of 330 million Hindu deities, Hindus might also agree that, in the end, there is just One.

Sushila Devi returns to her village by way of a *Tempo*, an awkward, three-wheeled platypus of a vehicle with a loud lawn-mower engine that commonly connects village to city throughout India. Arriving back at her home, Sushila Devi finds her family still asleep. Her grandson stirs on the mat as she hunches over the home fire to boil water for chai. Hanumān's name—and Ram's, by extension—is still on her lips. It is only 7 AM.

ISLAM

As we wend our way north from Assi, first through the thin *galīs* (street lanes), then to the main street linking the old city like an artery, we soon find ourselves in a new environment. Fewer women walk the streets, and the men walk them wearing a skullcap, a long white kurta or shirt, and the baggy pajamas common to northern India. Above the shops, one spies the ornate, if a bit dilapidated, architectural styles often associated with the Middle East. On the right stands a tall white mosque with green trim. Walking in the opposite direction across the street are women in full black *burqas*, holding the hands of daughters in frilly, sherbet-colored dresses. We are now in Madanpura, one of Varanasi's Muslim neighborhoods.

Turning back into a *galī*, we hear voices from inside a house. The dark entrance opens to an enclosed courtyard with a hand pump in the center. A *khārkāna* (weaving room) flanks both sides; narrow stairs lead to the second story. Peering up, one can hear (but not see) women speaking in the rooms upstairs. Following the steady, rhythmic clank, as of wood striking wood, and attendant conversation coming from the *khārkāna*, we look inside to see a young boy and an older man sitting at a loom, tending their latest sari creation.

As these weavers ply their trade, the owner of this house, Iqbal Rahman Ansari, a master weaver of the illustrious Banarsi textile industry, emerges from the mosque after his *āzān* (morning prayers) dressed in smart kurta pajamas, a cap, and a checkered cloth towel strewn over his shoulder. Stabbing his feet into leather sandals, he is approached by another septuagenarian, his friend. They take their places at a tea stall. It is March in Banaras, the weather is a cool 68 degrees Fahrenheit, and a gentle breeze blows in from the *Ganga*. The gentlemen continue their discussion over some *pān*, the ubiquitous betel nut that stains teeth a blood red. The seething hot summer is two months away, leaving Banarsis free to enjoy the outdoors. There is never a better time for some good *bātchit* (conversation) — not that the weather ever discourages Banarsi sociability. Among its inhabitants, the Madanpura *Mohallā* (neighborhood) where these men live is characterized by the practice of *ada/adab* — courtesy, grace, and culture.[28]

What they are exhibiting, in part, is called *Banarsipan*, a way of life among this town's inhabitants characterized by simplicity, carefreeness, contentment, and the love of nature.[29] It is a lifestyle cutting across religious boundaries, though Hindus and Muslims dip into different religious pools to understand, justify, and elaborate on their lifestyles.

Iqbal Rahman Ansari was not born a wealthy man. The name *ansārī* signifies the endogamous Muslim weaver community, and weavers, like all artisans, are especially known by their poverty. Perhaps only a quarter of weavers can read and write. Iqbal cannot remember a time when his family did not weave silk, though he speaks of a time in the 1950s when his father was temporarily forced to become a rickshaw *wāllā* (driver) during a silk shortage. And though he claims the sheikh descent associated with those Arabs who made their home in Banaras under the Delhi Sultanate and Mughal Empire, this is probably a fiction stemming from the nineteenth-century assertion by the *ansārīs* to higher status within the South Asian Islamic social or caste hierarchy. It is likely that most of the city's weavers are Hindu converts, though any knowledge of that past has long been forgotten.

Iqbal has become a rich man, due in large measure — by his rendering — to his own ambition, *Allāh kī marzī* (God's will), a little *kismat* (luck), and the creative drive to innovate—no small character trait at a time when China has siphoned away much of the Banarsi textile market. The vicissitudes of globalization weigh on the *ansārīs*, but apparently less so on Iqbal. His two sons, Kabir and Sayed, received a traditional education, attending one of the thirty Varanasi *madrasās* (religious schools) in their youth, and one receiving a bachelor's degree in commerce, later used to run his father's business. This education was forbidden his daughters, as it was his mother. His two grandsons, aged 9 and 13, attend an English medium school and therefore will likely attend college, but are less likely to continue their family trade. At home they are taught the Qur'an by a *maulvi* (Sunni Muslim religious teacher). Iqbal's own education was sporadic at best, having spent most of his youth apprenticing his father at the loom.

Today is Thursday. Thursdays are typically important days in South Asian Islam, when families travel to *pīr* (saint) and *shahīd* (martyr) shrines to venerate the tombs of Sufi saints and to receive some *baraqāt* (supernatural blessings and power). Having returned home, bathed, and checked in on the progress of his weavers, the entire family crams into Kabir's new Toyota Corolla to visit Chandan Shahīd, just moments away from their *mohallā* on the Varuna river. Young and old spill out of the car: two grandchildren; Iqbal; Iqbal's wife, Zubaida; Kabir and his wife, Fatima. The weaver-cum-servant, Alauddin, trails behind on a cycle rickshaw with snacks. All join scores of others, Muslims and Hindus, making their way to the *mazār* of the eighteenth-century Chishti Sufi saint and martyr.

The shrine is typical for its type: a green coffin-sized tomb adorned with silk *chādars* (covers or sheets); and an airy, white building enclosing the tomb. Each of the family members stands briefly in line outside the tomb to venerate Chandan Shahīd. Zubaida has brought some flower garlands to lie atop the flower-petaled tomb. As Zubaida begins to circumambulate the tomb with both palms facing the ceiling, Iqbal kneels before the tomb, kisses it, and raises his cupped hands to his face in prayer as he slowly stands. His grandchildren dutifully follow his example. A few feet away, a man sits kneeling before the Qur'an, reading it audibly.

Whereas Hindus call the practice of seeing and being seen by a deity *darśan*, Muslims call the practice of encountering a living or dead holy man *ziyārat*. Women are especially active in these practices. While the men depart to begin a picnic, Zubaida and Fatima join other women who are sitting at the foot of the tomb, praying for specific needs, and making certain pledges before the *shahīd*, who is known for his miracles and acts of healing. Zubaida has spent her adult life in *pardāh*, the custom of female seclusion from the public sphere. As a Muslim woman and as an *ansārī*, her life has consisted of housework, raising her children, and some of the work of weaving, especially when she and Iqbal were first married. But these bucolic trips to Chandan Shahīd or other *mazārs* are times of deep enjoyment and satisfaction.[30]

Outside the tomb, this small pilgrimage continues over some mutton, rice, and sweet delicacies. Meanwhile, other families enjoy this *saill* (outdoor trip), exhibiting the Banarsi love not just for visiting shrines and temples, but for openness—*khulāpan*, in speech, in the heart, and in the outdoors.[31] They eat while others enjoy some of the singing of wandering Muslim ascetics (*faqīrs*), colorful if culturally marginalized figures often associated with special powers and sometimes trickery. They may have some powers of some personal benefit, but one probably does not want to invite them over for dinner.

If these wandering *faqīrs* make some uncomfortable, it should be noted that almost all religious and economic Muslim elites in Banaras frown upon rituals surrounding tombs and shrines, and the "magical" behavior and benefit of *faqīrs*. Worship of *pīrs*, for example, is rejected by local Muslim clerics as idolatry. Asked why these practices are so popular, these *bare log* ("rich, influential people" in the eyes of those low on the social hierarchy) will blame it on lack of education and poverty, which makes people susceptible to the suspect influences of Hinduism.[32] This tension between high and low, wealthy and poor, reflects an important truth about Banarsi Muslims, Islam, and religion more generally: no religion is monolithic. In Banaras, Muslims do not self-identify primarily *as* Muslims, but first by their identity as *ansārī*, then as residents of a particular neighborhood, then as Banarsi. Their religion dwells within these identities. According to anthropologist Nita Kumar, who lived among the ansārīs for several years, this endogamous community never spoke in terms of "all we Muslims." In short, there is no one, primary "Muslim identity."

Islam came to South Asia by sea and by land. By sea, Islam was transported with Arab and Persian merchants to southern or peninsular India in the seventh century. Part of a vast trading network stretching from North Africa to Southeast Asia, these boatmen and traders settled in coastal areas and married local women. Over generations, these Sunni Muslims, with support of foreign traders, founded mosques and Qur'anic schools all along the southern west coast.[33] Over still further generations, their successors were likely responsible for penetrating the Deccan peninsula.

By land, Islam was introduced with the armies of so many opportunistic military leaders and dynasts from west[34] and central Asia. In 711 CE, Arabic-speaking Muslims from the Umayyad Dynasty based in Damascus seized control of the Sindh region in the lower Indus Valley. Two centuries later, Mahmud of Ghazni swept down into Sindh and Gujarat from what is now Afghanistan, plundering and destroying famous temples in places such as Somnath in Gujarat, Mathura, and Varanasi. He would be followed by waves of Turko-Afghan regimes entering the Subcontinent through the mountain passages of the northwest like so many invaders of the previous two millennia who changed the Subcontinent as much as they were changed by it. These regimes would come to be known collectively as the Delhi Sultanate, and they would control most of the northern Subcontinent for the next three centuries. To the local peoples these new groups were not known as Muslims, but rather as *turushka* (Turks), another ethnic group they assimilated into older categories such as *yavana* (Ionian), the term used for the Greek invaders led by Alexander the Great a thousand years earlier) or *mleccha* (barbarians), the Sanskrit term denoting those outside Indic civilization.[35] To South Asians of the time, they would have seemed little different from Indic peoples because their economic and military institutions shared common traits with non-Muslim states: among other things, they offered opportunities for individual achievement largely based on military prowess, and their goal was military success in securing access to agricultural surplus in the countryside.[36] These Turko-Afghans initially may have been enemies to indigenous peoples, but they operated using a common idiom. And over time, they would cease to be foreigners at all, creating a hybrid culture still evident in India, Pakistan, and Bangladesh today.[37] The goal of these military campaigns—and those of the Mughal Empire that would follow the Delhi Sultanate—was not conversion to Islam, but the extension of Muslim power.

Yet conversion did occur through various means. First, through the charisma of Sufis such as Chandan Shahīd, holy men who stressed a mystical unity with God even as they cleared land bequeathed by the sultans, introducing agriculture where once there was jungle or desert. In such places as eastern Bengal, western Punjab, and Kashmir, regions where Muslim communities would eventually predominate, "Islam gradually became identified as a religion of the axe and the plough, as well as a religion of 'the Book.'"[38] (Note here the unity of pragmatic and transcendent concerns.) Particularly charismatic Sufis, the aforementioned *pīrs*, were empowered with the transferable blessings of *baraqāt*. This power transcended even death, and *dargāhs* (Sufi shrines) became important centers for Muslims *and* Hindus who were little concerned with the origins of such power. A likely second mode of conversion is offered by historian Susan Bayly, who argues that in southern India conversion represented an opportunity to advance upwards in the social hierarchy. And we may finally credit intermarriage as a force for Islamic growth. Today South India's highest-ranking Muslim lineages are those claiming Arab descent from the early immigrants.[39]

We cannot, however, underestimate the significance of Sufism to the growth and flourishing of Indian Islamic culture and South Asian culture more generally. Sufis served as significant arbiters of Islamic culture. Centered around the *pīr* shrine rather than the mosque, these Muslim mystics communicated through local religious vocabulary and local styles of verse and music, thus accommodating Islam to local thought and practice.[40] In other words, religio-cultural cross-pollination was (and is) the South Asian norm.

Thus, by the time of the displacement of the Delhi sultans in 1526 by the first Mughal, Babar, the Subcontinent was peopled with mendicant ascetics, charismatic Sufi saints bestowing *baraqāt*, devotional poet-saints, Brahmin philosophers, Muslim lawyers, Arab merchants, Turko-Persian emperors, and warrior rulers. In these circumstances, religious affiliation could be anything but clear.

> In addition to the committed professing Muslims and those who were identifiable as "Hindus" (or members of the sectarian and cult traditions which we now call Hindu) there would be even larger numbers who fell in the great class of persons possessing mixed and overlapping communal identities.[41]

The Mughal[42] emperors continued the trajectory of the Delhi sultans they overthrew, furthering their military expansion, the settlement of agriculture, and the political integration of the Subcontinent. Like the sultans, they depended on the services of non-Muslim peoples, particularly the Rajputs, in military service and for the proper administration of vast territories. Unlike the Delhi sultans, the Mughal emperors enjoyed a quasi-divine status. If there was a unifying ideology, it was not Islam, but loyalty to the ruler expressed through Persianate cultural forms that included the Islamic.[43]

If the Mughal court was inclusive of peoples, it was also cosmopolitan and relatively ecumenical in outlook. The third and arguably the greatest of Mughal emperors, Akbar (r. 1556–1605), notoriously enjoyed interreligious debates in his court. He surrounded himself with learned Brahmins, yogis, Muslim scholars, Jains, and Jesuit priests from Portuguese territories on the southwest coast. He patronized the arts, ordered translations of the Sanskrit epics into Persian, and sought the council of both Sufis and Hindu sages. His son and grandson, Jahangir and Shah Jahan, continued (for the most part) in this vein, and are now remembered for their monumental art, stone masterpieces such as the Red Fort in Delhi and the Taj Mahal in Agra.

In contemporary Varanasi, the Mughals are remembered not for their cosmopolitanism, but for their intolerance. Under Shah Jahan and Aurangzeb—leaders less ideologically magnanimous than Akbar—so many temples were destroyed that today no major Hindu religious sanctuary predating the seventeenth century exists.[44] Scholars may remind us that the destruction of Hindu temples had more to do with the perceived disloyalty of nobles associated with these sites than with religious chauvinism or iconoclasm; and academic historians may remind us that Aurangzeb continued to patronize other Hindu temples even as he destroyed Varanasi's. Still, this means little to Hindus in Varanasi and beyond—those whose view of history and attendant rhetoric is colored by the growing rift between Hindus and Muslims in this postcolonial period.

Islam first came to Banaras in the eleventh century with the Central Asian invaders described above. Further growth occurred under the Mughals in the seventeenth and eighteenth centuries. This was the period of Varanasi's "mughalization,"[45] when an enduring cultural imprint was made—in architecture, in the establishment of the neighborhoods that exist to this day, and in the presence of Sufi shrines dotting the landscape. Given the corresponding mughalization of social relations, perhaps it was during this period that strong ties were forged between the Muslim powers-that-be and the city's low-caste weavers like Iqbal Rahman Ansari.[46] Today, Islam is the religion of more than one-third of Varanasi city's population, or half a million people. There are as many Muslims in the ancient city as there are Brahmins, the majority of which are *ansārīs* like Iqbal and his family.

CHRISTIANITY

South of Iqbal's home, a bearded man in a white cassock steps off his Hero Honda motorcycle in Shivalā Ghāṭ, less than a mile north of Assi. While wealthier children sit in school, barefoot ones with streaks of blonde, sun-bleached hair scurry about Fr. Anthony Thomas as he checks the mail placed on his stoop. Nearby, from another stoop, a bohemian French woman distributes chits from their nonprofit dispensary. Twenty people crowd around, their arms reaching for a ticket that will open the door to Western medical attention. And just down a few yards is the local headquarters of Mother Teresa's Missionaries of Charity, which tends to the mentally ill. All this social work betrays real poverty and sickness. Fr. Anthony lives with another priest in an apartment out of which they run a local Roman Catholic social service agency. He is not originally from Varanasi, though he was educated in Delhi and speaks Hindi and the local dialect, Bhojpuri, fluently. He was born in the state of Kerala, some 900 miles southwest of the Banaras region, in the town of Kottayam.

It may seem odd to be discussing Christianity in South Asia, for it is commonly assumed that Christianity is merely a *Western* religion. But as it happens, Indian Christians trace their history back to the first century CE and the Apostle Thomas, who is said to have converted Brahmins along the Kerala coast before being martyred in what is now Mylapore, Tamil Nadu, in 72 CE. Written evidence shows that in the fourth century significant numbers of Syrian Christians immigrated to Kerala. Afforded the status of high-caste Hindus, they eventually became an endogamous group like other Hindu subcastes, participating in the local spice trade and offering military protection to local *rājās* (kings). For centuries, the Persian church, or what is now called the Church of the East or the Assyrian Church, sent bishops to Kerala. For the most part, however, these Indian Christians were largely isolated from their coreligionist cousins thousands of miles west. All this changed with the late fifteenth-century arrival of the Portuguese and the Catholic Church, who would, after a period of some amity, force these "Thomas Christians" to accept their Latin form of Christianity in 1599. Fifty years later an official, ecclesial rift ensued. After more than 1,000 years of unity, the Thomas Christians faced their first of many divisions. With each new colonial regime—Portuguese, then British—came a new Christian splintering. In the meantime, Catholic then Protestant missionaries began their respective missions to Hindus of low and high status in the form of evangelization, education, and medicine. In the second half of the nineteenth century, at the height of the British Raj—and at a time of significant social, religious, and political upheaval—low-caste and Dalit groups began converting to Christianity by the thousands, a "mass movement" that largely subsided after Indian independence in 1947. Today, there are an estimated 35 million Christians in India, mostly in the southern states of Kerala and Tamil Nadu, in the western state of Goa, and in the tribal belt of Bihar, Jharkhand, and Assam. In the northeastern state of Nagaland, Protestants constitute 90 percent of the population. While Christians make up only 3–5 percent of the total Indian population, they surpass the number of Sikh, Buddhist, and Jain adherents.

There are roughly 25,000 Christians in the Banaras region. Catholics are in the majority, but other denominations include the Church of North India (which was formed by the unification of a number of Western Protestant denominations in 1970), the Methodist Church, and a growing number of Pentecostal groups, the fastest-growing body of Christians in India today. Fr. Anthony traces his Christianity back to the first century and Saint Thomas, prior to the divisions of the original Syriac-speaking Thomas Christians. Understandably, talk of Christianity as a "foreign religion" makes him chafe. And yet, he is the first to admit that the Catholic Church was late to indigenize or accommodate its practices (much less its teachings) to the Indian Subcontinent. In light of the momentous Second Vatican Council (1962–1965), religious elite members such as Fr. Anthony are eager to add various Brahminical Hindu aspects to Catholicism's traditional ways. New churches may be built with a distinctly Hindu architecture, *Yeshu* (Jesus) may be presented as a guru figure, and seminaries may foster the articulation of Catholic theological categories by employing Sanskrit terms and concepts.

Much of this makes little sense to the majority of Varanasi's Catholics, who were Dalits when they converted 50 years ago. For this community, Brahminical Hinduism is anathema. After all, Hinduism kept Untouchables in bondage for more than 2,000 years. So they ask, why would we want to adopt religious elements of the oppressor? For Dalit Catholics, the Western form of Christianity provides new forms of identity, non-Hindu beliefs and practices, foreign art and architecture, and an association with another civilization that, for better or worse, many find superior to their own. (Long after the colonizers go home, the mindset of the colonized remains.) Dalits traditionally have lacked a "place" in Hindu society, dwelling literally on the margins of towns and villages. Christianity, as well as Buddhism and Islam, provide a strategy for Dalits to assert their own identity in a traditionally hostile society, even if this strategy has often failed.

The difference between religious elite members such as Fr. Anthony and Catholics of Dalit origin is emblematic of caste, class, and regional tensions within South Asian Christianity. Although caste does not figure in official Christian theology, it has found its way into Christian India. The vast majority of Catholic priests in India come from high-caste backgrounds, especially from among the aforementioned Thomas Christians. And one still finds spatial divisions within local churches based on caste and class differences, albeit in muted and less explicit ways.[47] In southern Arcot, Tamil Nadu, "clean caste" Malaiman Udaiyan Christian males and children occupy the middle rows of seats, Udaiyan women sit in rows on the right, and Dalit Christians sit in rows on the left.[48] In Goa, processions are still organized by caste—reconfigured into confraternities in the sixteenth century—expressing relations of rank and status, hierarchy, and honor.[49] Such is often the case in South India as well.

There is then a definite hierarchy in Christian South Asia. In fact, Christians in the Banaras region, the vast majority of whom hail from Dalit backgrounds, have their own taxonomy for classifying Christians. "Real" Christians are those who never participate in *pūjās*, such as pig sacrifices or temple worship; "trapped" Christians are those who still adhere to certain customs of untouchability or Hinduism; and "fake" Christians are those who converted merely for financial gain.[50] In this region, where Christians represent a small minority in a historical position of social marginalization, proximity to Hinduism or the old marks of untouchability represent often willful acts of transgression. This is not the case in much of western and southern India.

Back in Fr. Anthony's home district of Kottayam, Christianity in its Orthodox, Catholic, and Protestant forms represent 60 percent of the total population. Here the fear of being subsumed into a sponge-like Hinduism is absent from common discourse, because Christians and Hindus, both religious communities of some size, have lived in relative harmony for centuries. Practically, this translates into shared sacred space, explicit adoption of customs deemed Hindu, and a context where it is often difficult to determine the religious origin of various practices. For example, upon examining Christian-Hindu inter-action in public religious *tēr* (chariot) processions southwest of Kottayam in the state of Tamil Nadu, one scholar admitted, "I could not distinguish easily whether the devotees were in fact Christian or Hindu, and somehow, in the atmosphere of the moment, this identification seems not to matter."[51]

In the course of centuries of interaction and exchange between Christians and Hindus in western and southern Indian villages, Indian Catholics have cre-ated their own divine pantheons, about which we might generalize. The Trinity is at the apex, belonging to a different universe than that of the Brahminical Hindu gods. On the second level, intermeshing increases with the Virgin Mary, the saints, and the Hindu village gods and goddesses dwelling together. "Christians participate to a greater or lesser extent in the worship of Hindus deities, particularly at annual temple festivals."[52] The greatest interaction occurs further down the hierarchy, where we find various and sundry divine beings, such as those examined under the "pragmatic" religion rubric above. For Protestant Christians, the pantheon will of course be more limited because the Protestant Reformers rejected saint veneration and saint intercession on the Christian's behalf.[53]

Christianity, like the Hinduism discussed above, is diverse and difficult to generalize about. Just as we speak of Hinduisms, we may also speak of South Asian Christianities. The tribal Baptists of Nagaland are different from the Syrian Orthodox of Kerala; the Dalit Catholics of Varanasi who converted to Catholicism in the 1940s are different from Goan Catholics who converted in the sixteenth century; and cosmopolitan Mumbai Methodists might share very little with Hyderabadi Pentecostals. Each adherent finds herself in a different religio-cultural, economic, and political context. Each must dwell in "messy" terrain in which religious identities, borders, and authority are not concrete and absolute, but often fluid and open to negotiation."[54] The messiness is more visible to the outsider, however, who all too often operates with universalized, institutionalized formulations of identity, boundary, and authority.[55] To the adherent this is simply... life. As we have seen, religion in practice in South Asia is anything but tidy, and upon closer inspection we may find that our lives seem equally baffling to outsiders, those who understand "the West" monolithically.

Nevertheless, knowledge of the particular can get us closer to the general. So we return to Varanasi. Fr. Anthony serves the Mass everyday in a village church five miles from Shivalā Ghāṭ. The most highly attended Mass occurs on Sunday at 8 o'clock in the morning. The church, built in 1985, is painted in bright colors. Like Sushila Devi, local Christians take off their shoes prior to entering. They cross themselves, entering as a family, and find a place to sit on a mat before the altar. In some village churches, one might find that men and women sit separately. The languages are Bhojpuri and Hindi; the mood is subdued. At the time of singing, it seems that only women are lending their voices. Then again, 80 percent of the 50 parishioners in Fr. Thomas's church are women, as is often the case. At the time of the "passing of the peace," Indian Catholics do not shake hands, nor would they ever dream of embracing, but offer the *namasté* gesture to one another, turning left to right with hands cupped in front of their chests. Unlike in the contemporary West, one will not see female acolytes. Officiating of the Mass is an all-male affair, although the number of female religious in this region is staggering. There are some 21 separate female religious orders in the Varanasi Catholic diocese, an astounding number given the tiny Christian population.

After the Mass, Fr. Anthony greets the congregants at the door, who then walk past begging lepers as they journey home, a common sight outside temples, mosques, and churches. A few women wait to speak with him. They are Hindus, but require his prayers. It is a familiar occurrence. They ask for healing, mostly. A son is sick, a spouse is suffering from mental illness, and another feels like she is being eaten alive by mosquitoes. Fr. Anthony prays aloud with these women, but he also gives them practical advice, referring them to local clinics run by the nuns, recommending medicine, and promising to visit their village to pray for the sufferer in person. Striking is the tremendous deference given to the priest, a customary lay practice afforded to holy persons in South Asia. There is power in the holy and it can be bestowed by glance or touch. And it generally matters little where that power originates, be it in a Catholic priest, a Hindu *sanyās*, or a Muslim *pīr*. This too is emblematic of popular religiosity in South Asia—that is, it is largely nonsectarian.

CONCLUSION

While focusing on the sacred center of Varanasi and the Banaras region, we have actually stretched beyond its hallowed borders—from Banaras down to Kottayam in the southern state of Kerala; from Kāśī to the region of Sindh in modern-day Pakistan; from the city of Śiva to Islamic communities along the shores of the Indian peninsula. The religio-cultural metropolis situated halfway between Delhi and Kolkata has been influenced historically by forces political, economic, and indeed religious. In turn, this ancient city and the Banarsis who populate it have influenced the world in ways both manifest and unseen. Ultimately, the story of religion in practice in South Asia is a story of the interaction and exchange of persons and communities—rubbing up against each other, competing with one another, borrowing practices and ideas both explicitly and unconsciously, and rather unglamorously trying to make it through the day.

Finally, we must realize that in this age of globalization religions in South Asia travel as never before. Pundits and priests once tied to Varanasi may now be found teaching or dedicating a temple in Edison, New Jersey. Once the destination of Christian missionaries, India is now often the source of Catholic clergy who may find themselves in diocesan churches in England or New England. And Sushila Devi's granddaughter, if she does well on that examination, could very well end up writing computer programs in Bangalore, southern India, or in Santa Clara in the Silicon Valley. A back and forth movement once confined to rivers or trade routes overland, now journey by means of air travel, satellite television, and the Internet. A result is a transformation in our notions of place and community. Is Varanasi merely a geographical location or—through temple feast webcasts and real-time webcams—an electronic one? Does one have to live in Varanasi year-round to be a proper Banarsi, or is it enough if one travels there once a year, considers the city her own, and visits it electronically on a daily basis? In an age of intra-Indian emigration and mass communication, can local identities, such as that belonging to Iqbal Rahman Ansari, still exist? These are some of the questions evoked by globalization, a process significantly influencing South Asian religion in practice now and in the years ahead. One thing is certain: given the realities of globalization, we in North America have never been as close to South Asia as we are right now; and South Asians have never been more aware of North America. The effect this reality will have on us and on people such as Sushila Devi, Iqbal Rahman Ansari, and Fr. Anthony Thomas defies prediction.

GLOSSARY

Baraqāt: blessing; in the Sufi tradition it is the blessings and powers bestowed by God and mediated through a saint.

Bhakti: Loving devotion.

Darśan: The act of seeing and being seen by a deity.

Grāmadevatā: A generic name for a deity associated with a community.

Jāti: An endogamous subcaste or caste within the Hindu hierarchical social structure.

Liṅgam: A cylindrical aniconic image associated with Śiva.

Madras: School, either secular or religious.

Pūjā: A form of worship in which offerings are made to a deity.

Purāṇa: "Ancient" or "old"; mythological and genealogical stories concerning gods and goddesses.

Rāmāyaṇa: An epic featuring Ram, Sītā, Lakṣmaṇa, and Hanumān, among others.

NOTES

1. A ghāṭ is a landing place or bank along the river or coast. In Varanasi they are between 30 to 200 yards in length.
2. *Hindooism* replaced the earlier designation, "Gentoo [from "gentile"] religion," borrowed from the Portuguese. See Jonathan Z. Smith, *Relating Religion: Essays in the Study of Religion* (Chicago and London: University of Chicago Press, 2004).
3. Jonathan Z. Smith points out the novelty of many religious designations that we now take for granted. For example, *Boudhism* was first used in 1821, *Taouism* in 1839, and *Confucianism* in 1862. (Ibid.) Highlighting this fact is not meant to suggest that these traditions are simply creations of the Western encounter, but that these words are not derived from the respective "traditions" themselves. And there are certainly political ramifications to the project of naming.
4. Richard H. Davis, "Introduction," in Donald S. Lopez, Jr., ed., *Religions of India in Practice* (Princeton, NJ: Princeton University Press, 1995), p. 5.
5. Ibid.
6. Ibid., p. 6.
7. Ibid.
8. Quoted in Davis, p. 7.
9. Ibid.
10. We may compare the use of the word *Hinduism* to that of *Protestantism*, because a diversity of beliefs and practices likewise is found under a rather broad designation.
11. David G. White, "Popular and Vernacular Traditions," in Denise Cush, Catherine Robinson, and Michael York, eds., *Encyclopedia of Hinduism* (London and New York: Routledge, 2008), p. 612.
12. Ibid.
13. Stephen Huyler, *Meeting God: Elements of Hindu Devotion* (New Haven, CT, and London: Yale University Press, 2000), p. 102.
14. White, p. 612.
15. Ibid., p. 613.
16. Ibid.
17. Ibid.
18. I use this term instead of the more popular *classical Hinduism*, which connotes a religion that is mostly unchanging. As it happens, "classical" really means the religion of Hindu elites, which is many things but certainly not above the vicissitudes of time

and space. The term *Brahminical Hinduism* therefore seems more appropriate. By using this term I am not suggesting that only Brahmins are implicated, for in fact all *dvijās* (twice-born classes, i.e., Brahmins and Kshatriyas) are part of this complex.

19. Since the medieval period, adherents of these "great gods" have tended to treat other deities as inferior, placing them in a subservient position within the divine pantheon. This process is known as superordination.

20. White, p. 10.

21. Bhakti can be found among Jains, Muslims, Buddhists, and Christians.

22. Davis, p. 29.

23. A. K. Ramanujan, trans., *Nammālvār: Hymns for the Drowning* (New York: Penguin, 1993), p. 107.

24. Barbara Stoller Miller, trans. and ed., *Love Song of the Dark Lord. Jayadeva's Gitagovinda* (New York: Columbia University Press, 1997), p. 94. Other intimate bhakti relationships are expressed in terms of father-son, master-slave, and prostitute-customer.

25. Āratī refers to the ritual whereby one displays the camphor flame or lamp before the divine image. Burning incense may also be used.

26. Within Hindu traditions there exist real differences of opinion concerning worship's relationship to the acquisition of boons. The great pan-Indian deities Śiva and Viṣṇu are generally thought to be impervious to human remonstrations. (Hence the rise in popularity of "bridge" deities such as Hanumān and Ganeś.) The many instantiations of the Goddess are considered more accessible. None of these deities, however, are thought to be cajoled by mere mortals. "It is . . . clear that there is considerable variation among Hindus about the feasibility and morality of seeking benefits from worship," (C. J. Fuller, *The Camphor Flame: Popular Hinduism and Society in India*. rev. and exp. ed., (Princeton, NJ: Princeton University Press, 2004), p. 72.

27. Philip Lutgendorf, *Hanuman's Tale: The Message of the Divine Money* (Oxford and New York: Oxford University Press, 2007), pp. 127–128.

28. Nita Kumar, *The Artisans of Banaras: Popular Culture and Identity, 1880–1986* (Princeton, NJ: Princeton University Press, 1988), p. 70.

29. Ibid., p. 82.

30. For an anthropological examination of contemporary South Asian women's lives, see Laura A. Ring, *Zenana: Everyday Peace in a Karachi Apartment Building* (Bloomington and Indianapolis: University of Indiana Press, 2006).

31. Kumar, p. 76.

32. Ibid., p. 137.

33. Jackie Assayag, *At the Confluence of Two Rivers: Muslims and Hindus in South India* (New Delhi: Manohar, 2004), p. 37.

34. In North America and Europe, West Asia is known as the Middle East.

35. Barbara D. Metcalf and Thomas R. Metcalf, *A Concise History of India* (Cambridge: Cambridge University Press, 2002), p. 4.

36. Ibid.

37. Sri Lanka, Pakistan, and India are the nation-states carved out of the Indian Subcontinent in 1947–1948, after the departure of the British. Claiming discrimination and economic neglect, Bangladesh seceded from Pakistan with the 1971 war of independence. As we envision India historically, we should take care not to equate the borders of the modern Indian nation-state with the entire Subcontinent.

38. Richard M. Eaton, ed., *India's Islamic Traditions, 711–1750* (New Delhi: Oxford University Press, 2003), p. 18.

39. Susan Bayly, *Saints, Goddesses and Kings: Muslims and Christians in South Indian Society, 1700–1900* (Cambridge: Cambridge University Press, 1989), p. 74.

40. Ibid., p. 75.

41. Ibid., p. 78.

42. The Mughals were distantly related to the Mongols. Babar was a scion of Timur (1336–1405) on his father's side and the Mongol Chingiz Khan (1167?–1227) on his mother's.

43. Metcalf and Metcalf, p. 17.

44. Diana Eck, *Banaras: City of Light* (New York: Columbia University Press, 1999), p. 84.

45. This is a term coined by Christopher Bayly and further employed by Sandria Freitag.

46. Sandria Freitag, ed., *Culture and Power in Banaras: Community, Performance and Environment, 1800–1980* (Berkeley: University of California Press, 1989), p. 9.

47. Rowena Robinson, *Christians of India* (New Delhi: Sage Publications, 2003), p. 75.

48. Ibid. In the nineteenth century, there was a continual lament by Protestant missionaries over the fact that subcaste differences and antagonisms were being imported into the Christian Church through baptism into different Western Christian denominations. Thus, one Dalit *jāti* would become Presbyterian, whereas another would become Methodist.

49. Ibid., pp. 73–75.

50. Mathew N. Schmalz, "Dalit Catholic Tactics of Marginality at a North Indian Mission," *History of Religions* 44 (February 2005), pp. 226–227.

51. Joanne Punzo Waghorne, "Chariots of the God/s: Riding the Line between Hindu and Christian," in Selva J. Raj and Corinne Dempsey, eds., *Popular Christianity in India: Riting between the Lines* (Albany: SUNY Press, 2002), p. 29.

52. Robinson, p. 113

53. Historically, there have been three ways that "other gods" have been interpreted by Christians: as demons (Hindi *śaitāne*) to be rejected, as figments of the human imagination, and as deities somehow subordinate to the Christian deity. See John Carman, "When Hindus Become Christian," in Anna Lannstrom, ed., *The Stranger's Religion: Fascination and Fear* (South Bend, IN: University of Notre Dame Press, 2005), pp. 133–153.

54. Selva J. Raj and Corinne G. Dempsey, eds., *Popular Christianity in India: Riting between the Lines,* (Albany: SUNY Press, 2002), p. 2.

55. Ibid.

BIBLIOGRAPHY

Assayag, Jackie. *At the Confluence of Two Rivers: Muslims and Hindus in South India.* New Delhi: Manohar, 2004.

Carman, John. "When Hindus Become Christian: Religious Conversion and Spiritual Ambiguity." In Anna Lannstrom, ed. *The Stranger's Religion: Fascination and Fear.* South Bend, IN: University of Notre Dame Press, 2004, pp. 133–153.

Cohen, R. S. "Nāga, Yaksinī, Buddha: Local Deities and Local Buddhism at Ajanta." *History of Religions* 37 (1998): 360–400.

Dempsey, Corinne G. *Kerala Christian Sainthood: Collisions of Culture and Worldview in South India.* Oxford: Oxford University Press, 2001.

Eaton, Richard M. "Approaches to the Study of Conversion to Islam in India." In Richard C. Martin, ed. *Islam in Religious Studies.* New York: One World Press, 1987, pp. 106–123.

Eaton, Richard M., ed. *India's Islamic Traditions, 711–1750.* New Delhi: Oxford University Press, 2003.

Eck, Diana. *Banaras: City of Light.* New York: Columbia University Press, 1999.

Freitag, Sandria, ed. *Culture and Power in Banaras: Community, Performance, and Environment, 1800–1980.* Berkeley: University of California Press, 1989.

Fuller, C. J. *The Camphor Flame: Popular Hinduism and Society in India,* rev. and exp. ed. Princeton, NJ: Princeton University Press, 2004.

Grimes, John. *A Concise Dictionary of Indian Philosophy: Sanskrit Terms Defined in English,* new and rev. ed. Albany: State University of New York Press, 1996.

Hawley, John Stratton, and Vasudha Naryanan, eds. *The Life of Hinduism.* Berkeley and Los Angeles: University of California Press, 2006.

Huyler, Stephen. *Meeting God: Elements of Hindu Devotion.* New Haven, CT, and London: Yale University Press, 1999.

Kumar, Nita. *The Artisan of Banaras: Popular Culture and Identity, 1880–1986.* Princeton, NJ: Princeton University Press, 1988.

Lawrence, Bruce B. "The Eastward Journey of Muslim Kingship: Islam in South and Southeast Asia." In John L. Esposito, ed. *The Oxford History of the Muslim World.* New York: Oxford University Press, 1999, pp. 395–431.

Lopez Jr., Donald S., ed. *Religions of India in Practice.* Princeton Readings in Religions. Princeton, NJ: Princeton University Press, 1999.

Lutgendorf, Philip. *The Life of a Text: Performing the* Rāmcaritmānas *of Tūlsīdas.* Berkeley and Los Angeles: University of California Press, 1991.

———. *Hanumān's Tale: The Message of a Divine Monkey.* Oxford and New York: Oxford University Press, 2007.

Mandelbaum, David G. "Transcendental and Pragmatic Aspects of Religion." *American Anthropologist* 68.5 (Oct. 1966): 1174–1191.

Parry, Jonathan P. *Death in Banaras.* Cambridge: Cambridge University Press, 1994.

Raj, Selva, and Corrine Dempsey, eds. *Popular Christianity in India: Riting between the Lines.* Albany: SUNY Press, 2002.

Ring, Laura A. *Zenana: Everyday Peace in a Karachi Apartment Building.* Bloomington and Indianapolis: Indiana University Press, 2006.

Robinson, Rowena. *Christians of India.* New Delhi: Sage Publications, 2003.

Schmalz, Mathew N. "Dalit Catholic Tactics of Marginality at a North Indian Mission." *History of Religions* 44 (Feb. 2005): pp. 216–251.

Singh, Rana P. B. *Towards the Pilgrimage Archetype: The Pañcakrośī Yātrā of Banāras.* Varanasi: Indica Books, 2002.

Singh, Rana P. B, and Pravin S. Rana. *Banaras Region: A Spiritual and Cultural Guide.* Varanasi: Indica Books, 2002.

Smith, Brian K. *Reflections on Resemblance, Ritual, and Religion.* New Delhi: Motilal Banarsidass, [1989] 1998.

Smith, Jonathan Z. *Relating Religion: Essays in the Study of Religion.* Chicago and London: University of Chicago Press, 2004.

White, David. "Popular and Vernacular Traditions." In Denise Cush, Catherine Robinson, and Michael York, eds. *Encyclopedia of Hinduism.* London and New York: Routledge, 2008, pp. 612–616.

———. *Kiss of the Yogini: "Tantric Sex" in Its South Asian Contexts.* Chicago and London: University of Chicago Press, 2003.

Chapter 4

Pacific Islands

Ramdas Lamb

INTRODUCTION

The Pacific Ocean is home to the largest number of islands and island-nations of any area of the world. Each location has its own history and individuality that tends to be a unique mixture of religion, culture, ethnicity, and politics. In most of the Pacific islands, there is more of a blending of these elements than a separation. Moreover, most of the native languages have no distinct term for *religion*, for that which is typically labeled such did not exist as separate from the rest of life. Thus, although the focus of this chapter is on religion in the lives of the peoples of the Pacific islands, the other elements—that is, culture, ethnicity, and politics—must be included to provide a context for understanding. Geographically, the Pacific is usually divided into three regions: Melanesia, Micronesia, and Polynesia. These names come from the Greek words meaning dark islands, small islands, and many islands, respectively. They will be used herein for the purposes of geographic convenience only.

Geologically, there are two basic types of islands in the Pacific. High volcanic islands, such as Hawai'i, are the tops of underwater eruptions of submerged volcanoes that over periods of thousands of years rose above sea level to their current heights. An example of this process can be seen in the waters southeast of the island of Hawai'i, where geologists are watching the growth of a new volcano they have called Loihi. Most Pacific islands, however, are coral islands and atolls, such as those found in Micronesia, but even these are built on volcanic or other cores. Most inhabited islands are in the ocean's southern portion and have climates that range from tropical to temperate and that support year-round growth of a diversity of fruits, small animals, and plant life. In addition, the waters in which the islands exist have long been the home of abundant populations of marine life, which have formed an integral part of the sustenance of islanders and which have consequently made the connection between most islanders and the ocean fundamental to the islanders' existence.

According to anthropologists and archaeologists, people from Southeast Asia began inhabiting the islands of the Pacific more than 40,000 years ago. The first to settle were in what is now called Melanesia. It was not until about 4,000 years ago that another wave of people from Southeast Asia entered Micronesia, while others from Fiji moved east into the islands that are now Polynesia approximately 3,000 years ago. Tahiti became a center of exploration, and over the next two millennia, navigators from there reached islands as far away as Hawai'i and New Zealand (circa 1200 CE). From the time the islands first became inhabited by humans until the late eighteenth century, the Pacific remained relatively isolated, resulting in very little contact with people from outside the realm. Instead, there was movement by native voyagers between the various islands, which led to a great deal of sharing of physical, cultural, and linguistic elements. This fostered the development and spread of a variety of beliefs, practices, and other traits that became relatively commonplace in the islands but relatively unknown outside them. However, once European explorers began venturing into the Pacific with regularity just over 200 years ago, the subsequent interactions functioned to almost rewrite much of the cultures and lifestyles of the peoples of the Pacific.

The present chapter begins with a brief look into the religious beliefs and practices as well as commonly found elements that predated the arrival of the Europeans and are labeled herein as **Pre-Contact**. It then turns to the religious cultures and currents that arose out of contact with the foreigners and particularly with Christian missionaries, labeled herein as **Post-Contact**. This is followed by three sections, each of which focuses on one of the geographic regions mentioned above, providing examples of elements more specific to the lives and practices of the peoples in that region. Also, among all the island-nations and cultures represented in the Pacific, none has a greater percentage of non-Christians than Fiji, and none has a greater religious diversity than Hawai'i. Consequently, these two are focused on more extensively.

TIMELINE

c. 40,000 years ago:	First Pacific islanders settle in Melanesia from Southeast Asia.
c. 2,000 BCE:	Second migration from Southeast Asia to Micronesia; migration from Fiji (Melanesia) east to Polynesia.

	Intra-Pacific travel to Tonga, Samoa, Tahiti, Rapa Nui, and Hawai'i. Development of shared cultural, religious, and linguistic traits within the Pacific realm.
11th century CE:	Migration to and settling in New Zealand from other areas of the Pacific.
1500s:	First European explorers arrive in Micronesia.
1600s:	First European explorers arrive in Melanesia.
1700s:	First European explorers arrive in Polynesia.
1795:	Creation of London Missionary Society (LMS), one of the first missionary groups (Protestant) to begin exploration and conversion of Pacific islands, started in Tahiti.
early 1800s:	Introduction of Western technologies, goods, and weapons. Local chiefs and rulers begin to adopt Christianity, followed by commoners. Strong influence on traditional religious and cultural practices.
1850s–1900s:	Importation of plantation laborers from China, Japan, the Philippines, and Portugal to Hawai'i. Buddhism spreads to Hawai'i.
1874:	Fiji becomes a British colony and begins importing Indians as laborers. Hinduism comes to Fiji.
Late 19th to mid-20th centuries:	Development of cargo cults in the Pacific, particularly in Melanesia.
20th century:	Independence from colonial authority by many Pacific island-nations.

In gathering information for a historical study of the Pacific, three primary source groups are available. The first consists of the diaries and other writings of early European voyagers into the Pacific. The second includes the writings of missionaries who began the quest for native souls beginning at the end of the eighteenth century, and which has continued up to present day. The third consists of written accounts by native islanders of the lives and traditions of their own peoples. Although all three have been used and are of great value, there is no assumption that any of these sources were compiled without an agenda, whether it be to justify capitalist or imperialist aspirations, religious conversions, fabrication of historical records, or the preservation of ancient traditions. It is important to keep in mind that because ancient lore and knowledge were passed on orally prior to the arrival of the Europeans, all written accounts, by both natives and foreigners, have been influenced by European methods and thought processes used in writing and recording. Even the oral traditions that have been preserved up to present day have been done so in an environment inundated with Western Christian influence in ways that have fundamentally altered how most islanders conceive of and interpret their past. The overlay of Christianity has also destroyed, for good or bad, fundamental aspects of the lives of the people that had been present for centuries, if not millennia. Although there are still unique elements to the beliefs and practices of islanders, they almost all function within the context of Christianity. Thus, any attempt to understand them cannot escape that influence. Lastly, most of the explanations provided here have been simplified and generalized; the reality is far more multivalent and complex and would require far more elaboration than is warranted in the context of this study. The information presented herein is instead meant to offer a cursory overview of the religious traditions and cultures referenced. For a more detailed study, the attached bibliography provides a variety of good textual and Internet sources.

PRE-CONTACT

Deities

Indigenous peoples throughout history have tended to perceive the divine in much of what is and what happens in their everyday lives, and this approach has typically led to polytheistic and/or animistic conceptualizations. Because most people in the West have been taught that monotheism is the more evolved theological view, which is a primarily Judeo-Christian perspective, an attempt to understand traditional indigenous beliefs systems is best accomplished by a suspension of such a judgment. Both polytheism and animism have been persistent and prevalent in the belief systems of most non-Abrahamic religious traditions for several reasons. First, humans tend to conceive of the divine in their own image and likeness and thus endow it with human-like characteristics in both form and function. Thus, images and idols are often anthropomorphic, with human personality traits ranging from loving and compassionate to jealous and vengeful. Second, most of us experience power, knowledge, and authority as being possessed by many, not one. Whether it be in a family, village, community, or nation, power tends to be in the hands of various individuals, with each having a specific authority and function. There are clear advantages to such a system, because there can be various avenues for seeking assistance from one or more of those who possess these powers and/or knowledge. Polytheism reflects this world experience in formulating its depiction of and approach to the realm of the divine. In the 1930s, anthropologist Peter Buck related the following comment he had heard in this regard:

> A Polynesian once informed an early missionary that he could not understand how one god could possibly attend to all the varied demands made upon him. In

his religion, a person consulted the god of his particular need and had more chance of receiving attention. Hence he considered that the Polynesian religion was superior to Christianity.[1]

Polytheism, then, mirrors common human experience and is frequently found in cultures with a clearly stratified social and/or political hierarchy. Different divinities, like different bureaucrats, have different powers and functions: there may be, for instance, a volcano goddess or a rain god. One approaches and propitiates those deities or spirits with the requisite powers to fulfill the needs or desires of the supplicant. One can also focus on a divinity who appeals to one's own personality. In many ways, then, polytheism is a more pragmatic theological view than is monotheism.[2] Animism adds to this concept by perceiving spirit or some supernatural existence or power in all animate objects (such as plants and animals), inanimate objects (such as rocks, rivers, and mountains), and natural forces (wind, sun, rain, etc.). Everything humans encounter is seen as being connected with the spirit world and therefore can have power that may be able to help humans.

Divinities and spirits often exist at the center of the cosmological world views of the cultures in which they are found. For most traditional islanders within these, gods, ancestor spirits, or demons are all immediate, present, and powerful, and almost everything that occurs is connected with the spirit world. Every action, then, has religious aspects and consequences, from what one eats to what one wears, says, or does. Disease, death, and other catastrophes are often the direct consequence of angered spirits or other problems in the spirit world. Prayers, rituals, and offerings to the various gods, goddesses, spirits, or ancestors have been seen as fundamental to the maintenance of the human realm. When the spirits are happy, then human life tends to function well.

At the same time, disease, death, and other catastrophes are believed to be the direct consequences of angered spirits. This makes regular communication with the spirit world important and necessary to keep the physical world in order. Included among the various ways in which communication occurs are dreams, visions, trances, and divination. The geography of the particular islands has influenced which gods and goddesses are present and propitiated. For example, Hawai'i has Pele, the powerful volcano goddess of the island chain. Many propitiate her for her blessings as well as her protection. This is especially the case on the Big Island of Hawai'i because it is her home and volcanic activity is frequent there. In the coral atolls of Micronesia, where there are no volcanoes, so Pele plays no role and is not even present in the spirit world of the people there.

One of the significant features of island cultures and belief systems is the ease with which most were able to incorporate new gods, myths, beliefs, and practices to which they were exposed through contact with other island cultures. This inclusion process is the reason why there are such similarities in many of the cultures and religious traditions in each region and even outside the region. Independent beliefs and practices would evolve in one area, spread with seafarers to new areas and islands, and become merged with existing concepts in the new lands. Genealogies and mythologies have also been adapted to include new theological and cosmological additions and changes. The mythology surrounding the deity Maui, for example, is quite diverse in the various islands of Polynesia, depending on how it was incorporated. In Hawai'i, he is said to have pulled the islands from the ocean with his spear, and he also helped to separate the sky from the earth. Samoan stories of Maui have him accomplishing the latter as well, but through a different method. In New Zealand, a fish that Maui pulled from the ocean became the northern island, whereas his canoe became the southern island. This process of adoption and adaptation is much more common than is the exclusivism that is the hallmark of Western religious thinking.

Tribal or clan chiefs have been prevalent throughout the Pacific. In some areas, they were seen as being either divinities or descendants thereof, and offerings to them were seen as similar to offerings to the gods. In others, chiefs were simply seen as humans who had more *mana* or who were believed to have the power to invoke or to communicate with the gods and the ancestor spirits. Some were deeply loved and respected; most were deeply feared. To incite the wrath of a chief could easily mean death, not only to an individual but to family members as well.

Mana, Marriage, and Sibling Relations

Families, genealogies, and family relations are all important to the peoples of the Pacific. This is especially so in Polynesia, where traditional hierarchies were most pronounced and where one's ancestry determined one's rank and status. In addition, there was a strong belief throughout the Pacific in a non-physical power that exists within people, animals, objects, and places. In some islands, this is known as *mana*. Because the concept varies greatly from place to place, there is no one definition that can be universally applied, and the idea can be greatly misunderstood when too broadly defined or generalized. Nevertheless, some type of unseen power of supernatural origin has been a part of the belief systems of the inhabitants of most islands, and it is almost always connected with the spirit world. This led to an often held belief that those who could communicate or were connected through birth with the spirits had access to that power, which would give them authority, sanctity, or prestige. Things and places have also been considered to have unseen power, rendering them sacred and/or dangerous. In Polynesia and some of the Micronesian islands, chiefly lineages were believed to have inherited *mana*, the level varying by lineage, and this justified their position of superiority in the social hierarchy. Although inherited, this power could also be gained or lost through activities such as warfare or marriage. To maintain and preserve the power within a lineage, marriages were often determined by priests. In some cases, priests would have those considered to be of the highest chiefly lineage intermarry to keep the *mana* within the family, which led to different types of incestuous unions. Generally, the first born (*hiapo* in Hawaiian) was believed to have the most *mana*. Once there was a male offspring to carry on the lineage, then a chief could have wives or sexual liaisons with women of less powerful lineages. However, any children thus begotten would be seen to have a lesser degree of *mana*. Incest was limited to royalty and seen as necessary for the maintenance of chiefly *mana*. When foreigners first came to the Pacific with their tremendous ships, possessions, and weapons, they were typically seen to possess great *mana*. Some natives also thought they must be gods. Even after islanders came to see the sailors and their captains as human, still the captains were believed to have great power similar to that of their chiefs, and the requisite deference was afforded them.

Religious Functionaries

Nearly every religion or religious denomination has individuals assigned to fulfill specific functions or ritual duties. In the Pacific, there have been many names in the various languages for those with such roles. These include *tohunga*, *tahuna*, *tahua*, *kahuna*, and *kahu*, among others. They can be grouped into two broad categories.[3] The first category is that of priests, and includes those persons connected to royal families through bloodline or marriage and who perform rituals, especially those connected with the chiefs. Among their traditional functions was the memorization and performance of chants, particularly those relating genealogy or telling of the greatness of a particular chief. Such chants would be used to help validate and affirm the position and authority of the chief. Traditional priests were, and still are, also seen as keepers of the ancient knowledge and ways.[4] The tasks and functions of members of the second group have been much more varied and would often have more qualified names depending on what their specific functions were. They have been referred to broadly by some scholars as "inspirational priests," whereas other have labeled them "shamans," "sorcerers," or "magicians." Because of the generally negative association that the latter two terms conjure up in the minds of Westerners, *shamans* will be used herein when referring to those who have served these functions.

However, it must be understood that their existence and roles are rather unique to the Pacific. One of the important tasks of Pacific island shamans has been communication between the human world and the realm of the spirits and ancestors. Divination, trance, and possession have all been used for this purpose. Some have had the role of healers, through the knowledge of herbs, but also of secret potions and rituals. In Hawai'i, the latter were known as *kahuna la'au lapa'au*, and their knowledge was seen as being of the spirit world. Some shamans were considered to have special powers of craftsmanship—for instance, some were good canoe makers. Other shamans might have the knowledge to make a curse or counteract one made by another. In Fiji, those known as *daurai* were believed to have unique access to the power of the spirit world that would afford them the ability to make love potions or know the future.[5]

Chanting

Writing was not a part of Pacific cultures until the arrival of the Europeans. Prior to that, experience and memory were the tools used for recording all that was important, whereas chants, prayers, and songs were the vehicles for disseminating them. Chants preserved and passed on ancient lore, mythology, history, and genealogy. Those who had the talent and authority to chant were given great respect, for the knowledge they possessed was sacred. However, many of the ancient chants were lost when the old gods and ways were abandoned, because Christian missionaries convinced the islanders to reject anything connected with them. In recent decades, however, there has been a growing attempt at reawakening traditional ways in many of the islands, and there has been a concerted effort to remember, revive, or recreate the chants that have been lost or forgotten. This occurrence is more likely where the actual chanting tradition was not necessarily lost, but incorporated into Christianity. Polynesian islands such as Samoa, Tahiti, and to some extent Hawai'i, are good examples of this. Moreover, in the Christianity of these islands, traditional style chanting has become an integral part.

Taboo

To understand the origin and usage of the words from which the English *taboo* derives (Tongan *tapu*; Fijian *tabu*), their broader meanings need to be discussed. Throughout much of the Pacific, there were a variety restrictions placed on people, places, objects, and activities. These regulations or controls were of two basic types. The first focused on that which was considered sacred—that is, reserved for the chiefs or spirits. The second dealt with that which was considered defiling, contaminating, or corrupting. Both categories were considered taboo. Thus, the English word is used herein to denote broadly different yet connected concepts. Sacredness taboos have been and continue to be prevalent throughout much of the Pacific. Many of the others have fallen into disuse, except by strong traditionalists.

Abrahamic religious traditions, especially Christianity and Islam, put strict limitations and control on what is considered sacred and on who makes these determinations. Indigenous traditions, on the other hand, tend to have much broader and less defined understandings. In the West, *sacred* is typically defined as that which is "set apart for a god," "dedicated or set apart for the service or worship of a deity," "not secular or profane," and so forth. It comprises half of a duality in juxtaposition with *profane*. Mircea Eliade notes that the sacred is "something of a wholly different order, a reality that does not belong to our world."[6] That which is sacred, either through its nature or through some form of sanctification or consecration, tends to ever remain set apart and reserved for that which is holy, and is also permanently distinguished as such. In essence, the sacred and the profane remain ever distinct.[7] In indigenous traditions, including those in the Pacific, the approach is much different. That which is sacred can be almost anything: a rock, a plant, an animal, a river, a person. Sanctity can also be either permanent or temporary and is not necessarily predefined. The concept that applies here is taboo, and it refers to elements that are in one's daily life.

Although priests and chiefs generally determined and controlled that which was sacred, it was not always the case. Taboos associated with chiefs and royalty were generally permanent and dealt with prohibitions against touching them, looking directly at them, or speaking their names. Their homes, property, and possessions were all taboo. At the same time, skilled artisans or dancers could make the tools of their craft taboo. In much of the Pacific, an unmarried female was relatively free to have sex with whomever she chose. However, once married, she became taboo for all but her husband. Some foods, such as pork, were taboo either year-round or at certain times of the year for women or commoners. Whom a woman could eat with was also determined by taboo rules. Some foods were taboo and could only be eaten by the chiefs or the priests. Generally, these were foods that could be offered in sacrifice to the gods. Food taboos could be seasonal or in preparation for certain ritual observations. Some taboos had practical bases, such as to protect against overpicking of crops or overcatching of certain fish. Others were the result of myths and legends. An example of the latter was a taboo against eating certain fish in Hawai'i because they were believed to have aided the Tahitian king Pa'ao when he sailed there.[8] Restrictions existed for some as to whom one could marry. Certain places were taboo because of events that have occurred or will occur there, both good and bad. A place that is taboo may be off-limits to most people, only a chief or a priest being allowed to enter it; some places were taboo even for chiefs. People could also become taboo based on activities in which they participated, such as handling or touching a corpse, or if they had a serious illness. A menstruating female was also taboo. These were temporary and may be ended with rituals of purification or rituals conducted by priests.[9] Punishment for breaking a taboo could be minimal or fatal. In Hawai'i, it is said that the punishment was often death, unless the transgressor was excused by the chief. Although most such rules have fallen by the wayside, some still exist and are followed. The primary influencing factor here is the degree of Westernization that has occurred. At the same time, many of those attempting to reawaken traditional cultures in the region have sought to force a rethinking of traditional taboos and their necessity or relevance today.

Tattoos

Tattooing is an ancient art found in most areas of the world. It has been present in one form or another in nearly all the Pacific islands, although it has been most common in Polynesia. The English term was coined from the Tahitian *tatau* (literally, "punctured marks on the skin") by Captain James Cook, the eighteenth-century English explorer in the Pacific.[10] Although they had once been prevalent in Europe, tattoos were banned once the continent fell under Christian rule.[11] Thus, Cook and the men with him had never seen tattoos prior to arriving in the Pacific. Eventually, some of the sailors got tattooed, and they began a tradition for sailors that has lasted to present-day.

Among the various reasons for being tattooed was the expression of identity, personality, lineage, or rank; as part of a puberty ritual; as a type of offering to a deity; as an expression of strength and virility; to help cure an illness; to secure protection; or to inspire fear in opponents. When done as a religious undertaking, preparation typically entailed ritual cleansing and/or fasting. Each island group developed its own designs and methods of tattooing. These may involve geometric patterns, or may include animals or symbols representing gods. Because tattooing was both an art and a sacred activity, those who knew the craft were considered to have sacred knowledge or power. Tattoos have long connected island people to their cultures, ancestors, and gods; thus, the practice has had both social and religious aspects to it.

Because tattooing was one of the traditional cultural practices that missionaries deplored as savage and pagan, and as a vain glorification of the body, they had the practice banned on many islands. As a consequence, tattoos diminished drastically in the more evangelized lands in the Pacific to the point that they became almost nonexistent, although recent decades have seen a resurgence of the practice. In a time when identity for many islanders is being questioned and challenged, tattooing is one way of seeking to maintain a connection with the past, with ancestors, and with one's ethnic community. Because almost all islanders are now Christian, they look to those elements of traditional culture that do not have direct conflict with the contemporary expressions of their adopted faith, and tattooing has become one of them. This is especially the case in Polynesia. However, the spiritual or ritual element of tattooing has been largely lost or forgotten for the vast majority of those who currently get tattoos. Now, the practice is done primarily either for body adornment, for following the Western trend among the young, or for ethnic and/or cultural identity.[12]

Another form of body altering for males in pre-Christian Polynesia was the practice of circumcision. Although commonplace throughout Polynesia, it was rarely practiced in other regions of the Pacific. There were also temporary forms of bodily decoration using various pigments that were applied for the performance of rituals or by ritual dancers. This is found to a large extent in Melanesia, especially among less Westernized tribes in the interior portions of the islands. In Papua New Guinea, one form of ritual dance is done by men who imitate the dead by wearing large masks made of clay painted white. They also coat their entire bodies with clay to resemble a corpse.

Dance

In the Pacific, chanting and prayer have often been accompanied by drums and dance, and together they have long played an important role in most cultures. Dance has been associated with a variety of rituals, including rites of passage and other important events in the lives of individuals and whole communities. Thus, from birth to death, there were occasions in which dance was performed. Dancers were traditionally adorned in various ways, often with plant products such a leaves, flowers, or woven coverings. The mud men of Papua New Guinea provide one of the more elaborate examples. Some performers would also dress to represent an animal that is either to be sacrificed or is a totem of a particular tribe. Certain dances could only been seen by people who had been initiated into a particular society or group.[13] Some Melanesian dances were part of a ritual that would go on for years at a time.

Dance was also used as a form of storytelling and entertainment, and the dancer's task was to make the audience experience the story. The music that accompanied dance was usually made with drums, conch shells, nose flutes, and shell or gourd rattles. Although both males and females participated in various forms of dance, they rarely danced together. Some cultures would restrict female dancers to those who were unmarried, often because of the sensual nature of the dance. Since dance had a ritual role and was often sensual, missionaries on many of the islands banned public dance performances and even tried to eradicate them completely. As a consequence, several forms have died out completely, and others were performed only in the countryside, outside the view and notice of Christians. In more recent times, there has been a resurgence of dance in many of the islands, often to attract tourists. Although many have been sanitized of their connection with ancient beliefs, various dance contests emphasizing traditional styles have been established. This has given both opportunity and legitimacy to those who want to use dance as a vehicle to reconnect with their ancient cultures.

POST-CONTACT

The first Europeans to enter the Pacific were Spaniards, in the early sixteenth century. They were also the first to attempt conversion of the natives and to practice genocide against indigenous people in the realm. Fortunately, the activities and scope of the early Spanish were relatively limited, although they were responsible for the deaths of nearly all the adult males on the island of Guam. The waves of European and American travelers into the Pacific that came in the late eighteenth and early nineteenth centuries exposed islanders to new ways of viewing reality, both human and divine, and also to new threats and powerful challenges to their traditional beliefs and practices. They experienced goods, tools, and weapons that amazed and enticed many, especially the chiefs. Whenever an isolated people first come into contact with individuals and things from the outside world, there is inevitably a mix of emotional reactions, from fear to awe to longing. Some of the early foreigners were thought to have nonhuman origins either demonic or divine. Because they were also believed to have nonhuman powers, many islanders looked to past legends and ancient prophecies to explain their appearance. Where the presence of the foreigners could be accommodated within the framework of existing beliefs, the newcomers had immediate power. An example of this was the arrival of Captain Cook in Hawai'i, where he was initially seen by the people as their god Lono. Unfortunately, in such situations, power was often abused.

An important aspect of contact that will not be dwelled on in this chapter is the spread of communicable diseases by whalers and other outsiders. Although this often happened inadvertently, it was also purposeful at times. Because diseases such as the flu, measles, smallpox, and sexually transmitted diseases (STDs) were nonexistent in the Pacific, natives lacked any natural immunity. As a consequence, some island populations were almost totally wiped out. In Micronesia, Pohnpei lost nearly half its population to smallpox in the 1850s. The following decade, the disease killed more than 90 percent of the people on the island of Kosrae. In the 1870s, the same disease claimed the lives of most residents of the Polynesian island of Rapa Nui (more commonly known today as Easter Island).[14] The list goes on. This was not the doing of the missionaries, and many of them devoted their lives to helping the islanders. Nevertheless, had the diseases not been introduced, and had vast numbers of people not been lost with all the collective knowledge and wisdom they possessed, the history and present-day reality of the Pacific would surely be much different than it is today. However, these events did occur, and they clearly helped to create an environment that made many islands and islanders weaker and more vulnerable to the influences of Christian missionaries.

Most of the early European travelers to the Pacific were from either Britain or France. The two colonial powers had been competitors in trying to "possess" the Americas in preceding centuries, and now both made their moves into the Pacific. The one advantage the British had was that they tended to make the journey a one-way trip and put in an effort to understand the people in the new lands where they planned to settle. The French adventurers into the region, on the other hand, typically longed for a return to their homeland and, for the most part, continued to act like foreigners during their sojourns there. As a consequence, the British were generally more successful in developing long-term relationships with their island hosts.

The first missionary group to begin exploration and conversion of the Pacific islands was the London Missionary Society (LMS). Inspired by William Carey, a British Baptist missionary in India, this group of strongly evangelical Protestants started the organization in 1795 to support missionary ventures in the lands of the East. The islands of the Pacific became the primary target of the society, with Tahiti its first destination. Well into the mid-1800s, LMS continued to search for new islands and new souls in the realm. It eventually began sending missionaries all over the world. Reorganization of the society in the latter part of the twentieth century led to its current form as the 31-member Council for World Mission.[15]

The missionaries who were willing to venture into the unknown lands of the Pacific, thousands of miles away from home and family, were impelled by an evangelical zeal and ideology. Upon arrival in the realm, their first impressions of the prevalent belief systems led them to label these as pagan and therefore evil. They immediately set about to bring salvation to heathens, which is the way the islanders were typically understood. European intellectuals of the time were influenced by the ideas of early nineteenth-century French social thinkers such as Henri de Saint-Simon and Auguste Comte. Comte asserted that the evolution of human thinking and beliefs can be seen in theological conceptualizations, the lowest being animism, followed by pantheism, then monotheism, the highest. This provided the missionaries in the region an intellectual rationalization to go along with their ideological rejection of indigenous beliefs. They found easy justification to destroy existing religious cultures without stopping to consider their context or the positive role they might play in the lives of the people.

Also about the time the foreigners began to visit the islands, many indigenous beliefs, practices, and gods were being questioned and were losing popularity, especially in Polynesia, where strict hierarchies tended to relegate the lives of commoners to a serfdom-like existence in relation to their chiefs and rulers. For the chiefs who were at the losing end of power struggles and wars, there was a questioning of the strength and potency of their old gods and their old ways. It was in this environment that the first foreigners, and then the missionaries, began making inroads into the lands and lives of the people. These outsiders soon came to be seen as having brought a powerful god who helped them in their battles with the natives, and who provided them with the goods and power they possessed. Clearly, this superior god was worthy of chiefly offerings and prayers. Also, the military might and technological superiority of the foreigners inspired many of the chiefs to seek access to the superior weaponry of the Europeans. Acceptance of the new European god was seen as the key. Once chiefs accepted the new deity, their people began doing the same. In many of the traditional belief systems, the afterworld afforded chiefs a paradise-style existence, whereas the one for commoners was uninviting. When the latter were told that they would be allowed into the same Christian paradise as their chiefs, this seemed an attractive proposition.[16]

From the earliest European accounts of the Pacific islanders, it is clear that the native peoples were for the most part friendly, open, giving, and curious. This is not to say that no problems existed prior to the arrival of the Europeans, for warfare with people from other islands has been an integral part of the history of most of the islands. At first, conversion attempts by the missionaries had mixed results. Some were warmly accepted, others were ignored as much as possible, and some were killed. Where the power and possessions of the foreigners made them attractive to ruling chiefs, the missionaries were allowed to remain. Even where the chiefs did not wish to accept the new deity, they would often allow the missionaries to settle in their islands so their power might be available to the chiefs when needed. In those islands where the belief in a dominant male creator god already existed, the teachings of the missionaries about the Abrahamic creator god could be more easily adapted to or identified with an existing island deity. Conversion in this case meant little more than applying a new name and form of worship to an ancient deity. When a powerful chief aligned with a particular Christian denomination, his rivals might align with an opposing denomination. For example, in Tonga when a major chief, Taufa'ahau, became a Methodist, several rival chiefs then affiliated themselves with Roman Catholic Marists. Here and in various other situations, affiliation had little or nothing to do with theological alignments and more to do with political and military interests and agendas. Prior to the arrival of missionaries, many chiefs ruled by the authority of their gods. After conversion, they ruled by the authority of their new god. Here again, Taufa'ahau is a good example. In the beginning of the law code he issued in 1838, he asserts, "It is of the God of heaven and earth that I have been appointed to speak to you."[17]

Some missionaries and other foreigners sought to learn the dominant languages of the areas where they lived. However, these were unwritten and very different in structure from any of the European languages with which the foreigners were familiar. This not only made the learning process arduous, but it also resulted in many misunderstandings and subsequent mistranslations of what they were told by natives regarding the existing traditions. Even if the foreigners had a sincere desire to learn and translate earnestly, problems arose. The difficulty with translating the words and beliefs of the islanders was exasperated by the fact that Europeans assumed the former to be uncivilized, savage, and/or barbaric. In the process, missionaries often failed to perceive subtle and nuanced elements of indigenous understandings and beliefs. This was clearly the case in the Pacific. Christian missionaries often berated or even punished natives for holding on to traditional religious beliefs. They attempted to diminish or ban dancing and other forms of sensual entertainment, tattooing, adultery, and polygamy. Although this censure led to the demise of these traditional practices in some areas, in others it simply caused such beliefs and practices to go underground. The history of the Pacific since that time has been marked by native attempts to address, accommodate, and incorporate all that has occurred in their relationships with the world that exists beyond their shores.

POLYNESIA

Polynesia refers to a triangular shaped region of the central and southern Pacific Ocean that contains more than 1,000 islands. At the northern tip are the Hawaiian Islands, with New Zealand in the southwestern corner and Rapa Nui in the southeast. Of the three geographic regions in the Pacific, it is by far the largest and most populated, and it has the greatest diversity of religious denominations and groups. Thus, it will be the area about which there will be the most discussion. The islands of western Polynesia are larger and more populous than are those of eastern Polynesia, and this fact affects the types of cultures and beliefs that are present. New Zealand is an exception in this regard, because although it is has the largest landmass, it was settled by peoples from eastern Polynesia. The Maori thus blend both Western and Eastern influences.

There are many theories about the origins of the Polynesian peoples, most of which have them migrating into Oceania from various lands of the Asian continent, starting as early as 2000 BCE.[18] They crossed through Melanesia in the process, which may account for certain elements the two regions share. Samoa is likely one of the places where migrants into the region first resided. From there, they sailed to Tahiti. Centuries later, Tahitian and other Central Polynesian navigators traveled to Rapa Nui, and later to Hawai'i. New Zealand became populated sometime after the eleventh century. Legends tell of native voyagers sailing between the various islands in the region in Polynesian-style canoes long before the arrival of Europeans. These navigators are believed to have been highly skilled at sailing over vast distances from island to island.[19] Some of the preserved ancient chants contain the astronomical information to guide seafarers to the various islands. Throughout the migratory process, the beliefs and practices now considered indigenous to the various islands were being developed and shared by native seafarers who traveled between the islands. As a consequence, the languages and myths found in many of the outlying islands in the regions share a variety of similarities. That traditions were maintained and passed on orally allowed greater flexibility in adapting them to geographic and historical situations, and the Polynesians made good use of this. At the same time, each island or island group had, and still has, its own unique traits.

Deities

Polynesians are said to have one of the richest, most diverse and complex collections of mythological tales and legends about deities, demigods, and heroes anywhere in the world.[20] There are literally thousands of deities and spirit beings that were worshipped in Polynesia, covering a broad spectrum. There were gods of war and of peace, of healing and protection, of sorcery, of natural forces such as wind and rainbows, of places on land and in the heavens, and of the vast realm of the ocean. Among the more common terms for gods and goddesses in Polynesia are *atua*, *akua*, and *aumakua*. Some of the deities and spirits—such as Ra (also called La), the sun god—have common roots in other places in the world. Some deities that are more specifically Polynesian can be found throughout the region, although they are not understood in the same way in each place. For example, in Samoa, Tangaloa (or Tagaloa) is the creator god who rules everything under the sky. In Tahiti and French Polynesia, Ta'aroa is similarly understood. For the Maori, Tangaroa is the powerful and important god of the sea and creator of the fish, whereas for the people of Manihiki (Cook Islands), he is the originator and source of fire. In Hawai'i, he is Kanaloa, and although said to be one of the four primary deities, he is the least important. In ancient Rapa Nui, Makemake was the creator of all humanity.[21]

There are several levels of divinities and spirits, including high gods and ancestral gods. Depending on their lives, accomplishments, lineages, and importance, deceased humans can become guardian spirits or family gods (called 'aumakua in Hawaiian) for their clans. Because of this, there is an interesting interrelationship between humans and gods. As a family or clan gains power and prestige, the power attributed to its departed ancestors similarly increases. Proper prayer and worship endow them with spiritual power and turns them into guardian spirits. Those from very powerful clans may be adopted by individuals and families beyond the immediate clan and thus become elevated in power through the increase in prayer directed to them. When prayer is directed to a god or ancestor, that being gains in power as a consequence, so those to whom the greatest amount of prayer is given become the most powerful. This function of prayer is reflected in the Hawaiian word ho'omanamana, which is a term for worship that can be translated as "to endow with spirit power." It is one of the reasons why ancestor worship was important and why it was, and still is, found in nearly all the islands in the realm. For many Pacific islanders, especially Polynesians, one of the reasons Jesus is believed to have such great power is that so many people pray to him.

Ancestors would often take the form of a powerful animal to communicate with the living, and mortals are not to harm or eat the ancestors' living representatives, who impart their wisdom through visions, dreams, and other signs. Among the animal forms most commonly used to represent ancestors were the owl, shark, turtle, eel, and water lizard. These animals, then, were seen as totem animals, and as such were sacred and not to be killed or injured. Because different tribes and islands had their own deities, intertribal warfare would lead to the decimation of the idols and temples of the conquered peoples, and their replacement with the victors' gods. This could also lead to a rearrangement of the hierarchy of gods.[22]

An example of a deity in the form of an animal can be seen in the myths of the mo'o (water lizard) that are prevalent throughout Polynesia. They were great magical lizard-like beings who served as guardians. The mo'o was one of the oldest and most powerful of the animal representations of the guardian spirit. They typically represented a female deity. The origins of *mo'o* worship are unknown. Early on, she was found in Tahiti, where she was worshiped by a royal family, the Oropa'a.[23] One of the first *mo'o* goddesses in Hawai'i was Kanekua'ana. Subsequently, there were a variety of other *mo'o* goddesses, who usually lived near or in bodies of water. According to Dennis Kawaharada, *mo'o* are ancestral deities. Traditionally, their function has been to protect their descendants from a variety of illnesses and other dangers, including sorcery. They were also believed to be able to guide the spirit of the dead to the spirit world of the ancestors.[24]

Deity worship, religious ritual, and other ceremonies, especially those involving royalty, would often occur at sacred sites (*heiau* in Hawaiian, *marae* in Tahitian). Offerings included foodstuffs and/or sacrificed animals. It is believed that some such sites were reserved for human sacrifice as well. In Hawai'i, these were known as *luakini heiau*. Throughout the region, the sites were square, bordered by a coral and stone wall, with an altar (*ahu*) near one end. The use of wooden, coral, or stone images (known as *ti'i*, *ki'i*, or *tiki*) to represent deities was relatively common throughout the region. Some images had symbolic functions, others were seen to possess power, either inherently or because they had been empowered by a priest or by ritual prayers offered to them. In some places, they are still in use. Recent archaeological excavations in many of the islands—such as Tahiti, Mo'orea, Bora Bora, and Hawai'i—have uncovered old and forgotten sites and images. Although government support for this process is primarily for cultural preservation and attracting tourists, islanders who wish to resurrect, at least in part, their traditional religious ways are beginning to utilize these sites once again for religious rituals and other purposes.

Starting in its first year of publication in 1891, the *Journal of the Polynesian Society* began printing historical accounts of the region, including traditional prayers, chants, stories, and genealogies. Several of the latter elements are presented both in their native languages and in English. The authors were nearly all nonnative, but their efforts to preserve these forms of ancient knowledge have been pivotal in more recent attempts to revive lost traditions.

Although the vast majority of Polynesians have adopted Christianity, many have continued to hold on to what they have considered important aspects of their traditional cultures. This is especially true in Samoa, where native islanders very quickly became ministers and took over control of the way Christianity developed in their islands. Unlike foreign missionaries who were willing to destroy all aspects of the old traditions, native converts were much more respectful of their past. Additionally, the retention and perpetuation of their native languages have been important parts of the cultural revival process, because language is, after all, the philosophy and beliefs of a people put into words.

Samoa

Samoa is the collective name of a group of 15 volcanic islands in Central Polynesia. Nine compose the Independent State of Samoa, referred to herein as Samoa, whereas the other six make up the unincorporated territory of the United States known as American Samoa.[25] The two island groups are approximately 60 miles apart. More than 90 percent of the peoples that populate both Samoas are ethnically Polynesian, and many families have members in both island groups. Being politically and economically more closely connected with the United States, American Samoa has been far more influenced by Western ways and values. Nevertheless, the people there still maintain many aspects of their traditional culture, albeit to a lesser extent than do the people of Samoa.

Pre-Contact

The Samoan islands were first inhabited by humans, most likely from Tonga, nearly 3,000 years ago. The traditional belief system was polytheistic animism with several versions of creation. In one of the most popular, the dominant deity, Tangaloa (or Tagaloa), created the universe out of nothing.[26] The earth, the waters, the islands of Samoa, humans, and other gods followed. Depending on the myth, the islands of Samoa came either down from the heavens or up from the ocean. In one version, Tagaloa's grandson, Lu, descended from the heavens to earth and named the place he lived Sa-ia-Moa ("sacred-for-Moa"), after his uncle Moa. From this came *Samoa*.[27] There is also a tale of a powerful warrior goddess named Nafanua, who is said to have helped the Samoan people win their freedom from Tonga. She also predicted the arrival in the islands of a newer and more powerful ruler and government, which she advised the people to follow.

Post-Contact

The first known European to visit the Samoan islands was Jacob Roggeveen, a Dutchman, in 1722. From the latter part of the century until the arrival of missionaries in 1830, the islands became a stopover site for a variety of European and American ships. The first missionaries to arrive were Tongan Methodist preachers, but John Williams and other members of the LMS are credited with the establishment of the new religion.[28] Shortly after Williams's arrival, converts began to point to the story attributed to Nafanua, claiming that Jesus and Christianity were fulfillments of her prophecy. That and the conversion of the dominant *malietoa,* or warrior chief, facilitated an easy and rather rapid conversion of the population to Christianity. The LMS continued to be integral in the religious life of Samoa until it became part of the Congregational Council for World Mission in 1966. In 1977, the name was shortened to the Council of World Mission.

Catholic missionaries arrived on the islands in the early 1840s and officially established themselves in 1845. Toward the end of the century, the Church of Latter-Day Saints began its proselytization efforts, and the Seventh-Day Adventists arrived several years later. Thus, by the turn of the century, Christianity in Samoa had become quite diverse, and the aforementioned groups remain the dominant denominations today.

The conversion of the Samoan peoples was fairly rapid and complete in comparison to what occurred in other islands, at least in the view of the LMS missionaries. From their first contact, LMS missionaries were uncompromising in their rejection of indigenous beliefs and practices. Thus, the overt expression of native traditions was almost completely annihilated in Samoa. The national crest (or coat of arms) adopted after Samoa's independence in 1961 has the words "FA'AVAE I LE ATUA SAMOA" ("Samoa is founded on God"). Clearly, "God" here refers to the Christian god, for at the top of the crest is a Christian cross.

At the same time, however, traditional beliefs have continued in those areas of life that Christian thinking did not or could not address, namely, the psychological conflicts that many Samoans were experiencing in the face of the relatively rapid changes their homeland was undergoing. Chiefs who converted were able to draw on both traditional and Christian approaches to dealing with various social and political issues and problems. Moreover, this utilization of indigenous culture continues to be a valuable resource for Samoan leaders as well as commoners.[29]

Contemporary Times

Most Polynesians are proud of their traditions and want to see them preserved as much as is feasible. As a consequence, there exists a theological struggle today between those who want to maintain an exclusive Christian Samoa and those who want to preserve and perpetuate indigenous beliefs and practices. In this context, a recent talk by Mr. Tui Atua Tupua Tamasese Tupuola Tufuga Efi, the current head of state of the country, is significant. In a keynote address he delivered at the National University of Samoa in December 2008, he gave indigenous beliefs equal status with Christianity and emphasized the need for openness and religious freedom. Some of the more staunchly Christian Samoans were upset by his words. His speech used theological beliefs drawn from both traditions to explain and justify contemporary legal concepts. In showing the influence of traditional beliefs in the Samoan understanding of themselves, he stated, "In the Samoan version, God is progenitor of man and so man is, therefore, God descended. This gives man genealogical links with the sun, moon, seas, rocks, earth, water, trees, and so on. . . . Whilst the Christian reference promotes man having dominion over nature; the Samoan indigenous reference promotes man in a younger brother-type relationship."[30] He makes it clear that Samoan Christian thinking, in his eyes at least, is equally Samoan and Christian. Clearly, the American concept of separation of church and state does not exist in Samoa. Religion can be relevant in many of the government activities. In the 1980s, for example, one of the dominant political parties was the Christian Democratic Party, and the current head of state, Tui Atua Tamasese, was a member of it. The current prime minister, Tuilaepa Aiono Sailele Malielegaoi, is an avowed Roman Catholic. Prayer begins all government meetings, and often ends them as well.

There has been, like in other areas of the Pacific, a concerted effort to bring back some indigenous practices. The continued use of Samoan as their primary language has been an important factor in the ability to maintain essential aspects of the traditional beliefs and practices, because language, beliefs, and culture all have an intimate relationship. Some practices have been resurrected because of their preservation in families, whereas others have been fabricated out of a contemporary understanding of what they had been in the past. The traditions associated with tattooing, which is part of a rite of passage for many young Samoan males, have been largely maintained, albeit without elements that would be considered anti-Christian. Some women also get tattoos, but with different designs and limited to the thighs. For many, the process is a family affair with strong religious overtones. According to author Liz Thompson, there is a belief that a person is "vulnerable to the influence of malevolent spirits" while being tattooed. The guests and family members in attendance provide a sort of spiritual protection until the ceremony is completed.[31]

Although the more conservative Samoan Christians like to say that their old beliefs are no longer followed in their islands, this is far from the case. While these beliefs may not be adhered to in isolation from Christianity in any large way, they are apparent in their influence on the way the adopted religion is practiced, especially in the family-oriented way in which most things happen. Sundays are important holidays with the church playing an integral role in everyday life, especially in the more rural areas. Ministers are important and highly respected members of the community, and their opinions carry a great deal of influence in family and community matters. There are usually several church services on Sundays, and these are typically followed by other church-related activities. Attendees dress in traditional post-contact attire, and families can be recognized by the color and design of their cloth. White is the most important color because it symbolizes purity. In much of Samoa, shops close and work typically ends at sunset, and families will often get together to sing or pray. All nonreligious activity is supposed to be suspended on Sunday, and on some islands fines are even given to those participating in activities seen as inconsistent with the sacredness of the day.

The predominant Christian denomination today is the current manifestation of the LMS, that is, Congregationalism (34.8%). This is followed by Roman Catholic (19.6%), Methodist (15%), and Latter-Day Saints (12.7%). Many smaller Protestant denominations are present as well.[32] For the most part, the leaders of all the denominations in the islands are ethnically Samoan, and this indigenous control and influence of Christianity has been the case for most of the last two centuries. Approximately 98 percent of those living in American Samoa are Christian. The motto of the land is "Samoa Muamua Le Atua," which means "In Samoa, God is First."

Tahiti (Society Islands)

Pre-Contact

Ancient chants tell of the arrival of humans to Tahiti thousands of years ago. They are believed to have traveled from Southeast Asia, through Fiji, Samoa, and Tonga. Already skilled navigators, they soon spread out into the surrounding islands. Over the next millennium, the ancestors of those first settlers found their way to new islands in every direction, including Rapa Nui, the Cook Islands, Hawai'i, and lastly New Zealand, the latter two being at a distance of more than 2,600 miles away. It is largely because of these mariners and their incredible navigating skills that there is a recognizable Polynesian culture of shared beliefs, practices, and values.

Tahiti developed a strongly hierarchical culture, which influenced most of the cultures in the islands to which Tahitian navigators traveled. Clearly, Polynesia is far more hierarchical than the other Pacific regions. At the top of the hierarchy was the *ari'i* (*ali'i* in Hawaiian), members of the royalty. They had total control over the political and social life of the people. The formal religious sphere was controlled by the priests (*tahu'a*). Other *tahu'a* (shamans) dealt with healing, divination, or sorcery. Anyone with a specific important knowledge or capability, such as navigation, would also be known as a *tahu'a*. The commoners were known as *manahune*. Their only power existed within the context of their immediate family.

Deities

As in much of the Pacific, the gods of ancient Tahiti were a combination of ancestor deities connected with particular tribal groups and the more ancient gods who transcended tribal limits and were worshiped on a broader scale. The various deities were of land and sea, and the forms they took could be human, animal, or plant. For example, the god Roro'o, who inspired the priests in their chanting, was represented by a *miro* tree, which was planted around the sacred sites (*marae*) where chanting would occur.[33] Ta'aroa was the supreme deity and creator of the universe, Oro was the war god, and Pere was the fire goddess. The physical representation of a god or goddess was referred to as his or her shadow (*ata*). It could be anything in nature, from a fish or other animal to a rock. A human-made representation was called *to'o* or *ti'i*. These were considered to have sacred power and thus were taboo.

Marae

A *marae* is a sacred place. It is where religious worship, offerings, and ceremonies take place. Traditionally, activities ranging from making political decisions to dancing were also said to have occurred here; yet there were definite taboos as to what could take place at these sites and who could attend. Human sacrifice also occurred at certain *marae*. Some sites were national, and some were only for a certain clan. Walls of stone or coral would demarcate them, and *miro* trees would be planted around their perimeters. The altar (*ahu*) was considered to be the most sacred spot in a *marae* and could only be approached by the priests. Use of wooden, coral, or stone images (*ti'i*) to represent deities was relatively common, and these would often be clothed with *tapa* (cloth made from bark) and sacred feathers.

Post-Contact

The first European to land in Tahiti was the British explorer Captain Samuel Wallis, in 1767. Exactly 30 years later, members of the LMS arrived with a strong determination to convert the "heathens." Although the missionaries were welcomed by the king at the time, Pomare I, they subsequently fled the main island with his successor, Pomare II, after the latter's defeat by a rival. A decade or so later, with the help of Europeans, Pomare II was able to take over control of many of the islands. Because of the missionaries' role in his success, he officially converted to Christianity in 1819, and ordered the destruction of ancient sacred sites throughout the islands.[34] He established his own law code, the Pomare Code, strongly influenced by the wishes of his missionary advisors. It firmly set Christian principles in place and secured a permanent spot for the religion in governmental affairs.[35] In addition, missionaries had tattooing and dancing banned as anti-Christian activities. The Tahitian Auxiliary Missionary Society was also established shortly after Pomare II's conversion. The Society was created as an affiliate of the LMS to oversee and promote conversion of all Tahitians as well as support conversions throughout the world. Protestant missionaries were easily able to establish themselves and secure power under the king and his heir, Pomare III. The legal environment was so affected by Christianity that some people were arrested for not going to Sunday church services.[36] The government also decided to prohibit alcohol possession and consumption, although LMS members were doing the distilling and selling. The prohibition law was eventually passed but foreigners, including missionaries, ignored it. Chiefs on the outer islands did likewise, so the prohibition remained ineffectual.[37]

During the reign of Queen Pomare, Pomare II's daughter, in the 1830s, French Catholics sought to make inroads into the islands. Once the British Protestants became aware of this, they convinced the queen to prohibit the Catholics and their evangelistic efforts. The French government subsequently applied pressure, and she relented. Within a decade, the French government had essentially taken over much of the governmental powers, giving Catholics free reign to proselytize their own sectarian beliefs. Tahiti officially became a French colony in 1877.[38] The first Mormons (Latter-day Saints, or LDS) arrived in 1844. A break-off denomination, known in Tahiti as the Sanito Church, is also active in French Polynesia, and it is estimated to have more than half the numbers of adherents as does the main LDS Church.

From the time of its takeover of the islands until the present day, France has exerted continuous control over the islands, which have remained strongly Christian. French Polynesia is one of the few island groups left in the Pacific that continues under the control of a colonial administration. Although secularism is a strong component of French law, the same is not the case in French Polynesia. Here, as in much of the Pacific, religion is closely intertwined with politics. Religious leaders play an active role in all aspects of the political process, from prayers at political gatherings to influencing laws that are passed. The number of evangelical Protestants is growing in Tahiti, and they have now succeeded, to some extent, in having input on various governmental policies.

Churches are the hubs of social life. As in Samoa, Sunday is the day when people dress up, attend mass together as a large family, and are on their best behavior. During almost any evening, there is some sort of church gathering or activity that draws crowds. Informal dress at these activities is discouraged. Christianity in Tahiti and the Marquesas Islands has been strongly influenced by Catholic devotionalism, so singing of hymns is important and traditional

A Catholic Church in Nuku Hiva, Marquesas, with ancient Marquesan tikis (holy deities) on either side of the entrance, c. July 2007. (Photo by Sachi Lamb.)

chanting style is often used. In the Marquesas, crosses and statues of the Virgin Mary dot the hilltops overlooking the valleys where people live. They are regularly cleaned and adorned with flowers.

The dominant language is French. Although many of the elders know and speak Tahitian, younger islanders tend to understand it but prefer speaking French to each other. They are proud to be Tahitian, but it is Tahitian Christianity with which they most strongly identify. Although very few want a resurgence of the old religion as such, they continue to see their islands as sacred, much as their ancestors did, and this sanctity makes them special. Most Tahitians find it important to follow traditions tied with the old religion and culture, and they feel no contradiction in doing so. Myths and stories of the gods and of the various places on the islands connected with them are commonly heard, and these myths continue to be part of the people's thinking. One can even see ancient *ti'i* on church grounds because of the sanctity of both. In the present-day religious makeup of French Polynesia, Protestant denominations account for nearly 60 percent of the population, followed by Catholics at just over 30 percent.[39] The bulk of the remainder follow native traditions or none at all. In the Marquesas Islands, however, Catholics are a strong majority, estimated to be over 90 percent.

Hawai'i

Of all the islands and island-nations in the Pacific realm, Hawai'i has the most diverse religious landscape. It is a multicolored scene in which all of the major world traditions play roles, exerting tangible influences on culture, economics, and politics. With the possible exception of California, Hawai'i encompasses a greater diversity of religious traditions than does any other U.S. state, and it also ranks among the most religiously diverse areas in the world. There are two principal reasons for this. The first is a consequence of plantation owners' importing cheap labor to work their sugarcane fields. The second is that the state is a part of the United States, which has been the destination and goal of immigrants from all over the world. As a consequence of these and other factors, the Hawaiian Islands are clearly a religious and cultural melting pot.

Pre-Contact

A belief among some in Hawai'i is that Tahitian navigators were the first to reach the islands, bringing with them their religious traditions, gods, social and religious hierarchy, and lineages of chiefs and priests. Others believe that Marquesans landed first but were subsequently defeated by later Tahitians. Either way, many of the Hawaiian gods originated in Tahiti, but their functions and roles changed slightly in their new land. The primary gods of early Hawai'i were Ku, Lono, Kane, and Kanaloa. Lono, the Hawaiian god associated with clouds, storms and agriculture, likely comes from the Tahitian Ro'o, the messenger of the gods. Kanaloa, possibly from the Tahitian Ta'aroa, has a different function in Hawai'i and is not so elevated. Although he is generally coupled with Kane in much of the mythology, there is one tale in which he rebels against Kane and is sent to the underworld as ruler of the dead. This caused some Christians to associate him with the devil.[40] Traditionally, there were different priests for different gods, especially for Lono and Ku. The Lono priests would pray for rain and abundant crops, but also to avoid sickness and trouble.[41] Ku was the god of war and thus important to all the chiefs. The primary female deities were Haumea (also known as Papa), Hina, and Pele. One tradition sees all Hawaiians as coming from the same original couple, Wakea and Papa. The subsequent division of people into royalty (ali'i) and commoner (maka'ainana) was the result of necessity so that society could function properly.[42] Hina was the wife of the first man, Ti'i, from whom Tahitian royalty are descendants. Pele, the goddess of the volcano, is by far the most popular goddess in Hawai'i, because of the regular volcanic activity there.[43] In Tahiti and the Cook Islands, she is Pere, the goddess of fire.

Heiau

Many religious activities and sacrifices occurred at sacred sites known as *heiau*, which were similar in construction and use to the Tahitian *marae*. There were a variety of *heiau*, each meant for a different purpose. At *heiau* dedicated to Lono, for example, offerings were primarily of food in hopes for rain and good crops. A *luakini heiau*, on the other hand, was dedicated to the war gods. Dominant among them was Ku (Kuka'ilimoku) on the Big Island, and the offerings were animal or human. Priests associated with the particular god were the only ones allowed within the *heiau*. Worship there was an integral part of the worship of the gods and closely connected with the system of religious taboos in Hawai'i known as the *kapu* system. Once the system was overturned in 1819, the sanctity and use of the *heiau* essentially ended.

Post-Contact

Captain James Cook was the first foreigner to land on the islands, in 1778, and he found a friendly but timid people.[44] The future King Kamehameha was a young warrior at the time, although he almost immediately saw advantages in gaining access to the foreigners' powerful weapons and to their knowledge of warfare. Several years later, upon the death of his uncle, Kamehameha was made guardian of the war god Kuka'ilimoku and also given rule over a northern valley on the island of Hawai'i named Waipi'o. From that time on, he began the process of defeating the other chiefs on all the islands so that he could become king. The dominant gods at the time were Ku, the favorite of the king, and Lono. Kamehameha completed his victory in 1810 and became the first king of islands of Hawai'i. By the time of his death in 1819, he had purchased over 30 foreign ships and munitions with the proceeds of his monopolization of much of the trade with foreigners. Although Kamehameha did not worship the foreigners' new god, his descendants allowed the missionaries to reside in the islands and proselytize.

Kamehameha's successor was his 22-year-old son, Kamehameha II (Liholiho). At Kamehameha II's coronation, the late king's favorite wife, Ka'ahumanu, surprised her stepson by claiming the deceased king wanted her to be co-ruler. She also named herself *kuhina nui*, a title she created. The inexperienced new king accepted. The queen did not like the *kapu* system and its restrictions on women, so she set about changing things. One of her early actions was to have Liholiho eat with her and his mother, Keopuolani, and thereby break an important food taboo. After doing so, he also put an order in place to destroy the *heiau*, burn all idols, and end much of the *kapu* system. For a brief period after the old traditions and beliefs were officially ended and the support that the traditional culture had provided the people was lost, there was pervasive despair and confusion among the commoners. Many felt a sense of anxiety, not sure of what they should believe or do. Alcohol consumption by members of the royal family increased tremendously. The following year, the first missionaries arrived and were immediately welcomed.[45] In 1824, Ka'ahumanu officially converted to Christianity and was baptized in the Congregationalist Church. She encouraged all Hawaiians at the time to do the same. The king, however, did not convert, unwilling to stop drinking alcohol or to give up four of his five wives. Nevertheless, he helped the queen create an environment for the missionaries to proselytize and prosper.

After the end of the *kapu* system, missionaries began imposing their own system of rules, prohibiting such actions as murder, adultery, and theft.[46] But they also utilized aspects of the old system by declaring themselves, their homes, and their possessions *kapu*, or sacred and off limits to all but the select few.[47] As the power of the Protestants increased, they set about removing any of the remaining old traditions that met with their disapproval. Hula, the ancient dance tradition, was one of the victims. In 1830, Ka'ahumanu forbade hula performance claiming that it was lewd and against Christian values. Nevertheless, hula continued to be practiced in private and away from the urban centers in which the missionaries were most active. In the process, hula waned considerably for most of the nineteenth century. Tattooing was also discouraged, and missionaries banned it for converts.

The first Roman Catholic missionaries arrived from France in 1827. Protestants did not want the competition, so Ka'ahumanu eventually ordered them to leave the islands, which they did in 1831 after limited success. She also issued a decree forbidding the spread of Catholic teachings. In 1839, King Kamehameha III issued the Edict of Toleration (1839), which allowed for the return and permanent establishment of Catholicism in the islands. One of the early Protestant missionaries was Titus Coan, a determined evangelist bent on converting all the natives he encountered on the island of Hawai'i. He would hold emotional revival meetings that would sometimes last for days. His success was relatively limited in his first two years there. Then, on November 7, 1837, while he was praying, a tidal wave hit the town near his home. Coan was able to convince many of the locals that the lethal wave was a sign from God and that they had better protect themselves against the devil. He was a fiery evangelist, like his mentor Charles Grandison Finney. The focus of their preaching styles was sin, the fear of damnation, and the need to have a savior. Crowds began to listen to Coan, and the number of his converts increased to more than 3,000 during the next six months.[48] He became a pivotal figure in the expansion of Christianity in Hawai'i during this era.

The Hawaiian Evangelical Association was formed in 1854, and within 10 years it had native Hawaiians as clergymen among its ranks. Also in the 1850s, the first Mormon missionaries visited the islands, and they were followed a few years later by Episcopalians. Hawai'i had become a Christian nation, and only remnants of the old religious beliefs and practices remained.[49] Nevertheless, there were those Hawaiians who did not take to the new religion, except for superficially, and they continued to adhere to their native traditions and preserve them through their descendants. It was not until well into the twentieth century that Hawaiians in any considerable number began to try to reawaken some of those beliefs and practices. After searching for a Hawaiian word to define their concept of religion, the missionaries chose *ho'omana*, which means "to confer *mana* on something." At the same time, they began to use the reduplicative *ho'omanamana*, in reference to the old religion, which they saw as evil.

About the time that missionaries from new denominations were expanding the diversity of Christian forms in Hawai'i, owners of the growing sugar plantations inadvertently began to increase non-Christian traditions as well. Starting in the 1850s and into the early 1900s, they sought cheap forms of labor. Unlike the British in Fiji who had imported a single ethnic group to work their plantations, Hawai'i plantation owners looked in various lands. The first to arrive in any significant number were Chinese. They were followed several years later by the Japanese, then Portuguese, and finally Filipinos. The new immigrants all brought their beliefs systems with them as well, and to the dismay of the missionaries, added non-Christian traditions and practices to a rapidly increasing multiethnic society. To help counter this, the government did not allow first-generation Asian immigrants, nearly all of whom were Buddhist, to become citizens. Their children who were born in Hawai'i could become citizens by virtue of their birth. These children were expected to become American, and the missionaries made sure that they were aware that an integral part of being American was being Christian. Christian missionaries expanded their effort into the plantations. An example of the view they promoted of Buddhism can be seen in an article in *The Friend*, a monthly publication by Chaplain Samuel Damon. In it, he writes, "As an ethical system, Buddhism is superior to the heathen Hinduism, although it has totally failed to elevate the Japanese people anywhere near to the current morality and decency of Christian peoples."[50] In 1906, when the largest Japanese Buddhist denomination in Hawai'i, the Jodo-shin, applied for a charter as a religious organization, then-governor George Carter rejected it as not being in the best interest of the territories. However, the next governor, William Frear, agreed to sign the application.

Because of the increase in wealth and power of the plantation owners during the last decades of the nineteenth century, there was an increasing attempt by them and other powerful figures in the kingdom to diminish the power of the existing government and put it more solidly under the control of the U.S. government. The 1887 Bayonet Constitution, which then-king David Kalakua was forced to sign, furthered that process. When his sister, Lili'uokalani, became queen in 1891, she sought to return to the previous constitution. The forces against her and the monarchy finally succeeded in overthrowing her government in 1893, when the U.S. government took over possession of Hawai'i. This was a sad time for most indigenous Hawaiians, but it did little to change the religious dynamics. The queen and the entire royalty since the time of Kamehameha III had been Christian, so this was not a missionary-motivated act. It was purely a move by business and political forces to take hold of power on the islands.

In 1916 there were approximately 100,000 Japanese in Hawai'i, but fewer than 2 percent had become Christian. As working conditions became less bearable, and Buddhist priests encouraged the Japanese to strike, Buddhists came to be seen by plantation owners as a threat to their success. At the same time, young Japanese were being taught adherence to traditional Japanese culture and reverence to the emperor of Japan. This increasingly came to be seen as un-American. In an attempt to become more accepted in the dominant Christian society of the day, Japanese-language teachers shifted their focus toward preparing their students to be good Americans. Nevertheless, some Americans in Hawai'i and on the mainland continued to see the Japanese as less than good citizens.[51] This fact made the interment of Japanese during World War II easier for the government to undertake.

The U.S. military presence on the many islands of the Pacific during Word War II led to various servicemen becoming enamored of both the islands and their women. Marriages ensued, and Hawai'i became a midpoint between the two worlds for many of them to live. Hawai'i was also the first stop for a new wave of immigration to America, this one primarily from Asia and the Pacific. After arriving in Hawai'i, many of the new immigrants decided to go no further. The result has been an expansion of ethnic groups from all over Asia and the Pacific. This process continues up to the present day.

Contemporary Times

Reflecting the prevailing nationwide trend, Christianity is the dominant religion. Three-fourths of residents who acknowledge religious affiliation are Christian; however, knowing exact percentages is difficult for several reasons. One is that a significant number of residents are immigrants from countries where government intrusion into their lives was often a negative experience. Thus, they are hesitant to divulge anything but the minimum about themselves to government officials, including census takers. Another is that non-Christian immigrants are even less likely to declare religious affiliations during censuses, fearing that their non-Christian beliefs will offend Christian officials. When a study of the religious makeup of the islands was done by faculty at the University of Hawai'i in 1998, many individuals and organizations refused to divulge even basic information. That said, best estimates have Catholics comprising about 22–25 percent of the population, and there are almost as many Southern Baptists. The other Protestant denominations with significant numbers are Church of Jesus Christ of Latter-Day Saints (Mormons), the Church of Christ, and the Methodist Church. At the same time, non-Christian organizations are prevalent all over the islands, with many Asians and Pacific islanders joining religious organizations whose members share their cultural background. Numerous Christian groups have adapted to this ethnic diversity by providing non-English-language services, most commonly in Japanese, Hawaiian, Korean, Samoan, or Filipino. Several distinct expressions of Christianity have likewise evolved to assimilate elements of other religious cultures. For example, some Christian groups formally participate in the Obon and Lantern Festivals, which are Japanese Buddhist rites performed for departed ancestors.

Buddhism is the largest non-Christian religion, and the variety of denominations has expanded greatly over the last several decades. Many immigrants from South, Southeast, and East Asia have brought their own forms of Buddhism with them. Whereas first- and second-generation immigrants generally remain strongly attached to their ethnic religious forms, often their descendants abandon these ties, choosing either to become Christian, or not to affiliate with any particular denomination. The outcome of this trend is that although the number of Buddhist sects has increased over the last two decades, the overall number of acknowledged Buddhists has dropped slightly.

The overriding presence of Christianity in Hawai'i has also influenced the way some forms of Asian religions are practiced and expressed. The Honpa Hongwanji Mission in Honolulu probably embodies this influence more obviously than any other group. From its inception, the Mission has sought to provide a religious atmosphere adapted to the dominant culture. Thus, the temple's interior—complete with a pulpit, prayer pews, and hymnals—in many respects resembles a church. Sunday worship service includes a sermon and a choir. The temple acquired the first pipe organ in the state and was the setting for the first non-Christian service in English.

The flourishing of many new religious movements continues to diversify the religious character of Hawai'i. These groups tend to have younger membership than the more established religions and often are marked by charismatic leaders. Such groups can be broadly grouped into two categories: new Japanese religions and New Age religions. Many of the former have established branches in Hawai'i, such as Tenri-kyo, Seicho No Ie, and Mahikari. New Age religions tend to be metaphysical and originate as either offshoots of older religions, eclectic reformulations of several religious traditions, or totally new movements. They typically blend elements of mystical Christianity, Buddhism, Hinduism, and psychotherapeutics.

Hula and the Reawakening of Hawaiian Culture

In Hawai'i, one of the stimuli for the reawakening of traditional religious and cultural thinking has been the rise in popularity of studies of Hawaiian language and arts. With respect to the latter, hula has been fundamental. King David Kalakaua, who led the Hawaiian Kingdom from 1874 until his death in 1891, was a strong supporter of the traditions and culture of his islands, including music, dance, and language. Even though he had been raised as an Episcopalian, his sentiments were strongly aligned with the traditional culture of his people. During his reign, he sought to help reawaken Hawaiian traditions and culture in their minds and hearts by inviting musicians, artists, and hula dancers to his new palace and by promoting their performances. Because of this, he came to be known as the Merrie Monarch. To honor him, the Merrie Monarch Festival was begun in 1964. Although a resurgence of hula had been going on more quietly for several decades, the festival gave a much broader forum for its display, and this led to a rise in its popularity. Since that time, the number of hula *halau* (dance groups) has increased significantly: there are now more than 1,000 all over the world. Those who participate cannot help entering the world of ancient Hawaiian traditions in the process. The more serious hula *kumu* (a teacher of traditional arts) immerse themselves and their students in those traditions and the beliefs connected with them. This includes acknowledgment of old deities, prayers, and practices, including the value and practice of many forms of *kapu*. For practitioners of *hula*, Laka is the most important deity. She is the sister of Lono and patroness of the arts. Many traditional hula performances include chants to her. Pele, the volcano goddess, is also an important goddess for many hula dancers. The annual Merrie Monarch Festival is held on the Big Island (the common name in the state for the actual island named Hawai'i), which is also the home of Pele. Many *halau* who journey to the island will first go to Halema'uma'u crater, Pele's home. There, they will make offerings to her while they chant and dance for her. Many *halau* members will also observe various *kapu* restrictions connected with preparation and dance.

When asked about his views regarding the gods and goddesses traditionally associated with the hula, a well-known and respected hula *kumu* recently discussed his approach to them. He admitted that although he cannot officially worship them because he is a "strong Christian," he believes in them. He used the metaphor of water, saying that just as it gives him life and strength even though he does not worship it, in the same way the gods and goddesses have great *mana* and give him strength. Because of this, he includes prayers to them in his performances, and essentially all of his dance students who are Christian do likewise.[52] Another Hawaiian Christian, Chaplain David Ka'upu, often sought to bridge the apparent gap between old Hawaiian traditions and Christianity. For 31 years, he was chaplain at Kamehameha Schools, a private Protestant school in Honolulu where students are exclusively ethnic Hawaiians. He believed it was important to acknowledge divine connection between humans and God.[53] Speaking of the future of his school at the time of his retirement, Ka'upu emphasized that it should be "grounded in Hawaiian and Christian values.... There are some things in our Hawaiian traditions that can allow us to become better Christians and teach us about the essence of Christianity."[54]

There is an official acknowledgment of the connection between the contemporary world in Hawai'i and the old religious and cultural traditions of the islands. Before any land is excavated for new construction, an investigation is conducted to see if ancestral bones or other artifacts are unearthed. Dissension and protests accompany any plans to build on sites considered sacred within the traditional culture. Whenever there is a new government or military facility built, or a special activity about to occur, a Hawaiian Christian leader or minister is invited to perform a traditional Hawaiian blessing. Ironically, in these situations prayers occur where normally they would not be included to avoid complaints about separation of church and state. Many Hawaiians who are involved in the environmental movement see it within the context of a traditional respect for the land, or *'aina*. In this way, their actions to preserve the earth for future generations are grounded in an emotional contact with the land rather than on a secular or intellectual view. John Charlot quite accurately notes that "ancient worldviews prove more effective than post-Enlightenment Western thinking."[55]

MELANESIA

Melanesia is geographically the smallest of the three regions of the Pacific, bordered by Micronesia to the north, Australia to the south, and Polynesia to the east. It spreads from the islands of Maluku and New Guinea in the west to the islands of Fiji in the east. It includes the Solomon Islands, Vanuatu (formerly New Hebrides), Bougainville, New Caledonia, and numerous smaller islands. Estimates place the earliest human inhabitants of the region in New Guinea nearly 40,000 years ago. Sometime in the second millennium BCE, Austronesian peoples from the islands and mainland of Southeast Asia began to populate the land as well, eventually moving to other islands in the region as far east as Fiji.

Small by comparison, Melanesia has a greater number of languages, ethnic groups considered indigenous, and cultural groupings than the other regions. Because of this, it is difficult to make generalizations, so they are done herein with the understanding that they may have little or no application at all to some of the islands or cultures in the region. Whereas some myths, legends, beliefs, and practices are found throughout much of the region, others are unique to one island or island group. Christianity has obviously had a powerful impact in Melanesia; but of the three Pacific regions, it retains the highest number of tribes and groups that have yet to be assimilated by the foreign religion. Many indigenous groups and their traditional beliefs and practices survived relatively intact until at least the latter half of the twentieth century. Among those groups that have only been recently exposed to Western ways and Christianity, there continue to be many individuals who practice, have personal connection with, or have remembrance of the old ways.

There was traditionally little belief in a supreme god or even a broadly accepted hierarchy of gods in the region. Animism and ancestor worship tend to have the greatest influence. There were also relatively few creation myths regarding the world, because the world was assumed to have always existed. Instead, creation stories focus primarily on the various islands, spirits, humans, and animals. One deity present in much of the region is Qat. He is a creator god in some of the northern islands of Vanuatu, but he has a different role in most other Melanesian islands. Other creator gods include Tagaro and Manuai.[56] A common theme in many of the region's myths tells of two brothers. Often, one is wise and the other foolish. Their interactions are responsible for much of the good and the bad that exists on earth. Some islanders understand the stories to suggest that humans have two souls, one that goes to an afterworld whereas the other may take on various forms.[57] In many of the Melanesian tales, wood is the material from which humans and some gods were fashioned.

Gods, Spirits, and Ancestors

Spirits, and the spirit world, have long been a part of everyday life. Most are either ancestor or tribal spirits that are limited in their breadth, responsibility, and function. There is also a belief in many of the islands in spirits known as *masalai.* These are neither gods, nor demons, nor ancestor spirits, although they are generally connected with different tribes and families as well. They function somewhat similarly to Christian guardian angels in caring for those with whom they are associated, provided the latter have followed all the necessary taboo rules. They live in jungles and are the main cause of fear for those who venture into the wild.[58] No myths are common throughout the region, as is the case in Polynesia, although there are common themes. One is that humans have the power to control spirits or natural forces through magic.

Ancestors play an important role in the traditional beliefs of Melanesians. Some are seen in a positive light and are believed to be available to assist their living descendants. Others are believed to be more dangerous to the living, depending on who they were as humans and how they died.[59] Nevertheless, ancestor spirits play an integral role in many aspects of human life, and they may occasionally return to the world in another form, human or animal. In the Manus religion of the Admiralty Islands, worship is almost entirely limited to ancestors. The departed act as guardian spirits over their descendants, provided a proper relationship is nurtured and maintained by the living. The most recently departed male elder of the family is worshiped as "Sir Ghost," and his skull is placed in the rafters of the home.[60] Within a few generations, ancestor spirits are believed to lose some of their power and tend to no longer be propitiated. The Manus also believe in evil spirits, who can cause illness, and they will go to their shamans to have rituals performed for protection. Although most Manus are officially Christian, their religion is clearly a mixture of traditional and imported beliefs and practices. Their origin myth parallels aspects of the Genesis creation story, and their legends tell of a heaven and a hell and of angels, who are their ancestors' spirits.

There is a less defined social hierarchy in the region as well, which possibly results from the lack of a strict hierarchy of gods, with each tribe being somewhat independent in its thinking and functioning. Here, *mana* was considered to be possessed by royalty and by commoners as well, albeit in less degree. Through efforts and attainments, such as success in a battle over a strong opponent or some other great accomplishment, commoners could gain *mana.* Another effect of the lack of a hierarchy of gods, and of an overall lack of deities in general, is that shamans and priests have traditionally been considered to have the most *mana,* sometimes even more than that possessed by certain spirits. They not only facilitate communication with the spirit world and ancestors but also have the power to cause or prevent the effects of curses, take over the soul of a living person (adult or child), change the weather, and help remove illnesses. Shamanic functions have been carried out primarily by adult males who have gained knowledge of rituals or the ability to communicate with the spirit world. They have usually been trained by elders in the techniques used. Unlike in Polynesia, the individuals who typically perform priestly and shamanic functions are commoners with special expertise, not individuals whose sole function is to perform these. Such individuals would typically perform their rituals and other functions for members of their own families. On occasion, an exceptionally strong or charismatic figure could come to be seen as a prophet by followers who were from other families, and even other tribes. This is one of the factors that has facilitated the popularity of the region's cargo cults (see below).

Cargo Cults

One of the more unique aspects of Melanesian religious culture is the presence of cargo cults. Although found in other areas of the world, their presence is concentrated in this region. Cargo cults are religious movements centered around the belief that some deity, god, or possibly ancestor will bring an abundant supply of goods (cargo) for the believers. The means to that end are different in each cult, but a common feature is that members often give up working, give away or kill their livestock, and throw away wealth, all in hopes that the expected "savior" will arrive soon with all the cargo they will need or want.

The earliest record of a cargo cult in the Pacific is from the late nineteenth century. Cargo cults began with the arrival of the Russian scientist and explorer Nikolai Miklouho-Maclay to Papua New Guinea (PNG) in 1871. He set up residence on the Madang Coast of PNG, was generous with his goods, and spent years in the region helping natives to keep their rights in the face of increasing colonialist pressures. The islanders were not sure whether he was a god or an ancestor, but he was surely a "big man."[61] They would come from great distances to ritually exchange things with him. Through his generosity and kindness toward natives, he had inadvertently "introduced new symbols of wealth, the cargo, that could be incorporated in local myths about divine beings and in local rituals of exchange."[62] Foreign cargo and goods came to have a spiritual dimension to locals. However, the German Lutheran missionaries who followed were quite different in the eyes of the islanders. They were seen as selfish, a trait very negatively viewed by natives, who thus found no reason to convert to Christianity. These outsiders were too powerful to be destroyed, and they would not teach the islanders their magic.[63] In 1914 Australian administrators took over control from the Germans. Although the Madang people had resisted the Germans for years and even revolted against them, now several local prophets directed the people to join the new foreigners and worship their god to learn their magic. Very quickly, thousands converted to Christianity. In the process, they also reinterpreted a variety of biblical stories to fit their worldviews and aspirations, including the belief that heaven was located somewhere near or above Australia, and Jesus lived there with their ancestors making cargo for them.[64]

The Tuka Movement, another cargo cult, began in Fiji in 1885. It was started by a charismatic traditional priest and his followers, who sought to counter the growing influence of the Methodist missionaries. Most of the population had converted by that time, at least nominally, and the Christians had set about destroying all the old temples to end the old beliefs. The Tuka leader, Ndugumoi, claimed to be a seer with magical powers. Mixing indigenous and biblical concepts, including turning Jehovah into a Fijian deity, he prophesied that a new age was about to come in which the roles of power would be reversed.[65] Whites would become the servants of the natives, chiefs would be inferior to commoners, and all the shops would be filled with goods of many varieties, but those goods would be available only for the faithful. Others would go to hell or become slaves of the Tuka followers.[66] In both of these early movements, the attainment of Western goods became a focus of attention of the followers. Neither lasted long, but they set the stage for the movements that would follow.

The presence of Europeans and European goods intensified later in the nineteenth and into the twentieth century, as colonialists expanded their control over various islands. From the early 1900s, Japanese also sought to gain a foothold in the region, and they also brought with them amounts and types of cargo not seen before by most islanders. Then, in the late 1930s, preceding World War II, there was an increase in military activity, construction, and the number of ships in the Pacific region. There was also an increase in the American military buildup during the war, which again brought in amounts of cargo unfathomable to the natives. From the late 1800s on, natives believed that the foreigners' ability to obtain such wealth must have been either because they were gods or because they possessed powerful magic, for such cargo could have come from no other source. Once they realized the foreigners were not gods, they reasoned that they must possess magic. This was validated by what they saw: with increasing regularity, huge ships would appear filled with cargo that was given to the foreigners without them doing any work for it. Occasionally, loads of cargo would also drop from the heavens by parachute for them. When Black American servicemen began to appear in the islands with cargo as well, this convinced many natives that the magic was not limited to whites, and that they, too, could learn the magic necessary to obtain cargo.

As a result, various cargo cults appeared in the region, especially during and just after World War II. Again, it was often charismatic leaders who would originate the ideas behind the cults. They were the ones who would "communicate" with the pending savior and assure the islanders that such a time would come. New situations would bring new "revelations." One was that all the goods that the foreigners possessed had been sent for the islanders, but they were being wrongly kept and hoarded by the foreigners. This led to additional beliefs, including one that their savior's arrival would also bring about a total change in the existing hierarchy. Commoners' lives would be prosperous, whereas white foreigners would become their servants, rather than the other way around. A consequence of this latter view was a developing resistance to the influence of foreigner powers in the islands. Among the better known and written-about cults in the region is that of John Frum, based on the island of Tanna in Vanuatu (see below).

Vanuatu

Vanuatu is an archipelago consisting of 12 main islands and a total of 83 mostly small volcanic islands. Inhabitants speak over 100 dialects and uphold innumerable distinctive religious and cultural beliefs that tend to be a blend of Melanesian and Polynesian elements. From 1774 until its independence in 1980, it was known as the New Hebrides. The islands were the setting for novelist James Michener's *Tales of the South Pacific*, from which the movie *South Pacific* was made.

Pre-Contact

As is the case with much of Melanesia, it is generally believed that the first humans to inhabit the islands, at least 3,500 years ago, were from Southeast Asia, or possibly Samoa or New Guinea. Some of the northern islands have one of the few creation stories found in Melanesia. In it, the deity Qat is the creator of the earth, of humans, and of day and night.[67] One of the favorite stories about him tells how he created night because his 11 brothers were tired of there only being day. To do so, he went to Night and purchased a large quantity of darkness, returned with it, and taught his brothers how to sleep. He then took a knife made of red obsidian and cut through Night to make a place for dawn.[68]

The spiritual beliefs of the islands' tribes have traditionally attributed all natural and human-induced bad luck or calamities to sorcery, and lavish festivals are staged to appease the gods. Maui and other Polynesian deities figure in the mythology of Vanuatu, although their stories tend to be primarily of local origin. Throughout the archipelago, supernatural powers exist in varying levels with the different types of spirits. Ancestral spirits are among the more popular and powerful beings in the spirit world. Additionally, various spirits and aspects of the material world, from stones to humans, are believed to have *mana*. As in some other parts of Melanesia, there is a belief in dual souls at the time of death: one takes on a new form whereas the other travels to the land of the dead. The ultimate state of the soul is determined by one's social status while alive. Evil beings and monsters are recognized as well. There is a story on the island of Tanna, the home of the John Frum Movement mentioned below, that an evil ogre ate all of the islands' residents, except a woman who had hidden herself under a tree. To survive there, she ate roots and in the process swallowed a rock. From this, she gave birth to twin boys. When they grew up, they killed the giant and brought all the people he had devoured back to life.[69]

According to legend, nearly 1,000 years ago, all the islands in the group were united under the great King Roymata. His people loved and respected him, but his brother was jealous and poisoned him. His body was buried on the island of Retoka. To honor him, a taboo was placed on the island so that no one would ever reside there. The taboo was upheld until 1967, when a French archaeologist was allowed to search for the burial place. Forty-seven skeletons were exhumed from the site, which suggests that the king was buried with 46 family members or attendants.[70] Since the death of Roymata, many of the islands have traditionally had no chiefs, but rather heads of family groups, each one tending to its own ways of life. In the central islands, there has been more of a hierarchical society with chiefs, similar to what one finds in Polynesia.

Many people on the island refer to the pre-Christian culture and traditions as *kastom*, a Pidgin English form of *custom*. These include dancing, easy and intimate relationships, kava drinking, and ancestor worship. All these were banned by the British Protestant missionaries once they took over power. For the most part, *kastom* disappeared from public view until the last several decades. One rather distinct feature of the islands was the existence of a high number of secret local cults, each with its own variety of myths and rituals. The rituals were almost entirely limited to males, but there were a few female cults as well. Membership in these influenced one's status in society.[71]

Post-Contact

The first European to visit one of the islands of Vanuatu was the Portuguese explorer Pedro Fernandes de Queirós, in 1606. Subsequent explorers came from Portugal, Spain, and France, including Louis Antoine de Bougainville, who stopped long enough to name one of the islands after himself as he was circumnavigating the globe. When Captain Cook visited the islands in 1774, he named the island group "New Hebrides." Cook's exploration of the islands were more thorough than that of previous European voyagers. The islanders seemed rightly suspicious of him and his crew, and resisted his attempts at exploration into the interior of the islands. Foreign seafarers did not bother the natives again until 1828, when they arrived in search of sandalwood and anything else that fancied their needs and greed. This led to inevitable clashes between the sailors and the natives. Because the former had guns, many islanders lost their lives in these encounters. Even Polynesians who visited the islands on foreign ships mistreated and killed natives who did not meet their demands. It was in this environment that the first two missionaries arrived in the archipelago in 1839. One of them was the well-traveled and respected John Williams of the LMS. The New Hebrides natives had experienced ample hardship at the hands of foreigners, so shortly after the missionaries set foot on shore, they were killed and eaten. The LMS, fearful of losing more European missionaries, began sending converted Samoans to evangelize the natives. These were viewed with the same distrust as the white missionaries, and consequently, many met the same fate as Williams.[72]

In 1848 the Presbyterian Mission was begun by John Geddie. During the next 50 years, its missionaries succeeded in establishing themselves and their denomination in almost all the islands in the archipelago. Reverend William Watt, a Presbyterian missionary who lived on the island of Tanna from 1869 until 1910, writes about cannibalism on the island. He acknowledges that although some likely exaggerate the prevalence of the practice in ancient times, others seem to purposely downplay it. He then relates a variety of tales, including that of some men in the past who were said to eat humans as a regular part of their food intake. The practice was apparently done to denigrate the dead, although there seems to have been times when it was done out of a scarcity of food. Those who were eaten might have been captured warriors from other tribes, someone with whom there was a feud, or innocent victims, including children. Watt sums up his comments by suggesting that cannibalism was still being practiced, but that it was far less common than in the past.[73]

Roman Catholic missionaries began a sustained process of proselytization of islanders in the late 1880s. Several Catholics had spent time there in the 1840s, but left before making any converts.[74] In 1898, a group of four Catholic nuns landed on Malakula Island, Vanuatu's second-largest island. They set up their mission and began ministering to the people. Their order has been relatively successful in inspiring islanders to become nuns, and they are an important part of the Catholic presence there.

During World War II, the islands of Efate and Espiritu Santo were used as military bases by the Allies. The 1960s saw the natives begin a concerted and sustained effort to take over control of a combined British-French administrative system that had ruled the islands since 1906. They finally obtained full independence in 1980, and the islands became the Republic of Vanuatu.

According to the 1991 census, Presbyterians compose the largest Christian denomination (31.4%), followed by Anglicans (13.4%) and Seventh-Day Adventists (10.8%). Roman Catholics number just over 13 percent, as do other Protestant denominations. It is estimated that almost 6 percent of the population (mostly the followers of John Frum) practice indigenous religions.[75] In 1978, Hussein Nabanga became the first known indigenous Vanuatuan to convert to Islam. He was a member of the Mele people, and others from his tribe converted as well. Currently, Muslims estimate their numbers to be somewhere between 100 and 200.[76]

Today, there are still areas of Vanuatu that are yet to be Christianized or Westernized. In his study conducted in the 1990s, Felix Speiser suggests that cannibalism was still occurring in some places.[77] Most islanders, however, have long ago rejected any aspect of the practice. Even though they are officially Christian, many islanders continue to be influenced by *kastom*, especially those who to live in rural areas in large extended families. Rites of passage, from birth to death, play an integral role in people's lives and maintain many *kastom* elements. These provide opportunities for people to reconnect with each other and with the old traditions, and they are highlighted with music, dance, and storytelling of the past greatness of tribes or families.

John Frum Movement

The best known and most documented of the twentieth-century cargo cult movements in the Pacific is the John Frum Movement, based on the island of Tanna. Its origins and development are shrouded in myth and legend. It is said to have begun in the 1930s, in response to a lack of faith in the Christian missions and missionaries. The primary denomination at the time was Presbyterianism, but Presbyterians did little, in the eyes of the natives, to help the latter in any way. All the missionaries seemed to do was to talk and make villagers obey them. Listening to talk about Jesus and heaven had little practical meaning to the islanders, because they were suffering economically, while the missionaries seemed to have all they needed. The natives wanted a savior who would help them now, someone who would provide for them in the same way the missionaries were being helped. Sometime in 1940 or 1941, influential and charismatic prophets began talking about John Frum. There are several theories regarding the origin of this name. One suggests it originated from a combination of "John the Baptist," who told of the coming savior, and "broom," which evokes the hope natives had that the savior would sweep away the whites from their land.[78] Another says the name may have come from an American serviceman, possibly a "John" from America, whom natives had met while helping to off-load cargo for the American military on the island of Espiritu Santo. Either way, the cult arose with the belief that if they got rid of all their Western money and goods, the whites would leave. John Frum would then come and usher in a new era in which the natives would become youthful, the ancestors would be reborn, sickness would be gone, and all the cargo of the whites would belong to the natives. However, first the whites would have to go or lose power. Followers of the movement began spending all their "foreign" money, convinced a significant number of natives to stop attending Christian church services or sending their children to the mission schools, and some even killed their cattle, all in preparation for the coming of John Frum. The missionaries became alarmed, and the New Hebrides government jailed and exiled several individuals seen as responsible for the uprising, but it did not stop. Soon, word spread that John Frum was king of America, and the country came to be viewed as a heaven-like realm.[79] Then, word spread that John Frum was living inside the main volcano on the island, or that he would be soon. The natives who had worked for the Americans on Espiritu Santo returned to Tanna with Red Cross arm bands, saying that the red cross was the symbol of John Frum. They began erecting red crosses at various sites around Tanna, where they would pray to him. They had also seen the Americans marching in formation, which came to be understood by them to be a religious ritual done to honor or please John Frum. When some American military men landed on the island, this fueled expectations that he would be coming soon. After the end of World War II and the departure of the Americans from the New Hebrides, the expectation of the coming of John Frum continued, to the exasperation of the colonial British and French rulers. In the 1950s, a John Frum army was created, and members began marching in formation as a "ritual dance" for John Frum. Others began wearing a red cross on their clothing, as well as carrying and saluting homemade American flags.

The John Frum Movement continues to exist on Tanna, and its few followers persist in their belief that he will return and fulfill all their needs and desires. There is an annual celebration on John Frum Day, February 15, which is said to be the day that John Frum will arrive. It is the largest festive gathering of followers, during which devotees perform a ritual march like soldiers with "USA" painted on their chests, salute an American flag, and relive their hopes and dreams of John Frum's return. Their current leader is Chief Isaak Wan Nikiau, and he continues to defend his movement and the faith they maintain in John Frum. When asked several years ago by an American journalist how long they would wait for John Frum to return, he replied, "You Christians have been wait-ing 2,000 years for Jesus to return to earth," he says, "and you haven't given up hope."

Fiji

The Republic of Fiji Islands (Fiji) is composed of over 300 islands, but only about a third of them are inhabited. The two major islands, Viti Levu and Vanua Levu, cover 87 percent of the landmass and account for approximately 75 percent of the population. Because it is within the easternmost section of Melanesia, Fiji shares a variety of ethnic and culture connections to Polynesia. Moreover, it is likely that the first peoples who migrated to Polynesia were from Fiji.

Pre-Contact

The traditional religious system contained a large variety of deities, both male and female. They were generally divided between the *kalou vu* (root gods), ancient gods, and *kalou yalo* (divinized ancestors). The supreme deity, believed by many to be a creator god, was known by various names, includ-ing Degi, Ove, and Ndengei. The gods were said to reside in the heavens, but they would visit humans, taking the form of creatures such as fish, snakes, plants, or other humans. However, their places of residence on the earth were considered far more sacred than any particular form they took. Thus, the images found commonly in Polynesia were not typically used here. Each sep-arate tribe also has had deities exclusive to it, in addition to those gods who were common to many of the natives.[80] Prayers were offered both to seek for-giveness of transgressions as well as to request success in areas from health to warfare. Offerings to the gods included the first fruits of a harvest, a hunt, or a battle.[81] The gods were believed to have all the human emotions. They were also believed to make mistakes and would occasionally be blamed when problems occurred.

Most deities were aligned with one chiefly lineage or another, and they were the latter's source of power and authority. This gave chiefs almost unlimited power over the lives of their subjects. A chief could have anyone killed for almost any reason and would, according to various legends and accounts, eat an opponent on occasion to show his power over that individual. Disrespect of a chief was one of the most serious offenses punishable by execution. Other serious crimes included adultery and theft, and requisite punishments were bestowed on offenders.

Multiple stories and legends suggest that cannibalism was among the traditional practices. Moreover, Fiji and New Zealand were said to be where cannibalism occurred with the most regularity in the Pacific. The Fijian word *bakola* (cannibal victims) is one of 70 terms and expressions in the language that refer to actions and items associated with cannibal activity. Revenge, warfare, and intimidation of the living seem to have been among the main reasons for the practice. However, offerings of *bakola* to the gods and to chiefs were also important.[82] Among those who were ritually sacrificed and eaten were defeated warriors and members of defeated tribes, including women and children. If a special occasion warranted it, and there were no *bakola* at hand, then a commoner from a neighboring village might be killed for the event. The dead may be ritually offered to the war god, prior to being cooked and eaten.[83] Consumption in more casual circumstances occurred as well. Cannibalism, tribal warfare, and the savagery and ferociousness of the natives are often mentioned in early missionary writings. Cannibalism became the main target of the missionaries for eradication. As a consequence, it is said to have stopped for the most part in Fiji within a few decades of the arrival of the missionaries, likely because of the conversion of powerful chiefs.

Post-Contact

The Dutch explorer Abel Tasman is said to be the first European to visit the islands, in 1640. No other contact is known to have taken place until well into the next century. Trading ships began visiting the islands around 1806. At the time, the islands were ruled by tribal chiefs, who frequently fought with each other over territory. In the 1820s, Europeans began to settle and establish themselves in the islands. Christianity initially spread to Fiji from Tonga through LMS evangelists. A few Methodist missionaries arrived in 1835, but John Hunt, a Methodist who reached Fiji in 1838, is primarily credited with the conversion of most islanders within two generations. In 1854, the process was greatly enhanced when King Cakobau, the chief of Bau, officially renounced the religious beliefs and gods of the past and converted to Christianity. He also encouraged—some even say commanded—his people to do the same. For a variety of reasons, including to avoid confrontations with Europeans, several tribal chiefs were early converts.[84] This facilitated and expanded the work of the missionaries. Despite Fiji's reputation for cannibalism, there is record of only one missionary to have been eaten. In 1867, the Reverend Thomas Baker, a Methodist missionary, was killed because he angered and possibly disgraced a village chief. According to Christian records, that was also the last time that anyone was eaten, although there continued to be stories of cannibalism occurring in the highlands in the interior and northern portions of the main island well into the twentieth century.

In 1874 Fiji became a British colony. After this, missionaries were more easily able to root out the remnants of the old religious beliefs and traditions that they encountered, and they did so with a vengeance. Old temples and worship sites were destroyed, and churches were built in their places to show the superiority of the new god, Jesus. Almost immediately, the British started transporting thousands of Indians to Fiji to work their sugarcane plantations. The colonists did so rather than exploiting indigenous Fijian labor and threatening the new relationship they were seeking to develop with the natives. The Indian laborers were mostly poor and illiterate Hindus referred to as *girmitiyas*. However, neither the British nor Fijian Christians wanted the Hindus to establish a stable religious and social community, which they saw as a potential threat to Christians. Consequently, they did not bring the families of laborers, and fewer than 10 percent of the transported Indians (hereafter referred to as Indo-Fijians) were females.[85] This was done to minimize the possibility of family formation, thus inhibiting the development of a Hindu community in the islands. The women who were brought were mostly prostitutes. The British apparently thought they could get the women to satisfy both the British and the Indian men's sexual desires, while keeping the labor force primarily male. However, because of extreme pressure from Hindu men who could not countenance seeing their countrywomen live this way, most such women eventually stopped their activities.

Christian missionaries sought to capitalize on the suffering that Indians faced in Fiji. They offered the Hindus better pay and living arrangements in this world, and heaven in the next, if they would convert. Missionaries in Fiji regularly denigrated in speaking and writing the beliefs and practices of the Hindus to support their claim that Christianity was the only moral religion and that Jesus was the only sinless being to have ever lived.[86] Although nearly all indigenous Fijians had converted to Christianity, most Indo-Fijian Hindus resisted the temptation. To this day, the vast majority of Indo-Fijians have remained Hindu.

By the late 1800s various Hindu organizations were established to help serve the needs of Indo-Fijians. When the system of indentured servitude finally ended in 1920, the Indo-Fijians were officially free, and the British had to accept that the Fijian Hindu community would, for the most part, remain Hindu. The government even arranged to have a copy of the *Ramayana* of Tulsidas, the main Hindu scripture in Fiji, at each court house for the swearing in of Hindu witnesses and defendants. Nevertheless, the Methodist Church of Fiji and Rotuma, the official Methodist organization in Fiji, remained largely unwelcoming of the Hindu community and continued to support aggressive evangelization of Hindus. It joined the Great Council of Chiefs, the official body of tribal chiefs that has all along been closely affiliated with the church, in supporting the suppression of Indo-Fijian rights in the recent coups.

A minority of the *girmitiyas* were Muslim. As in most other Muslim communities around the world, the majority of these are Sunni. From the early days, the Muslim community members in Fiji sought to remain close to one another and to their religious beliefs and practices. They tended to be more successful at this than their Hindu counterparts, partially because Christian missionaries spent less time trying to convert them than they did Hindus.[87] At the same time, Muslims had good relationships with their Hindu brethren because of their shared language and geographic origin. Intermarriage occurred from time to time, although many of these were not necessarily official. If official recognition was obtained, it was the Hindu who would have to convert to Islam, because conversion out of Islam is strictly prohibited and can be punishable by death. The first mosque was built in Fiji in 1900, and gradually others began to appear in the islands. In 1920, the Fiji Muslim League was formed, and it has served as a religious and political representative of most Muslims in the country. It has also been active in the conversion of Fijians to Islam. Today, Muslims make up approximately 7 percent of the population and have a generally cordial relationship with the Christian majority.

For most of their history, Muslims in Fiji have not faced any significant level of harassment or intimidation. However, in the wake of the 9/11 attacks in the United States, several Pacific island-nations tightened their policies in relation to Muslims. In August 2002, a Sudanese Muslim cleric who had lived in Fiji for 18 years visited Samoa with a government official from Saudi Arabia. Based on concerns that there may be an attack, the U.S. embassy there was closed, and Samoa issued a visa ban on visitors from 23 predominantly Muslim countries. A few months later, the Fijian government denied a visa extension to the cleric and made him leave the country.

Contemporary Times

Fiji remained a British colony until 1945. In 1970, it became independent but stayed a part of the British Commonwealth. Prior to independence, the British had fostered an environment in which indigenous Fijians and Indo-Fijians had little social or political interaction. There was very little intermarriage, because of ethnic and religious differences. The Fijians owned the land, but many of the Indo-Fijians were farmers or small-business owners. The 1961 census reported 51 percent of the population as Indo-Fijian and 42 percent as indigenous inhabitants. After the independence, tensions between the two groups began to increase. This was exacerbated by the total dominance of indigenous Fijians in the government, which allowed them to enact legislation that solidified their power and control. Many Indo-Fijians began to emigrate to other lands. In 1987, a newly elected multiethnic government came into office, in which Indo-Fijians had a dominant role. Within a month of its taking office, there was a successful coup led by a military officer who was also on the Great Council of Chiefs. He was supported both by the Methodist Church and by indigenous elements who wanted power to be held exclusively by their ethnic group. The prime minister was ousted, the country was declared a republic, and the constitution was suspended and eventually replaced by a racially biased one. A systematic oppression of Indo-Fijians, especially Hindus, began.[88] At the same time, a movement that had the support of the dominant Methodist Church was started to officially make Fiji a Christian nation. Over the last two decades, the religious rights of Hindus have slowly been undermined through attacks on them and on Hindu temples, and the government has done little to protect them.

Shortly after the first coup, an organization named Interfaith Search Fiji (ISF) was set up under the auspices of the World Council of Churches, and it has monitored and recorded the situation in Fiji ever since.[89] According to the ISF, after the coup, a series of violent attacks against Hindus and Hindu temples began, many of the latter being damaged or destroyed. Throughout the 1990s, the situation stabilized to a large extent. Then, in 1999, a Hindu named Mahendra Chaudhry was elected prime minister. This resulted in another coup the following year, in which Chaudhry was taken prisoner. The Fijian president removed Chaudhry from office, claiming that because he was a hostage he was not doing his job. During the five years that followed, police statistics list 134 incidents of desecration of Hindu temples, images, and holy books.[90] The Methodist Church of Fiji denounced the desecration but would not denounce those involved, including the Methodist ministers who supported such acts. The organization also endorsed the creation of a formal Christian state and increased efforts to convert Hindus.

Fiji today is close to being a theocratic state although it is not officially so. Methodist beliefs dominate nearly all areas of life, and many of its adherents continue to push for the official establishment of Fiji as a Christian nation. At the same time, Fiji continues to have the largest percentage of non-Christians of any Pacific island-nation. Evangelists and Christian leaders there are frustrated at this fact and continue to seek and receive government support in their aggressive attitude toward non-Christians more than is the case anywhere else in the Pacific. Though Christian writings remain highly critical of Hinduism and Hindus, they are neutral with respect to Islam. In the last few decades, a split arose within the Hindu community between those who follow the typical Hindu approach of tolerance and openness to other religions and those who see this as making them susceptible to the designs and deviousness of the missionaries.[91] This has created a great deal of tension between the nonaggressive Hindus and those Hindus who believe that they must fight for their rights or they will be slowly but surely decimated. The latter faction points to census statistics, according to which the percentage of Indo-Fijians has dropped from 51 percent in 1961 to under 36 percent today.[92] More than 100,000 Indians have left Fiji since 1987, fleeing the oppression and brutality that they experienced in the last two decades. Many who remain are fearful of their future in Fiji. The traditionally nonaggressive attitude that Indo-Fijians have had toward indigenous Fijians and toward political activity has made oppression of them relatively easy for the Methodist-dominated government. Indigenous Fijians own approximately 88 percent of the land, so many of the Hindus farm, rent the land, or do sharecropping with the knowledge that they can be removed from the land at any moment.[93] Partially because of the stressful life and social instability that they face today, Indo-Fijians commit suicide at a rate of nearly six times per capita of indigenous Fijians.[94] According to the 2007 census, 65 percent of the population are Christian. Of these, 54 percent are Methodist, 9 percent are Catholic, 5 percent are affiliated with assemblies of God, and nearly 4 percent are Seventh Day Adventist. The remaining Christians belong to other Protestant denominations. The percentage of Hindus has dropped to under 28 percent and is expected to continue falling. Muslims comprise approximately 6 percent of the population.[95]

MICRONESIA

Micronesia spans an area in the southwestern Pacific larger than the continental United States, but the collective landmass of its more than 2,000 islands and atolls is just over 1,000 square miles. The region is composed of small islets and atoll groups joined together by coral reefs that form perimeters around large lagoons. The highest land elevation on many of the islets and atolls is less than two feet above sea level and the highest point on land is the top of a coconut tree. There are a few larger volcanic islands, such as Guam, Kosrae, and Pohnpei. The total population of the region is approximately 500,000. The many languages spoken in the region are all classified in the family of Austronesian languages, but English is also spoken on almost all the islands and atolls. Most islands have traditionally had a decentralized chieftain system, in which each had relative independence. The larger islands generally had more of a stratified social hierarchy than did the atolls, with the exception of the atolls of the Marshall Islands.[96] Micronesian people today represent a multitude of ethnicities and cultures, and Polynesian and Melanesian influences are mixed in with more indigenous elements.

Gods, Spirits, and Ancestors

The cosmology of the region is filled with a variety of spirits. Some are heavenly, some are terrestrial, some are beneficial, and some may be harmful. There are also ancestor spirits. Micronesians have seemed to accept "anything that might have a prospect of satisfying their need for symbols appropriate for organizing and interpreting experience."[97] Creation myths are quite diverse. For example, in Kiribati, Spider, Turtle, and Eel are primal beings that created the earth and the sky by separating the original formless mass. The mythology of the Caroline Islands tells of the eternal goddess Ligoupup, who created the world and now sleeps under its surface. Earthquakes are caused when she stirs. On the island of Chuuk (Truk), it is either she or her husband, Anulap, who created the world. The various tribes were born from their children through incestuous sex. In the Marshall Islands, it was Loa who looked down from the heavens until the islands and plants appeared. Both the Marshall and the Caroline islanders say that the islands were created by an unnamed female who threw sand onto a primeval sea. Humans may be the product of sexual union of divinities, or they may be born out of any of various body parts of a deity.[98]

Each island has spirits that are limited to specific locations or specific functions. They are propitiated only for those functions. Spirit mediums and shamans may be contacted for that purpose. They may also be used to help make contact with ancestor spirits, who are highly revered. Their worship may be similar to that of the gods, which includes offerings of food, cloth, and the like. As in Melanesia, the most recent dead are often the ones most remembered and venerated. They are believed to assist their descendants, but they also demand that those seeking help be ethical, lest they be punished. Each home may have a shrine for their ancestor spirits where offerings are made. When necessary, mediums are called on to assist the living in communicating with the dead, with expectations that the latter will help with the curing of illnesses, family problems, and important decisions.[99]

Among the more important activities with regard to unseen powers and the spirit world are what can be loosely called magic and sorcery. These involve prayers and rituals done to bring about specific, usually beneficial, effects on individuals and even on an entire community. Magic can be performed for most aspects of human life, including physical health, marriage issues, construction of homes and canoes, protection when sailing and fishing, and allaying the effects of a pending storm. Amulets and talismans are useful in this regard. Amulets are also important for protection against a curse. Such items can be obtained from a sorcerer and are used to stop the negative effects of a curse, usually caused by another sorcerer. Curses may be against anything from individuals to families to homes to canoes, and they are often the consequence of an unsettled dispute between individuals. Those who perform magic and sorcery are usually men. Even though there tends to be a general lack of status for women in the religious sphere, they too can act as sorcerers. They are considered to have the ability to perform magic typically associated with home, family, and crops.[100]

Marshall Islands

The Republic of the Marshall Islands (RMI) is composed of two chains of atolls and a few islands that run roughly parallel from the northwest to the southeast. Majuro is the main atoll and the seat of the government. Collectively, the area of the islands is about 73 square miles, slightly larger in area than Washington, D.C., and it is dispersed throughout 375,000 square miles of ocean.[101] The islands are primarily of the coral-reef type and rise only a few feet above sea level. The islands were a trust territory of the United States from the end of World War II until 1986, when they officially became a sovereign nation. The RMI and the United States continue to have a close relationship under the provisions of the Compact of Free Association.[102]

Pre-Contact

The first Micronesian navigators began to populate the Marshall Islands between 2,000 and 4,000 years ago. The people of the islands have a rich mythology and corpus of legends about the birth of the various islands, the plants on them, and the gods and evil spirits who either improve or aggravate the lives of the people. There are also stories about historical beings and events and the many battles that occurred between the chiefs for control of the various atolls. A significant number of stories are about evil spirits and women. Each atoll tended to have myths and spirits unique to it, and this led to a great diversity of beliefs within the islands. Many of the spirits are seen as responsible for the formation of the various atolls and islets. Propitiation of the spirits was very important, but human sacrifice and cannibalism did not exist here as they did in other parts of the Pacific.[103] The various deities could take on many forms. Here, constellations were traditionally one of the forms in which many were seen.

The most persistent form of spirit worship has been that of ancestors, and many Marshallese continue to honor and pay respect to the departed, who despite having left their physical bodies, are believed to be still close by. A traditional practice on many atolls was to bury the dead near the home in which they lived. This made it easier to call on them for protection and assistance or to mediate between the living and the gods in case one of their descendants breaks a taboo or has otherwise angered a spirit. Ancestors and other spirits were also seen as helpful in case of physical or psychological affliction. Traditional shamans were used to help facilitate the communication and to provide protection from curses. Shamans can still be found on each atoll, but they are now much quieter about their activities, primarily because of the influence of Christianity. As a consequence in contemporary times, Christian ministers are called on for these functions, and some do practice aspects of the old ways. Marshallese family structure is matrilineal, so land rights are passed on through one's mother. Cheiftanships, on the other hand, are patrilineal.

Post-Contact

In 1521 Ferdinand Magellan became the first European to reach Micronesia. He is said to have stopped on Guam for a few days before going on to the Philippines, where he was killed by natives who were resisting attempts to be converted to Christianity. Subsequently, several more Spanish seafarers— Garcia de Loyasa in 1526 and Alvaro Saavedra, credited with "discovering" the Marshalls, in 1529—traveled to Micronesia. As a consequence of the Treaty of Tordesillas in 1494, Spain had already claimed ownership of all of Micronesia without even having had any prior contact with the region. This attitude toward Micronesia is reflected in much of what the Spanish would do to the people of the region in subsequent centuries. The British Naval Captain William Marshall sailed through the atolls in 1788, stopping long enough to name them after himself and establish a permanent contact between the Marshallese and the outside world.

American missionaries from the Congregational Church arrived in 1857. They were helped in the evangelization of the Marshallese by Hawaiian and, to some extent, other Micronesian missionaries. As in other island-nations, missionaries banned tattoos and dance, but the latter has made a comeback in recent decades, primarily for tourist purposes.

Not long after the arrival of the missionaries, Germans began to set up outposts for trading copra. They treated some of the Marshallese decently, but they saw many of the others as cheap labor for their plantations. Germany formally took possession of the islands in 1886, after it paid Spain for its nearly

400-year-old claim of ownership of the islands. Just before the turn of the century, German catholic missionaries made their way to the Marshalls. Because they had not trained many Pacific islanders as missionaries the way Protestants had done, they had a much more difficult time making converts.

From 1914 until World War II, the islands were under the control of the Japanese. Stories of this time period draw a horrific picture of the way the new imperialists treated the people, so when the American military showed up at the end of World War II, many Marshallese were very welcoming of their "saviors." The Marshall Islands became a trust territory of the United States for the next 40 years. Other Christian denominations began appearing shortly after the end of World War II.[104] A few decades later, members of the Bahai faith also began converting islanders. In 1982 then-president Amat Kabua declared the island group a republic, and this was officially recognized by the United States in 1986.[105] Since 2004, the Marshall Islands and the United States have participated in a Compact of Free Association, through which their relationship is officially maintained.

Nearly all Marshall islanders follow some form of Christianity, at least officially, and most are Protestants. The largest current denomination is the United Church of Christ–Congregational in the Marshall Islands (UCCCMI). More than half of all Marshallese are adherents of this denomination. The other large Protestant denomination is the Assembly of God (25.8%), whereas Catholics make up just over 8 percent of the population. Other denominations include Baptist, Seventh-Day Adventist, Bukot Non Jesus (also known as Assembly of God Part Two), and the Church of Jesus Christ of Latter-day Saints (Mormons).[106] Marshallese are very religious and church attendance on Sunday is a must for most. Because denominational affiliation has become so important and divisive, competition and tension between the Protestant groups can lead to family problems when there are members of different denominations in the same household, especially on the more populated Majuro Atoll. The Catholic Church is small and tends to stay out of such controversies as much as it can.

As is typical in much of the Pacific, the Christianity of the Marshallese is on their own terms. According to one of the old beliefs on Majuro, there were four primary divinities, one connected with each of the cardinal points. They supplied the people with everything they needed; however, they slept at night, so the islanders would remain indoors in fear of evil spirits wandering at night. With the coming of Christianity, the islanders were forced to stop many of the activities they enjoyed, including dancing, music, kava drinking, and enjoying other sensual activities. Although they adopted Christian ways to please their new god, Jesus, some of them applied to him as well the old understanding that gods sleep at night. As a consequence, many see themselves as good Christians in daytime, but once the sun sets, there are those who feel comfortable in returning to some of the native ways that bring joy and diversion to their lives. Clearly, many no longer spend much time worrying about demons at night.

CONCLUSION

Culture defines how people should live and what they should and should not think and do. Long-held traditions reflect the natural surroundings and the collective personalities of a culture. The traditions in the Pacific have developed over several thousand years and reflect the way the processes of culture have evolved. They are not simply fabricated constructs that can be adopted from the outside irrespective of history, land, and people. After the introduction of Christianity, the cultures took on a decidedly Christian flavor, although fundamental aspects of the process have continued to reflect much of the pre-Christian ways. Some of the missionaries understood and accepted this, but the more conservative ones did not. Many set about destroying as many elements—such as clothes, food, language, family relations, social activities, entertainment, government, and laws—of the traditional cultures as possible in an attempt to make the natives more like the European missionaries. While they were generally successful in making the natives adopt many of the external cultural expressions, they were much less successful in making them think or believe the same way.

In the Pacific, the external changes happened rather quickly because of the rapidity with which many chiefs adopted the worship of the new deity. Sometimes they included Jesus in their pantheon of gods, and sometimes he replaced the others and became the only god to be worshiped. Once chiefs became Christianized, others followed, and newly converted natives became the primary evangelists using native languages and traditional thinking to convert the rest of their people. The way most islanders came to understand Christianity, then, was that it dealt with the worship of a white man's god who seemed to have a great deal of *mana*, but who also seemed to be warlike in many ways. After all, he had given the people who worshiped him many things and great power, including strong weapons they could use to kill those who went against him. Adding Jesus to the islanders' pantheon was, in the islanders' eyes, both useful and necessary. First, it would hopefully keep the foreigners from killing more of them and taking over their lands. In addition, worshiping this new god might help them get access to the power and possessions that he obviously gave his foreign worshippers.

Many ruling chiefs could see benefits in the process of adopting European ways, but most commoners could not. They continued to practice much of their traditional culture outside the purview of the religious authorities, especially on the islands to which missionaries did not have regular access or on which they had no informants. The term *Christianity* came to designate the veneer that covered a multivalent reality, much like a plywood veneer that hides the true nature of the wood underneath. Jesus became the most, and often the only, visibly worshiped god of the multitude of gods and spirits in the islanders' world. His worship became the dominant external expression of a complex of religious beliefs and practices. Christianity became a new methodology for expressing long-held traditional beliefs and practices. That which was done and believed before the arrival of Westerners became Christianized for acceptability. The names of the gods in ancient chants and prayers were changed, but many of the same feelings remained. Where Catholicism was successful, prayer to various gods was replaced by prayer to various saints, with the understanding remaining largely unchanged. A cross worn on a string became a new and hopefully more powerful amulet. Churches and church grounds came to be viewed and treated much the same way as the sacred shrines of the old traditions. An image of Jesus was a powerful *tiki*.

As the value of multiculturalism is touted by many today, both native and immigrant Christians in the Pacific now acknowledge the value of traditional cultures in providing strength, continuity, community, and security. An increasing number of native islanders, especially the young, are openly attempting to bring back some of the less seen, suppressed aspects of their ancestral ways into the public arena. Although the form of Christianity practiced in most islands is neither conservative nor traditional in the Western sense, it is deeply imbued with local tradition, and it can easily accommodate a renewal of fundamental aspects of the old cultures. As the Samoan leader Tui Atua Tamasese noted, Samoan Christians are as much Samoan as they are Christian. The same can be said of islanders all over the Pacific.

GLOSSARY

Incest: The practice of sexual relations between persons who are closely related. Although it is looked down upon in much of the world, in the Pacific it was often seen as a means of maintaining sacred power in royal families. Thus, it was a preferred practice among some royalty, although discouraged or even prohibited for commoners.

Kahuna: This and various similar terms (*tohunga, tahuna, tahua, kahu,* etc.) found in the Pacific realm refer to religious functionaries. Some may be confined to performing rituals for royalty or for commoners; others have been masters of various arts, including herbal medicine and healing, canoe building, navigating, or dancing. All these activities are connected to the religious culture of the people. *Kahunas* have typically been considered to possess *mana* (see below), and they have a connection with one or more spirits or gods.

Mana: A term found in various indigenous religious traditions in the Pacific. Although there are multiple understandings of the term, it generally refers to a nonhuman power with which certain humans, places, and things are endowed or to which certain humans have access. Depending on the tradition, *mana* can be gained or lost through birth, marriage, or various deeds and accomplishments.

Polytheism: The term has traditionally been used to refer to belief in many divinities, gods, or spirits. In the West it carries a connotation of paganism and an inferior theological understanding, in comparison to the formal monotheism of the Abrahamic traditions. However, polytheism should also be understood to refer to a multivalent approach to the unknown that utilizes various concepts of that unknown. Thus, many indigenous peoples who have been converted to Christianity continue to supplicate a variety of spirit forms, including ancestors, in hopes of gaining protection and benefit. Although Jesus may be viewed by them as the most powerful form of the divine, he exists for many as one of multiple divinities from whom help is sought.

Taboo (Tongan *tapu;* Fijian *tabu*): Taboo refers to restrictions placed on people, places, items, and actions either because of a belief in their sanctity or in their defiling, contaminating, or corrupting characteristics. In either case, interaction with anyone or anything considered taboo was highly restricted by cultural and religious rules. Both types of taboos continue to be prevalent throughout much of the Pacific.

Tattoos (from the Tahitian *tatau,* literally, "punctured marks on the skin"): Tattooing has long been a religious ritual on the Pacific Islands. Tattoos have been used to express identity, personality, lineage, or rank; as part of a puberty ritual; as a type of offering to a deity; as an expression of strength and virility; to help cure an illness; to provide protection; or to inspire fear in opponents. Because tattooing was both an art and a sacred activity, those who knew the craft were thought to have sacred knowledge or power. Tattoos have long connected island people to their cultures, ancestors, and gods; thus, the practice has had both social and religious aspects to it.

NOTES

1. Peter Henry Buck, *Anthropology and Religion* (New Haven: Yale University Press, 1939), p. 14.
2. Ramdas Lamb, "Polytheism," in *Encyclopedia of Anthropology*, vol. 4, ed. James Birx (Thousand Oaks: Sage Publications, 2005).
3. The terms are used here with the caveat that they should be understood as having only partial similarity to the Christian concept of priest or the more contemporary anthropological definition of shaman.
4. S. Percy Smith, *Hawaiki: The Original Home of the Maori, with a Sketch of Polynesian History* (Christchurch: Whitcombe and Tombs Limited, 1904), pp. 19–20.

5. Anthony J. Marsella, Ayda Aukahi Austin, Bruce A. Grant, *Social Change and Psychosocial Adaptation in the Pacific Islands: Cultures in Transition* (New York: Springer, 2005), p. 116.

6. Mircea Eliade, *The Sacred and the Profane: The Nature of Religion*, trans. Willard R. Trask (New York: Harcourt Brace, 1959), pp. 10–11.

7. Ramdas Lamb, "Sacred," in *Studying Hinduism: Key Concepts and Methods*, ed. Sushil Mittal and Gene Thursby (London and New York: Routledge, 2007), pp. 339–340.

8. David Malo, *Hawaiian Antiquities (Moolelo Hawaii)*, trans. N. B. Emerson (Honolulu: Hawaiian Gazette Co., Ltd., 1908), pp. 25–26 and 206.

9. *Encyclopaedia Britannica*, "Taboo, Tabu," 10th ed., 1902. Available at http://www.1902encyclopedia.com/T/TAB/taboo.html (accessed March 4, 2009).

10. Tohu is the Tahitian sea god, or possibly shark god, and is associated with tattoos. He is said to be responsible for all the designs on fish. See Robert D. Craig's *Dictionary of Polynesian Mythology* (New York: Greenwood Press, 1989), p. 285.

11. There is a Hebrew Bible prohibition against the practice in Leviticus 19:28.

12. Unlike in most of the islands today, there is still a great deal of cultural tradition connected with tattoos in Samoa, and there are those on other islands who are attempting to use tattoos as another vehicle for cultural revival.

13. William H. Rivers, *The History of Melanesian Society* (Cambridge: University Press, 1914), p. 512.

14. Jared Diamond, *Collapse: How Societies Choose to Fail or Succeed* (New York: Penguin, 2006), pp. 90–91.

15. Council for World Mission, "Who We Are." Available at http://www.cwmission.org/who-we-are (accessed Feb. 2, 2009).

16. Stephanie Lawson, *Tradition versus Democracy in the South Pacific: Fiji, Tonga and Western Samoa* (New York: Cambridge University Press, 2008), pp. 88–89.

17. Ibid., p. 89.

18. In 1947, Thor Hyerdahl, the explorer and author of the famous *Kon Tiki*, used the currents and traditional navigation methods to sail from Peru to the Tuamotu Archipelago in French Polynesia to prove his hypothesis that South Americans were the first to populate the islands of Polynesia.

19. Craig, p. xiii.

20. Ibid., p. xvii.

21. Ibid., p. 63.

22. John Charlot, *Chanting the Universe: Hawaiian Religious Culture* (Honolulu and Hong Kong: Emphasis International, 1983), p. 144.

23. Martha Beckwith, *Hawaiian Mythology* (Honolulu: University of Hawaii Press, 1970), p. 128.

24. Dennis Kawaharada, "'Aumakua of Kona, O'ahu," Kapiolani Community College Web site. Available at http://apdl.kcc.hawaii.edu/~oahu/stories/kona/aumakua.htm (accessed Feb. 10, 2009).

25. Samoa was known as Western Samoa until 1997. American Samoa is also referred to by many as Samoa.

26. Charlot (p. 144) suggests that this elevation of Tangaloa probably occurred in the latter part of the first century CE.

27. Jane Resture, "Samoa: Origin of Name, the People, Navigators Islands, Language, Receptions and Insignia of Rank." Available at http://www.janesoceania.com/samoa_origin/index.htm.

28. Robert Mackenzie Watson, *History of Samoa* (Wellington, New Zealand: Whitcombe and Tombs, Ltd., 1918).

29. Charlot, p. 543.

30. Tui Atua Tupua Tamasese Ta'isi Efi, "Keynote Address for Pacific Futures Law and Religion Symposium," National University of Samoa, Lepapaigalagala, Samoa, Dec. 3, 2008. Available at http://www.samoalivenews.com/Editor-and-Reader-Opinions/Religion-Law-and-the-Samoan-Indigenous-Reference.html.

31. Liz Thompson, "The Samoan Tattoo: A Powerful, Positive Message to the Community," Pacific Arts Online. Available at http://www.abc.net.au/arts/artok/bodyart/s197594.htm (accessed Feb. 11, 2009).

32. Based on the 2001 census. Available at http://www.worldstatesmen.org/Samoa.html (accessed Jan. 18, 2009).

33. Craig, p. 234.

34. Some scholars have suggested that sailors took news of this event from Tahiti to Hawai'i, and it inspired Kamehameha to do the same to the old religion of his islands.

35. William E. Tagupa, *Legal Concepts and Crises in Tahiti, 1819–1838* (Honolulu: Hawaiian Historical Society, 1974), p. 112.

36. Ibid., p. 114.

37. Ibid., pp. 116–117.

38. Jane Resture, "The Tahitian Royal Family." Available at http://www.janesocea nia.com/tahiti_royals/index2.htm (accessed Jan. 23, 2009).

39. NationMaster.com. Available at http://www.nationmaster.com/country/fp-french-polynesia/rel-religion (accessed Feb. 18, 2009).

40. Beckwith, p. 60.

41. Ibid., pp. 31–32.

42. Malo, pp. 23 and 78. Some myths say the couple are the parents of all humans, like Adam and Eve.

43. There are many myths about Pele, her origins, her parentage and siblings, and her exploits on earth. They can still be heard regularly in Hawai'i.

44. Gavan Daws, *Shoal of Time: A History of the Hawaiian Islands* (Honolulu: University of Hawai'i Press, 1974), p. 1.

45. Gananath Obeyesekere, *The Apotheosis of Captain Cook* (Princeton, NJ: Princeton University Press, 1993), pp. 156–157.

46. Orramel Hinckley Gulick and Ann Eliza Clark Gulick, *The Pilgrims of Hawaii* (New York: Fleming H. Revell Company, 1918), pp. 114–115.

47. Ibid., p. 124.

48. Daws, pp. 99–102.
49. Ibid., p. 105.
50. As quoted in Daws, p. 308.
51. Daws, pp. 308–309.
52. An interview by Sachi Lamb about her *kumu* hula, Kaleo Trinidad, July 2007.
53. Charlot, p. 545.
54. David Kaʻupu, in a 2001 retirement speech at Kamehameha Schools, Honolulu. Available at http://www.ksbe.edu/allpdfs/01summer/IMUA_12-13.PDF (accessed Feb. 18, 2009).
55. Charlot, p. 545.
56. Roland Burrage Dixon, *Oceanic [Mythology]* (Boston: Marshall Jones, 1916), pp. 106–107.
57. Jane Resture, "Melanesian Mythology: Vanuatu." Available at http://www.janeresture.com/melanesia_myths/Vanuatu.htm (accessed Feb. 2, 2009).
58. Ann Chowning, "Melanesian Religions: An Overview," in *Encyclopedia of Religion*, vol. 9, ed. Mircea Eliade (New York: Collier Macmillan, 1987), pp. 351–352.
59. Ibid., 350–351.
60. Reo Fortune, *Manus Religion: An Ethnological Study of the Manus Natives of the Admiralty Islands* (Philadelphia: The American Philosophical Society, 1935), pp. 1–3.
61. Marvin Harris, *Cows, Pigs, Wars, and Witches: The Riddles of Culture* (New York: Vintage Books Edition, 1989), pp. 115–117.
62. David Chidester, *Christianity: A Global History* (San Francisco: Harper San Francisco, 2000), p. 474.
63. Harris, pp. 138–150.
64. Chidester, pp. 475–476.
65. Robert L. Winzeler, *Anthropology and Religion* (New York: Rowman & Littlefield Publishers, Inc., 2007), p. 237.
66. Peter Worsley, *The Trumpet Shall Sound: A Study of Cargo Cults in Melanesia* (New York: Schocken Books, 1968), pp. 20–21.
67. Dixon, pp. 124–125.
68. *Encyclopaedia Britannica: A Dictionary of Arts, Sciences and General Literature* (New York: The Henry G. Allen Company, 1890), p. 148.
69. Resture, "Melanesian Mythology: Vanuatu" (accessed March 10, 2009).
70. "Raymata—Ancient King of Vanuatu." Available at http://www.vanuatutourism.com/vanuatu/cms/en/history/roymata.html (accessed on Jan. 16, 2009).
71. Douglas L. Oliver, *The Pacific Islands* (Honolulu: University of Hawaiʻi Press, 1989), pp. 169–170.
72. Ibid., pp. 54 and 169–171.
73. Rev. William Watt, "Cannibalism as Practised on Tanna, New Hebrides," *Journal of the Polynesian Society* 4.4 (1895), pp. 226–229.

74. John Garrett, *Footsteps in the Sea: Christianity in Oceania to World War II* (Suva, Fiji: University of the South Pacific, Institute of Pacific Studies, in association with the World Council of Churches, 1992), pp. 90–101.

75. http://www.nationmaster.com/country/nh-vanuatu/rel-religion.

76. Ben Boehane, "Islam Is Spreading in Melanesia," *Pacific Magazine*, June 29, 2007, p. 2.

77. Felix Speiser, *Ethnology of Vanuatu: An Early Twentieth Century Study* (Honolulu: University of Hawai'i Press, 1996), p. 215.

78. Worsley, p. 153.

79. Worsley, pp. 152–156.

80. Mary Wallis, *Life in Feejee; or, Five Years Among the Cannibals* (Ridgewood, NJ: Gregg Press, 1967), pp. 55–57.

81. Laura Thompson, *Southern Lau, Fiji: An Ethnography* (Honolulu: The Museum, 1940), p. 110.

82. Marshall Sahlins, "Artificially Maintained Controversies: Global Warming and Fijian Cannibalism," *Anthropology Today* 19.3 (June 2003), p. 4.

83. Lewis F. Petrinovich, *The Cannibal Within* (Edison, NJ: Aldine Transaction Publishers, 2000), pp. 133–136.

84. Wallis, pp. 26–29.

85. The most current term of identity for Fijian nationals of Indian origin or ethnic heritage is *Indo-Fijian*. Other terms—such as *Fiji Indian*, *Fijian Indian*, and *Fiji Born Indian*—are used as well. In the latter half of the twentieth century, Indo-Fijians attempted to have the government officially recognize them simply as Fijians, claiming it would foster unity among all citizens of the nation. However, most native Fijians were vocal in their opposition to this, feeling such a move would erode the special government privileges they have enjoyed because of their exclusive ethnic identity.

86. John Kelly, *A Politics of Virtue: Hinduism, Sexuality, and Countercolonial Discourse in Fiji* (Chicago: University Of Chicago Press, 1992), p. 207.

87. Though there were some Christian writings that denigrated Islam, they were not openly disseminated among the people in Fiji. An example of this is Frank L. Nunn's deprecating article entitled "Islam in Fiji," which appeared in *The Muslim World*, ed. by Samuel M. Zwemer (New York: The Arthur H. Crist Co., 1919).

88. Michael R. Ogden "Republic of Fiji" (forthcoming in the *World Encyclopedia of Political Systems*, 3rd ed.). Available at http://www2.hawaii.edu/~ogden/piir/pacific/fiji.html (accessed March 3, 2009).

89. Tessa MacKenzie, "The Situation in the South Pacific Islands" Available at http://www.wcc-coe.org/wcc/what/interreligious/cd35-20.html (accessed Feb. 27, 2009).

90. Chris Hammer, "Fiji Desecration," Special Broadcasting Service, June 22, 2005. Available at http://news.sbs.com.au/dateline/fiji_desecration_130533 (accessed March 3, 2009).

91. Kelly, p. 210.
92. "Fiji Islands Bureau of Statistics." Available at http://www.spc.int/PRISM/ country/fj/stats/Census2007/census07_index2.htm. (accessed Feb. 2, 2009).
93. "Fiji Facts and Figures." Available at http://www.spc.int/PRISM/country/ fj/stats/FFF08.pdf (accessed Feb. 18, 2009).
94. Ibid.
95. "Population by Religion and Province of Enumeration, Fiji: 2007 Census." Available at http://www.statsfiji.gov.fj/Key%20Stats/Population/2.10Religion2007 .pdf (accessed March 18, 2009).
96. K. R. Howe, Robert C. Kiste, and Brij V. Lal, *Tides of History: The Pacific Islands in the Twentieth Century* (Honolulu: University of Hawai'i Press, 1994), p. 15.
97. William A. Lessa, "Micronesian Religions," in *The Encyclopedia of Religion*, vol. 11, ed. Mircea Eliade (New York: Macmillan Publishing Co., 1987), p. 498.
98. Ibid., pp. 504–506.
99. Ibid., 499–500.
100. Ibid., 500–504.
101. Jack A. Tobin, *Stories from the Marshall Islands* (Honolulu: University of Hawai'i Press, 2001), p. 1
102. "History of the Marshall Islands." Available at http://www.rmiembassyus .org/History.htm (accessed Dec. 18, 2008).
103. Tobin, p. 7.
104. Tobin, p. 6.
105. Tobin, pp. 3–4.
106. "2007 Report on International Religious Freedom—Marshall Islands." Available at http://www.unhcr.org/refworld/topic,464db4f52,46a70ae32,46ee67745f,0.html (accessed March 20, 2009).

BIBLIOGRAPHY

Books, Journals, and Magazines

Alerts, Theo. *Traditional Religion in Melanesia*. Port Moresby: University of Papua New Guinea Press, 1998.

Allen, Michael, ed. *Vanuatu: Politics, Economics and Ritual in Island Melanesia*. New York: Academic Press, 1981.

Ammann, Raymond, David Becker, and Helena E. Reeve-Brinon. *Kanak Dance and Music*. London: Taylor and Francis, 1997.

Anderson, Rufus. *History of the Sandwich Islands Mission*. London: Hodder and Stoughton, 1872.

Arens, William. *The Man-Eating Myth: Anthropology and Anthropophagy*. New York: Oxford University Press, 1980.

Attenborough, David. *Quest in Paradise*. London: Pan Books, 1960.

Baker, Paul T., Joel M. Hanna, and Thelma S. Baker. *The Changing Samoans*. New York: Oxford University Press, 1986.

Barker, John, ed. *Christianity in Oceania: Ethnographic Perspectives*. ASAO Monograph no. 12. Lanham, MD: University Press of America, 1990.

Beckwith, Martha Warren. *Hawaiian Mythology*. New Haven, CT: Yale University Press, 1940.

———, trans. *Kumulipo: A Hawaiian Creation Chant*. Honolulu: University of Hawai'i Press, 1981.

Best, Elsdon. *Polynesian Voyagers: The Maori as a Deep-Sea Navigator, Explorer, and Colonizer Melanesian Element in Polynesia*. Wellington, New Zealand: Dominion Museum, 1923.

Blong, R. J. *The Time of Darkness: Local Legends and Volcanic Activity in Papua New Guinea*. Seattle: University of Washington Press, 1982.

Boehane, Ben. "Islam Is Spreading in Melanesia." *Pacific Magazine*, June 29, 2007.

Bott, Elizabeth. *Tongan Society at the Time of Captain Cook's Visits*. Wellington, New Zealand: Polynesian Society, 1982.

Boutilier, James, Daniel Hughes, and Sharon Tiffany, eds. *Mission, Church, and Sect in Oceania*. Ann Arbor: University of Michigan Press, 1978.

Brandon, James R., and Martin Banham. *The Cambridge Guide to Asian Theatre*. New York: Cambridge University Press, 1997.

Buck, Peter Henry. *Anthropology and Religion*. New Haven, CT: Yale University Press, 1939.

———. *The Coming of the Maori*. Wellington, NZ: Maori Purposes Fund Board, 1950.

Burridge, Kenelm. *New Heaven, New Earth: A Study of Millenarian Activities*. New York: Schocken, 1969.

Chamberlin, Paul. *Can We Be Good without God?: A Conversation about Truth, Morality, Culture & a Few Other Things That Matter*. Downers Grove, IL: InterVarsity Press, 1996.

Charlot, John. *Chanting the Universe: Hawaiian Religious Culture*. Honolulu and Hong Kong: Emphasis International, 1983.

———. "Contemporary Polynesian Thinking." In Eliot Deutsch and Ron Bontekoe, eds. *A Companion to World Philosophies, The Blackwell Companion to World Philosophies*. Oxford, England: Blackwell Publishers, 1997, pp. 542–547.

Chidester, David. *Christianity: A Global History*. San Francisco: Harper San Francisco, 2000.

Chowning, Ann. "Melanesian Religions: An Overview." In Mircea Eliade, ed. *Encyclopedia of Religion*. Vol. 9. New York: Collier Macmillan, 1987, pp. 349–259.

Codrington, R. H. *The Melanesians: Studies in Their Anthropology and Folk-Lore*. New Haven, CT: Behavior Science Reprints, 1957 [1891].

Craig, Robert D. *Dictionary of Polynesian Mythology*. New York: Greenwood Press, 1989.

———. *Handbook of Polynesian Mythology*. Santa Barbara, CA: ABC-CLIO, 2004.

Cunningham, S. *Hawaiian Religion and Myths*. St. Paul, MN: Llewellyn Publications, 1995.

Dawkins, Richard. *The God Delusion*. Boston: Houghton Mifflin Co., 2006.

Daws, Gavan. *Shoal of Time: A History of the Hawaiian Islands*. Honolulu: University of Hawai'i Press, 1974.

Day, A. Grove. *Hawaii and Its People*. New York: Duell, Sloan and Pearce, 1960.

Diamond, Jared M. *Collapse: How Societies Choose to Fail or Succeed*. New York: Penguin, 2006.

Dixon, Roland Burrage. *Oceanic [Mythology]*. Boston: Marshall Jones, 1916.

———. *The Mythology of All Races in Thirteen Volumes*. Vol. IX, *Oceanic*. Boston: Marshall Jones Co., 1917.

Eliade, Mircea, ed. *The Encyclopedia of Religion*. Vols. 3, 9, 11, 13, and 15. New York: Macmillan Publishing Co., 1987.

———. *The Sacred and the Profane: The Nature of Religion*. Translated by Willard R. Trask. New York: Harcourt Brace, 1959.

Ellis, William. *Narrative of a Tour through Hawaii, or Owhyee*. London: H. Fisher, Son, and P. Jackson, 1827.

Emerson, Nathaniel B. *Unwritten Literature of Hawaii: The Sacred Songs of the Hula*. Washington, DC: Smithsonian Institute, 1909.

Encyclopaedia Britannica: A Dictionary of Arts, Sciences and General Literature. New York: The Henry G. Allen Company, 1890.

Enk, Gerrit J. van, and Lourens De Vries. *The Korowai of Irian Jaya: Their Language in Its Cultural Context*. New York: Oxford University Press, 1997.

Fortune, Reo. *Manus Religion: An Ethnological Study of the Manus Natives of the Admiralty Islands*. Philadelphia: The American Philosophical Society, 1935.

Fuchs, L. H. *Hawaii Pono*. Honolulu: Bess Press, 1961.

Garrett, John. *Footsteps in the Sea: Christianity in Oceania to World War II*. Suva, Fiji: University of the South Pacific, Institute of Pacific Studies, in association with the World Council of Churches, 1992.

Gifford, Edward W. *Tongan Myths and Tales*. Honolulu: The Museum, 1924.

Gill, William W. *Myths and Songs from the South Pacific*. London: H. S. King & Co., 1876.

Grey, Sir George. *Polynesian Mythology*. Auckland, New Zealand: Whitcombe and Tombs, Ltd., 1965 [1854].

Gulick, Orramel Hinckley, and Ann Eliza Clark Gulick. *The Pilgrims of Hawaii*. New York: Fleming H. Revell Company, 1918.

Gutmanis, J. *Na Pule Kahiki*. Honolulu: Editions Ltd., 1983.

Handy, Willowdean Chatterson. *Tattooing in the Marquesas*. Honolulu: The Museum, 1922.

Hardman, Keith. *Charles Grandison Finney, 1792–1875: Revivalist and Reformer*. Syracuse, NY: Syracuse University Press, 1987.

Harris, Marvin. *Cows, Pigs, Wars, and Witches: The Riddles of Culture*. New York: Vintage Books Edition, 1989 [1974].

Herbert, Christopher. *Culture and Anomie: Ethnographic Imagination in the Nineteenth Century.* Chicago: University of Chicago Press, 1991.

Heslin, Joseph. *A History of the Roman Catholic Church in Samoa, 1845–1995.* Edited by Michael B Tyquin. Apia, Western Samoa: J. Heslin, 1995.

Howe, K. R., Robert C. Kiste, and Brij V. Lal. *Tides of History: The Pacific Islands in the Twentieth Century.* Honolulu: University of Hawai'i Press, 1994.

Hutchison, William R. *Errand to the World: American Protestant Thought and Foreign Missions.* Chicago and London: University of Chicago Press, 1987.

Ivens, Walter G. "The Polynesian Word Atua: Its Derivation and Meaning." *Journal of the Royal Anthropological Institute of Great Britain and Ireland* 24 (Aug., Sep., Oct. 1924): 114–116, 133–136, and 146–147.

Jones, Stella M. "Economic Adjustment of Hawaiians to European Culture." *Public Affairs* 4.11 (Nov. 1931): 957–974.

Kane, J. Herbert. *A Concise History of the Christian World Mission.* Ada, MI: Baker Academic, 1978.

Kanahele, Edward, and Pualani Kanahele. "Hawaiian Religion." In *Atlas of Hawaii.* 3rd ed. Honolulu: University of Hawai'i Press, 1998, pp. 202–203.

Kelly, John. *A Politics of Virtue: Hinduism, Sexuality, and Countercolonial Discourse in Fiji.* Chicago: University of Chicago Press, 1992.

Kent, Janet. *The Solomon Islands.* Harrisburg, PA: Stackpole Books, 1972.

Koda, Tara K. "Aloha with Gassho: Buddhism in the Hawaiian Plantations." In *Pacific World.* Third Series. Mountain View, CA: Institute of Buddhist Studies, 2006, pp. 237–254.

Kuykendall, Ralph S. *The Hawaiian Kingdom.* Vol. 1, *Foundation and Transformation, 1778–1854.* Honolulu: University of Hawai'i Press, 1938.

Lamb, Ramdas. "Polytheism." In James Birx, ed. *Encyclopedia of Anthropology.* Vol. 4. Thousand Oaks, CA: Sage Publications, 2005, pp. 1889–1891.

———. "Religion." In *Atlas of Hawaii.* 3rd ed. Honolulu: University of Hawai'i Press, 1998, pp. 201–204.

———. "Sacred." In Sushil Mittal and Gene Thursby, eds. *Studying Hinduism: Key Concepts and Methods.* London and New York: Routledge, 2007.

Larkin, Barbara, ed. *International Religious Freedom 2000: Annual Report.* Washington, DC: U.S. Department of State, 2002.

Laroutette, Kenneth Scott. *A History of Christianity.* 2 vols. New York: Harper and Row Publishers, 1975 [1953].

Lawrence, P., and M. J. Meggitt. *Gods, Ghosts and Men in Melanesia: Some Religions of Australian New Guinea and the New Hebrides.* Melbourne, Australia: Oxford University Press, 1972.

Lawson, Stephanie. *Ethnic Politics and the State in Fiji.* Canberra: Australian National University, Peace Research Centre, 1993.

———. *Tradition versus Democracy in the South Pacific: Fiji, Tonga and Western Samoa.* New York: Cambridge University Press, 2008.

Le Tagaloa, Fanaafi Aino. *Tapuai: Samoan Worship.* Malua: Malua Printing Press, 2003.

Lindstrom, Lamont. *Cargo Cult: Strange Stories of Desire from Melanesia and Beyond.* Honolulu: University of Hawai'i Press, 1993.

Loeliger, Carl, and Garry Trompf. *New Religious Movements in Melanesia.* Suva: University of the South Pacific and University of Papua New Guinea, 1985.

Malo, David. *Hawaiian Antiquities (Moolelo Hawaii).* Translated by N. B. Emerson. Honolulu: Hawaiian Gazette Co., Ltd., 1908.

Mariner, William, and John Martin. *An Account of the Natives of Tonga Islands in the South Pacific Ocean.* London: John Murray, 1817.

Mark, Diane Mei Lin. *Seasons of Light: The History of Chinese Christian Churches in Hawaii.* Honolulu: Chinese Christian Association of Hawaii, 1989.

McGrath, Ken, and Hugh Young, "A Review of Circumcision in New Zealand." In George C. Denniston et al., eds. *Understanding Circumcision.* New York: Kluwer Academic/Plenum Publishers, 2001, pp. 129–146.

Mead, Hirini Moko. *Tikanga Ma-ori: Living by Ma-ori Values.* Wellington, New Zealand: Huia Publishers, 2003.

Melville, Herman. *Typee, and Omoo, or, The Marquesas Islands, and Adventures in the South Seas.* London: G. Routledge, 1850.

Middleton, John, ed. *Gods and Rituals: Readings in Religious Beliefs and Practices.* Austin: University of Texas Press, 1967.

Mirecki, Paul Allan, and Marvin W. Meyer. *Magic and Ritual in the Ancient World.* Vol. 141, *Religions in the Graeco-Roman World.* Leiden: Brill, 2002.

Montgomery, Right Rev. H. H., ed. *Mankind and the Church: Being an Attempt to Estimate the Contribution of Great Races to the Fullness of the Church of God, by Seven Bishops.* London: Longmans, Green, and Co., 1907.

Mulholland, J. *Hawaii's Religions.* Tokyo: Charles E. Tuttle and Co., 1970.

Munro, Doug, and Andrew Thornley. "Editorial Introduction: Retrieving the Pastors." In Doug Munro and Andrew Thornley, eds. *The Covenant Makers: Islander Missionaries in the Pacific.* Suva, Fiji: Pacific Theological College and The Institute of Pacific Studies at the University of the South Pacific, 1996, pp. 1–16.

———, eds. *The Covenant Makers: Islander Missionaries in the Pacific.* Suva, Fiji: Pacific Theological College and The Institute of Pacific Studies at the University of the South Pacific, 1996.

Narokobi, Bernard. *The Melanesian Way.* Boroko: Institute of Papua New Guinea Studies, 1983.

Newbury, Colin. *Tahiti Nui: Change and Survival in French Polynesia, 1767–1945.* Honolulu: University Press of Hawai'i, 1980.

Niukula, Paula. *The Triple Aspect of Fijian Society: The Three Pillars.* Suva: Research Group, 1994.

Norbeck, Edward. *Religion in Primitive Society.* New York: Harper & Row, 1961.

Northcott, Cecil. *Glorious Company; 150 Years Life and Work of the London Missionary Society, 1795–1945.* London: Livingstone Press, 1945.

Nunn, Frank L. "Islam in Fiji." In Samuel M. Zwemer, ed. *The Muslim World.* New York: The Arthur H. Crist Co., 1919, pp. 265–267.

Obeyesekere, Gananath. *Cannibal Talk: The Man-Eating Myth and Human Sacrifice in the South Seas*. Berkeley: University of California Press, 2005.

———. *The Apotheosis of Captain Cook*. Princeton, NJ: Princeton University Press, 1993.

Oliver, Douglas L. *Polynesia in Early Historic Times*. Honolulu: Bess Press, 2002.

———. *The Pacific Islands*. Honolulu: University of Hawai'i Press, 1989.

Papa Ii, John. *Fragments of Hawaiian History*. Bernice Pauahi Bishop Museum Special Publication. Honolulu: Bishop Museum Press, 1959.

Petrinovich, Lewis F. *The Cannibal Within*. Edison, NJ: Aldine Transaction Publishers, 2000.

Philsooph, H. "Primitive Magic and Mana." *Man* (New Series), 6.2 (June 1971); 182–203.

Pierce, L. W. *Hawaii's Missionary Saga*. Honolulu: Mutual, 1992.

Poignant, Roslyn. *Oceanic Mythology: The Myths of Polynesia, Micronesia, Melanesia, Australia*. London: Paul Hamlyn, 1967.

Premdas, Ralph R. *Ethnic Conflict and Development: The Case of Fiji*. Research in Ethnic Relations Series. Brookfield, VT: Ashgate Publishing, 1995.

Progue, Rev. John F. *Moolelo of Ancient Hawaii*. Translated by Charles W. Kenn. Honolulu: Topgallant Publishing Co., Ltd., 1978.

Prout, Ebenezer. *Memoirs of the Life of the Rev. John Williams, Missionary to Polynesia*. New York: M. W. Dodd, 1843.

Pukui, Mary Kawena, and Samuel H. Elbert. *Hawaiian Dictionary*. Honolulu: University of Hawai'i Press, 1957.

Rivers, William H. *The History of Melanesian Society*. Cambridge: Cambridge University Press, 1914.

Ryle, Jacqueline. "Roots of Land and Church: The Christian State Debate in Fiji." *International Journal for the Study of the Christian Church* 5.1 (2005): 58–78.

Sahlins, Marshall. "Artificially Maintained Controversies: Global Warming and Fijian Cannibalism." *Anthropology Today* 19.3 (June 2003): 3–5.

———. *How "Natives" Think: About Captain Cook, For Example*. Chicago: University of Chicago Press, 1995.

Schneebaum, Tobias. *The Asmat: Dynamics of Irian*. Jakarta, Indonesia: Asmat Progress and Development Foundation, 1991.

———. *Where the Spirits Dwell: An Odyssey in the New Guinea Jungle*. New York: Grove Press, 1988.

Seaton, S. Lee. "The Hawaiian *kapu* Abolition of 1819." *American Ethnologist* 1.1 (Feb. 1974): 193–206.

Sharp, Andrew. *Ancient Voyagers in Polynesia*. London: Longman Paul Ltd., 1963.

Sillitoe, Paul. *An Introduction to the Anthropology of Melanesia: Culture and Tradition*. New York: Cambridge University Press, 1998.

Silverman, Jane L. *Ka'ahumanu: Molder of Change*. Honolulu: Friends of the Judiciary History Center of Hawai'i, 1995.

Smith, S. Percy. *Hawaiki: The Original Home of the Maori, with a Sketch of Polynesian History*. Christchurch, New Zealand: Whitcombe and Tombs Limited, 1904.

Speiser, Felix. *Ethnology of Vanuatu: An Early Twentieth Century Study*. Honolulu: University of Hawai'i Press, 1996.

Spriggs, Matthew. *The Island Melanesians*. Cambridge, MA: Blackwell, 1997.

Steinbauer, Friedrich. *Melanesian Cargo Cults: New Salvation Movements in the South Pacific*. Translated by Max Wohlwill. Queensland: University of Queensland Press, 1979.

Tabrah, Ruth M. *Hawaii: A History*. New York: W. W. Norton and Co., 1980.

Tagupa, William E. *Legal Concepts and Crises in Tahiti, 1819–1838*. Honolulu: Hawaiian Historical Society, 1974.

Thompson, Laura. *Southern Lau, Fiji: An Ethnography*. Honolulu: The Museum, 1940.

Thornley, Andrew. "Heretics and Papists: Wesleyan–Roman Catholic Rivalry in Fiji, 1844–1903." *Journal of Religious History* 10(3) (1940): 294–312.

———. "On the Edges of Christian History in the Pacific." *The Journal of Pacific Studies* 20 (1996): 175–187.

———. "The Methodist Church and Fiji's Indians: 1879–1920." *New Zealand Journal of History* 8.2 (1974): 137–153.

Tobin, Jack A. *Stories from the Marshall Islands*. Honolulu: University of Hawai'i Press, 2001.

Tregear, Edward. *The Maori-Polynesian Comparative Dictionary*. Wellington, New Zealand: Lyon and Blair, Lampton Quay, 1891.

Talu, Sister Alaim, et al. *Kiribati: Aspects of History*. Suva: University of the South Pacific, Institute of Pacific Studies and Extension Services, and the Ministry of Education, Training, and Culture, Kiribati Government, 1984.

Turner, Victor Witter. *The Ritual Process: Structure and Anti-Structure*. The Lewis Henry Morgan Lectures, 1966. New York: Aldine de Gruyter, 1995.

Von Daniken, Erich. *Pathways to the Gods: The Stones of Kiribati*. Translated by Michael Heron. New York: G. P. Putnam's Sons, 1982.

Walls, Andrew F. "Haweis, Thomas." In Gerald H. Anderson, ed. *Biographical Dictionary of Christian Missions*. New York: Macmillan Reference USA, 1998.

Wallis, Mary. *Life in Feejee; or, Five Years among the Cannibals*. Ridgewood, NJ: Gregg Press, 1967 [1851].

Watson, Robert Mackenzie. *History of Samoa*. Wellington, New Zealand: Whitcombe and Tombs, Ltd., 1918.

Watt, Rev. William. "Cannibalism as Practised on Tanna, New Hebrides." *Journal of the Polynesian Society* 4.4 (1895): 226–230.

Westervelt, W. D. *Myths and Legends of Hawaii*. Honolulu: Mutual Publishing Co., 1987.

Williams, John. *A Narrative of Missionary Enterprises in the South Sea Islands: With Remarks upon the Natural History of the Islands, Origin, Languages, Traditions, and Usages of the Inhabitants*. London: J. Snow, 1845.

Williams, Thomas. *Fiji and the Fijians*. Vol. 1, *The Islanders and Their Families*. Edited by George Stringer Rowe. Suva, Fiji: Fiji Museum, 1982 [1858].

Williamson, Robert W. *The Religious and Cosmic Beliefs of Central Polynesia*. 2 vols. Cambridge: Cambridge University Press, 1933.

Winzeler, Robert L. *Anthropology and Religion*. New York: Rowman & Littlefield Publishers, Inc., 2007.

Worsley, Peter. *The Trumpet Shall Sound: A Study of Cargo Cults in Melanesia*. New York: Schocken Books, 1968.

Zink, Mary Lynn. "Gauguin's Poèmes barbares and the Tahitian Chant of Creation." *Art Journal* 38.1 (Sept. 1978): 18–21.

WEB SITES

Carando, Joanne. "Hawaiian Royal Incest: A Study in the Sacrificial Origin of Monarchy." *Transatlantica*, 2002. http://www.transatlantica.org/document525.html.

Council for World Mission. "Who We Are." http://www.cwmission.org/who-we-are.

Encyclopaedia Britannica. "Taboo, Tabu."10th ed., 1902. http://www.1902encyclopedia .com/T/TAB/taboo.htm.

"Fiji Facts and Figures." http://www.spc.int/PRISM/country/fj/stats/FFF08.pdf.

"Fiji Islands Bureau of Statistics." http://www.spc.int/PRISM/country/fj/stats/ Census2007/census07_index2.htm.

Hammer, Chris. "Fiji Desecration." Special Broadcasting Service, June 22, 2005. http://news.sbs.com.au/dateline/fiji_desecration_130533.

"History of the Marshall Islands." http://www.rmiembassyus.org/History.htm.

Islamic Human Rights Commission. "Islam under Threat in Papua New Guinea." http://www.ihrc.org.uk/show.php?id=134.

Ka'upu, David. "Going with God." http://www.ksbe.edu/allpdfs/01summer/IMUA _12-13.PDF.

Kawaharada, Dennis. "'Aumakua of Kona, O'ahu." Kapiolani Community College Web site. http://apdl.kcc.hawaii.edu/~oahu/stories/kona/aumakua.htm.

MacKenzie, Tessa. "The Situation in the South Pacific Islands." http://www.wcc-coe.org/wcc/what/interreligious/cd35-20.html.

Nation Master. "Oceania." http://www.nationmaster.com/region/OCE.

Ogden, Michael R. "Republic of Fiji" (forthcoming in the *World Encyclopedia of Political Systems*, 3rd ed.). http://www2.hawaii.edu/~ogden/piir/pacific/fiji.html.

"Population by Religion and Province of Enumeration, Fiji: 2007 Census." http://www.statsfiji.gov.fj/Key%20Stats/Population/2.10Religion2007.pdf.

Raffaele, Paul. "In John They Trust." *Smithsonian*, February 2006. http://www.smith-sonianmag.com/people-places/10021366.html?page=1.

"Raymata—Ancient King of Vanuatu." http://www.vanuatutourism.com/vanuatu/cms/ en/history/roymata.html.

"2007 Report on International Religious Freedom—Marshall Islands." http://www.unhcr.org/refworld/topic,464db4f52,46a70ae32,46ee67745f,0.html.

Resture, Jane. "Melanesian Mythology: Vanuatu." http://www.janeresture.com/melanesia _myths/Vanuatu.htm.

————. "Samoa: Origin of Name, the People, Navigators Islands, Language, Receptions and Insignia of Rank." http://www.janesoceania.com/samoa_origin/index.htm.

————. "The Tahitian Royal Family." http://www.janesoceania.com/tahiti_royals/index2.htm.

"Samoa." http://www.worldstatesmen.org/Samoa.html.

Tamasese: Tui Atua Tupua Tamasese Ta'isi Efi. "Keynote Address for Pacific Futures Law and Religion Symposium." National University of Samoa, Lepapaigalagala, Samoa, December 3, 2008. http://www.samoalivenews.com/Editor-and-Reader-Opinions/Religion-Law-and-the-Samoan-Indigenous-Reference.html.

————. Religion, Law and the Samoan Indigenous Reference." *Samoa Alive* News Line, December 6, 2008. http://www.samoalivenews.com/Editor-and-Reader-Opinions/Religion-Law-and-the-Samoan-Indigenous-Reference.html.

Thompson, Liz. "The Samoan Tattoo: A Powerful, Positive Message to the Community." Pacific Arts Online. http://www.abc.net.au/arts/artok/bodyart/s197594.htm.

Chapter 5

Indonesia

Monika Arnez

OVERVIEW

Indonesia, a vast archipelago stretching from the Indian Ocean to Melanesia, is a highly complex and diverse region, where several hundred regional languages and ethnic groups have developed. It can easily be imagined that such a geographically and linguistically diverse region also produced a rich variety of religious practices. Although the main religion in Indonesia is Islam (with 88% of its inhabitants adhering to it), the practices and beliefs associated with Islam are diverse. The same is true for Protestantism (6%), Roman Catholicism (3%), Hinduism (2%), Buddhism and Confucianism (1%), minority religions in the archipelago. This chapter will provide interesting examples illustrating this diversity. As far as Islam is concerned, I reveal how *slametan*, a syncretistic Islamic ritual often mentioned in scholarly works as a part of "Javanese Islam," is practiced in different contexts and by different groups. Furthermore, the chapter explores the relationship between Islam and Christianity, which has become more troubled in the last decade, including this author's firsthand experience with the matter. As an example of integration between Catholicism and local tradition (*adat*), I provide the *kéo rado*, a death ritual performed by the Ngadha people in Flores, East Indonesia, as analyzed by Susanne Schröter.[1]

The principle of "belief in One Almighty God" (*Ke-Tuhanan Yang Maha Esa*) was formulated on May 29, 1945, in Pancasila, the Indonesian state philosophy, which is part of the Indonesian constitution. Today, the

Indonesian state officially acknowledges six religions: Islam, Protestantism, Catholicism, Hinduism, Buddhism, and Confucianism. However, to access the variety of religious practices in Indonesia, it is necessary to realize that in many places Indonesians have adapted and transformed religions according to their local traditions. As Smith Kipp and Rodgers observe, the local ethnic religions can be seen as "*social creations* of the interaction of world religions and village ritual."[2] They argue that before having come into contact with Islam or Christianity, local rituals were not necessarily regarded as components of a distinctive system. The result was a continuing process of adaptation, transformation, and reconceptualization of religion. An important element of many *adat* practices is ancestor worship. One reason for the sustainability of *adat* in many places in Indonesia might be that these rituals belonged to village life before the big monotheistic religions gained ground. The indigenous people were animistic communities with death and spirit cults. People in West Papua or on the Mentawai Islands adhere to animism to this day.

HISTORY

Hinduism attracted many people from the Indonesian archipelago largely because it revealed ways to achieve religious goals that already existed in indigenous belief systems. For example, Indonesians had already been used to building terraced temples, which symbolized holy mountains, for honoring and burying the dead. Thus, the Brahmans' doctrine that Shiva dwelled on a holy mountain was not unfamiliar to them. An important symbol of the Shaivite Brahmans was the lingam. Linga is Shiva's phallic symbol and is associated with that god's creative power. The Brahmans were representatives of an increasingly influential devotional movement (*bhakti*) in Indian Hinduism, in which the rulers obtained Shiva's grace through devotional exercises offered to Shiva. These practices were thought to guarantee a superior status in the afterlife. The Shaivite cults were a source of prestige and royal authority.

The Buddhist kingdom of Srivijaya, a trading state, was founded on Sumatra about 500 CE. Srivijaya's power was centered in the region of present-day Palembang, Sumatra, and reached to coastal areas on the Malaysian peninsula and elsewhere, and Mataram, Central Java, where the great Buddhist and Hindu monuments Borobudur and Prambanan were established. The Shailendra Dynasty, the power behind the creation of Borobodur, promoted the Mahayana and Tantric forms of Buddhism. Set

The Borobudur temple in the heart of Java, Indonesia, was constructed around 800 CE. It is the largest sacred building of Buddhism and one of the best-preserved monuments in the world. The temple consists of six square platforms below and three circular on top. The upper platform displays seventy-two small stupas surrounding one large central stupa. The monument features 504 Buddha statues, carved from massive volcanic stone. (Photos.com.)

on a plain ringed by mountains, a pyramidal form was constructed around a natural rise in the terrain to become an artificial hill, symbolizing the cosmic hill, center of the universe. A Buddhist follower is to walk around each level of the temple, following the 1,460 narrative relief panels, as a symbolic path to enlightenment. Every year in May on the full moon, the Vesak celebration (called Tri Suci Waisak in Bahasa Indonesia) is held at Borobudur. This ritual commemorates the birth, enlightenment, and passing away of the Buddha. In contrast to Borobudur, Prambanan, the largest Hindu complex in Indonesia, is divided into a large number of small temples and eight larger ones, crowned by the Shiva temple. It is composed of eight main shrines and more than 250 individual shrines surrounding the main shrines. The three biggest shrines, Trisakti, are dedicated to the gods Shiva, Vishnu, and Brahma.

TIMELINE

c. 100:	Hinduism reaches Kalimantan.
c. 425:	Buddhism reaches Sumatra.
c. 500:	Beginnings of the Kingdom of Srivijaya.
c. 770:	Shailendra King Vishnu begins building Borobudur.
910:	Sanjaya King Daksa begins building major Hindu temples at Prambanan.
1292:	Wijaya founds a new court at Majapahit.
1297:	Pasai in Sumatra converts to Islam. Sultan Malek Saleh is the first Muslim ruler in what is now Indonesia.
1511:	Portuguese Admiral Albuquerque's forces take Malacca.
c. 1520:	Much of Java begins to convert to Islam.
1522:	Antonio de Britto establishes a fort on Ternate.
1602:	Companies combine to form the Vereenigde Oostindische Compagnie (VOC).
1861:	German Lutherans start to work among the Batak (Sumatra).
1883:	The first Confucian shrine, Boen Bio, is built in Surabaya.
1912:	Sarekat Islam and Muhammadiyah are founded.
1923:	Center for Confucian Religion Assembly is founded.
1926:	Nahdlatul Ulama are founded.
1948:	Kartosowirjo proclaims himself imam of Darul Islam.
1980s:	The Department of Religious Affairs restricts missionary activities by the Roman Catholics; period of Islamic revival in Indonesia.
2000:	Jemaah Islamiyah (JI) masterminds an organized series of bombings of Christian churches on Christmas Eve.
2002:	Jemaah Islamiyah attacks nightclubs in Kuta, Bali.

The greatest of the Hindu-Buddhist states was Majapahit, in East Java, claiming hegemony from the late thirteenth to the late fourteenth century. Majapahit was a trading and naval power.[3] It used its naval power to establish ties with different regions such as Champa, Cambodia, Siam, southern Burma, and Vietnam. The influence of Majapahit started to decline in the late fourteenth century. At the same time, the great Malay trading state of Malacca became a center for foreign Muslims and apparently supported the spread of Islam.

However, Islamization proceeded only slowly until the fifteenth century. According to Ricklefs, there were two processes of how Islamization occurred in Indonesia.[4] He argues that on the one hand foreign Asians came from India, Arabia, and China in the thirteenth century who were Muslims already and decided to settle permanently in an Indonesian area. On the other hand indigenous Indonesians came into contact with Islam and converted to this religion. These two processes were probably intertwined. By the end of the thirteenth century, Islam came to North Sumatra, and in the fourteenth century to northeast Malaya, Brunei, the southern Philippines, and to some East Javanese regions. Around the beginning of the fifteenth century Malacca, a new trading state, arose in the Western archipelago. In the seventeenth century, the southern midland of central Java became the dominant power on Java, and the sultanate Mataram was born.

In the seventeenth century, the Vereenigte Oostindische Compagnie (VOC) started to forcibly monopolize the spice trade. But it was not before the nineteenth century, when the Dutch Crown took over the trading company, that the colonial regime was systematized. An alliance of *priyayi* (aristocratic officials) and *ulama* (religious scholars) led the way in the Java war (1825–1830). Because the Dutch feared orthodox Muslims, they tended to employ *abangan* (syncretistic Muslims), instead of *santri* (orthodox Muslims).[5] The terms *abangan* and *santri*, popularized by the American anthropologist Clifford Geertz in the 1960s, are used to suggest varying degrees of Islamic piety. *Abangan* refers to nominal Muslims, who seldom attend Islamic devotions or lead syncretic religious lives, in which non-Islamic elements may be drawn from other religions (Hinduism and Buddhism) or folk beliefs.[6] *Santri* are orthodox Muslims, adhering strictly to the ritual and legal requirements of Islam. In the course of the nineteenth century, santrism became a religious and political anticolonialism doctrine that increasingly distanced itself from Hindu-Buddhist traditions. Both traditionalist and modernist Muslims, today mostly represented through the mass organizations Nahdlatul Ulama (NU) and Muhammadiyah, respectively, are classified as *santri*. Around 1910 modernism started to play an increasing role among the merchants in the urban centres. In 1912 Sarekat Islam, the first nationalist movement, was born, as well as the modernist Muslim organization Muhammadiyah. As a reaction to modernism, Nahdlatul Ulama (NU) was founded in 1926, based in rural areas. It represents the interests of traditionalist Muslim scholars.

Christianity came to Indonesia through the Portuguese. In the sixteenth century, Portuguese Jesuits and Dominicans operated in Maluku, southern Sulawesi, and Timor. In 1522 the first attempts were made to convert the local people to Christianity, but it was only in 1534 that local people converted to Christianity, through the proselytizing of the Portuguese priest Simon Vaz, who became the first local martyr. At the end of the sixteenth century, 20 percent of the inhabitants of Southern Maluku had converted to the Catholic faith. The southeastern parts of the archipelago—Larantuka, on Flores, and Dili, on the island of Timor—also became centers of Catholic life under the pastoral care of Dominican friars.[7] When the Dutch defeated the Portuguese, however, Catholic missionaries were expelled and the Calvinist Dutch Reformed Church became the only Christian influence in the region for 300 years. Only some small communities continued to exist in Java, Maluku, northern Sulawesi, and Nusa Tenggara (primarily Roti and Timor) until the nineteenth century. It was only after the dissolution of the VOC in 1800 that the Dutch permitted proselytizing in the territory. The more tolerant German Lutherans used this freedom. They started to work among the Batak of Sumatra in 1861, and the Dutch Rhenish Mission did so in central Kalimantan and central Sulawesi. In addition, Jesuits established successful missions, schools, and hospitals throughout the islands of Flores, Timor, and Alor.

In the course of the twentieth century, many new Protestant missionary groups came to Indonesia. Furthermore, Catholicism spread, and a considerable number of regional and reformed Lutheran churches were built. As a consequence of the 1965 coup d'état, all nonreligious persons were labeled atheists, and hence were easily accused of sympathizing with communists. At that time, Christian churches of all varieties experienced explosive growth in membership, particularly among those who felt uncomfortable with the political aspirations of Islamic parties. In the 1990s, the majority of Christians in Indonesia were Protestants, with particularly large concentrations found in North Sumatra, Irian Jaya, Maluku, Central Kalimantan, and North and Central Sulawesi. Catholicism could not spread so rapidly, partly because it relied heavily on European personnel. The Muslim-dominated Department of Religious Affairs restricted missionary activities by the Roman Catholics in the 1980s. Larger concentrations of Roman Catholics were located only in West Kalimantan, Irian Jaya, the Lesser Sundas, and East Timor.

The history of Confucianism in Indonesia has not been long. In 1883 the first Confucian shrine, Boen Bio, was built in Surabaya, East Java. In 1923, in a congress held at Yogyakarta, Central Java, the Center for Confucian Religion Assembly was founded, which was finally renamed as MATAKIN, for Majelis Tinggi Agama Khonghucu Indonesia (Supreme Council for Confucian Religion of Indonesia) in April 16, 1955. Confucianism was outlawed in Indonesia in 1965 in the wake of the failed communist coup attempt, communism being associated with China, and hence with the local Chinese population. In 2000, the Minister for Home Affairs abolished the 1978 Ministerial Instruction on Confucianism, thus making it Indonesia's sixth officially recognized religion. In 2000, then-president Abdurrahman Wahid declared Imlek, the Chinese New Year, an optional national holiday.[8]

As far as the relationship between Islam and other religions, especially Christianity, is concerned, we can observe an increasing tension in the last 20 years in Indonesia. As a consequence of emerging extremist forms of Islam in this period, which has deepened the religious differences between Muslims and Christians, the latter have felt increasingly threatened in the archipelago. The friction between these groups has led to repeated attacks against Christian and Muslim places of worship in the last decade. Violence especially hit the Moluccan Islands, Sulawesi, Java, and Sumatra. The growing intolerance made it easier for Islamist groups such as Jemaah Islamiyah to carry out their destructive plans. One of the most prominent attacks this group has allegedly masterminded was an organized series of bombings of Christian churches on Christmas Eve in 2000, and the Bali bombings in 2002, which claimed 202 lives.[9] However, this tension does not mean that Muslim-Christian relations are necessarily strained in daily life, although an increasing segregation of the Christian and Muslim communities can be observed, as will be shown later in this chapter.

This segregation between the religions is partly driven by the revitalization of Islamic thought in the 1980s.[10] In the last decade, religious pop culture, the use of visible symbols of piety such as the veil, the *burqa*, and the *niqab*, and televised sermons have become increasingly popular. Because of this Islamic revival, which has been accompanied by outward displays of piety, Islamic television programming has expanded, and Islamic books providing "self-help" advice are in high demand. As a consequence, some charismatic TV preachers (such as Aa Gym), who have succeeded in using religion to entertain and build the audience's confidence in the challenges of life and the hereafter, have become iconic figures.

DAILY LIFE

Indonesia has a rich repertoire of religious practices in daily life. It seems appropriate to start analyzing religious practices on Java, the island with the highest population density in Indonesia. Because the majority of the Javanese are Muslim, I will first describe Islamic practices and their context in daily life in Java.

One important ceremony in Javanese Islam is *slametan*, held for the purpose of achieving a state of physical and/or psychological *slamet* (safety, security). Although there is disagreement among scholars on the question whether *slametan* is mainly animistic or Islamic,[11] most scholars characterize it as a syncretistic ritual because Muslim and Hindu-Buddhist elements can be found there.

There are various types of *slametan*, used for different purposes. First, there are calendrical *slametan*, one of which is the Garebeg Maulud, held by the

palace family in Yogyakarta and Surakarta to commemorate Prophet Mohammad's birthday. It is one of the biggest *slametan* in Central Java. In this highly
institutionalized form of *slametan* a pair of royal gamelan and a traditional
Javanese orchestra accompany the ritual ceremony. The celebration is held at the
central mosque of the court, starting on the sixth day of Maulud (the lunar
month in which the Prophet was born) and for six consecutive days and nights
thereafter.

KYAI HAJI ABDULLAH GYMNASTIAR

Kyai Haji Abdullah Gymnastiar, known as Aa Gym, became an iconic
figure because of his humorous sermons on TV and the self-help message
of Manajemen Qolbu (Managing the Heart). His weekly television shows
had millions of viewers; hundreds of thousands made pilgrimages to
Daarut Tauhiid, his Islamic school and spiritual center. And in 2006, several political parties wanted Gymnastiar as their vice presidential candidate for the 2009 elections. He favored everyday anecdotes over deeper
theological discussion and was able to entertain his audience. In his
preaching, he included stories of his own success and tips on how to build
a harmonious family. By shifting away from traditional forms of religious
authority in Indonesia and presenting himself as an accessible, young,
flexible, and yet pious man, he won many hearts. But when he took a
second wife, he started losing his iconic status. To his female followers, Aa
Gym's polygamy was inconsistent with his public image as a virtuous
husband at the head of a harmonious family. They believed the messages
of his sermons to be inconsistent with his actions.[12]

Second, there are *slametan* held periodically by villages. As Sumastuti
Sumukti puts it, the purpose of the *bersih desa* (clean village) as a rite of inten-
sification is to "maintain or improve the village's natural, social, and economic
conditions, as well as the health of its people."[13] *Bersih desa* aims at either
appeasing the guardian spirit of the village or celebrating abundant harvests
granted by the gods. Most villagers celebrate this type of *slametan* only if some
misfortune hits their village, but there are also some prosperous villages that
hold *bersih desa* almost every year as a way to express their gratitude to God.
Hence, *bersih desa* may serve several purposes: to "cleanse" the village from evil,
to maintain agricultural production, and to preserve propitious relations with
God and the local spirits. In preparing for the *bersih desa*, each household in
the village contributes money for a *wayang* (shadow play) performance and

trays of prepared food. The trays are taken to the house of the *lurah* (village head), and at around 11 AM a group of men, who act as household representatives, assemble for the *slametan*. After a formal statement of intention (*ujub*) by the *lurah* and prayers led by an official religious leader, the prepared food is distributed among the participants. A *wayang* (shadow play) may be performed afterwards.

In a private context, *slametan* are conducted for rites of passage—such as pregnancy, birth (and after birth), circumcision, marriage, and death—especially among *abangan* (nominal, syncretistic Muslims). They are held to ensure that in critical moments of life the host family will not become upset, sad, poor, or sick.

Although *slametan* are typically associated with *abangan* Muslims, *santri* Muslims occasionally hold it, especially to celebrate important dates in Islamic history, such as the birth of Prophet Mohammad, his ascension to heaven, and the beginning and ending of Ramadan. Although there are differences as to why and how *abangan* and *santri* celebrate *slametan* (and sometimes tensions between the two groups may occur because of these differences), *slametan* also fulfills a unifying function. For instance, if an *abangan* family holds a *slametan* ceremony, family members always entrust the *santri* to lead the ceremony and the Islamic prayers. On the other hand, the *santri* will invite all of their neighbors, including the *abangan*, to their *slametan*. Thus, *slametan* is considered a significant social ritual in Java. Besides serving as a reconciling factor for the different ideologies of Javanese Muslims, *slametan* is conducted to pray for safety and welfare of a family in critical moments of life. In most cases the prayer session of the ritual is conducted by men, mostly religious leaders such as *kiai* (an Islamic teacher) or *modin* (an official religious specialist). It is common that a chosen messenger orally invites close kin and neighbors to the ceremony before the sunset prayer (*slametan* is usually carried out in the evening after sunset).

Before the *slametan* ritual begins, the guests typically engage in small talk, smoke, and wait for other guests to arrive. In *abangan* rituals incense is often used (*menyan* or *dupa*), in contrast to *santri* ceremonies ,where it is rejected as a part of the Hindu tradition. After the guests have gathered, the host welcomes them in High Javanese (*kromo inggil*) with the *ujub*, which plays a fourfold role: First, it is done to welcome the invited guests and to express gratitude for their attendance. Second, it fulfills an introductory function in explaining the specific reason for a particular *slametan*. Third, it explains the general reason for the *slametan*—for example, to provide safety or avoid bad luck. Finally, the *ujub* is uttered to apologize for the lack of eloquence in the speech and the inadequacy of the food.

Afterward, one of the guests (a *santri* living in the neighborhood) chants selected passages of the Qur'an. The most common passage chanted in a *slametan* is the opening passage of the Qur'an, the Al-Fatihah, the most common prayer in the Muslim world. After the Al-Fatihah, other passages of the Qur'an are chanted. When the prayers are finished, the guests rub their faces with the palms of their hands, symbolizing that they have absorbed the blessings descending from God, and the prayer leader is invited by the host to begin the meal, followed by the other guests. The food consists of cones of steamed rice (*nasi tumpeng*), with side dishes of meat, fish, eggs, vegetables, and fruits, usually covered with banana leaves. The existence of the *tumpeng* implies that the *slametan* is held to ask the sacred in the invisible world for blessings. The *gunungan* (mountain of food) represents the mechanism that opens the gate connecting the mundane and the sacred worlds for communication.[14] The hosts generally serve tea on trays containing kettles, glasses, bowls with fresh water for hand washing, and empty plates with which the guests serve themselves. Once the dishes are placed on trays in the center of the room, the invited guests sit cross-legged around mats on the floor. After the guests have eaten, they go home, often taking leftovers with them, wrapped in banana leaves.[15]

I will now give an example of a *slametan* for circumcision, an important rite of passage for boys, documented by Abdur Ghuffur Muhaimin in the city of Cirebon.[16] Almost everyone in Cirebon considers circumcision a requirement, which is also the case in other Javanese regions. Through this rite of passage a boy turns into a man and a Muslim. If a Javanese boy has not been circumcised between 7 and 10 years of age, peers will exercise group pressure, teasing him for "being a Chinese," for instance. This is embarrassing for the boy because being Chinese means having Christian faith. To be called a Chinese thus suggests not being a Muslim, and this is embarrassing for Muslims. The anthropologist Muhaimin writes that as a result of peer pressure, it is often the boy himself, rather than the parents, who proposes his circumcision.

When the decision to circumcise is made, the date for ritual is set, a matter usually decided among the boy's parents, grandparents, or other elderly close kin. Next, talks will be held concerning the approximate costs, the number of guests, and other organizational matters. When everything is decided, the house is cleaned and a practitioner—either a physician, a paramedic, or a traditional healer (*dukun*)—is contacted. A few days before the date of the circumcision, close kin and relatives contribute rice, sugar, beans, coconuts, and chickens.

Early in the afternoon on the day before the circumcision, the child is ceremonially bathed and dressed in aristocratic or *santri* clothes. If the family has decided that the boy will wear both, one set is worn in the afternoon and the other in the evening. The boy is treated like a king or a groom, called the *penganten sunat* (circumcision groom). Led by an elder, he is put on an ornamented horseback or a *becak* (trishaw), to put flowers on the graves of his parents' closest deceased relatives. On the way to and from the grave complex, he is publicly paraded in a festive manner, usually accompanied by drums or other musical performance. Participants are mostly boys and girls, especially his playmates, peers, and kin.

Most circumcisions are held either in the evening or in the morning (around 7 AM) of the next day. Some people prefer going to a physician or a paramedic to have their children circumcised, either for reliability or for prestige; others prefer a *dukun* for both reliability and cost. Traditionally, if the circumciser is a *dukun*, the operation is done in the yard of the house. The boy is put on his father's or an authorized individual's lap. The *dukun* squats down facing them, teaches the boy the proclamation of faith, utters a prayer, and circumcises the boy. In other cases the boy is taken by car to the operation room, lies down on a mattress, is circumcised and taken back to the house. After being circumcised, the boy is laid down on a mattress in the front room. His friends and peers come to congratulate him with presents, so do the adults who come and give him some money while saying, "Congratulations, you are called a real male."

The evening is the real celebration, the peak of the circumcision feast, at which, for those who can afford it, there is some sort of entertainment such as a *wayang* performance. Special guests, mostly men, go to the boy's house in the evening. They are welcomed, led to sit on chairs to enjoy the entertainment, if any, and served food. After asking for permission to leave, the guest shakes hands with the host and hands him a named envelope containing some money, which is his contribution to the feast. Women guests, on the other hand, mostly come in the afternoon, and they give their contributions to the hostess. All guests at the *slametan* are men and are especially invited to recite prayers led by an imam, who is usually the most prominent local *kiai*. After the *slametan*, the celebration of the circumcision is completed.

In the month of Ruwah (in the Javanese calendar; Syaban in the Arabic calendar) the Javanese prepare for Ramadan, a holy month during which Muslims are meant to purify body and soul by feasting. In Ruwah (derived from the Arabic word *arwah*, the soul of a deceased person), another form of *slametan* is held, the *slametan nyadran*. During this month people collectively carry out the Ramadan ancestor ceremony, by cleaning the graves of the deceased and putting flowers on them. People pray at the graves of their ancestors or deceased prominent local Islamic authorities. This ceremony reaches back to the Majapahit era.

Nyadran is believed to have similarities in ancestor worship with the *craddha* tradition practiced during the Majapahit period.

Village inhabitants in Java generally hold *nyadran* ceremonies in a communal manner. *Nyadran* processions are preceded by each family preparing *kue apem* (sweet rice fritter), *ketan* (glutinous rice), and *kolak* (fruit cooked with coconut milk and brown sugar). The food offered in *nyadran* ceremonies points to the importance of maintaining friendship, forgiving one another, and overcoming sins committed in the past. These ceremonies also suggest that the soul of the deceased will find its place beside God. Thus, *nyadran* can be interpreted as a ritual strengthening bonds between human beings and God, among members the community, and between the living and the dead.

In several villages in Central Java *nyadran* is held for two days and two nights before the end of the Javanese calendar's month of Ruwah; in others it lasts from lunchtime till evening. Some *nyadran* begin with the *tenong sepindah* (the first tray) ritual, with hundreds of villagers carrying a tray (*tenong*)—containing offerings of yellow rice cones, fruit, and snacks—from the house of the village elder to the graves of their ancestors. All villagers take part in the *nyadran* rite.

A *nyadran* ceremony can take place at a graveyard or a mosque. After the grave is cleaned, a ritual feast is then held either in a mosque or in a rural cemetery. The *nyadran* rite is performed at the rural cemetery where the ancestors are buried, at the graves of Muslims who have made significant contributions to the spread of Islam, or at locations that served as Islamic centers in the past.

The *nyadran* tradition, which is essentially a visit to a graveyard in the month of Ruwah, has become almost an obligation for the Javanese. Although *nyadran* and a visit to a grave both entail going to a cemetery, the former is different in meaning from the latter. For instance, the time for a *nyadran* rite is determined by the party who has authority over the area where the rite is practiced. In nearly all the villages, it is the caretaker of a cemetery/sacred place—a village elder or someone considered most senior in the community.

One day before Ramadan starts, the Javanese ritually cleanse themselves by bathing themselves with running water. This ritual, called *padusan*, is usually carried out at such places as wells, bathing places, rivers, pools, lakes, and ponds. During Ramadan there are certain days, called *maleman*, on which the Javanese hold *slametan*: the 21st, 23rd, 25th, 27th, and 29th day of Ramadan. Several rituals include elements formerly associated with Hinduism, such as the *wayang* and the gamelan orchestra. However, these elements have been acculturated into Islam over time. According to the legend, Sunan Kalijaga has played an important role in this context.

DAILY PRACTICES AT RAMADAN

During Ramadan, Muslims are not allowed to eat or drink from dusk until dawn; they are supposed to abstain from sexual relations as well. In this month religious activity is intensified. Evening prayers and Qur'an recitations are especially important in Indonesia at that time. The fast begins in the morning just before sunrise, at *Imsak*, and is broken at *maghrib*, which falls at sunset. Fasting during Ramadan is one of the five pillars of Islam and an obligation for devout Muslims. The fasting faithful awake early in the morning to have a meal before *subuh*, morning prayer. To awaken the faithful, the call to prayer is sounded from neighboring mosques. In addition, groups of young boys walk around, beating on drums and other noisemakers.

The breaking of the fast at sunset is a very social occasion for which special foods are prepared for gatherings with family or friends. Upon hearing the sound of the *bedug* drum on the television or the call to prayer from the neighborhood mosque at sunset, the faithful know it is time to break their fasting (*buka puasa*), usually with sweet drinks and snacks. People pray *maghrib* prayers before a full meal is served. Evening prayers (Javanese *traweh*; Indonesian *tarawih*; Arabic *tarāwīḥ*) are held in neighborhood mosques and at gatherings every evening at about 7:30 PM and last until dawn. These voluntary prayers are enjoyed by many.

SUNAN KALIJAGA

Sunan Kalijaga is one of the nine saints (*wali songo*), also known as Great Proselytizers, who are believed to have brought Islam to Indonesia. He is believed to have been born in 1450, and according to the legend he lived more than 100 years. He is said to have converted to Islam after encountering *wali songo* Sunan Bonang. He founded a religious center at Kadilangu, Demak, where he was eventually buried, but his activities reached far beyond that area. Because of his travels to Cirebon and even to Sumatra, he spread Islam in different regions of the Indonesian archipelago. His special contribution to Islam in Java was his method of proselytizing. It is a common belief that Sunan Kalijaga introduced the shadow theater, gamelan orchestra, and *slametan* and even the Qur'an and the Five Pillars. It is believed that his conversion was accomplished by meditation, ascetic practice, and communion with Sunan Bonang. A treasure Sunan Kalijaga left is a pair of gamelan he originally created for use in the Mosque of Demak. This pair of gamelan, known as gamelan Sekaten, is now preserved at the central Javanese courts of Yogyakarta and Surakarta.

Almost all Javanese Muslims agree that the *traweh* prayers are of immense importance to practicing Muslims and that they can only be performed during the fasting month. They further agree that these prayers can be performed either individually or congregationally. During the performance of these evening prayers, mosques and prayer houses are especially crowded in Java. The muezzin summons worshippers to the mosque, but those who are late often have no other choice but to look for a place in the parking lot next to the mosque.[17] Many people willingly spend about an hour at the mosque to follow the prayers lead by an imam. Most people participating in them do so at their local mosques just after the evening prayers. As the muezzin announces the call to prayer for the obligatory *isya* (evening prayers performed around 7 PM), people in the neighborhood begin to get ready. They are in no hurry as they know the prayer leader and the muezzin will allow a longer time than usual to elapse between the call to prayer (*adzan* in Indonesian, *adhān* in Arabic) and the actual prayer session. At the start of Ramadan the mosque is crowded and additional straw mats for worshippers are needed in the parking lot. From the middle to the end of the month, the mosque is half full at best. A one-meter-wide green cloth separates the mosque into two almost equal parts: one at the front and the other at the back. The front, the male domain, is generally slightly larger, but the area is adjustable should circumstances require it. The back is for women. The cloth is only a symbolic barrier as it does not prevent one group from viewing the other. But it is regarded as necessary by both men and women to maintain the two spheres during *traweh* prayers. This token cloth barrier is only used during Ramadan.

Upon arrival at the mosque, Muslims perform two *raka'at* (prayer cycles, in Indonesian), not mandatory but highly recommended prayers to be performed as one enters a mosque. Afterward, everyone sits down and either engages in small talk or recites quietly parts of the Qur'an. When the muezzin feels that he has waited sufficiently, he announces through the microphone that the evening prayers are to begin. The Ramadan prayers are no different from those of the rest of the year, consisting of four *raka'at*. Each *raka'at*, as always, consists of the recital of Al-Fatihah (the first chapter of the Qur'an), the bending of the upper part of the body, and the complete prostration.[18] Some may use the time before a short Islamic lecture (*kultum*) is presented to perform two additional and individual *raka'at*. In Masjid An-Nur, the Ramadan committee ensures that invited guests offer such lectures each night in connection with the *traweh* prayers. The subject of these sermons is often related to fasting during Ramadan or to some other aspect of Islamic worship. André Möller mentions one occasion when a local policeman gave the Islamic lecture, speaking on the work of the police in eliminating narcotics in Yogyakarta.[19] Often the *khatib* (deliverer of the sermon, in Indonesian) is a local religious authority and the topic chosen is explicitly related to Islamic ritual practices or basic theology. Javanese children use this time to run inside and outside the mosque, for they become restless after a few *raka'at*. Except during Ramadan, Javanese children rarely play outside the house after *maghrib* (sunset) prayers. At the end of the *kultum* the muezzin raises his voice: "Let us perform the nonobligatory *traweh* prayers in congregation, in hope that God will extend His Grace on you all." Some, but not all, reply by saying, "There is no god but God, Muhammad is the Prophet of God." This is the sign that the *traweh* prayers are about to begin, and the entire congregation rises and starts to murmur individually the prescribed intent for this: "I intend to perform the nonobligatory *traweh* prayers for God, the Exalted." Most Javanese can say this sentence in Arabic, but some utter it in Javanese. This done, the imam raises his two hands and utters, *"Allāhu akbar"* (God is greater), and commences the first *raka'at* by reading aloud Al-Fatihah and an additional Qur'anic chapter. The difference between the *traweh* prayers and their obligatory equivalent is that there is no break between the second and the third *raka'at*, as the imam and the congregation immediately proceed to the third and the fourth prayer cycles. As the fourth *raka'at* is over and the *salam*-greeting uttered, the congregation may again rest for a short while. The congregation then rises again and performs four more cycles of *traweh* prayers, following the imam. The rest follows the above-mentioned procedure, and then the *traweh* prayers are over.

Lebaran/Idul Fitri is the celebration day, the ending of Ramadan. It begins with mass prayer gatherings early in the morning at mosques, open fields, and parks, and on major streets. Muslim women are dressed in their *mukena* (white, head-to-toe prayer gowns) performing the synchronized prayer ritual. Muslim men tend to wear sarongs, traditional shirts, and *peci*, caps of Indonesian Muslim origin in the shape of a truncated cone, usually made of black felt, to Idul Fitri morning prayers. On the walk home from the mass prayers, quick visits are made to friends in the neighborhood to ask for forgiveness, a wish expressed in the phrase *Mohon Maaf Lahir Batin*, which means, "Forgive me from the bottom of my heart/soul for my wrongdoings in the past year."

Following the morning prayers and neighborhood visits, Muslims visit their close family members around town, starting with their parents, then moving on to the most senior relative's house, and finally visiting other relatives. At each house drinks and cookies or snacks are served.

Strongly held traditions to visit family at this time necessitate the exodus of several million people from Jakarta and other urban centers to rural villages and towns for the Lebaran holiday (*mudik*). During this period the streets in urban centres are nearly empty.

MUSLIM-CHRISTIAN RELATIONS IN DAILY LIFE

A week after this celebration, Indonesian Muslims usually gather for the Halal bil Halal, which is the last day of the seven-day Lebaran celebration, to share a meal and ask each other for forgiveness. These gatherings are designed to maintain social bonds. Today, these social bonds are mainly strengthened between members of one religion, and interactions between members of other religions have become more rare. In the past, Christians were included in the religious activities of Muslims and vice versa, with foods and visits being exchanged in the fasting month, at Lebaran, and at Christmas. But this practice has gradually changed since the 1980s, with the beginning of Islamic revival in Indonesia. In the 1980s Islamic development accelerated, helping Muslims to be more conscious of their own religious identity and that of others. Since that time the line between *umat* Islam (Islamic community)and *umat* Kristen (Christian community) has been drawn more clearly and the consciousness of each others' religious difference has grown. At the same time the idea of an "in group" and an "out group" took hold and extended into the social domain.[20] Thus, it has become an important matter whether Muslims should have a Christian friend or partner, or promote a Christian as a candidate for an election.

Although violence does not play a major role in everyday life, the relationship between Muslims and Christians can be described as strained. In his research on the village of Kolojonggo, Kim has observed that Muslim-Christian relations, which were probably harmonious in the past, have cooled off.[21] In this context he points out that the reciprocal movements of foods and visits between Muslims and Christians are no longer taking place.[22] It is no longer common practice to include Christians in the Muslims' exchange network of food after the fasting month or to invite them to *slametan* after the fasting month. In the past, Christians reciprocated at Christmas the food they had been given by sending food parcels to their Muslim neighbors, and some Muslim villagers attended the Christmas celebration held in the *kapel* (chapel).[23]

In my fieldwork in Yogyakarta, Central Java, in 2008, I observed that there is not much overlap between the Muslim and Christian *umat*, with Muslims and Christians mostly going separate ways. Ibu Projosuto, the Christian Catholic lady I stayed with, had close friendships with other Christians, who regularly came to her house for prayer gatherings in the early evening, at sunset. In turn, she also joined prayer gatherings in the neighborhood, organized by her Christian friends. Most of the participants were women, some of them nuns, but men also joined the group, including priests. Tea, snacks, and fruits were served at the prayer meetings, which took between one and two hours.

Because the hostess was over 80 years old, a young woman assisted her in serving the guests. Chanting and prayers were the core activities of each gathering. After the formal part of the meeting was over, the participants engaged in informal talk before going home.

Besides meeting for the regular prayer gatherings, the Christian *umat* also met for pilgrimages. During my stay, for instance, around 15 Christian women, belonging to Ibu Projosuto's circle of friends, organized a one-day pilgrimage to the cave Gua Maria Tritis, in the village of Giring, close to the central Javanese town of Wonosari. This is supposed to be the only natural cave where the statue of Virgin Mary resided. The grotto is a limestone cave with natural stalactites and stalagmites, situated close to the southern coast of Java and to the Indian Ocean. Outside the cave pilgrims pray to Jesus at the cross, inside to the Virgin Mary. Charity plays an important role in daily life, besides prayer gatherings, visits to the local church on Sundays, and pilgrimages to holy sites. Ibu Projosuto regularly goes to the nearby hospital several times a week to bear company to sick people. Her sister, who pays regular visits to her house, is the head of an orphanage on the outskirts of Yogyakarta. This orphanage takes care of children whose parents have died or who cannot take care of them because of economic problems. All children older than six years have the opportunity to go to school. Graces and visits to church are binding. The strengthening of social ties within the Christian Catholic community is an important aspect of daily practices. Although this community did not actively seek contact with Muslims and vice versa, encounters between these religious groups were not characterized by tension, but by a friendly and respectful atmosphere.

An explicit example of religious tolerance is in Jember, East Java. In Sumberpakem, for instance, a remote district in Jember, Christmas still is the peak of the religious and social celebration in church, with a call for all to bring peace to the world. On the night of December 24, hundreds of local people dressed in Madurese traditional attire walk to church to a chorus of ringing bells. Standing with candles in hand before a decorated Christmas tree, dozens of children recite the birth of Jesus Christ according to the gospel of Luke. After listening to a sermon by a church minister who calls on churchgoers to bring peace to the world, all lamps are extinguished and everybody present sings "Silent Night" in Madurese. On the following day, Christian families visit one another, bringing food and cake, and receive congratulations from their Muslim and Hindu neighbors.

In the following section we will leave Java to look at religious practices in Flores, to show how local variants of religion and Roman Catholicism coexist in daily life and how the Muslim minority is integrated into daily life.

CHRISTIANITY AND LOCAL TRADITION IN EAST INDONESIA

In Flores, East Indonesia, the ancestors still play an important role in daily practice. They are still regarded as the ultimate source of continuity, and communication with the ancestors is necessary to preserve the community.[24] Flores, a region with a majority of Roman Catholics, has a small Muslim minority. In the village of Ma'undai, in the eastern Keo region of the regency of Ngadha, Muslims constitute only 20 percent of the predominantly Roman Catholic population.[25] However, as Tule demonstrates, these people are part of the local Keo society, viewing "Islam and adat as siblings." They are well integrated into the social system, turning to typical Keo identity markers such as *peo* (sacrificial posts), *sa'o nggua* (ritual houses), and *tu'a 'eja* (kinship and marriage). This strong interrelationship between monotheistic religion and *adat* can also be seen in examples with the predominantly Roman Catholic population.

One such example are the Hoga Sara, people of the village Sara Sedu, in the Goléwa district of the Ngadha regency of Flores. They number only some 1,156 individuals and occupy the mountainous terrain of the southeastern part of the regency. The Hoga Sara practice subsistence agriculture on dry fields and mostly raise water buffalo, horses, pigs, chickens, and dogs. In Ngadha regency, 93 percent of the population are Roman Catholics. However, Andrea K. Molnar found that despite this seemingly clear devotion to Catholicism, traditional beliefs and ritual observances, especially ancestor cults, still remain highly significant. Being aware that local practices form an important part of collective identity in Flores, the Roman Catholic Church has launched "acculturation" programs, through which it shows itself sensitive to local customs and practices. Molnar argues that the Hoga Sara people tend to see Roman Catholicism as a form of religion supplementary to their own belief system that might achieve a continuous adaptation of cultural elements.[26] Giving an example from the Ngadha people, in Central Flores, who have been Roman Catholic since the early twentieth century, Susanne Schröter observes that they have achieved a successful integration between Catholicism and local practice. She refers to a death ritual called *kéo rado*, which is needed in case a *mata golo* (death inflicted by murder, accident, or diseases) occurred. The Ngadha believe that a *mata golo* symbolizes a disturbed relationship with the ancestors. To appease the ancestors and prevent further *mata golo*, they hold a *kéo rado* some time after the ordinary funeral.[27] In this ritual, the Ngadha invite the dead to join great festivities in the course of which many sacrificial animals are slaughtered and their blood is used to consecrate the sanctuaries. Among the sanctuaries is the hearth within the house, which is edged by stones and the utensils used for oracles such as bamboo sticks. The hearth is a central reference point for the ritual because its symbolic "hole" requires that it be repaired through the ritual practice of the *kéo rado*. The hole in the hearth symbolizes that the living have neglected their duties toward their ancestors. As a consequence, the latter do not protect the living from evil influences. In the course of the complex *kéo rado* ritual, Satan, who is believed to become manifest in evil spirits (*polo*) that are said to have caused the violent death, is fought against to restore the disturbed balance between a clan and its ancestors. For this ritual, the relatives of the deceased person have to make specific preparations. The relatives of the victim consult oracles to find out if the ancestors agree or disagree with the clans' proposals. The ancestors finally answer the question of who is responsible for the specific steps of the ritual. The culmination of the ritual is the symbolic hunt of the evil spirits by male members of the clan and the ritual act of symbolically cutting off its head, taking it home to the village. The Ngadha believe that after this act the balance between the ancestors and their descendants is restored.[28]

Although missionaries have categorized this ritual as heathen, the Ngadha feel this is an essential part of their culture. They do not think that their Christian belief is at odds with their *adat* rituals. Instead, to them *adat* rituals have simply been complemented by Christian practices in the course of history. Nowadays, both are essential for Ngadha identity and social structure, but *adat* rituals such as the *kéo rado* have a special place because without them it would be impossible to restore the social order between the ancestors and their descendants. The priests do not actively recognize this ritual out of respect for the local belief system, because active recognition by the Catholic Church would imply that the chain of misfortune will continue.[29] The Ngadha believe that God is not powerful enough to remove the fear of evil spirits in ordinary life and to counter the anger of the ancestors for transgressions against the *adat*.[30] The following descriptions are based on Susanne Schröter's fieldwork on the Ngadha, the result of which was published in 2000.

In contrast to the *kéo rado* ritual, Catholic Christian and local practices are equal parts of the religious system, going hand in hand in "common" death rituals that are held in case of a *mata ade* (natural death). When the death of a relative is recognized, the body is laid on a bed in the middle of the room for the reception of guests, white candles are lighted, and Christian devotional objects are placed beside the body. The relatives gather, loudly sobbing, and somebody hits a gong to inform relatives and friends in the neighboring villages of the death. Because governmental regulations stipulate that the dead must be buried within 24 hours, the following actions must be performed promptly. People have to bring rice, sacrificial animals, palm wine, sitting mats, and chinaware to organize the ritual. One or two people take the role of official mourners for the whole ceremony. These people are not always women; families with little children and young fathers also fulfill this task. The mourners sit beside the dead on the bed or stand beside the coffin, constantly sobbing and touching the body fondly. They recall memories and characteristics of the dead person, emphasizing the intimate relationship with the beloved person that has now been brutally cut off. Nobody prays during these moments. The Christian decoration of the room—which in the course of the day is supplemented by a wooden holy cross with the name and dates of birth and death of the deceased, and the initials R.I.P.—has no relation to the events taking place. Around lunchtime the house is filled with people who have brought sacrificial animals (mostly pigs and chicken), palm wine, and rice. Pigs are squeaking in death agony; chickens tied with ropes to poles are fluttering; and in the kitchen women are preparing coffee, rice, and coconut. This part of the ritual is not marked by silent mourning but a happy renewal of social relations. People who do not meet every day now readily take the opportunity for social interaction. They just gossip or talk about planned activities, future weddings, or sickness. Meanwhile, the people offer meat, blood, rice, and palm wine to the ancestors, thereby reinforcing spiritual bonds. In the late afternoon the community gathers for a Catholic burial. After the coffin is closed, men carry it on their shoulders, and everybody marches in a long procession to the local graveyard. Individuals start to recite "Hail Mary" or "Our Father," and the others follow. After a few young men have dug a grave, the coffin is lowered into the ground. A lay priest delivers a short speech and prays together with all participants. Afterward, everybody goes back and the *adat* festivities continue. On the following three nights and on the fortieth night after the deceased person's death, the mourners gather for prayers to God and Virgin Mary and make sacrifices to the ancestors. After these rituals, the deceased belongs to the category of the ancestors, and is offered blood and cooked food. At the same time, however, the Catholic tradition is important: the Ngadha pray for the dead and light candles for them on their graves.

CONCLUSION

In this chapter only a small part of the rich variety of religious practices in Indonesia could be covered. It has especially focused on describing Islamic practices in Java that, in some way or another, are linked to the fasting month Ramadan. This chapter has also explained the contexts in which *slametan*, a religious practice unique to Java, are held. The descriptions reveal that although *slametan* are mostly associated with nonorthodox

Muslims, *santri* play an important role in these rituals because they are thought to have wide knowledge about Islam, thus being accepted as authorities. Both *abangan* and *santri* invite each other if a family holds a *slametan*. Thus, the *slametan* both strengthens ties between *santri* and *abangan* and keeps evil forces away from a family by means of prayer, especially in critical moments of life.

Furthermore, the different ways in which religious communities and traditions interact with each other were analyzed. As we have seen from Indonesian history, Christianity, Islam, Hinduism, and Buddhism have always been interwoven with local traditional religious practices. These are marked by a continuing process of adaptation, reinterpretation, and acculturation. For instance, traditions originally associated with Hinduism, such as the *wayang* and the gamelan orchestra, were easily acculturated into Islam over time and are still used for some religious practices. The examples of Flores, East Indonesia, have revealed that in this region traditional practices are still vital to social life and do not necessarily collide with the religion of the majority—in this case, Roman Catholicism. Here, Christian faith has become a supplement to *adat*, and religious life includes both.

As far as interactions between religions are concerned, there are different tendencies. First, it becomes clear that over time Christian and Muslim communities have become more and more separate so that religious practices tend to be held within the group, rather than across groups. There are different factors accounting for the decreasing contact between the communities. One such factor is the influence of transnational developments on daily life. Emerging extremist forms of Islam in the last decade, for instance, partly resulting out of a transnational, postcolonial, anti-Western stance, have contributed to decreasing tolerance. Furthermore, reactions of Islamist Muslims against national politics during the New Order regime under ex-president Suharto play an important role in this context. After the fall of this president, Islamist Muslims saw their chance to implement Islamic law and seek constitutional recognition of sharia. They believed Christians had been favored in politics under Suharto's rule and now tried to increase their power, one means of which was the use of violence. When the repression the Suharto government had committed was over in 1998, Islamist groups that had gone underground seized their opportunity. For instance, the Islamist organization Jemaah Islamiyah—which launched a bomb attack on two Bali nightclubs on October 12, 2002, killing 202 people—sees itself as the heir of the Islamist organization Darul Islam, which operated in Indonesia from the mid-1940s to the late 1950s. Jemaah Islamiyah was founded in 1993 by Abdullah Sungkar and Abu Bakar Ba'asyir, two former Darul Islam leaders.[31]

The tendency of increasing segregation between the Christian and Muslim *umat*, however, is not a new phenomenon. When Islamic revival started to become strong in Indonesia in the 1980s, partly as a reaction to Suharto's repressive policies, this tendency already showed. As a reaction to banning political activity on campuses, for instance, several university-based movements—such as Hizbut Tahrir (Liberation Party), Gerakan Tarbiyah (Education Movement), and Jemaah Tabligh (Preaching Community)—were initiated on campuses. In the 1980s there were more religious activities reminding Muslims of the boundary of the *umat* Islam.[32] Furthermore, Christians have been accused of expanding their community at the expanse of the *umat* Islam. Since that time religious ideology has increasingly been used as a means to claim hegemony, which makes different religious communities distance themselves from one another.

Although these forces only give a small glimpse of Indonesian Islam, they are paralleled by an increasing segregation of the Muslim and Christian *umat*. This chapter has revealed that in today's daily practice there are not many points of contact between the groups, but some examples given in this chapter reveal that there are also efforts to practice exchange, religious pluralism, and tolerance among communities.

NOTES

1. Susanne Schröter, *Die Austreibung des Bösen. Ein Beitrag zur Religion und Sozialstruktur der Sara Langa in Ostindonesien* (Stuttgart: Kohlhammer, 2000).
2. Rita Smith-Kipp and Susan Rodgers, *Indonesian Religions in Transition* (Tucson: University of Arizona Press, 1987), p. 3.
3. M. C. Ricklefs, *A History of Modern Indonesia since 1300* (Stanford, CA: Stanford University Press, 1993), p. 19.
4. Ibid., p. 3.
5. Andreas Ufen, "Islam und Politik in Indonesien," in *Politik und Gesellschaft Online, International Politics and Society 2/2001*. Available at http://www.fes.de/ipg/ipg2_2001/artufen.htm.
6. Greg Fealy, Virginia Hooker, and Sally White, "Indonesia," in *Voices of Islam in Southeast Asia. A Contemporary Sourcebook*, eds. Greg Fealy and Virginia Hooker (Singapore: Institute of Southeast Asian Studies, 2006), pp. 39–50.
7. Karel Steenbrink, *Catholics in Indonesia 1808–1942: A Documented History*, Vol. 1, *A Modest Recovery 1808–1903* (Leiden: KITLV, 2003), p. 7.
8. Chang-Yau Hoon, "The Politics of Imlek," *Inside Indonesia* 95 (Jan.–Mar. 2009). Available at http://www.insideindonesia.org/content/view/1159/47/.
9. C. S.Kuppuswamy, "Jemaah Islamiyah. The Indonesia-Based Terrorist Organisation," in *South Asia Analysis Group*, paper no. 746 (2003). Available at http://www.southasiaanalysis.org/%5Cpapers8%5Cpaper746.html.

10. Robert W. Hefner, "Islamization and Democratization in Indonesia," in *Islam in an Era of Nation-States. Politics and Religious Renewal in Muslim Southeast Asia*, eds. Robert W. Hefner and Patricia Horvatich (Honolulu: University of Hawai'i Press, 1997), pp. 75–128.

11. Clifford Geertz, *The Religion of Java* (Glencoe, IL: The Free Press of Glencoe, 1960); Mark R. Woodward, *Islam in Java: Normative Piety and Mysticism in the Sultanate of Yogyakarta*, Monograph no. 45 (Tucson: University of Arizona Press, Association for Asian Studies, 1989).

12. James B. Hoesterey, "The Rise, Fall, and Re-Branding of a Celebrity Preacher," *Inside Indonesia* 90 (Oct.–Nov. 2007). Available at http://www.insideindonesia .org/content/view/1011/47/.

13. Sumastuti Sumukti, *Gunungan: The Javanese Cosmic Mountain* PhD thesis (Ann Arbor: University Microfilms International, 1998), p. 161.

14. Ibid., p. 210.

15. Masdar Hilmy, "Islam and Javanese Acculturation: Textual and Contextual Analysis of the Slametan Ritual" (master's thesis, McGill University, Institute of Islamic Studies, 1999), p. 58.

16. Abdul Ghoffur Muhaimin, *The Islamic Traditions of Cirebon. Ibadat and Adat Among Javanese Muslims* (Canberra: Australian National University, ANU E-Press, 2006).

17. André Möller, "Islam and Traweh Prayers in Java," *Indonesia and the Malay World* 33.95 (2005), p. 41.

18. Ibid, p. 43

19. Ibid.

20. I Iyung-Jun Kim, *Reformist Muslims in a Yogyakarta Village. The Islamic Transformations of Contemporary Socio-Religious Life* (Canberra: Australian National University, Research School of Pacific and Asian Studies, ANU Press, 1996), p. 226.

21. Ibid., p. 188.

22. Ibid.

23. Ibid.

24. Andrea K. Molnar, *Grandchildren of the Ga'e Ancestors. Social organization and cosmology among the Hoga Sara of Flores* (Leiden: KITLV, 2000); Susanne Schröter, "Death Rituals of the Ngadha in Central Flores, Indonesia," *Anthropos* 93.4–6 (1998), pp. 417–435.

25. Philipus Tule, "The Indigenous Muslim Minority Group in Ma'undai (Keo) of Central Flores: Between the House of Islam and the House of Culture," *Antropologi Indonesia: majalah antropologi sosial dan budaya Indonesia* 22.56 (1998), pp. 68–85.

26. Andrea K. Molnar, "Christianity and traditional religion among the Hoga Sara of West-Central Flores," *Anthropos* 92, 4 (1997), pp. 393–408.

27. Schröter, *Die Austreibung des Bösen*, 2000.

28. Ibid.

29. Schröter, "Death Rituals," 1998.
30. Schröter, *Die Austreibung des Bösen*, 2000.
31. Fealy, Hooker, and White, p. 49.
32. Kim, p. 226.

BIBLIOGRAPHY

Bowen, John. *Muslims through Discourse: Religion and Ritual in Gayo Society*. Princeton, NJ: Princeton University Press, 1993.

Chambert-Loir, Henry, and Anthony Reid. *The Potent Dead: Ancestors, Saints, and Heroes in Contemporary Indonesia*. Crows Nest, New South Wales: Allen & Unwin; Honolulu: University of Hawai'i Press, 2002.

Hauser-Schäublin, Brigitta. *Traces of Gods and Men: Temples and Rituals as Landmarks of Social Events and Processes in a South Bali Village*. Berlin: Reimer, 1997.

Hefner, Robert. *Civil Islam: Muslims and Democratisation in Indonesia*. Princeton, NJ: Princeton University Press, 2000.

Lukas, Helmut. *Theories of Indianization. Exemplified by Selected Case Studies from Indonesia (Insular Southeast Asia)*. Austrian Academy of Sciences, Commission for Social Anthropology, University of Vienna, Department of Social and Cultural Anthropology, 2003. http://www.oeaw.ac.at/sozant/images/working_papers/soa001.pdf.

Ramstedt, Martin. *Hinduism in Modern Indonesia: A Minority Religion between Local, National, and Global Interests*. London: Routledge Curzon, 2004.

Chapter 6

West Africa

Elizabeth Graveling

Eight AM. A woman in a black headscarf sits on a bench outside her little wooden shop at the side of the road, carefully measuring out sugar into twists of polyethylene, each just enough to sweeten a cup of tea. A man's voice chatters excitedly from the radio perched on a shelf, intermittently drowning out the bleating of goats, the pecking of chickens in the dust, the rise and fall of voices as people walk past and call out greetings across the street, and the rhythmic crash of waves on the beach behind the shop. The shop is next to the village taxi station and the drivers of two battered taxis sit in the shade eating a breakfast of maize porridge and chatting with a small group of men in faded shorts and T-shirts as they wait for their vehicles gradually to fill with passengers. A man dressed smartly in shirt and trousers climbs in, leaving just one place to be taken before the taxi will leave for town. Children on their way to school saunter past in their freshly ironed uniforms, some yellow and brown, others blue. A young woman with a baby strapped to her back stops at the shop to buy bread; the older woman finishes the last portion of sugar, serves her, then picks up a broom made from the fronds of coconut trees and bends to sweep up the granules she has spilt on the ground.

Scenes similar to this one are common in many countries in West Africa. This particular episode took place—and is repeated almost every morning with slight variations—in a village on the coast of Ghana. It is a snapshot of everyday life: nothing unusual happens and nothing stands out to identify this place as especially different from anywhere else. There is also no reference to religion: people get on with the business of daily life without giving much thought to religious matters. However, this does not mean that religion is not present. A more detailed examination of the scene depicted in this vignette reveals that religion, in multiple ways, is very much present in and relevant to the lives of the people portrayed. In this chapter we will look first at developments in the religious landscape across Africa over several hundred years before focusing our attention on religion in contemporary life in West Africa.

TIMELINE

1st century:	Egyptian and Ethiopian Christianity begins.
615:	Muslims flee to Ethiopia from Mecca.
8th century:	East African coastal trading centers lead to the arrival of Islam from southern Arabia and the Red Sea.
8th century:	Islam spreads south via trans-Saharan trade networks.
c. 1000:	First African ruler to accept Islam (king of Gao, present-day Mali).
11th century:	Islam expands in the Sahel (West Africa) and along the East African coast.
15th century:	First Catholic missionaries in Kongo (with Portuguese traders).
1730:	Moravian missionaries arrive in West Africa.
1787:	Freetown founded as Christian settlement for liberated slaves.
1792:	Moravian missionaries arrive in South Africa.
1864:	Samuel Crowther is the first African ordained bishop.
1884–1885:	Berlin Conference, Africa is partitioned among colonial powers.
1957:	Ghana becomes the first African country to gain independence.
2000:	Northern Nigerian states adopt sharia.

A BRIEF HISTORY OF RELIGION IN AFRICA

There are usually thought to be three main religions in sub-Saharan Africa: African traditional religion, Islam, and Christianity. Other religions (such as Hinduism, Baha'ism, Buddhism, and Judaism) are also present but with relatively tiny numbers of adherents. Although also recognizing the prominence and importance of Islam, this chapter will focus mainly on Christianity and "traditional religions," which represent an extremely broad and varied spectrum of experience, doctrine, and practice.

Historically, these three groups have very different origins. The first, "traditional religion," is of course not a single religion but rather an umbrella term for all the different cosmologies that are seen as indigenous to the African continent. Evolving throughout time and space, modified and adapted through migration, trade, and war, many of these cosmologies bear great similarity with each other in the ways they conceptualize the world. However, there is also enormous diversity. African "religions" are often thought of in terms of separate ethnic groups—for example, the religions of the Yoruba, the Maasai, and the Zulu. Because there are over 2,000 languages spoken across the continent, each related to a different ethnic grouping, the potential for variation is immense. Furthermore, these different groups are not necessarily discrete and static. Some are closely related; migration and intermarriage are common; and people often live side by side with or interspersed among other groups. Religious practices are interpreted and drawn on in a multitude of different ways as individuals and groups construct their own cosmologies. Therefore, while the word "traditional" is employed here for the sake of convenience, it should be borne in mind that this is a contested term that does not adequately represent the complex nature of religion in Africa.

Both Islam and Christianity have been introduced to Africa from elsewhere. Christianity grew from a deliberate and relatively short era of evangelization and was associated with the rise of Western (or Western-style, outside the colonial era) secular governance. Islam, on the other hand, gradually expanded over a period of many centuries through trade, settlement, intermarriage and some jihad. It brought with it its own legislative system and structures of authority, which were adopted and indigenized by the local population, so that Islamic culture became thoroughly embedded in the African societies in which it thrived. Muslims are recorded as having fled from Mecca to Ethiopia as early as 615 CE, although the spread of Islam in sub-Saharan Africa began in earnest in the eighth century, from two different directions in addition to expansion from the northeast into Sudan. Muslim traders began to travel south from North Africa via trans-Saharan networks to do business with the people of the Sahara and the Sahel, while merchant ships from Arabia and the Red Sea arrived on the East African coast to establish trading centers from the Horn of Africa all the way to what is now southern Mozambique. Muslim communities, comprising both settlers and indigenous Africans, grew around these coastal trading centers, which began to expand more rapidly from the beginning of the eleventh century. At roughly the same time the influence of Islam increased in the West African Sahel, with the king of Gao (present-day Mali) becoming the first ruler to accept Islam. The terms of conversion varied: although it was sometimes achieved by coercion, the primary driving force was trade. As Muslims were not usually permitted to enter into a business relationship with non-Muslims, anybody who wished to trade with them was required to convert to Islam. In practice this was not always the case, and Muslims often lived under the hospitality of non-Muslim kings. Other rulers and their entourage were often strongly influenced by Islam and sometimes adopted it nominally or even sincerely. However, this did not necessarily apply to their subordinates and subjects, who continued their indigenous traditions while also accommodating the new religion.

Ethiopia was also the site of the first appearances of Christianity in sub-Saharan Africa. Much of Ethiopian religious identity is bound up with Hebraic religion, in particular the claims to blood links with King Solomon via the Queen of Sheba, and to the location of the final resting place of the Ark of the Covenant. The Ethiopian church traditionally grew from the baptism of the Ethiopian eunuch by Philip (Acts 9 in the New Testament), although others attribute it to the influence of the Egyptian Coptic Church, dating its arrival in the kingdom of Aksum (northern Ethiopia) from Alexandria in the fourth century, when it came to be adopted as a state religion. Despite the expansion of Islam in this area, Ethiopian Christianity survived, largely in the form of the Ethiopian Orthodox Church, which is closely related to the Coptic Orthodox Church. The Ethiopian Orthodox Church was disestablished in 1974, when the Marxist military government, the Derg, toppled Haile Selassie. In contemporary Ethiopia most of the population is divided between Christianity and Islam, with Christians (mostly Orthodox, although Protestant churches are increasing) narrowly outnumbering Muslims.

Christianity existed in Ethiopia for over 1,000 years before it was encountered elsewhere on the continent, with the establishment of the Portuguese Empire in West and Central Africa during the fifteenth and sixteenth centuries. This was a Catholic and anti-Islamic crusade that succeeded particularly in the Kongo, the missionary strategy being first to target the king of each people group and then through him to baptize his subjects en masse. Although the structures of Kongolese Christianity were shattered by war in the seventeenth century, aspects of Christian rituals remained embedded in the local culture. On the East African coast, conflict raged between Muslims and Portuguese Christians, which resulted in Portuguese dominance from the mid-1500s to the mid-1600s, when it was overturned, with Christianity being all but eradicated from the area.

Protestant Christianity arrived in the 1780s with the rise of Britain in African affairs. As the slave trade became established, chaplains were sent out to slavers on the West African coast and, in 1787, Freetown was founded in

Sierra Leone as a Christian society for the returning African diaspora. The beginning of the Protestant missionary movement was marked by the arrival of a small group of Moravian missionaries in southern Africa in 1792. By the 1820s this movement had grown significantly, with various missionary societies founded mainly in Britain, Germany, and the Netherlands. Although the churches established by these societies were at first led entirely by White missionaries, from the 1840s African leaders began to emerge, including the Yoruba Samuel Crowther, who in 1864 became the first African Anglican bishop. With colonization came increased numbers of missionaries, but they did not consolidate their control over the church in Africa which, as it matured, became more self-conscious and independent. The beginning of the twentieth century saw secessions from missionary-controlled churches in Nigeria and South Africa, resulting in the birth of some of the African Indigenous (also referred to as Independent or Initiated) Churches (AICs), which expanded and multiplied in the run-up to the independence of African countries in the 1950s and 1960s. Since the 1980s, however, the most rapidly expanding sector of Christianity has been Pentecostalism, because of a combination of an influx of Western evangelical mission organizations and increased North American influence, and because of a strong African-initiated revivalist movement with renewed interest in reconciling Christianity with African culture.

The contemporary religious landscape in sub-Saharan Africa, then, consists of pervasive and diverse indigenous traditions that have neither remained static nor been eradicated by the introduction and growth of two world religions, Christianity and Islam. Islam is concentrated in areas north of the equator: West Africa, the Sudan, and the Horn of Africa, as well as more southern areas of the east coast. Christianity is found largely in southern, Central and East Africa and the southern, coastal strip of West Africa.

Categorizing religions in this way conceals an incredibly varied spectrum of religious experience within all three areas of Islam, Christianity, and indigenous religions. Christianity can be further divided into four broad sectors, each of which is internally diverse: the Catholic Church; historic or "mainstream" Protestant churches (usually mission related); Pentecostals (both "classic" Pentecostal churches from the mid-twentieth century and "neo-Pentecostal" or "charismatic" churches emerging since the 1980s); and hundreds of African indigenous churches (AICs), some of which have branches at a transnational level whereas others remain as single, independent entities. In addition to these there are other churches initiated by modern mission organizations as well as the oldest church of all, the Ethiopian Orthodox. The

Christian landscape in Africa therefore encompasses the ancient sacraments of the Orthodox, Catholic, and Anglican churches, the liturgy of AICs dating from the early to mid-twentieth century, and the spontaneity of the Pentecostal sector. It includes historic churches with organ music, modern Pentecostal charismatics working up a frenzy with brass bands, and across all denominations but particularly in the AICs, the rhythmic and frenetic beating of drums. Among those who call themselves Christians are members of ancient priesthoods and new self-styled charismatic bishops; members of AICs who seek to maintain or revive the customs of their forefathers and Pentecostals who strive to break with such "pagan" practices; as well as Pentecostal and AIC members who reject the modern world and material prosperity, and others of the same sectors who embrace them as part of their religious identity.

The Muslim population of sub-Saharan Africa is similarly diverse. The majority of Muslims in Africa are Sunnis, representing various movements. Sufism is a strand of Islam that emphasizes the mystic and spiritual aspects of the religion rather than the legal and structural dimensions. It has therefore been relatively easily adopted and adapted to local cultural forms and is now found across most of Islamic Africa in the shape of various brotherhoods or *tariqas*—such as the Tijaniyya, the Qadiriyya, the Sanusiyya, the Kahatmiyya and the Salihiyya—which derive from the teachings of their respective founders and some of which have adherents numbering in the thousands or millions. In recent decades, however, Islamist reformist movements have gained ground, advocating a more universal approach that emphasizes the implementation of sharia. This growing influence has been a factor in tensions both between different strands of Islam and between Muslims and Christians, for example in Nigeria, where since 2000 several northern states have adopted sharia as their official legal system.

Referring to religion in terms of categories also tends to misrepresent the blurred boundaries between groups. Although people may identify themselves—or be labeled by others—as belonging to a particular religion, this does not necessarily prevent them from also participating in elements of other religions. This may be on a dualistic basis, in which the religions remain separate but the individual adopts practices from two or more, or it may be the case that lines of division between religions themselves are blurred. To reach an accurate understanding of the ways in which people draw on religious discourses, it is very important to examine how religion is played out in the practice of daily life. In the following paragraphs, therefore, religions are not dealt with separately; rather, patterns are highlighted in different areas of life, drawing on examples from across the continent.

RELIGION IN THE PRACTICE OF DAILY LIFE

Let us return to the commonplace and apparently unremarkable episode described at the beginning of the chapter, where a woman sits at her shop measuring out portions of sugar and serving customers while the day-to-day events of village life take place around her. Where does religion appear in this scene and how does the vignette help us to understand the importance of religion in the practice of daily life?

Organization of Life

First, as in many societies of the world, much of life in West Africa is framed around religious structures—temporally, spatially, and socially. Lives are organized according to cycles of time marked by religious rituals and events, places denoted as more or less sacred, and relationships that connect human beings with spirits, all of which vary between different places and different religions.

Temporally, life is organized according to different cycles, punctuated by or based on religious traditions. In the scene described above, the woman who owns the shop is wearing a black headscarf, a sign of mourning. Somebody—probably a member of her family—has died. Stages of the life cycle—including birth, puberty, marriage, child bearing, and death—are marked by religious ceremonies that serve as rites of passage into the next stage. In this area of Ghana, funerals are often enormous and extravagant events that sometimes last several days and include customs associated both with traditional religion and with Christianity (in a context where Christianity has become embedded in society), as well as copious amounts of food and all-night music and dancing.

Traditionally, funerals—which are extremely large events and occur very frequently on one's social calendar—are the concern of the family, which in this culture primarily means the matrilineage of the deceased. As all members of the deceased's matrilineage are expected to attend. The family is often considered the abode of traditional religion, partly because this includes recognition of ancestors as playing an ongoing role in the community. Traditionally, the funeral rites entailed sending the deceased off to join the dead in an appropriate manner (for example, with gifts that are buried alongside the body), which would ensure his or her future blessings on the community. However, funerals in modern Ghana appear to be as much about consolidating and displaying family prestige as about honoring the person who has died. The religious rites still take place, but they are overshadowed, first by the enormous crowds of people who attend the "lying in state" of the body, the wake keeping

Coffins are created in all sorts of shapes and images in Ghana. The life of the deceased person is reflected in the choice of shape and decoration. Mourners carry the body in a procession through the community at the funeral. (Travel Ink.)

(normally on a Friday night), and the public gatherings over the following two days; and second by the massive amount of money spent on hosting the funeral (including mortuary fees, mortician's fees for dressing the corpse, the coffin, food and drink, hiring music bands, PA systems, canopies, chairs, and sometimes video-recording equipment). Perhaps partly because of this shift in emphasis, funerals are freely attended by Christians as well as non-Christians. The funeral of a Christian does not usually differ much from that of a non-Christian: in most cases it is still considered a family matter, and a thanksgiving church service is added on the Sunday following the other events.

Funerals are by far the most visible rite of passage in southern Ghana, although weddings, puberty rites, and baby-naming ceremonies are also performed. The baby strapped to her mother's back has recently been "outdoored," a traditional Akan ceremony performed within the family by an elder, normally the head of the family. The rite includes a few drops of water and then alcohol being placed on the baby's tongue while the elder names the baby and exhorts it to be honest, declaring, "If you say water, it must be water" and "If you say alcohol, it must be alcohol." Prayers and libation (pouring alcohol on the ground) are also offered to God, ancestors, and other spirits to acknowledge their presence and thank them for the gift of the baby. This baby, however, was born into a Christian family, so the customary libation was replaced with prayers led by a church pastor. The family ceremony was followed a few weeks later by a special Christian service in which the baby was presented at church. "Christianizing" of traditions in this way, either by adapting them or by establishing a parallel event, is common. Among Christians, female puberty rites in this area of Ghana are now often called "churching," and they include a church service as well as traditional customs. Marriage ceremonies are also likely to consist of two parts—sometimes performed on the same day—the "engagement," entailing the traditional handing over of the bride-price between the families, and the church wedding.

Other cycles of time pass simultaneously. Seasonal or calendrical religious events serve to structure the regular passing of the seasons. Christian and Muslim festivals are celebrated by their respective adherents and often more widely as public holidays, whereas other festivals are specific to localized ethnic groups. Many African cultures hold large celebrations at the beginning of the annual harvest. The Iri ji festival, for example, is celebrated annually by Igbo people in Nigeria, and the diaspora in July and August, when the first new yams are harvested. Besides being a staple food of the Igbo people, yams are considered sacred in Igbo culture, following a legend that tells of them springing up from the graves of the two children of one of the fathers of the Igbo race. The children were sacrificed by their father on the instruction of Chukwu, the highest spirit, to resolve the hunger that threatened the lives of the people. A deity, Ahianjoku or Ifejoku, was assigned to take charge of yams, and the uprooting of planted seedlings is considered an abomination toward the deity. Iri ji Ohuru, the New Yam Festival, is celebrated at the village level across Igboland, each community holding the ritual on its market day. There are many variations to the procedure; however, it usually involves ritual items including the largest yam tubers, a cockerel, kola nuts, gin, and palm wine. The *Okpala*, an elder, cuts a yam into four parts and, fixing them on a four-pronged *Otiri* branch, invites the ancestors to share the yam with the community and prays to certain spirits to provide them with an abundant crop of yams. He also sacrifices the cockerel at the shrine of the yam spirit, appealing for his blessing on their harvest, among other requests such as good health, fertility, and protection against illness and other misfortune. The yam is cooked and eaten by the elders. The festival continues with further prayers within households, singing, dancing, entertainment by music and masquerade groups, drinking of palm wine, and the consumption of large amounts of yams and soup.[1]

Cultural heritage is seen by many as being threatened by the forces of modernity: urbanization, globalization, secular education, and increased mobility are among the trends that combine to undermine traditional loci of power, understandings of the world, and the practices associated with those understandings. The result is often a deliberate, increased effort to sustain or to reinvent local customs and culture. The Ghanaian government, for example, has passed a law that requires all civil servants to wear Ghanaian rather than Western-style dress to the workplace on Fridays. In Nigeria, the Sacred Groves at the town of Osogbo have been developed, and the annual Yoruba festival has been popularized since the 1970s largely through the efforts of Susanne Wenger, an Austrian woman. Wenger, an artist who was initiated into and eventually became a high priestess of Orisha, created sculptures and shrines at the groves and lobbied to have them officially protected.

Besides through annual events, religion may also structure life on a monthly, weekly or daily basis. Muslims, for example, take Friday as their holy day, when they congregate at mosques to pray, whereas most Christian communities hold church services on Sundays. Indigenous religions are less likely to specify absolute holy days, although spirit possession cults—such as the cult of Olokun among the Edo in Nigeria and Mami Wata in Benin (and elsewhere along the West African coast)—also have weekly congregations, and individual spirits might proclaim days of rest over their own domain (see below). Although the seven-day week has been adopted almost universally for administrative purposes, indigenous time structures vary: traditionally, weeks are often arranged around local market cycles, which differ in length. At a local level religious organizations often arrange other regular activities such as weekly prayer meetings, youth and women's groups, classes and studies of holy texts, music groups, social action, and income-generating activities. The Seventh-Day Adventist Church in Ghana, for example, holds its main weekly service on Saturday mornings, but it has in addition a Bible study on Sunday evenings, youth meetings on Mondays and Fridays, choir practice on Tuesdays, a prayer meeting on Wednesdays, music band practice on Thursdays, and a "sundown worship" meeting on Fridays, along with daily early-morning Sabbath School meetings in which topics from the Bible are discussed. It should however be noted that this is a centrally planned program that is not always fully adhered to in smaller churches.

For Muslims the day is structured by five obligatory prayer times: *fajr* (dawn), *zohar* (noon), *asar* (afternoon), *maghrib* (sunset), and *isha* (evening). Although not adhered to by everyone, in multireligious societies these prayers can affect people of all religions, particularly when Muslims are employed in retail or service industries. For example, shops may be closed and public transport pulled over to the side of the road while the owner or driver pauses to pray. Christian prayers are generally less structured, although some churches prescribe set prayers to be recited at fixed times. The Musama Disco Christo Church is modeled after the structures of the Fante society in the south of Ghana and attended by the woman buying bread in the scene described above. Its Yinaabi prayer is composed of three elements widely used in Christian churches—the Ten Commandments, the Apostles' Creed, and the Lord's Prayer—and members are instructed to repeat this set of prayers three times a day, between 6 and 8 AM, between noon and 2 PM, and between 6 and 8 PM. In practice many people only adhere to this when with other members of the church; however, prayers associated with everyday events—such as before eating, on receiving a visitor and when setting out on a journey—are more widely practiced across the spectrum of Christianity.

As well as marking special times, religions set aside certain places as sacred: temples, churches, mosques, and shrines are all attributed special properties as spaces in which people can connect with spirits through prayer and ritual. Shrines are common throughout West Africa, and extremely varied. Many West African cosmologies include spirits—often referred to as gods or fetishes—that inhabit specific places such as rivers, lakes, trees, and islands; and shrines to these spirits may consist simply of the place in which they live—for example, a strangely shaped rock or a grove of trees. Near the chief's palace in the village in the vignette above is such a shrine, a cotton tree that continues to grow despite its trunk being split in two by lightning. These places are not necessarily set apart as sacred in themselves: this tree is surrounded by houses and people sit, work, and play under it. However, respect must be shown to the spirits that inhabit them and to any rules or taboos they impose. The men sitting and chatting with the taxi drivers are fishermen and would normally be out on their boats at this time of day; however, it is Tuesday, the day that the deity of the ocean has proclaimed as its weekly rest day. Fishermen respect this taboo and, for fear of drowning under the wrath of the spirit, do not put out to sea. Consequently, women of this village do not seek to buy fresh fish on Tuesdays, knowing that the search would be fruitless. Likewise, people from the same village do not visit their farms on Fridays, in accordance with the day of rest set by a different deity. As such spirits have limited jurisdiction, these are localized customs that vary from place to place. Other shrines, sometimes to ancestors, are marked by roughly or intricately crafted figures and tokens. They too are often found in mundane, everyday places such as within housing compounds, a part of daily life, although they may be located away from the center of the community and tended by priests and priestesses of the spirit they represent (the shrine is likely to form part of his or her residence). Shrines to Olokun in the homes of Edo chiefs, priests, and priestesses in Benin City, Nigeria, for example, are ornately decorated with abstract chalk designs re-created each morning on the ground around the entrance, and with sculpted figures forming a tableau representing Olokun surrounded by his entourage of chiefs, wives, and attendants.[2]

Religious experts are called on throughout West Africa to mediate communication with spirits and access to spiritual power, and in much of the continent social structures and relationships are organized around religious principles. The smartly dressed man climbing into the taxi is the pastor of a Pentecostal church in the village, on his way to visit the church's regional office in the city. In this village of about 2,000 people there are 11 different churches (two AICs, three historic mission churches, and six Pentecostal churches), each with its own authority structure.

Pastors enjoy a great deal of respect as "men of God," not only from their own congregations, but also from the wider society. As a moral authority they hold much influence over the behavior of the members of their churches, and as a spiritual authority they are perceived as having close links with God and therefore access to divine power. However, Christian pastors are not the only figures of authority with religious connections. In Islamic societies this role is performed by imams or other Muslim leaders, and throughout Africa religious experts associated with traditional religion can be found, such as seers and diviners, who use a wide range of techniques to explain, predict, and control their environment, and priests and priestesses of shrines, who mediate between humans and secondary deities. A common characteristic of such mediation is spirit possession, in which the body of an individual is appropriated as a tool of communication by one or more spirits. Another category of experts are those—such as some independent Christian prophets and *mallams* (holy men associated with Islam)—who have associations with mainstream religions but employ "traditional" spiritualist practices. Still others—such as herbalists who prescribe treatments for illnesses and are still widely used despite the increasing availability of modern biomedicine—are less directly connected with religion but draw on spiritual discourses to perform different roles.

Although religion is often considered to be strongly patriarchal, many religious structures in West Africa do provide some opportunities for women to gain power. Attendants of spirits are very often (and in some cultures, only) female priestesses. These women may be seen as enslaved to the service of their deity; however, they can also wield power in their status as mediators between human beings and the spirit they have come to petition. Priestesses in the Olokun cult of Nigeria mentioned above, for example, often give accounts of intense suffering until they agree to enter the service of Olokun, after which time they begin to prosper. Part of their role is to perform healing and divination, both of which services require payment from the patient or client. If a priestess gains a reputation for success in these areas, she will be visited by men and women from distant parts of southern Nigeria and can become very wealthy. This may allow her to move out of her husband's residence into her own house, and possibly also to acquire further properties to rent out to tenants. This economic independence combined with her ritual authority brings her personal autonomy, high social status, and extreme respect from both women and men.[3]

The perception of women as possessing particularly high spiritual capacity is reflected in many churches and especially in AICs, which tend to draw on local structures and cosmologies. The Musama Disco Christo Church for example, attended by the young woman in the vignette at the start of this chapter, has a dual system of authority based on pastors and prophets. Many of the prophets are women (prophetesses), and pastors can also be female. As with shrine priestesses, their authority is founded on their claim to have been called by and to act in the name of God. Women can also gain office in other types of churches: the Pentecostal pastor climbing into the taxi, for example, has a female deacon in his church who regularly preaches and leads Bible classes for mixed-sex congregations. Most widespread are the female worship leaders and choristers whose role is to lead the congregation in energetic singing, dancing, and prayers. The ratio of women to men in most West African churches is disproportionately high, allowing women the opportunity of gaining and exercising power within their congregations and denominations. However, with the exception of a few independent movements, men remain at the head—and therefore in ultimate control—of virtually every religious structure, whereas women are widely considered subordinate.

In many societies religion is not separated from social authorities: Islamist Muslim society, for example, is structured according to Islamic law so that legislative and judicial authorities are by nature religious. Many West African societies have a similar structure: in the village in which the woman sits outside her shop measuring sugar, for example, the chief is perceived as having spiritual as well as social authority, acting as a link between the people and the sacred. He is therefore respected not only for the position he occupies, but for the very essence of his identity: he is in effect a living shrine. Spiritual matters are not separated out from the rest of society and confined within their own domain; rather, they are pervasive and intrinsic to all areas of life. Societies where Western and Christian influence have been strong are generally organized according to the model of a secular state, independent of religious institutions. However, even supposedly secular politicians are widely seen as having close links with spirits, through which they are thought by many to obtain their power. These may be good spirits: power and prosperity are often interpreted as blessings from God, and politicians in predominantly Christian societies are likely to seek to cultivate this through emphasizing connections with churches; however, they may also be suspected of achieving their position through evil spiritual power such as juju and witchcraft, which is discussed below.

Context of Life

Religion therefore plays an important role in organizing people's everyday lives. It also strongly influences the context of people's lives, that is, the environment in which they live. First, in West Africa religious groups are often key providers of services, particularly in the areas of health and education. Some of the children in the scene depicted above wear yellow shirts or blouses and brown shorts or pinafore dresses, whereas others are in blue uniforms; however, they are all on their way to the same school. The reason for this is that the Ghanaian state decided in 2004 to hand back part of the running of many of its schools to the church denominations that originally founded them. The school in this village has been returned to the Ghanaian Methodist Church, thus the brown and yellow state uniforms are gradually being replaced with the blue of Methodist schools. Church schools or independent Christian schools are widespread across Africa, partly because of recent growth in Christianity (both African Christian groups and external faith-based organizations) and partly because of the legacy of the missionary movement dating from precolonial times. As well as education, Christian missionary organizations have historically taken on the role of providing health facilities, and a large number of hospitals and clinics continue to be run by Catholic, Baptist, and Seventh-Day Adventist groups, among others. Most of these are now locally staffed, although some are still controlled by or employ the skills of expatriate professionals, on either a short-term or long-term basis. Muslim organizations also provide health facilities, and in Islamic societies religion and education are intrinsically bound together, with study of the Qur'an forming a fundamental element of the education of boys in *madrassas*. In addition to these more established community services, the nongovernmental development organizations that are ubiquitous in sub-Saharan Africa include many religiously oriented groups (primarily Christian and Muslim), commonly labeled Faith-Based Organizations (FBOs). As well as seeking to promote their own religion, these carry out a wide range of development initiatives, from child sponsorship, microfinance services, and agricultural programs to lobbying governments and international institutions. Some of these development programs are extremely successful and beneficial, whereas others are less effective. As the children walk to school in their state or Methodist uniforms, most pass one of two disused wells (one is broken, the other too close to the shore and therefore salty) provided by World Vision, a Christian development organization seeking to bring the village better access to fresh water. Many of the children are sponsored through the same organization by citizens of Western countries who donate money to assist in their education.

Second, in West Africa religion is usually very visible. Eleven churches in a village of 2,000 people is not uncommon in southern and central Ghana, and churches are not shy of promoting themselves. Although more recently established—often Pentecostal—churches in urban areas are more likely to opt for modern buildings in the style of offices and conference centers (as opposed to traditional Western church architecture), these are often elaborately and expensively designed and adorned with enormous banners proclaiming the name of the church and a catchy tagline or slogan, such as "Home of Breakthrough" or "Stop Suffering—Come and Join Us." Rural churches, reflecting the relative size and poverty of their congregations, are usually smaller and less elaborate affairs; indeed, many remain as unfinished structures for a long time even while they are used for meetings, being gradually improved as and when church finances allow. This village, situated as it is in the south of Ghana, where Islam is not as strong as Christianity, does not have a mosque. Even where Islam is the predominant religion, mosques are generally not as numerous as are churches in Christian areas, because of the less fragmented nature of the religion—one is unlikely to find eleven different Muslim brotherhoods operating independently within one village. However, as sacred places of prayer, and particularly as the site from which the call to prayer emanates across the community, mosques are prominent buildings and often more ornate than their Christian counterparts. Traditional West African religions, on the other hand, usually do not have specific, designated places of worship. Because religion is likely to be intrinsic to social structures, meeting places within communities often have underlying religious value even when used to discuss matters of justice, legislation, or governance. As mentioned above, shrines and sacred groves are located wherever the spirits they are associated with reside, and there may be many of these in any given geographical area. Diviners and herbalists usually operate from their own homes.

As well as through buildings, the presence of religion is felt in many other ways. One of the taxis waiting to fill with passengers before leaving for town, has a sticker on its bumper proclaiming in red capital letters, "IN GOD'S TIME." This is extremely common in Ghana and Nigeria, among other countries: religious—particularly Christian—slogans are exhibited on the inside and outside of cars and minibuses, alongside local aphorisms and warnings against HIV and/or AIDS. Shops and businesses also display religious messages, often incorporating them into their names. The shop owned by the woman in the black headscarf has the words "Nyamınlı wʊ ɛkɛ" painted on the wooden frame running across the top of the hut, meaning "God is there." Many other businesses are given names in English—for example, "Jesus Loves Fashion," "Finger of God Bakery" and "New Life Motors."

People themselves often bear or embody religious symbols. In some West African cultures the body—often the face—is deliberately marked with scars, indicating the status of that person as belonging to a certain clan or worshipping a particular god. The Ifè people of Togo are identified by scars according to the god they worship: those worshipping the highest god, Bùkúù, have horizontal marks on the forehead and on both cheeks; males worshipping Tsànkpàná, the god of smallpox, are marked around the waist, and females worshipping either Tsànkpàná or Ògú, the god of iron tools and war, have an upturned V on their back. Ifè people who have adopted Muslim culture can be identified by a slanting mark on their left cheek.

Styles of clothing can also represent religion. Muslim societies are often identifiable by the long veils and scarves worn by women and the caps and robes worn by men. Religious groups, like other organizations and businesses, sometimes commission a special design of cloth incorporating the logo of the group—which is made available for members to buy and have sewn into clothing—to commemorate a particular occasion such as an anniversary. Colors can also be significant, with many Zionist and other "spiritual" churches across Africa using white as their preferred color of clothing for worship. Mourning has widely come to be symbolized by the color black or, in Muslim societies, white; however, there are many variations to this. Akan funeral attendees, for example, can also wear shades of red. Some groups have other symbols of membership: the young woman buying bread and her baby girl both wear copper rings with the engraving MDCC, the initials of the Musama Disco Christo Church, of which she is a member. This jewelry, along with a copper cross with the same engraving and worn around the neck, performs the double function of protecting the wearer from evil spirits and identifying her to other members of the church, thereby invoking an obligation of mutual solidarity and assistance in times of trouble.

The sounds of religion are heard frequently in West African daily life. The Muslim call to prayer is one of the most common, ringing out across towns and cities throughout much of the continent. Christian churches make themselves heard mostly through music: the nocturnal chants of Zionist congregations at prayer; the dawn choruses of Methodist singing groups; and increasingly common (and increasingly complained about), the noisy drumming, singing, and dancing of

Pentecostal churches. Local-style music and drumming have grown in popularity within historic as well as Pentecostal churches over the past two decades, possibly because of the rapid expansion of the latter and the need among mission churches to adapt to retain their members. However, this music continues to be used outside church contexts and is especially important in indigenous religions, often being used to invoke spirits and induce spirit possession and trances.

Another form in which religion is continually seen and heard in daily life in West Africa is through the media, particularly television and radio broadcasts and newspaper articles. The voice chattering excitedly on the radio in the shop is a participant in a discussion about appropriate styles of clothing to be worn in church, specifically the issue of whether women should be permitted to wear miniskirts. Discussion programs such as this one, often in the format of phone-in shows, are broadcast daily on national and local radio stations, which abound all across West Africa. Subjects vary widely but are often based on moral issues and are frequently religious in tone: if the matters they relate are not specifically religious, they are often discussed with reference to religion because of its prominent place in society. Radio stations also broadcast religious messages, including prayers and sermons. Radio and television media are especially and increasingly used by Pentecostal charismatic churches to disseminate their teachings and raise their profile either through short advertisements, highlighting their ability to effect miracles and solve problems, or in the case of the larger and wealthier churches, through broadcasts of church services. Advertisements and announcements are also placed in popular newspapers, adding to the numerous references to religion that abound in news stories, whether describing charitable initiatives of religious groups, scandals involving religious leaders (some of whom have celebrity status), or religious comments made by politicians.

Religion is therefore very prominent in West African society. It is also present in ways that are both less obvious and more fundamental to people's daily lives, forming the basis of their worldviews. The spiritual is central to many Africans' interpretations of reality. Spirits—God, deities, ancestors, witches, angels, demons, and evil spirits, among others—are perceived to influence lives in very real ways, and are therefore continuously taken into serious consideration. Moreover, although people may identify themselves with one particular religion, this does not mean they discount the existence and power of spirits that are not intrinsically associated with that religion. This tendency has led to descriptions of much religion in Africa as syncretistic, mixing Christianity and/or Islam with traditional religions. However, in many cases, rather than being a syncretistic combining of static religions, the spiritual landscape as a whole has been and continues to be reframed as new religions gain ground. In contexts in which Christianity has increased in popularity and influence, for example, there has been a notable change in the way that ancestors and secondary deities, in particular, are perceived. Once seen as either morally neutral or interested in upholding moral standards within society, they are now commonly considered to be evil and demonic. Because it is the nature of their power that has changed rather than its existence, such spirits are still perceived as powerful actors with the capacity to influence and intervene in people's lives.

Besides spirits intervening directly in one's life, there is also a constant awareness that other people can and do interact with different spirits. These interactions may be for good or for evil, and they can have direct implications not only for the person involved but also for others in the community, whether for their benefit or for their harm. Moreover, engagement with spirits may be performed openly, but it may also be—and in the case of malicious activity, is likely to be—covert. Relationships therefore operate within a context of uncertainty, where other members of society, even those to whom one is close, can potentially be enemies. This is intensified by the emphasis commonly placed on *intent* in explanations of events and situations. Rather than things happening by chance or through purely "natural" causes, events (and particularly major events) are commonly interpreted as being deliberately brought about by a specific actor, whether human or spirit. Thus, questions asked in the event of a death often relate not only to *what* killed the person, but also to *who* killed them. Poor health, crop failure, singleness, loss of money, and failure to pass exams or to obtain a visa are all examples of misfortunes that could potentially be attributed to the malicious intent of others, although the perpetrators often remain unidentified. The constant fear of harm by others, through spiritual or other means, results in an underlying current of distrust within relationships in some African societies. People are likely to be guarded about personal information, reluctant to reveal their plans and dreams to all but a very few people, and careful not to leave themselves vulnerable to harm in other ways. When preparing maize porridge for her baby, for example, the woman buying bread remains especially vigilant over the cooking pot when there are visitors to the household, for fear that somebody might deliberately contaminate the food either with poison or using witchcraft.

The sense of uncertainty and insecurity has increased with the onset of modernity. New markets, political systems, cultures, and technologies have opened up and mobility and communications have developed, creating opportunities of prosperity for some and frustrations for others who cannot take advantage of them. In such a context accusations of witchcraft have escalated, because people draw on spiritual discourses to interpret difficult situations. Witches tend to be portrayed as people who, rather than using their resources for the benefit of the community, seek to suck resources out of the community for their own advantage. Witchcraft is associated with jealousy: witches hate seeing others prosper. Rich and poor alike are therefore vulnerable to allegations of witchcraft, the former through accumulating wealth and the latter through potential jealousy. However, in practice it is the weaker members of society who are more likely to face accusations. Women, and particularly older women, are the most commonly accused, although recently accusations against children have increased in countries such as the Democratic Republic of the Congo and Nigeria. Family members are primary suspects of witchcraft because they have not only greater access to the supposed victim than outsiders but also higher potential for jealousy. Alleged witches may be chased out of their communities or face trials and exorcism either by traditional spiritual authorities or by other religious—often Pentecostal—leaders. Conversely, benign intent is also perceived to lie behind positive events and conditions, although it is less common for people to question the origin of good things that happen to them than that of bad things (which is not unique to Africa), and positive occurrences tend to be interpreted more generally as blessings from God.

Practice of Life

Daily life in much of West Africa is therefore played out in a context shaped and colored a great deal by religion. Not only does religion affect how life is organized—dictating to some extent which things should be done by which people, at which times, and in which places—it also forms an integral part of the environment within which lives are lived. The way people manage the structures and environment within which they live constitutes the practice of daily life. Religion consists largely in practice: it is so prominent in African society precisely because Africans practice it in their everyday lives. The clothes people wear, the radio programs they listen to, the names they give their businesses, the places where they assemble, and the rituals with which they mark new phases of life are all part of their practice of religion. Conversely, people's practice of religion—both the way they practice it and the fact that they practice it at all—is determined and informed by their social context and the structures that shape it.

Religion in West Africa is such an integral part of daily life because both are intensely practical by nature. Rather than being a conscious project of inner transformation of the self, much of religion—and much of life—is about problem solving. The range of problems faced by people in West Africa is wide. We have already encountered some examples: poor health, crop failure, poverty, exam failure, singleness, visa rejection, violence, war, infertility, lawsuits, school fees, marital infidelity, physical danger, unemployment, and debt constitute just a few instances of difficulties that religion is employed to solve. People seek both to avoid potential problems, protecting themselves from harm, and to solve actual problems and procure for themselves advancement or blessings. Religious discourses play a key role in both of these objectives, as people draw on them to implement a range of different strategies. Thus, in the churches in the village referred to at the beginning of this chapter, prayers frequently focus on thanks and requests for blessings, including business success and prosperity, educational achievement for children, domestic harmony, good health, and successful pregnancies. People also repeatedly give thanks and appeal for protection against illness, as they travel and in their daily work; women whose husbands are fishermen, for example, pray for their protection as they take their boats out on the ocean. In non-Christian contexts protection may be sought in other ways. For the Kapsiki of northern Cameroon, potential sources of harm and evil abound in everyday life, and to avoid them certain protective strategies must be applied. These range from carefully living one's life in accordance with the principles and regulations ordained by one's personal god (transgressions may include anything from engaging in illicit sexual relations to having a cock crow on one's granary) to performing specific rituals and taking medicine for protection against difficulties such as drought, war, or illness. However, possibly the greatest threat is from other people, whether thieves, those who have inherent spiritual capacities (such as witches) and whose spirits or shadows leave their bodies at night to cause physical harm to others, or those who perform *beshèngu* (black magic), whose practice is a learned profession. It is important to minimize the danger by managing relationships with care not to arouse jealousy or ill-feeling. Magic or medicine is also used (*rhwè*), either self-administered or obtained from a diviner, which usually consists of a bundle of special ingredients (such as grasses), specifically concocted for the issue in question, to be buried or hidden at a certain place. A protection against burglary placed in one's compound, for example, will make a thief forget his intentions to steal as soon as he crosses the threshold.[4]

Thinking of religion as something practical helps to understand apparent conflicts and contradictions in the ways that it is played out in people's everyday lives. As we have seen, religion in most of West Africa is by no means homogenous and consists of an ever-changing myriad of different concepts and groups that coexist and interconnect in multiple and fluid ways. In practice, then, people do not live within a single, internally coherent religious system, but rather within a broad landscape of religious teachings and practices that originate from different sources and do not necessarily concur with each other. This may result in or exacerbate conflict and violence, as in the case of Muslim-Christian tensions in Nigeria; it may lead to different religious groups coexisting peace-fully and separately within society, or to religions being adapted, mixed, and merged with other beliefs and practices; and it may also create eclecticism and fluidity in the way people draw on religion in their everyday lives as they com-bine and move between religious discourses.

Conflict between religions often means that people have to make important and continual decisions at all levels of life regarding what sets of values and practices they will follow. The Ifè people of Togo, for example, consider them-selves to live under the protection of the local deities they worship according to clan. Christianity, which has been introduced over the past 30 years through a Bible translation project, is seen by many as a threat not only to the lives of converts—because betrayal or neglect of Ifè religion is expected to result in either death or madness—but also to the whole community as the deities are threatened by the risk of converts revealing important secrets intrinsic to religious ceremonies. And social order is disrupted as converts are accused of embracing a foreign religion and thus betraying their own culture and showing disrespect toward parents, elders, and the interests of the community as a whole. Ifè Christians may therefore face intense persecution—in the form of disownment, mockery, expulsion from their village, spiritual attacks, and attempts on their lives—from family and community members. Dilemmas Christians face include the extent to which they should participate in cere-monies and festivals associated with traditional religion, which in turn affects areas of daily life. Even one's name may change: upon baptism into a Christian church, converts often choose or are given French "Christian" names, although in practice their original Ifè name usually continues to be used outside church circles. Within households the custom of men and women eating separately is abolished by many Christians. Indeed, a Christian marriage is highly desirable for women insofar as Christian men are held fully accountable to the church for their actions and moral attitudes. Christian marriages are modeled on monogamy, the pooling of resources, and consideration toward (although not equality with) spouses, rather than polygamy, sexual license for men, and unequal access to resources. In practice, however, this is not always the case, and women within a Christian marriage may find themselves more isolated than their non-Christian counterparts.

The extent to which one should participate in one's own culture is a question constantly faced by Ifè Christians, and one approached differently by different churches. The Catholic Church is the denomination most accepted by non-Christians, mainly because of its tolerant approach to traditional prac-tices, permitting its members to continue worshiping Ifè divinities as well as attending Mass and confessing. Ifè Catholics can in effect live a dual identity, with traditional and Christian practices kept in separate cultural spaces. The initial Protestant missionary approach contrasted starkly with this, rejecting all forms of Ifè culture—including music, clothing, and even to a certain extent language—as unholy. To convert to Christianity, people were required to make a complete break with their "pagan" culture. Over the past 20 years and largely as a result of the Bible translation project, a third approach has developed mainly within Protestant churches. Although still denouncing traditional religion, there has been a conscious effort to "indigenize" Christianity, particularly through the use of Ifè language and music styles. This is an ongoing process of negotiation, as Christians try to reconcile their culture with their faith.

Where practical issues are concerned people are likely to be pragmatic in their approach to solving them. Just as citizens of Western countries who have no interest in or knowledge of the workings of Chinese medical theory may visit an acupuncturist as well as their doctor to treat a bad back, many Africans are pragmatic in how they draw on religion to solve their problems. In Ghana and in other West African countries, for example, it is not uncommon for people to attend a specific church because of the reputation of the pastor as an extraordinarily powerful "man of God" who possesses the ability to effect miracles. Problem solving is one of the most common reasons for attending church, and if the prayers and practices of one church do not appear effective, attendees may switch to a different church, or go to weekday meetings of other churches while continuing to attend the church of which they are a member. Perceived effectiveness and reputation may also lead them to consult traditional religious experts such as herbalists, diviners, practitioners of juju, and *mallams*, or visit shrines of local *abosom* (small gods). Such choices are constrained less by conceptual matters of whether or not these spirits exist, and more by moral frameworks: a Christian may be reluctant to visit a *mallam* because he has been taught by his church that it is morally wrong. However, if he is facing a pressing or persistent problem, practical concerns may override moral issues. A student, for example, who has repeatedly failed his exams despite studying hard, may well consult a non-Christian spiritual practitioner if his prayers appear to go unanswered. For a woman who experiences difficulties with conception or delivering a healthy child, a potential source of help is likely to be an *obosom* who is represented by a priest or priestess and who usually requires payment of some type for services rendered, often in the form of a sacrificial bird or animal. Severe and minor illnesses and injuries are often treated with remedies administered or advised by herbalists, sometimes simultaneously with other types of therapy, such as biomedical drugs and prayer. Some herbal treatments—particularly those that involve consultation with a herbalist—are associated with spiritual powers. Others—for example, the use of specific plants as liniments—are seen simply as practical indigenous knowledge and used commonly throughout society, or rejected by some as myth.

Central to much religion in West Africa is the notion of interaction with spirits, whether God, ancestors, secondary deities, or otherwise. Rather than formless and impersonal forces, spirits are usually understood as persons or as personified beings with their own volition and with which people can and must interact to get along in life. One of the most obvious and widespread methods by which people communicate with spirits to resolve their problems is prayer. Specific techniques are diverse, both within and between religious traditions: prayer can be a corporate or an individual activity; it can be performed directly by the supplicant or through the mediation of a religious expert; words may be spontaneous or shaped by prescribed liturgy; prayer may be integral to or accompanied by ritual actions, or it may consist solely of speech or unspoken thoughts. For many people prayer is practiced in several or all of these ways at different times. The woman with the baby who attends the Musama Disco Christo Church in southern Ghana may or may not recite the *Yinaabi* prayer three times a day—perhaps she is more likely to do this when she has a specific, urgent request to make of God—but she participates in group performances of the prayer at church meetings. All prayers at her church are performed corporately, sometimes in the form of sung liturgy, sometimes with all members praying aloud and simultaneously on themes directed by the pastor, and other times with one person petitioning God for something while the others punctuate her (the church membership is nearly all female) prayer by saying "Amen!" At evening prayer meetings it is the pastor who takes the leading role: often in a state of semi-trance and as her congregation sing, drum, and dance, she prays for each member individually with rough movements, employing candles, water, and oil as she deems appropriate or is prompted by the Holy Spirit. Before this woman gave birth to her baby, she visited the pastor and an elder of the church daily for prayers of protection for her child, which involved a ritual entailing massaging her belly with oil. However, to tackle another problem, the infidelity of the father of her child, she attends a weekly prayer meeting at a Pentecostal church in a nearby city, which has a reputation for powerful answers to prayer. She also prays at home, both for specific issues such as her domestic situation and as part of her daily routine, for example before meals.

Prayer is generally considered communication with spirits through words. However, a great deal of communication is also carried out through actions. Fasting, for example, is considered a powerful accompaniment to prayer within many strands of Christianity and Islam in West Africa. Actions may be self-prescribed or recommended by an expert—such as a pastor, imam, or diviner—whose advice is often sought over difficult issues. Depending on immediate social structures, different experts vary in status: in predominantly Islamic societies Muslim leaders are the most acceptable mediators between humans and spirits, a role performed by pastors in Christian societies. Traditional experts—diviners, fetish priests and priestesses, and herbalists—may be respected and revered as having a close relationship with spirits or viewed as agents of evil powers, depending on the society in which they operate and the perspective of community members. As already noted, it is common for people to visit more than one type of expert, particularly if their problem does not appear to be solved immediately. The role of religious experts is often to suggest both the cause of the problem and its solution, arrived at through the knowledge and reasoning of the expert as well as through his or her ability to inquire of the spirits, usually through prayer or ritual. Problems are often deemed to be the result either of misdemeanor on the part of the petitioner or of malicious activity initiated by another actor, whether human or spirit. The solution may involve one or more of a range of remedies, including behavioral change; prayer; fasting; protective "medicine" or amulets; sacrifice of animals, crops, or money; and rituals involving incantations and materials such as oil, fire, and water.

Because problems often originate from offense against a spirit, part of interacting with spirits involves evaluating one's standing with them and seeking to consolidate and improve these relationships. People are likely to reason that if they are requesting something of a spirit, it is in their favor to live and act in a fashion pleasing to that spirit. They may therefore start to pray; to attend worship regularly; and to make sure that they have performed all the appropriate rites of passage, that they continue to uphold customary rituals such as pouring libation to ancestors at communal gatherings, and that their behavior does not contravene the moral standards required by the power they are petitioning. All these things, of course, are also practices that people employ in their daily lives: rather than necessarily being targeted at a particular issue or problem, they are employed as general strategies by which people place themselves in the best position to receive blessings and to protect themselves from harm. Many practices, such as compliance with rules and taboos dictated by spirits, are habitual patterns of behavior sometimes learned in childhood, sometimes adopted later in life (for example, joining a church). They are an integral part of the practice of everyday life, constituting and shaping areas of life such as the clothes people wear, the time they get up in the morning, their daily routine and activities, how they eat, and how they relate to others.

CONCLUSION

Religion in West Africa is extremely diverse. The three main areas of Islam, Christianity, and traditional religion alone conceal a complex arena made up of a multitude of different groups, practices, and values that both vary enormously within different categories and interconnect across them. Although Christianity and Islam originated outside Africa, both have been present on the continent for several centuries and have become deeply embedded in local culture, in some areas indistinguishable from or superseding previous traditions. Although local religious customs have been to varying extents influenced by Christianity and Islam, these religions have also been indigenized and debates around acculturation continue in both.

Whatever the specific religious environment, it is clear that religion plays a fundamental role in shaping everyday life in sub-Saharan Africa. It strongly influences the *organization* of life temporally by defining rites of passage, calendar events, and monthly, weekly, and daily structures of life; spatially, by assigning sacred value to particular places; and socially, by attributing power through religious expertise to certain members of society. Religion is also an integral factor in forming the *context* of daily life: its presence is strongly felt through services it provides (especially health care and education); through religious buildings and places, such as mosques, churches and shrines; through titles of businesses and slogans on bumper stickers; through the physical appearance of different members of society, including their clothing, jewelry, and body markings; through sounds of prayer, music, and drumming; and through media broadcasts and reports via television, radio, and newspapers. Moreover, religion is intrinsic to people's cosmological understandings of the world, that is, their worldview. There is a deep sense of awareness of the existence of spirits and the ability of other humans to tap into spiritual power, whether for good or for evil purposes.

Because religion is intrinsically related to the organization and context of daily life, it is also crucial to its practice, influencing what different people do, and when, where, and how they do it. Prayer and ritual are usually considered by commentators as particularly "religious" practices, although religion is also fundamental in determining everyday behavior. Indeed, religion in Africa is often understood as underlying and pervading life in its entirety: everything is seen in spiritual terms and organized around religious principles. However, this notion of religion as totalizing and all-encompassing may be misleading. As we have seen, much religion in Africa is largely practical by nature, oriented around solving problems, protecting from harm, and receiving blessings, rather than around abstract theological questions or self-transformative projects. Even though people may spend a lot of time "doing" religion, this does not mean that religion or religious issues are uppermost in their minds all the time: they do not necessarily spend a lot of time "thinking" religion. Furthermore, religion in Africa tends not to be separated out from the nonreligious or secular. Residences of spirits, for example, may also form part of everyday life and are used for mundane purposes such as cooking, washing, and sheltering one from the sun. Spiritual, political, and administrative authorities are often closely related or embodied within the same persons. Ancestors are spirits, but they are also social actors, elders who happen to have died. The continuity between physical and spiritual and between sacred and secular makes it hard to define what is religious and what is not religious, and this difficulty in identifying and separating out religion exists precisely because it is so intrinsic to the practice of daily life.

GLOSSARY

Juju: Occult activity.

Mallam: Islam-associated holy man, spiritualist.

Matrilineage: Line of descent traced through the female side of the family; all the members of one's extended family on one's mother's side.

Obosom (sg.), *Abosom* (pl.): Secondary deities (in the Fante language of Ghana).

Sharia: Islamic code of law based on the Qur'an.

Yinaabi: Ritual prayer of the Musama Disco Christo Church.

Zionist Churches: Indigenous, "spiritual" churches, often seeking to withdraw from mainstream society and/or establish countersocieties based on the notion of the coming Kingdom of God.

NOTES

1. Chris M. Ukachukwu, "The Sacred Festival of Iri Ji Ohuru in Igboland, Nigeria," *Nordic Journal of African Studies* 16.2 (2007), pp. 244–260.
2. Paula G. Ben-Amos, "The Promise of Greatness: Women and Power in an Edo Spirit Possession Cult," in *Religion in Africa: Experience and Expression*, Blakely et al., eds. (London: Currey, 1994), pp. 126–130.
3. Ibid., pp. 130–134.
4. Walter E. A. Van Beek, "The Innocent Sorcerer: Coping with Evil in Two African Societies (Kapsiki and Dogon)," in *Religion in Africa: Experience and Expression*, Blakely et al., eds. (London: Currey, 1994), pp. 196–228.

BIBLIOGRAPHY

Bartle, Philip F. W. "The Universe Has Three Souls: Notes on Translating Akan Culture." *Journal of Religion in Africa* 14.2 (1983): 85–114.

Blakely, Thomas D., Walter E. A. Van Beek, and Dennis L. Thomson, eds. *Religion in Africa: Experience and Expression*. London: Currey, 1994.

Brenner, Louis. " 'Religious' Discourses in and about Africa." In K. Barber and P. Farias de Moraes, eds. *Discourse and Its Disguises: The Interpretation of African Oral Texts*. Birmingham: University of Birmingham, Centre for West African Studies, 1989, pp. 87–105.

Ellis, Stephen, and Gerrie Ter Haar. *Worlds of Power: Religious Thought and Political Practice in Africa*. London: Hurst and Co., 2004.

Evans-Pritchard, Edward E. *Witchcraft, Oracles and Magic among the Azande*. New York: Oxford University Press, 1937.

Hastings, Adrian. *The Church in Africa: 1450–1950*. Oxford: Oxford University Press, 1994.

Levtzion, Nehemia, and Randall L. Pouwells, eds. *The History of Islam in Africa*. Oxford: Currey, 2000.

Chapter 7

Muslim Middle East

Mashal Saif

In 610 CE a man named Muhammad received a revelation from God. Meditating in a cave on the outskirts of the city of Mecca, in Arabia, Muhammad was confronted with a voice commanding him to recite. The voice, deep and arresting, was accompanied by the sudden materialization of a piece of silk with words embroidered on it. Startled at the command and the voice Muhammad stammered, "I cannot recite." The voice just repeated the command, "Recite," and the piece of silk was thrust at him again. Again, Muhammad could only reply, "I cannot recite."

Muhammad was unlettered, unable to read, and hence unable to decipher the words on the brocade before him. The mysterious voice commanded him for the third time, "Recite," and Muhammad, repeated himself yet again, "I cannot recite." These words had only just escaped his lips when he was inspired to say out loud:

> Recite: In the name of thy Lord who created,
> created man of a blood-clot.
> Recite: And thy Lord is the Most Generous
> who taught by the pen,
> taught Man that he knew not. (Qur'an 96:1–5)[1]

And in this way, on this momentous night in the month of Ramadan in 610 CE, Islam was born. However, the idea of the "birth" of Islam is misleading for a number of reasons. First, Muslims do not understand Islam to be a new religion. Instead, it is perceived as the reconfiguration and purification of the monotheism that God had commanded his prophets to preach from time immemorial. In the Islamic tradition, the line of prophets starts from Adam and comprises 124,000 prophets in total. These prophets include Abraham, Moses, Noah, and Jesus, among others. Muhammad is the last of this long line; consequently, Islam is perceived as the eternally true religion, and the culmination of God's messages to humanity.[2]

The Arabic word *Islam* literally means "to submit." Religiously interpreted, it means "to submit or to surrender to God." The term *Muslim* is a derivative of *Islam*, and it means "one who surrenders (to God)." In the Qur'an, the word *Islam* and its derivates are used in approximately 70 verses. However, only in a few of these verses is the term used in an exclusivist sense—that is, to mean specifically the religion established by Muhammad and the Qur'an. Instead, we see the term *Muslim* being employed in the Qur'an to refer to individuals who follow any of God's numerous prophets. For example, one Qur'anic verse states:

> And when I revealed to the Apostles [of Jesus], "Have faith in Me and My messengers," they said, "We have faith, and we bear witness that we are muslims." (Qur'an 5:111)

Despite the existence of many thousands of prophets since Adam's time, the miracle and blessings of revelation ended with Muhammad. Consequently, for Muslims the Qur'an is the last divine book. Other divine books include the Torah, the Gospels, and the Psalms of David—however, all these scriptures are understood to have been corrupted over time. The Qur'an, on the other hand, is the unchanged word of God as revealed to Muhammad by the angel Gabriel over the 23-year course of Muhammad's prophecy (610–632 CE). Qur'anic revelations are often divided into Meccan and Medinan chapters (*surahs*)—Mecca and Medina being the two cities in which Muhammad lived and received divine messages during the period of his prophethood.

EVERYDAY USES OF THE QUR'AN[3]

The Qur'an is perhaps the most universally accessible verbal and material object to which Muslims can turn for divine blessings and intercession. In a formalized manner, the Qur'an is used in the performance of Qur'anic recitation (*tajwid*) and the act of ritual prayer (*salat*). However, the scripture is also employed in many other ways, such as the following:

- In performing a range of personal prayers.
- In many ways in daily speech; for example, saying *insha' Allah* (If God wills) as part of everyday speech or performing the *tasliya* (the act of calling down

blessings) on the prophets (especially Muhammad), on Sufi saints, and Shi'ite imams is a basic part of the everyday life of many Muslims.

- In spells, verbal charms, and incantations.
- In physical talismans and amulets that are meant to provide protection from evil eye—that is, from ill feelings and the envy of men and jinn.
- For the purposes of healing and fertility. A common method that is employed is to write down Qur'anic verses in ink made from natural ingredients. The writing is then washed off and the water is given to the sick person to drink. This practice traces its roots back to medieval times and is still popular in many regions, especially the Sudan.
- For divination (*istikhara*) through interpreting the Qur'anic text and for the divining of dreams that are interpreted through the Qur'an.
- In physical representation of the text in calligraphy, engraving, and the decoration of everyday objects. Wall hangings, mosaics, painted murals, car stickers, and carpets, for example, all routinely evidence Qur'anic inscriptions.

After the Qur'an, the second most important source text for Muslims is *hadith* literature. In contrast to the Qur'an, which is the unchanged word of God, the *hadith* are simply human recordings of Muhammad's utterances, actions, and approvals. This copious body of literature serves as an important reference for Muslims wishing to know how to best practice their faith and emulate the life of the perfect human being, Muhammad.

There exist many sects within Islam and each group emphasizes different dimensions and interpretations of the faith. One method of distinguishing between Muslims is to see whether they privilege the mystical dimension of Islam (Sufism) over the ethical and religious law of Islam (the Shari'a). Muslims who emphasize the juridical dimensions of the faith usually align themselves with one of the five major schools of Islamic law. These legal schools represent a diversity of opinion regarding the configurations and interpretations of Islam's religious and ethical system of conduct.

Another way of distinguishing between different groups of Muslims is by dividing them along sectarian lines. There exist two major branches of Islam. The larger of these is Sunnism, adherents to which make up approximately 85 percent of Muslims today. The other major branch of Islam is Shi'ism. Shi'ites can be distinguished from Sunnis in terms of their legal school as well as their doctrines and practices. The most significant doctrinal difference between these two groups is the Shi'ite belief in the Imamate, that is, that particular descendents of Muhammad, called Imams, are infallible human beings who act as intermediaries between the rest of the Muslim community and God.

Despite differences in legal schools and sects, almost all Muslims agree that Islam is defined by its Five Pillars, which are the basic practices by which one's belief is expressed.[4] These pillars are the confession of faith (*shahada*), prayer (*salah*), fasting (*saum*), alms giving (*zakat*), and pilgrimage (*hajj*).

THE FIVE PILLARS OF ISLAM

The first pillar, the confession of faith, requires the formal utterance of the statement "There is no God but God and Muhammad is the messenger of God." As a consequence of this statement, a Muslim is also required to believe in the existence of angels, God's books, His messengers, the decrees of good and evil, and life after death.

The ritual act of prayer is understood to be the second most important practice in the tradition, following the confession of faith. Muslims are required to pray five times a day facing the holy shrine in Mecca (the Ka'ba). Each prayer must be performed at a designated time during the day. The prayer entails a specific set of postures and utterances that can only be performed once the believer has entered a state of ritual purity, which is reached by performing the ablution (wudu').

The third pillar is fasting, which entails abstinence from food, water, and sexual relations. This act of abstinence must continue from dawn till dusk (after sunset one is free to eat, drink, and indulge in sexual intercourse). The lunar month of Ramadan is designated as the month for fasting, and it culminates with the celebration of the religious holiday of 'Id al-Fitr.

The act of alms giving is considered compulsory in Islam. This pillar emphasizes social commitment and requires individuals above a particular economic bracket to aid the underprivileged and contribute to social uplift. This monetary donation attests to one's belief in an afterlife removed from the materialism of this world. It also invokes God's blessings and benevolence on the donor.

The fifth and final pillar of Islam is the hajj, that is, the pilgrimage to Mecca at a particular point during the Islamic lunar year. Pilgrimage to Mecca once during the course of a lifetime, is considered obligatory for those who can afford the journey. The ritual of hajj extends over several days and it constitutes an honoring of God's symbols, especially the Ka'ba, which is the shrine in Mecca built by the prophet Abraham.

THE FORMATION AND EXPANSION OF ISLAM

Initially, it took Muhammad a while to win over supporters to his new faith. However, by the time of his death in 632 CE, most of the inhabitants of the Arabian peninsula had embraced Islam. After Muhammad's demise, political power was handed down through the institution of the caliphate. Although different sects within Islam dispute the authority and order of succession of the caliphs, the dominant sect, Sunnism, accepts the first four caliphs as "rightly guided." Under the authority of these caliphs, the Muslim empire expanded at a remarkable rate.

The Arab conquest of the Near East—an area that stretches from Egypt to Iran—took place in the forth and fifth decades of the seventh century. This conquest came as a shock to the unsuspecting inhabitants of Iraq, Syria, and Egypt. The surprise and bewilderment of the conquered populations persisted for an extended period, and the Muslim armies and their new monotheistic faith were not integrated into the culture of the Near East for some time.[5] The Muslim conquerors made little attempt to impose their faith on the inhabitants of the conquered territories. During this early period, Islam was seen as a badge of privilege exclusive to the Arab conquerors, and these new rulers had little desire to share this privilege with their subjects.[6] However, the confrontation with the inhabitants of the conquered territories provided the impetus for the Muslim armies to define a distinct Muslim religious identity for themselves. Consequently, Muslim identity began to sharpen in the latter half of the seventh and the beginning of the eighth centuries, and the conquering Arabs of the peninsula gradually became incorporated into the larger social and cultural configurations of the Near East.[7]

This period of the sharpening of the contours of the Islamic tradition was also a time of political upheaval for the Muslim empire. The fourth caliph, Ali, was murdered in 661 CE, and upon his death, his rival, Mu'awaiya, established his own caliphate. This event marked the advent of the Umayyad Dynasty—a dynasty premised on one family's (the Banu Umayya) hereditary right to rule. The Umayyad period was a time of transition. On the one hand, the Muslim community during this time was still predominantly Arab; on the other, the state itself was experiencing a series of evolutions and becoming increasingly centralized and imperial. During this time, a small but growing number of non-Arab converts began occupying important posts in the administration, in the army, and in religious scholarship. Moreover, the foundations of Muslim society shifted as the Arab rulers settled down to routine life in the lands that their fathers had conquered.[8]

The art, architecture, and placement of the grandiose palaces constructed by the Umayyad Dynasty reflect both the underlying "Arabness" of the Umayyad state as well as its transitional character. The placement of the palaces in the countryside, beyond the reaches of city life, depicts the political realities of that era. It was only at a distance from the heavily Christian urban centers that the Muslim Arab commanders could interact freely with the nomadic and seminomadic soldiers and army personnel who constituted the backbone of the state's defenses. In contrast, an examination of the art and

The Umayyad Mosque in Damascus, Syria is often referred to as the Great Mosque. Beautiful, intricate mosaics intersperse the white interior of the mosque. The mosque houses a magnificent courtyard containing ablution fountains and a number of domes supported by columns. (Flemming Pless/iStockphoto.com.)

architecture of the magnificent Umayyad palaces reveals a high degree of interaction with the aesthetic understandings of various non-Arab cultures. The sculptures, wall painting, and floor mosaics that embellished the dwellings of the Umayyad officials drew freely on Iranian and Roman imagery. The art in the palaces reveals an emphasis on geometric and vegetal designs, on figures clothed in Byzantine or Sassanian royal costumes, and on scenes of merry making and song and dance.[9]

Despite its ostentatiousness (or possibly as a result of it), the Umayyad Dynasty did not last long, collapsing in 750 CE, when it was replaced by the 'Abbasids. As these political transitions continued on the higher playing fields, in the eighth-century at the grassroots level, Islam was developing more formally as a tradition while simultaneously becoming increasingly integrated into the larger Near Eastern culture. In fact, by the advent of 'Abbasid rule a distinct Muslim tradition and society had emerged. But although non-Arabs were increasingly converting to Islam, Muslims were still a minority in the Near East, at least outside of Arabia.[10]

Although initially the Arab conquerors made little effort to facilitate conversions among the non-Arabs, by the end of Umayyad rule, the focus on conversion became characteristic of the attitude of certain pious Muslims. In fact, after some time, it became common for biographies of famous preachers to boast of the number of infidels converted by the holy men.[11] The conversion of the conquered inhabitants of the Near East was a gradual process whose impetus was not always strictly religious. Public preaching sessions, which non-Muslims attended either out of curiosity or by invitation, facilitated conversion.[12] Informal teaching sessions, especially at Sufi lodges (khanqahs), were also integral in contributing to the adoption of Islam by non-Arabs. Additionally, the social and psychological factors leading to conversion cannot be ignored. In some cases the motives were economic—for example, non-Muslims were required to pay a poll tax (jaziya), and conversion meant freedom from this economic hardship. Scholars of the Umayyad period have documented acceleration in conversion rates, especially in Iraq, during periods in which tax collection was more strictly enforced than usual.[13] In other situations, the desire to escape prejudice as a result of stigmatization or the wish to marry a Muslim woman were the reasons for conversion. Conversions were also facilitated by the fact that the inhabitants of the conquered lands knew that they could never completely integrate themselves into Muslim society unless they embraced Islam.[14]

The aforementioned reasons for conversion hold true for the spread of Islam in both the Middle East and Africa. However, with regard to Africa, it is best to understand the diffusion of Islam in the continent as a multistaged process. On the one hand, Muslim armies had already introduced Islam to North Africa by the mid-seventh century. However, the impact of Islam was not felt in Sudanic lands until the eleventh century, when contact was facilitated through trade. The eleventh-century invasion of the Almoravids, a group of Berber nomads who emphasized adherence to the Shari'a, gave the conversion process a new impetus in Ghana and beyond. By the thirteenth century, trading interactions with Muslim lands had increased, and a number of merchant traders as well as rulers of Sudanic kingdoms (specifically Ghana and Mali) had converted to Islam. The general population, however, remained mostly unaffected. Islam continued to infiltrate into the African continent over the centuries, and gradually sub-Saharan African developed its own brand of Islam, characterized by distinct religious sects, beliefs, and practices.[15] For example, compared to the practice of Islam in other regions, African Islam is often more mystical in terms of its emphasis. Moreover, African Islam is often described as organized into brotherhoods. These institutions reflect the communal nature of societal organization in the continent. A more specific example of the distinctly native character of African Islam would be the reverence attached to a particular stone phallus in Mogadishu, Somalia. In a study conducted in the 1980s the phallus was seen to be surrounded by offerings by Muslim Somalis. Questioning revealed that the phallus both symbolized the visit of the prophet Khidr and acted as a fertility symbol for sterile women.[16] The rituals and reverence surrounding this phallus evidence religious integration and syncretism in addition to demonstrating the native character of African Islam.

As Islam in Africa was garnering more converts, undergoing changes, and developing its own distinct brand, the Muslim Near East was experiencing transitions of its own. The 'Abbasid Dynasty was replaced by the Fatimids in Egypt, and over the course of the centuries the Muslim world saw the rise of dynasties such as the Ayyubid, the Seljuk, the Mamluk, the Ottoman, and the Mughal. The power of these political families rose and fell: each dynasty had its heyday and then was inevitably replaced. By the nineteenth century much of the Muslim world had been colonized. With the rise of colonialism, these dynasties came to an end, and eventually in the post-colonial era, Muslim nation-states were born.

Although Islam was born in Arabia, its development took place, and continues to take place, in lands stretching from Nigeria to Indonesia and beyond. Within a century after God's first communication with Muhammad, Islam had already spread to Mesopotamia, or the Near East. These lands were populated by members of various faith associations, ranging from paganism to Zoroastrianism, Judaism, and Christianity. Consequently, it is impossible to understand the development and content of Islam without keeping in mind the religious history of these other traditions.

As detailed above, very early in the history of Islam, its center shifted from beyond the Arabian peninsula to the religious and cultural traditions of the Near East. These regions stretching from Egypt to Iran played a critical role in forming and circumscribing Islam and Muslim identity as we understand it today.[17] In terms of religious influences on Islamic practices, there was strategic borrowing by Islam from a number of religious traditions. Certain pre-Islamic Arabic pagan cultic rituals and practices were reconfigured and adopted by the new Islamic faith, including animal sacrifice and pilgrimage to shrines, especially the Ka'ba.[18] In fact, the history of the *hajj* can be traced back to pre-Islamic pilgrimage practices to this very destination. In addition to paganism, Christianity and Judaism also had a large stake in Arabia at the time surrounding the birth of Islam. Even Zoroastrianism was known to the Arabs and informed the cultural context of Arabia at the time of the emergence and initial development of Islam.[19]

One must not be taken aback at the realization that Islam was not a fully developed entity at the time of its inception or even at the time of the death of the Prophet Muhammad in 632 CE. Islam, like all historical abstractions, is a complex and constantly evolving phenomenon that continues to adapt itself to this day with the birth of new religious movements and understandings. The early generations of Muslims felt comfortable with the idea of constant development of the tradition, and many considered borrowing and adaptation to be unproblematic. The tenth-century Muslim historian Mas'udi explained in his works that Islamic civilization had learned and appropriated many disciplines from those peoples who the early armies had conquered—science and philosophy were learned from the Greeks, statecraft from the Persians, and so on.[20] Moreover, it would be naive to understand borrowing and exchange with other traditions as a one-way process. Throughout history, there have been many occasions in which Islam has inspired developments in Christianity, Judaism, Zoroastrianism, Hinduism, and other faiths. For example, the unexpected burst of Arab conquerors from the desert who announced themselves as abiding by the new monotheistic faith of Islam, forced the older faith traditions to sharpen and rearticulate the boundaries of their faiths in increasingly distinct ways.[21]

Finally, the borrowing that occurs between traditions is not without its own creative impetus—concepts, ideas, institutions, and practices are not simply taken as is and integrated into the host tradition. Rather, they are modified to suit the spirit of the host tradition and the culture in which it is housed. Thus, the pre-Islamic pagan practice of pilgrimage to the Ka'ba was modified and given a distinctive flavor in the Islamic reconfiguration of this ritual. Similarly, although pre-Islamic art and architecture informed the development of Islamic artistic conceptions, a distinct Islamic flavor colored these reworkings, and it gave birth to a decidedly Islamic artifact—the mosque.[22]

TIMELINE

570 CE:	Muhammad is born in Mecca.
610:	Muhammad receives the first revelation.
622:	Muhammad and his followers migrate to Medina following persecution in Mecca.
630:	Muhammad and his followers conquer Mecca, whose inhabitants then embrace Islam.
632:	Muhammad dies.
632–661:	The four Righteous Caliphs rule the rapidly expanding Muslim empire.
661–750:	Rule of the Umayyad Dynasty.
750–1258:	Rule of the 'Abbasid Dynasty.
909–1171:	Rule of the Fatimid Dynasty in Egypt.
1380–1918:	Turkish Ottoman Empire.
1501–1722:	Rule of Safavid Dynasty in Iran.
1526–1857:	Mughal Dynasty rules in India.
1800s–1900s:	European colonization of North Africa, the Middle East and South Asia.
1900s:	End of colonial rule in North Africa, the Middle East and South Asia. The formation of Muslim nation-states.

ELITE AND POPULAR ISLAM: INSTITUTIONS, KNOWLEDGE SYSTEMS, AND INDIVIDUALS

As detailed above, the development of Islam was a gradual process that took place over a large geographical expanse. In each region, Islam developed in conversation with local traditions and cultures. Concurrent with the formation of Islam was the protracted process of conversion of the inhabitants of the conquered lands. Consequently, different formulations of Islam entered into the daily lives of individuals through a variety of ways.

The permutations of Islam in the various regions of the Near East were not always greeted with open arms by the Muslim scholarly elite—the *ulama*. In the pre-modern period, the *ulama* were not an exclusive group. Generally, the *ulama* included scholars who had undergone thorough training in fields such as the science of Islamic jurisprudence, theology, Qur'anic exegesis, and *hadith* literature. For the *ulama*, jurisprudence was the centerpiece of religious learning and a written canon was soon compiled and utilized in the training of budding scholars.[23] Given their rigorous scholarly training, the *ulama* were cautious of diversity and emphasized the maintenance of the contours of the Islamic tradition. Thus, discussions about Islam often bifurcate the religion into the two distinct forms in which the faith manifested itself: elite Islam and popular Islam. Islam and religious authority entered the lives of Muslims through engagement with the institutions, knowledge systems, and individuals who represented either one or both of these two formulations.

On the one hand, the adjective *popular* is apt for all forms of Islam in that (1) religion impacts social life and shapes the identity of the population and (2) religion permeates daily life and serves as a resource in times of crisis.[24] However, the term *popular Islam* has a distinct meaning and refers to those religious beliefs and practices that are different from, and possibly even in opposition to, the elite Islam defined by the scholars, jurists, and respected mystics. Consequently, popular Islam is understood to be a permutation of Islam that is shaped by the priorities and concerns of the masses.[25] In addition, the term *popular Islam* often serves as an index for the assertion of authority by raising questions about orthodoxy, legitimacy, and authenticity.

In opposition to popular Islam, elite Islam was, and continues to be, defined by an emphasis on aspects such as the legal dimension of Islam, Qur'anic exegesis, the study of *hadith*, and accepted forms of mysticism (Sufism). Elite Islam's focus on the juridical dimensions of the faith results from the influence of other Near Eastern religious traditions. It is widely accepted that the Jewish legal model that developed in rabbinical academies in Iraq in the period just following the Muslim conquests influenced the development of Islamic law, especially because many Muslim jurists lived in Iraq.[26]

The elite scholarly tradition of Islam thrived, and continues to flourish, in urban centers. Because this tradition housed itself in cities, and currently defines the urban religious landscape of the Near East, Islamic doctrines and practices permeate into the lives of city dwellers either by their participation in or association with this tradition—especially its figures of authority and its institutions.

There was no institutional structure for the transmission of religious knowledge at the inception of Islam. Scholars who study this period conjecture that mosques served as the loci of congregation and intellectual discussions.[27] This role of the mosque as the center for religious learning continues to this day. Following historical precedent, both formal and semiformal study circles still form at many mosques in the Middle East. In West Africa today, the mosque courtyards are often the setting for a Qur'anic school for young children. Similarly, all over the Muslim world, nightly congregations at mosques mark the month of Ramadan as preachers and scholars indulge in public exegesis of the Qur'an and deliver religious instructions to the faithful.[28]

THE MOSQUE

The English word *mosque* refers to the Muslim place of prayer known in Arabic as *masjid*. Translated literally, the word *masjid* means "a place of prostration." Mosques vary in size and grandeur and evidence the artistic and architectural conventions of the time and region in which they were built. Most mosques have a minaret from which the call to prayer (*adhan*) is announced five times a day to summon the believers to worship. Other structures of the mosque include the *minbar* and the *mihrab*. The *minbar* is a pulpit or raised structure from which sermons are preached and announcements are made. The *mihrab* is a semicircular niche in the center of the wall that faces the *qibla,* that is, the direction of prayer. Facilities for ablution (*wudu'*) are usually part of the mosque structure.

Mosques serve many religious and social functions. 'Id prayers, prayers to beseech for rain, and prayers during solar and lunar eclipses, among others, are also performed at mosques, besides the five daily prayers. Moreover, during Ramadan, some mosques collect and distribute charity. Mosques also serve as centers of religious education. More recently, a number of mosques have taken on political roles.

Today, in addition to the mosque, there exist specific institutions devoted to learning known as *madrasas*. More so than the mosque, the *madrasa* characterizes the scholarly tradition of Islam. Some scholars situate the advent of the *madrasa* in Khurasan, in Eastern Iran; others cite the Nizamiyyah *madrasa*—built in Baghdad in the late eleventh century by Nizam al-Mulk (d. 1092), the Persian vizier to the Seljuk Dynasty—as being the first of its kind.[29] Within a few centuries following its inception, the *madrasa* became a typical feature of the urban landscape of the Middle East and Muslim North Africa. In fact, the proliferation of *madrasas* is understood to be one of the defining features of religious life in the medieval Muslim world. Among the most famous *madrasas* of the Muslim world is al-Azhar in Cairo, Egypt. Established initially as a mosque in the ninth century during the reign of the Fatimid Dynasty, al-Azhar soon became a thriving center of learning because of its geographical position and political unfoldings. The fall of Baghdad in 1258 made al-Azhar increasingly prominent among intellectual circles. From the eighteenth century onward, the organization of al-Azhar was consolidated and the institute came to be understood as "the principal religious university of the Islamic world."[30]

Individuals who graduated from al-Azhar and other smaller *madrasas* were held in high religious esteem and were considered the authorities on Islam. In the medieval period, they engaged with the public in a variety of ways: by delivering sermons to the masses at mosques, by issuing juridical pronouncements, and by making public statements. Through these means, the scholarly elite tradition of Islam permeated the lives of ordinary Muslims. This public role of the 'ulama continues to this day as this scholarly elite propagates religious doctrines to the masses through new modes of technology such as television broadcasts and the Internet. In Egypt, cassette sermons have become a common device by which 'ulama reach out to the public. Similarly, in Yemen some 'ulama now deliver their juridical pronouncements over the radio.

Despite the reverence accorded to the 'ulama even in the contemporary period, institutions and structures of knowledge associated with these scholars are under threat. In the modern Muslim world the madrasa is being increasingly marginalized by secular institutions of learning, and the brightest among the students often opt for more lucrative secular professions, instead of devoting themselves to religious causes. However, the modern period has witnessed the rise of a religious elite that in some ways is more diverse but in other ways is more systematized and regulated than its medieval counterpart. For example, ever since the time of the Ottoman Empire, the 'ulama have been inscribed into precisely defined ranks and employed by the state. This process of regularization of the 'ulama continues to this day.[31] On the other hand, in the contemporary period attitudes toward female religious competence have changed and women are increasingly allowed to participate in the elite scholarly tradition. For example, in 2007, Morocco officially appointed 50 female preachers to mosques in various provinces.[32]

The Moroccan example evidences larger transitions in the scholarly tradition of Islam. In the modern period, the rise of the printing press and the jump in literacy rates has shifted engagements with knowledge and debates over intellectual authority to a different playing field. Additionally, over the past three centuries madrasas have undergone substantial shifts. Colonialism and globalization have made education in madrasas a systematic process: curricula have been set, examinations have been implemented, and a complicated system of degrees and awards has been established. For example, the Egyptian government was strict in imposing reforms at al-Azhar. A governmental decree passed in 1872 instituted a diploma at the end of the course of a student's study. It further legislated that only six students a year could sit for a long and excruciating exam focusing on 11 different subjects. Success granted them the title of alim, assured them of material success, and allowed them to teach at al-Azhar.[33]

Historically, the 'ulama's focus on jurisprudence and the intricacies of theological issues, has held little appeal for the masses. After all, in the medieval period, 98 to 99 percent of Muslims were illiterate, and the majority of them lived in rural areas where scholars and institutions associated with the elite scholarly tradition hardly ever ventured.[34] Given this inaccessibility of the elite scholarly tradition, a parallel mystical tradition of Islam soon emerged. This mystical tradition, known as Sufism, appeared in the eighth and ninth centuries in regions such as northern Mesopotamia, Syria, and southeastern Anatolia. The distance of these regions from the larger metropolises of Baghdad and Damascus allowed for figures such as 'Abdallah ibn al-Mubarak (d. 797) and Ibrahim ibn Adham (d. 777) to forge a distinctive Islamic ascetic tradition that eventually took on a mystical dimension and evolved into the movement that came to be known as Sufism.[35]

A good representative of early Sufism is the mystic Ibn al-'Arabi, popularly known as al-Shaykh al-Akbar, that is, the Great Shaykh. Born in Murcia in 1165, Ibn al-'Arabi emphasized the personal nature of his religious experience. He described the spiritual seeker as a traveler on a journey, writing that the traveler must observe four conditions: (1) silence, (2) withdrawal from society, (3) hunger, and (4) wakefulness and/or alertness. When sincere intentions were coupled with the observance of these conditions, there would be awakened in the spiritual traveler's heart a love (*mahabba*), which would grow into a passion (*'ishk*). This passion would transport the traveler to God, and unison with the divine (the ultimate goal of Sufism) would be achieved.[36]

With figures such as Ibn al-'Arabi providing impetus to the movement, within a short period of time, the Sufi ethos came to infuse the entire fabric of popular religious life in medieval Muslim lands. This tradition unabashedly drew inspiration from Jewish, Gnostic, Christian, Hindu, and animist sources, while simultaneously engaging with the learning of the *'ulama*. The engagement between the *'ulama* and the Sufis was a two-way process, since the *'ulama* were often drawn to the charisma and lore of the "holy men" (*salahun*). The appeal of Sufism was so great that the majority of scholars agree that it was through Sufism, and not the elite scholarly tradition (with its focus on the Shari'a), that Islam spread across sub-Saharan Africa, Central Asia, India, and Indonesia.[37]

Although popular Islam and Sufism are not direct equivalents, the two are very closely intertwined.[38] Sufism is often characterized by a folk piety that adapts itself to local circumstances. This formulation of Islam was, and continues to be, considered dangerous by the *'ulama* because of its ability to shape the contours of the tradition and to define Islam in a manner oppositional to that of the scholarly elite. Moreover, many Sufi adherents undermined the importance of the Shari'a and in doing so challenged the authority of the *'ulama* because these scholars' authority is intimately tied to the authority of the Shari'a.[39] The less rigorous and less disciplined path available to Sufi practitioners also opened doors to mystical ecstasy by accepting the use of chemical stimulants, charms, magic, and other practices frowned upon by the scholarly elite.[40] Opposition to such practices, the lack of emphasis on the juridical dimension of Islam, and the acceptance of doctrines and rituals considered questionable by the scholars were expressed by the *'ulama* in the language of "innovation" (*bid'a*). Deviant practices and beliefs were labeled as *bid'a*—that is, something for which there existed no precedent in the practices of the Prophet and his revered companions. Many medieval scholars such as Ibn Taymiyya (d. 1328) and Ibn al-Hajj (d. 1336) critiqued the practice of popular Islam and considered it a threat to the religion. Over time, a tirade against popular religion became an integral part of medieval Islamic scholarly discourse. The language of innovation (*bid'a*) and acceptable practice (*sunna*) can be traced back to the early scholars of Islam, whose clearly articulated and nuanced discourses distinguished between acceptable and praiseworthy innovations and reprehensible ones.[41] These distinctions continue to provide the framework for analysis for many Muslim scholars to this day.

Sufism and popular religion entered the lives of Muslim practitioners in a variety of ways. Initially, Sufism, like the transmission of juristic knowledge, flourished without any institutional structure. Later, Sufism was characterized by the emergence of institutions such as *khanqahs, ribats,* and *zawiyas.* Although the specific meanings of these terms vary according to the location and time period, all three terms can roughly be translated to mean Sufi lodges or Sufi hospices. These lodges and hospices came complete with buildings and endowments, and they housed and supported mystics and ascetics. Such structures are thought to reflect the effect of Iranian civilization on the Islamic polity, because the roots of these institutions lie in ninth- and tenth-century Iran.[42]

All over the Near East, but especially in Egypt and Syria, *zawiyas* flourished both in urban and rural areas. In rural areas, the heads of *zawiyas* often mediated in local factional disputes or disagreements between tribes and the political authorities. The proliferation of *zawiyas* in Libya and the eastern Sahara in the nineteenth century led to each tribe identifying with a particular *zawiya.* Similarly, in the sixteenth and seventeenth centuries, during periods of weak authority of Moroccan rulers, *zawiyas,* such as the Nasiriyya one in Tamgrut, were local centers of power, functioning almost as antonymous principalities. Some *zawiyas* sought to supplant central governments, whereas others such as those under the Husaynid Beys in nineteenth-century Tunisia received government support and patronage. State support for *zawiyas* can be traced back to a much earlier period in Islamic history. In Morocco *zawiyas* were introduced under the Marinid Dynasty (1217–1465). One of the largest and most elaborate *zawiyas* in Morocco is the complex built in Marrakesh in the sixteenth century CE for the *shaykh* Djazuli (d. 1465). The Moroccan ruler of the time was the patron of this complex. The *zawiya* includes a mosque, the tomb of *shaykh* Djazuli, a cemetery for his followers, a hospice for pilgrims and individuals who revered the *shaykh*, a school, a residence for the superintendent, ablution facilities, and a bath.[43]

Of course, not all *zawiyas* were as lavish as that of *shaykh* Djazuli of Morocco. *Zawiyas* varied in size and most amounted to small mosques or hospices associated with local *shaykhs*. The majority of rural *shaykhs* lacked the rigorous scholarly training of the *ulama* and the figure of the unlettered *shaykh* (*shaykh ummi*) is characteristic of the medieval period. *Shaykhs* were intimately tied to the communities in which they lived. In these communities they served as immediate local religious resource to the masses. Sometimes, these *shaykhs* were even financed by local donations. In serving their community, *shaykhs* led prayers, facilitated religious education, delivered sermons, and performed *dhikr*, that is, the ritual of repeatedly reciting the names of God while practicing rhythmic breathing and bodily motions such as turning from side to side. Sufi *shaykhs* were not the only religious authorities who posed a threat to the *ulama*: popular preachers and storytellers who lacked the rigorous scholarly religious training that characterized the *ulama* were also common figures in the medieval Islamic era. Similarly, in thirteenth- and fourteenth-century Damascus, marginal holy men known as the *muwallahun* held great sway over the majority of the population.[44] These local and more immediately accessible figures who configured Islam in a manner that rendered it palatable to the population were held in high religious esteem by the masses. However, the *ulama* questioned the character and training of these figures and competed with them for religious authority. For example, the *ulama* criticized storytellers and preachers for transmitting *hadith* that they had not learned through the personal authority of a religious scholar.[45] In the medieval period, female preachers were also critiqued and viewed as a danger to the authority of the patriarchal scholarly tradition.[46]

Another defining feature of the religious experience of the masses in the medieval period was the focus on particular individuals celebrated for their saintly character and learning. This eventually led to the establishment of rituals such as pilgrimage to the gravesides of these revered figures and yearly celebrations of the death anniversaries of these saints. This emphasis on, and reverence of, saintly figures continues to thrive till this day. Practices associated with saint reverence are discussed in detail later in this chapter, in the section titled "*Mawlids*."

Another historical characteristic of the religious practices and expectations of the Muslim populace was an unabashed attitude toward syncretism and borrowing. At the grassroots level, where members of different religious traditions intermingled without the supervision of the 'ulama, many Muslims blurred the boundaries between their practices and those of members of other faith traditions. The medieval period of Islamic history is peppered with reports of Muslims sharing in the religious festivities and celebrations of their Jewish and Christian neighbors. Muslim scholars inveighed against such practices, and the works of jurists such as Ibn Taymiyya (d. 1328) and Ibn al-Hajj (d. 1336) evidence their criticism against Muslims who participated in Christian festivals such as Palm Sunday or Easter, or imitated the Jewish practice of keeping the Sabbath by resting on Fridays.[47] Similarly, Abu Bakr al-Turtushi (d. 1126), a Spanish Muslim who settled in Egypt, wrote a treatise condemning "innovations," such as chanting the Qur'an in a manner that imitates Christian practices, or decorating mosques so that they resemble churches and synagogues.[48]

Although the aforementioned scholarly critique of Sufism and popular religion makes it appear that the scholarly and popular traditions of Islam were diametrically opposed, such was not always the case. In fact, in the medieval period, in urban centers, Sufism and elite juristic modes of Islam became increasingly intertwined. Many medieval Muslim scholars were identified simultaneously as jurists and mystics. And it was occasionally difficult to distinguish madrasas from zawiyas because both institutions were serving similar functions and imparting similar types of knowledge.[49] Moreover, during this time, various Sufi groups came to coalesce into specific turuq (the plural of tariqa), that is, the ways and paths that mystics followed in their spiritual journeys. Typically, a tariqa was an order of mystics who traced their spiritual genealogy back to a revered figure (a shaykh), and through him back to his spiritual masters and eventually to the Prophet Muhammad.[50] The turuq reflected the existence of contrary religious pressures. On the one hand, there was a desire to centralize authority and keep it confined to specific individuals and institutions; on the other, there was a move to infuse authority among the broader population.[51]

A good example of a popular mystical tariqa is the Naqshbandiyya order of Persia, founded in the fourteenth century by Baha' al-Din Naqshband. The cause of the Naqshbandiyya tariqa was taken up by 'Ubayd Allah Ahrar (d. 1490), who spread the tariqa to most regions of Transoxiana. During this time the influence of the tariqa also spread southward to Herat, in present-day Afghanistan. In Herat and Transoxiana the Naqshbandiyya has become permanent, but it lost most of its following in Persia soon after its inception. The Naqshbandiyya also figures prominently in contemporary Turkey.[52] In contrast to other turuq, the Naqshbandiyya tariqa emphasizes the practice of silent dhikr.

In the medieval period, the increasing popularity of the *turuq* brought under the fold of Sufism many individuals who were otherwise only tangentially involved in mystic discipline. Moreover, the routinization of the *turuq* gave Sufism a catholic appeal in the medieval Islamic world.[53] This mass appeal of Sufism evidences itself in the Middle East and North Africa to this day. For example, the Moroccan Jazuliyya order, which thrived in the early modern period, influenced Sufi practices and doctrines as far away as South Asia. Similarly, the eighteenth-century Moroccan order known as the Tijaniyya is prominent in West and North Africa today and is becoming increasingly visible in Europe. As in the medieval period, even individuals who do not associate themselves explicitly with any of these orders continue to share in the festivities and celebrations that are held to honor the great figures of these traditions. These practices are discussed in more detail in the "*Mawlids*" section of this chapter.

As already stated, the elite scholarly tradition emphasized the strict delineation of the contours of Islam. This scholarly tradition was marked by an emphasis on jurisprudence, theology, Qur'anic exegesis, discussions on *hadith*, and the acceptance of certain austere forms of mysticism. However, the hierarchical nature of knowledge transmission and the specificities of the knowledge being discussed by the scholars were not part of the daily religious experience of the masses. Although the elite formulation of Islam and the individuals and institutions associated with it (i.e., the *'ulama* and the *madrasas*) defined the urban Muslim landscape, the situation in the rural regions was very different. In fact, even in the urban centers, mystical and popular formulations of Islam posed a considerable challenge to elite articulations of the religion. The same is true for formulations of Islam in the contemporary period. The *'ulama* continue to rail against the "innovations" of the populace and decry their practices and doctrines as deviations from the true faith. However, such local expressions of Islam and the figures and institutions associated with them continue to hold sway over much of the contemporary Muslim population because of the immediacy of access and the ease of relatability and comprehension.

In the medieval period, Sufism and popular Islam were defined by the local contexts in which they operated—the same can be said for how Islam is defined today. This is because at the grassroots level, the masses have the ability to influence what is considered Islamic. Popular opinion's ability to shape formulations of Islam is evident in an anecdote cited by the fifteenth-century scholar al-Suyuti. In a treatise condemning popular preaching and religious storytelling, al-Suyuti narrates his encounter with one particular popular storyteller. The storyteller had been narrating fabricated *hadith*, and al-Suyuti confronted him, stating that untrained storytellers must confirm the authenticity of *hadiths* with reputable scholars such as al-Suyuti. Fuming, the storyteller spitted out, "You expect the likes of me to verify my *hadith* with the scholars. Rather, I will verify them with the people!" He then spurred his audience against al-Suyuti, until the mass of listeners threatened to stone the scholar.[54]

This ability of the masses to influence Islam was not limited to the popular formulations of Islam; it manifested itself also in its interactions with the scholarly tradition. For example, custom and customary understandings of law (*'urf*), although not one of the formal sources of law in classical Islam, had gained almost formal recognition by the sixteenth century. The sixteenth-century scholar Zayn al-'Abidin ibn Nudjaym (d. 1563) writes, "Know that custom and usage are so frequently taken into consideration in the law that they [the jurists] have made it a formal source." Moreover, from the sixteenth century onward, legal literature came to contain special chapters on custom. This tradition has continued to this day and contemporary Muslim jurists who write books on law generally devote a chapter to custom, in addition to penning sections on classical sources. The emphasis on writings on custom implies the jurists' acceptance of custom as a source of law.[55]

TEMPORALITY AND CELEBRATIONS

Having discussed the spread of Islam, the multiple forms in which the religion evidenced itself, and the individuals and institutions associated with these formulations, let us now look at some of the concrete ways in which Islam impacted and regulated the lives of Muslims. The daily life of an individual involves a plethora of practices—for example, the performance of daily or weekly rituals such as prayer and fasting; attitudes toward purity and cleanliness; the intricacies of domestic architecture; food and drink; attitudes toward clothing, ornaments, and beauty; relations between different classes of individuals, men and women, merchants and slaves, the religious elite and the political elite, and husbands and wives; the world of women; and the nuclear family. It would be impossible to discuss all of these issues, but this chapter will touch on a few of these topics to give readers an idea of the manner in which religion came to inform the lives of Muslims in the Middle East and North Africa.

However, before launching into a discussion on how Islam regulated and affected the daily lives of its practitioners, the reader is again reminded that not everything Islam introduced into the lives of Muslims involved a break from past traditions. Islam not only generated new customs, rituals, events, and celebrations but also gave a specific flavor to events and celebrations that had already existed in individuals' lives. Thus, rites of passage such as birth, marriage, and death came to be understood through a religious framework.

Let us begin our examination by looking at the new practices and celebrations introduced by Islam and then turn our focus to how Islam changed the understandings of its followers regarding preexisting customs and rites.

Arguably, the most significant influence of Islam on the daily lives of Muslims was the religion's impact on individuals' temporal configurations. With the spread of Islam, the lunar Muslim calendar was adopted in the Muslim Middle East and North Africa. The adoption of this method of temporal ordering went hand in hand with the organization of life according to the festivals and events that marked this calendar. These included celebrations of events and individuals who figured prominently in Islam's sacred history. Although the Qur'an does not use the term 'id (holiday), this term began to be utilized to mark two specific feast days: the feast marking the end of Ramadan ('Id al-Fitr) and the feast of sacrifice marking the end of the rites of pilgrimage ('Id al-Adha). Other celebrations were soon added to the religious calendar, including the commemoration of Muhammad's birthday, the celebration of the death anniversaries of saints, the commemoration of the martyrdom of Husayn, Muhammad's grandson, to name just a few.

Prayer

The reordering of temporality that was characteristic of Islam made its effect obvious on a very immediate level with the adoption of the five daily prayers. The ritual of five daily prayers was instituted during the middle of Muhammad's prophecy. Its specificities developed partly as a reaction to increased hostility by Medinan Jews toward Muhammad. As a consequence of the Jews' antagonistic and disparaging attitude toward Muslims, the qibla (the direction faced by Muslims during the formal prayer) was changed from Jerusalem to Mecca, midway during Muhammad's prophecy.[56]

In fulfilling their religious obligation to pray five times a day while facing Mecca, Muslims must to wake up at dawn to perform the early morning prayer, and throughout the day, Muslims are expected to be conscious of performing their prayers at the appointed times. During Muhammad's prophecy, the Friday afternoon prayer (salat al-jum'a) was designated as the weekly congregational prayer, and Muslims continue to observe this practice to this day. In fact, it is considered obligatory for every free male Muslim adult to perform the Friday afternoon prayer in congregation at a mosque. The act of praying in congregation is not limited to Friday afternoons; from the beginnings of Islam until today the more religious minded among the population frequent mosques to partake in congregational prayers on a daily basis. This impetus for mosque visitation comes from the understanding that communal prayers at mosques are designated as 25 times more meritorious than solitary prayers.[57] Thus mosques, from the medieval period until today, serve as important institutions for public worship and as structures for maintaining the cohesiveness of the community.

Ablution

The institutionalization of the ritual of prayer also led to changes in attitudes toward cleanliness and purity. The Jewish obligation to purify oneself before worship was institutionalized in a modified manner by Islam. Because prayer was considered impermissible without performing the ritual ablution (*wudu'*), Muslims began to enact this ritual cleaning as an integral part of their daily routine. *Wudu'* entails the washing of the hands, arms, feet, and face of with clean water. The washing must be performed in the systematic order adopted by Muhammad. In case water is not available, it is acceptable to perform dry ablution (*tayammum*), which is performed by rubbing the hands and face with sand. A more thorough ablution, known as *ghusl*, becomes obligatory after indulging in sexual and intimate acts, after the emission of sperm, after the end of a menstrual cycle, and in the period following childbirth. *Ghusl* entails the uninterrupted washing of the whole body, including the hair. These particular practices of ablution and prayer form an integral part of the daily lives of Muslims to this day.

Ramadan, 'Ashura', and 'Id al-Fitr

The temporal regulation of Muslim life as a result of religious obligations was, and continues to be, especially apparent during the month of Ramadan. The lunar month of Ramadan, as discussed briefly in the first section of this chapter, is designated as the month for fasting. The Qur'an states, "Fasting is prescribed for you as it was for those before you, that you may learn piety." (Qur'an 2:183) Before the institutionalization of fasting during Ramadan, Muslims, emulating the Jews, observed the fast of 'Ashura'. The word 'Ashura' is an adaptation of the Hebrew 'asho-r, with the Aramaic determinative ending: a. 'Ashura' marks the day on which God rescued Moses and his followers from the Egyptian pharaoh. The 10th day of the Islamic lunar month of Muharram is mentioned in early sources as the day of 'Ashura'. It is conjectured that the 10th day of the first Muslim month was chosen as 'Ashura' to harmonize with the 10th day of the first Jewish month. Possibly in an attempt to distinguish themselves from the Jews, some Muslims deem the 9th day of Muharram, either along with or in place of the 10th, as a day of fasting.

After fasting in the month of Ramadan was made obligatory, the fast of 'Ashura' was deemed optional. However, devout Sunni Muslim still fast on this day, and the door of the Ka'ba is open on 'Ashura' for visitors.[58] 'Ashura' has special significance among Shi'ite Muslims - they commemorate the day with a variety of rituals.

During the month of Ramadan, Muslims refrain from eating, drinking, and engaging in sexual intercourse from dawn until sunset. After sunset all these activities are permitted. Many Muslims also observe extra prayers at night (*salat al-tarawih*) and other forms of religious devotions such as Sufi *dhikr* and folk dancing during this month. The breaking of the fast at sunset is often a time for communal celebration and feasting. However, the real feast is at the end of the month. Ramadan culminates with the celebration of the religious holiday of 'Id al-Fitr, an event marked by the donning of fine clothes and the visiting of family and friends.

SHI'ITE COMMEMORATIONS OF 'ASHURA'

'Ashura' has a different significance for Sunnis and Shi'ites. Shi'ite Muslims celebrate the 9th day of Muharram as the day of fasting, and for them the 10th day of Muharram ('Ashura') is regarded as a day of deep mourning. For Shi'ites, 'Ashura' marks the anniversary of the day on which the Prophet's grandson, Husayn, fell fighting against the armies of the caliph Yazid bin Mu'awiya at the battlefield of Karbala in 680 CE. Shi'ites commemorate the day by pilgrimaging to sacred sites, especially Karbala. On 'Ashura', many wear mourning attire, listen to elegies, and refrain from celebrating joyous events such as weddings. The ritual of passion play (*ta'ziya*) reenacting the death of Husayn is widespread.

Ta'ziya as a form of ritual theater emerged in the eighteenth century, with the fusion of ambulatory and stationary rites. Initially, *ta'ziya* plays were performed at town squares and marketplaces; later, at inns and private establishments. Finally, special structures called *takiyas* (or Husayniyyas) were built for the performances. These structures were paid for either by local citizens or by wealthy benefactors. The size and grandeur of the *takiyas* varied: some could seat thousands, others could only accommodate a handful of people. Many *takiyas* were temporary, erected only for the Muharram commemorations and dismantled after the 40th-day observances for the dead were completed.

Takiya Dawlat, the Royal Theatre in Tehran, was the most famous *ta'ziya* theater. It was built in the 1870s by Nasir al-Din Shah. Unfortunately, the building's structure was weak and the entire edifice had to be torn down in 1946.[59]

Hajj, 'Id al-Adha, and Animal Sacrifice

The other major yearly festival in the Muslim calendar is the feast of sacrifice ('Id al-Adha). The holiday marks the celebration of the pilgrimage to Mecca (*hajj*). Muslims the world over celebrate this feast in unison with the pilgrims in Mecca. The *hajj*, as briefly discussed earlier, is a religious obligation on all Muslims who can afford the journey to the birthplace of Islam. *Hajj* takes place once every lunar year, and it involves rites such as circumambulating the Ka'ba (the shrine built by Abraham), running between the mounds of Safa and Marwa, stoning pillars representing Satan, holding a daylong vigil at the plain of 'Arafa, and sacrificing an animal. The performance of the *hajj* includes regulations on sexual activity and permissible garments, among others. As mentioned earlier, many of the rituals involved in the *hajj* bear traces of the pre-Islamic pagan pilgrimage to the same site.

One of these pre-Islamic rituals that now constitutes an integral part of the *hajj* is the old Arab custom of offering an animal in sacrifice. Islam modified this custom to make animal sacrifice on 'Id day obligatory not only for pilgrims but for all free adult Muslims who can afford the act. Sheep or goats (one for each person), or camels and cattle (one for ten people according to some schools of thought) are sacrificed. The animals must be of a certain age and free from defects. A number of practices are recommended for the sacrificers: (1) starting the act with the *tasmiya*, that is, the utterance "In the name of God, Most Beneficent, Most Merciful"; (2) voicing blessings on the Prophet; (3) turning toward the *qibla*; (4) uttering "God is Great" thrice before and thrice after the *tasmiya*; and (5) requesting God to accept the sacrifice. If the sacrifice is offered on account of a vow, all the meat must be given away for pious purposes. If the sacrificer performed the animal offering freely, as is usually the case, he may keep up to one-third of the meat, but must distribute the rest among the needy and deserving.[60] A saying in the Muslim world celebrating the charity of 'Id al-Adha declares that as a result of the meat distribution on this day, poor Muslims get to taste meat at least once a year.

Mawlids

In addition to these two 'Id celebrations, the celebration of Muhammad's birthday and the days that mark the deaths of saints are also occasions of festivity. The term used to describe these events is *mawlid*, which literally means birthday but in most cases is used to denote the death anniversary of a saint. The celebration of *mawlids* began around the twelfth century in Egypt, under the Shi'ite Fatimid Dynasty, when the rulers officially celebrated the birthday of the Prophet (*mawlid al-nabi*) during daytime. In contrast, the modern *mawlid* celebrations are marked by a nocturnal carnival.

The adoption of the *mawlid* celebration by the majority Sunni sect is traced back to the celebration held in 1207 in Ibril, in modern-day Iraq. The celebration, influenced by Christian rites, was arranged by Muzaffar al-din Kokbori, a brother-in-law of Saladin. With the proliferation of Sufism in Egypt under the Sunni 'Ayyubid Dynasty (1171–1250), *mawlid* celebrations became the norm and expanded to the rest of the Muslim world. During this period *mawlid* came to be celebrated in Muslim Spain and northern Morocco as a way of countering the Christian influence. *Mawlid* celebrations of that era were sponsored by the political elite and attended by prominent government officials. This practice of state sponsorship of the *mawlid* continues in many Muslim countries to this day.

In addition to celebrating the birth of Muhammad, the death anniversaries of local saints (*awliya*) were also days of festivity in the medieval period. Lavish public festivals and visitations to the shrines of the dead saints often marked such days. For example, the popular Sufi order of Ahmad al-Badawi (d. 1276) attracted visitors from all over the Nile Delta to the shrine of al-Badawi in the Egyptian city of Tanta on the day of the *mawlid* of the great saint.[61] This visitation of shrines was a practice common not only to Muslims but also to Near Eastern Jews and Christians. The shrines of pious individuals were understood as spiritual centers where the body of the saint lay in a state of constant connection with God. Saints were perceived as intermediaries between the masses and God, and the populace began visiting their graves seeking blessings (*baraka*) and divine intercession and appealing for solutions to problems. The devotees of certain saints even claimed that the visitation of saints' tombs could replace the religious obligation to visit Mecca.

Upon arriving at these saints' shrines, visitors circumambulated the tombs, muttering prayers and vowing to make animal sacrifices and food donations to the needy in the event that their prayers were answered. Visits to tombs were often accompanied by the performance of *dhikr*. The very public nature of such celebrations drew in Muslims from all walks of life and introduced marginally practicing Muslims to the experiential dimensions and mystical traditions of Islam as evidenced in the Sufi practices of *dhikr*, dancing, and singing. Moreover, such festivals familiarized Muslims with local institutions and figures of religious authority.[62]

This practice of shrine visitation, especially at the time of the *mawlid* of the saint, continues in virtually all parts of the Muslim world to this day. In modern-day Egypt, *mawlid* celebrations extend for weeks. During this period people camp outside shrines for weeks as different smaller celebrations lead up to the carnival on the night of the *mawlid*. As in the medieval era, in the modern period many Muslim scholars of a puritanical bend have critiqued this popular practice of visiting shrines and seeking intercession from saints: like their medieval counterparts, modern puritans emphasize the innovated nature of such practices and label them un-Islamic and idolatrous. However, Shi'ites consider visitation of the tombs of imams much less controversial than do Sunnis.[63] Despite the critique of these practices, they continue to be an integral part of the religious experiences of many Sunnis and Shi'ites today.

RITES OF PASSAGE: BIRTHS AND DEATHS

In addition to introducing new rituals, celebrations, and methods of temporal ordering, Islam also reconfigured earlier ritual practices and modes of celebrations. The life of any individual is marked by many important events, including birth, the onset of puberty, engagement, marriage, motherhood, the loss of one's parents, and one's own death. Because of space constraints, this chapter will examine only two of these events: birth and death.

Birth

With the onset of Islam, births came to be conceptualized and celebrated in specific ways. For example, the Prophet's practice (*sunna*) of reciting the call to prayer in the newborn infant's right ear was adopted. Similarly, *'aqiqa*, the pre-Islamic custom of shaving the infant's head within a few days of its birth, became integrated into certain formulations of Islam and spread across the Middle East and North Africa. The same is true for the ritual of sacrificing a sheep or distributing alms to the poor (if one's finances permit) as an act of thankfulness to God on the occasion of a birth in the family. Male circumcision (*khitan*) was a common practice in pre-Islamic Arabia—Islam came to designate this as a religious obligation and the practice spread throughout the Muslim world. In some places, the ritual of female circumcision also became common.

Death

Conversion to Islam led to a change in attitudes and practices toward death. Islamic law lays down regulations about the handling of the body of a deceased individual and specifies that the dead should be buried. Islamic burial rites (*jana'iz*) have four distinct features: (1) specific procedures for washing the body, (2) shrouding or wrapping the body in cloth, (3) funeral prayers, and (4) prompt burial, with the deceased laid in the grave on his or her right side, facing the Ka'ba. It is recommended that the person closest to the deceased should wash the body. For example, Muhammad's body was washed by his son-in-law and cousin, Ali. The body of Fatima, the daughter of Muhammad, was washed also by Ali, her husband. The place where the body is washed should be private and secluded. As part of the washing, the ritual ablution (*wudu'*) should be performed on the deceased's body. The body should then be covered in a perfumed white shroud. No more than three pieces of shroud should be used for males (Muhammad's body was wrapped in three shrouds), and no more than five for females.

There are also directives about the manner in which mourners should act at the cemetery and about the specific funeral prayers that are to be performed by the living for the deceased before the burial. The deceased should be placed in front of the congregation and the prayer leader. Following the prayer, the body of the deceased should be carried to the graveyard and buried. It is recommended to raise the grave a little above the ground so that it can be recognized. It is part of the tradition to bury the deceased within 24 hours of death. These specific practices continue to be followed by Muslims today when their loved ones pass away.

Moving past temporality, let us shift our discussion to two other integral aspects of the daily lives of Muslims: dress and food and drink.

DRESS

According to a frequently quoted *hadith*, Muhammad forbade men (not women) from seven things: silver vessels; gold rings; silk garments; brocade; satin; *kassi* (a striped fabric from Egypt containing silk); and tanned hides. Other writings in traditional literature add much more detail to this list and specify the exact types of fabrics and garments that are considered impermissible. Although the early Muslims observed these austere regulations, Muhammad's recommendations in terms of dress were soon abandoned with the rise of the Islamic empire. With an increase in the wealth of the empire and its rulers, there emerged a whole corpus of counter-*hadith* testifying to the permissibility of wearing luxurious garments. The Umayyad caliphs were famous for the sumptuousness of their garments, and members of the Fatimid Dynasty in Egypt exceeded even the Umayyads in all manners of pomp and ceremony as reflected in their attitudes toward dress. The first Fatimid caliph, al-Mu'izz (d. 975) spent tens of thousands of dinars in founding a special government costume supply house. The costume supply house was overseen by an official bureau that ensured that every official and functionary down to governmental clerks was supplied with a ceremonial costume.[64]

During the medieval period, ostentatiousness in dress was the norm even for the middle class. This period was characterized by an emphasis on the turban as the mark of "belonging." A person's turban size corresponded with his status in society, and people wore increasingly elaborate headdresses to distinguish themselves from others. This was specially so for scholars who were occasionally criticized even by their fellow *ulama* for their extravagance in dress. However, the idea of the turban as a mark of religious erudition was so ubiquitous that Chinese Muslim literature in the sixteenth and seventeenth centuries makes frequent reference to encounters with turbaned men from the West as a trope alluding to meetings with erudite Middle Eastern Muslims.

Dress was an important marker of identity in the medieval period, and non-Muslims were often required to dress in a manner that made their religious affiliations explicit. Laws specifying that non-Muslim subjects of the Islamic empire (*dhimmis*) needed to don distinguishing clothing originated during the Umayyad period; however, such legislation was not always implemented or followed. Supporting such legislation, the thirteenth-century scholar Ibn Qayyim al-Jawziyya cites and agrees with the opinion of an earlier scholar, Abu Qasim, that *dhimmis* must not be allowed to wear turbans. For these scholars, the turban was understood as a mark of honor and prestige reserved for Muslims alone. However, documents from the Geniza archives (see sidebar) reveal that this view was not always enforced and members of Jewish communities living in the Middle East occasionally wore elaborate headpieces.

According to the historian Ibn al-Fawati (d. 1323), during the rule of the 'Abbasid caliph al-Muqtadir bi-Amrallah (who reigned in Baghdad from 908 to 932), Christians "had to wear black or grey garments, a special belt around the waist, and a cross on their breast."[65] Similarly, Jewish men were required to wear yellow turbans and a badge, whereas Jewish women were required to wear yellow veils and mismatched shoes—one white and the other black. However, a fourteenth-century Muslim writer, commenting on the status of *dhimmi* women in Egypt, states that the religious affiliations of these women are not apparent in their manner of dress. He writes, "They go into the bazaars and sit in the shops of the merchants, who pay them respect on account of their fine clothes, unaware that they belong to the *dhimmis*."[66] Similarly, documents from the Geniza archives attest that Jewish and Muslim women dressed alike during the Fatimid and Ayyubid periods.[67]

Poetry gives us some insight into the manner of dress of Near Eastern women. Pre-Islamic Arabic poems testify that the practice of veiling was observed before the time of Muhammad. At that time the veil was the prerogative of women of a certain rank. The practice of veiling, regardless of religious orientation, continued in the medieval period. In medieval Cairo, women covered their faces, but left apparent their ornaments. The Spanish poet Judah ha-Levi, who spent a winter in Egypt in 1140–1141, composed the following verses in Hebrew describing the girls on the Nile shores: "For heavy are the bracelets on their arms / And their steps are narrowed by anklets."[68]

The characteristics of female ornamentation described in these verses are still apparent today in parts of the Middle East and North Africa. However, over time, fashions and manners of dress and ornamentation evolve, and with the onset of globalization and the modern era, many of the earlier specifically Middle Eastern forms of dress are being abandoned for those of the West.

Conversely, certain Islamic attitudes toward dress still remain strong. The Islamic emphasis on modesty continues to inform the dressing practices of many Muslims even though the forms and shapes of dresses have changed over the centuries. For example, many young women in Morocco today wear Western-style dresses and skirts with nothing on their head, except possibly sunglasses. In Nigeria, Muslim Hausa women continue to wear their traditional colorful Hausa outfits; non-Muslim Hausa women also wear the same outfits. In the contemporary period, the Kingdom of Saudi Arabia has legislated veiling as mandatory for women, and the showing of any body part other than the face, the hands, and the feet is deemed illegal. In Iran, veiling is also state enforced, although women have more leeway in deciding the color and form of their dress. Even in Middle Eastern and North African countries where clothing regulations are not state enforced, many women continue to wear the veil; and the modern era has been marked by the emergence of several pro-veiling movements. Similarly, the more legal-minded religious men among the population today are careful to observe the religious injunction against wearing silk garments and gold adornments.

In the same vein, customs associated with dress that emerged in Muhammad's era continue to inform the imagination of Muslims today. Many Muslims still follow Muhammad's practice of bestowing felicitations and congratulations on someone wearing a new garment. Similarly, as in Muhammad's time, Muslims continue to make an effort to wear new garments or their best clothes on religious festivals. For example, many Muslims wear new outfits on 'Id.

CAIRO GENIZA[69]

Geniza is a Hebrew word designating a storage place where Hebrew documents could be deposited to prevent the desecration of the name of God, which was penned on them. The Cairo Geniza (often called simply "the Geniza") refers to documents that were discovered in a storage room in the 1890s in the Synagogue of the Palestinians, in Fustat, Egypt. Some of the documents of the Cairo Geniza were excavated from the cemetery al-Basatin, near Fustat.

The Cairo Geniza has been described as possibly the greatest daily-life archive in world history. Although Hebrew is prominently represented in the Cairo Geniza, many of the its documents were also written in Arabic, with the utilization of the Hebrew script. Writings in the Arabic script also made their way into the Geniza. The importance of the Geniza as a source of the cultural, linguistic, social, and economic history of medieval Islam is increasingly being recognized. Documents such as letters, court records, contracts, and accounts are of immediate interest to scholars of Islam. Many of these documents are from the Fatimid and Ayyubid periods (the Mamluk period is scantily represented); from the sixteenth century onward the Geniza appears to have been used more frequently, albeit in an inconsistent manner.

In addition to Egypt itself, Tunisia and Sicily find substantial representation in the Geniza. The prominence of the latter two in the Geniza documents is a result of their importance in the Mediterranean trade in the eleventh century and of the migration of many Maghrabis to Egypt in the same period. Most of the Geniza documents related to the Indian trade are from the twelfth century. Spain finds little representation in the Geniza in the twelfth century, and even less in the eleventh. Correspondences from Palestine and cities on the coast of Lebanon and Syria are well represented in the Geniza. Additionally, thousands of juridical responsa (*fatwas*) from Baghdad are contained in the Geniza. Writings from Damascus, Syria, and other Mesopotamian cities do not figure prominently.

FOOD AND DRINK

One of the most drastic ways in which Islam affected the daily lives of believers was its prohibition against the consumption of alcohol. Despite poetry and anecdotes about caliphs in drunken stupors attesting to the contrary, scholars agree that this prohibition was honored more than it was transgressed. As religious identities sharpened and religious sentiments deepened among the population, substitutes for alcohol, both in terms of stimulants and with regard to taste and nourishment, began to be produced. Simultaneously, there was a rise in disparaging attitudes toward other religious communities, such as Christian and Jewish, that utilized alcohol in their religious rituals. The Geniza archives attest to a proliferation in wine substitutes made from flowers, vegetables, spices, fruits, and other ingredients. These drinks figured largely in the diet of the middle classes, indicating the replacement of wine by such nonalcoholic substitutes. However, wine continued to be sold openly. Documents reveal the existence of "A Street of the Wine Sellers" in Cairo in 1038, and in Fustat in 1156.[70]

In addition to banning alcohol, Islam also declared the consumption of pork as religiously impermissible. No distinction was made between domesticated pigs and wild boars. This prohibition also rendered illegal the buying or raising of these animals, and their very presence near a praying Muslim was thought to invalidate the prayer.[71] Also impermissible is the consumption of the meat of already dead animals, and of meat sacrificed to idols or to deities other than God.

Islam also prescribes rules for the slaughter of animals. The act of slaughtering animals in accordance with these rules renders the meat permissible for consumption. Small animals such as sheep and goats should be slaughtered by slitting the throat, cutting through the windpipe, the gullet, and the jugular veins. For larger animals, it is permissible to slit the throat, without necessarily cutting in the manner described for smaller animals. In all cases, the animals should be allowed to bleed to death. Smaller animals should be laid on their left side, facing the *qibla* (the direction faced during the ritual prayer), at the time of slaughter. The animal's life should be taken in the quickest, most humane manner possible. Some scholars consider reciting the name of God at the moment of slaughter to be essential to rendering the meat permissible for consumption. These ritual requirements for slaughter do not apply to fish, locusts, or other similar creatures.[72]

Given the vastness of the Middle East and North Africa and the ethnic and cultural diversity of the regions, it should come as no surprise that there existed, and continue to exist, a variety of opinions and attitudes toward food. In the medieval period, certain elites enjoyed pontificating on food and drink in a secular manner—commenting on its taste, texture, and other physical characteristics. However, the majority of the population, informed by religious understandings, viewed the act of partaking in meals as enjoying the sustenance given to them by their God. Thus, at the start of the meal, praise was given to God, the Provider (the human preparer of the meal often remained unacknowledged). Refraining from commenting on the meal was understood to be part of good table manners. Instead, as per the advice of al-Ghazali (d. 1111), discussions at mealtime were ideally limited to spiritual and religious topics.[73] Such understandings regarding food continue to manifest themselves among the more religiously inclined members of the population to this day. The same is true for attitudes toward alcohol and the consumption of impermissible meats.

Over time, certain foods and drinks have acquired special religious significance. The Prophet's practice of breaking his fast with a date is widely adopted across the Muslim world. In the Middle East, *kunafa* (a sweet prepared from cheese, cream, and nuts) has acquired the status of a staple dish during Ramadan. The Qur'anic mention of the healing powers of honey has led to a special reverence for the substance. Similarly, many Muslims ascribe blessed properties to the water from the Meccan spring of Zamzam because of the miracle associated with it.

CONCLUSION

As this chapter shows, Islam has historically informed the lives of Muslims in many ways. Of course, a complete examination of the impact of Islam on the daily lives of Muslims would require the production of a multivolume book. However, this chapter has provided basic insights and interesting points of departure for further reading and examination.

To sum up, there are multiple permutations of Islam that enter the lives of Muslims through a variety of institutions and individuals. Two basic divisions are (1) the scholarly legal tradition as characterized by the 'ulama and madrasas and (2) the Sufi tradition, which often resonates with popular Islam, or Islam as it is lived and practiced by the masses. Of course, only a marginal number of Muslims are 'ulama, grow up attending madrasas, affiliate themselves with particular Sufi orders (turuq), or actively seek the intimate guidance of Sufi shaykhs. However, these figures of religious authority, and the institutions associated with them, inform the daily lives of Muslims in multiple ways—for example, madrasa graduates serve as prayer leaders and religious scholars at local mosques. The average Muslim approaches 'ulama and Sufi shaykhs when he needs religious and spiritual guidance, wants a Islamic legal ruling on a dispute, seeks a cure to a medical ailment, or wishes to banish the effects of an evil eye. Moreover, these figures of religious authority try to disseminate their views among the population and emphasize their public presence as religious leaders. They give sermons at mosques; lead prayers; emphasize the strength of their personal connection (and occasionally communication) with God or Muhammad; publish manuals and books for lay Muslims; and distribute their speeches via CDs, cassettes, and the Internet. Large local festivals and commemorative events such as mawlids and 'Ashura' also facilitate interactions between lay Muslims and religious authorities. These interactions with religious authorities color and inform the daily religious practices of lay Muslims.

The differences between the elite and popular traditions of Islam allow a wide variety of practices to be concieved as religious rituals. Two differing examples of these diverse practices would be the somber act of learning hadiths and the possibly carnivalesque act of consuming intoxicating substances in order to reach a state of spiritual ecstasy. Similarly, practices that are in explicit violation of the *sunna*—such as the piercing of one's genitals, the public smoking of hashish, and the deliberate eschewing of prayers, all of which characterized the behavior of ascetics in Damascus and elsewhere in the Middle Ages—were, and still are, understood as Islamic. The reason for this classification is that in particular contexts, these uncustomary practices are understood to have religious motivations. On the other hand, the scholarly and legal-minded Muslim elite condemn such acts and emphasize that Islam provides rules for the most mundane of daily acts: how frequently to cut one's toenails, what parts of the body to cover, what to do when entering a mosque, how to greet a stranger, when and with whom to have sexual intercourse, and so on.

Despite the existence of outliers and exceptions, it is safe to say that certain everyday Muslim practices are intimately tied to, or reflect, the influence of Islam. As discussed, these include the temporal ordering of one's daily, weekly, and yearly life; manners of dress; and attitudes toward food and drink, and filth and purity. Of course, many other practices remained unexamined—for example, ways of engaging with different animals; the place of art and conceptions of beauty; and attitudes toward marriage and the domestic sphere. Moreover, in examining the genealogy of the practices, institutions, and structures that inform the daily lives of Muslims, this chapter has focused more on the pre-modern period than on the developments that have characterized the past four centuries. (For more information on the contemporary period, the reader is advised to refer to Volumes 2 and 3 of this encyclopedia.)

Lastly, I would like to emphasize that Islam and Islamic practices are constantly contested and vary in their manifestation across different geographical regions and between socioeconomic strata. Though Muslims emphasize theological unity, there are many differences among them, especially in terms of cultural practices and interpretations. Furthermore, even secular practices in Muslim lands are often influenced by religious history.

ISLAMIC PRACTICES

For Muslims, Muhammad was the perfect human being. They believe that the ideal way of fulfilling their religious obligations is by emulating the Prophet. In addition to performing the five pillars, for some devout Muslims, this means implementing even the seemingly mundane and trivial practices of Muhammad into their daily lives. Some of Muhammad's practices that are observed by Muslims to this day include the following:

- Greeting both fellow Muslims and strangers with *al-salam 'alaykum* (peace be upon you).
- Giving to charity on a regular basis.

- Saying *insha' Allah* (if God wills) when talking about events that have yet to occur, even in situations where their occurrence is virtually confirmed. For example, a man with every intention of seeing his brother the next day might say, "I will see you tomorrow, *insha' Allah.*"
- Keeping a beard.
- Uttering "All praise belongs to God" when someone sneezes in one's presence.
- Rolling up one's pants so that they do not reach below the ankles (this only applies to men.)
- Trimming one's pubic hair on a regular basis.
- Waking up in the middle of the night to perform the supererogatory late-night *tahajjud* prayers.
- Using the right hand when eating and drinking.

GLOSSARY

Five Pillars: The fundamental rituals by which Muslims express their belief and practice their faith. These pillars are the confession of faith (*shahada*), prayer (*salah*), fasting (*saum*) alms-giving (*zakat*), and pilgrimage (*hajj*).

Hadith: After the Qur'an, the second most important source of text for Muslims is *hadith* literature. In contrast to the Qur'an, which is the unchanged word of God, the *hadiths* are simply human recordings of Muhammad's utterances, actions, and approvals. This copious body of literature serves as an important reference for Muslims wishing to know how to best practice their faith and emulate the life of the perfect human being, Muhammad.

Qur'an: The Qur'an is the unchanged word of God as revealed to Muhammad by the angel Gabriel over the 23-year course of Muhammad's prophecy (610–632 CE). Qur'anic revelations are often divided into Meccan and Medinan chapters (*suras*)— Mecca and Medina being the two cities in which Muhammad lived and received divine messages during the period of his prophethood.

Shari'a: Literally, the word *Shari'a* means a path leading to water. In common religious parlance the word refers to the ethical and religious law of Islam.

Shi'ism: In contrast to Sunnism, the other major branch of Islam is Shi'ism. Shi'ites can be distinguished from Sunnis both in terms of the legal school that they follow and certain beliefs and practices. The most significant difference between these two groups is the Shi'ite belief in the Imamate, that is, that particular descendents of Muhammad, called Imams, are infallible human beings who act as intermediaries between the rest of the Muslim community and God.

Sufism: Sufism is the mystical dimension of Islam. Practitioners of Sufism are referred to as Sufis. Sufis often coalesce into *turuq* (the plural of *tariqa*), that is, the ways and paths that mystics followed in their spiritual journeys. Some *turuq* emphasize asceticism and renunciation of the material world.

Sunnism: Sunnism is the largest sect of Islam. Adherents to this sect make up approximately 85 percent of Muslims today. As opposed to Shi'ites, Sunnis believe in the justness of the order of succession of the four caliphs immediately following Muhammad.

'Ulama (singular alim): Traditionally educated Muslim religious scholars. Generally, the 'ulama include scholars who have undergone thorough training in areas such as Islamic jurisprudence, theology, Qur'anic exegesis, and hadith literature.

NOTES

1. Translation by Arthur John Arberry.
2. Ebrahim Moosa, "Islam," in *A Southern African Guide to World Religions*, ed. John W. de Gruchy and Martin Prozesky (Cape Town: David Philip, 1991), p. 203.
3. Most of the information contained in this sidebar is taken from Kathleen Malone O'Connor, "Popular and Talismanic Uses of the Qur'an," in *Encyclopedia of the Qur'an*, ed. Jane Dammen McAuliffe (Leiden: Brill, 2009). Brill Online, Duke University. Available at http://www.brillonline.nl/subscriber/entry?entry= q3_COM-00152 (accessed April 2, 2009).
4. Moosa, p. 230.
5. Jonathan P. Berkey, *The Formation of Islam: Religion and Society in the Near East, 600–1800* (New York: Cambridge University Press, 2003), p. 73.
6. Marshall Hodgson, *The Venture of Islam: The Expansion of Islam in the Middle Periods*, vol. 2 (Chicago: University of Chicago Press, 1974), p. 533.
7. Berkey, p. 75.
8. Ibid., p. 77.
9. Ibid., p. 78. Berkey also makes similar arguments regarding the evolution of iconography on coins.
10. Berkey, pp. 57–58.
11. Hodgson, p. 535.
12. Ibid.
13. Berkey, p. 118.
14. Ibid.
15. Hodgson, pp. 551–555.
16. Timothy Insoll, *The Archaeology of Islam in Sub-Saharan Africa*, Cambridge World Archaeology (Cambridge: Cambridge University Press, 2003), pp. 66–67.
17. Berkey, p. 39.
18. Ibid., p. 42.
19. Ibid., pp. 46–47.
20. Ibid., p. 62.
21. Ibid., p. 57.
22. Ibid., p. 62. See also the many writings by Oleg Graber on Islamic art and architecture.
23. Robert W. Hefner, "Introduction: The Culture, Politics and Future of Muslim Education," in *Schooling Islam: The Culture and Politics of Modern Muslim*

Education, eds. Robert W. Hefner and Muhammad Qasim Zaman (Princeton: Princeton University Press, 2007), p. 10.

24. Berkey, p. 248.
25. Ibid.
26. Berkey, pp. 143–144.
27. Jonathan P. Berkey, "*Madrasas* Medieval and Modern: Politics, Education and the Problem of Muslim Identity" in *Schooling Islam: The Culture and Politics of Modern Muslim Education*, eds. Robert W. Hefner and Muhammad Qasim Zaman (Princeton: Princeton University Press, 2007), p. 42.
28. J. Pedersen, R. Hillenbrand, J. Burton-Page, P. A. Andrews, G. F. Pijper, A. H. Christie, A. D. W. Forbes, G. S. P. Freeman-Greenville, and A. Samb, "Masdjid," in *Encyclopedia of Islam*, 2nd ed., eds. P. Bearman, T. Bianquis, C. E. Bosworth, E. van Donzel, and W. P. Heinrichs. Leiden: Brill. Available at http://www.brill online.nl/subscriber/entry?entry=islam_COM-0694 (accessed March 1, 2009).
29. Berkey, 2007, p. 43.
30. J. Jomier, "Al-Azhar (al-Djami' al-Azhar)," in *Encyclopedia of Islam*, 2nd ed., eds. P. Bearman, T. Bianquis, C. E. Bosworth, E. van Donzel, and W. P. Heinrichs. Leiden: Brill. Available at http://www.brillonline.nl/subscriber/entry?entry= islam_COM-0076 (accessed March 29, 2009).
31. Berkey, 2007, p. 57.
32. Richard Hamilton, "Islam's Pioneering Women Preachers," *BBC News*, February 25, 2007. Online International Edition, available at http://news.bbc.co.uk/2/ hi/africa/6392531.stm (accessed February 25, 2009).
33. Jomier.
34. Hefner, 2007, p. 11.
35. Berkey, 2003, p. 120.
36. A. Ateş, "Ibn al-'Arabi, Muhyi'l-Din Abu 'Abd Allah Muhammad b. 'Ali b. Muhammad b. al-'Arabī al-I Iatimi al-Ta'i, known as al-Shaykh al-Akbar," in *Encyclopedia of Islam*, 2nd ed., eds. P. Bearman, T. Bianquis, C. E. Bosworth, E. van Donzel, and W. P. Heinrichs. Leiden: Brill. Available at http://www.brill online.nl/subscriber/entry?entry=islam_COM-0316 (accessed March 29, 2009).
37. Patrick D. Gaffney, "Popular Islam," *Annals of the American Academy of Political and Social Science* 524 (Nov. 1992), p. 43.
38. Berkey, 2003, p. 249.
39. Ibid., p. 253.
40. Ibid., p. 249.
41. Ibid., p. 252.
42. Ibid., p. 157.
43. J. G. Katz and C. Hamès, "Zāwiya (a., pl. zaw āyā)," in *Encyclopedia of Islam*, 2nd ed., eds. P. Bearman, T. Bianquis, C. E. Bosworth, E. van Donzel, and W. P. Heinrichs. Leiden: Brill. Available at http://www.brillonline.nl/subscriber/entry ?entry=islam_COM-1384 (accessed March 29, 2009).
44. Berkey, 2003, p. 254.

45. Jonathan P. Berkey, *Popular Preaching and Religious Authority in the Medieval Islamic Near East* (Seattle: University of Washington Press, 2001), p. 73.
46. Ibid., p. 32.
47. Berkey, 2003, p. 251.
48. Ibid., pp. 197–198.
49. Ibid., p. 241.
50. Ibid., p. 236.
51. Ibid., p. 238.
52. Hamid Algar and K. A. Nizami, "Nakshbandiyya," in *Encyclopedia of Islam*, 2nd ed., eds. P. Bearman, T. Bianquis, C. E. Bosworth, E. van Donzel, and W. P. Heinrichs. Leiden: Brill. Available at http://www.brillonline.nl/subscriber/entry ?entry=islam_COM-0843 (accessed March 29, 2009).
53. Berkey, 2003, p. 239.
54. Ibid., pp. 255–256.
55. G. Libson and F. H. Stewart, "'Urf," in *Encyclopedia of Islam*, 2nd ed., eds. P. Bearman, T. Bianquis, C. E. Bosworth, E. van Donzel, and W. P. Heinrichs. Leiden: Brill. Available at http://www.brillonline.nl/subscriber/entry?entry=islam _COM-1298 (accessed February 18, 2009).
56. Berkey, 2003, p. 64.
57. Pedersen et al.
58. A. J. Wensinck and P. Marçais, "Ashura," in *Encyclopedia of Islam*, 2nd ed., eds. P. Bearman, T. Bianquis, C. E. Bosworth, E. van Donzel, and W. P. Heinrichs. Leiden: Brill. Available at http://www.brillonline.nl/subscriber/entry?entry =islam_COM-0068 (accessed March 28, 2009).
59. P. Chelkowski, "Ta'ziya (a.)," in *Encyclopedia of Islam*, 2nd ed., eds. P. Bearman, T. Bianquis, C. E. Bosworth, E. van Donzel, and W. P. Heinrichs. Leiden: Brill. Available at http://www.brillonline.nl/subscriber/entry?entry=islam_SIM -7476 (accessed March 28, 2009).
60. E. Mittwoch, "'Id al-Adha," in *Encyclopedia of Islam*, 2nd ed., eds. P. Bearman, T. Bianquis, C. E. Bosworth, E. van Donzel, and W. P. Heinrichs. Leiden: Brill. Available at http://www.brillonline.nl/subscriber/entry?entry=islam_SIM -3472 (accessed March 28, 2009).
61. Berkey, 2003, p. 239.
62. Ibid., p. 240.
63. Valerie J. Hoffman, "Festivals and Commemorative Days," in *Encyclopedia of the Qur'an*, ed. Jane Dammen McAuliffe (Washington, DC: Georgetown University and Brill, 2009). Leiden: Brill. Available at http://www .brillonline.nl/subscriber/entry?entry=q3_COM-00066 (accessed February 18, 2009).
64. Y. K. Stillman and T. Majda, "Libas," in *Encyclopedia of Islam*, 2nd ed., eds. P. Bearman, T. Bianquis, C. E. Bosworth, E. van Donzel, and W. P. Heinrichs. Leiden: Brill. Available at http://www.brillonline.nl/subscriber/entry?entry=islam _COM-0581 (accessed February 27, 2009).

65. Bat Ye'or, *The Dhimmi: Jews and Christians under Islam* (Rutherford, NJ: Fairleigh Dickinson University Press, 1985), p. 191.
66. S. D. Goitein, *A Mediterranean Society: The Jewish Communities of the Arab World as Portrayed in the Documents of the Cairo Geniza*, Vol. IV, *Daily Life* (Berkeley: University of California Press, 1983), pp. 199–200.
67. Stillman and Majda.
68. Goitein, 1983, p. 200.
69. Information for this sidebar has been taken from S. D. Goitein, "Geniza," in *Encyclopedia of Islam*, 2nd ed., eds. P. Bearman, T. Bianquis, C. E. Bosworth, E. van Donzel, and W. P. Heinrichs. Leiden: Brill. Available at http://www.brillonline .nl/subscriber/entry?entry=islam_SIM-2433 (accessed March 28, 2009).
70. Goitein, 1983, p. 254.
71. F. Viré, "Khinzir," in *Encyclopedia of Islam*, 2nd ed., eds. P. Bearman, T. Bianquis, C. E. Bosworth, E. van Donzel, and W. P. Heinrichs. Leiden: Brill. Available at http://www.brillonline.nl/subscriber/entry?entry=islam_SIM-4289 (accessed February 27, 2009).
72. Ersilia Francesca, "Slaughter," in *Encyclopedia of Islam*, 2nd ed., eds. P. Bearman, T. Bianquis, C. E. Bosworth, E. van Donzel, and W. P. Heinrichs. Leiden: Brill. Available at http://www.brillonline.nl/subscriber/entry?entry=q3_COM -00186 (accessed March 28, 2009).
73. Goitein, 1983, pp. 432 (footnote 15) and 229.

BIBLIOGRAPHY

Bat Ye'or. *The Dhimmi: Jews and Christians under Islam*. Rutherford, NJ: Fairleigh Dickinson University Press, 1985.

Bearman, P., T. Bianquis, C. E. Bosworth, E. van Donzel, and W. P. Heinrichs, eds. *Encyclopedia of Islam*, 2nd ed. Boston: Brill, 2009.

Berkey, Jonathan Porter. *Popular Preaching and Religious Authority in the Medieval Islamic Near East*. Seattle: University of Washington Press, 2001.

———. *The Formation of Islam: Religion and Society in the Near East, 600–1800*. New York: Cambridge University Press, 2003.

———. *The Transmission of Knowledge in Medieval Cairo: A Social History of Islamic Education*. Princeton Studies on the Near East. Princeton, NJ: Princeton University Press, 1992.

Francesca, Ersilia. "Slaughter." In Jane Dammen McAuliffe, ed. *Encyclopedia of the Qur'an*. Leiden: Brill, 2009. Brill Online, Duke University. http://www.brillonline .nl/subscriber/entry?entry=q3_COM-00186.

Gaffney, Patrick D. "Popular Islam." *Annals of the American Academy of Political and Social Science* 524 (Nov. 1992): 38–51.

Goitein, S. D. *Mediterranean Society Jewish Communities of the Arab World as Portrayed in the Documents of the Cairo Geniza*. Berkeley: University of California Press, 2000.

Hamilton, Richard. "Islam's Pioneering Women Preachers." *BBC News*, February 25, 2007.

Hefner, Robert W., and Muhammad Qasim Zaman. *Schooling Islam: The Culture and Politics of Modern Muslim Education*. Princeton, NJ: Princeton University Press. 2007.

Hodgson, Marshall G. S. *The Venture of Islam: Conscience and History in a World Civilization*. Chicago: University of Chicago Press, 1974.

Hoffman, Valerie J. "Festivals and Commemorative Days." In Jane Dammen McAuliffe, ed. *Encyclopedia of the Qur'an*. Washington, DC: Georgetown University, 2009.

Insoll, Timothy. *The Archaeology of Islam in Sub-Saharan Africa*. Cambridge World Archaeology. Cambridge: Cambridge University Press, 2003.

Makdisi, George. *The Rise of Colleges: Institutions of Learning in Islam and the West*. Edinburgh: Edinburgh University Press, 1981.

Moosa, Ebrahim. "Islam." In John W. de Gruchy and Martin Prozesky, eds. *A Southern African Guide to World Religions*. Cape Town: David Philip, 1991, pp. 203–237.

Murata, Sachiko, and William C. Chittick. *The Vision of Islam*. New York: Paragon House, 1994.

O'Connor, Kathleen Malone. "Popular and Talismanic Uses of the Qur'an." In Jane Dammen McAuliffe, ed. *Encyclopedia of the Qur'an*. Washington, DC: Georgetown University and Brill, 2009. Brill Online, Duke University. http://www.brillonline.nl/subscriber/entry?entry=q3_COM-00152.

Chapter 8

Eastern Orthodox Christianity

Stephen R. Lloyd-Moffett

OVERVIEW

Orthodox Christianity is often a mystery to those who live in the West, for whom Protestant and Catholic are the two best known branches of Christianity. However, there are approximately 300 million Orthodox in the world (though determining the precise number of active adherents is difficult), about the same number as that of Protestants and one-third the number of Catholics. Part of its mysteriousness derives from its connection with geographic areas that have a long history of being close but exotic for Western Europeans, such as Greece, the Balkans, Russia, Palestine, and Egypt. Its mysteriousness is further amplified by the struggle to fit it into known religious categories: its focus on mysticism, incense, and elaborate rituals reminds observers of Eastern religions, but its creeds form the basis of all Western theology; it has priests and bishops like the Catholics, but it has no Pope and clergy marry as with Protestants; at times it can feel closely tied to specific ethnicities, but it claims a universal message that spans across space and time. Learning about Orthodoxy will clarify some of these points of difference, and it will also lead to the recognition that mysteriousness itself is central to the Orthodox worldview.

CATHOLIC AND ORTHODOX—WHAT A DIFFERENCE A CAPITAL LETTER MAKES!

- *orthodox* means true belief or true doctrine.
- *Orthodox* refers to a specific group of churches that originated in the Eastern part of the Mediterranean, such as the Greek Orthodox Church, the Antiochian Orthodox Church, and the Coptic Orthodox Church.
- *catholic* means universal.
- *Catholic* refers to the Roman Catholic Church led by the pope in Rome.

Thus, Orthodox churches consider themselves catholic, and Catholic churches consider themselves orthodox. But Catholics are not Orthodox, and Orthodox are not Catholics!

The Orthodox community comprises the following three parts:

1. **Clergy (deacons, priests, bishops, patriarchs).** The Orthodox Church follows the doctrine of Apostolic Succession, in which each bishop is consecrated within a line of bishops that can be traced back to one of the original apostles of Jesus. The lower clergy of deacons and priests are most often married in the Orthodox Church, though one must be unmarried to be a bishop or a higher official. As a result, many of the bishops are chosen from the monastic ranks.

2. **Laypeople.** Everyone who is not ordained clergy is considered a layperson in the church. Laypeople can teach in the church and help with its administration, but they cannot perform any sacraments (including offering communion to others), preach the homily during the liturgy, or be considered one of the governing hierarchy of the church. Historically, laypeople play a more significant role in the Orthodox Church than in the Catholic Church as protectors of the faith. This article will focus on the religion of Orthodox laypeople, unless otherwise noted.

3. **Monastics (monks and nuns).** A special category of laypeople are monastics, who dedicate their entire lives to their faith. Unlike in Catholicism, there are no monastic orders in Orthodoxy such as the Jesuit, Benedictine, or Franciscan orders. The monastic life has four phases generally: the novice period, a time of trial during which one can leave the monastic life; the *rassaphore* (robe-bearer) period, which starts after one is tonsured a monk; the *stavrophore* period (cross-bearer), which designates maturity in the monastic life and preparedness for leadership; and the Great Schema period, which is reached by those who achieve the highest levels of spiritual maturity. If a monk is ordained a priest, he is called a hieromonk, and higher-ranking priest monks are given the title of archimandrite. Throughout history, there has been a close connection between monastic and nonmonastic laypeople, even at times in opposition to the hierarchy of the church.

The Beliefs of the Orthodox

Orthodox Christians trace the origin of their beliefs to the earliest apostles of Jesus and stress the continuity of doctrine and Traditions across time. Most Orthodox beliefs are no different from those of other Christians, and they are preserved in the Nicene Creed, which is repeated in each liturgy:

> I believe in one God, Father Almighty, Creator of heaven and earth, and of all things visible and invisible.
> And in one Lord Jesus Christ, the only-begotten Son of God, begotten of the Father before all ages;
> Light of Light, true God of true God, begotten, not created, of one essence with the Father through Whom all things were made.
> Who for us men and for our salvation came down from heaven and was incarnate of the Holy Spirit and the Virgin Mary and became man.
> He was crucified for us under Pontius Pilate, and suffered and was buried;
> And He rose on the third day, according to the Scriptures.
> He ascended into heaven and is seated at the right hand of the Father;
> And He will come again with glory to judge the living and dead. His kingdom shall have no end.
> And in the Holy Spirit, the Lord, the Creator of life, Who proceeds from the Father, Who together with the Father and the Son is worshipped and glorified, Who spoke through the prophets.
> In one, holy, catholic, and apostolic Church.
> I confess one baptism for the forgiveness of sins.
> I look for the resurrection of the dead
> and the life of the age to come.
> Amen.

A close analysis of this statement of faith reveals the beliefs of Orthodoxy in six critical areas: God the Father, His Son Jesus, the Holy Spirit, the Church, Sacraments, and the End Times. Most of these are shared with the Roman Catholic Church and the majority of Protestant denominations. However, as will be seen below, there are also some important differences.

Differences between Orthodoxy and Catholicism

+ Orthodoxy rejects the Catholic doctrine that states the primacy of the pope over all other Christian jurisdictions.
+ Orthodoxy encourages priests to marry (bishops are celibate), whereas Catholicism requires celibacy for all clergy.
+ Orthodoxy rejects the addition by Catholics of "and the Son" (filioque) to the Nicene Creed.

Differences between Orthodoxy and Most Protestant Denominations

+ Orthodoxy claims that both the Scripture and the Church Tradition are valid sources of faith and practice, whereas Protestantism seeks to follow Scripture alone.
+ Orthodoxy interprets the Bible through the collective teachings of the saints, whereas Protestantism tends to favor individualized interpretation.
+ Orthodoxy values the intercessory power of saints, a position rejected by Protestantism.
+ Orthodox bishops connect themselves to the earliest followers of Christ through Apostolic Succession, which is rejected by Protestants.

Although the lists above highlight the traditional differences between Orthodoxy and the primary Western Christian branches, Orthodox writers often cite the "Orthodox mind" as a more fundamental but perhaps less tangible difference. The Orthodox mind is a deep-seated worldview shared by most Orthodox, regardless of ethnic background, that defines their general orientation to the world. While composed of many elements, the Orthodox worldview has five aspects that stand out in comparison to those of Western Christians:

1. **Stress on the community over the individual.** For Orthodoxy, the Church community is not limited to those active members of a church but is rather composed of *all* Christians across time and place who hold firmly to the Orthodox faith. Thus, the saint who lived 1,000 years ago in a land far removed is just as much part of the community as the individual next to one in the pews. This robust view of community is physically indicated by the many icons that adorn the walls of all Orthodox churches. Upon entering Orthodox churches, one often feels as if one has walked into a family gallery, because the pews are literally surrounded by images of saints. Icons in Orthodox churches are not merely aesthetic ornamentation; they are windows into this broader community that is mystically present during all services. Furthermore, the frequent prayers directed toward saints reflect the belief that saints are just as much part of the community as friends or relatives. Thus, Orthodoxy is grounded on a view of community that stands counter to the more individualistic orientation of the modern West.

2. **Stress on the mystery of God over the rationality of God.** All Christians recognize the rationality of God and the fact that any human attempt to encapsulate or circumscribe God is limited. However, Orthodoxy tends to stress the mystery over the rationality when conceptualizing God. This mysterious quality of God is said to engender theological humility toward God. The Orthodox Christian life is most often conceptualized as an unending

journey into richer appreciation of the mystery of God, rather than as a logical procession into clearer knowledge of Him, which is often the case in the West.

3. **Stress on the mystical encounter with God over the emotional and intellectual encounter.** Historically, Christian worship has affected many aspects of the individual, but worship in the modern West usually targets the emotions and the intellect. Although Orthodoxy values the heart and the mind, it ultimately aims for a deeper, mystical encounter with God that goes beyond the world of the senses and the limits of the rational mind. Underlying this emphasis is recognition that there are many layers to reality and that the encounter with God may begin with the five senses but needs to transcend them.

4. **Value of asceticism as an important spiritual discipline.** Asceticism—the training of the body for spiritual ends through fasting, celibacy, and other forms of bodily control—has been central to Christianity from its inception. Asceticism has declined in importance in the modern West, but Orthodoxy preserves the belief that control of the body is an essential spiritual discipline through which one reorients oneself to God and destroy the habits that keep one from him. The centrality of the body is also apparent in prayer techniques such as the one used in the Jesus Prayer, during which one aligns one's prayer to the natural biorhythms of the body.

5. **Stress on the salvation that comes from victory over death.** For Orthodoxy, the goal of life is to return to a state in which the very energies of God flow unimpeded through humans. This goal is called *theosis*, or deification. The fall of Adam and Eve is usually understood in Orthodoxy as the story of how death entered the world, and through death, sin. There is no acceptance of the Western doctrine of Original Sin, according to which humans are born guilty and stained. For Orthodoxy, the cosmic state of mortality is the cause of the separation from God and the source of all sinful action; the disease is death and the universal symptom is sin. Humans sin in response to the fear of death, not because of a guilty and entirely corrupt nature. Jesus's destruction of death through his resurrection is the source of salvation. The focus then tends to be on the victory over death through resurrection, as opposed to the Western focus on the fact that Jesus's suffering and crucifixion atones for the debt humans owe to God but cannot pay. As a result, theologians have often noticed that Orthodoxy highlights the resurrection, whereas Western Christianity tends to focus on the crucifixion as the primary moment of salvation. In the Orthodox worldview, humans, no longer faced with the threat of extinction, have a chance to be restored to the True Life discovered in *theosis*.

Grasping the Orthodox Mind is often one of the most challenging elements when encountering Orthodoxy for the first time. However, it is often noted that for many people growing up in traditionally Orthodox regions, it is a natural part of their outlook: it is not taught in Sunday School or public schools but seeps into the consciousness of those who grow up there. Many contemporary Orthodox writers have noted that as some traditionally Orthodox regions fully embrace Western cultural norms, this mindset is weakening.

Church Governance

Orthodox Christians consider themselves part of one church insofar as they share the same faith, theology, Byzantine liturgical tradition, canons, and spiritual practices. For historical reasons, the following three different forms of governance exist within Orthodoxy:

1. **Eparchy, or direct patriarchal rule.** Some Orthodox churches are patriarchal eparchies, that is, ecclesiastical provinces that are directly under the auspices of one of the four senior patriarchs, or in certain cases, other patriarchs or archbishops. These include the large emigrant churches formed in the West, such as the Greek Orthodox Archdiocese of North and South America (formed in 1922; 1.5 million members) and the Greek Orthodox Archdiocese of Australia (formed in 1924; 400,000 members). The leaders of these churches are usually given the titles of eparch, metropolitan, or archbishop. Most eparchies in non-historically Orthodox areas are within the jurisdiction of an ecumenical patriarch, who can directly influence the daily life and practices of the people within the eparchy through his own behavior or by appointing leaders of eparchies who support his views.

2. **Autonomous.** Autonomous churches operate with full administrative independence but have leaders who are chosen or affirmed by a patriarch. Autonomous Orthodox churches include the small but important Church of Sinai—which is limited to the famous Monastery of St. Catharine, built below the site in which Moses received the Ten Commandments.

3. **Autocephaly.** As self-governing churches, autocephalous churches have hierarchies independent of the patriarch and operate with complete independence. While maintaining ecclesiastical and theological communion with the patriarchs, these autocephalous Orthodox churches are responsible for all church matters affecting the life and administration of the church, with the exception of doctrinal and canonical positions.

   Historically, these churches often emerged as a result of nationalistic movements, and they are closely identified with the local national ethos. The largest Orthodox autocephalous churches are the Russian (110 million members), Romanian (18 million members), Greek (8 million members), Serbian (8 million members), and Bulgarian (6 million members).

TIMELINE

33 CE:	The Orthodox Church is born on Pentecost.
312:	Roman emperor Constantine converts to Christianity.
325:	The Nicene Creed is formulated at the First Ecumenical Council at Nicaea.
349:	Basil of Caesarea and Gregory of Nazianzus study together in Athens.
431:	Schism of Assyrian churches.
451:	The Council of Chalcedon leads to a major schism, causing the separation of the Coptic Church of Egypt.
787:	Supported by the laity, the Second Council of Nicaea restores the religious use of icons.
860:	Brothers Cyril and Methodius begin their missionary trips to the Slavic lands.
988:	Prince Vladimir of Russia converts to Orthodoxy.
1054:	Mutual bulls of excommunication are exchanged between churches of the East and the Roman Catholic Church in the West.
1204:	Western Christians sack Constantinople in the Fourth Crusade.
1453:	Fall of Constantinople to the Ottoman Turks.
1794:	America's first Orthodox parish is founded in Kodiak, Alaska.
1917:	Communist Revolution takes place in Russia, which leads to creation of the officially atheistic USSR.

HISTORY

According to the Orthodox Church, history is divided into the following six eras.

1. Creation of the World to the Resurrection of Jesus Christ

Although most Orthodox do not take the Genesis account of creation literally, there is a belief that the universe and everything in it was directly created by God out of nothing. The history preserved in the Old Testament (the Hebrew Bible) is the story of God's relationship with his chosen people, the Jews. However, for Orthodoxy, this era culminates when God the Father becomes incarnate in the person of Jesus Christ, who ministered to the people of his area, was crucified, and then resurrected on Easter morning. The resurrection of Jesus inaugurated a new era in which humanity's relationship with God was restored and the promise of the primordial unity with God was once again possible.

2. The Persecuted Church (33–312 CE)

The "birthday" of church according to Orthodoxy is Pentecost—50 days after the resurrection, and when the original disciples are said to have received the Holy Spirit, the third person of the Trinity. Over time, this movement spread beyond the original audience of Jews to gentiles (non-Jews) and from Palestine to the Roman Empire and beyond. Contrary to popular perceptions among Christians today, this growth was not particularly rapid or well noticed by those outside it, but it was steady over the centuries. With rare exceptions, the church was not actively persecuted by the Roman Empire during its first three centuries, except for specific local persecutions when Christians would be blamed for some natural or unnatural disaster. However, in the self-identity of the church, this era came to be identified with persecution and the martyrs became the public symbol of this era.

3. The Imperial Church and the Era of the Councils (312–787)

The conversion of Roman emperor Constantine (272–337) to Christianity in 312 inaugurated a new era for Orthodoxy. The fourth century began with the most severe and widespread persecution of Christians, but by the end of that century, Christianity had become the official religion of the empire and the once-persecuted began persecuting other religions and heresies. The center of religion, politics, and culture shifted from Rome to New Rome, later named Constantinople, where it would remain almost until the fall of Constantinople in 1453. Though power was officially shared by the emperor and the patriarch, in many cases the imperial throne and the imperial church intertwined and became almost indistinguishable. The Church had become a powerful spiritual, social, and political institution.

The church defined and clarified the essential doctrines of the Orthodox faith through ecumenical councils held throughout this era in response to doctrinal challenges. The goal of the ecumenical councils was to bring representatives of the universal church to a single place to decide on its authentic doctrine. Orthodoxy recognizes the following seven such councils:

1. **The First Council of Nicaea (325)** defined the relationship of Jesus to God the Father, disagreeing with the heresy of Arianism, which argued that Jesus was not fully divine in essence but had a lesser divinity derived from the Father. It also composed the primary tenants of the Nicene Creed and defined the date of Easter.
2. **The First Council of Constantinople (381)** defined the Holy Spirit as divine and as a coequal part to the Trinity, against those who argued that it was not divine.

3. **The Council of Ephesus (431)** delineated the precise definition of the human and divine natures of Jesus, disagreeing with the heresy of Nestorianism, which claimed that Jesus had two persons with two natures instead of one person with two natures. Those who rejected this council formed the Assyrian Church, which still exists today and is deemed the heretical "Nestorian" church by the remainder of Eastern Christians.

4. **The Council of Chalcedon (451)** clarified the teaching of the previous councils by repudiating the "monophysite" (one nature) doctrine—declared by the leadership of the church in Alexandria, Egypt—which claimed that Jesus effectively had only a divine nature, not a divine and human nature. Those who rejected this position of the church formed churches that are known historically as the non-Chalcedonian churches, more recently called Oriental Orthodox churches.

5. **The Second Council of Constantinople (553)** interpreted previous teachings regarding the nature of Christ and confirmed the use of the term *Theotokos* (Mother of God) as appropriate for Jesus's mother Mary (a doctrine established in the Council of Ephesus).

6. **The Third Council of Constantinople (680–681)** rejected two attempts at forging a compromise with those who denied previous councils. Monothelitism attempted to argue that Jesus's divine and human nature shared a common will and monoenergism argued that the divine and human nature shared a common energy. Both were rejected by the council.

7. **The Second Council of Nicaea (787)** restored the proper veneration of icons after the emperor banned them for a period with the support of a few church leaders.

This era is often called the golden age of patristics, after the church fathers who collectively provided the theological backbone that supports Orthodoxy even today. Among these are the Three Hierarchs: Basil of Caesarea (330–379), Gregory of Nazianzus (329–389) and John Chrysostom (347–407). Writing in their native Greek, the theology of the Three Hierarchs was never as influential in the Latin West, where Augustine (354–430) quickly overshadowed all others.

A FRIENDSHIP FOR THE AGES

Basil of Caesarea and Gregory of Nazianzus both grew up in privileged families in the fourth century in the region of Cappadocia, in present-day Turkey. In 349, at the age of twenty, the young men followed the ancient tradition of seeking wisdom in Athens. Gregory had arrived first and was thus aware of the rowdy initiation rites through which various intellectual circles harangued all newcomers. When Basil arrived, he protected his fellow Cappadocian, and there, in the shadow of the Acropolis, one of the most beautiful and important friendships in Christian history arose. The two shared a passion for philosophy, rhetoric, and Christianity. Eventually, they would both return to their homeland, be ordained priests, and later become bishops. During trials— personal and ecclesial—they would resort to each other for counsel and friendship.

Although at times their lifelong friendship was challenged by the pressures of being leaders of the church, Gregory was the first to laud his friend Basil as St. Basil the Great—a distinction that remains today. Their combined contributions form the foundations of much of Orthodox Trinitarian theology, canon law, liturgical rites, ecclesiology, and spirituality. Perhaps their greatest and most lasting legacy, however, is the friendship, which continues to be memorialized in every icon of the Three Hierarchs.

---

4. Orienting toward the East (787–1453)

Cultural and linguistic differences between the Greeks and the Romans predated the rise of Christianity, but for the first eight centuries of the Common Era, the Church identified with a larger unity that bound all Christians together. As the Nicene Creed (325) declared, the church is "one, holy, catholic, and apostolic." With the spread of Islam in the eighth century and the gradual conversion to this faith of many Christians in the Levant and North Africa, Christianity became predominant in two primary regions: Greek East and Latin West. Signs of a breakdown between these two essential groups can be traced to the fifth century or earlier, but the eighth and ninth centuries mark an important shift in the Christian polity for two reasons.

First, the Christianity of the Greek East began to expand dramatically north and northeast. Two brothers, Cyril and Methodius, began their missionary efforts in the 860s by developing the Cyrillic alphabet to translate the Bible for Slavic audiences. Their first stop was Moravia (modern-day Czech Republic), where despite initial success, German missionaries eventually persuaded the local people to look to Rome. However, the orientation to the north and northeast continued. The Bulgarians converted to Eastern Christianity in 860. The Serbs, Romanians, and Ukrainians followed. In 988 Prince Vladimir of Russia converted to Christianity and aligned himself with the East by marrying the sister of the Byzantine emperor. Eastern Orthodoxy thus became the state religion of Russia until 1917. By the end of the tenth century, the Greek East had expanded its influence throughout Eastern Europe and Russia.

Second, the simmering rift between the Roman power centers of East and West came to a boiling point during this era. In the ninth century, a series of issues surrounding claims to papal supremacy, additions by the West to the

Nicene Creed, and differences in worship practices, among other disagreements, increased tensions. In 1054, a conflict between the patriarch of Constantinople and a visiting Catholic representative led to the proclamation of mutual bulls of excommunication. Few thought such a dramatic schism would last. However, despite many attempts at reunification, the relationship was permanently damaged in popular opinion when the Fourth Crusade (1204) brought Latin Christians into the Eastern Christian capital of Constantinople to sack and destroy it. The lingering anger and strident derisiveness remain to this day for many Orthodox Christians.

By the end of the eleventh century, a recognizable and distinct Eastern Christian block had formed. Although employing diverse languages, differing governance forms, and a kaleidoscope of cultural norms, these countries shared a common vision of Orthodoxy, forging a single Christian polity that stood in contrast to the more uniform Latin West.

5. The Russian Era (1453–1917)

After the fall of Constantinople to the Ottoman Turks in 1453, the nucleus of Orthodoxy shifted north to Moscow. The four patriarchs of Eastern Orthodoxy remained in their respective districts, but Moscow

St. Basil Cathedral, a Russian Orthodox cathedral erected on the Red Square in Moscow in 1555–1561, represents the architectural pinnacle of the Russian Era. It's flame-like design gives Russian churches their unique styles. (Photos.com.)

assumed the title of "Third Rome," and its patriarch quickly became the standard-bearer for Orthodoxy. The Church had relative independence until the patriarchate was abolished by Tsar Peter I in 1721, after which the church effectively became an agent of the state. Meanwhile, the Eastern Orthodox of modern-day Greece, Turkey, and Cyprus struggled merely to preserve their faith within the Ottoman system, often facing persecution. For example, on December 16, 1803, twenty-two women were cornered on a cliff in Zalongo, in western Greece, by the famous Ottoman leader Ali Pasha. Because they did not want to be taken captive, the women kissed their children tenderly, pushed them off the cliff, and then joyfully sang and danced off the cliffs themselves. Christianity in Ottoman lands struggled under persecution, but the Russians continued to spread Orthodoxy to new areas, arriving in Alaska in the eighteenth century. This era concludes with the Communist Revolution of 1917, when increasingly strict control over religion slowly strangled Orthodoxy in Russia.

6. The Modern Era (1917–Present)

The twentieth century was a difficult time for Orthodoxy. The persecution of Orthodoxy in Russia after 1917 severely suppressed its spiritual and intellectual vitality. To a lesser extent, religion declined throughout the Eastern Orthodox areas of the communist bloc, such as Bulgaria, Yugoslavia, and Romania. The ecumenical patriarch in Istanbul as well as the patriarchs of Jerusalem, Antioch, and Alexandria all faced often hostile local environments. Monastic populations declined rapidly throughout the world. Bright spots included the Church of Greece and the Church of Cyprus, which thrived again after years of stagnation under the Turkish yoke, but increasingly became identified with nationalistic endeavors. However, the final decades of the twentieth century and the first of the twenty-first revealed promising signs for the future of Eastern Orthodoxy. A new intellectual movement with roots in a group of exiled Russian thinkers in Paris in the 1930s flourished in America and the West so that the contemporary state of Orthodox theology is stronger than in any time in the past millennium. After the fall of communism, Orthodoxy is returning to Russia and other former communist countries and being embraced with great fervor. The Ecumenical Patriarch Bartholomew, nicknamed "the Green Patriarch," gained worldwide recognition for his initiatives and leadership in care for the environment, including convening biannual symposia dedicated to threatened bodies of water such as the Amazon River, the North Sea, and the Aegean Sea. As a result, contemporary Orthodoxy is experiencing a global resurgence.

RELIGION IN DAILY LIFE

Orthodox often remind visitors that the daily life of Orthodoxy needs to be experienced, not analyzed. The best way to see this life is to visit a small town in Lebanon, Greece, Serbia, or Russia that still preserves the ancient traditions. One might see the following if one visits such a place.

A Day in the Life of an Orthodox Town

The morning begins with the sound of church bells proclaiming the beginning of service. With so many saints with feast days, most churches have liturgy nearly every day. The older women arrive first, usually wearing black if they are widows. As they shuffle down the street and the sun offers its first rays, they "cross" themselves when they first glimpse the church, as all Orthodox do whenever they see a church. The most pious among them may have woken up even earlier to say prayers in front of their home altar before the sun rose. The home altar reflects the life of the family—with pictures of loved ones, mementos from travels, and past joyful announcements—and shares space with traditional icons of the Virgin Mary, Jesus, and saints. The morning prayers are second nature to these women after decades of repeating them; they offer a familiar beginning to the day, before making their journey to the local church in the quiet, early morning.

The local church is their second home. They are comfortable there and immediately get to work, rummaging through boxes to fill up the brass box that holds candles that people will light in memory of loved ones missing or gone. Once the box is filled and the leftover candles from the previous night lit, they pause, cross themselves, and watch the smoke glide by the face of the patron saint of the church, whose icon stands illumined behind a cadre of flames. Next to the candle stand is a gem-encrusted gospel, whose brass is tarnished from centuries of being kissed by the faithful. The women once again cross themselves and kiss the gospel as one kisses an old friend. Turning toward the doors of the sanctuary, a waft of sweet incense is detected. Opening the door, the low drone of the chanter singing the psalms fills the near-empty room. These halls are large open spaces, with no pews, surrounded by walls lined with ancient captain's chairs for the impaired. A woman carries some flowers from her garden and places them in front of the image of the Virgin Mary that stands on a wall that separates the main area from the altar area. Another woman carries a special loaf of bread—baked in her own oven, according to an ancient recipe—that will be used for communion. Yet another woman grabs a broom and begins to sweep the floor as the service carries on. The women are preparing their "home" for visitors.

Many people filter in and out during the next hour—some on their way to work or school stay for 15 minutes, listening to the familiar hymns and readings; others wander in to light a candle or kiss an icon, and leave just as quickly. These people are deeply connected to the building that houses the church: their names derive from those of the saints whose images adorn the wall; the fount in which their children, parents, and grandparents were baptized stands lonely in the corner this morning; the slightly damaged dome stands as a reminder of more worldly battles that the previous generations waged to defend their people and religion. On great feasts and some Sundays, locals will fill the church and spill out into the street, but the midweek services of lesser-known saints attract only the most faithful. By the time the main liturgy begins, a handful of stalwarts are standing, as they will for the whole service.

Outwardly, the faithful participate little during service—perhaps singing along to a favorite hymn, saying the Nicene Creed or the Lord's Prayer, and kneeling at appropriate times. Yet, they know the service as well as they know the creases in their wrinkled hands. As with a dramatic play with whose perfection one does not want to meddle, the liturgy is largely the same each and every time down to the very syllables. There are few elements that change—such as the Gospel and Epistle reading and the hymns to the saints—but most of the service is precisely the same every time, as it has been for over 1,000 years. The older women could repeat it by heart—even the priest's parts—and murmur whenever the young priests miss a syllable or stumble over a reading. The words are soothing, like a familiar nursery rhyme, and they connect the faithful with something that transcends time and place.

The highlight of the service is not the sermon, which is short and general, but the taking of communion, the mystical cup of immortality, as the ancients called it. Taking communion used to be rare when the worshipers were children, but at the urging of the patriarch, the young priest has been encouraging frequent communion, as priests did in the early church. Though the older women are uncomfortable with this new practice, they oblige. When the service concludes, the faithful cross themselves one final time as they exit the church and return to their daily tasks.

Leaving the church does not mean that the believers leave their faith behind. Orthodoxy shapes their day in ways that almost seem quaint to many modern Westerners. The church is located on the town's central square, which is lined with cafes filled with people talking politics and religion, two subjects always intertwined in Orthodox countries. When the priest exits the church, many people leap up to kiss his hand and receive a blessing. Even an older man who has not set foot in church in decades seeks out a blessing; he is not sure if he believes in God, but the blessing cannot hurt, he reckons. He returns to his coffee and his worry beads—which look remarkably like Western rosary beads—praising the priest as he sits.

At the corner of the square is a baptismal store filled with everything an Orthodox family needs for baptizing a child. Its white outfits—many with ornate bows and intricate designs—spill out onto the street. Religious sacraments are an industry in Orthodox countries. There are dozens of baptismal candles to consider, many of which are bigger than the infant being baptized and bear images—such as those of Disney characters, Barbie, and toy trucks—that betray Orthodoxy's ancient reputation. Everyone who attends a baptism will receive a gift, and there are many to choose from. Everything must be just right for the child's special day, or so the salesperson argues.

A young man whizzes through the central square on a scooter with a large jug of olive oil on the back. He is taking the jug up to the monastery on the hills overlooking the city. The monks have been up since before dawn, praying first in their cell and then walking under a chorus of stars at three in the morning to an ancient, cold church where they will begin their day dedicated to God with five hours of community prayers. The olive oil the young man is bringing comes from ancient trees that surround his family home in a remote village where his grandfather grew up, before the family moved to town. As long as anyone can remember, his family has supplied the olive oil for the monastery, as part of an ancient tradition according to which the local people support the monks. This young man can rarely be seen in church—few young people go to church nowadays—but his faith is evident as he delivers his gift to monks who have known him since he was a baby. He kisses the hand of the abbot, whose long white beard and hunched posture reflect his nearly 50 years as a monk. The abbott embraces the young man and warmly strokes his cheek, more like a caring grandparent than a sanctified agent of institutional Christianity. They talk about the young man's life and the world while sipping some homemade ouzo and nibbling at a sweet often referred to as Turkish delight. The young man is part of the family that the monastery is.

Back at the central square, led by their teacher, children from the local elementary school walk in single file to the church. The local priest teaches monthly lessons on morality and church doctrine to the children. The state, which pays the priest's salary, has consistently maintained that it expects a social benefit from the priest's activities, not just a spiritual one. A century ago, Orthodoxy would have been the only religious option for these young people, but the church's monopoly on religion is over. Protestant missionaries are now in town; a prominent actor in the country just became a Buddhist; and secularism is no longer receiving the public scorn it once has. The young priest seems aware of these changes and makes an effort to be more relevant and "hip," at least compared to previous generations of priests. The children listen respectfully, though they rarely make eye contact with him so as not to be noticed or questioned.

A few hours later in an apartment above the square, a family gathers around the table for lunch. It is Wednesday, a fast day in Orthodoxy, which means that no meat or dairy is served. The culinary cultures have adapted ably to these restrictions, and long-held family recipes ensure appealing food for all. The young children and the breast-feeding mom, who are exempt from fasting requirements, add a few slices of cold cuts to their plates. Before the meal, the father leads the family in the Lord's Prayer and blesses the food. The family begins to eat, and the conversation drifts seamlessly between news from the church, politics, and church politics. It seems the church is intertwined with society in ways that would seem unfamiliar to most in the West.

Later that evening, the town's young people dress up for a night out. They hop on a bus to a new discotheque outside of town, where they will spend all night flirting, drinking, and dancing. Along the way, they pass a church and nearly all of them instinctively cross themselves—the bus is quiet for a brief moment and then returns to the normal din of youthful indiscretions. When they return just before sunrise, they run into the bishop, who is walking with his gem-encrusted cane toward a church that will host a feast in a few hours. The bishop inquires with a grin, "Are you returning from your all-night vigil?" Everyone laughs as the nearly sober young people seek his blessing before going to bed. One day they will be heading to vigils, but not today. A day in the life of the Orthodox town is completed, and a new one begins.

Orthodoxy at Home

Orthodox spiritual life is as likely to be practiced in the home as in a church. Each year after the feast of the Epiphany (January 6), which commemorates Jesus's own baptism by John the Baptist (called the Forerunner in Orthodoxy), the priest visits homes to bless them. This practice reaffirms the house as dedicated to God, extending the sacred space of the church altar to the domestic realm.

In Greece, the blessing of the house is given a secondary, colloquial meaning as well. A tradition says that little demons or goblins (*kalikatzaroi*) arise from the earth after Christmas and wreak havoc until the home is blessed by a priest. The *kalikatzaroi* are not evil and do not usually cause harm, but they are known for mischievous pranks. When the priest comes to bless the house, he dips basil into holy water, sprinkles the house with it, and makes the sign of the cross in every room. This act scares the *kalikatzaroi* away, at least until the next year.

The remainder of the blessed water is often kept at the home altar, which may be as simple as a few icons on a wall or as elaborate as a whole room. The home altar resembles the church altar. It has icons of the Theotokos (the Virgin Mary), Jesus, John the Forerunner, and various saints. Usually, an oil lamp perpetually illumines the icons. Holy water, baptismal candles, relics, and other religious items are often found. However, home altars also often develop unique qualities. Alongside the more traditional religious items, people often include pictures of loved ones, mementos from vacations, or other items that hold personal significance. The home altar becomes in this way a mirror of the believer's life as well as the spiritual center of the home.

The kitchen is also a central piece to much of Orthodox spiritual life. Food is prepared at home for liturgical services and religious festivals. Baking bread is one of the most important spiritual functions of laypeople. Holy bread used for communion is usually baked by parishioners at home. Consisting of two parts of white leavened bread, it is stamped with a cross and the letters IC, XC, and NIKA, which together represent the phrase "Jesus Christ Conquers." Parishioners also bake and bring five loaves of spiced bread for special occasions such as feast days. Special unleavened bread is often baked for the first day of Lent in the Greek traditions and the fourth week of Lent in the Russian tradition. Even ordinary bread retains spiritual significance because of its potential as the body of Christ. Older women in particular are careful not to set loaves upside down, and they usually make the sign of the cross over it before cutting it. Any bread crumbs remaining are not thrown away, but fed to animals. There is even a folk belief in some parts of Russia according to which all the bread crumbs wasted over a lifetime will be weighed on Judgment Day, and if collectively they weigh more than the person who wasted them, his or her soul will be condemned!

Food often is connected to religious festivals. The most important feast of the year is Easter, called Pascha or Passover in most Orthodox countries. Boiled eggs dyed blood red are said to represent Christ's crucifixion and resurrection. Numerous traditions are associated with these eggs, including popular competitions to see whose egg remains unbroken after hitting another egg. This game also has been given spiritual significance: if the egg represents the tomb of Christ, then breaking it represents the resurrection.

In addition to the red-dyed eggs, Russians and Ukrainians also produce elaborately painted Easter eggs. These eggs are usually made by applying hot wax to the egg and then subjecting it to a series of dye baths that imbue color to the egg. The patterns, colors, and designs are revealed when the wax is melted off. The eggs become a source of pride for Orthodox families.

The resurrection service in Orthodoxy happens at midnight on Saturday night. In the early hours of the morning, the first meal of the resurrection includes *magyeritsa* (a special soup made from lamb innards), sweet bread, cheese, hard-boiled eggs, and rolls. On Easter day, the roasting of lamb is ubiquitous in Orthodox countries, so much so that the name of the day in Greek translates as the day of "the turning of the spit."

Pork is the most common meal associated with the other major feast day, Christmas. One can read about "Christmas hogs" slaughtered on Christmas Eve and prepared following traditional recipes that make it possible to consume them entirely. Today, however, turkey often replaces hog because of traditions from the West. There are a number of other traditions associated with Christmas. In Slavic countries, people fast on Christmas Eve until the conclusion of the evening service, after which they eat a special porridge made with boiled wheat, barley, or rice with honey. In Ukraine and the orthodox areas of Poland and Lithuania, a feast including 12 dishes (none with meat or dairy) celebrates the 12 apostles. Greeks, by contrast, are used to a specially prepared sausage, seasoned with orange rind (*loukanika*), a rose-water–flavored shortbread, and sweet honey cakes (*melomakarona*). Many Orthodox countries have a special bread for Christmas, usually sweetened with honey and consumed on Christmas Eve.

As the list below indicates, food is also intimately tied with other main feasts:

- New Year's Day in Orthodox countries coincides with the popular feast day of St. Basil. On this day, a cake called *vasilopita* is ceremoniously cut by the head of the household. The first slice is reserved for Jesus, the second is set aside for the poor, and the remaining slices are distributed in a variety of traditional schemes—for example, they can be distributed starting from the youngest member to the household to the oldest. Hidden in the cake is a coin said to bring good luck to the one who finds it.
- On the first day of Great Lent (the fasting period before Easter), people eat unleavened bread (*lagana*) topped with sesame seeds. Meat and dairy are prohibited, but octopus and squid are common in Mediterranean Orthodox countries, along with lentil soup. The most common sweet of Lent is *halva*, a tahini-based sweet that probably originated in the Middle East.
- Palm Sunday, the Sunday before Easter, is a festive day in the middle of Great Lent. The traditional meal on Palm Sunday is fried cod (or some other fish) with garlic sauce.
- Good Friday commemorates the death of Christ, and the typical meal on this day is a bitter soup made with vinegar and sesame paste or lentils.

Another liturgical item usually prepared at home by lay people is *koliva*, boiled wheat sweetened with honey and sugar, often mixed with nuts, seeds, or raisins. *Koliva* is most commonly associated with memorial services, both on the day of the funeral, and 40 days, 1 year, and 5 years later (and also at other intervals). The wheat and seeds are said to symbolize the fruit of the resurrection.

Orthodoxy in the Week

Religions often pattern the daily existence of adherents, and Orthodoxy is no different. The Orthodox week begins at sunset on Saturday, with the service of Vespers or the beginnings of a vigil in Russian traditions. These services prepare the space for the highlight of the week, which occurs Sunday morning, when the community comes together for worship. The most common service is the Divine Liturgy of St. John Chrysostom, whose roots are in the fourth century, though it has evolved over time. Sunday worship, as with most liturgies, typically has the following three parts:

1. **Matins (or Orthros)** is both the culmination of the evening services and a preparation for liturgy. In the Greek tradition, it directly precedes the Divine Liturgy, which usually happens on Sunday morning. In Slavic traditions, it is usually held the night before, and on special occasions it can be an all-night vigil. It concludes with the Great Doxology or Great Blessing. During this period, the priest performs a special service in private that prepares the bread and wine for the Eucharist.
2. **The Liturgy of the Word** is the first part of the liturgy proper. It follows traditional Jewish worship practices through prayers, psalms and hymns, scripture readings, and a sermon. In the past, those who were not baptized Orthodox were asked to leave at the conclusion of this section, though this practice is becoming increasingly rare.
3. **The Liturgy of Eucharist** begins with the Great Entrance, when the priest, surrounded by the altar boys, brings into the sanctuary of the people the bread and wine that will be consecrated. It includes the communal saying of the Creed and the Lord's Prayer as well as the special prayer for the consecration of the gifts. The highlight is the receiving of the Eucharist, also called Communion.

After the Liturgy of the Eucharist, traditional communities continue the worship experience through fellowship around a common table. This practice of breaking bread as a community is frequently mentioned in the earliest texts about Christianity and remains an important part of the Orthodox experience in many places in the world.

With the exception of major feasts, most Orthodox do not regularly attend full services during the week. However, it is very common for people to stop by a church to light a candle or have confession during the week. Orthodox churches are usually less formal than their European Catholic counterparts, with people freely wandering in and out. One of the surprising elements for many people visiting an Orthodox service for the first time is that people will often walk in late, sometimes very late. Although the clergy members do not condone this practice, it reflects a realization on behalf of the people that Sunday service is not primarily a time for personal worship—it is a time when the entire community of Christians across time and place are brought together to transform the universe through common worship. Thus, the community is present, even if some of its members are physically absent.

The remainder of the week is often patterned by the fasting requirements of the church, which are intended to instill a sense of self-discipline and serve as frequent reminders of one's faith. All Orthodox are expected to fast on Wednesdays and Fridays, in addition to the four major fasting periods discussed below. Definitions of proper fasting differ among Orthodox, but the general pattern is similar: no eating of meat, dairy, and sometimes olive oil on Wednesday, Friday, or before communion. Relaxation of fasting prescriptions is allowed for pregnant women, those traveling, those ill, children, and at others times, when advised by a priest.

The weekly fasting requirements are often trumped by the four main fasts of the year, during which the fasting requirements extend to every day of the week.

1. **Great Lent** is the period of seven weeks preceding Orthodox Easter.
2. **The Nativity (or Advent) Fast** is the period from November 15 to December 24 (forty days), in anticipation of Christmas.
3. The **Apostles' Fast** is the period from the week following Pentecost to the feast day of Saints Peter and Paul, on June 29.
4. The **Dormition Fast** is the period of the first two weeks of August, in anticipation of the feast of the Dormition of the Theotokos.

Orthodoxy in the Year

Eastern Orthodox countries use two different calendars that are currently separated by 13 days. In 1923, following the lead of the Patriarch of Constantinople, the churches in Greece, Romania, Cyprus, and a few years later, Bulgaria introduced a revised Julian calendar that mirrored closely the Western Gregorian calendar. The remainder of the Orthodox world maintained the older Julian calendar. This decision to align the Eastern calendar with that of the West created one of the most important modern schisms of the church. Today, "Old Calendarists" Orthodox sects that reject the existing church hierarchy because of their decision to adjust the calendar are present in nearly every country that introduced the new calendar.

The Orthodox Ecclesial Calendar begins on September 1st each year. In recent times, the Ecumenical Patriarch Bartholomew has encouraged adherents to pray for the protection of the environment on this day. A special service dedicated to the Preservation of Creation is now celebrated in many parts of the world. Afterward, there are often ecological projects that remind the Orthodox of their sacred duty to care for the earth. These events usually coincide with the new Sunday School year and the beginning of a new liturgical calendar.

In Orthodox countries, the most important religious celebration is Pascha (or Easter). Pascha preparations begin nearly two months before the feast is celebrated. Paschal preparations begin unofficially with carnival, called *apokries* in Greek, and last for two weeks, and it reaches its climax the weekend before the fasting period begins. This festive affair includes costumes, parties, parades, confetti, and a variety of other traditions. The most famous carnival in Greece takes place in the city of Patra and ends with a ceremonial burning of an effigy of Judas. In Russia, the celebration is called *Maslenitsa*, and it draws on pagan roots and includes pancakes, masquerades, snowball fights, and sledding. It concludes with the embodiment of the festival, Lady Maslenitsa, being ceremoniously burned symbolizing the end of festival and the beginning of a period of penance.

The period immediately prior to Pascha is called Great Lent, which commences with Clean Monday, when the fasting period begins. The celebration of Clean Monday is marked by special Lenten foods and special church services. In Greece, a custom from ancient times includes picnicking with one's family and flying kites. Children traditionally make a "Lady Lent" paper doll that has seven legs, representing the seven weeks of Lent. Every week, a leg is cut off to show how many weeks remain until Easter.

Palm Sunday, the Sunday before Easter, celebrates the arrival of Jesus in Jerusalem. Palm branches are often held by laypeople this day (pussy willow branches sometimes substitute for palm branches in colder Slavic countries). Arab Christians hold candles decorated with flowers during the procession. Fish is the traditional meal of Palm Sunday.

Good Friday is a day of mourning in most Orthodox countries, with flags flown at half-staff. Arab Mediterranean Orthodox Christians do not use their customary greeting "peace be with you" on Good Friday, because it reflects how Judas greeted. Instead, they use the phrase "the light of God be with your departed ones." For Greeks, the center is the evening, when ornately decorated symbolic tombs of Jesus are carried in procession from the various churches in town to a central location, accompanied by songs of lamentation. There, the city as a whole sings songs together in a symbolic burial of Jesus. In Russia, an image of Jesus is placed in a silver coffin bearing a cross and surrounded with candles and flowers. The faithful creep on their knees and kiss and venerate the image of Christ's body painted on the shroud.

The highlight of the religious year occurs at the Resurrection Service that commences at midnight on Pascha. Just before midnight, the lights of the church are extinguished and the priest comes forth from the altar with a single candle. He utters the sentence "the Light of Christ illumines all" and then transfers the flame of his candle to the attendants' candles until a bright, warm glow fills the church. Everyone then leaves the church singing a hymn that proclaims that Jesus has risen from the dead, bring death to death. At midnight, the priest, surrounded by the faithful holding candles, pronounces "Christ is risen!" The people shout back, "Truly, he has risen!" In modern times, fireworks often go off at this moment and pandemonium breaks out as all seek to embrace their loved ones. When the service concludes, it is customary in some Orthodox areas for the faithful to bring the paschal fire back to their homes, unextinguished. At the door of the houses of the faithful, three crosses are formed with the soot of the candle, and the crosses will remain there throughout the year as a memorial to this event. The week following Easter is called Bright Week, during which there can be no fasting. In Bright Week all church services are altered to reflect the joyous season.

WHY IS ORTHODOX EASTER A DIFFERENT DATE?

According to the ruling of the First Ecumenical Council in 325, which is accepted by Western and Eastern Christians, Easter Sunday should be celebrated on the first Sunday after the first full moon after the first vernal equinox, which happens on March 21. If the full moon happens to fall on a Sunday, Easter is observed the following Sunday. As a result, Easter can never occur before March 22 or later than April 25. If both branches agree to this formulation, why is Orthodox Easter often different?

The answer lies in what calendar is employed to determine the first vernal equinox, March 21. Since the sixteenth century, Western Christianity has used the Gregorian calendar, developed in response to problems with the traditional Julian calendar system, which is 13 days behind. In 1923, most Orthodox churches around the globe accepted a revised Julian calendar that mirrors the Western Gregorian calendar until 2800! The original Julian calendar was maintained for the determination of Easter, however. Thus, whenever the first full moon appears within 13 days of March 21 in the Gregorian calendar, Western Christians and Eastern Christians celebrate Easter on different days.

Although Pascha is the most elaborate and important celebration for Orthodox, there are 12 other important feasts, which are usually referred to as the Great Feasts.

1. Nativity of the Holy Virgin (September 8) celebrates the birth of Mary, Jesus's mother.

2. Elevation of the Cross (September 14) commemorates the recovery of the Cross on which Jesus was crucified.

3. Presentation of the Holy Virgin in the Temple (November 21) celebrates the presentation of Mary to the Temple in Jerusalem, where, according to tradition, she lived until her betrothal to Joseph.

4. Nativity of Christ or Christmas (December 25) celebrates the birth of Christ in Bethlehem.

5. Theophany (January 6), literally, the "manifestation of God," recalls when Jesus was baptized by John and his earthly ministry began.

6. Presentation of Jesus in the Temple (February 2) commemorates when Mary and Joseph took their newborn child to the Temple in Jerusalem.

7. Annunciation (March 25) celebrates the moment when the Angel Gabriel appeared to Mary to announce that she would bear a son, Jesus.

8. Entrance of the Lord into Jerusalem or Palm Sunday (Sunday before Pascha) marks the beginning of the final week of Jesus's life.

9. Ascension (40 days after Pascha) remembers when Jesus blessed his disciples and ascended into heaven.

10. Pentecost (50 days after Pascha) commemorates the day when the Holy Spirit came upon the original followers.

11. Transfiguration (August 6) recalls the transformation in Jesus's appearance before the disciples Peter, James, and John.

12. Dormition of the Holy Virgin or Assumption (August 15) marks the "falling asleep" of Jesus's mother and her ascension into heaven.

Many regional customs are associated with these feasts. For example, on Christmas Eve at midnight in Bulgaria, groups of boy carolers called *Koledari* stroll through villages visiting neighbors, family, and friends. The *Koledari* carry sticks that they use to pat the backs of their audience to wish them good luck. On Christmas in Serbia, families go out and find or purchase an oak log, called a *badnjak*, which is then taken to church and blessed by a priest. The branches on the *badnjak* are stripped from it, and together with wheat and other items symbolizing resurrection, the *badnjak* is burned in the fireplace on Christmas day.

Though the festal calendar is consistent throughout Orthodoxy, certain other feasts can gain such prominence in specific countries that they come to equal or surpass the Great Feasts. For example, the Republic of Georgia celebrates St. George's Day (*Giorgoba*) each year with tremendous fanfare. In Serbia, St. George is such a popular family saint (called a *slava*) that St. George's Day (celebrated on a different date than in the Republic of Georgia) has effectively become a national holiday as well. In some countries, the feast days of popular names such as George, Constantine, John, Nicholas, Mary, and Eleni have also nearly become national holidays. These yearly celebrations usually include going to liturgy to receive communion and then throwing a party or having an open house for visitors. In some countries such as Greece, it is common for the name-day celebrant to give gifts to those who attend the celebrations.

Orthodoxy in the Cycle of One's Life

The Catholic Church often speaks of seven sacraments, but there has never been a fixed number of sacraments in the Orthodox East. Nearly all historical commentators have identified baptism and the Eucharist (Communion) as core events in the Orthodox life, but marriage, confession, holy unction, holy orders, and funeral services are also important. Despite never being systematized, Orthodox rites of passage influence a person at every stage of life.

MYSTERY VERSUS SACRAMENT

When the earliest Christian practices spread from Palestine into Greek and Roman lands, they inevitably were shaped by the cultural conditions found locally. This adaptation is clearly evident in the terms that were used to describe the Christian rites such as baptism and the Eucharist.

Romans in the West used the term *sacrament* to refer to Christian rites. Sacrament was the term used to refer to the vow or pledge a Roman soldier took to the emperor. As such, Christian practices were seen a pledges to God made in return for some spiritual benefit. One can see this most clearly in wedding ceremonies in the West, in which the central goal is the exchange of vows before the community and God.

Greeks in the East, by contrast, view Christian rites in terms of a mystical transformation of the individual that were ultimately beyond full comprehension, yet revealed the divine. The term employed is *mysteries*. As a result, the Orthodox wedding, called properly the Mystery of the Crowning in Marriage, contains no vows, but rather a mystical service that unites bride and groom in an everlasting bond.

Children in Orthodox countries are always named after saints, who come to be seen as their guardian throughout their life. In Serbia and nearby Orthodox lands, the family, rather than the individual baby, has a patron saint. The *slava* is usually passed down from father to son, with females usually taking the *slava* of her husband's family.

In numerous Orthodox countries, a name is not given to a baby until he or she is baptized, which usually happens before the baby is two years old. Officially, the godparent supplies the name, though there are different customs in each country. For example, in Greece, the first boy is usually given the paternal grandfather's name; the second boy is given the maternal grandfather's name; the first girl receives the paternal grandmother's name, and so forth. However, despite the custom, sometimes godparents surprise the family by choosing a different name.

After birth, a 40-day period begins in which the mother and baby are to be kept out of public spaces. In Russia, mothers often do not show their newborn baby to anyone other than the father for a month, but in other Orthodox countries many relatives visit. On the 40th day, the mother and child reenter society through a ceremony at church during which the baby is dedicated to God and the mother is welcomed back into the community.

Given the historic high rate of infant mortality, the first years of a child's life often include local superstitions to ward off potential malevolent forces. For example, in Greece, newborns and infants are often outfitted with talismans (*filahta*) such as small medallions or small pieces of cloth sewn into sachets inside of which there may be images of saints, olive branches, candle shaving from a church, dirt from Jerusalem, or any number of other holy items.

Baptism is the first major sacrament or mystery for a child and usually occurs within the first couple years of life. Because the Orthodox Church does not accept the Western doctrine of Original Sin (according to which a newborn baby is born stained with sin and guilty before God), there was never a rush to baptize children. The baptismal service was developed during a time when most people being baptized were adults, so it includes many elements in which an infant cannot participate, such as public rejection of the devil and the recitation of the Nicene Creed. As a result, the godparents play an important function in the service as the surrogate of the child, agreeing to raise him or her up in a manner consistent with his or her Orthodox baptism. The Orthodox baptism includes a threefold immersion in the name of the Holy Trinity, and it usually accepts baptisms by others churches that are performed in the same manner. Chrismation, which has become a separate rite of confirmation in the West, is performed immediately after baptism and is seen as the descent of the Holy Spirit into the newly illumined.

The next major life-cycle rite is the wedding service. Marriage is the norm in Orthodox society, though celibacy has a long and prominent history in monastic circles of the church. The wedding service, called the Mystery of Crowning in Marriage, does not include formal vows as in the West. Rather, the imagery expressed is the forging of a higher unity between two individuals. The centerpiece of the service is the wearing of two crowns linked by a ribbon that unite the couple as they walk around a table, led by a priest holding an ornate copy of the gospels. The newly married couple forms a new relationship between each other, God, and the church.

Orthodox tend not to use the term *death*, rather calling the end of life "falling asleep in the Lord," which reflects their belief that the individual has not ceased to exist. Burial rites have several stages. Shortly after someone expires, the priest will say a short prayer for the release of the soul, followed by a small memorial service performed for loved ones. Orthodox are never cremated, and the body, after being cleaned and clothed, is traditionally brought into the church the evening before the funeral service. The family and friends can then spend the night with the body in the church, reciting psalms and invoking memorial prayers. A divine liturgy may follow. The funeral service proper contains numerous prayers and readings, returning to a familiar refrain: "With the saints give rest, O Christ, to the soul of Thy servant where there is neither sickness, nor sorrow, nor sighing, but life everlasting." The body and the faithful travel in procession to the cemetery where the body is interred to the sound of bells. In the Russian tradition, a series of bells called *Perebor* are struck, from highest to lowest, symbolizing the life of the person from birth to eternity. Russian tradition has individuals buried with funeral "bundles" that include the cloth that covered the coffin, two crosses (one to hold and one around the neck), a *provodynychok* (a blessed paper wreath), written prayers, and candles from the funeral service.

Memorial services for the dead are an important part of Orthodox life. Even though their frequency varies across Orthodox areas, they are usually performed on the third and fortieth days after death, and then again on the yearly anniversaries. It is a common belief in popular religiosity that the soul wanders the earth for 40 days after death; as a result, the families occasionally leave a glass of water, a piece of bread, or a fruit to sustain the earthbound soul.

Orthodoxy and the Management of Evil

The official Orthodox worldview exists alongside a more diverse, less unified series of local traditions surrounding the management of evil and bad luck. Though officially shunned by the church, these practices are often condoned by the local clergy. Their roots are often pre-Christian, though they usually take on a Christian veneer or symbolism. Many Orthodox, especially from rural areas untouched by the modern world, hold these practices as seriously as any.

Perhaps the most famous such practice in the Mediterranean region is known as the "evil eye," or *matiasma* in Greek. It can be brought on by jealousy or envy and causes both physical and psychological harm. Babies and young people are particularly susceptible to the evil eye, as they are so often the focus of lavish attention. To avoid the evil eye, people will wear a little blue marble glass pendant or a necklace or bracelet with an eye painted on it. Blue is said to be the color that wards off evil. Spitting is also said to ward off evil. Older Greeks, for example, often spit when they hear bad news for the first time. In Russia, spitting is usually in the direction of the left shoulder, where the devil is said to reside. Many local prayer books contain prayers to rid a person of the evil eye, most of which call on Jesus's mother to protect those "infected."

Warding off evil with various techniques has a long tradition in Orthodox countries. In Russia, whistling indoors is said to lead to misfortune, and evil spirits can be summoned by bragging or calling attention to good health. Throughout the Orthodox world, garlic is said to ward off evil; hence the braided garlic outside houses or the single garlic clove in people's pockets. In parts of Bulgaria, Romania, and Serbia, costumed men perform a ritual dance that is said to ward off evil spirits. Called *Kukeri* in Bulgaria, these men usually don animal masks and ring bells in the hopes of scaring off evil spirits.

IMPACT OF DAILY LIFE IN HISTORY

In the summer of 726, the great volcano island of Santorini in Greece erupted, causing significant damage and fear. The Byzantine emperor at the time—a general named Leo III, who made his name fighting the expanding Islamic armies—decided that the eruption was a warning sign from God that needed to be heeded if further devastation were not to come upon the Byzantine Empire. Leo, perhaps influenced by his encounter with the strong iconoclasm of Islam, determined that God was punishing the Greeks for their veneration of images of Jesus and the saints. In his mind, these images violated the second commandment, "You shall not make for yourself an idol, whether in the form of anything that is in heaven above, or that is on the earth beneath, or that is in the water under the earth." He immediately had soldiers remove the great icon of Christ that marked the entrance to the imperial palace for centuries. The images, however, were beloved by the people, for whom they became concrete representations of the divine. Immediately, the historians report, a mob gathered in protest. An elderly woman shook the ladder of the soldier who went up to remove the icon, leading to his death. The people thus made a religious stand against the emperor.

Initially, the religious leader of Constantinople, the Patriarch Germanos I, defended the proper use of images, but the emperor exiled him and assured a replacement who was more agreeable to his views. With the patriarch and the emperor pushing the iconoclast (breaker of icons) agenda, all worldly power was aligned against the iconodules (supporters of icons) and iconophiles (lovers of icons). It then became law that every citizen of Constantinople was to bring his icons into the public square to be burned, under threat of death, but few ordinary people complied. The lines were drawn: the powerful and the people were at odds.

Leo's son Constantine V (718–775) called for an ecumenical council in 754 to settle the matter. The 338 bishops present—an attendance rate higher than that of any ecumenical council previously—condemned icons. The people, however, never embraced this council. As had so often happened before, the people found a champion in the monastic ranks: a monk from Palestine named John of Damascus. He became the voice of the people. As a Christian living in Muslim lands, the emperors had no control over him, which allowed him to write freely without any fear of reproach. Moreover, he was fluent in Arabic, so he was very aware of the debate that was happening in Islam at the time regarding images. In his defense of icons, he argued not only that icon veneration was permissible but that it was central to the Christian proclamation.

The emperors responded harshly against the monks within their jurisdictions who were supporting John of Damascus. They confiscated their land, threw their famous relics into the sea, and publicly mocked them. In one famous incident, the emperor forced the dissenting monks of Constantinople to parade in the central hippodrome, each hand in hand with a woman, in violation of their vows. With such persecution, many of the people hid their icons from authorities. There are many stories passed down about icons that were miraculously preserved or were sent out to sea only to find their home in a protective monastery. For the church community, the saints represented by the icons were not heroes of a bygone age, but active parts of their community. They did not merely worship them but rather recognized the saints' ongoing presence through veneration.

In 787, a woman named Irene ruled the empire while her son Constantine VI (780–797) grew into maturity. She worked for the restoration of icons, often against military units that had been loyal to her iconoclastic husband. Eventually, she convened a new ecumenical council in 787, with the support of the people. This council reversed the decrees of the previous iconoclast council and has since appropriated its title as the Seventh Ecumenical Council. There would still be iconoclastic emperors in the ninth century, but despite their worldly power, they could never convince the people or the monks to embrace iconoclasm.

Today, on the first Sunday of Great Lent, Orthodox Christians from all over the globe join together to commemorate the triumph of the people over the emperors and patriarchs who attempted to dictate iconoclasm. They bring icons to church, have them blessed, and then move in procession around the building. It is a family reunion of sorts, when the distant members of the Orthodox family come together with the current ones. The images themselves draw the believer into a holy embrace with the past pillars of the church, who are still present. These icons are not memorials in paint, but living windows into a heavenly realm. As the community members walk around the church displaying their icons, one is reminded that the Orthodox community transcends place and time.

GLOSSARY

Filioque ("and the son"): A Roman Catholic addition to the Nicene Creed referring to the source of the Holy Spirit that has been a cause of division between Eastern and Western Christianity.

Hieromonk: An Orthodox monk who is also a priest.

Icon: A painted image of a saint, Mary, or Jesus that is used as a "window into heaven," especially during worship services.

Jesus Prayer: A prayer ("Lord Jesus Christ, Son of God, have mercy upon me, a sinner") used as a spiritual exercise, particularly by monks.

Pascha: The Greek word for Passover and the traditional word for Easter in the East.

Eucharist. Literally means thanksgiving, but it is the named employed for the body and blood of Christ and the name of the service that culminates in partaking of it.

Slava: The patron saint for families in the Serbian tradition.

Theosis: Deification through Christ, often presented as the goal of Orthodox life. Derived from 2 Peter 1:4, which calls on Christians to "participate in the divine nature."

Theotokos (Mother of God): The traditional title for Jesus's mother in Orthodoxy.

BIBLIOGRAPHY

Anonymous, *The Way of a Pilgrim*. Translated by R. M. French. New York: HarperOne, 1991. A classic Russian tale about the importance of the Jesus Prayer in Orthodox spirituality. Available in multiple translations.

Clendenin, Daniel B. *Eastern Orthodox Theology: A Contemporary Reader*. Grand Rapids, MI: Baker Academic, 2003. A commendable collection of some of the best essays on Orthodoxy in the last several decades.

Gilquist, Peter. *Becoming Orthodox*. Brentwood, TN: Wolgemuth and Hyatt, 1989. A modern classic that traces the journey to Orthodoxy of prominent Evangelical Christians and their struggles to reconcile their own evangelical background with their increasing understanding of history and tradition of the Church.

Ouspensky, Leonid, and Vladimir Lossky. *The Meaning of Icons*. Crestwood, NY: St. Vladimir's Seminary Press, 1982. One of the foremost interpretations of the history and use of icons in the Orthodox Church.

Schmemann, Alexander. *For the Life of the World: Sacraments and Orthodoxy*. Crestwood, NY: St. Vladimir's Seminary Press, 1973. A classic book about the liturgical life of the Orthodox Church and the nature of the Orthodox mindset.

Ware, Timothy. *The Orthodox Church*. 2nd ed. New York: Penguin, 1993.

Ware, Bishop Kallistos. *The Orthodox Way*. Crestwood, NY: St. Vladimir's Seminary Press, 1995. A classic introduction to Orthodoxy written by a man who would become a prominent bishop and Oxford professor. His companion volume, *The Orthodox Way*, examines the critical beliefs of Orthodoxy.

Chapter 9

Medieval Europe

Peter Collins

INTRODUCTION: MEDIEVAL FAITH AND BELIEF

Although medieval Europe was officially Catholic, individuals and groups frequently invented variations and alternatives. Such groups include the Mozarabs, Templars, Vilgards, Leutards, Petrusians, Humiliati, Tondrakians, Paulicians, Messalanians, Albigensians, Waldenensians, and Cathars. These groups, sometimes led by charismatic individuals and sometimes not, themselves demographically and theologically diverse, called into question the pervasive worldview—often in the certain knowledge that persecution would follow. Sometimes this questioning led to schism, sometimes not. And, of course, the Roman Catholic Church has itself never been entirely unified and homogeneous—because people act as though they believe the same thing, that does not mean that they believe the same thing.

Consider the case of Domenico Scandella, called Menocchio, the sixteenth-century Italian peasant whose life is brilliantly described by Carlo Ginzburg in *The Cheese and the Worms* (1980). We know about Menocchio's ideas because of the careful record kept of his several interrogations by his inquisitor, Canon Giambattista Maro. In Ginzburg's account, we catch a glimpse of the peasant as an individual, one who is able to reflect on his position in society and the cosmos. Consciously and purposely, Menocchio subjects the religion of the day (Catholicism) to a constant and concerted barrage of criticisms. He developed an overtly idiosyncratic personal theology and, despite the dangers, was able and willing to discuss his ideas with others. The record suggests that sometimes he accepted the main tenets of Catholic doctrine, and sometimes he veered away from them in interesting ways. Was he a Lutheran, Anabaptist, or a (rather free-thinking) Catholic? From Menocchio's own account of his faith and practice, it appears that he was simultaneously both all and none of these; certainly, it is better to talk about his cosmogony rather than his theology. He believed that the Host contained the Holy Spirit, that Christ did not die so that the sins of mankind might be purged, that the Gospels contained truth but also the personal ideas of the apostles, that the Mass was on the whole a good thing, and that the idea of the virgin birth was irrational. As these examples show, his belief system displays a striking individuality. The record further suggests that Menocchio had a flair for metaphor and simile, likening the universe to a vast cheese from which the angels emerged: "They were produced by nature from the most perfect substance in the world, just as worms are produced from a cheese, and when they emerged received will, intellect, and memory from God as he blessed them."[1] As in many of his explanations, Menocchio draws on everyday experience in making sense of his beliefs. At first sight, Menocchio appears an extraordinary man, determined to maintain an extraordinary faith and practice. But is this the case? Ginzburg argues the contrary: "Rather, we should ask if they [unorthodox believers like Menocchio] don't belong within an autonomous current of peasant radicalism, which the upheaval of the Reformation had helped to bring forth, but which was much older."[2] Menocchio, despite accusations of heresy, prosecutes his own life course with a degree of single-mindedness and determination that we might think few others could achieve. But then we have before us the record of just one individual and that record suggests that such idiosyncrasy is at least universally possible. Where is social structure here? How can we understand the faith and practice of Menocchio (or of any woman or man) without paying careful attention to his individuality?

Much of medieval religion had little to do with the spiritual or devotional, but rather with administration, celebrations, and the overt display of wealth and power. There is a plethora of material relating to such matters, but very little indeed relating to the religious faith and practice of ordinary men and women. Medieval people tended not to celebrate publicly their individuality. When we come across examples of such behavior, it is rarely that of the ordinary person happy with their lot. Generally speaking, evidence of individual spiritual development is most often associated with the extremes of sainthood or heresy. The sources that we draw on in the pursuit of individual spirituality—such as archives of ecclesiastical courts, visitations records, heresy trials, and so forth—tend naturally to focus on the unusual. And generalizing from single instances is to be guarded against. With that in mind let us proceed to describe religious life during the Middle Ages.

The medieval age is sometimes presented as that period of (mostly Western) history beginning at the end of "the Classical period" around 350 CE and merging into the pre-modern period at around 1550: this might be called "the long Middle Ages." Apart from the temporal vastness of the subject, we are dealing here with the whole of Europe—though I will focus on Western Europe. Clearly, then, it is dangerous to generalize in such circumstances because the social changes that took place within these 1,200 years were immense and varied hugely across the continent. Let us break the period up into three parts: the Early Middle Ages (350–1000 CE), the High Middle Ages (1000–1300), and the Late Middle Ages (1300–1550).

Besides the spatial and temporal enormity of the task before us, there is another major challenge in discussing "medieval religion," and that is the inevitable paucity of data. That is not to say that data do not exist, but that evidence relating particularly to "ordinary folk" is sparse indeed. With the advent of printing in the fifteenth century, the situation changes considerably, of course. As might be expected, the information that most readily comes to hand, especially relating to the Early Middle Ages, is concerned with the "big issues" of empires and emperors, of invasion and war. In terms of religion, once again, we can glean quite a lot about princes and popes, but next to nothing about the faith and practice of ordinary people. The one guarded assertion we can make, however, is that the medieval period is characterized, perhaps above all else, by the steady rise of Christianity across the continent, and by the steadily increasing grip of Catholicism in particular. This is not to homogenize either the process or the product. As we will see, Catholicism can be counterposed to "heresy," of one form or another, throughout the Middle Ages. Because of the greater availability of evidence, I will focus on the period from 1000 to 1500.

The medieval Church imposed a morality and ethic on all adherents through its disciplinary and penitential structure, its preaching, and its promises of hell, purgatory, and paradise. It oversaw the continuance of the moral structure in this world and also cajoled people into self-regulation. The detailed organization of Christian life was an important element in the totality of the Christian experience, because people adopted specific lifestyles that indicated degrees of commitment. From minimal to considerable and very personal, this range might seem incoherent, unless we view the whole as a conglomerate of discrete communities. All varieties seem subsumed under the unity of "the Church." Though regulation was not adopted by everyone, everyone was subjected to the same degree of regulation through the liturgy, which established the timetable for the religious and spiritual Christian life and dictated the opportunities for worship and the means for communing with God.

TIMELINE

5th century:	Collapse of the Roman Empire with the conquest of Rome by Germanic tribes. The early medieval period (the "Dark Ages") sees the growth of a powerful Christian (Catholic) Church.
500:	Clovis, founder of the Frankish state, conquers most of France and Belgium, converting his territories to Christianity.
590:	Pope Gregory establishes a religious system for Western Europe by fusing the Roman papacy with Benedictine monasticism. He creates the Latin church, which serves to counteract the subordination of the Roman popes to Eastern emperors.
700:	Benedictine missionaries complete the conversion of England begun by St. Gregory the Great.
800:	Charlemagne is crowned emperor by the pope in Rome, marking an autonomous Western culture based on Western Christianity and the Latin language.
955:	John XII becomes pope at the age of 18. His rule typifies the decline in value of the Church in the early medieval period. Local lords establish control over churches and monasteries, and Church officials are often unqualified. The majority of priests are illiterate and live with concubines. The majority of popes, mostly sons of powerful Roman families, are corrupt or incompetent.
1054:	Great Schism: separation of (Western) Catholic and (Eastern) Orthodox churches.
1095:	Byzantine Emperor Alexius Comnenus requests help to reconquer the lost territory of Asia Minor, initiating the First Crusade. Western Europe sends large armies to rescue Jerusalem from the control of Islam.
1164:	Henry II returns power to civil from ecclesiastical courts. The archbishop of Canterbury, Thomas Becket, opposes Henry's reforms and is murdered in Canterbury Cathedral. He is martyred and revered as the greatest saint of English history.
1198:	Pope Innocent III, founder of the Papal State, is elected pope. He is trained in canon law and theology. His primary concern of administration is the unification of all Christendom under the papal monarchy, including the right to interfere with the rule of kings. He is the organizer of the Fourth Crusade, ordered to recapture Jerusalem from Islam. Pope Innocent III

initiates the Albigensian Crusade to destroy the heretical threat of the Albigensians. Seven years later, he organizes the Fourth Lateran Council, which recognizes the necessity of the Eucharist and penance as sacraments for salvation. This council exemplifies the power of the papacy over kings and Church. In 1216, he authorizes St. Dominic to found the Dominican order, which sets out to convert Muslims and Jews and to put an end to heresy. The Dominicans become the main administrators of the medieval Inquisition.

1212: Christian Spain reconquers the Iberian Peninsula from the Muslims.

1244: Jerusalem is lost by the West and is not recaptured until 1917.

1300: Boniface VIII calls the first papal jubilee, recognizing pilgrimages to Rome instead of Jerusalem, no longer accessible to the West.

1305: The papacy is moved from Rome to Avignon. For most of the fourteenth century, the papacy is subordinate to French authority.

1347: The Black Death appears during a time of economic depression in Western Europe and reoccurs frequently until the fifteenth century. The Black Death is a combination of bubonic and pneumonic plagues and has a major impact on social and economic conditions. Religious flagellation is practised by lay groups to appease divine wrath.

1399: In England, the death penalty becomes the punishment for heresy, and many Lollards, John Wycliffe's lay followers, convert.

1417: The Council of Constance, the largest Church meeting in medieval history, ends the Great Schism.

1439: Johannes Gutenberg of Mainz, in Germany, develops a movable type printing technology, initiating the European age of printing.

1509: Henry VIII succeeds his father, Henry VII, as king of England, and in 1534 instigates the Reformation in England, despite previously defending Catholicism against attacks from Martin Luther.

THE INSTITUTIONAL ORDER, 350–1550

Let us begin by describing the social, political, and economic order of medieval Europe as feudal, though this term has been increasingly contested (and not used by those alive during the Middle Ages). To generalize somewhat, feudalism represents the typical medieval European political system. The system comprised an array of reciprocal legal and military obligations among the warrior nobility, revolving around lords, fiefs (revenue-producing property such as land and hunting rights), and vassals who exchanged military service for the use of fiefs. Fiefs were occupied mainly by peasants, freemen who received land in return for their labor. Following the Black Death and the rise of the middle class (or bourgeoisie), the pyramidal feudal system broke down and was replaced by the modern, capitalist system: the lord became landlord; the vassal became tenant farmer or landless laborer; the landed gentry lost their grip on power; and popular assemblies grew in strength across the continent. Finally, land became less central in economic affairs than money, which became the key symbol of power. The old conception of the feudal force had completely disappeared.

The Church, too, had its place in the feudal system. It was also granted territorial fiefs, became a vassal, and possessed immunities. The Church gained a foothold in new regions outside the Roman Empire, to which many Christians thought it was irrevocably bound. For example, the baptism of Clovis, the Frankish King, indicated that the baptism of Constantine had not tied the Church to any one nation-state. There was to be not so much a universal Church as a number of national churches under their territorial princes. But there was also an overlap between secular and ecclesiastical systems of power: the younger sons of nobles were consecrated as bishops, even becoming popes, and within the empire there were several prince-bishops and senior abbots, whose power and authority was greater than that of many secular barons. Indeed, the Church was in danger of becoming an annex of the state, and the pope of becoming the chaplain of the emperor. These abuses were primarily the result of secular interference in the monasteries, and of the Church's tight integration with the feudal and manorial systems. By 1100, the papacy wished to reassert control of all clergy and stop the investiture of bishops by secular rulers. The Reforms of Cluny, the impetus of which was corruption within the Church, particularly the denial of celibacy by the priesthood, eventuated in the greater separation between church and state.

The rest of this section presents an overview of medieval canonic religion that is necessarily sketchy and schematic but also crucial to provide the ideological backdrop against which everyday religion was enacted.

The medieval Church was considerably more than simply the fount of coercive power; the Church was human society in its entirety, subject to God's will. Whether or not any rational social order might exist outside the Church was a matter for dispute. Such an order could, in any case, be no more than an attenuated and relatively insignificant order. One's sense of identity and belonging depended on one's membership in the Church because it provided one's home in the world. The Church was not only a society but society itself, not one ideology but *the* ideology across most of Europe, certainly after 1000. But that is to talk only about this world; the Church also offered the gift of salvation, extending its reach into the next world and thereby determining not only this life, but life eternal—of all people, everywhere. The medieval Church developed in extraordinary detail the idea of a universal human society as an integral part of a divinely ordered universe in time and in eternity. A person's life was lived in the context of a worldview established by the Church and which combined the Judeo-Christian and the Greco-Roman to form a coherent and comprehensive cosmology. There were of course major social, political, and sociocultural changes over the course of these 10 centuries, but the Church remained relatively constant, not merely as a backdrop but as both cause and effect of social action. Moreover, throughout the period the dominant institution was the papacy, at least across the Western half of the continent.

The patristic age (fourth to sixth centuries) was fertile for the development of distinctive ideas and practices of Christianity. The writings of Basil, Ambrose, Jerome, and Augustine, for example, provided the intellectual framework of Christian thinking for the entire Middle Ages, the Reformation, and even for modern times. The distinctive Christian emphasis on virginity and the organization of monasticism first appeared in the Early Middle Ages. These vital and formative processes were directly relevant to the current faith and practice of Islam as well as to contemporary economic and political processes more generally. In the West, the Roman Empire expired in the fifth century, but its legacy is apparent through the Middle Ages, and indeed it has been said that the Roman Catholic Church was an attempt at its re-creation. The end of the Early Middle Ages witnessed the major rift between the Latin and Greek churches, due to theological and other differences. The rift lasted a very long time, indeed until the Second Vatican Council, known as Vatican II (1962–1965), at the conclusion of which Pope Paul VI and Orthodox Patriarch Athenagoras issued a joint expression of regret for many of the past actions that had led up to the Great Schism between the Western and Eastern churches, and lifted the mutual excommunications dating from the eleventh century.

The ideological framework of the papacy was strengthened by Leo I (440–461), who, citing Roman law, argued that an heir inherited all the rights and obligations of the testator—that is, in a legal sense, the former became the latter. Leo argued that Peter had been the bishop of Rome and had passed on his authority to his successor, Clement, who in turn passed on what he had received from Peter to his successor and so on, down the line to Leo and beyond, each incumbent receiving what Christ had given to Peter. Indeed, he insisted that each pope could be said to *be* Peter and therefore had both the right and the duty to make final and binding decisions on matters of doctrine.

Between 700 and 1050 the West was in effect the poor relative of Byzantium, inferior in many ways to its Greek and Muslim neighbors. The crucial weakness of the West was its poor socioeconomic condition; however, when circumstances improved the population began to grow. In religious terms the period is dominated by the Benedictine Order. The monastery at Monte Cassino was established in Italy around 529, and it was the first of a dozen monasteries founded by St. Benedict of Nursia, though there is no evidence to suggest that he intended to found an order. Indeed, the Rule of St. Benedict presupposes the autonomy of each community. However, most monasteries founded during the Middle Ages adopted the Rule of St. Benedict, and it thus became the standard for Western monasticism. Many great men of the age were Benedictine monks or their patrons. To enter Holy Orders was generally regarded as the best chance of salvation. The Benedictine monasteries were the symbol of stability and immutability in a world of flux; they were the gate to heaven, replicas of heaven on earth. The Benedictine monasteries went on to play an important role in the spiritual, economic, and political life of Europe, so much so that the years from 550 to 1150 have been called "Benedictine centuries."

The Muslim-Christian conflict was played out most energetically in the Iberian Peninsula. Although the Arab conquest of Spain was more or less accomplished by 750, parts of northern Spain remained Christian, and Christian resistance was unceasing during the next 750 years. The Christian reconquest of Spain was virtually complete by 1212. By the end of the Middle Ages, Arabs (and Jews) who had not converted to Christianity were expelled from Spain. Violent anti-Semitism prevailed by the time of the Plague (1391), which Christians blamed on Jews, whom they accused of poisoning wells.

Pope Gregory's assertion of universal papal authority, especially concerning the investiture of bishops, provoked collision with kings and rulers who still regarded bishops as feudal inferiors. The drive toward greater uniformity was expressed in the systematizing of canon and doctrine: the Fourth Lateran Council (1215) under papal auspices asserted the doctrine of the transubstantiation at the mass, a miracle that only the priest could perform. As doctrine became more tightly controlled, so was the cult taken out of the hands of the local episcopacy by 1200—the concentration of decision-making powers on the papal curia in Rome included a claim to the exclusive right to bestow the accolade of sainthood. Innocent III (1198–1216) adopted the title "vicar of Christ," which was purloined from the emperor. Universal cults tended to be promoted over local ones. Devotion to the mother of Christ was also strengthened through the creation of new cults. New international orders such as the Cistercians encouraged neither cults of local saints nor relics. Newer cults,

such as miraculous crosses, did not need them—Marian cults were embodied
in statues and images rather than relics. The emphasis on a universal Church
was contained within Western Christendom because this process was opposed
by the Orthodox Church in the East. Feelings toward the universal Church
were ambivalent, and local churches refused to deny the validity of local cults.

The Late Middle Ages (1300–1550) have been called "the age of unrest,"
partly because of the attacks on popes by kings—for instance, on Boniface
VIII by French troops in 1303. Urbanization gathered pace, towns found their
voice: Florence grew from a population of around 10,000 before 1300, to over
120,000 in 1345. This affected the Church because urban growth provokes
dissent, including increasingly articulate lay opinion about religion. Hierarchical stability faltered. Thomas Aquinas believed that the more self-sufficient a
community was, the more perfect it was—trade promoted avarice and instability. As towns grew, they made religious institutions seem less important,
provoking a new intensity of personal religion. Increasingly powerful laymen
recognized that the pope was much like themselves. The idea of the necessity
of a universal lord was urgently questioned; and if necessary then should the
universal lord be the pope? And should he pronounce on both the secular and
spiritual affairs? The continued interaction of theory and practice produced a
new emphasis on individual experience, on the values of secular life, and on the
role of the community as the source of political and spiritual authority. But to
cause the established order to topple would surely lead to something infinitely
more terrible. The scattered numbers of radical thinkers were not sufficiently
knowledgeable or unified to bring about major change. And why bring down
the papacy? By 1500 the institution had already ceased to be a major political
player. Strangely, England contained simultaneously the most radical men and
the most conservative church, a state of affairs achieved largely through the
support of the aristocracy, which established social stability through ecclesiastical authority. The alliance of secular and Church hierarchies survived, at least
for the time being.

The beginning of the early modern period is not clear-cut, but it is generally accepted to be in the late fifteenth or early sixteenth century. The Renaissance included a flourishing of art and science in Western Europe,
demonstrated most spectacularly in the universal genius of Leonardo da Vinci.
A key moment was the invention of the first European movable type printing
process by Johannes Gutenberg in 1436—a device that fundamentally
changed the circulation of information. The conquest of Constantinople by
the Ottomans in 1453 signaled the end of the Byzantine Empire. The first
documented European voyage to the Americas by the Italian-Spanish explorer
Christopher Columbus took place in 1492. The Reformation began in 1517,

with Martin Luther nailing his 95 theses to the door of the church in Wittenberg, Germany; and in 1545 the Council of Trent marked the end of the medieval Roman Catholic Church. The year 1550 might seem an arbitrary place to end the Middle Ages, and of course it is. The foundations of the Reformation were already being laid and there can be no doubt that significant changes in the practice (if not the faith) of ordinary people were taking place. In England, at least, the transition from the Middle Ages and Catholicism to the early modern period and Anglicanism was less seismic than might be imagined.

THE CHRISTIAN WORLDVIEW

Although it may seem that there was a shared worldview among the peoples of medieval Western Europe, there certainly was not a single, unified cosmology, and everyone did not believe the same thing. However, clearly, enough was shared for these populations to consider themselves sharing the same world. What they shared, for the most part, was an inherently religious worldview, undergirded by the political and military might of church and, increasingly, state. The generally accepted worldview was Catholic. Of course, whereas a few learned men would know about and fully comprehend Catholic theology and Church structure in its entirety, the vast majority of people would grasp only fragments of the overall picture, and their understanding of these fragments would in most cases have been partial. Every person would have known that there was one God and that God was three persons—the Father, the Son, and the Holy Spirit—and that they were immortal and omnipotent, all-seeing and all-powerful.

The First Council of Nicaea met in 325 with the clear intention of defining and unifying the beliefs for Christendom as a whole. The Nicene Creed clarified the relationship between the Son and the Father—which from then on was seen as the hallmark of Orthodoxy—declaring that the Son and the Father are "of the same substance." The doctrine of the divinity and personality of the Holy Spirit was developed by Athanasius (c. 293–373) during his final years, and by 400 the doctrine of the Trinity was more or less complete. In contrast to the warring deities of the pagans, there is just one and the same God in the Old and New Testaments. The Holy Trinity sat in heaven as the crowning glory of a well-defined celestial hierarchy. The council declared Arian and non-Trinitarian doctrines heretical and excommunicated those who defended them.

Some would further know that God's first act was to create the angels, incorporeal beings who could in various ways affect the lives of ordinary people.

Angels are organized into nine tiers or choirs, headed by the seraphim and cherubs. Representations of angels in the art and sculpture of the time are extraordinarily consistent: they are winged, of indeterminate gender, and bathed in heavenly light. The symbolism of the angelic choir, because so visual, would probably have been grasped largely, if not in its entirety by all of those who worshiped in all but the smallest churches. In the great celestial drama, some angels fall from grace, and the greatest among these is Satan himself, who commands his force of demons in hell. Angels and demons might have been incorporeal, but their effects on human being were believed to be dangerously real.

During the Middle Ages, heaven and hell were regarded as real, physical places: above the earth, heaven, and hell below. Such inversion is characteristic of such representations: whatever "good" is, "evil" is its opposite. Purgatory (God's waiting room) has been depicted both as material and nonmaterial at various times. In Dante's fourteenth-century work *The Divine Comedy*, the Earth is placed at the center of the universe and hell at the center of the Earth. The planets and stars revolve around Earth and Heaven (or the Seven Heavens), encircling Creation in celestial spheres. Purgatory is represented as a mountain in the southern hemisphere. When, according to Dante, Satan rebelled against God and was defeated, he was cast out from Heaven and fell to Earth. The impact crater from the fall was so great that it reached to the Earth's core. Satan's being held at the center of the center of the universe (Earth) was proof of his selfishness. The crater was filled over, becoming a dark and fiery cavern, Hell, with Jerusalem directly over Satan. But the force of Satan's impact created such an uplift that it produced a mountain "beneath" Satan, on the opposite side of the Earth. Souls given a second chance find themselves at Mount Purgatory, and should they reach the top they will find themselves at Jerusalem's antipode, the Garden of Eden itself. Cleansed of all sin and made perfect, they wait in earthly paradise before ascending to Heaven.

Although the idea of punishment, penance, and absolution were familiar to all by that time, the distinction between purgatory and hell was new. The chantry movement was a direct outcome of the development of the idea of purgatory. The chantry was established to offer prayers and masses for the dead to speed their passage through purgatory. The day of judgment is represented with particular vigor in the twelfth-century Winchester Psalter. This extraordinary book was most likely illustrated for a house of nuns. The pictures are shockingly graphic and would probably have had the desired effect. Ladies, including queens, are portrayed tumbling into the jaws of hell, and brutal medieval torture equipment is depicted being used on men, with monks and bishops standing by. The focal illustration depicts Christ in majesty, indicating the wound in his side, while angels carry the cross onto the altar. The final picture is of angels shutting the gates of hell. Images of Christ in judgment were common in churches throughout Western Europe in the thirteenth century, on numerous tympana over the doors of French cathedrals and abbeys, and in sculpture. Christ is typically placed in the center, with heaven to his right and hell to his left (the sinister), depicting all the horrors in store for the unrighteous. The terror of those facing death might be assuaged by the idea of a merciful God who would receive prayers on their behalf.

VERNACULAR RELIGION IN TOWN AND COUNTRY

In this section we will consider the various ways in which religion bore on the daily lives of individuals. First we need to look a little more closely at the relationship between the local church and the laity. We will then go on to look at some of the many ways in which the lives of ordinary people, in particular aspects of everyday life, were driven by religious motivations.

Liturgy and the Mass

To understand the most vital component of medieval religion—the mass— we need to place it within the wider context of both parish life and the liturgical calendar. The latter consisted of three temporal cycles. First, the divine office included a series of daily prayers and praises that defined the hours and was especially important for those committed to formal, regular existence. This series was based on the monastic *horarium*, or daily schedule, which was divided into a series of celebrations (Lauds, Matins, Prime, Terce, Sext, Nones, Vespers, and Compline), each involving the chanting of psalms and biblical readings. The material changed so that all psalms would be sung during the week and the entire Bible recited during the year. Although this was a primarily monastic system, clerics might have participated as might laypersons. Second, the weekly round clearly focused on Sunday, dedicated as it was to God; work and entertainment were prohibited on this day except in unusual circumstances. Saturday might be dedicated to the Virgin. Friday was significant, and the eating of meat prohibited as a regular reminder of God. Wednesday was also important but less so than Friday. These special days may have caused a certain fragmentation of the week but were more likely to serve as a reminder that religion was not to be relegated to Sunday only. And third, there was the annual calendar, which was long established but not immutable. The tendency was toward addition rather than subtraction, which made the liturgical timetable increasingly crowded. Although the liturgical round grew increasingly uniform, the result was not liturgical uniformity, and the evident liturgical variation is most explicit in the regional liturgies of the several "uses," that is, different formats for what were essentially the same rites. These distinctions were generally the result of diocesan arrangements enforced in the thirteenth century by synodal legislation. Pressure from Rome ensured that greater standardization slowly emerged.

The liturgical round included a diverse range of celebrations but none was as important as the Mass. By 1300 only the priests received both bread and wine, whereas the laity received the Host only, and annual Communion probably sufficed for most people. Those who chose to receive Holy Communion more than once a year showed a greater devotion—even especially devout women in late medieval England, such as Margery Kempe, thought annual Communion sufficient. In many cases, laypersons were mere spectators at liturgical events, including the Mass. This was offset by the development of what might be called a "private liturgy," most highly developed in books of hours. These texts were not universally available and were too difficult for most people to follow, some straying a considerable distance from Church liturgy. Such books proliferated from the thirteenth century on. Their most important function was to stimulate prayer, and they certainly encouraged a private devotional tradition, providing laypersons with a means of structuring their lives through a personal liturgy. There is considerable evidence pointing to the gendered use of the books and the development of a domestic female spirituality from the thirteenth century on.

The Mass was primarily a rite that involved the priests and God, and although worshippers were encouraged to attend, they were more or less irrelevant for the right ordering of the rite. Although the Mass was generally a public event, it was held in the chancel and may not have been directly observed by many. The elevation of the Host and chalice was standard practice by the thirteenth century, and worshippers very much wanted to see the event, to witness the moment when God was in the Host, even if it was not to be consumed. They understood that at this moment in the Mass they would be in the direct presence of Christ. This spiritual communion provided a key component of the personal devotion for some, though probably not for others. The elevation of the Host became so central to the rite that people increasingly made the effort to be present at that point, sometimes rushing in at the last minute and even from church to church in the hope of witnessing as many as possible. Such enthusiasm can be seen either as profound devotion or a rather utilitarian view of the elevation as a means of curtailing time in purgatory. The clerical view was that the laity should remain passive but the laity may well have disagreed. In the parish church, laypersons would have been aware of the sacrificial purpose of the Mass but probably considered it to be something more, an opportunity for celebrating the local community and for bringing together

God, the Church, and the people. Mass would also have been seen as a powerful act for securing divine intervention and as a means of worship. The causal efficacy of the mass was taken for granted, even though theologians held that God was not to be persuaded. The Mass was understood by the laity to contain a type of magical energy; it was a life preserver, a source of miracles; it was world-influencing and a soul saver for those who had died. The Mass grew increasingly complex in its choreography after 1300. The greater use of light, incense, and music, explicitly for the greater glory of God, would have been more engaging and might possibly have generated a deeper emotional response.

Parish, Clergy, and Laity

From 1100 onward, the Church of Rome dictated to an increasing degree the religiosity of the rich and poor alike. The papacy, through a burgeoning system of Church councils, kept a tight rein of the episcopacy, resulting in an increasingly unified Church both in terms of doctrine and practice. Greater weight was placed on the parish as episcopal government set out to ensure the presence of a properly equipped and morally upright clergy at the local level. The Windsor Council (1070) required archdeacons to ensure that churches kept a careful stock of vessels, and that priests knew the correct way to celebrate Mass. A well-educated and resident clergy would help ensure improvement in the religious awareness of laypersons and prompt a greater dedication to the Church.

The Church determined the duties of laymen with increasing clarity after 1100. Bishops ordered their archdeacons to enforce customs such as Pentecostal processions and commitment to a devotional life, and urged them to maintain careful records of contributing parishioners. Laypersons were pressed to help build churches as remission for their sins and, most significantly, tithe became institutionalized. In England, canon law decreed that every individual should give a tenth of their total annual income. The tithe was a regressive and thoroughly inequitable tax, and it is easy to imagine the tensions generated between the parish priest and the local community by tithe demands. Records indicate that there was, in all places, a constant battle in which laypersons tried to minimize their payment and priests tried to maximize their return. The recipients of tithes regularly complained to their bishop that tithe payments were withheld, stolen, or wrongly measured, whereas farmers complained that they were being systematically overtaxed. Noncontributors were humiliated by being forced to make their payment in a public place; the payment was then destroyed in front of their kinsmen and neighbors. Entire villages were excommunicated on account of non- or partial payment. For example, Bishop Sutton of Lincoln excommunicated the entire population of Berkhamstead in 1290 merely for obstructing the tithe collectors. The tithe, supported by biblical text, came to be generally understood (grudgingly, on the part of the taxed) as a spiritual investment—an idea that made particular sense in association with the then recently developed doctrine of purgatory. Tithe payment clearly colored the relationship that ordinary people had with the Church and consequently with institutional religion more broadly.

The parish was increasingly defined as the central focus of lay worship, and by the twelfth century attendance at the parish church on Sunday morning was regarded as mandatory. The priest, himself more thoroughly trained, was given greater responsibility for instructing parishioners. Hearing confession was now understood as a skill to be learned, the question being how to draw out the penitent and prescribe appropriate penance. The thirteenth century saw an increase in the number of manuals, provided primarily by friars. The Fourth Lateran Council (1215) emphasized the need for regular confession, stipulating that all congregants confess annually, preferably at Eastertide. This simple rule established the central role of the priest in parish life and the dependence on him of the parish laity. The obligations of parishioners to maintain the ornaments and the fabric of their church were gradually expanded upon (and minutely detailed by various synodal councils) throughout the Middle Ages, at least until the Reformation. The performance of parochial duties by priests was inspected lightly until the twelfth century. However, the greater responsibilities required of clergy and laity began to be monitored more systematically from then on, via a new system of visitation.

The system of ecclesiastical government was more or less complete across Western Europe by the fourteenth century and percolated down into the parish, effectively regulating the lives of ordinary people. A tension existed between established and traditional forms and the introduction of new ideas. The ideals of a universal Church continued to flourish: universal cults were promoted over local ones (although these continued to prosper) and new feast days were introduced, many of them Marian or Christocentric, including Corpus Christi, the Compassion of the Virgin, the Transfiguration, the Five Wounds, and the Holy Name of Jesus.

The attempt to enrich the inner life of the laity was taken further, though pastoral objectives were seriously curtailed by famines in the early fourteenth century, and then, catastrophically, by the Black Death, which reached England in 1348 and which wiped out around half of the population of Europe. Indeed, the Plague had a significant effect on the practice of religion across Europe. Some believed that God was punishing mankind for their incorrigible sinning and that the end of the world was imminent. There seems to have been an increase in processions of flagellants, whipping themselves until the skin on their backs was in strips. Such processions were rare in England, where the bishops and clergy preferred a more measured approach, urging laypersons to pray, attend Mass, and avoid irreligious behavior. There was an increase in the incidence of pilgrimage, as suggested by the accounts of major shrines such as St. Thomas's in Canterbury, though records are not so complete that we can be certain of pilgrims' motives. At any rate, pilgrimages had settled back into a pre-Plague rhythm by 1400. There was also a growing enthusiasm for testamentary practice, amounting to what might be called a "cult of remembrance." Others threw themselves into bouts of unbridled hedonism in an attempt to escape the constant threat of death. And though representations such as the Dance of Death existed before the Plague years, they certainly multiplied thereafter. However, we should not exaggerate, and perhaps continuity was more prominent than a significant obsession with the morbid. Throughout the medieval period, the focus of the Church at the time of death was on the condition of the soul, not of the physical body. The idea of "the good death" did, however, gain ground, and *The Book of the Craft of Dying* provided a meditation on the Church's instruction on how to die well. Death lurked around every corner and so it was important to be prepared.

The Plague resulted in a severe shortage of priests and a corresponding and energetic attempt to recruit clergy. Considerable thought was given by the Church authorities to increase lay knowledge directly. The "Lay Folks' Catechism," written by Archbishop Thoresby of York and circulated in 1357, provide a comprehensive guide to belief and practice structured around the Creed, the Ten Commandments, the Seven Works of Mercy, the Seven Virtues and Vices, and the Sacraments. The text is in verse so that laypersons might commit the verses to memory.

By 1400 papal control was great indeed, though ecclesiastical control at the lower levels was limited by the demands of wider groups of laypersons, some of whom were powerful in political circles. Pastoral reform was as much due to lay demand as to central decision making. The growth and character of parish churches was conditioned by local circumstances and shaped by local parishioners. The increasing number of homiletic and devotional texts was a response to demands from an increasingly literate laity. The universal Church was shaped to a considerable extent by the laity—for example, the celebration of fasts and feasts. Though we have some idea of the practical organization of feast days, it is far more difficult to ascertain the types of beliefs that underpinned them. The clergy could be critical of celebrations on saints' days, describing them as resting on superstition and perhaps even rooted in paganism. There were many saints' days listed in the *Cisio Janus*, a medieval composition of 24 verses with a syllable for each day in the year and whose function was to help people memorize the most important feasts. This calendar of liturgical feasts originated in northern Germany in the twelfth century. It lists, for instance, 18 possible feast days in January and 21 in July. Local parishes would celebrate their patron saint's day and perhaps one or two other feasts. The day was determined, generally speaking, by the bishop—and such feasts were movable. It became common practice in the late fifteenth century to celebrate patron saint's days in early October, during the weeks between harvest and autumn plowing. Such festivals were time consuming and could be costly. Work was forbidden and there would be a high Mass in honor of the saint, followed by processions. The afternoon was generally spent dancing and playing raucous games, and in the evening there might have been a religious play.

The question of Sunday observance is altogether different. Sunday had long been accepted as a day of rest and rejoicing in the early medieval Church. Sunday as a day of rest received canonical recognition by the early councils (in England the Council of Clovesho (747) condemned work on Sundays). The only thing that varied was the penalty for nonobservance and the zeal with which the law was applied. Medieval observance was for the most part fairly lax. Although most people would have attended Mass, the rest of the day would have been spent relaxing: playing games and doing gardening and small jobs around the house. Little encouragement was given by the Church to games, though many villages had a field or areas given over to rowdy, often violent games, including early forms of football. The Christian calendar had been grafted on the seasons of the year, and feasts sometimes seem to be more obviously connected with the season than the Christian event. The bishops' biggest concern was not so much the saturnalian character of such practices but their unduly secular nature. By the fifteenth century such complaints are not so much heard, and ales and other celebrations generally receive clerical support.

It will come as no surprise that the experiences of rich and poor were not the same. Communal celebrations seem designed to mark out the social contours of the parish. The Brookes describe how processions on Palm Sunday ended up at the door of the local lord's aisle or at the east end of the Lady Chapel: the canopy of the holy sacrament was carried by four yeomen, and the drinking on feast days was held at the manor.[3] The extent and type of participation in parish life was partly determined by social position. Brooke suggests that the term *community* is best avoided in describing the medieval parish because it connotes shared values and a degree of social harmony that was probably absent.

Evidence suggests that women were more overtly and devoutly attached to their parish than men. Certainly, religious practice was gendered. The liturgy itself contained gendered distinctions in baptism and funerals, for instance, and churching was clearly restricted to women (and was postponed further if the newborn was a girl). Spatial boundaries within the church were potentially more restricting on women than on men. The chancel was the preserve of the clergy, but excluded particularly women. When seating was introduced it was probably reserved for women. Their economic status was lower, and few of the significant parish roles (churchwarden, warden of guilds, or altar light) were open to women. But women did participate in communal celebrations. And records show that women were more likely than men to give to the poor. Maybe their devotion was deeper. Men were more likely to leave bequests outside their parish, indicating their greater economic mobility. Greater stress was laid on women's than on men's attendance. Women were assumed to run their household, including its spiritual well-being and it seems likely that the parish church was taken as an extension of that domain. Life in the parish exhibits a very clear division of labor based on gender. "Hoggling" (collecting door to door on occasions such as New Year's), for example, was a distinctly male activity. However, there was no single gender identity for all women. Churching was for those who bore children. Class cross-cuts the gender division of labor, and the few women who did become churchwardens were of a higher social status. Fixed seating soon became allocated by social rank rather than gender. It is hard, then, to determine a "feminine" type of piety that characterized all women in the parish. Women's roles were based, more than men's, on the life cycle.

The parish was the focus, but it was not the only locus. Although the position of guilds or fraternities peaked in the fourteenth and fifteenth centuries they were already becoming established in England in Anglo-Saxon times. Guilds were voluntary associations composed of laypersons, and they were popular because of certain specific religious services they performed, especially the commemoration and suffrage for the souls of their members, again a service prompted by the new theological thinking on purgatory and penance. Being a member of a guild would allow one to accommodate devotional needs within the context of one's daily life. Thousands of guilds came to exist, in many types of social contexts. During the Early Middle Ages, they were criticized by the Church as unchristian, but later were praised for generating the type of piety encouraged in the laity by churchmen. Pastoral reform saw the guilds contributing to many aspects of parish life (candles, vestments, extra masses, etc.). Some guilds were involved in religious instruction, funding events such as the performance of plays. A guild in Thetford was, by 1289, offering services for those coming to town on market day, and a guild in Boston provided service for traders who had to leave town early. The relation between priest and guild was often complex, the one often complementing the other.

Popular Devotion

Expressions of popular devotion included the votive Mass, pilgrimage, and the innumerable cults of saints and relics. Clergy and laity alike agreed that the Mass was the most powerful form of intercession that could be offered to God and it was customarily celebrated for the needs of the entire congregation. The funeral mass was celebrated by the priest for the repose of the soul of an individual (or sometimes several individuals). By the High Middle Ages votive masses were being requested for a variety of reasons. Laypersons paid priests to say them often in private, the donor himself often absent. The chief role of the medieval clergy was not to lead prayers, but to offer prayers on behalf of the whole of society.

Most ordinary people were aware of Christianity as an intrusion of the supernatural into their lives in the form of miracles and ritual—for instance, in judicial ordeals, life-cycle rituals (at time of birth, marriage, and death), and the liturgy. They sought the association with eternity through the relics of saints, perhaps the most important feature of the religious landscape.

When in need, laypeople found it hard to approach God directly. They experienced Christ's presence during the Eucharist and this filled them with awe. In times of great need they paid priests to offer Mass on their behalf, but in their private prayers they preferred to turn to saints for assistance. The Holy Virgin Mary was the primary saint; many accounts of miracles performed by her circulated around medieval Western Europe. Saints were once human and therefore approachable—and they enjoyed heavenly patronage. It could have been that newly converted people retained their polytheism in the cult of saints, but it is clear that converts did eventually accept the Church's ruling that God alone should be worshiped. Saints were revered but not usually worshiped. But saints were believed to have power in their own right: they could perform miracles such as cure sickness, save petitioners from storms and earthquakes, preserve women from sexual assault, and help defeat stronger foes. Generally, they were prayed to, perhaps as minor divinities, in the hope that they would intercede with God on the believer's behalf. Saints helped ward off natural disasters and diabolical malice. They were very real to medieval people: they moved through the world and could manifest themselves to mortals. In the Early Middle Ages, saints were chosen by popular acclaim although bishops reserved the right to veto a new cult. Generally, there was no disagreement, saints were known to have led exemplary lives and died exemplary deaths. In several important instances, their place of death was marked by a miracle of some type and subsequently established as a site of pilgrimage. When the papacy assumed control of canonization in the twelfth century, it became more difficult to sustain popular cults that had no historical foundation, though much depended on the strength of local commitment. The Church has never accepted the veneration of animals, the only nonhuman creatures lawfully invoked being the angels; however, in the mid-thirteenth century, the Dominican inquisitor Stephen of Bourbon found that women in the Dombes, in the diocese of Lyon, venerated St. Guinefort as a child healer. The inquisitor was pleased to hear this until he discovered that this saint was not a holy man, but a greyhound. Despite sustained Church disapproval, the holy greyhound Guinefort continues to be venerated in the Dombes area up to the present day.

Relics were everywhere and were especially valued by those with secular power. In the relic collections of the king lay the safety of the kingdom: they compensated for his powerlessness before man and nature. This was the power of relics and rituals that intertwined in the lives of men. People were powerless in themselves and could only survive through reliance on the supernatural. Relics were the main channel through which sacred power was available for the needs of ordinary people. In this way, relics prepared the path for pilgrimage, and at first, pilgrimages were made to places in which holy relics were stored.

Relics come in two varieties, primary (physical remains) and secondary (personal items or places where the saint stayed), and both manifest the saint's spiritual powers. People have long collected memorabilia, but for medieval people, relics were more than sentimental and nostalgic: they contained tangible power for the good. And this was no pagan vestige, but a Christian innovation. (Pre-Christians were horrified by the polluting effects of relics.) The cult of relics had long been a popular devotion before it was assimilated by the Church, which licensed the cult of relics but reserved the right to authenticate items and to destroy those it considered spurious. The most revered were those associated with Christ, the greatest of all being the Cross, which was excavated in Jerusalem in 330 and whose parts have circulated ever since. Such relics were universally revered but unevenly distributed, and there was soon a lively market and traders were not especially scrupulous in their dealings. Theft and plunder was common, especially during the Crusades. St. Francis was considered a saint during his lifetime, and when he fell sick at Cortona in 1226 and expressed a wish to die at Assisi, the city council sent an armed escort to accompany the litter to prevent other towns from appropriating his relics should he die en route. Fake relics became a major industry driven by demand and the need to believe. The West is full of shrine churches built to house the more important of these relics—that is, the remains of the bodies of saints such as bones, hair, or blood.

Relics were often "toured," usually with a view to raising money for church restoration. An example is the traveling relics of Laon Cathedral, whose church was destroyed in 1112, after the town had rebelled against the tyranny of the bishop. During a trip to the town of Buzançais in the district of Tours, the monks carrying the relics preached and told the crowd about the destruction of the church. When the monks saw that the lord and his garrison were listening to them with evil in their hearts and were planning to plunder them as they left the place, the man whose duty it was to speak was placed in a tricky position. Although he did not entirely believe his promises, he said to the people standing there, "If there is an infirm soul among you, let him come to these holy relics, and, drinking the water which the relics have touched, he will assuredly be healed." Then the lord and the men of his castle were glad, thinking the monks must be caught for liars out of their own mouths, and they brought forward to the monks a servant about 20 years old, who was deaf and dumb. At that the danger, the dismay of the monks could not be described. After they had prayed with deep sighs to the Lady of all and her only son, the servant drank the holy water, and the trembling priest asked him some question or other. He immediately replied, not with an answer to the question but with a repetition of the exact words that the priest had used—words that he had never heard before. The hearts of the people of that poor town became larger than their means. The lord of the town immediately gave the monks the only horse he had, and others gave them what they could. And so the men who had planned to attack the monks became their greatest advocates, many in tears, praising God their helper, and they freed the cured servant so that he may stay with the holy relics forever. News of the miracle spread far and wide.[4]

Pilgrimage, sometimes undertaken as a penance, was a common practice, though not an essential part of Christian practice (unlike Islam). The immediate aim of the pilgrim was to visit a shrine, but the motivations of individuals were many and varied; some traveled on behalf of themselves, others on behalf of friends or relatives. Some went in thankfulness, others in penance, some to fulfill a vow made at a time of crisis, others most likely to enjoy the trip, much like contemporary backpackers. Typically, the difficulty of the journey depended largely on the extent of one's resources. The rich traveled in relative luxury; the poor traveled on foot and roughed it.

After 1200, the chief pilgrimage center was Rome, the burial place of St. Peter and St. Paul. Next in importance came Compostela (where the remains of St. James have been kept), Canterbury (martyrdom of St. Thomas Becket, archbishop of Canterbury), and Cologne (home of the bones of the Magi). Soon after the death of Thomas Becket in 1170 (probably instigated by Henry II), Pope Alexander canonized him, and the murdered archbishop was elevated to sainthood. Becket's shrine at Canterbury has became the most important place in the country for pilgrims to visit. When Becket was killed, local people apparently managed to obtain pieces of cloth soaked with his blood. Rumors soon spread that, when touched by this cloth, people were cured of blindness, epilepsy, and leprosy. Before long, the monks at Canterbury Priory were selling to visitors small glass bottles containing Becket's blood. The keeper of the shrine would also give the pilgrim a metal badge, stamped with the symbol of the shrine. The guardians of his tomb worried that Becket's body might be stolen, so they moved the marble coffin to the crypt of the cathedral. The monks also built a stone wall in front of the tomb, leaving two holes through which pilgrims could insert their heads and kiss the tomb. In 1220, Becket's bones were moved once more, to a new gold-plated and jewel-encrusted shrine on a raised platform supported by pillars, behind the high altar. Canterbury, because of its religious history, had always seen a large number of pilgrims, but after the death of Thomas Becket, the number of pilgrims visiting the town grew rapidly, and at times the crowds were difficult to manage.

Indulgences

An indulgence is the full or partial remission of temporal punishment due for sins already forgiven. With each additional indulgence, the prospective pains of purgatory could be partially offset, and heaven brought that much nearer. Medieval charity was rooted in self-interest but no more so than the demand for indulgences, which provided an easy way to build up credit for the afterlife. Parishioners, in return for gifts to the parish (for example, for church repairs), would receive a partial dispensation for one's past sinful deeds. Indulgences were dispensed by a wide variety of institutions, including fraternities and guilds. Many were dispensed on behalf of religious institutions and church-sponsored hospitals, including St. Anthony's in London. The theory of indulgences seems simple, resting on the idea of the treasury of merits, an eternal sinking fund against which penances to be satisfied in purgatory could be offset. Indulgences aided individuals ascend to heaven with as little delay as possible. However, their practical operation is less easy to follow: how could allocations of time operate in a nontemporal purgatory? This conundrum left even the best theologians baffled. Aquinas simply stated that the Church would not offer them if they did not work. The base tariff was that of the old penitentials, which before 1200 defined the penance due for each confessed sin. In fifteenth-century England it was generally accepted that indulgences might be cashed in against terrestrially imposed penances. In other regions it was thought proper that earthly penances be performed even if harsh and that the indulgences be saved for purgatory on the assumption that the earthly penance would not cover the full amount due. Lay understanding of indulgences was vague. Indulgences were commonly traded and their value often wildly inflated; such an indulgence, if acquired by the credulous, would be seen wrongly as securing total release from the effects of sin. The demand for indulgences was impressive—in 1498 a Barcelona printer was contracted to provide 18,000 copies of an indulgence peddled for the maintenance of the abbey of Monserat, and the London hospital of St. Anthony sold over 30,000 a year around 1500, whereas lesser institutions had a more limited appeal.

These vast sales were a result of many individuals touring Europe collecting contributions. Pardoners, those licensed to sell papal pardons and indulgences, earned a bad reputation for trafficking in forged grants, a dubious trade dating back at least to the twelfth century, when monks and canons toured Europe with their relics touting for building funds, along with questors acting on behalf of holy orders. Buyers and sellers invested hugely in what had become a commodity, and the condemnation of indulgence mongering was widespread long before Martin Luther's scathing criticism of the practice. However, though the sellers were heavily criticized, the buyers cannot be ignored, and they were clearly happy with what was on offer. In the early 1500s, a "unit" of indulgence cost four pence, still a substantial sum for a craftsman, so purchases were probably from wealthier individuals with poorer people making do with indulgences that were paid for by effort, such as visits to church or repeated prayers, rather than by money. They were often more expensive: during the jubilee of 1500 the rate was £2 for those owning assets worth more than £1000, down to one shilling for those with assets valued between £20 and £200. There was, though, great regional variation, Italy providing a smaller market than Germany. Indulgences were a major feature of the economies of salvation in medieval Europe.

Rites of Passage

The key Christian rites (the sacraments) are Mass attendance, Holy Communion, confession, fasting, and abstinence. Apart from these were those rites which marked the transition from one status to another, that is, the life-cycle rituals, which for the medieval Catholic man and woman were baptism, churching, confirmation, marriage, the last rites, and burial.

Infant baptism varied in form but was universal in Christian Western Europe. Parish priests were generally allowed to baptize, though in some regions the rite was performed in the baptistery of the main church. The holy oils used in baptism were blessed by the bishop each year on Maundy Thursday and distributed to his clergy, while priests blessed the waters of their fonts on Easter eve. Baptisms were performed throughout the year, and it was the sacrament of salvation, which freed a child from original sin. It was believed that if a baptized baby died, it would go straight to heaven because it had committed no sins, whereas an unbaptized child would go to purgatory or Limbo. Because infant mortality rate was extremely high throughout the period, parents were anxious to have their children baptized as soon as possible after birth. The baptismal liturgy had been designed for adult converts and was long and elaborate. When used for infants, responses were made on the child's behalf by its godparents, of whom there were at least two, one of each sex. The godparents' duty was to ensure that the child was instructed in the faith, but they also assumed secular obligations. Medieval godparents took their job seriously and treated godchildren as kinfolk. For that reason baptism was an important social as well as religious occasion, and it was the time at which a child was given his or her name. The liturgy began with exorcisms, and the godparents were then required to make a brief profession of faith on the child's behalf. The central part of the rite consisted of pouring water three times on the child's head while pronouncing the words "*Baptizo te in nomine Patris et Filii et Spiritus Sancti*" (I baptize you in the name of the Father and of the Son and of the Holy Spirit), at which point the child was named. Lastly, the child was anointed with holy oil and marked with the sign of the cross. If the child were dying then a shortened form of service might be used, which could be administered by anyone, even a non-Christian. Canon law also permitted a Christian woman living in a frontier region to arrange for the baptism of a sickly child if she were attended only by a Muslim midwife. Many children must have been baptized by laypersons—chiefly women, because men were generally absent during labor. All married women and midwives must have been taught how to baptize in an emergency and very few children were left unbaptized.

The earliest account of a church wedding in the West dates from the ninth century, but such ceremonies were not common until the eleventh century. Before then marriage was a secular rite. Theologians taught that marriage was the oldest sacrament and agreed that it was not an ecclesiastical sacrament: the ministers were the bride and groom. The Church did not devise a marriage rite but merely adapted that of Roman civil law. The role of the officiating priest was as chief witness. The marriage rite was much the same as it is today. After the couple exchanged vows, the priest blessed them. A marriage accompanied by a Mass was described as being solemnized. It was not essential to be married in church, unless (as in some countries in the Late Middle Ages) this was required by civil law. The ceremony generally took place in the churchyard or in the porch (entrance to the church), which marked it as a non-Church rite. In an attempt to prevent clandestine marriages, the Fourth Lateran Council (1215) ordered that marriage banns should be called in the churches of the bride and groom prior to marriage. This was hard to enforce because if two people who were free to do so took marriage vows and then slept together, they were legally married. The marriage could be regularized by being publicly blessed by a priest but could not be annulled. This might have been a problem for parents who wanted to arrange their children's marriage. The Church maintained its position, though, and ruled that marriage was a natural sacrament that need not take place in church, but laypersons encouraged church weddings for social and legal reasons.

When a man was dying, a priest would be summoned to administer the last rites. He would hear the dying man's confession and give him the *viaticum*, or "provision for the journey (to the next life)," that is, Holy Communion from the reserved sacrament. He would then administer extreme unction, a sacrament of healing in preparation for the afterlife used exclusively for the dying from the tenth century on. Extreme unction conferred the forgiveness of sins, even if the man was unconscious and could not confess his sins. If a man died suddenly the assumption was that he had made his peace with God, unless there was evidence to the contrary. The Church very rarely denied a baptized member a Christian burial.

The bodies of noblemen and rich burgesses were received into church on the night before the funeral and placed on a catafalque, surrounded by tall candles of unbleached wax, while clergy and kinsmen kept vigil beside them all night. In many parts of Europe older customs were followed by the common people: the body remained in the house overnight and a wake was held in honor of the dead. A requiem was said at every funeral for the repose of the dead person's soul. Most people wanted further masses said to ensure the deceased's journey on through purgatory. In the early medieval period, monasteries were the main intercessors for the dead, and there was no limit on the number of masses that could be said in a day. In the thirteenth century, priests were forbidden by cannon law to say more than one Mass on most days. So, laymen began to endow chantry chapels, served by one or more priests who were bound to offer the Mass and recite the office of the dead every day for the souls of those listed in the deed of foundation. Many chantries were founded across Europe, some in churches, others as separate foundations. Indeed, the multiplication of prayers for the dead became a prominent feature of late medieval piety. Further insurance was provided by the masses said on All Souls' Day (November 2). It could be said that medieval people valued the institutional Church above all else as intercessor for the dead. Laypersons could baptize their own children, and they did not have to get married in church; some of them rarely went to Mass or received the sacraments; and others did not even receive the last rites, because they knew that their salvation was not contingent on doing so; but everybody recognized that the Church alone could pray them out of purgatory.

The Iconography of Art and Architecture

Beyond the verbal, the innumerable concrete forms of representation must have been a major channel for reinforcement of individuals' appreciation of the content of the faith. The most obvious survivors of such concrete forms are the ecclesiastical buildings themselves, in which colorful decoration, wall paintings, glass, and statuary provided a "book for the unlearned." As the face of a building to the outside world, doorways had always been a focus for sculpture in the Middle Ages, but a great explosion of sculpture on church portals occurred in the mid-eleventh century, expanding over time to include entire facades. In many regions of medieval Europe, the semicircular tympanum—the space between the lintel and arch over a doorway—became the site of spectacular medieval sculpture. The Last Judgment, showing events from the end of time, was a particularly favored theme. Depicting the fate of the righteous and the sinful as they appear before Christ as judge, the door served as a powerful reminder of the ultimate authority of God and the earthly authority of the Christian Church.

The intention behind such representations is not always clear, and on occasion, the position of some images must have prevented the message from reaching laypersons. Though instructional and devotional, they were primarily crafted to the glory of God. Their function was not merely to serve dogma, then. Even though they depicted heaven and hell, the crucifixion, and so forth, a statue might also represent a man's life, his spirituality and earthly attributes, which generated a specific emotional response. However, much iconography was indeed instructional. Paintings of judgments pointed not only to the fact of the Last Judgment but also to the preparation for it here and now. Stained glass often dealt with historical issues; narratives could be implicit, depending on subtle juxtapositions as in a number of French and English cathedrals. Such images were occasionally found also outside the church; alabaster figures were privately owned, as were rosaries. Private houses were sometimes decorated with instructive paintings or hangings. Printing greatly extended biblical and other religious knowledge through pictures as well as text; most woodblock prints were simple but some were com-

A section of stained glass depicting the *Massacre of the Holy Innocents*, from the east window of the church of St. Peter Mancroft in Norwich, England. (Photo by Peter Collins.)

plex, such as the print produced by Wold Taut of Nuremberg in 1510, depicting the seven sacraments and many other allusions to the faith. Other prints were more obviously didactic than devotional, including those in series, such as those depicting the seven deadly sins and the Ten Commandments.

The Catholic faith was all around and was all-encompassing, especially if its allegorical content is taken into account. In a world where almost anything might be taken to mean something else, opportunity for the reinforcement of faith was great. The response to these representations is hard to guess, though.

A typical alabaster figure could well have meant different things to different individuals, depending on their status, knowledge, gender, and class, for example. Furthermore, it is likely that complexity of imagery might have served to obscure meaning, especially if there was a code that needed to be known before it could be deciphered. It is also possible that images were known better then than now, and readings would probably also change over time. For example, at Moissac, in France, the Christ of the Apocalypse on the abbey portal was interpreted in the fourteenth century as a depiction of Clovis (c. 466–511), the first Christian king of France, whose cult was then popular. The intellectual power of the images may have been greater during the "missionary" period (1215–1515), and indeed, by 1500 the function of the images may have changed from historical to more affective and doctrinal concerns. There is some evidence for a growing revulsion during this time toward overdecoration and gaudiness. The Lollards began to complain about the misleading and superstitious impact of images, demanding a reduction in ecclesiastical decoration, which served only to distract worshippers from the building's main function, an iconoclastic reaction that gathered force through the Reformation.

The Book

During the early centuries of the Middle Ages, very few people indeed would have even seen a book; by the end of the period many if not most people would have at least seen a book, and growing numbers of people would have read and possibly owned them. The Bible gained an increasingly central place in day-to-day religious practice during the Middle Ages. Early Latin translations of the Bible date from the third century. In 382 Pope Damasus I commissioned St. Jerome to make new translation of entire Bible from the Greek and Hebrew originals. Completed in 404, the Vulgate (that is, the Bible in "common speech") was intended for all churches, but this was impossible before the age of printing. In the early eighth century, Alcuin (in Northumbria, England) produced a revised version widely used in theological schools across northern Europe. The Vulgate was meant for popular use, whereas the Latin was standard among the educated. However, vernacular language became widespread after the collapse of the Roman Empire, especially in Germanic Northern Europe, and after 600 the Vulgate was no longer widely read. Churchmen were encouraged to adapt biblical stories for popular consumption, producing a genre that spread across Western Europe after 830, including poems designed for public recital. At the same time, literal vernacular translations were made of parts of the Bible, often interspersed with Latin text, and used in theological schools as teaching texts. By 1000 the Gospels had been translated into West Saxon, and in the twelfth century the four Books of Kings were translated into Old French.

Until 1200, the Church tolerated laypeople owning and reading copies of the Bible, but it was considerably less tolerant thereafter on account of heretical groups producing their own translations alongside unorthodox interpretations. In places where such movements were strong, the Church banned people from both owning and reading vernacular versions. The synod of Toulouse (1229) proscribed lay ownership of the Bible in any language. During the fourteenth century, vernacular Bibles circulated freely in France, Italy, Aragon, Castile, Germany, and Burgundy. Heresy had declined and Bible reading was no longer assumed to be the province of the unorthodox. England was the exception; the first complete translation of the Bible was by John Wycliffe in the late fourteenth century—shortly afterward his followers (Lollards) were condemned as heretics. The Council of Oxford forbade the use of vernacular scriptures made during Wycliffe's time unless a bishop's license was first obtained—the reason for this was, again, the unorthodox interpretations published by Lollards. By 1400, elsewhere in Western Europe there were no restrictions of lay reading of the Bible. A growing number of devout laypersons owned the Bible, which indicates an improvement in book production after 1350. Bibles were in short supply throughout the Middle Ages, primarily because of the cost of production; materials were expensive (parchment was the base until 1300) and low literacy meant there were few who could scribe. Because of their status as luxury goods, many medieval versions of the Bible are lavishly decorated and, therefore, unique. After 1300 paper began to be used, which was far cheaper to produce, and literacy rates began to increase. Printing did not immediately produce cheap books, but they were now affordable by some clergy and well-off laymen. However, many churches, especially in more remotes places, were still without a complete text even by 1500.

The medieval Church inherited much biblical commentary from the Church of late antiquity. There were four senses in which biblical text could be understood: (1) the literal sense, including grammatical study and consideration of meaning as statement of fact; (2) the moral sense; (3) the allegorical sense; and (4) the anagogical or mystical sense, according to which the scriptures were understood as symbols of ultimate realities. Not all passages could easily be rendered meaningful in each sense, but such multilevel analysis was the norm. The first standard commentary was written by the brothers Anselm and Ralph of Laon (Glossa Ordinaria), and further commentaries soon followed. Although few laypersons would have read the commentaries, the fourfold interpretation colored all Christians' understanding of the Bible stories. The same fourfold interpretation also influenced religious iconography, though only the educated could understand all the allusions contained in such esoteric symbolism. However, this detailed, multileveled way of interpreting scripture did in some measure influence everybody. The Bible was very important for the medieval Church and its members. It was different from all other medieval texts because it was divinely inspired. Only the Bible expressed the mind of God, and the Church could not be selective in its reading. The role of the Church was merely to interpret the revelation it contained. But the authority given those interpreters was critically important in ensuring a unified understanding by most people.

Demons and Witches

The medieval world was rife with evil in material form. Apart from witches and sorcerers—those "weird" individuals who had somehow assimilated supernatural powers—people took it for granted that they shared their world with legions of demons and spirits, penumbral beings drawn both from biblical reference and the pagan traditions. Satan stalked the earth as the anti-Christ, shadowed by demons both major and minor. Betwixt and between were the changelings, elves, fairies, giants and ogres, ghosts, gnomes, goblins, vampires, werewolves, and dragons that confounded ordinary people going about their everyday affairs. They varied in their impact from the benign to the murderous. Fortunately, there were an array of Christian defenses that could be employed in defense against these forces of darkness. The least obviously human of these tormentors were repelled by prayers, incantations, and charms. Witches and sorcerers, however, were avoided until the Late Middle Ages, when they were confronted and tested in public. Accusation of witchcraft during the Late Middle Ages was an extremely serious affair in that the consequences for those convicted were always painful and sometimes fatal.

Tales of ghosts and demons were widespread throughout the period. In one unnamed English village in 1397 it was said that there was a malevolent spirit who was the stillborn daughter of a widow in the village. The spirit castigated the woman for her bringing about the stillbirth and claimed that the woman would be damned for her evil deed. For her part, the widow replied that she could not be damned to hell, because she had confessed her sin at the time and undertaken a penance that would remove the threat of eternal damnation. The widow accused the spirit of deceitfulness and the two were often involved in fractious dispute in the village. The spirit, energetic in its haunting, also attacked the widow's son, a priest, accusing him of spending too much time hunting, and put forward thoroughly rational arguments why he should stop. The priest recalled that one of his dogs had been killed during a hunt, though the cause of its death remained unknown. The spirit remained with the widow and her son, making a nuisance of itself, for three years.[5]

A second account involves the ghost of a wage laborer from Rievaulx, England, who helped a villager to carry his beans.[6] After watching his horse go lame, a man took the beans off his animal's back and loaded them onto his own. A little further down the road the man saw what he took to be a horse standing erect on its hind legs. The man was horrified and ordered the horse "in the name of Jesus Christ" not to harm him. Eventually, the horse was transformed into a rolling pile of hay with a light in the middle, at which point the man said, "Begone, for you bring me evil!" The hay then took the shape of a ghostly figure who began to explain his strange form and how he might be helped, requesting that the man let him carry his beans. When they reached a stream the ghost disappeared, and the man realized that the beans were once again on his back. Later, the man had the ghost absolved and had masses said for him, which helped him. These accounts suggest that medieval people lived among the demoniacal. Thus, they might be confronted by specters of one sort or another in any place and at any time, and given that their major defense was to invoke the Trinity, it paid to uphold a Catholic way of life.

Although providing an apparently similar challenge, the existence of witches and sorcerers posed a different type of threat, one which was even more dangerous because so much more intrusive. There was good and bad magic. Bad magic was practised by witches and sorcerers who consorted with demons with a view to harming others and/or furthering their own interests. Given that the medieval worldview accepted that heavenly bodies could influence human beings, it is hardly surprising that the Church accepted the likelihood that demons would tempt men and women and even take their form to practise their evil deeds. All churchmen and some others were familiar with the biblical injunction "Thou shalt not suffer a witch to live" (Exodus 22:18), but the incidence of witchcraft during the Middle Ages was far lower than that during the sixteenth and seventeenth centuries. However, although witchcraft and sorcery as defined by the Catholic authorities had been practiced since pagan times, it was nowhere near as rife as is sometimes thought. In many cases, men and women (though mostly women) accused and convicted of witchcraft were in fact practicing pagan rituals—for the fertility of the land, for example—with no malicious intent. Church authorities took an increasingly hard-line on such rituals, however, establishing that because they were not Christian rites then they must be heathenish, therefore necessarily evil and heretical. The Inquisition, established by the Church in 1258, was delegated only to deal with cases of witchcraft that were clearly heretical. Only after 1398 was all witchcraft deemed to be heretical. Still, the Inquisition remained an instrument of last resort throughout the Middle Ages.

The trial of Lady Alice Kyterler of Kilkenny (Ireland) took place in 1324. Along with her son and ten associates, she was accused of practising witchcraft, although throughout their trial they are described as heretics and sorcerers, rather than witches. This early trial became something of a template for the trials that followed. For instance, Alice was accused of having sexual intercourse with her demonic familiar. Of the seven charges laid against her, the first was that she rejected Christ and refused to attend church. They were also accused of seeking advice from and making sacrifices to demons, mocking the Catholic Mass, and casting spells. Despite considerable evidence that the accusations were a result of social malice rather than genuine fear of witchcraft, Alice was found guilty and was excommunicated in absentia (she had fled before the end of the trial). One of her "accomplices," Petronella of Meath, was burned at the stake.[7]

The science of witch finding reached a peak with the publication in 1486 of the *Malleus Malificarum* (*The Hammer of the Witches*), by the Dominican friars Henry Kramer and Joseph Sprenger. This was the ultimate "how-to" manual for those whose obsession with witchcraft had peaked in the mid-fifteenth century. The authors were extraordinarily systematic in their classification of acts of witchcraft and of ways and means by which the accused could be tested. They begin, in Part One, with the following statement: "Whether the belief that there are such beings as witches is so essential a part of the Catholic faith that obstinately to maintain the opposite opinion manifestly savours of heresy."

CONCLUSION: HERESY AND TOLERATION

Let us return to where we began, to the heterogeneity of faith and practice that existed even during the centuries in which the Catholic Church played an overwhelmingly dominant role in the lives of ordinary people. Throughout that period, ordinary people determined the details of their own faith and practice. If they chose to push against the boundaries of orthodox Catholicism, then they could expect to face the consequences, from more or less severe harassment by church or state officers to execution. As far as the Church was concerned, heresy (deviation from the one true path), was less a matter of individual error and more a result of the intervention of Satan in everyday life. In the first instance, heretics would be given the opportunity to recant, and minor heresy was often overlooked. Major heresy was taken far more seriously and the punishment for it could be severe. Schism was present to some extent throughout the Middle Ages, and major heretics include the Donatists, Cathars, Waldensians, and Lollards. The heretics were often extremely tenacious, but no more so than their prosecutors. Pope Gregory IX established the Inquisition during the 1230s in areas where heretics were tolerated. Lambert describes the case of the Cathars in Languedoc, recorded by Bernard de Caux in 1246.[8] He interrogated over 5,000 people, most suspects were Cathars, and a minority were Waldensians. The questioning focused less on belief and more on practice. This suggests that heretics, so long as they kept their beliefs to themselves, might have been largely ignored. Medieval Inquisition could be harsh but was rarely as harsh as it has sometimes been represented. Some 207 sentences were imposed, but less than 10 percent of these involved imprisonment, and the rest involved compulsory pilgrimage, crosses worn on clothing, and other light punishments. A burned heretic could not be converted, and churchmen would not readily support such a punishment. This was largely a game of cat and mouse; the Inquisitor had a long memory, and his inquiries were extremely thorough. The heretical community was slowly worn down. The range of the medieval Inquisition was limited, and it never operated in England or in medieval Castile.

Religious pluralism existed in the Medieval West from 1000, though dissent could not be openly practiced in most places most of the time. However, there were during these 500 years many clandestine alternatives to Roman Catholicism. Some were large movements involving many thousands of people, well organized and bravely led. But then, to come full circle, there were also more or less isolated individuals such as Menocchio, who plowed their own furrow, popping in and out of the Church and developing their own version of Catholic faith and practice. It is certain that there were many more like Menocchio whose stories were never and will never be told.

GLOSSARY

Bible: The multiauthored text that Christians and Jews take to be most sacred. The exact composition of the text varies according to tradition. The Christian Bible comprises the Old Testament and New Testament. In the Roman Catholic, Protestant, and Eastern Orthodox traditions, there are 39 books in the Old Testament and 27 in the New Testament.

Clergy: The group, in most cases traditionally dominated by men, that comprises the class of leaders in any religious group. This leadership tends in most cases to be hierarchical. Clergy members are in most cases responsible for ritual practice, including important life-cycle rites marking childbirth, baptism, circumcision, coming of age ceremonies, marriage, and death. Clergy members induct people into the faith and disseminate the religion's doctrine and practices, though they may or may not have received theological training.

Heresy: A belief or practice at variance with established religious beliefs. Although the term is most often used with regard to dissension from Roman Catholic dogma, heretics have been identified in all of the world's religions, and it sometimes happens that one section of a religious group will exchange accusations of heresy with another section.

Iconography: A term deriving from the Greek word *ikon*, meaning image. Originally, an icon was a painting of Jesus Christ (usually on a wooden panel) and an object of devotion in the Orthodox Greek Church from the Early Middle Ages. The term *icon* has since come to signify an object or image that is exceptional, especially for its religious meaning. For instance, the iconography of Christianity includes images such as the lamb, which represents Christ; the dove, which symbolizes the Holy Spirit; grapes, which refer to the Eucharist; and the blue mantle or cloak, which represents the Virgin Mary. Such symbolically loaded images are found in virtually all major religions, often forming a complex iconography developed over centuries.

Indulgences: In Roman Catholic theology, the complete or partial remission of temporal punishment for sins already forgiven, that is, after the sinner has confessed and received absolution. Indulgences draw on the storehouse of merit acquired by Jesus's sacrifice and on the virtues and penances of the saints (see below). They are granted for specific good works and prayers and came to replace the severe penances of the medieval Church. Roman Catholics can gain partial or plenary indulgences for themselves or have them granted to the dead. The system was increasingly abused during the later medieval period, when the sale of indulgences became primarily a money-making operation. The increasingly corrupt system of indulgences was a significant component of Martin Luther's attack on the Roman Catholic Church in the early sixteenth century. Today, only the pope can delegate the power of granting indulgences to others.

Liturgy: A regularly performed religious rite, generally led by a priest or someone specially sanctioned to do so, often involving a combination of prayer, hymn singing, recitation of the Creed, homily, and sermon or some similar form of instruction. Movement is generally incorporated into the performance of liturgy, and timing or tempo often plays a significant part. The structure and content of liturgy varies considerably from one religious group to another, the only common characteristics being that each form has a beginning and an end. Liturgy is often scripted, as in the Roman Catholic missal, but need not be.

Middle Ages: The term generally applied to the period in history that starts with the fall of the Western Roman Empire, in the fifth century, to the Reformation, in the early sixteenth century.

Papacy: An ecclesiastical system defined by the Second Vatican Council in which the pope, as successor of St. Peter and Vicar of Christ, leads the Catholic Church. Besides describing the office of the pope, the term also denotes the sociopolitical influence of this office as a historical reality.

Roman Catholicism: The preeminent of those Christian churches that identify themselves as "catholic," characterized by a specific set of beliefs regarding the relationship between God and humanity and the sacraments. Roman Catholicism embraces monasticism, a communal understanding of sin and redemption, missionary activity, and the papacy.

Saints: A saint is an exemplary holy person. In the Christian tradition, a saint is one who resides in heaven or an individual who has been martyred or who has given exceptional service to the Church and has been formally canonized by the Church. John Coleman[9] suggests that saints tend to have the following characteristics: they are supreme examples of holiness; they are extraordinary teachers; they have special powers for the good; they can intervene on others' behalf before God (the gods); and they have a special relationship to God (the gods). There are over 10,000 Roman Catholic saints. In traditional Christian iconography saints are generally depicted with halos.

NOTES

1. Carlo Ginzburg, *The Cheese and the Worms* (Baltimore, MD: Johns Hopkins University Press, 1980), p. 55.
2. Ibid., p. 21.
3. Rosalind and Christopher Brooke, *Popular Religion in the Middle Ages* (London: Thames and Hudson, 1984), pp. 109–110.
4. J. Shinners, ed., *Medieval Popular Religion, 100–1500: A Reader* (Peterborough, Ontario: Broadview Press, 1997), pp. 151–152.
5. Ibid., p. 220.
6. Ibid., p. 229.
7. Ibid., pp. 238–241.
8. Malcolm D. Lambert, *Medieval Heresy: Popular Movements from the Gregorian Reform to the Reformation* (Oxford: Wiley Blackwell, 2002), p. 148.
9. John Coleman, "Conclusion: After Sainthood," in *Saints and Virtues*, ed. J. S. Hawley (Berkeley: University of California Press, 1987), pp. 214–217.

BIBLIOGRAPHY

Brooke, R., and C. Brooke. *Popular Religion in the Middle Ages.* London: Thames and Hudson, 1984.

Coleman, John. "Conclusion: After Sainthood." In J. S. Hawley, ed. *Saints and Virtues.* Berkeley: University of California Press, 1987, pp. 214–217.

Ginzburg, Carlo. *The Cheese and the Worms.* Baltimore, MD: Johns Hopkins University Press, 1980.

Hamilton, B. *Religion in the Medieval West.* London: Edward Arnold, 1986.

Le Roy Ladurie, E. *Montaillou: Cathars and Catholics in a French Village 1294–1324.* Harmondsworth, England: Penguin, 1980.

Lambert, Malcolm D. *Medieval Heresy: Popular Movements from the Gregorian Reform to the Reformation.* Oxford: Wiley Blackwell, 2002.

Shinners, J., ed. *Medieval Popular Religion, 100–1500: A Reader.* Peterborough, Ontario: Broadview Press, 1997.

Tanner, N. *The Ages of Faith: Popular Religion in Late Medieval England and Western Europe.* London: I. B. Tauris, 2008.

Chapter 10

Modern Europe

Alberta Giorgi and Roberto Marchisio

INTRODUCTION

Describing religions in Europe throughout the last two centuries is a difficult task because they have undergone important changes and are highly differentiated from country to country. The relations among churches, states, and society, for example, are deeply connected to the constitutional path and the legal framework of individual states, and this connection affects the daily life of believers. For instance, the role of religion in Italy and in other southern European countries is quite different from that in northern Europe. There is often a gap between the institutional level of religions, including relations between churches and states, and the personal level of religious feelings and practices.

Furthermore, religion has participated in many different ways in the growth of national and regional identities. For instance, some national identities, such as that of the Irish, are rooted in religion. More broadly, public and political debates have been carried out to discuss the role of religion in a united Europe. Finally, the link between religions and politics appears whenever new states are considered for membership in the European Union.

Several historical processes and events, as well as recent social and political issues, have affected religions in Europe. The secularization process, the Holocaust, migration flows toward Europe, biotechnology, and terrorism have all hugely affected daily religious life in Europe. This chapter will provide a broad overview of religion in modern Europe.

OVERVIEW OF RELIGIONS IN EUROPE

A quick rundown of religions in Europe in the third millennium shows the situation to be similar to that of Europe near the end of the eighteenth century, when the continent was under the influence of the changes brought about by the French Revolution. As in those days, present-day Europe is still strongly influenced by Christian churches of the Catholic, Protestant, and Orthodox traditions, and we can begin our analysis by describing the geographical and doctrinal differences that distinguish these three branches of European Christianity.

Its presence in Europe going back to ancient times, Judaism has also had an important role in the religious history of the continent. In the twentieth century, widespread persecutions of the Jews and the Holocaust constituted a terrible turning point in the history of Judaism in Europe. Nowadays, Judaism is almost absent in Spain, and quite widely spread in France, the Netherlands, and the United Kingdom.

During the second half of twentieth century, the religious composition of Europe began to change. With increasing intensity since the 1970s, migration flows have caused the diffusion of non-Western religions throughout Europe. Asian religions and especially Islam have spread almost everywhere, albeit in very different ways and forms. Moreover, this introduction of non-Western faiths triggered religious hybridization and the rise of new religious movements.

Islam mainly diffused in France because of immigration flows from North Africa, and in Germany because of flows from Turkey and the former Yugoslavia. A huge Islamic presence is also found in Bosnia and Albania.

European Christianity can be geographically distinguished between southern Europe, which is mainly Roman Catholic; northern Europe, which is mainly Protestant; and Central Eastern Europe, where Orthodoxy is the main Christian tradition. In southern Europe, Catholicism has for a long time been the state religion in Italy, Portugal, and Spain. According to survey data gathered by the European Values Study and World Values Survey, Catholicism is still the most diffused European religion. In Italy, a large majority of the population is Catholic, even if there are other religious minorities, such as Protestants, Jews, and more recently, Muslims. In the twentieth century, a charismatic movement developed in the Catholic Church. Protestant churches include the Waldensians, who are diffused in the northwest regions, and the Evangelical Methodists, who were unified in 1979. There are also small communities of Baptists and Pentecostals, established in the nineteenth century, and of Jehovah Witnesses, established in the twentieth century. Immigration from Africa and Asia also brought new Christian migrant communities.

A small but important Jewish community has long existed in Italy. For historical reasons, the Iberian Peninsula has no important Jewish communities. In Spain, Protestants organized themselves into the Spanish Evangelical Church and the Spanish Reformed Episcopal Church, whereas in Portugal, they have joined the Evangelical Presbyterian Church of Portugal and the Lusitanian Church of Portugal, both of which grew out of nineteenth-century missionary work. In both countries, there are also a few Anglicans. In the twentieth century, some new Protestant groups emerged, mainly Pentecostals. Because of migration flows, Islam diffused in Spain, whereas the controversial Universal Church of the Kingdom of God (from Brazil) and the Mana Church from South Africa were established in Portugal.

In southeastern Europe, the dominant Orthodox tradition plays an important role in national identity. In Greece and Romania, the population is mainly Orthodox, though there are important religious minorities, such as Catholics, Protestants (both Lutheran and Reformed), and Pentecostals. Romania has Catholics—who are members of the Uniate (oriental rite) churches, which are in communion with Rome—and an important Baptist minority. In the Balkan countries, religious minorities are mostly composed of national minority groups. In Albania, adherents of Islam and Christianity are almost equal in number. Among Christians, the Orthodox and the Catholic are the largest churches, though there is also a small Protestant presence.

In many of the former socialist countries of Eastern Europe, including the former Yugoslavia, religions were nearly banished from public space. However, when these regimes collapsed in the 1990s, religion served as a source of identity. For instance, the former Yugoslavia divided into Muslim Bosnia Herzegovina, Catholic Croatia and Slovenia (though the latter has granted political asylum to several Bosnian Muslim refugees), Orthodox Montenegro and Serbia (though Serbia has a strong spatially bounded Catholic community), and the pluralistic Republic of Macedonia (where there is a consistent presence of Orthodox, Catholics, and Muslims). A controversy still exists between Serbia and the autonomist Muslims of Kosovo.

Central Europe is divided into Catholic and Protestant majority nations. Catholics are the main religious group in Austria, although there is a small group of Protestants (mainly Lutherans, though also some Reformed, Baptists, and Methodists). Poland is a Catholic country, with Orthodox and Lutheran minorities. Slovakia and the Czech Republic are also mainly Catholic, though the latter has important Protestant churches, including Pentecostal groups, the Czechoslovak Hussite Church, and the Evangelical Church of Czech Brethren. Near Prague is also a Baptist theological seminary that serves the whole of Europe. Hungary's largest church is Catholic, though

Lutherans and Calvinists have played important roles historically, and Ortho-doxy remains in the minority.

In France, the Catholic presence is preponderant, though religions are forbidden a public role, according to the concept of secular society that distinguishes between the religious and the public spheres. France also has a Protestant Reformed minority that is historically significant. As a result of immigration, Islam is now the second-largest religion in France. Immigration has also brought to France diverse African Evangelical and Pentecostal Christian groups.

Protestant churches are most widespread in northern Europe. In the Scandinavian countries of Sweden, Norway, Denmark, Finland, and Iceland, the Lutheran tradition is the most popular, whereas in other northern European areas the Reformed tradition is more significant. In Switzerland, Catholicism and Protestantism (organized in a Protestant Federation that groups the Reformed churches of the different cantons) have about the same number of adherents. There is also a small presence of Methodist groups. Through immigration, Orthodox and Pentecostal churches have increased their presence in northern Europe.

Lutheran churches became the national churches in most Scandinavian countries in the sixteenth century, and in some countries, they are still the national or state churches today. In Denmark, the Lutheran Church is the national church, though there is also a small Baptist union and several Charismatic groups. In Iceland, the Evangelical Lutheran Church is the national church, and it plays a huge role in terms of national identity. Scandinavia also has a small percentage of Pentecostal groups and Catholic believers, as well as extra-European religions diffused among migrants' communities.

In Finland, because of its closeness to the former Soviet Union, there is also an important Orthodox presence, mainly in the northern part of the country. In the second half of the nineteenth century, several smaller Protes-tant denominations, such as Baptists and Methodists, diffused in Finland. In the twentieth century, Pentecostal groups also established themselves in Finland, becoming the largest non-Lutheran denomination in the country. The Church of Norway (Lutheran) used to be the state church and is still the majority church. Norway also has small free Protestant, Catholic, Orthodox, Pentecostal, and Charismatic churches. Sweden has strong Orthodox and Pentecostal minorities because of immigration and the revival movements of the nineteenth and twentieth centuries. Although, the Lutheran Church is the majority church in Sweden, there is also a small Methodist community. Because of migrations, Islam is growing, thus becoming an increasingly important presence in the Scandinavian countries.

In modern Germany, Catholicism seems to be the most widespread religion. Catholics are a majority in southern Germany, whereas Protestants (Lutheran, Reformed, and United churches) are the majority in northern and eastern Germany. Of course, because Germany was the birthplace of Martin Luther and the Lutheran Reform, German Protestantism has played an important role in the country's history.

In the Netherlands and Belgium, religious separation follows the borders of geographical and linguistic differences. Southern Belgium has a Catholic majority, but the Netherlands to the north is historically a bulwark of conservative reformed churches based on Calvinist doctrine, though there is also a small Lutheran presence. The twentieth-century migration flows increased the presence in both countries of Christian migrant churches from Africa, Asia, and Latin America. Nowadays there is also an important diffusion of Muslims in both countries. The Catholic Church is the majority church in Belgium, despite the historical importance of the Reformation in the area. However, the Protestant presence is still high, and divided into the United Protestant Church of Belgium (Reformed), the Evangelicals, and Pentecostals, together with a small percentage of Charismatic groups. There is also a small but growing presence of Orthodoxy.

Among the Baltic republics, Estonia has a great majority of Protestants, an increasing presence of Charismatic and Pentecostal groups, and a small minority of Orthodox churches. Latvia is mainly Orthodox, with a strong Catholic presence, especially in the western area. Since the breakup of the Soviet Union in the 1990s, a religious revival has diffused Protestantism in the country through the Evangelical Lutheran Church and a small Pentecostal presence. Finally, Lithuania is mainly Catholic.

Among the European Protestant churches, the Church of England (or Anglican Church) is unusual in that it defines itself as both Catholic and Reformed. As a result, it is sometimes divided into a high church (or Anglo-Catholic) tradition, which emphasizes its Catholic characteristics, and a low church (or Evangelical) tradition, which emphasizes Protestant characteristics. The United Kingdom consists of England, Scotland, Wales, and Northern Ireland. In England, the Anglican Church is the established church, whereas in Scotland the Presbyterian Church is the national church. Protestantism is the most diffused religion in the United Kingdom, but there is also an important Catholic and Jewish presence, and because of migrations, a growing Muslim, Hindu, and Sikh presence. The independent African and Afro-Caribbean churches are very lively and strong. In the struggle for Irish independence from the United Kingdom, the Catholic religion has played a huge role in terms of national identity, making Ireland the only northern country with a Catholic majority.

TIMELINE

1869–1870:   The Roman Catholic Church holds the First Vatican Council.

1905:   Separation between church and state achieved in Portugal and France.

1910:   The Conference of Edinburgh, a Protestant missionary conference, is held in Scotland.

1914–1918:   World War I takes place in Europe.

1917:   October Revolution overthrows the Russian czar.

1922:   Russia becomes the USSR and officially atheistic.

1922–1945:   Fascism rules in Italy.

1933–1945:   Nazism rules in Germany.

1934:   The Theological Declaration of Barmen (Protestant) is issued.

1936–1939:   The Spanish civil war takes place.

1939–1975:   Francisco Franco's nationalist regime rules in Spain.

1939–1945:   World War II takes place.

1948:   The Universal Declaration of Human Rights is issued.

1962–1965:   The Roman Catholic Church holds the Second Vatican Council.

1968:   World Contentious Movement.

1989:   The Berlin Wall falls.

2000:   The Roman Catholic Church Year of Jubilee.

CHRISTIANITY IN EUROPE: DIFFERENCES BETWEEN PROTESTANTS AND CATHOLICS

From a historical perspective, Europe is considered Christian territory, with three main traditions: Orthodoxy (southeastern Europe), Protestantism (central and northern Europe), and Catholicism (central and southern Europe). Until the second half of the twentieth century (and in some cases even afterward), Christian culture permeated European societies, popular thought, and peoples' daily activities. There was regular Sunday worship attendance, the observance of religious rituals, and a widespread recognition of the religious foundation of moral value. Nevertheless, there was—and still there is—an enormous variety in traditional practices. Religious beliefs are embedded in several physical forms of faith expression, and popular religion is deeply rooted in local traditions. The material expressions of religious membership are too numerous to be listed; however, they are mostly variations of the same codified models of worship.

The majority of Christian beliefs are the same in the different traditions. Christians believe in the Trinity: God ("the Father"), Jesus ("the Son") and the Holy Spirit. God is unique and is recognized as the creator of the world. He embodied himself in Jesus, who was sent to save humanity from death and sin. Jesus was, at the same time, human and divine. He taught humans to love God and each other. The Holy Spirit is God's manifestation in daily life as well as in the actions of believers.

In Christianity, the dimension of daily life is crucial—religious belonging involves both beliefs and practice. The latter does not simply involve attendance at rites and rituals. To be a good Christian, every action should be "Christian"; Christianity has a strong practical and collective dimension. This is especially true for Protestantism and Catholicism; Eastern Christianity particularly stresses worship.

Religiosity marked the social values of almost the whole of European society. There was a strong sense of religious piety toward the poor, and religious decorum defined the respectable citizen, both in Protestant and Catholic societies. On the other hand, in everyday life the religious ethos dominated in different ways. In both Catholic and Protestant traditions there was an undemanding ethos, involving a certain obedience to Church authority, periodic devotion, and a general adherence to Christian values and behaviors. However, there was also a more active ethos, involving a deeper commitment to religious life. In Protestantism, this ethos can be defined as evangelical, involving both regular practice and active religious behavior to live religiously. For instance, it entailed the commitment to community life as well as participation in social-care–oriented groups and associations. In the Catholic tradition, this attitude was more common because of the stronger claims for regular attendance and Christian piety, and also because of the fact that Catholicism was a more public religion than Protestantism. Participation in religious associations was widespread and represented a fairly important requirement for being a "good Catholic." Furthermore, there was an important social pressure for the respect of religious values and behavioral codes. Until recently, for instance, abortion was morally and firmly condemned. Nevertheless, there was a great variation among European countries. As a matter of fact, Christian tradition had different historical paths in different countries. Therefore, several Christian traditions developed on territorial basis. Furthermore, in many cases, these differences within the same denominations were markers of linguistic, cultural, and even class identity.

Different periods during the twentieth century witnessed waves of religious revivals promoted by movements aiming at a deeper religious life in terms of emotional involvement and religious activities. In this perspective, sinners were encouraged to reconnect to religion by accepting Jesus and converting or reconverting (in some way, "rebirthing"). Revivalism was presented in a missionary fashion, which also affected traditional religious style. Religious evangelism was also accompanied by vigorous moral campaigning.

Indeed, during the twentieth century, both Catholicism and Protestantism adopted a missionary attitude toward European societies as a reaction to different historical processes. In the Protestant tradition, missions have always been important. The Mission Conference of Edinburgh of 1910 was only the first step along a path of massive reflection that involved all Christianity and led to an awareness of the necessity for European re-evangelization. Decolonization, the aftermaths of the two world wars, and the effects of secularization triggered reconsideration of religion as a mission. In the twentieth century, European Protestantism often took the shape of a "church of opposition." In general, Protestantism was reshaped as a church without a submissive spirit; religion promoted a critical attitude toward society and a political and civil commitment to social justice, truth, and democracy. In this light, Europe was seen as a place in need of re-evangelization.

A similar attitude affected Catholicism, mainly in relation to social issues and the effects of secularization. The Catholic Church has usually been very committed to social issues. On the one hand, the Church opposed the dissemination of socialist theories, but on the other, it tried to be more connected to workers, even recognizing in some instances the working class as the main target of re-evangelization. The Church even proposed to build a few Christian missionary communities in poorer communities. In accordance with this spirit, the mission of Paris was established in 1944. Priests participating in the Paris mission wanted to share the conditions of life of those whom they sought to evangelize. From these communities developed the experience of the Working Priests, who worked in factories and shared the life and working conditions of believers. The French working priests also shared the social struggles of the workers, and some of them even joined Marxist workers' unions. In 1954, the Vatican ended this experiment by forbidding priests from working in factories and forcing them to return to a more traditional apostolate to avoid the risks of socialist influence. But thanks to the working priests, faith became increasingly important in the daily behavior of working-class believers; it was the expression of a daily commitment based on actions (orthopraxis). In Christianity, the clergy has an important role, although there are some denominational differences.

The Role of the Clergy

The Church is God's body on Earth and the hinge of the Christian community. Although the whole of Christianity includes the idea of specialized clergy, its role is different in the three European religious traditions. Catholics believe in the key role of clergy and are especially devoted and obedient to the papacy.

The Catholic Church is a pyramid, with the pope at the top, followed by cardinals (who have the right to elect a new pope at the death of the incumbent), archbishops, bishops, priests, and laity. The pope, based in the Vatican State, is considered the successor of Saint Peter, on whom Jesus conferred the headship of His Church. Until the war for Italian unification (known as the *Risorgimento*—"the revival") in the mid-nineteenth century, the pope was a temporal ruler, governing a part of central Italy from Rome as the Papal States. In September 1870, after a cannonade that breached the Aurelian walls bordering the city, the Italian army entered Rome, which one year later became the capital of the Kingdom of Italy. Because the pope refused to officially recognize the Italian kingdom until 1929, Catholics were prevented from getting involved in Italian politics, an interdiction that lasted until the foundation in 1919 of the Partito Popolare (Popular Party) by the priest Don Luigi Sturzo. In other countries, this interdiction was not applied.

In the Catholic tradition, the pope has a central role. He can speak infallibly on matters of faith and morals. During the nineteenth and twentieth centuries, all popes, except the two most recent—John Paul II, elected in 1978, and Benedict XVI, elected in 2005—came from Italy. The role of the pope is both temporal and spiritual. Especially during the twentieth century, the papacy increasingly intervened in European and world politics. The pope has the ultimate authority on issues of faith and Catholic morals, and he has become an increasingly familiar figure in the life of Catholics, particularly after the Second Vatican Council (1962–1965), and to non-Catholics around the world, thanks to the mass media. The pope has the right to choose the cardinals, who are members of the Sacred College. Since 1962, all cardinals have had to be bishops. The bishops are considered the successors of Jesus's apostles; they are appointed by the pope and lead the local Catholic dioceses. The diocese is the key geographical unit of authority. Important dioceses are called archdioceses and are governed by archbishops. The bishops and archbishops ordain new priests and confer the sacrament of Confirmation. Every diocese is divided into vicariates (or deaconries), and then further divided into parishes, which are governed by priests.

Priests administer sacraments, including the celebration of the Mass (or Divine Liturgy), and hear Confession, also known as the Sacrament of Penance. Only bishops can ordain priests, who should be at least 25 years old and celibate. The Second Vatican Council was very important in defining the role of laity within Catholicism. It promoted their involvement during liturgical services, introducing "lectures" during the Sunday Mass, and in the Catholic community. The mobilization of the laity was historically rooted in the Catholic tradition. Between the end of the nineteenth and the beginning of the twentieth centuries, the role of the laity within the Church was reorganized in a new form of apostolate following territorial borders (see Religious Associations and Organizations, below). Nevertheless, the role of the clergy is crucial in Catholicism. Priests are the hinge and the moral guide of Catholic communities and the local parishes were, for a very long time, the center of Catholic life.

The other Christian traditions do not obey the pope, and even if they have a similar internal organization to that of the Catholic Church, the relationship within them between obedience and authority is quite different. Because of the lack of a central head, Protestant churches exhibit differences in their internal organization. Protestants, in fact, assert that there is no intermediate authority between God and their church (considered a community of believers). This affects their internal structure, which is not organized as a pyramid. There is a wide range of organizational forms within the Protestant Church, from a totally congregational model to a more synodal one. The main Protestant churches in Europe are the Lutheran, Reformed, Methodist, and Anglican. By and large, most have a Presbyterian or synodal structure.

Lutheran, Methodist, and Reformed churches generally adhere, with some variations, to an organizational form based on the community life of local churches. The community is led by ordained pastors and elders, or presbyters (laypersons). Local churches gather in regional and wider (national or international), assemblies and the ultimate authority rests with the synod. The laity has an important role in the church's organization; laypersons are totally involved in the structure of the church and contribute to the decisions and life of the religious community.

The Evangelical Methodist and Waldensian churches are organized in a synodal Presbyterian system. In some countries, as in Italy, Waldensians and Methodists merged, establishing unified Protestant churches. The Church of Scotland is also Presbyterian. Other Protestant denominations, such as the Baptists, have a more congregation-oriented constitution, without a centralized structure. Baptists affirm that the church, as the body of Christ, is the communion of the faithful; they recognize only the Bible as a binding authority, and under the guidance of the Holy Spirit each church may interpret the scriptures and design the life of its community.

The Church of England, which is the established or state church in the United Kingdom, has an intermediate position between Catholicism and Protestantism, and its own hierarchy. The head of the Church of England is Jesus, but the British monarch is the supreme governor. He or she has to approve the appointment of archbishops, bishops, and deans, on the recommendation of the prime minister, and formally opens the sessions (every five years) of the General Synod, the Church's governing body. The Church of

England's hierarchy includes 43 dioceses in England plus the Diocese in Europe. Each diocese has a bishop and at least one suffragan (or assistant bishop), and it is divided into archdeaconries, run by archdeacons. Archdeaconries are, in turn, subdivided into deaneries, which are collections of parishes. The Church of England is episcopal (led by bishops) and synodally governed.

The Orthodox churches are self-governing, either being autocephalous (meaning having their own head) or autonomous. Each church has its own geographical title, which usually reflects the cultural tradition of its believers. Because of their autonomy, not all Orthodox churches are "in communion." For the same reason, they have several internal differences. Orthodox churches are mostly spread across Eastern Europe, where they developed from the Christianity of the Eastern Roman Empire (this is the reason they are sometimes called Byzantine). Eastern Orthodox churches differ from Oriental Orthodox churches from a theological point of view; the latter form a separate group. The nominal head of the Eastern Orthodox churches is the Patriarch of Constantinople. He is the first among equals and has no real authority over churches other than his own. There are 15 autocephalous churches: the churches of Constantinople, Alexandria, Antioch, Jerusalem, Russia, Serbia, Romania, Bulgaria, Georgia, Cyprus, Greece (1870), Poland (1924), Albania (1937), the Czech and Slovak lands (1951), and the Orthodox Church of America. The first nine are led by patriarchs, whereas the others are led by archbishops or metropolitans. The orthodox communion also includes a number of autonomous churches: those of Sinai, Finland, Estonia, Japan, China, Ukraine, and the Archdiocese of Ohrid.

Although the Orthodox Church is a self-governing community, it recognizes the diaconate, presbyterate or priesthood, and the episcopate (bishops). As in Catholicism, the bishops are considered successors of the original apostles and should be celibate. Priests in the Orthodox Church are permitted to be married, but they may not marry after ordination. Orthodox priests normally do not shave their beards, in accordance with the Bible.

Whereas in Catholicism only unmarried man can be ordained, in Protestant churches married clergy are the norm. In recent decades, the ordination of women has become a hotly debated issue. The pope and Catholicism strongly reject this idea, as does the Orthodox tradition, but Protestantism has a more open attitude. Nevertheless, within Protestant traditions there are also some differences. In northern Lutheran countries, the ordination of women is the norm, even if some scholars argue that they have less prestigious roles and are subjected to congregational stereotypes; scholars also state that large congregations seem to prefer male clergy. The Anglican Church (Church of England) recently approved female ordination, as did the Waldensians. The ordination of women began in the nineteenth century in Protestant denominations with a congregational polity, thus their authority resided at the local level. After World War II, a second wave of female ordainment arose, becoming a public issue.

Recently, Christian denominations have become sharply polarized on whether clergy should be ordained regardless of sexual orientation. The Catholic, Orthodox, and conservative Protestant churches are quite strict about the ordination of non-heterosexual clergy. This position has been strengthened by recent scandals of involving clerical sexual abuses. Apart from some Protestant congregations or individual Catholic bishops, most Christian churches oppose the ordination of homosexuals.

Besides the ordained clergy, Christian denominations include other forms of membership. For instance, Europe has several religious orders, which are institutes of consecrated religious life where people live a common life following religious rules. Many are closed monastic orders, whereas others are open to laity. There are both male and female orders. Protestantism has few religious orders (in Europe the best known is the French-based Taizé), but orders perform an important function in the Catholic and Anglican traditions.

There are several differences among the more than 300 Catholic religious orders and even some differences within the same order. However, in spite of these differences, the orders share basic features, such as community prayer, community meals, community labor, private prayer and study, and religious vows (typically of poverty, chastity, and obedience). Most orders have a similar formation process, which is characterized by four stages: postulancy, novitiate, simple profession, and solemn profession. The process of discernment usually lasts about five years, until solemn vows are taken. The daily schedule of common-prayer time usually includes Lauds (or Prime) at waking (morning prayer); Terce (midmorning prayer); Sext (midday prayer); None (midafternoon prayer); Vespers (evening prayer); and Compline (night prayer). Orders can be either contemplative or active. Contemplative orders—such as the Benedictine, Carmelite, Trappist, Carthusian, and Cistercian—focus primarily on God and His love, and they have little interaction with society. Active orders—such as the Franciscan, Dominican, and Missionaries of Charity—live side-by-side with society and devote more time to services to the community. They typically organize such activities as feeding the hungry, teaching and preaching, participating in missions, and assisting those in need in many ways. Active orders are called mendicant because their members usually subsist on charity.

There are also several important Catholic communities and movements. In the nineteenth and twentieth centuries, the most important Catholic movements in Europe were the Neocatechumenal, the Charismatic, Communion and Liberation, Opus Dei, the Community of Sant'Egidio, the Focolare, and the Legion of Christ. Communion and Liberation (reorganized in 1969) played a particularly important role in twentieth-century Catholicism. Indeed, this lay ecclesial movement promoted an extremely communitarian and committed way of religious life, while at the same time lowering the level of institutional mediation of faith in a manner similar to Protestantism, thus inserting some features more typical of the Protestant faith within Catholic worship. Protestant churches have no religious orders, but believers are organized in several volunteering and socially oriented associations and organizations. Monasticism is a central part of Orthodox faith. Mount Athos, in northeastern Greece, is considered the center of Orthodox monasticism, and is completely devoted to prayer and worship of God.

Daily Life of Christians: Differences in Rituals and Organizations

The daily life of Christians revolves around prayer and the ceremonies and rituals of worship. In recent decades, because of the process of secularization (see Secularization, below), some material expressions of faith have been gradually losing importance. Nevertheless, other marks of church membership, such as the sacraments or participation in the main religious festivals of the liturgical calendar, still remain important in the life of believers.

Christianity organizes the time and space of individuals and communities. The life of Christians is marked by sacraments, called "mysteries" in the Orthodox tradition, which are signs of the relationship between God and the believer. Although there are differences in the ritual practices of sacraments and in their number (seven in the Catholicism and Orthodoxy, and two in Protestantism), the first sacrament (or mystery) in the whole of Christianity is Baptism, which is the sign of inclusion in the religious community. The Baptism ceremony usually takes place during the Sunday service. It includes a rite of public rejection of Satan and of evil by the parents (if a child is being baptized) and a public vow of faith. The infant or adult is bathed with holy water, an act that represents both inclusion in the believers' community and the forgiveness of sins.

In the Catholic tradition, baptism is usually administered to infants during their first year of life, and includes the forgiveness of original sin. To be baptized and introduced into the Catholic community, it used to be compulsory that at least one of the child's names be that of a saint, and even nowadays this is still a common requirement. Children usually wear a white dress, symbolizing their rebirth in purity, and the ceremony entails the pouring of water on their heads. During the ceremony, the godfather and godmother (usually uncles, aunts, cousins, or close friends of the parents) take the public vow to involve the child in the life of the Church and make a public commitment to be the child's guide. Especially in southern Europe, the role of godfathers and godmothers is very important. They usually give the child a golden object as a gift, such as a golden bracelet or a necklace.

In the Orthodox tradition, the baptism of adults and infants is by immersion in water three times in the name of the Holy Trinity, and it represents both initiation and forgiveness of sins. The rite involves the undressing of the child, which symbolizes the act of divesting the child of all sins. After the immersion, the child is dried with a white sheet and the priest immediately gives him or her the Confirmation and cuts three wisps of his or her hair as a gift for God. The child is then dressed in white, and all attendants walk three times in front of the baptismal font with a candle, singing hymns of joy.

In some Protestant denominations—such as the Baptists, Pentecostals, and Anabaptists—only adults can be baptized. For Baptists, only those who have personally and voluntarily made a decision to follow Christ through baptism are members of Christ's church. Thus, in the Protestant tradition, baptism represents the inclusion into the believers' community. For Baptists, baptism can only be by submersion; in Lutheranism, Methodism, Anglicanism, and other Protestant traditions, baptism can be by immersion, pouring, or sprinkling. The rite of baptism has a profound significance in Christianity, and even though such significance is weakening, the majority of children are still baptized, and their baptism involves a big ceremony with the child's whole family.

The Eucharist—which is also called Holy Communion, the Lord's Supper, or the Divine Liturgy—is a sacrament accepted by almost all Christians and constitutes a sign of Christian unity. The Eucharist is a reenactment of the Last Supper, the final meal that Jesus Christ shared with his disciples before his arrest and crucifixion. During the Catholic Mass, the priest recalls the action of Jesus, who asked his disciples to consume bread and wine in memory of Him. Those who take part in the ceremony drink a sip of wine (or grape juice) and eat a tiny piece of bread, both of which have been consecrated.

Although all denominations acknowledge the importance of the Eucharist, they differ about its meaning and practice. Catholics believe that during Mass, bread and wine become Christ's body and blood (a doctrine known as "transubstantiation"). During Mass, the priest gives the Eucharist to churchgoers, who line up in the church's main nave to receive the sanctified bread. In the Catholic ceremony, the ordinary Sunday communion usually does not include wine. In general, the priest puts the sanctified bread directly into the mouths of believers, whereas in Protestant denominations it is usually placed into the believers' hands. For Catholics, the Eucharist is the most important act of worship. All Catholics are encouraged to receive communion at least once a week during Mass. Some Catholics may receive the Eucharist every day. Protestants believe that Jesus made his sacrifice on the Cross, and they simply follow the tradition of the sacrament in memory of the event, recalling its symbolic importance in the life of Jesus. In Protestantism, the believers usually take the wine in individual communion cups. Other denominations receive Holy Communion less frequently, and services usually are held once a week or every few weeks. Like Catholics, the Orthodox believe in the transubstantiation. During the Orthodox service, believers, standing, are given the Holy Communion in a spoon containing both the bread and the wine.

For Catholics, becoming an effective part of the Christian community involves a path toward Confirmation. The first step is Confession, then comes Communion, and eventually Confirmation. The First Confession and First Communion are publicly celebrated. First Communion involves a ceremony that usually takes place in spring, during the Sunday service. Boys and girls—usually 10 or 11 years old—wear a white suit or dress and are introduced into the Christian community through their first Holy Communion. One adult, a female for girls and a male for boys, is required to be the godfather or godmother. Preparation for First Communion involves attending usually weekly classes. A layperson, called a "catechist," teaches children the main aspects of religion and religious behavior. Catechism classes begin one year before First Confession and last until Confirmation. After having celebrated First Communion, boys and, more recently, girls are allowed to attend the priest during the celebration of Sunday Mass or altar service. The presence of acolytes is also common in the Anglican and the Orthodox traditions. Apart from Baptism and the Eucharist, Catholics and Orthodox believers accept five other sacraments: Confession, Confirmation, Marriage, Holy Orders, and Anointing of the Sick.

Confession (or Penitence) has been recently renamed Reconciliation, because the sacrament leads to the person's reconciliation with God. This sacrament consists of three rites: confession, penitence, and absolution, granted by a priest, for sins committed after baptism. As a sacrament, Reconciliation takes place one or two years before First Communion. Believers are encouraged to confess at least twice a year, usually before the two main Christian feasts of Christmas and Easter. But as a rule, Confession should be given every time before celebrating Eucharist. Entering the confessional ensures anonymity, and the believer is required to openly admit his or her sins. At the end, the priest absolves the sinner and gives him or her a penance, usually consisting of some prayers. All Orthodox churches use the Mystery of Penance, or Confession, but in the Greek-speaking churches only priests who have been blessed by the bishop as Spiritual Fathers are allowed to hear confession. Children may be admitted to the sacrament of Confession as soon as they are old enough to know the difference between right and wrong. Through this sacrament, sinners may receive forgiveness. They enter into confession with a priest often in an open area in the church (not in a confessional, as in the Roman Catholic tradition, or separated by a grille). Both the priest and penitent stand and cross themselves, and a book of Gospels or an icon is placed in front of the penitent, with the priest standing slightly apart. This arrangement stresses the fact that the priest is simply a witness and forgiveness comes directly from God, not from the priest. The priest listens to the confession and sometimes gives advice. After confession, the penitent kneels down before the priest, who places his stole on the penitent's head, saying a prayer of absolution. In the Orthodox tradition the believer's spiritual father prays together with the sinner at the end of confession, without giving him or her absolution.

Reconciliation and the Eucharist are the only sacraments (or mysteries) celebrated more than once during the Christian life. Baptism, and for Catholics and Orthodox, Confirmation, Marriage, Ordination, and Anointing of the Sick should be celebrated only once. In the Orthodox tradition, Confirmation follows immediately after Baptism and is followed by the Holy Communion. This means that in the Orthodox churches children are immediately full members of the Church. Chrism can only be consecrated by the patriarch, or chief bishop of the local church. Some of the old chrism is mixed with the new, thus linking the newly baptized to their forebears in the faith. Chrism is used to anoint different parts of the body with a sign of the cross: the forehead, eyes, nostrils, mouth, ears, chest, hands, and feet.

Confirmation is a sacrament, ritual, or rite of passage practiced by several Christian denominations. In Catholicism, Confirmation requires a path of consciousness, involving the attendance of religious classes to learn about the sacrament, the faith, and Christian responsibilities. Confirmation preparation helps candidates have a proper understanding of how to live as followers of Christ. For this reason, children are usually 13 or 14 years old when they are confirmed. During the ceremony, they traditionally wore white dresses, similar to those worn for the First Communion ceremony. In the last decades, however, the custom has changed, and they have been allowed to wear other types of clothes. Confirmation is usually celebrated by bishops, who ask the believers to refuse evil, anoint their foreheads with chrism, and then give them a little cuff. The latter symbolizes that the confirmed have become a Soldier of Christ. In the Anglican Church, the sacrament of confirmation is conferred through the laying of hands. In English- and German-speaking countries, during Confirmation the child adopts the name of a saint, who becomes his or her patron saint. Whereas the Catholic branch of Anglicanism considers Confirmation a sacrament, the Protestant branch, together with other Protestant denominations, regards Confirmation as a mature expression of faith by an already baptized person. Nevertheless, Methodist and Presbyterian churches recognize confirmation as a "coming-of-age" ceremony, an acceptance of full religious responsibility. It is a symbolic act that allows the baptized person to make a mature statement of faith.

Christian marriage is a solemn and public covenant between a man and a woman in the presence of God. Getting married in a church, in front of God, is very important. A marriage is a public declaration of love and commitment. This declaration is made in front of friends and family in a church ceremony. It is an essential prerequisite that at least one of the parties be a baptized Christian. Moreover, the ceremony must be attested by at least two witnesses, and the marriage must conform to the laws of the state and the canons of the church. Anglicanism, Catholicism, and Orthodoxy consider (heterosexual) Holy Marriage a sacrament, thus sex outside marriage is a sin, and divorce is not allowed. Before the marriage is celebrated, couples are required to attend religious classes, which usually last one year, to verify their mutual commitment. Holy Marriage is still an important event in people's lives, especially in southern Europe, where, for traditional reasons, it is common to celebrate religious marriages even though church attendance levels are low. In recent years, Catholic priests have called for more sober and religiously grounded ceremonies, inviting believers to be more present in the Catholic community. However, the religious marriage rate is decreasing in favor of civil weddings. Although marriages outside the faith are nowadays common in Catholicism, they are discouraged in the Orthodox tradition. Although marriage is seen as a permanent commitment in the Orthodox tradition, divorce and remarriage are permitted in certain circumstances.

In Protestant churches, marriage is not considered a sacrament, though it has great importance in the life of the community and in that of believers. Given the importance of this rite, Episcopal churches ask the couple to follow, as in Catholicism, a path of religious counseling. In the Church of Scotland, nonmembers of the church as well as divorced people may be married, if the minister agrees, whereas in other denominations it is more difficult, if not explicitly forbidden.

The last sacrament in a Christian's life is the Anointing of the Sick (called until a few decades ago Extreme Unction), which is administered only when death is approaching. The sacrament can represent the extreme forgiveness of sins for the salvation of the sufferer's soul, or simply a religious support to suffering believers. It can be administered during Mass, at home, in a hospital or institution, or at church. The rite involves the sprinkling of all those who are present with holy water, and the anointing of the sick on the forehead. It is permitted, in accordance with local culture and traditions regarding the condition of the sick person, to anoint also other parts of the body, such as the area of pain or injury. The Anointing of the Sick is a sacrament in Catholicism and Orthodoxy and has a sacramental character in Anglicanism. Protestant communities greatly vary; in the main Protestant churches, it has fallen into disuse, whereas in Charismatic and Pentecostal denominations it is a more common practice. (Among the sacraments, Holy Orders are something aside because they are a celebration reserved for the ordination of clergy and do not affect the ordinary life of believers.)

Sacraments mark believers' lives, standing as rites of passage. But in daily life there are other religious events. The Christian liturgy, for instance, has a liturgical calendar that contemplates several religious events and festivals throughout the year.

Liturgical Year

The liturgical year comprises various festivals and seasons. Festivals are deeply interconnected with the traditions and habits of each country. They are events that express popular religiosity and vary from place to place. Some festivities are common to all Christian traditions, whereas others are typical to some traditions only. Christmas, common to the whole of Christianity, commemorates the birth of Jesus, and in Europe it is a festivity also in the civil calendar. Generally speaking, Christmas is the Christian festival most celebrated by non-churchgoers. In European countries, it is the most important festivity during the liturgical year, and churches usually are full for the midnight service. In Spain, Midnight Mass is referred to as Misa del Gallo. The contemporary forms of Christmas celebration emerged in the early twentieth century, and their importance as a festival grew remarkably in the last century. During World War I, for instance, several brief unofficial cessations of hostilities occurred on Christmas Eve or Christmas Day—they were called "Christmas truce." Although Christmas giving was particularly difficult during wartime, it became a very rich and consumerist habit in the boom years and especially in recent decades, so much so that religious authorities often call for a return to the true religious spirit of Christmas.

In the Catholic tradition, the days in December leading up to Christmas constitute the season of Advent, during which believers set up a crib in their home. Usually, Jesus's statuette in the crib is covered by a tissue until the Christmas day. In small towns, communities often perform "living cribs" on Christmas Eve. Traditionally, Advent is a penitential season; however, nowadays Christians are no longer required to fast. Usually, Christians do not eat meat on Christmas Eve, but they do eat it on Christmas Day. Christmas is a truly family-oriented celebration, and families traditionally eat Christmas Eve dinner or Christmas lunch together. Protestants also celebrate the traditional midnight Mass. Particularly in Scandinavia and Germany, Lutherans celebrate Christmas with traditional festive music and candlelight services. In Germany, there was the tradition of *Christmette*, a Christmas vigil taking place in the early morning of December 25. In both Protestantism and Catholicism, the civil and religious traditions are mixed together—for example, we can find Santa Claus together with the Crib as part of the symbolism of Christmas. Christmas is celebrated by Orthodox Christians in Central and Eastern Europe on January 7 in the Gregorian calendar—13 days after all other Christians celebrate Christmas. After World War I, various Orthodox churches, beginning with the Patriarchate of Constantinople, began to abandon the Julian calendar (or Old Calendar), and adopted a form of the Gregorian calendar (or New Calendar). Today, many Orthodox churches—with the exception of Jerusalem, Russia, Serbia, and Mount Athos—use the Gregorian calendar for fixed feasts and holy days and the Julian calendar for Easter and movable feasts. In the East, Christmas is preceded by a 40-day fast, beginning on November 15. Usually, observant Orthodox Christians fast until late evening on Christmas Eve, waiting for the first star to appear. When the star is spotted in the sky, people lay the table ready for the Christmas supper. On Christmas Day, people take part in the divine liturgy, after which many walk in procession toward the sea, rivers, and lakes. Everyone gathers around in the snow for outdoor ceremonies to bless the water.

The other important religious festival of the liturgical calendar is Easter, commemorating the resurrection of Christ. The date of Easter changes each year, and it is considered a holiday also in the civil calendar. Easter is preceded by 40 days of Lent, which begins on Ash Wednesday and lasts until Holy Saturday, the day before Easter. The Archdiocese of Milan, which follows the Ambrosian Rite, is an exception in this regard. During Lent, believers are required to fast, which takes different forms in different Christian denominations. In the Orthodox tradition, abstention from meat is still commonly practiced during the whole Lent period. Conversely, Catholic tradition imposes abstention from meat only during Lent Fridays, but in the last decades only traditional believers have rigorously observed this practice. In Protestantism, fasting is perceived nowadays as a choice; this means that Protestants may decide to abstain from a favorite food or drink.

The last week of Lent is Holy Week, which begins with the Palm Sunday celebration commemorating Christ's triumphal entry into Jerusalem. Holy Week celebrations vary by country, each having its own traditions. In the United Kingdom and Sweden, Holy Thursday (charity day) is an important event; in other countries—notably, France, Italy, and Spain—Holy Friday (or Good Friday) celebrations include processions. In northern Lutheran countries, Easter festivities are associated with spring's arrival. Nevertheless, Easter, or Holy Sunday, is the most important single day; people celebrate Jesus's resurrection by decorating their homes with palms (Spain and Sweden), olive (Italy), or willows and birches (Finland). Especially in the Catholic and Orthodox traditions, people bring to the churches their Easter Sunday lunch dishes for the priest's benediction. National traditions affect Easter celebrations, and there is a great variety of popular festivals. In Spain, for instance, Easter is the most important religious festival, and in many towns, especially in the south, Holy Week (*Semana Santa*) processions take place. In Seville, holy processions last an entire week, and members of the city's religious brotherhood, wrapped in white clothes, with big hoods covering their faces, carry in procession wooden sculptures representing religious subjects, followed by penitents.

Three hooded sinners participate in the *Semana Santa* (Holy Week) procession on April 4, 2009, in Seville, Spain. Holy Week is the last week of Lent and includes the holidays Palm Sunday and Good Friday. (Dreamstime.)

Apart from Christmas and Easter, other important Christian festivals during the liturgical year include Assumption, Candlemas, All Saints, Corpus Christi, Epiphany, the Feast of the Immaculate Conception, Pentecost, and the Week of Prayer for Christian Unity. Festivals are more or less important according to the tradition of each country. Epiphany, for instance, is not a civil holiday in the whole of Europe. It commemorates the visit of the Magi to Jesus. For many Protestant traditions, the season of Epiphany extends from January 6 until Ash Wednesday, when Lent begins. In other traditions, including the Catholic, Epiphany is celebrated only on January 6. Furthermore, Candlemas, 40 days after the birth of Jesus, is mainly celebrated in Northern Europe. Among the religious festivals, the Week of Prayer for Christian Unity, a recent development that aims at Christian unification, has a special role. It was introduced by the World Council of Churches in 1966 and has become a practice also within Catholicism. Traditionally, it lasts eight days and is celebrated in the days between January 18 and January 25.

Besides the great variety of expressions of faith in national traditional celebrations, Protestants and Catholics assign different importance to different celebrations. For instance, within Catholicism, saints have an important role, and almost all Catholic cities and towns celebrate the day of their patron saint. These festivals of popular religiosity retain a profound importance in the religious calendar, in particular in southern Europe. In some Catholic countries, Marian piety—that is, devotion to the Virgin Mary—is widespread and important. In spite of the effects of secularization (see Secularization, below), attendance at Christian festivals is still high throughout Europe. But even though religion and religious festivals are important markers during the year, Mass attendance is decreasing.

In the whole of European Christianity, the Mass includes communion service and it is a very dignified occasion—people proceed in lines toward the priest and elders who serve him. The rite is usually accompanied by music and hymns. The Mass, especially Sunday Mass, is the event celebrating the Church, and is the basis of the Christian community life. The week is religiously organized, and Sunday is the day devoted to rest. Although Mass takes place every day, the good Christian is required to attend at least one Mass weekly. Therefore, Sunday Mass is the basis of Christian liturgical life.

Sunday services are divided into two general types: Eucharistic services and services of the Word. Both types of service include hymns, music, readings, and prayers, but whereas the Eucharistic service is focused on the Holy Communion, the service of the Word does not include this rite, and features a much longer sermon. Different churches, even within the same denomination, use very different styles of worship, assigning different roles and places to music and hymns, to the minister, and to congregational participation. Despite the different structures (pyramidal, congregational, and so forth) in Christianity, the parishes are the center of community religious life and have a certain degree of autonomy in the organization of local religious life.

Within Catholicism, diverse types of worship can be singled out. In 1912 Pope Pius X published the *Catechism of the Christian Doctrine*, which became a reference textbook in Italy and deeply influenced the catechisms of other European countries. Nevertheless, some differences still remain. The *Catechism* promoted the role of the laity in ritual practices and underlined the importance of celebrating Sunday as a moment of community aggregation and construction in the Catholic liturgy. Even though traditional believers, especially the elders, often participate in daily Mass, the Sunday Mass is the crucial weekly event during which the whole religious community gathers. During Mass, which lasts about one hour, the celebrant mentions what happened in the week, such as births and deaths, and in some cases, comments the news. Within the liturgy, which can take different forms, prayers are addressed to saints who have great importance. In the Church of England and the Church of Scotland, the singing of hymns is an important feature of services, and most members own a copy of the hymn book. After the Second Vatican Council, the Catholic Mass began to be celebrated in vernacular languages to encourage greater participation and better understanding. Nevertheless, some Catholic branches have called for a return to the traditional Latin Mass, and Pope Benedict XVI, who came to the papacy in 2005, has allowed this option.

In the Orthodox Mass, hymns and gospels as well as processions and the profession of the Creed (as in Catholicism) play a crucial role. Liturgy follows the liturgical calendar and there are therefore four different liturgies: the Liturgy of St. John Chrysostom (used on Sundays and weekdays); the Liturgy of St. Basil the Great (used 10 times a year); the Liturgy of St. James, the Brother of the Lord (sometimes used on St. James's Day); and the Liturgy of the Presanctified (used on Wednesdays and Fridays during Lent and on the first three days of Holy Week).

Within the Protestant churches, differing forms of worship have developed over the centuries in interaction with local cultures. Lutheran worship tradition has sought to maintain liturgical continuity with what is called "ancient church" (the original church of the apostles and early Christians) in the reading and proclamation of the word of God and in the celebration of the sacraments of Baptism and Holy Communion. Each parish can decide whether and when to celebrate the Eucharist. Congregationalist denominations assign a greater role to the hymns and music, and in some cases they introduce the believers' interventions during the celebration. On the whole, the Protestant Mass includes hymns, readings, and sermons, but the liturgy varies depending on the denomination, country, and even locality.

Besides adherence to a religious ethos, participation in religious festivals, and attendance to services, material expressions of faith in daily life also influence dietary and dress codes. For instance, until the huge wave of secularization following World War II, food was an important marker of religious belonging, especially for religious minorities. Nowadays, dietary codes are strictly respected only by very traditional believers and by religious minorities (e.g., Jews) or migrant religious groups (e.g., Muslims in Europe). Apart from the clerical dress, Christianity does not impose dress codes. Even the norms that prevent people from entering churches and sanctified buildings wearing unsuitable clothes, such as shorts or miniskirts, are traditional norms referring more to a common morality than to a specific religious ethos.

Religious habits involve several different practices, both individual and collective, rooted in the traditions of each country. Some religious habits are common to the whole of Christianity. For instance, prayer has great importance in both the Protestant and Catholic traditions. In the past, families offered a common prayer of thanks to God before meals, and children prayed before bedtime. In recent decades, however, these habits have largely lost their importance in the daily life of believers. But they are still practiced by traditional families or on some special occasions, such as religious festivals. Other habits are based on religion or on each country's specific traditions. Furthermore, some religious festivals or popular expressions of religiosity are not initiatives led by the clergy or the Church, and sometimes popular religiosity clashes with the view of religious hierarchies. One recent case is that of the Catholic popular devotion to Padre Pio (1887–1968), a controversial modern "saint" who became famous because of the stigmata on his hands. Despite the tension within hierarchies, which are usually against excesses of popular devotion, Padre Pio is still very popular, especially in southern Italy. Another example involves the images of saints. It is very common to see small saints' images hidden in wallets, hanging in taxis, or framed in restaurants. These images of saints or the Holy Virgin are lucky charms, and their use is widespread among Catholics. In some cases, devotion to saints is closely connected to pagan or non-Christian practices embedded in a form of popular religiosity, which, despite being related to institutionalized religious forms, has aspects rooted in popular traditions.

Protestantism and Catholicism aside, other religions have helped shape the European religious landscape. Some Christian denominations outside the mainstream, such as Jehovah's Witnesses, are widespread. Other non-Christian religions have a long-standing history in Europe, such as Judaism and Islam. Judaism played a particularly important role in European history. The Holocaust, and the processes of Jewish persecution during World War II, indelibly marked the European conscience. As a result of the genocide, and after the creation of the state of Israel in 1948, the number of Jews in Europe drastically diminished. Jewish communities remaining in Europe are mostly located in big cities. Differences within Jewish communities are based on geographical, liturgical, and linguistic factors. In central and eastern Europe, the Ashkenazi community—characterized by a specific liturgy and, for a long time, the use of Yiddish—was widely disseminated. The Oriental Jewish communities were the most affected by persecutions. In southern Europe, the Netherlands, and the United Kingdom, the Sephardim spread. Ashkenazi and Sephardi Jews differ in customs and liturgy. For instance, Ashkenazi Jews usually refrain from eating legumes such as corn, millet, and rice. Conversely, Sephardi Jews do not have any legume restrictions, but they have stricter requirements for meat. The main celebration day is the Sabbath (the day of rest), during which believers are prevented from work and all other activities, which must be finished before midnight on Friday. The liturgy includes hymns and prayers from the Torah, which are led by the community's rabbi. The celebration takes place in the synagogue, and it is an important moment for the community, above all for Jews of the Diaspora. On Friday night, candles are lit and placed in candlesticks, marking the beginning of Sabbath. In the late nineteenth and early twentieth centuries, Austrian Jewish communities launched a political movement named Zionism, which supported the idea of a homeland for the Jewish people in the land of Israel. This movement sought an end to the Diaspora and the creation of a new Jewish nationalist attitude. Jewish communities represent religious minorities in Europe; thus, religious festivals and celebrations are important identity events that gather the community, enforcing network relations.

More generally, the European landscape is shaped by Christianity, and other religions have been religious minorities and, for a long time, religious enclaves. Apart from specific cases of interrelation, members of other religions lived in territorially separated worlds from those of Christians. The secularization process deeply affected European religions, especially believers and religious hierarchies.

SECULARIZATION

Introduction

During the nineteenth and twentieth centuries, religions in Europe, as well as religiosity and the personal way of faith, interacted with a series of relevant political, economical, and social transformations. All European societies were affected by an exceptional acceleration of transformational processes that involved pervasive changes and simultaneously affected the political, economic, and legal spheres. In particular, this modernity involved a modification of the social structure, which was characterized by institutional differentiation. With the establishment of the nation-state, the political sphere became independent from the religious one. In addition, the economy, from the Industrial Revolution onward, gradually moved away from traditional small-scale artisan production and cottage industries. Each sphere came to be organized by its own distinct internal logic. Nevertheless, these remarkable economic, social, and political transformations affected and were themselves influenced by transformations in the cultural, artistic, scientific, and ethical spheres. These changes disrupted traditional societies and altered the daily life of millions of people. The relationship between the individual and society changed radically; the human being became the only point of reference. The individual's role in the world and his or her relationship with society marked the transition from the medieval to the modern age. The idea that an individual person could be the sovereign of his or her own existence, be free to choose his or her own destiny, and be responsible for his or her own choices and actions characterized the shift to modernity. This wave of innovation dramatically affected also religious life. In the Catholic world, for instance, the absolute obedience to the dogmas, rituals, and commandments of the Church were the basic criterion of religious belonging. There was no room for individual initiative, and individual religiosity was allowed only to the virtuous (e.g., friars, ascetics, and mystics). The emergence of capitalism and the Protestant Reform stressed both individual autonomy and independence. Within religious life, individual religiosity started to gain ground, influencing the institutional way of religious believing: the idea that the individual's own conscience, personal experience, and direct relationship with the Divine could be as valid as the institutional way of faith slowly emerged.

Generally speaking, such institutional changes were the result of a long historical process characterized by sudden accelerations, slowdowns, and turnabouts. Nevertheless, this process was successful in establishing a new civil, temporal order, separate from religious traditions. This process of emancipation, which affected the multiple relations between religion and society, is defined as the secularization process.

In general terms, religions reflect and at the same time influence the character of societies. To better frame the relationship between religion and society, consider the distinction between (a) the individual sphere of religion in terms of values and beliefs, and (b) the social and public spheres. The public sphere of religions does not merely involve the relation between clerical institutions and the political apparatus; the history of the relations between states and churches has been determinant in shaping the political history of religion in Europe. Moreover, between the level of individual feelings and that of political and legal relationships, there is the social level. At this level, religions are common points of reference, part of a common sense.

The secularization hypothesis claims that the role of religion becomes progressively less relevant. This means that social life becomes increasingly emancipated from religious rules. Although there has been a shift from a common Christianity to what is called a secular society, this does not mean that traditional or pre-modern societies were completely submitted to and driven by religious values, observances, and rituals. What really changed is the separation between the Christian and the citizen. Moreover, religions no longer pretend to rule people's lives. Every citizen can decide about religion, and about religious affiliation. Additionally, rituals and religious belonging have ceased to be a reason of exclusion from social, professional, or political life. More precisely, this distinction is related to the separation between the public and the private spheres theorized by the Enlightenment.

Christianity strongly affected European time and space. The European landscape is marked by churches, places of worship, and monasteries. Everywhere crosses were raised, from the humble ones placed at street corners to those erected in beautiful churches and cathedrals. The timing of daily life was shaped by the introduction of the liturgical calendar. If this was the initial situation, over the centuries, Christianity became instead a factor of division. Disagreements between Eastern and Western churches, and the Protestant Reform of the sixteenth century led to different religious configurations.

Before the French Revolution, in the late eighteenth century, Europe was religiously fragmented in opposing confessions. There were a few religious "Europes" interacting and overlapping. The relationship between religion and the *ancien régime* societies was structured on deep connections and reciprocal interpenetration. Religion was pervasive and ruled individual and collective life; moreover, it organized time within the social sphere, legitimized social functions, and managed education and social assistance. In this perspective, Christianity characterized the whole of Europe. Especially for Catholicism, in the seventeenth and eighteenth centuries, the establishment of an articulated system of religious conformity based on Church attendance was crucial. The true believer should attend religious services every Sunday, celebrate all the religious festivities, and receive all seven sacraments. Furthermore, he or she should receive the Eucharist at least once a year, usually on Easter. The disciplinary character of the Council of Trento, which defined and reformed Catholicism in the sixteenth century, rested on the transformation of the

Catholic Church into a parish-based institution. For over 200 years, in those places where catholic bishops ruled with open jurisdiction, religious obedience was the rule until the collapse of the *ancien régime* in the late eighteenth century. The parish's obedience was a real silent revolution that greatly modified Catholic Europe. In Protestant countries, this revolution did not take place, even if Anglican bishops made a similar attempt at reorganization.

Despite the institutional framework of unity, at the individual level there was a huge difference in terms of authenticity of practices and personal beliefs. Recent historiography underlines the fact that in this period principles began to be differentiated from daily life. Nevertheless, the crucial turning point was the *Declaration of the Rights of Man and of the Citizen* (1789), which stated that individual rights should not be given on the basis of religious belonging. The citizen was differentiated from the Christian. One of the first steps of the secularization process was the establishment of a civil and secular state, which took over functions traditionally performed by religion. For instance, baptism and religious marriage lost their civil and social meaning and were replaced by official registrations or civil marriage. The separation between religious belonging and citizenship became the basis on which relations between religions and societies were eventually built. The separation concerned not only laws and politics but also private individual life. Finally, what was at stake was the autonomy of society from religious influences, that is, the secularization of society. Secularization processes affected all European societies, and had different effects according to the religious and political traditions of each country.

The reconfiguration of church-state relations concerned all religious traditions. Two main frameworks opposed each other in the public sphere: the notion of a religiously based state versus the idea of a civil autonomy from religion. This struggle heavily affected the everyday life of citizens, with controversies erupting over such issues as the sounding of bells, the propriety of religious processions in public spaces, and the passage of anticlerical laws and regulations. Secularization also dramatically impacted morality, which became a battlefield where secular laws opposed religious laws. In some cases, however, the state imposed respect for religious morals and traditions. In Victorian Britain, for example, citizens were not allowed to work on Sunday, which was considered a "holy day." The main tensions arose from regulation of the private sphere (e.g., marriage, sexuality, reproduction, and death). Among the European religions, the Catholic tradition is most likely to raise controversies around these issues. Protestant churches are more cautious and maintain a more positive attitude toward modernity. Finally, the Orthodox churches were less eager to become independent from the state.

The Roman Catholic Church severely condemned the modern world. The teachings of early nineteenth-century popes (e.g., Pius VII [1800–1823], Leo XII [1823–1829], Pius VIII [1829–1830], Gregory XVI [1831–1846]) sought to restore the influence of Christianity in the cultural, social, and political spheres. In 1869–1870, the First Vatican Council restated the principles of Catholic faith and condemned what it saw as the main errors of modernity—rationalism, atheism, and materialism. Furthermore, it reaffirmed the sovereignty of the papacy not only on Catholic doctrine, but even on government and discipline. The Protestant attitude toward secularization and the religious neutrality of the state was different: it cautiously approved of the principles of religious freedom and religious pluralism.

Secularized Religious Practices

Secularization processes heavily affected European religions. Whereas Protestantism was involved in a deep reformulation of its theology and practices that influenced the everyday life of believers as well as of the role of Protestant religion in European political and social life, Catholicism promoted an antimodernist attitude, even if an important sector of its hierarchies and believers welcomed the effects of secularization in the social and political spheres.

Deeply religious at the start of the twentieth century, most European societies were only weakly religious at the start of the twenty-first century. Religion weakened in different dimensions, including the diminishing of service attendance, a growing detachment between believers and religious authorities, and a weakening of beliefs, as well as phenomena of hybridization of faiths. Christianity lost its dominance of public culture and private morality, non-Christian religions increased, and European societies embraced other faiths. Churches and religious ideas lost influence on government, education, and social welfare.

The main effect of secularization processes was on religious practice. Christian worship traditionally involves a weekly celebration on Sunday, some holy days during the year (especially Christmas, Epiphany, Easter, Ascension, and All Saints), and administration of the sacraments. Furthermore, individual Christians can also worship God on their own by praying. While individual prayer and sacraments, though decreasing, are still important in daily life, weekly attendance at services has been diminishing since the 1970s; however, festival attendance maintains high levels throughout Europe. On the whole, the expression of religiosity has become more personal and individual, and less linked to institutionalized expressions of belonging. For instance, according to an international comparative survey carried out during the 1990s (the *International Social Survey Programme*), the practice of individual prayer is more

Table 10.1
Religious Affiliation in Europe

	Buddhist	Evangelical	Free Church	Hindu	Jew	Muslim	Orthodox	Other	Protestant	Catholic
TOTAL	0.1	0	2.4	0.1	0.2	5.6	18.4	1.4	20.4	51.4
Albania [2002]	0	1.5	0	0	0	66.9	20.8	0.7	0	10.1
Austria [1999]	0	0	0.4	0	0	0.3	1	0.9	6	91.4
Belgium [1999]	0	0	1.8	0	0.1	2.8	0.5	3.3	0.9	90.7
Bosnia and Herzegovina [2001]	0	0	0	0	0.3	54.4	27.8	0.1	0.1	17.3
Bulgaria [1999]	0	0	0.2	0	0	15.6	82.9	0.1	0.9	0.3
Croatia [1999]	0	0	0.5	0	0	0	0.1	1.6	0	97.9
Czech Republic [1999]	0	0	2.2	0	0.2	0	0.2	2.3	10.8	84.3
Denmark [1999]	0.1	0	0.4	0.1	0	0.5	0	1.1	96.8	0.9
Estonia [1999]	0	0	0	0	0.4	0.4	41.1	2.7	53.9	1.6
Finland [2000]	0	0	1.5	0	0	0	1.2	2.1	95.1	0.1
France [1999]	0.4	0	0.7	0.2	2.4	0.2	1.9	0	2.4	91.8
Greece [1999]	0	0	0	0	0.5	0	97.7	0.3	0	1.6
Hungary [1999]	0	0	3.2	0.1	0.3	0	0.5	0	26.2	69.5
Iceland [1999]	0	0	0	0	0	0	0	4.4	95.1	0.4
Italy [1999]	0	0	0.1	0	0	0	0.1	0.2	0.4	99.3
Latvia [1999]	0	0	7.4	0	0	0.2	28.3	2.3	28.6	33.2

Table 10.1 (Continued)

	Buddhist	Evangelical	Free Church	Hindu	Jew	Muslim	Orthodox	Other	Protestant	Catholic
Lithuania [1999]	0.1	0	0	0	0	0	3.5	1	2.9	92.5
Luxembourg [1999]	0	0	3.5	0	0.8	1	0.7	0.4	0.3	93.3
Netherlands [1999]	0.5	0	16.6	0.3	0.7	2.1	0	8	21.8	50
Poland [1999]	0	0	0.6	0	0	0	0.3	0.3	0.4	98.3
Portugal [1999]	0	0	0	0	0	0	0	2.8	0.6	96.7
Romania [1999]	0	0	1.4	0	0	0	87.7	1.1	2.1	7.7
Slovakia [1999]	0	0	0.3	0	0.3	0	1.1	0.4	14.6	83.3
Slovenia [1999]	0	0	0.9	0	0	1.6	2.3	0	0.4	94.9
Spain [2000]	0.2	0	0	0.1	0.1	0.1	0.1	1.3	0.7	97.4
Sweden [1999]	0	0	3.6	0.4	0	0.6	0.7	0.5	92.4	1.9
Great Britain [1999]	1	0	8.2	0.8	1.1	1.2	0.2	5.5	66.8	15.4
Germany West [1999]	0	0	2.5	0	0	3	0.8	1.4	47.8	44.6
Germany East [1999]	0.5	0	3.9	0	0	0.3	0.5	3	81.3	10.5
Northern Ireland [1999]	0.1	0	31.7	0	0	0	1	1.8	17.7	47.6
Serbia [2001]	0.1	0	0	0	0.2	4.7	85.5	2.6	0.4	6.5
Montenegro [2001]	0	0	0	0	0	21.8	72	0.1	0.2	5.9

Source: European Value Survey.

common than service attendance. Although the measurement of religiosity is extremely complex, and certain issues do not perfectly fit into the dimensions they are supposed to analyze, survey data allow a general description of the European religious landscape and highlight some differences.

The expression of belonging is high all over Europe, except in certain countries in the former Soviet bloc, such as East Germany, the Czech Republic, and Estonia. In some European countries, such as France and the Netherlands, the levels of church membership are lower than the European average. The great majority of Europeans say they believe in God, but citizens of countries characterized by a strong institutionalization of religion say they believe in a personal God (in general closer to the Christian God), whereas elsewhere there are expressions of the belief in a God represented as vital force. What is interesting to note is not the content of the vital force concept, which greatly varies, but the fact that there is a progressive broadening of ideas about God among religious Europeans.

There are differences in the attendance rates of the Catholic countries of southern Europe (and Ireland), where levels of regular attendance at weekly services are still high, on average, and northern Europe, where the percentages are lower. Poland shows high levels of regular service attendance, mainly because of the importance of religion—especially Catholicism—in the collapse of the Communist regime in the 1980s. The different rates between northern and southern Europe, or between traditionally Protestant and Catholic countries, is quite relevant. For instance, in Ireland more than half the population attends religious services at least once a week; in Denmark, regular churchgoers do not reach the rate of 3 percent. The largely Protestant Scandinavian countries are characterized by high levels of faith and low levels of church attendance; belonging is linked to a form of membership that is more cultural and national than religious. In the United Kingdom and the Scandinavian countries, levels of church attendance are decreasing.

Multiconfessional societies show differences between different religious denominations. In the Netherlands, Protestant denominations are the most active, but the country has important Protestant religious communities that express a religiosity that is reconfigured and revitalized; a large secularized population; as well as a small percentage of traditional religious people. Therefore, within all Christian denominations there is a large nonregular churchgoing constituency that only attends special festivals, such as Christmas or Easter.

There is a great difference between southern and northern Europe. In northern Europe, the casual churchgoing constituency largely disappeared during the last century, and there is now a large chasm between the committed religious people, who regularly go to church, and those who do not go at all. In southern Europe, the casual churchgoing constituency grew, making church attendance levels drop even though a strong level of church membership was maintained.

Religion is still important to a large majority of the population, even though concrete commitment has decreased. An increase in the abandonment of sacred buildings throughout Europe bears witness to a decrease in both church attendance and vocations. Sacraments are still important communitarian events in the life of people, especially those sacraments that represent a moment of change, such as Baptism and Marriage. Although sacraments continue to have great importance in people's lives, their administration is decreasing among all European denominations, except those serving migrant religious communities. Additionally, there is a dramatic fall in levels of religious marriages, baptisms, and attendance at Sunday schools or at religious classes. But these rates differ among countries and denominations. At the same time, religious festivals such as Christmas and Easter play an important role in marking the religious as well as the civil year, and people's involvement in them indicates their importance.

As for sociodemographic features, women are more likely to believe in God and to practice religion than men; and adults (especially elders) are more likely to be religious than young people. Young people tend to be more secular, exhibiting less feeling of religious belonging and less dependence on ritual practices or spirituality. Adults and elders have always decried the decline of Christian practice. Nevertheless, in recent years, probably because of multiculturalism and uncertainty, there has been a small reversal in this trend—some young people are more religious than their parents, though it is difficult to identify a uniform trend. Even the religious socialization of the young is decreasing. Though most babies are baptized, involvement in religious youth organizations and attendance at religious schools are steadily declining. On the whole, adherence to religious associations that focus on territory or class has fallen considerably over the last century.

Other European religious denominations were also affected by the weakening of religiosity. For instance, there has been a decline in the observance of the Jewish Sabbath, which prohibits work, sports, or games; nowadays people tend to disregard these restrictions. In Islamic communities, the maintenance of religious behaviors are being challenged by hybridization and secularization processes. Attendance at religious services has long been considered the main expression of religiosity, and it is decreasing in the whole Europe and within European religious denominations, with the exception, to some extent, of migrant religious communities.

However, religiosity, as well as the declaration of membership, are still high in Europe. Religious expression is changing form, from a collective and institutionalized expression, such as Sunday Mass attendance, to more individual and "spiritualized" forms of membership and religiosity. The collective and public dimension of faith is now less important than individual and private spiritual practice.

In the whole of Europe private prayer rates are higher than those of service attendance. The practice of prayer is a form of relationship with the sacred dimension, characterized by an individual attitude and individualized features. It is interesting to notice that there has also been a decline in thanking God before meals and in saying prayers before bedtime, the most common forms of private prayer. Thus, also prayers were reshaped into a more personalized and spontaneous form.

In general, the feeling of religious belonging and key beliefs are more widespread than practice. The number of people who declare themselves believers remains large, but adherence to traditional religious practice, such as Mass attendance, has strongly decreased. Moreover, in many instances, religious belonging does not go hand in hand with identification with a specific church, but rather with a religious tradition or with an unspecific form of spirituality. Therefore, the number of people who believe without belonging is growing. This is the choice of the majority in some countries, such as the Netherlands, Belgium, and Great Britain. The number of religious people has not changed, but there has been a decrease in identification with a church. This is an important transition in the history of religions because faith is lived more individually and spiritually, with less attention to ritualization and public collectivity. Growth in the number of people who claim a personal relationship with God hints at a change in the type of religious culture, notably in Catholicism, where an institution acts as a mediator in the relationship with God. In Eastern European countries, the situation is different; in many cases, the feeling of national identity is built around the Orthodox Church. Poland is an exception because Catholicism is prevalent and because it has a particularly high religiosity level.

Lastly, religious beliefs sometimes combine traditional elements of a doctrine with those of other faiths. For instance, many southern European Catholics declare that they believe in reincarnation, which is an alien concept to the traditional Catholic faith system; such belief shows the hybridization of elements of different religious traditions. A growing deregulation of beliefs emerges in the doctrines of traditional religions, appearing as a divergence between the doctrine's central elements and the corpus of institutionalized beliefs. The rupture of beliefs and their re-formation on an individual level is called bricolage. The competences of bricolage are differentiated by class, gender, age, and generation. Indeed, these competences require a wide knowledge of religious elements typical of different denominations, as well as the ability of compare and merge similar features. In particular, highly educated people tend to intellectualize beliefs by reinterpreting them in a modern way to make them consistent with a secular setting. On the other hand, those belonging to disadvantaged social classes, together with the least educated members of the privileged classes, tend to express a more traditional religiosity that is linked to a process of desymbolization of beliefs along with a reconciliation with the powerful, conservative core of professed religion. Under these circumstances, a rebuilding by an individual or group of a system of meanings occurred; it configures itself as a reform that modifies the ways of belonging to a religious identity. Thus, the redefinition of religion does not happen to occur in individual processes only, but also in collective rebuilding.

Therefore, religious syncretism has broadened. The idea of God appears to gradually detach itself from traditional concepts and becomes a relevant reference, though undetermined and generic. This happens mostly in those countries that are not religiously uniform; in less pluralist nations, beliefs are closer to traditional faith references. Finally, codified religious traditions change and undergo processes of hybridization and transformation so that the contents and the modalities of worship expression are changed through collective processes.

Considering social survey data, a great majority of Europeans believe in God and identify themselves with a church or religion. The data concerning church membership show that some part of the population feel a traditional or ethnic affiliation to the church. In this perspective, religion is considered as part of cultural and traditional belonging, so that it represents a basis for each country's community. Former Soviet-bloc countries, whose populations express a different attitude, are a case in point. While some countries, such as Poland, display a high level of religiosity, others, such as the former East Germany, have a low level of faith. Even if practice seems to fall, religion is still an important point of reference for the population of European countries. Indeed, religion is not only part of a country's tradition, but it also becomes an element of identity; faith and religiosity are present in the whole population, and only a very small percentage is atheist or agnostic. In religiously uniform states, such as southern or northern European countries, beliefs are less uncertain and generic than those of pluralistic central European countries. In European countries, religious belonging and regular practice seem no longer closely linked to each other; people define themselves as religious even without regular church attendance.

Anglicanism, for instance, is an important cultural element in the United Kingdom, even if Anglicans are secularized and nonregular churchgoers.

Particularly in northern countries, Protestant churches developed modernity-oriented attitudes, supporting civil and social reforms. For this reason, churches in those countries retained an important role in the public sphere. Another sign of changes in faith expression is the growing importance of community life, such as membership in religion-rooted associations with social aims. As a matter of fact, the involvement in Christian associations engaged in solidarity and assistance does not suffer this crisis or, at least, is affected to a smaller extent. This practice symbolizes some sort of personal involvement for Protestants, of testimony for Catholics, and sometimes is an alternative to religious services. Even the emotional dimension holds great importance both in the practice of new religious movements and in contemporary revisiting of traditional religions. From this point of view, the immediacy of sharing experiences is more privileged than the appeal of tradition. In this perspective, it seems that religious attitude is becoming more private, meaning that both individual and collective dimensions are important in religious life, representing a communitarian character. The public expression of religiosity seems to weaken in favor of a more community-oriented religious life. Though church hierarchies intervene in the public sphere, individual believers tend to live their religiosity in a private way.

Nevertheless, there are also opposite tendencies to traditional and old-fashioned attitudes and behaviors, such as the spreading, in some places, of the Tridentine (Latin) Mass, in order to defend a traditional vision of worship, calling for the return to the "original roots" of Christendom. At the same time, there is a proliferation of associations in defense of traditional values, which try to rediscover and reaffirm some basic religious values in terms of ethical and moral choices (acting publicly). In this regard, religious minorities show a higher degree of religiosity in all the dimensions considered: worship, feeling of membership, adherence to religious values, and behaviors. This is not a Christian revival, but rather a specific religious commitment of some religious groups, either belonging to the main churches or to religious minorities or enclaves. Indeed, affiliation to a country's majority religion is more flexible and volatile, being more a general acknowledgment of a traditional belonging than a specific religious attitude.

When ideological and political crises occur, religions are an identity reference. A relevant number of people remain anchored to traditional faith for ethnic and cultural reasons, rather than for conviction. Religions have an important role in everyday life as cultural reference in terms of values and behavioral orientations, and churches are considered important public actors by a large number of Europeans. On the other hand, there is a strengthening of active minorities expressing a "militant" faith. They aim to vigorously reassert a specific religious identity by fighting against cultural relativism and growing secularization. In this perspective, though it is true that the number of worshipers in the traditional meaning is decreasing, the remaining ones are deeply involved in religion. This applies to both Catholicism and the Protestantism, mainly in the charismatic movements of the 1990s. It is thus possible to detect an expansion of the religious ethos in Europe, related to the transformations occurring in the religious landscape.

Considering religion in general, all these transformations have various consequences, both on the internal structure of organized religions and on society. The ever-growing role held by testimony and example in the Catholic religion, rooted in Christian tradition and influenced by Charismatic revivalism, is a symptom of the diminishing role of the institution as the mediator of beliefs in organized religions. In this case, proselytism is based on examples and on the immediacy of empathy rather than on words. A second example, which has always been a concern for the Catholic Church, is the growing internal pluralism regarding the system of truth and authority. The loss of hegemony suffered by religious institutions, as well as their role of intermediation among the believers and the cult system, is evincible in the growth of integralist movements that generally refuse traditional religious authorities by creating new ones.

However, it seems that "faith privatization" and the decline of the communitarian dimension are counteracted by a growing public presence of the churches, notably in the last decade. Religion takes care of various issues, always pertaining to the ethical and moral dimensions of community life. Anyway, there has been a redefinition of the Christian religious message. First, organized religions do not accept an exclusively private role; they demand a public role, chiefly in ethical issues—for example, in the application of such scientific discoveries as food biotechnologies and genetic research, as well as in euthanasia. The strong presence of religious organizations in the public sphere and in public debates regarding such issues raises a complex controversy about the meaning of religious freedom and about the role of religion in the public and political spheres of contemporary society. Therefore, organized religions have often been accused of undue interference.

The situation is different in Eastern European countries that were under the control of the former Soviet Union, where religion now has an important role in both the public and private spheres. For instance, the late pope John Paul II was from Poland, and he contributed to the collapse of the communist regime in that country. Catholicism became a feature of Polish identity, and the Catholic Church in Poland plays an important public role and is highly politicized. Despite its rigidity of positions, however, the Polish Catholic Church is affected by a process of internal pluralization, and the media identify two different Catholic churches: one modern and one traditionalist. Furthermore, the Polish people are experiencing the effects of the secularization process; therefore, their membership does not affect the modernization of individual behavior. Other countries, such as Romania or Bulgaria, recovered the Orthodox tradition, which is claimed as part of a national identity that needs to be reconstructed. In countries that were part of the former Soviet bloc, religion is often politicized by political parties to obtain legitimization.

Religious Associations and Organizations

The main and more visible effects of the secularization process affected the traditional practice of religious belonging (namely, religious service attendance). Nevertheless, other paths of faith expression are relevant within European societies. Indeed, Christianity promotes believers' engagement in the social and political spheres. In the twentieth century, the democratization processes triggered the organization of religious-inspired political parties and associations.

Despite the decreasing numbers of worshippers, Christian churches remain amply embedded in the structures of European states. Throughout Europe, religions are involved in social welfare activities in different ways. Faith-based agencies act in partnership with governments to deliver social services. They are supported by public funds and provide services on behalf of the state. Their involvement in social welfare varies from country to country, but these agencies are important and influential actors in all European states. Some faith-based agencies are large, bureaucratic organizations, and others are small. What these agencies share is their religious ethos, and the large involvement of volunteers. Because of the strong social attitude of both Protestantism and Catholicism, many believers are involved in these agencies, which represent a way of expressing a religious ethos through a social commitment.

The social engagement of Christianity has a long-standing history. In the twentieth century, a deep theological meditation within Protestantism led to important changes in the daily life of believers. During the first years of the twentieth century, Protestantism was marked by a liberal theology, which identified the essence of Christianity in its historical original meaning, that is, Jesus's teachings, including faith in God the Father. In the view of Protestant liberal theology, Christian religion is also, and mostly, inner life and dwells in the individual relationship with God. Within this framework, a crucial element is the claim for justice taking precedence over contingencies and as a true moral guide. In this context, religion plays the role of lever for social transformation. Protestant theology came to an important turning point with the so-called dialectical theology (due to stress on the transcendental nature of God) or theology of the crisis, developed around Karl Barth and, later, the magazine *Zwischen den Zeiten* (1922–1933). The dialectical theology recalls the central meaning of religion: the absolute supernaturalism of God, something totally and incomparably different from human beings. Karl Barth's theological reflections are combined with a strong political commitment; indeed, he is the author of the *Theological Declaration of Barmen*, which condemned Nazism. Dietrich Bonhoeffer, another important figure in twentieth-century Protestantism, introduced into Protestant theology the idea of God as weak, impotent, and suffering, and of Jesus as a man who lived for others, a token for a Christian life. For Bonhoeffer, God is not beyond the world, but inside it. Bonhoeffer's death in a Nazi concentration camp and his project of a "non religious Christianity" inspired twentieth-century Protestantism and had a strong influence on general philosophical debate. Apart from the important figures of Barth and Bonhoeffer, there was in the Protestant world a common need for living faith through individual political and social commitment.

Some theologians who were particularly sensitive to social issues focused especially on the origins of Protestantism as a "protest." From this perspective, the Protestant ethic is antiauthoritarian and refuses any absolute power. Thus, Christianity has a strong egalitarian and social component, which emerges as a strong groundwork for activism. This is the standpoint of religious socialism, which tries to reinterpret Christianity from the perspective of a working-class movement. The fathers of Christian socialism, Charles Kingsley and Fredrick Maurice, both belonged to the Broad Anglican Church. In Germany, Wilhelm Weitling supported a Christian Communism that was to be achieved without violence. In France, the social Christian movement (Christian left) focused on the cooperative movement as a third way between social collectivism and private capitalism. Other expressions of social-oriented attitudes more openly refer to socialism and the Soviet Union, although they are not taken seriously by Marxist movements and are ignored by church hierarchies. Christian socialism was an ethical movement rather than a political one, and Christian socialists concentrated especially on the promotion of an ethical economic system.

These movements, which sought a more social-oriented Christianity, were reintegrated into contemporary Christianity, mostly through ecumenical conferences. In the twentieth century, Protestantism in Continental Europe often took the shape of a "church of opposition." In general, Protestantism developed as a church without a submissive spirit, according to which religion should promote a critical attitude toward society and greater political and civil commitment, seeking social justice, truth, and democracy. During the twentieth century, social Christianity grew rapidly, and many associations and organizations were established that promoted believers' engagement with the needy and marginalized.

In the twentieth century, Catholicism also experienced a massive renewal, involving a special focus on the "social question." The twentieth century began with a crisis within Catholicism that is usually referred to as "the crisis of modernity." Hierarchies condemned calls for religious renewal supported by some Catholic groups, and confirmed the necessity of re-Christianization of the civil consortium. Already at the end of the World War II, the papacy recognized that a democracy based on Catholic values should be the groundwork of the new international order. For this reason, Catholic hierarchies supported "the Western world" by, for example, denying the sacraments to those who collaborated with Communist regimes, while at the same time condemning the West for increasing atheism and materialism excesses. In addition, the Catholic Church (both believers and hierarchies) felt the need to reorganize its codes, practices, and social actions.

The social question is a crucial element in twentieth-century Catholic culture. Both the most conservative and the most progressive wings within Catholicism consider preferential attention to the poor and vulnerable to be one of the main duties of the Roman Catholic Church. Thus, throughout the last century many centers of social assistance developed in relation to parish churches, Catholic Action, and other groups and organizations into which Roman Catholicism was organized for intervening in the public sphere. Catholic social thinking, defined through various papal encyclicals, consists of three basic ideas. First, human beings, as God's creatures, are defined as the center of the economical, political, and social order, and for this reason have fundamental rights to life and its necessities. The sanctity of human life is closely related to human dignity, which should be defended and guaranteed. In particular, a person has a right to a religious life, a family, employment at a living wage, and freedom. Catholicism does not necessarily oppose war, but it does oppose racism and discrimination and calls for the preservation of the human being. Second, humans are intrinsically social, and the first and basic unit of society is the family. Families form communities, which organize themselves into states that pursue the common good. Society must have as a goal economic justice; everybody has the right to a job, fair wages, and safe working conditions. Third, and more importantly, the Catholic Church should care for the poor and vulnerable. The Christian believer should promote social justice and show solidarity with poor persons. Solidarity is one of the most important values for the Roman Catholic Church in the twentieth century.

In this light, the Second Vatican Council was a key event for European Catholicism. Even if its results were considered disappointing by groups that had called for complete renewal, and strongly criticized by the most conservative factions, there is no doubt that it was a turning point for Catholicism in the twentieth century. One of the outcomes of the council was an increasing decentralization and diversification at the territorial level. National churches gained more autonomy from the Vatican, and they have different paths of development in different countries, but the pope retained a leading role in the Catholic Church. The council also promoted the role of the laity within ecclesiastic life. The mobilization of the laity was historically rooted in Catholic tradition. Between the end of the nineteenth and the beginning of the twentieth centuries, the role of the laity within the Church was reorganized into a new form of apostolate following territorial borders.

Along with the Catholic Action, which was divided according to gender and age and maintained an interclass structure, many organizations oriented toward specific socioeconomic sectors developed in different European countries. The working class, in particular, became a "place for mission" to resist socialist ideologies. In Belgium, the Young Christian Workers (Jeunesse ouvrière chrétienne [JOC]) was established in 1924; like the Catholic Action the JOC addressed the working class as a social category instead of as a territory. This experience spread beyond Europe, and other groups were created that addressed other working sectors—such as rural society (JAC), workers of the sea (JMC), students (JEC), independent professionals (JIC), and those involved in academia (JUC)—all of which worked side by side with Catholic Action. At first, this type of experience aroused fierce resistance from those parts of the hierarchy interested in maintaining an aggregative apostolate with an interclass profile. However, these organizations soon became an important element in the associative landscape of the Catholic world, especially after the crucial encyclical *Quadragesimo anno* (1931).

Many tensions existed, at both the national and central levels, between conservative Church hierarchies and groups committed to the idea of direct association. In 1968, the authority of the Catholic hierarchies was frontally challenged by the activities of several priests' and believers' associations. In Italy in 1969, the lay ecclesial movement Communion and Liberation was reorganized. It promoted a religious way of life that was communitarian and committed, and it also lowered the role of institutional mediation of faith in a manner similar to Protestantism. Additionally, the Basic Ecclesial Communities spread and became more important in the daily life of believers. Furthermore, although hierarchies promoted a center (or center-right) political orientation, most Catholic movements were more left-oriented; the movement of Christian workers in Italy and elsewhere in Europe openly chose left parties as political references. Catholic movements closer to the hierarchies, such as the Catholic Action, promoted religious engagement rather than a social-oriented commitment. Associations and organizations of laypersons developed all over Europe, thanks to the deep changes in Catholicism introduced by the Second Vatican Council. Catholic Church hierarchies faced the tensions cause by growing internal differences and plurality. Thus, the history of the Roman Catholic Church in the last years of the twentieth century became more precisely a history of the Catholic churches, with unitarian events, such as the Jubilee of 2000, but mainly differentiated at the national and organizational levels. The political sphere has also been an important space for faith expression. After World War II, several religious-inspired political parties were established, promoting an ethical and moral commitment in the civil and political life of European countries. Both Catholic and Protestant parties were created.

Christian democratic parties spread throughout Europe. Those established immediately before or during World War II collected some of the political legacy of previous Christian democratic movements. However, seeking political consensus, they included almost all elements of the Catholic world. Christian political parties had different political orientations. The Austrian party, the Belgian PSC, the Irish Fine Gael, and the Swiss CVP/PDC were more socially oriented and progressive; the Belgian UDB, the French CDS, the German Parties, the Italian Christian Democracy, the PCS of Luxembourg, and the Christian Parties of Portugal and Spain were more conservative. In general, political attitudes of Catholic-inspired parties was consistent with the position expressed by Catholic Church hierarchies. They were moderate and interclass parties, usually with a centrist orientation, and promoted a specific attention toward social policies. In spite of remarkable internal differences, all Christian parties joined the European People's Party in 1976.

Christian parties are important in European societies. First, in many countries they played important roles in the governments formed after the World War II, especially in Italy, Belgium, and Germany. Catholicism played a key role in the legislative and cultural spheres, and not only in social life. Second, the party's life often merges with the life of parishes as one of the forms of public and collective commitment that religiosity takes. For instance, all Christian parties have youth organizations. Moreover, the boards of directors of Christian political parties often come from the top management of Catholic associations and organizations involved in the civil and social sphere (such as Catholic Action), and vice versa. In Ireland, where Catholicism is strongly connected to nationalism, all parties are Catholic because Catholicism permeates Irish society. Because all parties openly refer to Christian values, the main differences between parties lie in the political support of the hierarchies and in the social background of the parties.

Scandinavian Christian parties are not comparable to Catholic or other European Christian parties. The latter, in fact, are mass parties and have the open approval of ecclesiastic institutions. Conversely, the Scandinavian Christian parties are the expression of specific national or social identities and strong religious values. The Lutheran Church is most widespread in Scandinavian societies, where the majority of the population traditionally belongs to the Protestant confession. The history of these countries is characterized by the absence of religious struggles and by the institutionalization of the Protestant churches, which are national in character, part of the established order, and not criticized by the population. Nevertheless, the secularization process also affected Scandinavian societies. Therefore, Scandinavian Christian parties could be seen also as a reaction to secularization and an instrument for reaffirming the importance of Christian values in society and public policies. In some countries, such as Denmark, Christian parties are grounded on a religious popular belonging, which is still rooted in the society, even though the rates of religiosity and church attendance are diminishing. They are a reaction to permissive laws regarding regulation of sexuality and reproduction. These parties are not always openly supported by national churches, not because of occasional ideological differences, but because the entire political system could be considered religiously oriented, so that believers do not express a clear preference for one or another political party. Therefore, the religious world as a whole does not necessarily join Christian parties, mainly because its commitment is more social than political. The parties are important political actors, though not crucial for the political sphere of their own countries.

In a few European countries, religious differences merge with political ones. In Belgium, for example, especially at the beginning of the twentieth century, linguistic differences combined with religious and geographical differences to separate Catholic Flanders, where Flemish is spoken, from francophone Walloon areas, which were considered de-Christianized. For a long time, the party had two different wings organized along geographical and linguistic lines. More frequently, religious fractures consisted of confessional differences; this was the case in the Netherlands, where three Christian parties were connected to different religious traditions in the Catholic agricultural south and the trading Calvinist north.

Even if Christian parties are based on religious traditions, ecumenical movements promoted experiences of ecumenism. A significant example of local-based ecumenicity is the experience of the Christian German parties. German parties are interconfessional, although the Catholic component is predominant. Two geographically articulated parties, the CDU and CSU (in Bavaria), stand as one group in parliament, though they are growing progressively apart. Interfaith parties form around (1) geography, with internal migrations mingling two confessions; (2) a shared anticommunism; and (3) a convergence of social and public actors that frame the churches as trustworthy and not compromised by association with the previous regime. Religious institutions gave their support to these interfaith parties after some minor difficulties were overcome. Initially, the German Catholic Church distrusted the opportunity of a "democratic" commitment; however, it supported the project. On the contrary, in the Protestant world criticism was raised by the "Christian" side of the project, especially because they were supported by progressives led by the important theologian Karl Barth. The Protestant critique rests on the conviction that Christians should commit themselves as free men and believers. They should not use their religious belonging as a flag, trying to collect support based on common religious feelings. On the contrary, being religious should be something completely transcendental, everybody should "translate" their religiosity in the actions of daily life. The common flag should not be religion, but a shared idea for a better life in this world. In this way, political agreement will not be built on religion, but rather on a vision of common values. Nevertheless, several Protestants managed the German parties. The German Catholic Church was quite conservative, but after some initial hesitations, fully supported the Christian German parties, marginalizing the internal elements of critique. However, in the experience of the German Christian democratic parties, some frictions occurred between the wishes of Church hierarchies and the political choices of the parties.

Currently, only in such countries as Ireland (both Northern Ireland and the Irish Republic) and the former Yugoslavia religious adherence continues to strongly influence voting. Nevertheless, in Europe, Christian parties are important faith-based initiatives. Indeed, within European Christianity, the public commitment of believers covers a wide range of activities, and the intervention in the political sphere is rooted in those dimensions of the European religious ethos that underline the importance of the believers' action within society.

Youth and Others Forms of Faith Expression

As an expression of religious commitment in the public sphere, religious associations and organizations and religion-inspired political parties played an important role in European societies and in the daily life of believers. Young people were a main target of organized religion. Both Protestantism and Catholicism had (and still have) youth organizations aimed at socialization and the transmission of tradition. Educational focus first involves religious schools, such as Protestant Sunday schools and Catholic catechism. In religion classes, priests, elders, or catechists teach children the main elements of religious traditions, and children often act as attendants to clergy during Sunday services. In many countries, primary and secondary public schools offer religion classes. Levels of attendance are generally high, probably because parents still consider religion classes, whether at church or in school, to be an important feature of education. However, because the next generation of parents show lower levels of church attendance and religious involvement, this trend seems likely to change.

Churches also organize youth-oriented religious associations. Within Catholicism, the most important has been the Catholic Action, which was established in Italy in 1923 by Pope Pius XI and then exported to other European countries to serve as a model organization. It spread throughout European society, deeply influencing the everyday life of citizens. The Catholic Action was divided according to gender and subdivided according to age, with a specific affiliated organization created for universities. The organization of the Catholic Action varied somewhat by country. In Germany, it was a federal agency, not an independent organization. Political attitudes also varied by country. In France, it had a leftist political orientation, like the other religious organizations active in French social life, especially those related to the working class. The activities of Catholic Action mainly concerned those areas of social life having religious and spiritual aspects, such as social assistance. Throughout the twentieth century, youth organizations increasingly mixed with other types of organizations, whether religious or not, that were active in criticizing consumerism, promoting peace, or assisting the needy. Youth associations have been revitalized by such recent global, media-driven events as the World Youth Day, which, with its concluding papal visit, can be seen as a form of modern pilgrimage.

The main changes in the material expression of faith and religious feelings are connected to such technological developments as cable television and the Internet. In many countries, public television broadcasts Sunday Mass or the pope's Sunday speeches, and cable television offers channels especially devoted to religion, such as the Catholic Church's SAT2000. The diffusion of Internet has significantly changed the individual religious landscape, especially in its most recognizable form, the World Wide Web. In the last two decades, all churches and religious organizations have connected to the Web. Besides the provision of religious information and discussion forums, religion on the

Internet offers a variety of online religious practice, such as the streaming of services. The most popular use of the Internet remains the use of e-mail and the reading of news, but online networking connected to specific aims is increasing. Whether the Internet can provide a space for building stable communities is uncertain, but there is increasing evidence that New Age religions and migrant religious communities offer many Web activities and exchanges.

Public Controversies

The emergence of modernism in Europe was the combined effect of scientific, technological, industrial, and democratic revolutions that began with the Enlightenment. These processes challenged religion in various ways. Despite the consequences of the secularization process and the diminishing importance of religion in everyday life, religious issues are often at the top of the political agenda. Besides the ethical and moral aspects of public policy, they are often related to such matters as migration into Europe and the consequent rise in Europe of non-Christian religions (see Decolonization: Multifaith and Multicultural Societies, below). One Christian reaction to secularization has been a redefinition of the Christian message in modern terms. In a context of pluralization, religious institutions make an effort to deal with modernity, above all intervening in ethical issues.

Ethical choices, mainly in family and sexual areas, show a growing detachment with regards to religious references. Western Europe has seen the remarkable growth of relativism and individualism, even in the ethical field. The process of separation of ethics from the public sphere of religious control is relative. In fact, churches have maintained great relevance in European societies; some recent research has indicated the possibility of a religious revival. However, since the 1960s and 1970s, European countries have undoubtedly gone through deep cultural and even legislative changes in the field of family and sexual morality. Premarital sex, though still frowned upon by churches, has become widespread. Whereas religious marriages have decreased, civil ones have increased. Almost every European country has approved laws that allow divorce and legalize or decriminalize abortion. These issues are particularly relevant, especially for the Catholic Church, which strongly opposes both practices. Southern Europe, which is Catholic and relatively more practicing, shows less open-mindedness toward family and individual ethics, while Protestant northern Europe, with its pluralism and lower level of religiosity, is more tolerant and permissive. Nevertheless, secularization processes have heavily affected public and private morality, and Christian behavior has become unenforceable by the state as traditional Christian-based laws on homosexuality, abortion, divorce, suicide, censorship, blasphemy, and Sunday trading and entertainment have been repealed.

The 1960s was the most important decade for the decline of religion in Europe. In that decade, pop music, extreme fashion, and student and worker revolts initiated radical changes in sexual attitudes and the dismissal of conventional authority. A cultural revolution among young people, women, and immigrants targeted the churches, the older generations, and government. The old Christian culture was shattered, and liberalization, diversity, and freedom of individual choice in moral behavior came into favor. Religion was in a crisis. The 1960s were critical for the modification of patterns of popular religious behavior in relation to mainstream churches. The religious crisis affected both cities and rural areas, fostering a real cultural reshaping. Apart from the sexual revolution, the exodus from churches took the shape of a widespread boredom with organized religions. In this perspective, lack of religiosity was directly associated with the loss of communitarian traditions. De-Christianization was expressed as something related to society, not to individual behavior. The secularization process, in this regard, can be seen as a gradual shift from community to society.

There was also a huge revolution in ideas about women and their control over their own bodies and fertility. In previous centuries, women were supposed to be virtuous and their femininity was established in religious terms; in the second half of the twentieth century, a deep change transformed their role within the family and society. They started to be considered autonomous, and even within religion their role changed from that of moral guardian of their families to that of activist. Their role in believers' communities also changed, as they became animators of religious associations and parish life. They were more involved in social-assistance activities and the organization of religious events and campaigns.

Together with the emancipation of women, moral changes affected religious ethics and priorities. One of the most important aspects was the sexual revolution of the 1960s. Sex before marriage became the new critical indicator of de-Christianization. Furthermore, the spread of techniques of birth control, such as condoms or the contraceptive pill, contributed to the separation of sex and procreation, raising deep questions about the relation between religious values and individual behaviors. Whereas Protestant churches were divided on contraception, Catholicism usually condemned these instruments. Sex changed the religious agenda, and despite concerns over class alienation from faith, churchmen started alleging that declining sexual morality was undermining the religious condition of the nation. There was a huge debate over sexual matters within Christianity as well as in the public sphere.

In the 1960s and 1970s the de-Christianization of European society was signaled by the passage of controversial legislation permitting abortion and divorce. In some countries, these acts were government decisions; in others, large movements called for changes in existing laws. These changes deeply affected the concept of family, challenging the traditional Christian idea of a society based on heterosexual, married families. While divorce allowed the rupture of families, abortion interfered with the relation between sex and reproduction, important issues for many religions. Furthermore, scientific innovations, especially in biotechnology, raised several issues within Christianity. Through biotechnology, science became able to intervene in reproductive processes, and several questions were raised about the limits of science in bioethical matters. The main points in debate are the protection of the embryo and the family, and the relationship between science and nature. The Catholic Church, in particular, refused the possibility of what is conceived as an "external intervention" in reproduction. Family is defined as the fundamental and basic unit of the Catholic community and as the basic nucleus of society; the family is meant to ensure reproduction. Society is thus conceived and regarded as a network made up of families. As the fundamental nucleus of society for Catholics, the family is sacred and has to be impenetrable.

Public debates involving religion are often related to moral controversies over the family and the role of religious ethics within society. The broad revolution in habits and morality triggered several similar issues, setting in opposition different religious traditions and views within religious denominations, and altering the relationship among governments, public policies, and religions. These debates and controversies became more complex because of the presence of a non-Christian religious ethos.

DECOLONIZATION: MULTIFAITH AND MULTICULTURAL SOCIETIES

Migrations were another important phenomenon that contributed to the change in the European religious outlook. Eric Hobsbawm, a major contemporary historian, defined the twentieth century as the "century of migrations." Thousands of people moved from southern to northern Europe and from Eastern to Western Europe to improve their living conditions. Furthermore, population displacements that were sometimes defined as "forced migrations," such as the deportation of Jews, added to these migration movements. Finally, extra-European populations, fleeing poverty and war, chose Europe as their destination. During the 1960s, European colonies in Africa and Asia achieved independence through either rebellion or negotiation. Migrations from these former colonies increased, spreading many Oriental and African religions throughout Europe. These non-European religions interested those Europeans who were tired of traditional religious organizations. During the 1960s, many young people rejected Christianity, claiming that it was tied to an old cultural system that was badly in need of innovation. They turned to foreign religions based on different world visions. By untying spirituality from authority, these religions symbolized the discovery of an alternative. The development of New Age cults went hand in hand with interest in foreign religions, cults, and disciplines. Various spiritual and animistic disciplines spread throughout Europe, especially during the1970s. On the whole, these teachings ascribed some spirituality to natural forces and they invited one to discover a new relationship with nature and with one's own body. The term *New Age* has been used to identify various religious movements, cults, or self-development techniques that promote well-being and transcendental experiences. On one hand, New Age groups and many non-Christian cults promoted an everyday spirituality and a sacral vision that was not limited to specific places or practices and that had a strong mystical component. On the other hand, they allowed a community vision of religiosity to take shape, encouraging a deep sharing and less institutional mediation than traditional Christian religions. Because of their focus on personal, charismatic, and immediate components of faith, some studies define increased interest in these religious forms as a "spiritual revolution."

In fact, religious diversification took various forms. One of these was Oriental mysticism, tied to transcendental meditation or to groups such as the Hare Krishna. These groups promoted a vast spirituality that was far from conformity and social order. The dawn of new religious movements inside Christianity marked a second type of development. These movements felt the effects of external suggestions and rediscovered medieval Catholic mysticism.

Though these phenomena were minor, they furthered the creation of a cultural system whose religious references expanded to include not only Christian elements, but also different ways of imagining spirituality and divinity. One reason of their success was the fact that some actors, singers, and other famous people belonged to such cults. Their adherence brought these cults public attention, while fueling much emulation. The European religious outlook broadened as syncretism and hybridization began to occur among both traditional religions and new religious movements and cults.

Therefore, the most important issue faced by contemporary European religions is the coexistence of different religious traditions inside the same territory. In many ways, it is a new phenomenon. Although different religions had coexisted in Europe and although every culture is the result of hybridization and the encounter of different customs, the extent of this phenomenon in the twentieth century is unprecedented. Starting in the1970s, the immigration of people from former Asian and African colonies created a sudden and significant shift in the religious makeup of European society. Immigrant groups usually settle in urban areas. They often introduce chains of migration that create heavy religious concentrations in certain city districts. Increasing migration broke the relative correspondence between religious affiliation and territory through the pluralization of religious references. Apart from historical religious enclaves, such as Jewish communities, European countries were, in terms of religion, quite homogeneous until the first half of the twentieth century. Twentieth-century migrations significantly altered the religious landscape of Europe, drawing in non-Christian immigrants who were more likely to be religious than the native population. These migrants practice formal religion, which is deeply embedded in migrant cultures. The migrants' sense of self was often strongly imbued with a religious identity that was becoming increasingly alien to secularized Europeans. Indeed, Europeans were largely affected by secularization, whereas migrants largely maintained their religiosity.

Migrants brought religions, traditions, symbols, and worldviews that were the hallmark of their identity, and European religions were influenced by these non-Christian elements. In some cases, European believers adopted migrant religious traditions, beliefs, or habits, combining them with their own beliefs in various ways; in others, Europeans converted to non-European religions. Fearing that their religious traditions would be altered or weakened by contact with the secular European societies in which they had settled, migrants strengthened their adherence to their religion, which they viewed as a key component of a cultural system that they wished to preserve. Within contemporary European democracies, the management of cultural differences is complex. In recent years, Europe has seen many religious controversies and clashes, arising mainly over religious buildings and codes.

Most religious tensions in modern-day Europe involve the so-called second-generation of migrant believers, who are often significantly more religious than their parents. In some cases, the parents have been secularized, whereas their children try to reaffirm their religion as part of their identity. In other cases, religious parents have to deal with secularized children, who were schooled in their adopted countries and became increasingly alienated from their parents' religion. Such children, often referred to as "the cross generation," are less involved in their community life and find their parents' older tribal loyalties to be less relevant.

Immigration issues differ according to the country of origin. For instance, immigration from Christian countries or regions, such as the Philippines or Eastern Europe, matters less than Black, Asian, or North African immigration. Chinese migration shows a different pattern because it dates back many centuries, and Chinese communities have always constituted separate religious and ethnic enclaves. Protestant migration came from former British or Dutch colonies (e.g., Afro-Caribbean immigration) and brought a Christian culture that was mainly evangelical and Pentecostal. Although European Pentecostalism is mostly diffused among migrants' communities, Pentecostalism has also spread among Europeans seeking a renewal of their faith. Migrants often brought new lifeblood to traditional churches that had seen decreased attendance by natives. Indeed, many migrants came from Christian (or Christianized) countries, and their religion became an instrument for integration. Sometimes, migrants and natives attended the same parishes. For the most part, however, migrants, even if they shared the same faith, gathered in different places, thereby creating full-blown ethnic churches. Besides being places of worship, these churches are also meeting places for people coming from the same geographical area. Moreover, they are spaces where newcomers can find support and a mutual-aid network. Non-Christian migrants established similar ethnic and religious communities that were both worship places and meeting rooms.

One of the main issues that rose in the regulation of different religious traditions is linked to the definition of religion itself, because the religious legislation of the European countries is based on Christianity. The development and spreading of other religions caused various difficulties in the regulation of cult expression and practice, notably in the case of "new religious movements" that were not legally acknowledged by all European states. In general, Great Britain, Denmark, Sweden, and Spain are more open. Other nations, without legally acknowledging such forms of spirituality as religion, give them the status of cult organizations. Lastly, there are particular circumstances in which some forms of spirituality are allowed in some countries and banned in others. This is the case with Scientology, a movement with a religious background that is banned in Switzerland, Belgium, and Germany, and considered dangerous in France.

The acknowledgment of religions and cult practices is particularly relevant because there is a need to find a balance between what is prescribed by doctrines and what is allowed by the law of individual nations. The issue lies in the regulation of dress and dietary codes and religious festivities as well as in practices that affect the integrity of one's body, such as excision, infibulation, or circumcision. In 2007—the European Year of Equal Opportunities for All—the European Union published an important guide concerning nondiscrimination and carried out research about the difficulties and the possible routes for legislative integration of different cult practices and religious doctrines.

In Europe, the organization of time is directly linked to Christianity. In spite of the effects of the secularization process, the civil calendar shows its Christian roots. In every European country, common festivities are Christmas (on December 25), Easter Sunday (the date of which varies each year), and Assumption (on August 15). In Orthodox Christianity the civil calendar is the same as in the rest of Europe, but the liturgical calendar follows the Julian calendar, which differs by 13 days from the Gregorian calendar, which is used by the rest of Christian Europe. Epiphany (on January 6), the day of the first manifestation of Jesus's divinity, is considered a civil festivity in Italy, Austria, Croatia, Finland, Greece, Slovakia, Spain, Sweden, as well as in some Swiss cantons and German states. In recent decades, public debate has arisen about whether or not to reckon the holy days of non-Christian religions as civil holidays, or at least as public religious festivities. For instance, in the primary schools of many European countries, teachers and parents argue about Nativity scenes in classrooms at Christmas or the scheduling of events connected to such non-Christian festivities as Jewish Hanukkah or Islamic Ramadan. The weekly calendar also poses problems. The days of rest of the three monotheistic religions are different: Sundays for Christians, Saturdays for Jews, and Fridays for Muslims. Some European countries are trying to adjust their legislation to resolve such problems.

Besides the calendar, dietary and dress codes are also issues. Both businesses and the educational system are adjusting themselves to these new circumstances. Controversies have arisen over the Islamic veil and the placing of a crucifix in classrooms. Religious dress codes, such as the wearing of the veil, blur the separation of the public and private spheres because they are visible marks of religious belonging. Are visible religious symbols compatible with a secular society? The use of crucifixes in public schools relates to the secularization of institutions. Physical elements, such as religious symbols on the wall, could frame a space in such a way that it discriminates against those who do not profess that particular religion or who do not believe in any religion at all.

Dietary prescriptions based on religion can also be markers of specific religious belonging. For Jewish communities, the preparation and consumption of kosher food (especially during the Friday night meal) is an important tool for maintaining religious identity. Therefore, all public offices and services have introduced faith-based menus, as have several private companies. However, some dietary religious habits, such as Ramadan, have raised problems for those jobs in which it is hard to respect religious prescriptions.

The main difficulty is that religions are not fixed and static; they change and transform themselves, and the same denominations can have a wide variety of manifestations in different countries. For this reason, issues related to migrant religion interact with processes of religious transformation in the countries of origin as well as in those of arrival. In public discourses, religions are often represented as monolithic entities, but European Islam, for instance, has specific features grounded in the context of migrations. For instance, most second-generation Muslims do not strictly adhere to Islamic practices, such as the five daily prayers. These groups also engage in such forbidden activities as drinking, dating, and dancing.

Among non-Christian religions, Islam occupies an important place in Europe. Several scholars have shown that in the last decades the public discourse of European societies has progressively introduced the term *Muslim* to identify migrants coming from countries where Islam is the prevailing religion. Therefore, instead of a national or ethnic identification (Algerian, Turkish, Pakistani, etc.), migrants from those countries are identified by religion, whether or not they are religious. Furthermore, in public discourse, the idea of a religious community, characterized by deep interconnections and relations among members, is usually associated with Islam. This association signals the importance of Islam as a public issue in European societies. Its importance increased particularly after the September 11, 2001, attacks on the United States. A feeling of fear and mistrust toward Islam spread among some European populations. This feeling was stirred up in subsequent years by other incidents, such as the murder, by a fanatic, of Theo van Gogh, the Dutch film director who made a movie about violence against women in some Islamic societies. Other examples are the Al-Qaeda train bombings in Madrid in 2004 and the attacks on the London Underground in 2005. However, at the same time, Islamic imams in European cultural centers and national and local heads of Christian sects are building relationships based on cultural encounter and mutual knowledge to overcome mistrust and find methods of peaceful coexistence.

Islam in Europe takes different forms. Religions of the diaspora, as they are called to underline the globalization of religions in the contemporary world, often lose connection with their countries of origin. Consequently, believers in the diaspora express their faith in different ways. First, many Muslims in Europe have had their faith expression subjected to a process of hybridization. Sufism, for instance, is quite widespread, but it does not intervene in the public sphere and is thus less visible. Other Islamic groups in Europe try to revitalize their faith by calling for strict observance of values and practices. It is a sort of identity recomposition based on the idea of a global Islamic community. This leads to different attitudes—for example, toward the use of the Islamic veil. For women, it is a symbol of religious membership and faith. Nevertheless, in some cases, young women who wear the veil as a sort of rebellion against their parents are accused of being too "Westernized."

As we can see, religion can be a cause of conflict in European societies. In Ireland, for instance, religion is an element of national identity, being deeply entwined with the long conflict between the English and the Irish. In the countries that once formed Yugoslavia, religion is a factor in clashes between different ethnic groups.

CONCLUSION

The fall of the Berlin Wall and the slow collapse of the Soviet Union profoundly changed the face of Europe. No longer split into two opposing blocs, European countries now share the same democratic goals. In this framework, the politicization of religion is less common, because religion is no longer used as an alternative to socialism. Moreover, religion is not only and simply a reference for order and social conservatism. Though many acknowledge that the papacy had a major role in the fall of the Soviet system, Orthodox Churches have regained power and converts in Eastern Europe.

Today, churches retain or have even increased their public presence in spite of growing secularization, which is attested to by a declining number of active attendants of every religion and by low levels of compliance with proper Christian values. Two main changes affected religion in Europe: the focus on individuality, first and foremost, and the transformation of religion from an element of identity permanently acquired by birth into an individual choice.

Generally speaking, at the beginning of the twenty-first century, European religions found themselves facing many challenges: secularization, but also a renewed public importance; multiculturalism and competition with different cult traditions; tension and syncretism; the growth of new forms of more personal and spiritual religiosity; and the simultaneous strengthening of the collective commitment of believers. Under these circumstances, two main dimensions of European religions have emerged. First, there is no longer uniformity in religious views; they are highly diverse, either because of the increasing coexistence of many religious traditions in the same territory, or because of changes and reconfigurations within religious denominations. Contemporary Europe includes multicultural and multifaith societies. The second dimension is that in many cases religion weakened as an element of everyday identity and culture, occupying only a small part of people's thoughts and behavior. The role of religion in daily activities is therefore comparatively small compared to what it was in the eighteenth and nineteenth centuries, when Christian culture planned seasons and weeks and determined private morality, from what wear to what to think. And this was true not only for believers but also for dissidents and nonbelievers. Nonetheless, religion still matters, as the rise in religious conflict suggests.

Since the 1990s, Europe has been characterized by a growing religious pluralism. Other cults have joined the traditional Christian religions, ranging from those faiths that were already present, such as Islam and Judaism, to the religions imported by migrant groups and the "new" esoteric and mystical religions. This heterogeneity derives not only from the coexistence of different religious professions in the same area, but also from the great variety of positions expressed by various individuals about religious issues. First, there is a growth in the number of agnostics and atheists apart from the majority of people who still declare themselves religious. In addition, there are growing differences among those who declare themselves as such. These differences lie in the way those people think of their affiliation to a church or a group, as well as in their beliefs about traditional faith systems and in the way people express their religiosity.

In contemporary Europe, religions are confronted with several changes affecting societies and their role within them. First, the establishment of the European Union and the debate on its constitutional roots showed that there is no agreement about the role of religions in European laws and states. Therefore, both religions and states should work out a common regulation. Religion no more means only Christianity; pluralism, which affects the traditional way of believing, is growing. Several centers of faith close to Christian churches have been established in the last decades.

Second, the social sphere is characterized by debates involving religious issues. Current scientific innovations raise issues over biotechnology; social movements raise the issue of the rights of homosexual couples; migrations emphasize problems concerning citizenship and cultural rights. All these issues underline differences between religions and cultures.

In spite of decreasing numbers of churchgoers, religion still plays a crucial role in public life and represents a point of reference for many people. The traditional framework of separation between religion and the state is increasingly challenged, raising issues such as whether or not a democracy should promote common values enforced by law and what kind of mediation politics could represent. At the same time, Christian churches in Europe are perceived as references of certain values, as public actors expected to be engaged in social assistance and in public affairs related to social matters. The majority of Christian believers in Europe, as reported in many surveys, accept the church's involvement in public affairs, above all in those concerning ethical issues linked to biotechnologies, social assistance, and migration. What seems to be clear is that in spite of the secularization processes, religion is still a crucial aspect of daily life for Europeans, both as a practice and a point of reference for values and behavior.

GLOSSARY

Bioethics: Bioethics studies the ethical, moral, religious, philosophical, and political controversies surrounding scientific discoveries. Scientific developments raise ethical questions about the limits of science in intervening on the human body and on its possibilities. Bioethical questions are, for instance, controversies surrounding medically assisted procreation or euthanasia.

Globalization: Globalization refers to the process of increasing flows of people, goods, and ideas between countries. This process affects the permeability of national borders and the authority of nation-states, which manage the local effects of global processes. For that reason, several new global institutions have been created, and processes of governance rescaling have taken place worldwide. Globalization processes facilitate networks of believers, migrations, and hybridization between religious traditions. Religions also are affected by a rescaling process.

Holocaust: The word *holocaust* comes from the Greek word *holókauston*, which means "sacrifice by fire." Holocaust (Shoah in Hebrew) refers to the genocide of about six million Jews during World War II by the Nazi regime of Germany and its collaborators. The Nazis believed in racial purity and considered the Jews a threat to that. Besides Jews, the Nazi regime killed and persecuted other ethnic groups, such as the Roma and some of the Slavic peoples; political and ideological groups, such as communists and socialists; and groups targeted because of their behavior (e.g., homosexuals), racial inferiority (e.g., handicapped people), or religious affiliation (e.g., Jehovah's Witnesses).

Laicity: The word *laicity* derives from the French *laïcité* and indicates the institutional separation between church and state. It narrows the term *secularization* (see below), referring only to its institutional implications.

Multiculturalism: Multiculturalism alludes to the increasing cultural diversity within the same territory. Because of globalization (see above) and the migration processes in contemporary societies, there is a lack of cultural, ethnic, and religious homogeneity and increasing pluralism. Processes of cultural hybridization take place. Multiculturalism affects the everyday life of believers because there is a progressive religious diversity in previously religiously homogeneous nations (such as those in Europe).

New Religious Movements: This expression refers to religious doctrines or spiritual organizations that are not part of traditional churches and denominations. It includes a wide range of movements, cults, and communities.

Second Generation: This expression often refers to the children of migrants to highlight their being at the crossroads of different cultures.

Secularization: Secularization is the historical process by which religious and political spheres become progressively separated from each other within contemporary societies. This process started with the modernization of European and North American societies, where religious institutions have experienced a weakening of their authority in the public sphere. Within the social sciences, secularization is referred to as a theory, maintaining that there is a decline in religiosity in modern societies. According to the secularization theory, modernization affects the role of religion in contemporary societies in many different ways: religious and political institutions are strictly separated; religious institutions lose their importance in the public sphere; individual religiosity declines, as shown by the decreasing levels of religious-service attendance; individuals refer to a lay ethic rather than to religious morality in making private choices; and religious traditions have increasing levels of internal differentiation. In recent decades, secularization theory has been increasingly challenged by empirical analysis showing the lasting importance of religions in everyday life, and a change in the practices of believing toward an increasing rather than a declining individualization.

BIBLIOGRAPHY

Beckford, J. A., and Demerath, J. N., eds. *The SAGE Handbook of the Sociology of Religion*. Thousand Oaks, CA: SAGE Publications, 2007.

Capelle-Pagacean, A., P. Michel, and E. Pace. *Religion(s) et identité(s) en Europe: l'épreuve du pluriel*. Paris: Presses de Sciences Politique, 2008.

Davie, G. *Religion in Modern Europe—A Memory Mutates*. Oxford: Oxford University Press, 2000.

Inglehart, R., and P. Norris. *Sacred and Secular: Religion and Politics Worldwide*. Cambridge: Cambridge University Press, 2004.

McLeod, H. *Religion and the People of Western Europe, 1789–1970*. Oxford: Oxford University Press, 1981.

Rémond, R. *Religion and Society in Modern Europe (Making of Europe)*. Oxford: Blackwell Publishers, 2003.

Willaime, J. P. *Europe et religions: Les enjeux du XXIe siècle*, Paris: Fayard, 2004.

Chapter 11

Native North America

Michael Guéno

INTRODUCTION

The native cultures of North America have developed a variety of sacred narra-tives, symbols, and ritual practices that help them orient themselves in the cos-mos, add purpose to life, and structure social and family relationships. Each distinct culture includes its own language, identity, and sense of common his-tory, as well as its own religious traditions, practices, and beliefs. Scholarly esti-mates indicate that there were more than five hundred distinct Native American societies and languages in North America prior to European contact. As recently as the middle of the twentieth century, approximately 150 Native American languages were still in use within the borders of the United States.[1] However, Native American diversity was not confined to linguistic variation. Such diversity also typifies Indian cultural characteristics. Native societies could be rigidly structured or loosely bound, and the majority existed somewhere between the two extremes. Native North America included small communities of Inuit, the larger and more complex Iroquois Confederacy, and the widespread Mississippian cultural empire dominated by the city of Cahokia. The Cofi-tachiques passed their rights and authority through the male parent's lineage, whereas the Hopi prioritized women in social organization and the Iroquois included women in the exercise of power. The Naskapi primarily subsisted as hunter-gatherers and the Pima on agricultural industry, but most cultures blended the two. The Zuni constructed permanent structures of adobe, the Mohawk semi-permanent log longhouses, and the Apache temporary wickiups of wood and grass or hides. Some cultures of Native North America embraced warfare or trade, others were isolationists, and others viewed the shedding of human blood as an affronting form of spiritual pollution. Despite the incredible diversity of religious practices and understandings of religion found in native cultures, some generalizations regarding Indian conceptions, and thus practice, of religion are possible.

Native American religions include symbols, actions, and concepts that express and define the structure and nature of the cosmos, including the role and purpose of human life within those boundaries. However, for the inhabitants of Native North America religion regularly occurred in "stories of creation, heroes, tricksters, and fools; in architecture, art and orientations in the landscape; in ritual drama, costumes, masks, and ceremonial paraphernalia; and in relation to hunting, farming, and fishing."[2] That is, the most transcendent and sublime of religious ideas and experiences may be found in highly complicated, formally articulated intellectual and artistic forms as well as among the most crude and mundane environments and elements of life. Many Native American communities over time have considered religion and the religious as beyond and distinct from mundane or ordinary existence. However, religion is also recognized as lived and practiced in the most common elements of life. Hunting, farming, food preparation, art production, and the daily routines of households are reinforced and taught through religious stories and associated with wisdom revealed by nonhuman spirits to generations past. Although practitioners and many contemporary scholars do not explicitly recognize such activities as religious, nearly all daily practices are informed, influenced, and contextualized by a religious worldview and dramatic, recognizably religious practices. Such a diffuse view of religion multiplies the abundant examples of religious practice to nearly infinite variety. By examining the performance of commonly recognized religious actions, one may glimpse the similarities among different religious traditions and understand the way in which religion framed each moment of daily life in Native North America.

Although such categories are admittedly oversimplified, modern scholarship tends to recognize several common themes and characteristics running through Native American religious practices. In general, Native Americans have understood the world they found themselves in as constructed and governed by ties of kinship. Their concepts and relationships with that which is held to be sacred is directed by a strong sense of interrelation and of behavioral ethics rooted in familial interactions. That is, Native American individuals and communities primarily situate themselves in reality through everyday family relationships writ large and reflected in the cosmos. These ties of kinship bind all creatures found in nature, human beings, and those beings that Western culture would call supernatural. Thus, some Native American cultures have recognized the nonhuman spirits known as Thunder Beings as Grandfathers, and others have understood the potent spiritual beings called *katsinas* as beneficent rain spirits and deceased ancestors. Other peoples have revered the wisdom of Grandmother Spider or expressed thanksgiving for the gifts and succor of the Corn Mother. Animals could frequently take on human form and were similarly engaged according to familial relationships. These included trickster figures such as Coyote, Hare, and Raven, as well as sacred animals such as White Buffalo Woman. The Moon, Sun, and Rattlesnake were likewise understood and related to through the metaphor of familial bonds for various indigenous cultures. All of existence comprised one very large extended family network where Native Americans usually existed as the younger and ideally more humble siblings surrounded by their wiser and more venerable family members.

In a worldview in which metaphors of kinship formed the basis for a reality that recognized no distinction between humans, animals, and nonhuman spirits, the material world was correspondingly important and infused with the sacred. Whereas Euro-American religions frequently sought to distinguish and delineate all things material from that which is spiritual and privilege the spiritual, Native American religions expressed a sense of the sacredness of the material world or nature through a variety of religious practices and ideas. Native American communities recognized powerful and awesome religious forces manifest within each aspect of nature. Rarely were these powers understood to be abstract forces that were ultimately distinct from nature. Often, sacred beings manifested as animal or plant guardians that had long ago bound the bodies of their species to serve as prey and food for humans: "Thus, Pacific Coast Indians had to be careful in taking flesh from the salmon, for they believed that the skeleton, when placed in the river waters, would receive new flesh as the sacred beings reproduced themselves."[3] Scholars and Native practitioners have noted that, because of the sacredness of the natural world, Native American communities developed elaborate rules and manners of respect and courtesy that governed the way in which Indians could hunt or plant. They were expected to ask permission from or apologize to the spirits of the creatures whose lives they took. Native Americans would frequently make offerings of thanksgiving and appeasement to these spirits, and they were expected to treat the parts of the creature with respect and humility. Native American practitioners assert that their ancestors were careful to use every portion of what they killed and killed only what was needed. Thus, Native American religions are often associated with the practice of ecological conservationism in an era before Western culture had developed a similar concept.[4] Native Americans experienced the sacred and mysterious within the boundaries of daily existence, or the natural world, conceived as a continuous space and time containing human and mythical action.

The religious practices of Native North America were generally overseen and directed by religious professionals called shamans or medicine men. Shamans were human beings that were responsible for maintaining the spiritual order and proper relationship between Native American peoples and spirits. They possessed knowledge of the proper ceremonies for realigning these relations and were skilled in spiritual feats such as mediumship, travel outside the body, and the physical healing of the ill. Among the Huron, they were called *arendiwane*—men and women who experienced a powerful dream of vision of a spirit and emerged with the abilities necessary to ensure the prosperity of the community. The spiritual capabilities varied among *arendiwane* but could include abilities to manipulate the weather, avert catastrophe, bring success in hunting and fishing, heal the sick, and extract evil powers used by witches.[5] Although Native terms for and understandings of the role of shamans vary, shamans are recognized as holy people who serve as sacred healers, mystics, and religious leaders. Shamans had a prominent role in maintaining social order and cohesion and resolving any social tensions or misfortunes plaguing their communities that may have resulted from the exercise of spiritual powers by a mistreated and angered spiritual being. Shamans were not the only Native Americans capable of spiritual feats and experiences, nor were they enforcers of religious orthodoxy. Among the Plains Indians, even common people were believed to be able to speak to guardian animal spirits during the ritual of vision quests. Indians of the Great Lakes region respected the spiritual potency of dreams and heeded the power and advice that anyone had the potential to receive through them.

To more fully understand any particular belief of Native American religions, it is important to attempt to engage as fully as possible the worldview in which that element is found. A worldview is the conceptual framework that gives shape to the whole of reality and sets the boundaries within which reality is perceived and mundane life is negotiated. Given that every facet of the material world has culturally designated attributes such as time, space, and authority, virtually anything can reveal these delineations of cultural value. Indeed, any product of a culture or element of its environment can be a symbol of a culture's worldview and understanding of the form or content of some portion of reality.[6] Evidence of Native American worldviews can be found in stories, religious symbols, and social structures, but most immediately in ritual actions. Religious rituals from the extraordinary and rare to the daily and mundane concretize and make real the worldview, giving the cosmos and local society its order and shape. Whether a practice is performed frequently in private or in annual public ceremonies, the worldview is reinforced, personal meaning is attained, and cultural implications of the ritual define daily life throughout the year.[7] Religion in the daily life of Native North America is defined and reinforced by rituals performed daily, seasonally, or according to unique scheduling guides; these give meaning to life and structure to the experience of reality. Each of the practices presented below demonstrates one of the ways in which the essential elements of Native American religions were and are evoked and utilized to define cultural understandings of space, time, and authority and to shape human life in North America.

TIMELINE

400 BCE– 200 CE:	Maya Late Pre-classic Era.
16th century CE:	*Popul Vuh*, a highland Maya sacred document, is written.
1519:	Spain begins its conquest of Mexico.
1535:	Practices using the sacred pipe are first observed by European explorers.
1620:	The use of peyote is banned by the Spanish Inquisition.
1830:	U.S. Congress passes the Indian Removal Act.
1830–1839:	The Trail of Tears—forced removal of various tribes from the southeastern United States.
1866:	The Sun Dance is first observed.
1883:	The Sun Dance is banned.
1890:	The Massacre at Wounded Knee in South Dakota.
1918:	The Native American Church is organized.
1932:	*Black Elk Speaks* is first published.
1947:	Black Elk relates *The Sacred Pipe* to Joseph Epes Brown.
1952:	The full practice of the Sun Dance resumed after the ban is lifted.

NATIVE AMERICAN PRAYER

Prayer is a central religious practice that is found at the dramatic climaxes of the ritual performances of many Native North American cultures. Many Native American peoples recite prayers as part of larger ceremonies or as ritual practices unto themselves. It has been through the analysis of the practice of prayer by Sam Gill that modern scholarship has begun to explore the intricate system of practices and ideas that compose Native American religions.

Gill's study of Navajo prayer reveals the central role of prayer in Navajo cere-monial life and illuminates the interconnectivity between the practice of prayer and other elements of Native American religiosity. The structure and intent of prayer connect the ceremonial practice to larger ritual elements as well as the culture and religious worldview upon which the practice is founded.

The performance of Native American prayer is a ritual act that is inherently creative. The practice creates or strengthens the bonds of relation or kinship between human and spiritual powers. These relationships are essential to defining individual and group identities, traversing unfortunate circumstances, and ensuring the continuation of life. This is especially true in the Oglala rit-ual for the Making of Relatives, a ceremony intended to promote peace and familial relations between two peoples. While making an offering of sweetgrass and a buffalo bladder, the officiate prays, "Grandfather, *Wakan-Tanka*, Father, *Wakan-Tanka*, behold us! Upon this earth we are fulfilling thy will. By giving to us the sacred pipe, You have established a relationship with us, and this rela-tionship we are now extending by making this peace with another nation with whom we were once at war. . . . Through this offering we shall be bound to You and to all Your Powers."[8] The relations forged through prayer are binding upon and compulsory for both parties according to the religious practices and beliefs of many Native American cultures. This compulsion is not mechanistic, nor is it based upon coercive pressure. However, prayer instills common Navajo prac-titioners with authority and provides them with a medium to negotiate the inherent responsibility for reinforcing the order of their universe. Although this tremendous power is deftly demonstrated by shamans in public and pri-vate rituals, it is wielded in the practice of daily life by Native Americans in common prayers.

The structure of prayer is simultaneously formulaic and a medium for per-sonal creativity. The framework of prayer is inviolable, and variation from tra-dition is rigidly renounced to maintain cosmic order and stave off disaster. However, the underlying purpose of prayer is to serve as a vehicle for meaning-ful self-expression that is inherently creative. Gill has demonstrated that despite the constraints of a set framework and only twenty distinct elements, Navajo prayer is capable of nearly infinite variation and may be modified to express a creative range of intent and content. The prayers in the Navajo Flintway ritual process have the same structure: an invocation of a spiritual being, a mention of a prior sacrifice to the being, a request by the petitioner to be restored to health or wholeness, and a description of the experience of restoration. However, by changing the name of the spirit, the description of its home, and references to its related phenomenon in the invocation, the prayer may address a variety of beings. By altering the description of the unfavorable condition of the petitioner and its resolution, the same prayer may be used to achieve a solution to any unpleasant misfortune. Even when the words or ritual pattern is set or even formulaic, Native American prayer expresses the desires, hopes, and affects of common practitioners.[9]

The public recitation of prayer often follows a rhythmic pattern. Prayers are often performed as litanies sung by a medicine man and the patron for whom the ceremony is conducted. In many Navajo ceremonies, the singer and the one-sung-over sit (i.e., the patient) on the floor of the Hogan while the singer carefully recites a prayer with a brief pause between each phrase. During the pause, the one-sung-over echoes the holy man's words, and the singer begins to overlay the next phrase while the patient is still chanting. This timing creates an echo effect that is often performed with little intonation. Despite the roughly monotone recitation, the linguistic patterns and tones create a rhythmic structure.

The performance of prayer frequently involves more than the simple articulation of prescribed litanies. Prayer in Native North America often includes song, bodily movements and positions, the use of ritual artifacts, and sometimes the accompaniment of performers or religious assistants. During many ceremonies, singers demonstrate mastery of prayer performances by using the formulaic elements of prayer to compose the songs that the patron of the ceremony requires. The ritual mastery of these religious professionals extends to the arrangement and use of the proper ritual artifacts and accompanying ceremonies to express the desired sentiment and evoke the appropriate response. The combinations of ceremonial objects, prescribed gestures, and prayer syntax are as infinitely varied as the motivations and ideas expressed through prayer.

Prayer, however, serves as more than a mere description of circumstances and a request for a desired outcome. Prayer is a form of speech and, as such, engages a culture's worldview, framework of symbols, and aesthetic principles. The performance of prayer is an act that is tied to communicative elements of style. In some Native cultures, prayer utilizes changes in verb tenses to indicate and effect a transition in time. The performance moves from a request for assistance or a desired action from spiritual powers to a present-tense description of the desired results occurring, and it concludes by describing the effects of and appreciation for the previously granted boon. The shift in verb tenses conforms to indigenous aesthetics of literary composition, indicating the ritual and message communicated as a prayer, but it also frames the enacting of the invoked blessing within the flow of time, strengthening the likeliness and reality of its occurrence.

Prayer functions as a means of communication between human beings and supernatural powers. However, the "style of the language used in prayer suggests that it has a performative function as well as a petitionary function, that is, that it evokes and affects as well as informs."[10] That is to say that, though prayer serves as a medium for intelligible communication between humans and higher powers, it is also a ritual act that engages a mythopoetic network of symbols to evoke a variety of associated emotions and understandings. This evocation is intentionally and unintentionally performed through symbolism woven into the prayer and accompanying mythoi and, more intensely, through the sensuousness of rhythmic repetition and the other sounds, images, scents, and bodily articulations that contextualize and define the performance of a given prayer.[11]

Native American prayer is a common act of communication oriented toward achieving practical ends. It is also a ritual practice that engages a complex structure of symbols and myths to contextualize a moment and create a system of relationships between practitioners and supernatural powers. It expresses the heartfelt desires and feelings of the performer while evoking powers capable of transforming affects, motivations, and the context of the practitioner. The practice of prayer serves as both a means of intelligible communication with the anticipation of a pragmatic effect and a performance that may achieve the desired results. It empowers religious practitioners with the authority and ability to reinforce the structure of the world and functions to transform it.

MAYA BLOODLETTING

Blood was central to many aspects of Maya daily life and their beliefs about the world in which they lived. Blood bound ancient Maya ritual life into a cohesive whole. The Maya let blood during rituals for each important life stage of the individual and to note important events in the life of the community. Blood was the official offerings that kings and other nobility can and did offer to seal ceremonial events. The majority of the surviving art from the Classic Maya kingdoms serves to document the bloodlines of their kings and rulers. The legitimacy of Maya kingships was traditionally determined by descent and bloodlines as kingship passed from father to son. Because of the importance of blood and bloodlines, a significant majority of Maya imagery and writing is consumed with documenting records of parents and ancestors transferring power to their heirs. To celebrate and bless the birth of his heir, a Maya king offered a personal blood sacrifice to his ancestors. According to Maya accounts, human sacrifices were typically offered to sanctify, and they realized the accession of an heir to a king and were occasionally depicted as a vital component of accession rituals and subsequent imagery. Warfare and the taking of captives are common among the events recorded on Maya monuments. Although the

motivations for and consequences of Maya warfare were numerous and complicated, its primary ritual function was to provide Maya communities with
sacrificial victims, whose blood would be offered to the gods. In death, Maya
kings were honored by being placed in handsomely appointed tombs that were
frequently painted the color of blood and ordained with imagery of blood and
the Underworld. From birth to death Maya and their rulers were associated
with and surrounded by blood and blood rituals. It is important to note that
in the religious practice of the Maya, the centrality of blood was not viewed as
bizarre or exotic but rather necessary to sustain and invigorate the world.[12]

Blood was the mortar of Maya ritual life from Late Pre-classic era through
the arrival of Spanish explorers and missionaries. The Spanish were immediately appalled by the practice of bloodletting and attempted to purge it as a
form of idolatrous worship. Fray Diego de Landa Calderón described with
horror bloodletting during rites of human sacrifice, when "the foul priest in
vestments went up and wounded the victim with an arrow in the parts of
shame, whether it was a man or woman, and drew blood and came down and
anointed the faces of the idol with it . . . struck with great skill and cruelty a
blow between the ribs seized the heart like a raging tiger . . . and snatched it out
alive."[13] Although scholars have long recognized the importance of blood sacrifice in Mesoamerica, the practice was attributed to the larger Mexican culture
rather than essentially to the Maya. However, the more recent translation of
event glyphs and the deciphering of iconography associated with bloodletting
by epigraphers in the past few decades have revolutionized this view. It is now
generally accepted that the Spanish reaction to, and obsessive description of,
blood rites was not exaggerated. Bloodletting did indeed permeate Maya daily
life and was fundamental to their religious practice. Bloodletting was foundational to the institution of rulership, a great variety of public rituals, and the
myths through which Maya articulated the order of the world.

Though not practiced in Maya communities today, personal bloodletting
was a frequent and common ritual of ancient Maya life. Through bloodletting
rituals, Maya sought visions that they conceived of as the manifestations of an
ancestor and/or god. The Maya articulated their personal religious piety by
letting blood from various parts of the body. Bloodletting ceremonies could be
performed in private, individual practices or in large, public rituals for a community officiated by religious professionals from formal priesthoods. Though
bloodletting was often undertaken voluntarily by ruling elite and common citizens, it was not uncommon to let the blood or even sacrifice the lives of captured enemies. The Maya elite demonstrated their legitimacy and worthiness
to rule by communicating with their deceased ancestors who were believed to
reappear as visions during bloodletting rituals. These rituals could and did

occur under a variety of circumstances, most commonly as part of significant life events, including birth, marriage, accession, and warfare. When buildings were erected and dedicated, crops planted and blessed, children born and couples married, or when the dead were buried, blood was offered by common Maya to express their piety and call the presence of the gods into the world. For kings, however, every stage in life, every event of political or religious importance, and the ending of every significant period of the sacred calendar required sanctification through bloodletting. Indeed, kings would let blood "with greatest regularity . . . at the completion of the twenty-year period, the katun."[14]

In time even the instrument for drawing blood, the lancet, became understood as a religious artifact infused with sacred power. Simulacra of stingray spines were fashioned from rare stone and considered precious by the Maya. These sculptures were not used as lancets but rather as symbolic manifestations of the power inherent in the stingray spine. The transcendent power of the lancet was personified in the form of the Perforator God: "The triple and double cloth knots tied around the forehead of the Perforator God became the most pervasive symbol of the bloodletting rite."[15] During bloodletting rituals, the Maya wore paper cloth strips with knotted bows in their hair and clothing, on their arms and legs, and through freshly pierced earlobes. This sacrificial paper cloth was manufactured from the felted bark of the fig tree and was used as cloth. The paper cloth and the cotton cloth were cut or torn and used in the bloodletting rite to collect the fresh sacrifice offered up by the Maya. When the paper cloth was properly saturated with blood, it was ceremonially burned in a brazier to transform the blood into smoke so that the gods might consume it. The cosmological symbolism accompanying the Maya glyphs for sacrificial objects and ritual sacrifice suggests that Maya understood blood to be the basic and essential element of this world as well as its most sacred and precious substance.

The Maya creation story found in the Popol Vuh illuminates a limited context for the importance of bloodletting rites. In the beginning, after the creator gods had ceased their labor, they desired to be recognized by their newly living creations. The creatures of the air and Earth responded to the gods with a meaningless cacophony of noise were thus fated to be the prey of mankind and one another. The gods sought to create *special* creatures that could know them but after several attempts were unsuccessful. Ultimately, they created human beings that were able to recognize the gods and their own relationship to these creators by using maize for flesh and water for blood. The gods had desired creatures "to 'name [their] names, to praise them'" but also to serve as their providers and caretakers. The gods wanted creatures that could worship them,

but—more important—they needed humankind to provide them with sustenance. According to the art and inscriptions of the Classic Maya Period as well
as the Popol Vuh, blood drawn from all parts of the human body, but especially
from the earlobes, tongue, and genitals, was vital sustenance for their gods.

Perhaps the most descriptive representation of the Maya ritual of bloodletting, and also the most dramatic, can be found on two series of lintels among
the buildings of the Mayan city of Yaxchilan, in what is currently the state of
Chiapas, Mexico. The images found on these lintels portray distinct points
within one cohesive narrative of the performance of a ritual. However, the text
accompanying the scenes records widely disparate dates and likely indicates
that the same ritual was performed on several distinct occasions. The series of
panels begins above the left-hand door of a building referred to by archaeologists as Structure 23 and continues to narrate the bloodletting ritual of Shield
Jaguar, a distinguished Maya ruler, and his wife. Shield Jaguar is shown dressed
in the regalia of royalty, including a small mask or shrunken head atop his
head. His primary wife, Lady Xoc, is depicted kneeling before him in an huipil
woven with an intricate, traditional design with an ornate headdress decorated
with signs and symbols that indicate she is performing a bloodletting rite that
will culminate in captive sacrifice. She pulls a ceremonial rope, lined with
thorns, through a wound recently inflicted in her tongue, trailing the rope into
a basket piled with paper strips. The paper strips as well as her lips and cheeks
are spotted or shown with the dotted scroll sign that indicates the presence of
her freshly offered blood.

The second image of the sequence, found on Lintel 25, depicts the result
and hypothesized purpose of this bloodletting rite. Lady Xoc is still kneeling,
but now her gaze is fixed upon an apparition of a warrior ornamented with
symbols of Tlaloc, who is emerging from the unhinged jaws of a Vision
Serpent. She holds in her left hand a bloodletting bowl, which contains the
bloody paper strips and now a stingray spine and obsidian lancet, and in her
right hand she holds a symbol of a skull and serpent. The Vision Serpent
bearing the Tlaloc warrior emerges upward through a blood scroll from a
bowl placed upon the floor in front of her. Thus, the serpent, warrior, and
visions in general materialize from blood that is let. Although the warrior is
not named, the purpose of this bloodletting rite appears to have been effecting the materialization of this vision so that she might communicate with
him. Modern scholars believe that as part of the accession rituals of a Maya
king, his principal wife would submit to a bloodletting ritual to summon this
or a similar warrior, who may have been an ancestor or symbolic manifestation of the king's importance in the symbolic cluster of warfare, sacrifice,
rulership, and the evening star.

According to the pictorial records gleaned from Bonampak and elsewhere, a vibrant, public phase of the bloodletting rites sometimes took place in the colossal open-air plazas throughout Maya cites. Crowds of participants would cluster on terraces around the plaza vested with bloodletting paper cloth ritually tied in triple knots. A sixteenth-century Catholic missionary to the region, Bishop Diego de Landa, noted that such participants would have engaged in several days of fasting and abstinence to prepare themselves for the rite. Across the heart of the plaza and along the surrounding terraced platforms, elaborately costumed dancers would perform to the music drums, whistles, rattles, and trumpets. Their ritual costumes usually included large front panels that were decorated with abstract designs or religious imagery, and were dyed red by the blood flowing from the dancers' recently perforated penises to which the panels were tied. Over these panels dancers wore blood-splattered loincloths that, like the panels, would only become more saturated by blood as the dancing progressed. To the native Maya, the opportunity to participate in this dance and in such bloodletting rites was an opportunity to demonstrate their piety before their ruler and their gods. Indeed, the continued existence of the universe was dependent upon human beings willing to offer their blood and sustain the gods. Toward the climactic end of the ceremony, the ruler and his wife would emerge from their private preparations and stand high above the plaza. While the assembled participants and spectators observed, the king would lacerate his penis and she would pierce her tongue. Both then drew ropes through their wounded appendages to guide the flowing blood onto waiting paper strips. The newly saturated paper would be burnt along with other offerings, such as chicle resin and incense, in large braziers, creating billowing columns of smoke.

The best extant depictions of bloodletting rituals are associated with the accession of kings. Bloodletting was the earliest and most frequent royal action documented in public art. The calling of the apparition, depicted on Lintel 25, coincides with the accession of and inaugurated the reign of Shield Jaguar. In addition, one of the earliest-dated monuments of the Maya Lowlands, the Hauberg Stelae, portrays the same bloodletting ritual associated with an accession. Thus, the performance of bloodletting rituals, either before or as a conclusion to accession rites, was a longstanding Maya religious practice. The need to commemorate an actual royal bloodletting in stone monuments reveals the correlation between letting blood and the concretization of time. The monuments portray the rituals, recall the king's contact with the supernatural, and link the particulars of a specific ritual to the chain of facts and events that constitute Maya written history.[16] Kings let blood not only to call and sustain the gods, but also to reinforce the continuity of time itself and maintain the stability of civilization against entropy. Thus, the writing found on Maya public monuments not only functioned to cement events in the collective memory but also functioned as public propaganda by reinforcing the link between kings and gods and affirming the special place of their blood in the universe.[17]

Native Maya believed that the regular practice of bloodletting called and materialized deceased ancestors and supernatural beings within the confines of space and time inhabited by living humans. The practice of bloodletting called the desired god or ancestor, birthed him or her within the physical realm, and maintained the manifestation until the ritual ended and the supernatural vanished. The king was understood to be a vessel for various gods that could be invoked and dwell within his body for the duration of the ritual. During each ritual, a different supernatural being could be incarnated and reside within the king only to depart at the end of the ritual. It is possible that the Maya recognized all humans as able to host or at least invoke the presence of supernatural beings, as many participants in public rituals wore masks and body suits to represent the gods. However, because of the iconography associated with kingship and the consistent depictions of kings subsumed within the dress and identity of various supernatural beings, it is likely that the authority of the king and the elite was intricately bound if not dependent upon their religious duties and religious authority. Within the boundaries of the ritual, the letting of their blood enabled them to become the gods they impersonated: "Through his gift of blood, the king brought the gods to life and drew the power of the supernatural into the daily lives of the Maya. As the bearer of the most potent blood among humankind, the king was the focus of tremendous power" and bore the weight of the continued existence and prosperity of the human world.[18]

NAVAJO SAND PAINTING

Sand painting is a ceremonial practice that has been and is part of many religious rituals practiced among the Navajo, Apache, Arapaho, Cheyenne, and Pueblo peoples as well as many Native American cultures of southern California. It is performed by artfully and delicately sprinkling handfuls of a dry substance onto a prepared surface, usually a ritually cleansed and specified location on the ground, to form the patterns and figures of a painting. Sand paintings vary in size from a foot or less across to more than 20 feet in diameter, and they appear in a variety of shapes. The time and number of artists required depend on the size and complexity of any given painting. Four to six painters may create a six-foot painting in approximately three to five hours.

A Navajo medicine man during a sand painting healing ritual (ca. 1994). The patient in a sand painting ceremony is purified through sweating, vomiting, sexual abstention, ritual baths, and herbal medicines and ultimately is identified with the Holy People, supernatural beings invoked during the ceremony. In the sand painting ceremony, a symbolic picture is made by strewing finely powdered pigments on the floor of a hogan covered by fine sand. The patient sits on the painting and eats the given medicine. The evil spirits enter the painting and are dumped outside the hogan. Each illness requires a special painting, and the Navajo use more than a thousand different designs. (© Danny Lehman/Corbis.)

Each Native culture creates its dry paint from various materials and during different ceremonies. The Pueblo peoples craft their sand paintings from sand as well as richly colored ocher, corn pollen, or pulverized flower petals during a series of ceremonies performed in dedicated underground sacred structures called *kivas*. The cultures of southern California construct sand paintings upon the prepared earth as a central element of all puberty and initiation ceremonies. The ornate paintings depict both the abstract forces of the cosmos and more concrete astronomic phenomena. The Apaches, over the course of one day, fabricate a singular, highly detailed sand painting across the earthen ground contained within a circular space enclosed by tree boughs, and they ritually destroy the sand painting before sundown.

The Navajo often create multiple sand paintings during many of their ceremonies and are often noted for the intricacies of the large sand paintings that
they produce.[19] These sand paintings are a ritual component of many but not
all religious ceremonies, including rites performed to heal the sick and injured,
cast evil out of a person, invoke the blessings of spirits, and re-harmonize an
individual with the holistic universe. They serve as depictions of sacred stories,
invitations to the spiritual forces on the cosmos, and a temporary, sacred altar
upon the floor of the ceremonial Hogan, or primary religious structure. The
colors for the Navajo paintings are usually crafted from ocher, gypsum, ground
charcoal, and sandstone of various colors. Navajo religious professionals, often
called singers, bless these temporary artifacts and the ground upon which they
dwell by making offerings of cornmeal and pollen. Singers speak with the
patient and consult his or her family to determine the cause of the illness and
select the most relevant and appropriate sand painting for the particular
circumstance or illness from among the various paintings associated with a
given ceremony. During the selected ceremony, the singer or his assistant holds
some of the colored materials in his hand and generates a controlled flow to the
surface of the pattern from his hand, positioned close for greater precision. The
singer directs the painting according to the dictates of his memory with minimal alteration to adhere as closely as possible to the original sacred designs
passed down through the generations from the original chant heroes, who
inaugurated ceremonies for the use of human beings. No visual record or written text documents the patterns, and hundreds of distinct sand paintings have
been observed.

Each of the patterns is associated with a specific ceremony that is rooted in
a particular segment of the religious tradition's creation story.[20] The Navajo
understood that the *diyin dine'é*, or holy people, designated the ritual patterns
of each of the paintings as well as the proper construction of each in the beginning time. Sand paintings symbolically depict the creation and history of the
spirits and human ancestors and narrate relevant segments in the life of various chant heroes. The original designs and prescriptions for each sand painting were bestowed upon a chant hero, the protagonist of each story, who in
turn taught the humans on Earth how to properly re-create the sacred forms.
Thus, each sand painting re-creates one of the original patterns given by holy
people to the chant hero and passed down through the ages.

The sand painting is a component practice of and altar for several religious
ceremonies as well as the designated seat for the patient while the singer and
his assistance perform various rites. Each completed sand painting provides a
material medium through which the holy people may manifest their power and
presence. During each ceremony the singer offers cornmeal to purify, bless, and

inaugurate the ritual by sprinkling it around the painting and over the person for whom the ceremony is conducted. The person suffering illness or misfortune is positioned in the center of the painting and oriented east. The singer transfers sands from parts of the holy people in the painting that have some association with the diagnosed cause of suffering to corresponding parts of the one-sung-over's body to strengthen the association and identification between patient and spirit. The pictorial representations of the spirits invite them to the ceremonial Hogan and invoke them to instill the painting with some measure of their sacred power, healing the ailing in exchange for the prepared offerings. When the ritual identification and healing is accomplished, the sands are dispersed. The painting is made, the ceremony performed, and the pattern destroyed in one day. However, the ritual painting in combination with the associated rituals can last between one to nine days.[21]

To understand the way in which the various sand-painting ceremonials influence the everyday religious worldview of the common Navajo, one can examine and analyze the performance and implications of the Nightway ceremonial and the Whirling Logs sand painting that is often associated with it.[22] The Nightway ceremony is performed for a person who is suffering from a misfortune or illness that has been caused by one of the Navajo's holy people. Thus, the purpose of the ritual is to recognize the interconnection between the human and the spirit and reestablish the proper relationship between the suffering practitioner, also called the one-sung-over, and various holy people. According to the Navajo, once the ties are renewed and the relationship repaired, the misfortune will be removed, as the one-sung-over is re-created properly. The Nightway ceremonial lasts for nine nights, and the sand painting rites occur on the fifth through eighth days.

The Whirling Logs sand painting is created in the center of the ceremonial Hogan after it is cleared and the fire moved to one side. To prepare the space, a clean layer of sand is spread across the ground with weaving battens. The painters begin in the center and radiate out under the supervision and direction of the singer. To create the Whirling Logs pattern, they begin by painting a black cross, centered within the prepared area, to represent the whirling logs from the associated segment of myth. Sometimes a bowl of water is embedded in the center of the cross to represent the lake that the logs float upon. The black cross is outlined in red and then white. Next, corn plants with roots in the central lake are drawn in each of the four quadrants using yellow, blue, white, and black paint and outlined in a contrasting color. Each corn plant is depicted with two ears of corn on each stalk. The painters then draw two yé'ii, or masked holy people, on each length of the whirling logs cross. The inner holy figures are depicted as females with spruce branches in each hand, and the male *yé'ii* are shown with rattles and spruce branches and wear masks with plumes of eagle and owl feathers.

Once the interior segment of the pattern is laid down, the singer directs the painters to depict *yé'ii* figures adjacent to each end of the whirling logs. The holy person to the west is known as *hasch'é ooghwaan*, or Calling God, and is painted wearing black and a blue mask with eagle and owl feathers. The easternmost figure, *hasch'étti'i*, is Talking God. He is drawn in white, wearing a white mask ornamented with eagle feathers, a yellow tuft of owl feathers, and a fox skin. The painters place *ghwáá'ask'idii*, or Humpback holy people, in the north and south. They are presented in blue masks decorated with white lightning patterns and red feathers that symbolize sunbeams. Finally, an anthropomorphic rainbow, the Rainbow Guardian, is drawn around the circumference of the sand painting, leaving a gap on the eastern quadrant. The ritual practitioners complete the painting by erecting plumed wands to represent holy people around the periphery of the painting.

With the ceremonial space ritually prepared, the one-sung-over is brought into the Hogan, and the singer initiates the songs associated with the Whirling Logs ceremonial. The suffering patient then sprinkles an offering of cornmeal to the east of the painting, repeating the offering to the south, west, and north. He or she then circumscribes the painting with an offering of cornmeal. As the one-sung-over prepares to enter and take a seat upon the painting, a *yé'ii* makes an appearance in the Hogan by means of a masked impersonator, who then carefully scatters an herbal medicine mixture across the painting using a cedar branch. Once the patient is seated, the holy person presents him or her with a shell cup of medicine to be imbibed. The *yé'ii* places some of the remaining medicine on his hands and uses it to pick up grains of sand from the extremities of each of the depicted figures and apply them to the corresponding body parts of the suffering patient. After the application of the sands the holy person shouts twice into each of the one-sung-over's ears and departs the Hogan. The one-sung-over then stands and exits the painting. Finally, the plumed wands are removed and the singer uses a feather wand to ceremonially erase the picture. The remaining paint materials are carried out of the Hogan and disposed of properly. Throughout the entirety of the ceremony the singer, or medicine man, continues his choral performance until the *yé'ii* leaves.

The Whirling Logs painting and the Nightway story linked to it reveal the common Navajo's perception of the shape of the cosmos. Moreover, the ceremony was intended to transform a person from an unfavorable to a favorable condition as well as reaffirm and cement reality by reflecting the structure of creation and the relationships that bind it together. The shape and foundational pattern of the sand painting reflects the shape of the ceremonial Hogan and the quaternary division of the universe. It is a geometric reflection of the pattern and order in the cosmos. During the ritual, the Hogan is associated with the mythical Hogan in which the universe was originally created and is thus unconsciously linked with the essential framework of reality. Sand paintings created within its boundaries are similarly tied to the primal era and original events that the chant hero experienced. The Whirling Log painting recreates the pattern revealed to him by the holy people on the shore of the whirling lake and the logs whirling in the lake upon which he rode with the *yé'ii*. The painting not only represents but also cosmically re-creates the stories depicted. The creation of a sand painting constructs an echo of the events from the mythical era and re-realizes that sacred time and a degree of the sacred power of the holy ones in the story. It is simultaneously a visual recollection of the mythical story of the hero who obtained the Nightway ceremonial and experienced the original mystery of the whirling logs and passed the ritual on to the Navajo as well as re-creation of this primal event and a reflection of the shape of the universe.

The Nightway story also reveals the existence of two distinct but interdependent worlds in the daily lives of the Navajo: the world of humans and animals, and the world of holy people and the keepers of the game. This dualistic model of reality is vibrantly presented throughout the Nightway ceremonial. A male or female holy person tops each extension of the whirling logs cross. The Humpback *yé'ii* are paired opposite one another, just as Talking God and Calling God are juxtaposed across the division formed by the quaternary division. The cornstalks of each quadrant are outlined in and placed across from the cornstalk of its contrasting color—white and black, yellow and blue.

The implications of this dualistic tension are increasingly apparent and relevant in the ritual actions performed atop the painting. The holy person, through the costumed impersonator, presents the one-sung-over with medicines that have been previously offered and applied to each of the holy people depicted in the ceremonial art piece. Through the transfer of sands, the ritual strengthens the bonds between the patient and the holy ones, identifying each with the other. Thus, the one-sung-over is identified and united with the holy ones, the original chant hero that experienced the primordial vision, and the powers and structure of the universe itself.

The tension caused by the duality of existence is resolved within the person upon whom the ritual is focused. The complex dual imagery and cosmic associations in the sand painting and the ritual actions lead the one-sung-over to an experience of unity and transcendence beyond this dualism. This religious experience, according to tradition, enables the patient to experience reality and achieve unity with it and thus touch the sacred powers of which it is composed. During the course of the ritual, the one-sung-over experiences what the Navajo believe is "the truth in the stories, which is that there are not two worlds, but one world composed of parts which are complexly interrelated and interdependent. Order and disorder are interdependent, as are health and sickness, life and death, spiritual and material."[23] Within the Navajo worldview, once a person experiences reality in such a way, the sand painting is no longer necessary because the cosmos depicted has become an integral part of the one-sung-over. The patient confirms this experience of unity and transcendence of the misfortune afflicting him or her through the destruction and dismissal of the spent sand painting.[24]

VISION QUESTS AND DREAMS

The vision quest is a ceremony in which children and adults voluntarily enter an episode of isolation characterized by fasting to seek the religious experience of a vision. Although the pursuit of vision quest may be found in many Native American cultures, in some societies this practice serves a central role in rituals of transition and initiation that accompany puberty. For several Indian cultures, the vision quest serves as the central practice of indigenous religious traditions.

In the Ojibwa cultures of the Great Lakes region, parents traditionally began to prepare children for vision quests and the accompanying vision fast early in a child's life. Children were taught early how generate and recognize a good vision. Children learned the necessity of living one's life according to the vision to procure the power and proof of the vision, prosperity and guidance through life. When an Ojibwa elder deemed a boy the appropriate age, the child would be led to a wooden platform built high in a tree and located a considerable distance from any village. There the youth would lie, abstaining from food, drink, and speech. If the young boy endured the fast without returning home prematurely or receiving a bad vision, he was usually rewarded with a vision and journey to the realm of spirits. There he would interact with spiritual beings and receive a physical token of the sprit that would serve as his guardian throughout the rest of his life. The religious experience endowed the youth with a heightened awareness of the importance and presence of spiritual forces, spiritual power, and local respect. The long period of preparation taught young males their gender roles and responsibilities as adults while inuring them to the mental and physical ordeals of adult life. The vision transformed boys into the men they must become and imbued them with the authority necessary to assume their new role.[25]

The practice of the vision quest is widespread among the cultures of North America. Native American cultures from the Maya to the Sioux to the Blackfeet incorporate the practice of vision or dream quests. These visions or dreams do not always focus on the acquisition of guardian spirits, and they vary in significance and purpose. Preparation rituals differ greatly across cultural boundaries, with some societies privileging spontaneous visionary experiences and others seeking a vision for several years. The experience is intensely individual and yet expresses the worldview of their culture, further binding an individual to society while allowing for personal expression and a degree of religious authority.[26] As many Native societies, such as the Shawnee and Sioux, experienced greater pressure from Western culture after European contact, the visions of their holy men and common practitioners began to include more symbols, figures and concepts that engaged, paralleled, or hybridized well with Christianity.[27] Although contemporary forms diminish the asceticism within the practice, the respect for dreams and the desire of many individuals for a vision remains an undercurrent of Native American communities.

THE CREEK GREEN CORN CEREMONIES

Within the religious practices of native North America, the symbols through which one expressed and experienced religion and reality were drawn from mundane elements of daily life. Elements of the environment were drafted and applied to communicate and reinforce understanding of the shape and forces of the universe. Patterns reflected in the natural world took on transcendent meanings, and the fundamental activities necessary for daily existence expressed religious truths just as their proper performance was imbued with religious truth and prescriptions. In a society of hunters "living on the flesh of animals, equipped with tools and sheltered by structures made of animal bones and skins," the religious practices and symbols are likely intertwined with the characteristics, habitat, and techniques required to hunt their chief game. Likewise, the daily religious practices of fishing societies and agriculturally specialized cultures tend to project their modes of sustenance and elements of the environment that surrounds them upon the cosmos. The religious is frequently understood by reference to the mundane and the supernatural expressed through symbolism rooted in nature.[28]

The Creek, one of the many southeastern cultures of North America that were subjected to the forced displacement in the 1830s now referred to as the Trail of Tears, traditionally tied the perceived cosmic cycle of renewal and the progression of time to the annual production of corn. The Green Corn

Ceremony, though tied to the symbolism and environments of eastern and southeastern North America, migrated with the displaced Creek and was adapted to the Creeks' new natural environment and circumstances. The ritual practice was consistently performed in varying forms from before European contact through the nineteenth century. Influenced by both the divergent cultural background and time periods of the observers, the written accounts of Native American practitioners, Euro-American travelers, and early ethnographers who recorded their experiences after witnessing the ceremony differ considerably.

However, despite the differences, the performance of the Creek Green Corn Ceremony or busk, generally followed a common structure. The ritual was usually enacted each July or August, when the green corn began to ripen and change color. The four- to eight-day ritual performance was focused within a ceremonially prepared sacred space a short distance from the village of local practitioners. The square space was framed on each side by a low log structure that opened onto the central square. The various categories of ritual performers resided within these buildings for the duration of the ceremony. Creek households were a secondary locus of the Green Corn Ceremony. Creeks cleaned their homes, especially the hearth, forgave most crimes and offenses, and repaired friendships in preparation for the imminent ritual of renewal. Finally, all fires were extinguished in the village and the more dramatic, public phase of the ritual commenced. Four hewn logs were oriented toward the cardinal directions within the center of the ceremonial space, strengthening the connection between the sacred area and fundamental cosmic structures. A fire was set in the center, upon which the religious professionals brewed an emetic elixir for the ritual performers, who remained within the consecrated area for four days, fasting and frequently partaking of the drink to assist their physical and spiritual purgation. The entire community practiced a more modest period of religious dietary regulation and abstained from consuming any corn during the course of the ritual, to honor the corn and delineate the time of the ceremony as distinct from the rest of the year. Creek practitioners also refused to imbibe salt and restricted relations between men and women.

The newly kindled fire, called the breath master, received offerings of green corn, a black drink made from roasted corn, and other precious items. Medicine men prepared infusions of medicines over the new flame before inviting the women of the village to enter the sacred space and rekindle their hearth fires from the new fire. For the first three days of the ritual performance, Creek men fasted and purged themselves while dancing, sometimes accompanied by women. The final day of the ceremony witnessed the breaking of the fast and dietary taboos as the new foods and corn were eaten. Frequently this feast was accompanied by a celebratory day of mock battles and dancing to honor the renewal of the world and inaugurate the new year.

The ritual performance of the Green Corn Ceremony demonstrates the correlation between the ripening of corn and the realization of the new year. The performance of the ceremony instituted the coming year and renewed the vital forces that made life possible. However, the repercussions of the annual rite were experienced each day the following year. It made each day possible and imbued each day with meaning. The Green Corn Ceremony celebrated peace and forgiveness as it concretized community and the cosmic powers of renewal. It strengthened kinship ties and recognized the dependence and inter-connectivity between human life and the processes of nature. Using the sym-bolism of the green corn, the busk celebrated life, reinforced the religious order of world, and initiated a new time. It was a time for reparation and new begin-nings that renewed the material and spiritual world, renewing the structures of the universe and filling it with vibrant, transformative powers of renewal.[29]

DELAWARE BIG HOUSE

The patterns and categories by which Native American cultures construct and negotiate their lives and universe are usually readily discernible. Myths and sacred stories naturally reflect and articulate such distinctions of value. However, the understandings that Native Americans used to frame and com-prehend their temporal-spatial reality are also revealed in culturally con-structed social hierarchies, architectural forms, and geography.[30] The Zuni erect their villages to reflect the patterns of the cosmos, and the Navajo mir-ror the universe in their understanding of their ancestral territories. Land-scapes, village layouts, and the architectural structures from ceremonial lodges to the homes of common villagers replicate the way in which Native American cultures perceive the forms and functions of the world about them. However, despite the complex diversity and rich cultural value systems manifest in relationships that articulate understandings of space, generations of observers of Native North America have shown a propensity to oversim-plify these conceptions into inaccurate universal statements applied generally to all Native American cultures.

To more fully understand the way in which religious worldviews are fre-quently expressed spatially and concretized in many Native American cultures and glimpse the polyvalent symbolism that can be expressed in native architec-ture, one may examine the temporal and spatial structure of the Delaware/Lenape Big House. The term that is translated here as *Big House* refers to both a religious ritual and the physical structure in which the rite takes place. For the Delaware, the origins of the religion of the Big House are found in the origins of the world itself, and thus the resulting ceremonial structure mirrors the universe with which it shares its birth.

The lodge is constructed of four walls that support a roof that is open in the center. A central pole erected in the floor of the lodge rises to penetrate this opening. The Delaware equate the floor of the lodge with the earth and the roof with the vault of the sky. The walls thus symbolically correlate with the four quadrants of the world. The central post bears a carved visage of the supreme being and creator of the Delaware, *mesi'ngok*. This figure is recognized as the central axis of the lodge structure and of the religion. The pole, grounded in the earth, extends through all of the 12 levels of reality in which *mesi'ngok* resides. Each of the support pillars along the walls displays the carved faces of the Manitou, or spirits, that correspond to the respective region of the cosmos. Below the earthen floors and the Earth that they represent are the various underworlds. To the east and west are doors associated with the rising sun, symbolic of the beginning of all things, and the setting sun, indicative of the end of things.

During the Big House ceremonies, movements within this ceremonial space are carefully prescribed and performed. Participants enter the lodge through the east door, move toward the north around the central post in a circular motion, and exit through the west door. The movements of the ritual participants reflect and reinforce the path of the sun and the white path, or the cycle of life. Within the boundaries of the lodge, and symbolically the cosmos, there are distinct places set aside for the people of each of the three clan structures. Within the seating spaces of the Wolf, Turtle, and Turkey clans, men and women are distinguished and separated.

The ceremony of the Big House ritually enacts the progression through one solar year. The ceremony is spread over 12 nights, each correlating to one of the 12 lunar months of every year. The ritualized dancing across the floor of the lodge traces the east-to-west movement of the sun and, more abstractly, the path of life from birth to death. The categorization of space within the lodge recognizes the distinct place and relationship between clans and men and women and designates a place for each within the schema of reality. The construction of the categories and designations represented in the Big House not only reinforces the concepts that structure the perception of the world but also offers a brief glimpse of the manner in which a people create and traverse their reality. Participation in annual rites such as the Big House ceremony is a reaffirmation of cultural values and identity and a reminder of one's place within the religiously structured geography of the cosmos.[31]

LAKOTA SUN DANCE

Perhaps the most commonly known ritual practice of Native North America is the dramatic Sun Dance. Variations of the Sun Dance were practiced among most of the Native American cultures of the Plains region of North America that regularly hunted buffalo, including the Arapaho, Blackfeet, Cheyenne, Crow, Dakota, Kiowa, Lakota, Plains Cree, Plains Ojibwa, Shoshone, and Ute. The performance, and even the name, of the rite varies among the peoples that observe the practice. Translations of the indigenous names of ritual vary from The Offerings Lodge and New Life Lodge to the Abstaining from Water Dance. Scholars usually trace the English term, Sun Dance, to the Lakota name for ceremony, *Wi wanyang wacipi*, or Sun Gazing Dance.

Although Native American peoples have divergent understandings of the origin and purpose of the sacred dance, the most diffuse interpretation belongs to the culture that is most often associated with the ritual, the Lakota. The Lakota understand the Sun Dance to be one of the Seven Sacred Rites spoken of by White Buffalo Calf Woman and passed to humanity through the visions of a prominent shaman. According to the holy man Black Elk, the visionary Kalaya was the first to perceive and give the Sun Dance to humanity. According to tradition, the ceremony is performed to initialize a renewal of the Earth and its people, to fulfill a previous vow, to express thanksgiving to spiritual powers, and to entreat those powers for prosperity, safety, or healing. The Sun Dance was performed annually. However, various cultures and different Euro-American observers of the ritual record different natural indicators of the appropriate time to perform the ceremony, such as when the trees are with leaf, when the buffalo are appropriately fattened, or when the chokeberries begin to ripen. Traditionally during the summer, usually the later part of June, geographically diffuse tribal groups gathered to perform the Sun Dance as well as renew and strengthen friendships and family ties, and conduct games and official tribal business. For many groups of practitioners, the sacred ceremony included several days of preparatory rites, followed by four days of rituals. Despite the infrequency of the annual ritual, the Sun Dance remains relevant to the practice of Lakota religiosity throughout the year. The ceremony reinforces the kinship relationships, between individuals and between humans and supernaturals, which form such a prominent role in many Native American religions and reinforce the communal commitment to the shared religious vision of the world.

The component elements of the Sun Dance similarly differ across cultural lines but usually include ritual purification in sweat lodges, the instruction of male pledgers, and prolonged fasting followed by dancing about a sacred pole erected in a ceremonially prepared space. The dance usually instills and reinforces the cultural values of bravery, honesty, and generosity. However, there were some ritual components not found in the practices of all participating cultures. During the Kado (the Sun Dance of the Kiowa), flesh piercing was taboo and the shedding of blood during sacred rites was understood to bring misfortune. Buffalo hunts and feasts, mock battles, and the ritual piercing of children's ears in associated puberty rites are also found in the Sun Dance practices of some peoples and not others.

According to Lakota tradition, each Sun Dance is overseen by a Leader, or Leader of the Dancers, who is charged with obtaining the necessary objects for the ceremony, and abstaining and fasting in the days leading up to the ceremony. This leader is also expected to dance, give away property, and submit to scarification and torture during the Sun Dance itself. The leader defines the "first degree" of commitment and involvement with the rite, which only one person can occupy. The leader spends the winter before the performance of the Sun Dance procuring the necessary items and living a life of ascetic discipline. The following June, he selects an assistant and entreats a holy man to take charge of the dance. This officiating priest directs the leader and his assistant. Each of the other dancers must also choose an assistant and request the guidance of a holy man. The Sun Dance likely played a prominent role in the income of holy men, or shamans, given their necessarily extensive participation in the ceremony.

Traditionally, the four days immediately preceding the Sun Dance were dedicated to making the necessary preparations for the ceremony. The participants spent these days preparing the required objects, learning the requisite holy songs, selecting those persons who would search the nearby territory for a sacred cottonwood, choosing an individual for ritually cutting and transporting the tree to the ceremonially prepared space. The leader spent his days consecrating the ritual artifacts for the rite and praying with a sacred pipe. The ceremonial ax had to be purified by the smoke of burning sweetgrass before it could be used to prepare the ritual space. The other artifacts were rubbed with sage and similarly purified in the smoke from the sweetgrass. The leader was also tasked with painting the sacred tree and preparing the buffalo calfskin, small chokecherry tree, bag of tallow, and symbolic representations that were required for the dance. Once the felled tree was erected in the ceremonial area, a holy man directed the construction of a sacred lodge around to symbolize the universe. During intensive sweat lodge purification ceremonies, the participating practitioners received additional instructions to properly perform the dance and vowed personal flesh-offering sacrifices on behalf of a variety of entities and for diverse reasons.[32]

The Sun Dance was usually performed amid a great communal gathering with other religious ceremonies planned around its performance. An individual's pledge to participate in the Sun Dance was often a voluntary fulfillment of vows made during times of misfortune or illness to obtain transformative healing from spiritual powers. Other practitioners participated to secure spiritual power to aid in approaching military endeavors. Frequently, men announced their intentions to perform the Sun Dance during a winter feast, after visiting a sweat lodge. Through the ceremony, dancers expressed a mix of thanksgiving and an anticipation of imminent boons. The dance was intended to lead participants to an understanding of the majesty and essential necessity of supernatural powers as they fulfill their personal vows.

The participants in the dance were classified according to a various levels of commitment and the different tasks of each. The second degree of involvement required the practitioner to perform the same tasks as the leader with the exception of acquiring and preparing the artifacts for the dance. The third degree involved all of the obligations of a second-degree participant but excluded torture. The fourth degree demanded the same responsibilities as the third degree except scarification. Usually, only two to five dancers were pierced at any given ceremony.

According to the outsider reports of an early professional anthropologist who observed a Sun Dance in 1882, the ceremonial encampment of over 9,000 Native Americans was three-fourths of a mile across and oriented so that it was open to the east. Other reports note that the camp was open to the north. The assembled host came from nearby tribes that had each been invited. The camp structures were all round constructions and were completed within the first several days of encampment by all available men and boys. Marshals, appointed by the officiating priest, or holy man, for the duration of the ceremony, oversaw the temporary settlement.

The Sun Dance ceremonies began with the purification rituals performed by the leader and officiating priest at a specially constructed tipi. Every morning of the ritual, the dancers assembled at the tipi to prepare and rehearsed the next evening's performance. On the third day, a party of experienced, possibly battle-wounded, warriors with reputations for bravery were selected to find or "hunt" the sacred tree used in the rite. They dressed for battle and rode ritually decorated horses while searching for the tree. These warriors would then recount their notable kills three times while reenacting them through pantomime. The warriors further imposed a martial presence over the proceedings, which was reflected in ritual symbolism and has led many scholars to heighten the association between the Sun Dance and successful military endeavors.

The pole was located and the center of the ceremonial area was designated on the fourth day. The appointed tree was the focus of the morning's ritual efforts. The leader, officiating holy man, and various assistants journeyed to the selected tree and presented a pipe as offering, consecrating a circle of the surrounding earth with an offering of calico. At noon, seven holy men and two singing societies accompanied the appointed warriors that returned to the tree to cut it. However, five designated men and three girls performed the actual felling of the tree in one recorded account. The tree was ceremonially cut to ensure that it fell toward the west and then carried to the ceremonial area. After the pole was painted, the assembled people sometimes attached offerings before it was finally erected. With the sacred center of the ritual space finally in place, the Lakota would perform women's puberty rites and ear-piercing ceremonies. These associated ceremonies involved extensive gift giving, resulting in the vast redistribution of wealth. The association of transformative initiation ceremonies at such important transitional periods in a person's life and the transfer of wealth between all the assembled Lakota strongly implies the overarching importance of kinship and connectivity in the Sun Dance ceremony.

The following day, the warriors assembled and charged an erected artificial shade. As they exited the shade, the dancers emerged dressed in ceremonial skirts, blue rawhide horns, and crowns of sage while carrying sprigs of artemisia. The leader then entered the ceremonial space with the buffalo skull in hand, followed by the officiating shaman and the assistants. Although they had fasted since the felling of the sacred tree, they danced until noon of the following day with only occasional breaks. The dancers were accompanied by two singing societies, a hide drum, and an eagle bone whistle.

On the morning of the final day, the piercing occured. This is the most dramatic aspect of the Sun Dance. The buffalo skull painted with sigils representing the four winds and the god of motion and release, *Taku Skanskan*, was positioned before an area of packed earth marked with the symbol of the four winds. The participants made an offering of tobacco before painting both tobacco and skull with red ocher. The dancers then offered a pipe, a bowl inset with a buffalo chip, artemisia, sweetgrass, and food offerings by placing them before the skull in a ceremonial pattern. At this time the dancers could be painted and the personal flesh offerings made through scarification. The leader was brought before the pole and pierced just above the nipples by a knife while a stick was inserted into the wound. The dancers bound themselves to the pole with rawhide ropes as the leader was led eastward to the end of a rope that yoked him to the pole by his fresh piercing. The congregated witnesses give away more goods, and ceremonies were performed to ensure the leader's timely release. When a designated song was performed, the leader began to struggle against his binding, attempting to break the piercing loose one side at a time. Once free, the participants offered thanksgiving and the Sun Dance was concluded.

The account of the Sun Dance detailed above has been synthesized from several highly variable records of Lakota and Oglala ceremonies. Despite the diversity of form of these Sun Dances, many of the essential themes and culturally relevant roles of the dance remain consistent. The Lakota performance of the Sun Dance was always individual, based on the voluntary fulfillment of individual vows, and communal, involving obligations from the dancers' families and the assembly of several tribal groups to witness the ceremony. The dance involved the preparation of circular sacred space, the erection of a central pole and nearby shaded area, and the binding of dancers to the pole in some fashion. The ceremony was symbolically linked to hunting and the buffalo through the buffalo skull, buffalo fur robes, and rawhide ropes as well as to warfare through the involvement of veteran warriors, kill talks, mock charges, and war symbolism. The dance required sacrificial offerings—often through personal flesh offerings and ceremonial torture—and rigorous discipline, frequently in the form of fasting.[33]

The importance of kinship within the Lakota religious world was revealed in the religious obligations of a voluntary dancer's family. After a man vowed his intention to participate in the Sun Dance of the following summer, usually during a winter feast after frequenting a sweat lodge, he was treated with heightened respect, and all members of his household were obligated to abstain from certain behaviors. The pledged dancer's family was expected to provide him with support, the finest food, a new ornamented pipe, and a new tool for his exclusive use. Within his tipi, an altar was erected with care and his pipe ash respectfully placed upon it. While the Sun Dance participant prepared for the ceremony by preserving the skull of each animal that he killed and dedicating a tobacco pouch and robe for sacrifice, his family was expected to give especially generously at the coming dance. In addition, the prominence and frequency of gift giving, the redistribution of wealth in Sun Dance ceremonies, and the importance of reciprocal vow fulfillment between humans and supernatural beings reflected the Lakota understanding of the religious importance of kinship relationships.

The Sun Dance of the Lakota reinforced communal identity and the kinship ties that bound tribes and the universe together for the rest of the year.[34] It also ritually marked the passage of time through its annual repetition. Practitioners and volunteers involved with the Sun Dance were treated to increased importance and often leadership in their tribes. Thus, one could interpret the

Sun Dance as serving an important role in the maintenance of group identities and the transition of tribal authority to those who would likely influence their lives for the next year. Participants danced in thanksgiving or in anticipation of an imminent blessing from spiritual power. The dancers understood their pledge and performance as pleasing to the sacred powers. Moreover, the correct performance of the dance demonstrated proper respect and knowledge of ceremonial customs and thus stemmed the misfortune and ruin that could otherwise result.[35]

CONCLUSION

The religious practices of Native North America demonstrate the incredible diversity and variation among Native American religions and peoples over time and across geography. Although many rituals were practiced by several peoples in a geographical region, each native culture possessed its own, unique religious tradition. Variations in the performance of common rituals between neighboring societies make it difficult to recognize many shared ceremonies. Even within a society, ritual productions differ according to the shaman in charge, motivation for the ritual, and the time and place of the performance. Ritual differentiation and definition is further complicated by the highly adaptable character of Native American religiosity. Although medicine men have frequently sought to meticulously recreate rituals according to inherited traditions, religious practices have changed in response to changes in geography, as likely occurred in the Green Corn Ceremony, or have been altered to express the religious worldview, expectations, and heartfelt needs of their specific peoples, which partially accounts for the differences in accounts of the Sun Dance. Other practices demonstrate responsiveness to the religious challenges of Western contact by dissolving, as did the regular practice of Maya bloodletting and consequently the reign of Mayan monarchs, or incorporating the imagery and religious influences of Christianity, as did Ojibwa vision quests of the nineteenth and twentieth century. On Native American reservations, in contemporary Native American neighborhoods, and through the practice of individual Native Americans, many of the traditions and practices continue to exist, engage new ideas, and adjust to their contemporary environment.

Regardless of the era or region, Native American religions incorporate the symbols and actions through which human life, society, and the world is structured, given meaning, and expressed. The religious practices of Native North America express the height of human desire and ability along with the basest elements of existence. Quotidian practices of subsistence and industry were understood and experienced within a reality defined by religious worldviews that tied human activity to sacred narratives. Native American worldviews reveal themselves through religious myths, symbols, religiously reinforced sources of social authority, and, most explicitly, in ritual performances. The regular religious practices presented in this chapter include examples from cultures from coast to coast and from pre-contact to the present. Each practice reveals one of the polyvalent means through which Native American religious elements, including imagery and concepts, and Native American themes, such as kinship and nature, were engaged and employed to define perceptions of space, time, and power that contextualized each moment of the experience of life. Although some of these practices were performed frequently by individuals and others were regular but infrequent group ceremonies, the religious experience, identity, and understanding of the relationship between humans and the rest of reality shape daily practices and life throughout the year. Native American religious rituals from the dramatic and infrequent to the individual and mundane reinforce and realize collective worldviews, giving the universe and communities order and structure and giving meaning to human experience in North America.

GLOSSARY

Big House: Refers to the Delaware religious ritual that re-creates the religiously structured geography of the cosmos; also refers to the physical structure in which the rite takes place.

Bloodletting: The act of making a deliberate incision into the skin with the purpose of causing blood loss, understood in a religious setting to serve as an offering to supernatural beings.

Green Corn Ceremony: The annual Creek ritual of renewal, also called the busk, which was observed to commemorate the ripening of corn, reinvigorate the vital forces of creation, and realize the New Year.

Prayer: The act of communication between a human being and a spiritual being.

Sand Painting: The ceremonial practice and resulting artwork created by sprinkling dried, powdered paints upon a prepared surface, usually as part of a larger religious ritual.

Shamans: Native American religious professionals gifted with the ability to interpret the source of social or individual misfortune and endowed with the ceremonial or spiritual abilities necessary to rectify the situation.

Sun Dance: A common practice involving sweat lodges, the instruction of males who had previously pledged to take part in the ceremony, and prolonged periods of fasting and group dancing around a sacred pole erected in a ritually prepared space. It had varying meanings and interpretations but was practiced by most of the Native

American cultures of the Plains region of North America, whose way of life was tied to the hunting of buffalo.

Vision Quest: A ceremony in which practitioners enter a voluntary period of isolation and deprivation to initiate a religious experience or vision.

NOTES

1. Catherine L. Albanese, *America: Religions and Religion*, 3rd ed. (Belmont, CA: Wadsworth, 1999), p. 25.
2. Sam D. Gill, *Native American Religions: An Introduction*, 2nd ed. (Toronto: Wadsworth, 2005), pp. 7–9.
3. Albanese, *America*, pp. 26–27.
4. Catherine L. Albanese, *Nature Religion in America: From Algonkian Indians to the New Age*, Chicago History of American Religion (Chicago: University of Chicago, 1990), p. 23.
5. Bruce G. Trigger, *The Children of Aataentsic: A History of the Huron People to 1660* (Montreal: McGill-Queen's, 1987), pp. 79–80.
6. Albanese, *America*, 26.
7. For the relevance and social implications of ritual practice, see Åke Hultkrantz, *Belief and Worship in Native North America*, ed. with an introduction by Christopher Vecsey (Syracuse: Syracuse University Press, 1981).
8. Black Elk, *The Sacred Pipe: Black Elk's Account of the Seven Rites of the Oglala Sioux, Recorded and Edited by Joseph Epes Brown* (Norman: University of Oklahoma, 1989), p. 106.
9. Gill, *Native American Religions*, pp. 4–7, 36–37; Sam D. Gill, *Sacred Words: A Study of Navajo Religion and Prayer*, Contributions in Intercultural and Comparative Studies (Westport, CT: Greenwood, 1981), pp. 179–187.
10. Gill, *Sacred Words*, 43.
11. Åke Hultkrantz, "A Decade of Progress: Works in North American Indian Religions in the 1980s," in *Religion in Native North America*, ed. Christopher Vecsey (Moscow: University of Idaho Press, 1990), p. 183.
12. Linda Schele and Mary Ellen Miller, *The Blood of Kings: Dynasty and Ritual in Maya Art* (Tokyo: Perpetua Press, 1986), pp. 14–15.
13. Diego de Landa, *Landa's Relación de las Cosas de Yucatan: A Translation*, ed. Algred M. Tozzer (New York: Kraus Reprint, 1966), pp. 118–119.
14. Ibid., p. 17.
15. Linda Schele and Mary Ellen Miller, *The Blood of Kings: Dynasty and Ritual in Maya Art* (New York: George Braziller, 1986), p. 176.
16. Linda Schele and Peter Mathews, *The Code of Kings: The Language of Seven Sacred Maya Temples and Tombs* (New York: Scribner, 1998), pp. 106–108.
17. For more on the association between ritual and political authority in urban Native North America, see Gregory D. Wilson, *The Archaeology of Everyday Life at Early Moundville* (Tuscaloosa: University of Alabama Press, 2008).

18. Schele and Miller, p. 184.
19. For more on the origins and history of the Navajo, see Peter Iverson, *Diné: A History of the Navajos* (Albuquerque: University of New Mexico Press, 2002).
20. Robert L. Hall, *An Archaeology of the Soul: North American Indian Belief and Ritual* (Chicago: University of Illinois Press, 1997), p. 161.
21. Arlene Hirschfelder and Paulette Molin, *The Encyclopedia of Native American Religions: An Introduction* (New York: Facts on File, 1992), pp. 253–255.
22. Discussion of the Nightway ceremony and descriptions of the Whirling Logs sand painting is possible due to the observations and analysis in Washington Matthews, *The Nightway Chant: A Navajo Ceremony* (New York: American Museum of Natural History, Memoirs vol. 6, 1902).
23. Sam Gill, *Native American Religious Action: A Performance Approach to Religion* (Columbia: University of South Carolina Press, 1987), p. 56.
24. Ibid., pp. 38, 56–57.
25. Gill, *Native American Religions*, 72.
26. Guy H. Cooper, "Individualism and Integration in Navajo Religion," in *Religion in Native North America*, p. 68.
27. For further study of the incorporation of Christianity into Native American traditions through Native American prophets and medicine men, see Gregory Evans Dowd, *A Spirited Resistance: The North American Indian Struggle for Unity, 1745–1815* (Baltimore: Johns Hopkins University Press, 1992), pp. 124–129; Daniel K. Richter, *Facing East from Indian Country: A Native History of Early America* (Cambridge: Harvard University Press, 2001), pp. 228–230; and Michael Hittman, *Wovoka and the Ghost Dance* (Lincoln: University of Nebraska Press, 1990), p. 63.
28. Gill, *Native American Religions*, p. 85.
29. Ibid., pp. 97–98.
30. For more on the importance of spatial understanding in Native American religions, see Vine Deloria Jr., *God Is Red: A Native View of Religion*, 3rd ed. (Golden, CO: Fulcrum, 2003).
31. Gill, *Native American Religions*, pp. 21–22.
32. Hirschfelder and Molin, pp. 285–286.
33. Clyde Holler, *Black Elk's Religion: The Sun Dance and Lakota Catholicism* (Syracuse: Syracuse University Press, 1995), pp. 68–73.
34. Hultzkrantz, *Belief and Worship in Native North America*, pp. 245, 260.
35. Holler, pp. 76–83.

BIBLIOGRAPHY

Albanese, Catherine L. *America: Religions and Religion*. 3rd ed. Belmont, CA: Wadsworth, 1999.

——. *Nature Religion in America: From Algonkian Indians to the New Age*. Chicago History of American Religion. Chicago: University of Chicago Press, 1990.

Black Elk. *The Sacred Pipe: Black Elk's Account of the Seven Rites of the Oglala Sioux*, *Recorded and Edited by Joseph Epes Brown*. Norman: University of Oklahoma Press, 1989.

Cooper, Guy H. "Individualism and Integration in Navajo Religion." In Christopher Vecsey, ed. *Religion in Native North America*. Caldwell: University of Idaho Press, 1990.

Diego de Landa. *Landa's Relación de las Cosas de Yucatan: A Translation*. Edited by Algred M. Tozzer. New York: Kraus Reprint, 1966.

Deloria, Vine Jr. *God Is Red: A Native View of Religion*. 3rd ed. Golden, CO: Fulcrum, 2003.

Dowd, Gregory Evans. *A Spirited Resistance: The North American Indian Struggle for Unity, 1745–1815*. Baltimore: Johns Hopkins University Press, 1992.

Gill, Sam D. *Sacred Words: A Study of Navajo Religion and Prayer*. Contributions in Intercultural and Comparative Studies. Westport, CT: Greenwood Press, 1981.

———. *Native American Religions: An Introduction*. 2nd ed. Toronto: Wadsworth, 2005.

———. *Native American Religious Action: A Performance Approach to Religion*. Columbia: University of South Carolina Press, 1987.

Hall, Robert L. *An Archaeology of the Soul: North American Indian Belief and Ritual*. Chicago: University of Illinois Press, 1997.

Hirschfelder, Arlene, and Paulette Molin. *The Encyclopedia of Native American Religions: An Introduction*. New York: Facts on File, 1992.

Hittman, Michael. *Wovoka and the Ghost Dance*. Lincoln: University of Nebraska Press, 1990.

Holler, Clyde. *Black Elk's Religion: The Sun Dance and Lakota Catholicism*. Syracuse: Syracuse University Press, 1995.

Hultkrantz, Åke. *Belief and Worship in Native North America*. Edited by Christopher Vecsey. Syracuse: Syracuse University Press, 1981.

———. "A Decade of Progress: Works in North American Indian Religions in the 1980s." In Christopher Vecsey, ed. *Religion in Native North America*. Moscow: University of Idaho Press, 1990, p. 183.

Iverson, Peter. *Diné: A History of the Navajos*. Albuquerque: University of New Mexico Press, 2002.

Matthews, Washington. *The Nightway Chant: A Navajo Ceremony*. Memoirs, vol. 6. New York: American Museum of Natural History, 1902.

Schele, Linda, and Peter Mathews. *The Code of Kings: The Language of Seven Sacred Maya Temples and Tombs*. New York: Scribner, 1998.

Schele, Linda, and Mary Ellen Miller. *The Blood of Kings: Dynasty and Ritual in Maya Art*. Tokyo: Perpetua Press, 1986.

Trigger, Bruce G. *The Children of Aataentsic: A History of the Huron People to 1660*. Montreal: McGill-Queen's University Press, 1987.

Wilson, Gregory D. *The Archaeology of Everyday Life at Early Moundville*. Tuscaloosa: University of Alabama Press, 2008.

Chapter 12

North America since 1492

Joseph Williams

INTRODUCTION

In 1922 a letter penned by E. C. Gault was sent to the editor of a Pentecostal periodical. It recounted the harrowing story of a woman who had been informed by doctors that she had cancer of the stomach and would live only a few more days. Searching for some type of answer, the woman's husband requested that Gault pray for his wife. When Gault arrived at this friend's home, he believed that God told him to read aloud the biblical story in which Jesus raised a man from the dead. After reading the story, Gault asked the woman, "Sister, now do you believe that He can heal you?" She replied, "I know He can do all things." Following prayer, Gault wrote, the woman was able to swallow water, something she had been unable to do for several days, and eventually she overcame her illness.[1]

Gault's letter appeared next to another letter to the editor entitled "Healing When Doctor Was Dismissed." Written by a Mrs. George Martin, this second letter told the story of Delscenia Bolt, a woman who had lost all feeling in her legs and suffered from convulsions. After exhausting all traditional medical routes to healing, Bolt turned to chiropractic and osteopathic medicine—two healing traditions that have since largely moved away from the explicit religious teachings of their founders, but that nevertheless were born out of what is sometimes referred to as metaphysical religion. When those failed, Miss Bolt requested ritual prayer and anointing with oil. Afterwards, she reported, she regained feeling in her legs and experienced no further symptoms.[2]

Although these claims of divine healing may appear atypical at first glance, both testimonies illustrate perennial themes that have shaped the practice of religion for countless individuals in North America ever since Columbus crossed the Atlantic. Gault's utilization of prayer coupled with his reading of the biblical story of one of Jesus's miracles reflected the dominant role of Christianity and of the Bible in the religious lives of many North Americans since 1492, and at the same time Martin's references to osteopathy and chiropractic medicine highlighted the fierce religious competition and cross-pollination that resulted from the extensive diversity of religious—and nonreligious—opinions that historically also have existed in Canada, Mexico, and the United States. Of course, these stories reflect only a handful of the numerous trends that have shaped the everyday religious rituals of North Americans, including trends in politics, economics, gender relations, and the interaction between different ethnic and racial groups, to name a few. Before we attempt to clarify some of these key characteristics of religion in the daily lives of North Americans, however, it is important to get a clear picture of just how diverse the religious landscape on the continent has been ever since Europeans first embarked across the Atlantic Ocean.

TIMELINE

1492:	Christopher Columbus lands on the island of San Salvador.
1519:	Hernán Cortés lands on the Mexican coast, paving the way for Catholic missionaries in Mexico.
1531:	Aztec peasant Juan Diego sees Latina incarnation of the Virgin Mary at Aztec goddess shrine.
1607:	English Anglicans arrive in Jamestown, Virginia.
1619:	First Africans brought to English America.
1620, 1630:	Two groups of English Puritans settle in what will eventually become the Commonwealth of Massachusetts.
1630–1649:	Jesuit missionaries in present-day Canada work among the Huron Indians.
1634:	Colony of Maryland founded as a safe haven for English Roman Catholics.
1654:	First Jews in North America arrive in New Amsterdam (present-day New York).
1791:	The First Amendment to the U.S. Constitution, which protects religious freedom in the United States, is formally ratified.
1820–1865:	Number of Catholics in the United States increases from 160,000 to 3.5 million.

1830:   Joseph Smith first publishes the Book of Mormon and organizes the Church of Jesus Christ of Latter-day Saints.

1860–1914:   Number of Jews in the United States increases from 150,000 to 3 million.

1906:   William Seymour founds Pentecostal Christianity in Los Angeles, California.

1917:   New Constitution approved in Mexico restricts the political activities of the Catholic Church.

1960:   John F. Kennedy becomes first Catholic U.S. president.

1964:   Malcolm X visits Mecca and breaks with Elijah Muhammad's Nation of Islam.

1965:   Immigration and Nationality Act of 1965 passed in the United States, loosening restrictions on the immigration of non-Europeans, who would bring with them a variety of new religious traditions to the continent.

1982:   Canadian Charter of Rights and Freedoms passed in Canada, explicitly guaranteeing Canadian citizens' right to freely practice their chosen religion without government interference.

HISTORICAL OVERVIEW OF RELIGION IN NORTH AMERICA

When Columbus landed on the island of San Salvador in 1492, he envisioned himself as much more than just an explorer expanding the political and economic influence of Spain. Instead, he specifically referred to the Spanish monarchs as "Catholic Christians and Princes devoted to the Holy Christian Faith" who sent him across the ocean "to see the said princes and peoples and lands and [to observe] the disposition of them and of all, and the manner in which may be undertaken their conversion to our Holy Faith."[3] In this manner Columbus and his successors initiated a period of contact between a wide variety of religious traditions on the North American continent that was sometimes violent, sometimes peaceful, but always transformative for the parties involved.

As it happens, diversity of religious practices in North America already existed well before 1492. When Columbus arrived on the scene there were approximately 15 million indigenous Americans representing hundreds of different language groups and societies. The distinctive myths, rituals, and ways of life among Native Americans varied greatly, frequently reflecting the geography, climate, and history informing the ways of life followed by particular tribes. For example, the religious symbolism of the Oglala Sioux, whose well-being directly depended on their ability to hunt the buffalo in North American prairies, would have made little sense to the Inuit, who inhabited the Arctic regions of North America.

The Europeans who colonized North America brought with them their own share of religious diversity. Spanish and French Catholics colonized different regions of the continent and created very different models for interacting with Native Americans. Spanish ministers accompanied by Spanish soldiers frequently set up missions modeled on Spanish towns, whereas French priests typically traveled in small numbers to indigenous villages. By the early 1600s, Protestants from Europe arrived, establishing settlements along the entire East Coast. Though the Puritans (so named because of their desire to purify the Church of England) who settled in and around Boston frequently receive a lot of attention, numerous other Protestant groups eventually arrived in the colonies, including non-Puritan Anglicans, Presbyterians, Baptists, Mennonites, Moravians, German Reformed, Dutch Reformed, and others. Further adding to the diversity, by 1634 Maryland became a haven for British Catholics, and in 1654 a small number of Jews settled in New Amsterdam (present-day New York).

Not all of the religious newcomers arrived of their own free will. In one of the darkest chapters of North American religious history, the slave trade brought 10 million Africans to the Americas, with approximately 427,000 arriving in the colonies. Most of the individuals who survived the brutal journey across the Atlantic followed traditional West African religious customs, though some were followers of Islam. Regardless of the particular religious affiliation of those brought to the New World, slave owners systematically sought to strip them of their religious beliefs and practices as part of a broader attempt to stamp out any resistance. To be sure, some traditional practices survived, but for the most part the slave owners were successful in effecting what one historian has labeled an "African spiritual holocaust."[4]

The injustice of slavery stood in sharp contrast to the ideals of religious freedom enshrined in the Constitution of the United States when the Bill of Rights was ratified in 1791. The First Amendment stipulated that "Congress shall make no law respecting an establishment of religion, or prohibiting the free exercise thereof." Ever since these words were penned, the U.S. courts have grappled with the implications of the First Amendment for the religious lives of the country's citizens. What exactly constitutes "establishing religion" and giving one religion special privileges above another? How should the government balance the public good with individuals' right to freely practice their religion? Clarifying the government's approach to these questions became all the more urgent as the country grew increasingly diverse from a religious standpoint.

RELIGION AND THE U.S. CONSTITUTION

By forbidding the "establishment" of religion in the First Amendment, the founding leaders of the United States made it very clear that no one religious group should receive preferential treatment from the federal government. Along similar lines, the framers of the U.S. Constitution stipulated in Article VI that "no religious test shall ever be required as a qualification to any office or public trust under the United States." An individual's religious beliefs and practices (or lack thereof), in other words, were not to be used as a formal qualification for government service. Significantly, for roughly 150 years after the founding of the United States, relatively few court cases related to the First Amendment's religion clauses made their way through the federal court system for the simple fact that the law applied only to the federal government; most cases related to religious freedom and government neutrality regarding religion fell under the jurisdiction of local and state governments.

This situation changed dramatically in the twentieth century when, in 1940, the Supreme Court ruled that the free-exercise clause applied equally to federal, state, and local governments (the Supreme Court made a similar ruling in relation to the establishment clause in 1947). Since that time, numerous Supreme Court opinions touching on issues of church and state have been handed down, a number of which have had a significant impact on the daily religious lives of Americans. The courts have established guidelines, for example, clarifying when prayer is and is not acceptable in public schools, when it is appropriate or inappropriate to display religious symbols (such as the Ten Commandments) on public property, and whether or not the national motto "In God We Trust" violates the First Amendment. For court cases touching on each of these particular issues, see the following: on school prayer, see *Engel v. Vitale* (1962), *Lee v. Weisman* (1992), and *Santa Fe v. Doe* (2000); on public displays of religious symbols, see *Stone v. Graham* (1980) and *Lynch v. Donnelly* (1984); for the reference to God in the national motto, see *Aronow v. United States* (1970).

In time, as Mexico and Canada took shape as independent nations, both countries would eventually join the United States in protecting the basic religious freedoms of their citizens, though battles over state sponsorship of religion frequently differed in significant respects from the United States. Canada's continued ties with Britain, as well as the influx of British loyalists following the American Revolution, nurtured the presence of Protestantism within the region, as can be seen in the continued influence into the twenty-first century of the

Anglican Church, the United Church of Canada (a denomination formed in 1925 uniting a large number of Presbyterian, Methodist, and Congregationalist Canadians), and the Lutheran Church. At the same time, the large presence of French Catholics in Québec ensured a significant degree of diversity of religion (by 1971, in fact, Catholics outnumbered Protestants in Canada), and also helped to establish a pattern of laws confirming the ability of the Canadian provinces to support particular religious establishments, such as public schools, associated with particular denominations. When the Canadian Charter of Rights and Freedoms passed in 1982, it explicitly guaranteed Canadian citizens' right to freely practice their chosen religion without government interference, but it lacked the type of establishment clause found in the First Amendment to the U.S. Constitution, which explicitly prohibited the government's endorsement of particular religions.

Despite these examples of the official establishment of religion in Canada, religious participation has declined among Canadians by the early twenty-first century to a much greater degree than it has among the two North American powers to the south. One 1995 survey found that only 70 percent of Canadians believed that there is a God, which is all the more striking considering the fact that, as recently as 1971, 99 percent of Canadians identified themselves as religious.[5] Not surprisingly, declining membership within most mainline denominations during the second half of the twentieth century accompanied the increased secularization of Canadian culture. That said, not all religious groups experienced declines during this period. A number of evangelical churches, for example, experienced significant growth during the latter decades of the twentieth century, including the Pentecostal Assemblies of Canada, the Christian and Missionary Alliance, and the Church of the Nazarene. Non-Christian groups, though still a very small proportion of the population, also grew as a result of immigration, including Islam, Hinduism, Sikhism, and Buddhism, which together composed nearly 5 percent of the population by 2001.[6] (*For more information see Chapter 14 in this volume, on religious pluralism in contemporary Montréal.*)

In Mexico the key point of debate regarding religious freedom has typically involved the powerful role of the Catholic Church in Mexican society. Catholic priests accompanied Hernán Cortés when he first landed on the Mexican coast in 1519, and Catholicism has played a significant role in the region ever since; in the year 2000 close to 90 percent of the population identified themselves as Catholic.[7] Despite the numerical dominance of Catholicism in Mexico, bitter conflicts have taken place, especially in the nineteenth century, between liberal political leaders who sought to curtail the Church's political and economic influence and more conservative leaders who fought to protect the Church's privileged status. Secularists eventually won these battles, cementing restrictions within the constitution of 1917 on the political activities of religious groups, and in particular on the political activities of the Catholic Church. These restrictions were eventually lifted.

Catholics were by no means the only religious group operating within Mexico, however. Individuals frequently combined Catholic symbolism with indigenous practices, for example, and the presence of other religious traditions was strengthened by missionary activity. Some of the other religious groups with a significant presence in Mexico included evangelical Christian groups such as pentecostal and charismatic Christians, mainline Protestants, Jehovah's Witnesses, Seventh-day Adventists, and Mormons.

Unlike Mexico, where Roman Catholics dominated the religious scene, in the United States Protestants remained the most prominent religious group into the twenty-first century both in terms of the number of adherents and in terms of public influence. At the same time, beginning in the nineteenth century in particular, they increasingly had to make room for Americans from other religious backgrounds. The phenomenal growth of Roman Catholicism serves as a case in point. Though Roman Catholics were a small minority within the American colonies, after the Revolution their numbers grew exponentially. From 1776 to 1820 the number of Roman Catholics in the United States jumped from 25,000 to 160,000, as believers arrived on American shores from countries such as Ireland, Germany, Italy, and Poland. By the end of the Civil War in 1865, 3.5 million Catholics called the United States their home; in fact, by this time Roman Catholicism represented the largest single denomination in the country. Immigration would continue to build the Roman Catholic presence in the United States into the twentieth century.

The growth of Judaism in the United States followed a similar pattern. In 1800 only 2,500 Jews lived in the United States. Various waves of Jewish immigrants throughout the eighteenth and nineteenth centuries, however, greatly increased the visibility of Jews within American cities. By 1860 the Jewish population mushroomed to 150,000, and by 1914, 3 million Jews resided in the United States. In particular, during the nineteenth century Ashkenazi Jews hailing from Germany sparked reform efforts, bringing with them more liberal forms of Judaism developed in their home country. Another large of wave of immigration lasted from 1880 to the dawn of World War I. Drawn to the United States as a haven from persecution in Eastern Europe, many of these immigrants brought with them more traditional, orthodox forms of the faith, though others promoted more radical visions of social reform that were indebted to modern thinkers who were often very critical of religion's role in society.

Religious diversity in the United States also increased as more and more Americans crafted their own religions. To varying degrees, many of these traditions offered modified forms of traditional Christianity, though as time went on more and more traditions reflected the influence of other religious forms of practice. During the nineteenth century representative traditions included utopian experiments such as John Humphrey Noyes's Oneida Community, Mary Baker Eddy's mind-cure teachings, known as Christian Science, and the popular Spiritualist movement, which revolved around mediums who communicated with the dead. Mormonism, another prominent newcomer on the American religious scene, was based on revelations Joseph Smith received from the angel Moroni regarding hidden golden tablets that told the story of Christ's appearance to the Nephites and Lamanites, forgotten peoples that Mormons believed populated the North American continent long ago. By the twentieth century such religious creativity had only increased. Though many African Americans eventually adapted to Christian forms of belief and practice, frequently joining Baptist and Methodist churches in particular, others created their own alternative traditions, such as the Nation of Islam, often in explicit repudiation of the so-called "white man's religion." New Age religions drew on currents associated metaphysical traditions in the United States as well as other trends such as the burgeoning feminist movement, while other Americans felt more and more comfortable borrowing practices from multiple traditions as they crafted their own unique style of spirituality.

As the twentieth century progressed, Americans had more and more traditions to draw from. Changing immigration laws during the 1960s, such as the Immigration and Nationality Act of 1965, loosened restrictions on individuals from non-European countries, which helped expand the number of adherents in the United States to traditions such as Buddhism, Hinduism, and Islam. Both Buddhism and Hinduism have been particularly effective in spreading meditative practices in the United States associated with their traditions. For their part, by the early twenty-first century Muslims represented one of the fastest-growing religions in the United States.

RELIGION IN THE DAILY LIVES OF NORTH AMERICANS

As the brief history of North American religion detailed above demonstrates, religious traditions associated with Christianity have typically been dominant on the continent since Columbus sailed to the New World from Spain, but this should not detract from the remarkable diversity of religious traditions—both within and outside of Christianity—that have taken root in North America. This diversity makes it difficult to summarize how religion has shaped the daily lives of North Americans, and although many developments within North American religion are touched on in other chapters (see, for example, Chapters 16, 21, and 22 in Volume 2 on the impact of science, consumerism, and civil religion on religious practices), the following trends provide one possible avenue for exploring major themes in the region. First and foremost, the everyday religious practices of North Americans reveal the significant degree of adaptation and what I will refer to as "combinationism" that occurred as different religious traditions came in contact with one another and borrowed from other religions' ritual repertoire. Second, the democratic ideals of equality and freedom of conscience unleashed following the American Revolution also exerted a profound impact on North Americans' daily religious lives as individuals felt empowered to craft their own unique religious beliefs and practices. Finally, the increased pluralism and secularization within certain aspects of North American societies beginning especially in the twentieth century likewise have reshaped believers' religious lives in significant ways.

Adaptation and Combinationism in the Daily Religious Lives of North Americans

The presence of numerous different religious traditions on North American religious soil since 1492 ensured a significant degree of contact between individuals with very different perspectives on the world. This contact frequently transformed the practice of religion for individuals. At times, the contact led to a peaceful exchange of religious ideas and practices as religious groups interacted with one another and even incorporated aspects of other traditions into their own. At other times the contact was more antagonistic and violent, leading to the repression of particular religious rituals and ideas or to the creation of new religious practices meant to resist the dominant tradition.

On the one hand, the initial encounter between Europeans and Native Americans illustrated the ways in which contact between different religious groups frequently led to violent attacks on the daily religious practices of indigenous tribes. As was explicitly argued by figures such as Juan Ginés de Sepúlveda of Spain, many of the colonizers who arrived in the New World saw the original inhabitants of North America as intrinsically inferior to Europeans, and they believed that the Native Americans' way of life was uncivilized and demonic. Such assumptions facilitated the enslavement of Native Americans by the Spanish in particular, and early Catholic missionaries frequently sought to strip Native Americans of a wide variety of customs, including their sexual practices and norms, their shamanic healing rituals, and their reliance on dreams to predict the future. (See Chapter 11.) Missionaries then sought to replace these indigenous practices with traditional Christian rituals and values, focusing especially on rites associated with baptism, communion, and the basic tenets of the Christian faith.

Despite the violence that frequently accompanied the initial encounter between Europeans and Native North American tribes, such encounters also initiated a long tradition within North America in which individuals willingly combined religious practices from the different traditions to which they had been exposed. The celebration of the Day of Dead (*Día de los Muertos* in Spanish), which continues to the present, serves as a case in point. Initially observed among indigenous tribes in present-day Mexico as a month-long celebration revolving around the goddess Mictecacihuatl ("The Lady of the Dead"), Catholic priests eventually moved the celebration to coincide with All Saints' Day and All Soul's Day in the Catholic calendar, which fall on the first two days of November. As the new dates suggest, though the holiday derives from indigenous religious practices, significant Catholic elements have been incorporated into the celebration. Meant as time to honor and communicate with deceased relatives, individuals visit and decorate the gravesites of loved ones, or engage in festivities. In a clear sign of Catholic influence, participants frequently construct altars in their homes that include explicit Catholic symbols such as crosses and images of the Virgin Mary in addition to other items such as candles and images of the deceased.

The Virgin Mary herself serves as another great example of the intermingling of indigenous practices with Catholicism, as can be seen in Mexicans' devotion to Mary ("Our Lady of Guadalupe") as the divine patron of Mexico. The first signs of such combinationism[8] date back to 1531, when it is said that Juan Diego was walking near a shrine at Tepeyac for the mother goddess Tonantzin. Unexpectedly, a young woman met Diego and instructed him to collect flowers and deliver them to the Catholic bishop. Diego did as he was told, and when he unwrapped the cloth with the flowers in front of the bishop, the image of an Indian Virgin Mary appeared on the cloth—a visible symbol of the merger of indigenous conceptions of a mother Goddess with the Christian imagery surrounding Mary. Ever since this time the shrine for Tonantzin became a place to honor Mary, the "Virgin of Guadalupe."

Examples of both the violent repression of believers' daily ritual practices and of combinationism involving different religious traditions in North America only multiplied as the continent became more and more religiously diverse. As mentioned above, the religious systems brought over from West Africa during the slave trade were systematically suppressed by plantation owners, yet specific practices survived and merged with Christian practices to form a new religious amalgam. Such religious creativity flourished in particular within the secretive religious world constructed by slaves, a world that operated without formal leadership or buildings, and, most importantly, beyond the control of slave owners. It was here that the African American musical tradition referred to as spirituals was born. Combining elements of Christian hymnody and African music, black Christians perfected a call-and-response singing style that frequently utilized biblical imagery—such as references to the Hebrews' enslavement by the Egyptians—that simultaneously spoke to the deplorable conditions of slavery. As one spiritual proclaimed, "Oh! Fader Abraham/Go down into Dixie's land/Tell Jeff Davis/To let my people go./Down in de house of bondage/Dey have watch and waited long,/De oppressor's heel is heavy,/De oppressor's arm is strong./Oh, Fader Abraham."[9]

Whereas African American spirituals illustrate the way in which many of the combinative forms of religious practice in North America reflected the strong influence of Christianity, in addition to explicit combinationism, at times members of smaller, less dominant religious traditions simply adapted religious practices to better accord with the habits and lifestyles followed by their Christian neighbors. Many Jewish immigrants to the United States, for example, consciously shed some of their distinctive practices to fit in better with the broader society. Traditionally, Jewish dietary laws strictly regulated not only what Jews could or could not eat but also how the food was prepared. According to the Jewish law, for instance, eating shellfish such as shrimp was forbidden, and all meat and dairy products were to be kept apart both in the preparation and consumption of food. If strictly followed, these dietary laws affected much more than what a Jewish person could or could not eat; rather, they also helped shape Jews' interactions with outsiders, as Orthodox Jews would find it difficult to follow such guidelines when eating in non-kosher homes or at non-kosher restaurants. Building on reforms already under way among Jews in Germany, some American Jews thought such restrictions unnecessary, and they decided to focus more on the ethical demands within the Jewish tradition. In addition to challenging traditional kosher laws, these reformers loosened requirements regarding distinctive articles of clothing traditionally worn by Jews, such as the *kippah* (yarmulke); they began to incorporate organs into their synagogues; and they typically were less strict in their observance of the Sabbath.

THE PITTSBURGH PLATFORM

The Pittsburgh Platform, which appeared in 1885, served as a classic statement of the principles guiding the Reform movement within American

Judaism, which sought to adapt traditional Jewish practices in ways that allowed Jews to more fully participate in their surrounding cultures. The following extract from the document illustrates the rationale supporting key elements of the Reform movement's agenda:

> We recognize in the Mosaic legislation a system of training the Jewish people for its mission during its national life in Palestine, and today we accept as binding only the moral laws, and maintain only such ceremonies as elevate and sanctify our lives, but reject all such as are not adapted to the views and habits of modern civilization. We hold that all such Mosaic and rabbinical laws as regulate diet, priestly purity and dress originated in ages and under influences of ideas altogether foreign to our present mental and spiritual state. They fail to impress the modern Jew with a spirit of holiness; their observance in our days is apt rather to obstruct than to further modern spiritual elevation. . . . We recognize in Judaism a progressive religion, ever striving to be in accord with the postulates of reason.

At the same time that smaller religious traditions were adapting to fit in with the Christian majority, Christians themselves also frequently reconfigured their religious practices after encountering other religious traditions, as can be seen in many Christians' interest in the supernatural abilities associated with magicians and practitioners of metaphysical forms of religion (sometimes referred to as occultism). Almanacs, for example, which could be found in every corner of the colonies, contained astrological charts that helped individuals decide everything from when to plant certain crops to when to treat certain parts of the body. Colonists also relied on "wise men" and "wise women" to help them locate lost items or heal diseases. Ministers frequently warned their parishioners that magical and metaphysical practices invited Satanic activity, and for a time such fears helped spur witch trials, such as the infamous Salem witch trials of 1692. Try as they might, however, Christian leaders never succeeded in stamping out such practices.

In one of the clearest examples of the impact of metaphysical spirituality on the daily ritual lives of Christians in North America, the nineteenth-century teachings promoted by Mary Baker Eddy known as Christian Science specifically combined Christian and metaphysical sensibilities. On the one hand, Eddy drew on traditional Christian symbols and language, but her understanding of these symbols took on a distinctly metaphysical cast. For Eddy, God was more of a divine Principle or divine Mind than a personal being, and she went so far as to claim that the physical, material world was only an illusion. If humans really understood their true nature, she taught, they would recognize their immortality and their connection to the divine Principle. Here, none other than Jesus Christ served as the ideal role model who demonstrated for others how to live a life in connection with Love and the divine Mind. In terms of Christian Scientists' ritual lives, Eddy's teachings gave rise to distinctive healing practices, and in particular to a form of mental healing premised on the illusory nature of pain and illness. Eddy believed that individuals could remove all sickness as well as all roadblocks to living in connection with God by continually transforming their thoughts and concentrating on the Truth, often with the help of a Christian Science practitioner. At the same time, physical discipline was also necessary to reduce any reliance on human, physical aid, which has often led to restrictions among Christian Scientists on medicines and other substances such as alcohol and tobacco.

By the twentieth and early twenty-first centuries, the combinative, adaptive tendencies in the everyday religious practices of North Americans as described above persisted in ever more visible ways. The daily ritual lives of a wide variety of Americans pointed to a perennial willingness on the part of many North Americans to incorporate a wide variety of religious practices into their daily routines. Before we assess these more recent trends in the practice of religion in North America, however, it is important to clarify another important factor that contributed to the ever-increasing diversity of religion on the continent: namely, the democratizing effects of the American Revolution and in particular of the First Amendment's guarantee of religious freedom in the United States.

Democratization of North American Religious Practices

In a stroke of a pen, the authors of the U.S. Constitution's Bill of Rights formally granted religious freedom to the nation's citizens. Though this ideal has been imperfectly realized on the continent since the late eighteenth century, and despite the fact that religious institutions have continued to wield powerful influence in the lives of individuals into the present, the First Amendment nevertheless opened the door for a dramatic democratization of religious practices in which individuals openly celebrated their ability to craft their own spiritual pathways apart from the control of religious authorities. Not surprisingly, the early republic became a hotbed of religious innovation and experimentation as individuals confidently promoted their newfound religious insights.

To a certain degree, the democratizing impulse within North American religion was already visible within the colonies. Considering the large number of Protestants in the colonies, this should come as little surprise. Protestants typically highlighted the responsibility of all believers to search the Scriptures for themselves. This emphasis facilitated higher literacy rates, and it also had the unintended consequence of encouraging religious creativity as individuals challenged the consensus view on a variety of matters. The life of Anne Hutchinson serves as a case in point. Shortly after arriving in the Massachusetts Bay Colony in the 1630s, Hutchinson drew the ire of the colonial leadership by interpreting the Bible on her own and then teaching large groups of individuals in her home on religious topics. Considered a threat to social order, Hutchinson was placed on trial. During the proceedings, Hutchinson confirmed her ability to hear directly from God. This admission helped seal her fate; following her trial she was banished from colony.

Instances of individuals such as Anne Hutchinson charting their own religious paths and challenging the religious lifestyles of their neighbors increased exponentially by the late eighteenth and early nineteenth century. Nurtured by a fresh sense of optimism and excitement that accompanied the fledgling years of democracy in the United States, religious innovators often found receptive audiences as they advertised their new religious wares. A classic example of such trends can be seen in the Shakers. Founded by Ann Lee (known to her followers as Mother Ann), an Englishwoman who first arrived in New York in 1774, the Shakers eventually established a communitarian society where property within the community belonged to everyone equally. Though by no means the only communal experiment in the early republic, the Shakers stood out because of a number of distinctive practices that set them apart from their neighbors. For example, Shakers believed that the origin of all sin lay in sexual intercourse. Accordingly, those who joined the community agreed to live a celibate lifestyle. The Shakers were also known for their ritualized dances that could last into the night and culminate in an ecstatic union with God and Mother Ann. (The Shakers believed that Jesus Christ represented the male manifestation of God, and that Mother Ann represented the female manifestation of God on earth.) By 1837 mediums who conversed with spirits had become an important part of Shaker ritual life. As it happens, mediums unassociated with the Shakers, most of whom were women, would become more and more visible within American culture as the nineteenth century progressed, as can be seen in the popularity of the Spiritualist movement.

Whereas Shaker communities declined following the Civil War and consisted of only about 4,000 members at their height, another new religious movement born during the early nineteenth century, the Mormons, would manage to establish a more permanent presence on the American religious map as it introduced its own set of innovative ritual practices. Formally referred to as the Church of Jesus Christ of Latter-day Saints, Mormonism originated in the teachings of Joseph Smith during the early nineteenth cen-

The ritualized dances practiced by the Shakers, pictured above, often lasted into the night. For practitioners, the dances could culminate in an ecstatic union with God and Mother Ann, the founder of the movement. Mother Ann (as she was known by her followers) first arrived in New York in 1774, and eventually established a communitarian society where property belonged to everyone equally and each individual agreed to live a celibate lifestyle. (Library of Congress.)

tury. Though outsiders often associate Mormons with the practice of polygamy—a practice that church leaders formally abandoned in the late nineteenth century—other, lesser-known rituals and practices continued to shape the daily lives of adherents into the twentieth and twenty-first centuries. One of Smith's most important contributions to the daily lives of numerous North Americans was the Book of Mormon. According to Smith, the angel Moroni appeared to him and revealed the location of buried golden plates containing the long-forgotten religious history of North America. Along with the Bible (as well as continuing revelations given to Smith and subsequent leaders of the church), the Book of Mormon formed the bedrock of Mormon belief and practice. Other distinctive Mormon practices derived from their emphasis on the sacredness of the material world, and their tendency to collapse sharp distinctions between spirit and nature. Such beliefs reinforced practices aimed at physical health and well-being, such as restrictions on alcohol, tobacco, caffeine, and to a certain degree meat. In addition, marriage was considered by Mormons to be an eternal commitment between a man and a woman. Not only would husbands and wives be united to one another for all time, but such a bond was necessary if individuals were to fully progress in their spiritual development. In another illustration of the importance of the physical world in Mormons' daily lives, devout Mormons committed to wear a special undergarment both day and night. Received during special ceremonies conducted in Mormon temples, these undergarments reminded believers of their commitment to obey God.

It is important to note that new religious movements were by no means the only site of democratization within Americans' religious practices. Adherents within more established religions also grappled with the new energies let loose at the founding of the United States. Some of the most profound changes in the ritual lives of Americans during the early history of the United States occurred among black Christians in the North, who were free but nevertheless experienced significant discrimination. African American Christians in the North, for example, suffered a variety of injustices ranging from the denial of burial spots on church grounds, to segregated seating within sanctuaries, to being offered communion only after white members had been served. By the early nineteenth century independent black denominations such as the African Methodist Episcopal Church had been formed, providing many African Americans with independent control over key aspects of their religious lives.

The experience of American Catholics likewise served as a conspicuous example of democratization in the religious practices of Americans. In fact, Catholicism in the colonies already bore significant marks of democratization because of the paucity of priests. The few priests who were in the colonies often itinerated, making interaction with a priest an infrequent affair. In such a climate a form of domestic Catholicism developed wherein many of the rituals that normally would occur within a church were instead conducted in homes, and the formal sacramental rituals of the church became less prominent as believers had to cultivate more private, devotional forms of the faith that they could practice on their own. Following the American Revolution, Catholic leaders, such as John Carroll, who embraced the ethos of the new nation built on the pre-Revolutionary trends in American Catholicism to fashion a uniquely American brand of the faith, emphasizing for example the importance of a separate educational system for Catholic Americans, as well as churches run by lay trustees who were elected by church members instead of appointed by the church hierarchy. Because of papal opposition as well as criticism from foreign-born priests, many facets of Carroll's vision never took permanent hold, but the democratic, individualistic tenor of American Catholicism when compared with the official positions of the Church in Rome would continue to manifest in the daily lives of American Catholics up through the present, as can be seen in many adherents' disagreement with the Church's condemnation of birth control measures as well as the Church's restrictions on female priests.

Not surprisingly, American Protestants also evidenced the impact of democratizing forces in their daily lives, as can be seen in the proliferation of voluntary societies beginning in the first half of the nineteenth century. Though several of the initial voluntary societies were organized to plant new churches, a host of societies sprang up with wide-ranging missions. Bible societies published literature for missionaries; other societies worked to provide biblical instruction for children; and others focused on the development of colleges and seminaries built to provide a steady supply of clergy to the churches. Another set of societies fought everything from slavery, to alcohol consumption, to war. In each case, these societies provided an avenue for laypersons to translate their religious sense of duty into practical action without any need of formal approval from a formal denomination. As such, the growth of voluntary societies illustrated the powerful pull of democratizing forces in the daily lives of American Protestants.

The Spiritual Marketplace of North American Religion during the Twentieth and Twenty-First Centuries

By the twentieth and twenty-first centuries, new developments on the North American continent only increased the diversity of an already diverse religious landscape. Previously marginalized groups increasingly found their voice within a wide variety of religious traditions. At the same time, immigrants from different parts of the globe brought new forms of religious practice to North American societies. The rapid modernization and, in certain respects, secularization reshaping North American culture also added to the religious and nonreligious options available to individuals on the continent. To be sure, many North Americans resisted the increasing pluralism and relativism characteristic of North American religion, and Christianity retained its position as the faith of the vast majority of North Americans. Nevertheless, it is also fair to say that the "spiritual marketplace"[10] of North American religion during the twentieth and twenty-first centuries proved as diverse—and competitive—as ever.

Protestant and Catholic forms of Christianity remained central in the lives of the majority of North Americans. In a very significant development for

Catholics, in 1960 the United States elected its first Catholic president, John F. Kennedy. Around this same time major reforms in the Catholic Church connected to a special church council referred to as Vatican II helped set in motion new patterns in the ritual lives of many North American Catholics. Representative of these changes, following Vatican II significant changes were introduced in the way adherents experienced the Catholic Mass. For example, the Mass was conducted in the local language instead of Latin; priests began facing the congregation instead of facing the altar; and greater participation on the part of laypersons was encouraged.

Whereas Catholics outnumbered Protestants for the first time in Canada in the 1970s, Protestants remained the larger tradition in the United States during the twentieth century. Despite Protestant groups' shared heritage, however, sharp divisions emerged pitting various North American Protestants against one another, often as a result of very different reactions to modernizing trends. Resistance to religious change during the twentieth century was especially apparent among opponents of modernized forms of Christianity who defended more traditional forms of the faith against the growing impact of pluralism and secularization. Numerous North American Christians had for centuries sought to harmonize their religious practices with the rapid scientific progress transforming modern societies, and by the early twentieth century the conflict between so-called fundamentalist and modernists came to a head. On the one hand, conservative evangelical Christians in particular resisted trends in biblical scholarship that tended to treat the Bible as a product of human creativity as opposed to the divine words of God; they also repudiated attempts to reconcile the Biblical account of creation with such developments as Darwin's theory of evolution. For Christians on the liberal side of this divide, on the other hand, concerted social action and social justice increasingly stole the spotlight away from the more traditional emphasis in evangelical circles on converting non-Christians to the faith, as can be seen in the efforts of figures such as Martin Luther King Jr. to organize nonviolent protests against the racial injustice in the South. As the century progressed, similar liberal versus conservative disagreements played out between various religious groups in North America in relation to a host of issues ranging from school prayer, to abortion, to homosexual marriage, to the teaching of intelligent design rather than evolution in the public schools.

AIMEE SEMPLE MCPHERSON

When Aimee Semple McPherson first encountered Darwin's theory of evolution in her high school geology class during the early 1900s, his ideas shocked her religious sensibilities and in particular her confidence in the accuracy of the Bible. Having been raised in a conservative Christian home in Canada, McPherson accepted a literal interpretation of the biblical creation account in the book of Genesis, wherein God created the world and everything in it over a one-week period. If evolutionists were correct about natural selection and the descent of all living organisms from a common ancestor, she realized, then a literal reading of the creation story must be false. In McPherson's eyes, a stark decision between the Bible and evolution lay before her. "[I]f the Bible is mistaken in one place," she later explained, "it is very apt to be mistaken in others."[11] McPherson decided to trust the Bible. Indicative of the cross-fertilization of religion across national boundaries in North America, in the ensuing years McPherson joined the Pentecostal movement and moved to the United States, eventually becoming a very outspoken critic of anyone who she thought undermined traditional religion and in particular conservative forms of Christianity. With her church, Angelus Temple, listed as tourist attraction in Los Angeles guidebooks, McPherson was the first woman in the United States to obtain a radio broadcast license, and she perfected the art of Broadway-like performances known as illustrated sermons. Dressed as a police officer, McPherson rode on a motorcycle into a service and placed sin under arrest. She prayed for the sick in her audience wearing a nurse's uniform, and at another time terrorized the devil using a pitchfork. "Whether you like it or not," the Hollywood star Charlie Chaplin told McPherson, "you're an actress."[12] Although McPherson's life may appear atypical, her early dilemma over the authority of the Bible and her later willingness to experiment with new forms of religious rituals illustrated classic themes that have shaped the practice of religion for countless individuals in North America.

At the same time that Christianity remained the religion of choice for most North Americans, the combinationism as well as the democratization evident in North American religious practices continued unabated into the twentieth and twenty-first centuries. Take, for example, the twentieth-century ritual lives of participants in the Peace Mission Movement. Founded by George Baker, later known as Father Divine, the Peace Mission Movement drew both black and white adherents who lived together in a community directed by Father Divine. Reflective of trends associated with the holiness movement in North American Christianity, Father Divine taught his followers to avoid tobacco, alcohol, and drugs, while also providing food, shelter, and even jobs for those in need. The influence of New Thought, a metaphysical tradition that emphasized the power of the mind, can also be seen in Father Divine's teaching; he frequently instructed his followers regarding the power of the mind and of speech, directing adherents to avoid negative words. For example, Father Divine encouraged members of his community to refrain from the common salutation "hello," given the reference to "hell" embedded in the term. He recommended a simple greeting of "Peace" instead.

As the twentieth century progressed, numerous North Americans felt more and more comfortable not only modifying the cultural inheritance bequeathed by the dominant Christian tradition, but also directly challenging it. In one of the most prominent examples of such trends, New Age spirituality during the twentieth century tapped into many North Americans' dissatisfaction with Western forms of religion. Though their practices are difficult to summarize because of the movement's lack of institutional structure, many New Age practitioners embraced a set of religious practices strongly influenced by non-Western religious traditions that reflected metaphysical assumptions celebrating the spiritual power coursing through nature. Often, individuals in the New Age movement drew on feminists' criticisms of what they saw as misogynistic assumptions embedded in traditions such as Christianity that demeaned women as well as the natural world. Such believers frequently substituted female symbolism such as the Earth Goddess for the male-centric imagery associated with monotheistic religions. Common rituals associated with the movement included Reiki palm healing imported from Japan, shamanistic spirit journeys borrowed from Native American spirituality and other similar traditions, and extensive use of objects, such as crystals, that provided access to the spiritual energy pervading the universe.

Considering the strong connection between Christianity and slavery in the South, it should come as little surprise that a number of African Americans during the twentieth century likewise grew disenchanted with Christian forms of belief and practice. Instead of turning to New Age traditions, however, many simply embraced a rival form of monotheism, Islam. Early signs of this development appeared in the late nineteenth century; the Presbyterian minister Edward W. Blyden, for example, encountered Islam during his travels to Africa and became convinced that Islam afforded black Americans better opportunities than did Christianity. Though the majority of African American Muslims would eventually identify with more traditional forms of Sunni Islam, initially a significant proportion of these converts accepted the teachings of the Nation of Islam. In highly racialized rhetoric demonizing whites, the movement's leaders, Wallace D. Fard and Elijah Muhammad, promoted Islam as the key vehicle for restoring black power on the earth. Though the Nation of Islam perpetuated mainstream Islamic emphases such as prohibitions against the consumption of pork and alcohol, it was quite unlike traditional Islam in that adherents considered Fard a messianic figure and called for the formation of a separate nation composed solely of African Americans.

MALCOLM X

One of the most recognizable adherents to the Nation of Islam was Malcolm X. Born as Malcolm Little, Malcolm X discovered in the Nation of Islam both an explanation for and a means of resistance against the racially motivated injustice he experienced in American society. Following a pilgrimage to Mecca in 1964 (a duty required of all Muslims), however, Malcolm X embraced a more inclusive vision of Islam, and he began to distance himself from the Nation of Islam. Though Malcolm X was murdered in 1965, beginning in the 1970s Elijah Muhammad's son, Wallace D. Muhammad, followed in Malcolm X's footsteps as he sought to bring the organization in line with more traditional forms of Islamic belief and practice. Those still committed to message of black superiority, on the other hand, typically followed such figures as Louis Farrakhan.

The growing presence of religious practices unaffiliated with Christianity during the twentieth century was also a result of new immigration patterns, and in particular the arrival of more and more non-Europeans on the continent. The number of immigrants from Asia during the twentieth century, for example, grew exponentially, especially in the final third of the twentieth century. This development greatly increased the presence of Buddhism and Hinduism in both the United States and Canada. The impact of these religions in the daily lives of North Americans is especially apparent in the wide appeal of meditative practices frequently associated with the two traditions. Through the efforts of figures such as Paramahansa Yogananda and Daisetz Teitaro Suzuki, books and classes teaching the basic principles behind yoga and Zen meditative techniques spread the influence of these religious traditions throughout the continent. As it happens, though Buddhism and Hinduism attracted a growing number of converts, many North Americans practiced the meditative techniques associated with these traditions without relinquishing previously held religious commitments, creating their own new combinative forms of religious practice in the process.

In addition to increased immigration from Asia, the arrival of significant numbers of Arab American Muslims exemplified the adaptations numerous twentieth-century newcomers themselves made to their everyday religious practices. Many Arab immigrants found themselves for the first time in a culture largely indifferent to Islamic patterns of life. Pressing questions arose: Should Muslims attend public schools? Given North Americans' heavy reliance on credit to obtain everything from homes, to education, to transportation, should Muslims discard traditional prohibitions on interest-bearing loans? What about dietary restrictions? What should Muslims do if ritually prepared Halal meat is unavailable? Should women attend the mosques? What is the proper role of the role of imams? Should they simply lead prayers, as is often the case in the Middle East, or should they mirror pastors and rabbis in the United States who frequently counsel adherents and conduct funerals, baptisms, and so forth. On many of these questions a majority of Arab American Muslims found it necessary to adapt their traditional practices simply to survive. Other, more conservative Muslims, however, lamented the eroding effect of American culture on what they perceived as true Muslim piety.

As the experience of more conservative Arab American Muslims suggests, the movement away from traditional forms of religion evident in the daily ritual lives of many North Americans has not been warmly received by all religious believers in Canada, Mexico, or the United States. Despite the strength, at the turn of the twenty-first century, of conservative and fundamentalist traditions in North America who condemn the increasing pluralism and secularism on the continent, and despite the continued numerical dominance of Christianity, the mind-boggling number of religious options available to the citizens of Canada, Mexico, and the United States will only increase as the forces of globalization increasingly reshape North American societies into the twenty-first century. Thus, the religious competition so characteristic of North American religion, as well as the religious creativity it engenders, will undoubtedly continue to define the daily ritual lives of numerous North Americans for the foreseeable future. The spiritual marketplace of North American religion, it seems safe to say, will remain as lively as ever.

NOTES

1. E. C. Gault, "God Wonderfully Heals," *Church of God Evangel* 13(32) (1922), p. 3.
2. Mrs. George Martin, "Healed When Doctor Was Dismissed," *Church of God Evangel* 13(32) (1922), p. 3.
3. Quoted in Samuel Eliot Morison, *Admiral of the Ocean Sea—A Life of Christopher Columbus* (Alcester, UK: Read Books, 2007), p. 154.
4. Jon Butler, *Awash in a Sea of Faith: Christianizing the American People* (Cambridge, MA: Harvard University Press, 1990), pp. 129–163.
5. See George Gallup Jr. and D. Michael Lindsay, *Surveying the Religious Landscape: Trends in U.S. Beliefs* (New York: Morehouse, 2000), pp. 120–121, cited in

Christopher Eisgruber and Mariah Zeisberg, "Religious Freedom in Canada and the United States," *International Journal of Constitutional Law* 4(2) (2006), p. 245; see also "Religions in Canada," http://www12.statcan.ca/english/census01/Products/Analytic/companion/rel/canada.cfm (accessed January 7, 2009).

6. For further discussion of statistical trends in Canadian religion, see Roger O'Toole, "Religion in Canada: Its Development and Contemporary Situation," *Social Compass*, 43(1) (1996), p. 119–134.

7. For a breakdown of the Mexican census in 2000 according to religious identification, see http://www.inegi.gob.mx/prod_serv/contenidos/espanol/bvinegi/productos/censos/poblacion/2000/definitivos/Nal/tabulados/00re01.pdf (accessed January 7, 2009).

8. I borrow the term "combinationism" in particular from Catherine Albanese's *America, Religions and Religion*, 4th ed. (Belmont, CA: Thomson Wadsworth, 2007), pp. xvii–xviii.

9. David Macrae, *The Americans at Home* (Edinburgh: Edmonston and Douglas, 1870), 2:100, quoted in Albert Raboteau, *Slave Religion: The "Invisible Institution" in the Antebellum South* (New York: Oxford, 1978), p. 249.

10. I borrow the term "spiritual marketplace" from Wade Clark Roof's *Spiritual Marketplace: Baby Boomers and the Remaking of American Religion* (Princeton, NJ: Princeton University Press, 2001).

11. Aimee Semple McPherson, *This Is That: Personal Experiences, Sermons, and Writings*, ed. Donald W. Dayton (1919; repr. New York: Garland Publishing, 1985), p. 30.

12. Quoted in Edith Blumhofer, *Aimee Semple McPherson: Everybody's Sister* (Grand Rapids, MI: Eerdmans, 1993), p. 230.

BIBLIOGRAPHY

Albanese, Catherine L. *America, Religions and Religion.* 4th ed. Belmont, CA: Thomson Wadsworth, 2007.

Camp, Roderic Ai. *Crossing Swords: Politics and Religion in Mexico.* New York: Oxford University Press, 1997.

Corrigan, John, and Winthrop Hudson. *Religion in America: An Historical Account of the Development of American Religious Life.* 7th ed. Upper Saddle River, NJ: Pearson/Prentice Hall, 2004.

Moore, R. Laurence. *Religious Outsiders and the Making of Americans.* New York: Oxford University Press, 1986.

Noll, Mark A. *A History of Christianity in the United States and Canada.* Grand Rapids, MI: Eerdmans, 1992.

Porterfield, Amanda. *The Transformation of American Religion: The Story of a Late-Twentieth-Century Awakening.* New York: Oxford University Press, 2001.

Chapter 13

Latin America

Eloísa Martín

LATIN AMERICAN RELIGION:
MORE THAN JUST CATHOLICISM

Catholicism was brought to Latin America during the fifteenth century by the Spanish and Portuguese, and it went on to become the most widespread religion in Latin America. By the 1990s Latin America was responsible for 42 percent of the world's Catholic population. Nevertheless, Catholicism goes far beyond stating one's affinity, obeying church rules, or going to church; it is more of a cultural identity that unifies heterogeneous practices across the region.

Despite their common Catholic identity, Latin Americans also have Amerindian, African, and popular non-Christian religious traditions inherited from Spain. Even today many Catholics incorporate practices and beliefs that are not accepted by the Roman Catholic Church, including devotions to Gauchito Gil[1] in Argentina and Jesús Malverde in Mexico, Brazilian Candomblé and Umbanda religions, the Pachamama and the Ekeko cults in Bolivia, Maria Lionza worship in Venezuela, and the Vegetalists' religious practices in the Amazonian and Andean regions.

Over the past few decades, the religious map of Latin America has been further enriched by the presence of new religions, predominantly Protestant denominations. The novel aspect of such groups is the way in which they expand rapidly or suddenly attain visibility; in addition, many such groups have a strong presence in the region. The growth of Evangelist churches among the lower classes[2] in countries traditionally known for Catholicism has been attributed to many diverse factors: while some claim that Evangelism is a U.S. imperialist conspiracy, others argue that it is the result of increasingly impoverished living conditions among the poorest Latin Americans. Because Pentecostalism shares various cognitive and emotional ties with African and indigenous religions, this may help to explain its popularity among indigenous inhabitants of rural areas and for those with a history in Afro-Brazilian religions.

When researching religious practices in Latin America, we find stories of miracles and different ways of soliciting the saints for help and later giving thanks; different hierarchies of "supernatural" or "sacred" beings to whom such requests are made; reciprocity, which includes promise and sacrifice; pilgrimages; popular celebrations; and a colorful variety of devotional practices. These practices are shared by diverse social sectors, in that religious folk as well as nonbelievers often participate, and these practices are common to both men and women, though in different ways.

TIMELINE

Sixteenth century:	María Lionza is worshiped in Venezuela.
Sixteenth–nineteenth centuries:	The Catholic Church is the only legal religious institution in most Latin American countries.
1830:	The first *terreiro* of the Candomblé is founded in Brazil.
Mid–nineteenth century:	Deolinda Correa and Gaucho Gil die and become popular saints in Argentina.
1895:	Vatican crowns the Virgin of Guadalupe "Empress and Patron Saint of the Americas."
Late nineteenth century:	Jesús Malverde dies in Mexico and becomes a popular saint; Niño Fidencio begins to cure in Mexico.
1909:	First Pentecostal church is founded in Valparaiso, Chile.
1911:	The God's Assembly Church is founded in the north of Brazil; it becomes the largest Protestant church in that country.
1920:	Umbanda religion appears in the southeastern Brazil.
1923:	Francisco Pancho Villa dies.

1928:	Padre Toribio Romo is killed by the federal army in Mexico.
1938:	Niño Fidencio dies.
1955:	CELAM's first General Conference is held in Rio de Janeiro, Brazil.
1960s:	Afro-Brazilian religions are introduced into Argentina.
Mid-1960s:	Mexicans begin worshiping Saint Death in Hidalgo.
1968:	CELAM's second General Conference held at Medellín, Colombia.
1969:	Catholic Charismatic Renewal arrives in Brazil.
1970s:	Jesús Malverde becomes the saint of drug traffickers.
1970:	Catholic Charismatic Renewal arrives in Perú.
1971:	Catholic Charismatic Renewal arrives in Bolivia.
1972:	Catholic Charismatic Renewal arrives in Colombia and Chile.
1973:	Catholic Charismatic Renewal arrives in Venezuela.
1973:	First Latin American Catholic Charismatic Conference, in Bogotá, Colombia.
1977:	God's Kingdom Universal Church is founded in Rio de Janeiro.
1980s:	Pentecostalism is transformed into "Neopentecostalism."
1995:	Selena Quintanillo is murdered and becomes an object of devotion among Mexicans and Americans.
1996:	Gilda is killed in a car accident and becomes a popular saint in Argentina.

HISTORY

Although there were relatively few Catholic parishes in Latin America between the sixteenth and nineteenth centuries, the Catholic Church was the only legal religious institution in the majority of South American countries during the colonial period. In the mid-nineteenth century, the Church was separated from the national government in most of the newly drafted national constitutions. Gradually, some of the church's powers were taken over by the state (especially tasks related to personal records and education). However, toward the end of the nineteenth century and as part of nation building in the region, Catholicism's power began to grow once again. In some countries, in fact, the Catholic Church became one of the main pillars of national identity. This is the reason that the Vatican crowned the Virgin of Guadalupe "the patron saint of the Americas" at the start of the twentieth century. On the one hand, this represented the Church's efforts to make Catholicism "national" and to distance itself from colonialism because the Church wanted to appear as an ally in the institutional reorganization of the new states. On the other hand, countries sought a figure that could make sense of its heterogeneous identity, a figure that could represent both native populations, as well as waves of immigrants from different lands, including Africans during the period of the slave trade and Europeans starting at the end of the nineteenth century.

At the beginning of twentieth century, almost all Latin American countries were independent republics that guaranteed religious freedom to their citizens. At that time, the Catholic Church was officially separate from the national states, but it remained an important ally. Thanks to the supposed Catholic identity and culture of the residents, Catholicism was seen as the "official religion" of these former Spanish colonies. By imposing religious homogeneity, the state attempted to unify a geographically and ethnically diverse population.

From the beginning of the century until the mid-1950s, the Catholic Church was concerned with consolidating its position in national politics. To counter secularism, communism, and Protestantism, the Church brought in clergymen from Europe and also invested in schools to educate the children of the middle class and the elite. During this period, however, there were almost no anticlerical and secularization movements. In some countries, such as Chile, the Catholic Church had its own political party.

After World War II, the fight against communism and projects related to regional development created links between Catholic leaders and left-wing intellectuals. Important for Latin American Catholicism was the creation of the Latin American Episcopal Council (*Consejo Episcopal Latinoamericano* [CELAM]). Its headquarters was installed at Bogotá, Colombia. After the Second Vatican Council, political concern with social justice and poverty grew among Latin American bishops, young priests, and laity. They were responsible for the main positions taken by CELAM's second general conference in 1968 in Medellín, where the "Theology of Liberation" gained an important pastoral influence. This socially committed position, more open than traditional Catholicism to ecumenism and modernity, was defined as the "option of the poor." During the 1970s, and following this path, Basic Christian Communities were founded across the region; here, laypersons got involved in religion and participated in social movements.

At the same time, Catholic Charismatic Renewal was brought from the United States to Chile, Colombia, and Perú. Although the first Latin American Catholic Charismatic Conference took place in 1973 in Bogotá, the movement did not become widespread in South America until the 1990s. Charismatic Catholic groups have a special affinity with the media, and they have opened their own radio and TV stations. The Colombian priest Darío Betancur is very well-known; his show *Hablemos con Dios* is aired on *Televida* and his books on intercession prayer and healing are top sellers. At the turn of the twenty-first century, many Catholic Charismatic priests and laypersons stood out in the region because of their diverse contributions to regional liberation. Prophecy and healing are two fundamental features of the Catholic Charismatic priests, and leaders are often skilled preachers and singers.

Since the second half of the twentieth century, there has been a marked decline in the number of Catholics in Latin America. Regional estimates for 1999 show that Ecuador (90%), Perú (89%), and Colombia (88%) are the countries with the highest Catholic population, whereas Argentina, Mexico, and Venezuela (70%), and Guatemala (60%) have lower percentages.[3] Uruguay is the least Catholic country, with just 52% of the population declaring itself Catholic. In any case, despite the Catholic majority, populations across the continent continue to maintain Amerindian, African, Spiritualist, and folk traditions. In Mexico, Bolivia, and Perú, aboriginal movements and cults based on ancestral beliefs continue to flourish. In Ecuador, there are more than a thousand religious institutions of all sorts and many diverse indigenous religions; this is also the case in Guatemala, where Mayan worship is still practiced by a high percentage of the population.

Popular Pentecostal Christianity

During the first decades of the twentieth century, most Latin American Protestants were European immigrants, and their descendents had no interest in converting the locals. However, there were also various "Protestant mission churches." In 1909 the first Pentecostal church was founded in Valparaiso, Chile, after an Episcopal Methodist church was closed. From that year on, many Pentecostal missionaries arrived, setting up churches across Latin America.

Even though the Pentecostal churches were built during the first half of the twentieth century, they received little attention until the 1970s. The flexibility and simplicity in the structure of the first Pentecostal churches, such as the *Assembléia de Deus* (God's Assembly), allowed them to adapt to different locations. Pentecostalism can be seen as the syncretism of Protestants and ecstatic religious traditions; the emphasis is on experiencing the supernatural.

By the 1990s the growth of Pentecostalism in Latin America had become much more evident. In fact, it has transformed into what some have called "Neopentecostalism," which involves the use of the mass media for the church's own purposes. Media presence and involvement in politics are trademarks of various Pentecostal and Neopentecostal churches across Latin America. Several other Brazilian, Argentine, and Colombian Neopentecostal churches also use the media and send missionaries abroad.

Founded by Edir Macedo in 1977 in Rio de Janeiro, the *God's Kingdom Universal Church* has stood out in Brazil and in Latin America as an exemplary Neopentecostal church. Besides owning radio and TV stations, this church has influenced elections in Brazil by lending its support to candidates favorable to its cause; it has also sent missionaries to other continents.

Afro-Brazilian Religions

Afro-Brazilian religions are urban phenomena that date back more than 150 years. Brought in by African slaves (especially the Yoruba of Nigeria and the Ewe from Benin and Togo), their religion syncretized with Spanish Catholicism, Kardecist spiritism,[4] and local aboriginal beliefs. The different combinations of these four elements led to regional variations: *Catimbó, Tambor de Minas, Xangó, Candomblé, Macumba,* and *Batuques.*

The *orixás* (Afro-Brazilian saints or personal deities) have different Catholic saints as their counterparts and syncretize with them. The correspondence between *orixás* and catholic saints varies by geographical setting. Catholic St. George, for instance, is syncretized with Ogum in Rio de Janeiro and with Oxossi in Bahia. And Iansã, a female warrior *orixás*, is syncretized with Catholic St. Bárbara, St. Lucy, or St. Joanna D'Arc. Virgin Mary appears syncretized in two different *orixás*: Yemanjá (Our Lady of Navigators, Our Lady of Glory) and Oxum (Our Lady of Fátima). Even Jesus Christ is syncretized in Oxalá *orixás*, the humankind Creator.

The first *terreiro* (Afro-Brazilian religious temple) of the Candomblé, which is considered the most African and most traditional of these religions, was founded in the Brazilian city of Bahia in 1830. Another expression of Afro-Brazilian religions, the Umbanda, originated in the southeastern Brazil in the 1920s. Although the 2000 Brazilian census reports that only 0.34 percent of Brazilians claim to practice religions with African roots, most analysts assume that a greater percentage of such believers are actually listed as Catholics. These individuals prefer to identify themselves as Catholics even when they participate in both religions because the followers of Afro-Brazilian religions are often subject to discrimination: hegemonic social representation of this religion considers its followers as "poor, black and ignorant people because of its use of magical practices, which include rituals with animals' blood, baths with special herbs, offerings for *orixás* in public open places, and other such practices."

Mãe de santo (mother of saint) designates the female leader of an Afro-Brazilian religion temple, and *pai de santo* (father of saint) when he is a man,

This picture is from the Gauchito Gil Sanctuary in Corrientes, Argentina, during his annual feast day in January. It shows an ex-voto wall that displays messages from devotees giving thanks for the miracles performed by Gauchito Gil. (Courtesy Sebastian Hacher.)

because they are understood to be the parents of the *orixás*. Participation within these religions involves many steps and different degrees of commitment that are manifested in initiatory rituals. Those who go through all these rituals became *filhos de santo* (sons or daughters of saint).

Since 1980 participation in Afro-Brazilian religions has dropped. There has been a 20 percent drop in Umbanda followers according to the last census. At the same time, practitioners of Candomblé are on the rise. This is due, in many cases, to followers migrating from one such religion to another. The Brazilian sociologist Reginaldo Prandi attributes this movement to the social changes in Brazil over the past century. Umbanda reflects the type of society that gave birth to these religions, one characterized by nationalism and the aspiration to rise up the social ladder. Candomblé, in contrast, attracts a greater audience because it shares the values of the contemporary postmodern society: individualism, hedonism, and narcissism. The popularity of Candomblé, then, has been facilitated by the music and the media since the 1960s. The rediscovery of African culture, on the other hand, attracted the middle (and white) classes to Candomblé centers, and these new followers also helped the religion earn its legitimacy.

RELIGION AND DAILY LIFE IN LATIN AMERICA

In Latin America religion is constantly present in everyday practices. Religious practices accompany people in the broad cycle of life and in daily life as well, through rituals, feasts, promises, and miracles. It is commonsensical to examine this kind of religion in terms of its "function" for the poorest segments of the population. When religious practices are viewed as the result of poverty, they serve as a way to cope with educational, material, or spiritual deficiencies in contexts where there are no institutions such as the state or the Catholic Church to take responsibility for their welfare. Religion is often used to solve problems pertaining to other spheres. If there is no public hospital, for instance, then folk healers are visited. Similarly, where free, public, lay, and compulsory education fails in its mission, then beliefs in deceased people who perform miracles, cartomancy, or Afro-Brazilian priests will appear. In this respect, popular saints, pilgrimages, folk healers, and the new religious movements are not merely answers to anguish, privations, and despair. Nor is their use limited to protesting and resisting capitalist domination, the power of the state, or ecclesiastical control. Popular religion is more than an epiphenomenon in that it goes beyond political, economic, or even psychological needs. It reflects another way of inhabiting the world and another logic for understanding it. This cultural logic assumes the immanence and superordination of the sacred in the world as the relationships between heaven, nature, and human beings are articulated in a unique totality. The profane and the sacred are not considered separate, but are instead combined in a cosmic and harmonic whole.

Devotions

Within religion, devotion is the word used to refer to people's relationship to the saints. It is based on a triangle that involves a request, a miracle, and a promise made in return. The devotee asks the saint for a favor and offers something in exchange (the "request"). When the favor is granted (the "miracle"), the devotee is obliged to fulfill his or her promise to the saint (the "promise"). The devotee looks upon the image as if it were alive and facilitating direct and personalized contact. Such devotion is not limited to a mere exchange of favors, but may be understood from the perspective of a specific cultural logic.

Neither a life crisis nor structural privation can fully explain popular devotion to the saints. A modern-day approach could posit that subjects turn to religion to make sense or deal with loss, mourning, or despair. For Latin American popular sectors, any success or failure immediately enters a sacred dimension of reality, which includes God, the supernatural, the saints, and mystic elements. This dimension is not the ultimate answer or option when everything else is lost, but rather a variable that is always present in the world in which they live. A problem, illness, and personal or social crisis are reasons to appeal to the saints for help as opposed to variables that lead one to develop devotion. In turn, crises do not involve changes to one's faith or an increase in the religious practices per se. On the contrary, popular devotion remains steady over time and adapts to the new mores of the historical moment.

Although they all fall under a single generic term, there are different degrees of the "miracles" granted by the saints. Gabriel, a Gilda devotee (for more on Gilda, see the sidebar titled "Two Singers Who Became Saints: Selena and Gilda" later in the chapter), explains it clearly:

> There's a difference between a miracle and some help that She could give you to solve a problem you have. Maybe you meditate about, hear Her music, think on Her and you find the solution. . . . You ask Her for help and suddenly your path is opened . . . or you find inspiration to solve your problem. Another different thing is that case, the one of that little boy who was cured of meningitis. He asked Her to be cured. And I think this is a miracle, because the doctors said he wouldn't relief. And suddenly, he got better and better and they [the doctors] didn't find a reason why he was recovered. So, there's something that tells you that it is not possible. . . . It's believe it or not![4]

Evidently, passing a test is not the same as recovering from a major illness. Losing weight cannot be compared to getting a job after a long period of unemployment. Obtaining the clarity one needs to solve a problem is not the same as meeting one's ideal mate. The differences among different types of miracles could be more a question of impact than of quality. Obtaining a favorable ruling in a lawsuit thanks to a good lawyer, winning the lottery when you are in debt, and receiving positive inspiration to solve a problem are also miracles. Some of these miracles are not visible to others because they occur within an intimate and subjective realm. In any case, there is no question as to the value attributed to the saints. No matter how small the miracle, granted requests make saints present in the daily life of their followers.

Miracles are regular, not extraordinary, events. Far from exceptional, the saint—be it a deceased miracle worker, Jesus, Gilda, or the virgin—is present and involved in the lives of his or her followers. The origin of daily problems and the solution to these problems can be attributed to the sacred, and the requests and promises made to the saints fall within the range of everyday options to address such problems. In this regard, the saints are considered to open up possibilities, grant permission, and lend assistance, which is more necessary than "extraordinary" in making good things happen and putting an end to bad things. It is the close collaboration between humans and saints that makes miracles possible as part of the "natural" and rational order, as opposed to an oddity or last resort when other theories fail. As Daniel explains, referring to St. Cayetano, Patron of Labor and Bread:

> If you go to San Cayetano and you ask him for work, that doesn't mean that tomorrow the job is going to show up looking for you at your house. If you don't go out to look for a job, you'll never find work. . . . It depends on you, too . . . . Whether you're looking for work or something else, if you don't push for it, don't bother asking God to help!

God, saints, the deceased, and other extraordinary beings are sacred forces that participate in everyday life in a regular way and form a "natural" part of the world. Yet the presence and action of these forces is possible only when humans are also involved. From this perspective it is possible to understand, for example, the requests and promises made to the saints. Most of these are related to everyday aspects of life that could be resolved outside the scope of religion: "In general, devotees do not ask the saint to change the world, stop death or change the course of a river. Their requests are not related to nature's 'laws.' Instead, they are related to the insecurities of individuals or specific groups in a given situation" (Fernandes, 1982: 46–47). In exchange, the devotees do not commit to making a radical change in their lives, such as abandoning their worldly goods; however, they do promise to take actions or offer gifts that fall within their abilities.

Although there are no written rules for how to relate to the saints, the ways in which devotees interact with them are not entirely free or "spontaneous." The practice of dealing with the saints involves certain rules of etiquette and standards, which can bring undesired consequences when broken. The rules vary depending on the saint, and what is allowed among some saints is prohibited for others. While the devotees to Odetinha, a young girl worshiped at a cemetery in Rio de Janeiro, can take roses from her grave to prepare healing infusions, Gilda's devotees are warned that taking something from the deceased brings bad luck.[6] If drivers do not stop "to say hello" when they pass by the sanctuary of Gauchito Gil, they know that they may suffer an accident or a breakdown, whereas in the case of Deolinda Correa, there is no such interdiction.

The likes and dislikes of the deceased miracle worker, or the specific circumstances surrounding his or her life or death, are also taken into account when making an offering. In the case of prostitute saints, hair clips and makeup are among the offerings, whereas for DC, who died of thirst, bottles with water are the mainstay. Red objects are left for Gaucho Gil in homage of his spilled blood. Beer and cigarettes are the offerings preferred by Gardel and Pancho Villa, while marijuana cigarettes are left for Jesús Malverde.

MIRACLE WORKERS

Deolinda Correa lived in San Juan, Argentina, in the mid-eighteenth century. Following her husband, who had been recruited for the war, she crossed the desert on foot, carrying her child in her arms. After she got lost in the desert and died of thirst, soldiers found her body in the desert. Her son was alive and feeding from her dead breast. The *Difunta* (Deceased), as she is commonly called, is buried at the spot in Vallecito where her body was found, and a sanctuary was erected there in her memory. However, hundreds of altars have been constructed in homage to her along routes across Argentina and these altars are surrounded by bottles of water.

Francisco Pancho Villa (1887–1923) was the most popular and charismatic figure of the Mexican Revolution. He was also known as a social bandit who stole from the rich to help the poor. Currently, he is worshiped in several states in Mexico and by Mexican immigrants in Texas. Devotees ask for his assistance with regard to health and money, but also in love, as he was known for his luck with the women. His image is often found on domestic altars, next to Jesús Malverde's.

Antonio Gil was believed to have lived in Corrientes, Argentina, during the second half of the nineteenth century. According to some versions, he was a social bandit who was killed by an estate owner who was after him for robbery. In other versions, he was a heroic deserter of one of the internal wars who was killed by a provincial army because he refused to take up arms against his fellow citizens. However, both versions concur that he was brutally murdered in spite of his innocence. He was beheaded, strung up by his feet, and then abandoned without a burial. His first miracle, saving the life of the daughter of one of his murderers, led the assassins to hang a cross at the spot where he was murdered in Mercedes. Nowdays, there are countless altars that pay homage to *Gaucho Gil* in the homes of migrants from Corrientes in the lower-class neighborhoods of Buenos Aires.

Promises

Generally speaking, flowers, candles, cigarettes, and gifts are offered to win the favor of a saint. In some cases, the devotee makes a promise to do something that will be difficult, though never impossible. The importance of the promise lies in the possibility of fulfilling it, thereby maintaining the saint's trust in the devotee.

Of all the promises made, those that involve some type of personal sacrifice are the most common. A larger request or sacrifice inspires greater admiration among other devotees and pride for the devotee who has fulfilled the promise.

In one instance, Jorge, a 40-year-old unemployed father of nine, promised he would visit the sanctuary of Difunta Correa on his knees if she granted his request. When he reached the sanctuary, his knees were bloody from the rough terrain. This pilgrimage was made to save his son who was dying. When Jorge returned home, his son was sitting up in bed. This type of promise is possible because of the close bond between Jorge and his son and because illnesses ultimately have a sacred explanation. Human beings are not considered autonomous (and thus responsible for their own destinies) here, but as links of a chain that binds them to a world in which sacred forces are constantly at work. Because of the blood ties that join them, Jorge's body is the place where the cosmic order broken by his son's illness is restored. By ripping his own flesh in his offering to Difunta Correa, and thanks to her intervention, his son's body was restored. Regardless of the medical explanations for his son's illness, Jorge understood that there could be something more in the etiology of the illness; something attributable to the sacred realm. And this cause could be addressed only within this sacred realm. This argument will be further developed below in the analysis of healing practices.

Personal sacrifice plays a central role in devotions to saints. Devotional actions can be both propitious (depending on the saint's will) and consecratory (on the part of the person making the request). They vary depending on the gender of the devotee and the seriousness of the issue at hand. When the promises are made by a woman, different personal sacrifices are involved. Graciela, a 45-year-old housekeeper who is married with two children and lives in a middle-class neighborhood in Buenos Aires, recounts that when her son was five years old, he fell down, hit his head, and suffered a cranial fracture. He was in critical condition, and his doctors predicted that he would suffer terrible neurological consequences. When asking for her son's recovery, Graciela promised the hair of her daughter Cecilia, then an infant, to the Virgin of Itatí. According to her mother's promise, her daughter would not cut her hair until the age of 15 and she would then take it to the virgin. Diego was cured, and Graciela constantly mentions how intelligent he is—the paradigmatic sign of his intellectual capacity being that he is "a genius with computers," making it clear that the virgin amply responded to her request.

As in the case of Jorge, the miraculous cure of the boy in exchange for the hair of Graciela's daughter reestablishes a cosmic order that falls within the family sphere and is made evident there as well. Through her mother's promise, Cecilia has inherited her mother's devotion to the virgin and at the same time, she *has grown up* as a woman and become a devotee. Devotion is transmitted by family ties that are gender marked. What is more, religious and gender experiences are constitutive of the self in a dissociated way. A girl learns to become a woman by making a promise. Furthermore, attributes that are considered feminine, such as self-abnegation and patience, are appreciated by the saints. A boy learns that becoming a man involves making heroic sacrifices and risking one's physical integrity. Another lesson is that saints do not forgive devotees who do not keep their promises. In one's personal relationship to the sacred—in each singular practice—masculine and feminine are defined. And it is through gendered performances and contexts that individuals interact with the sacred.

Instead of fulfilling a single promise, Nilda, a mid-40s separated housewife and mother of two girls, "became a *promesera*." (The term *promesera* comes from the Spanish word for promise, *promesa*, and refers to a promise maker or someone who is constantly exchanging promises and favors with a saint.) This defines her connection to Gilda because she became stricter in terms of her self-discipline; taking her responsibilities more seriously and extending them over time and for life. In the case of a promise, the debt to the saint is paid off once the promise is fulfilled. There is always a possibility of making additional promises, but the devotee may also opt not to do so or to make promises to another saint. Becoming a *promesera* creates a stronger and more lasting bond, as it involves a passage, or change of status based on one's personal devotion to the saint. *Promeseras* reveal their status by wearing special clothes during celebrations for the saint or visits to the sanctuary. Those devoted to Gauchito Gil, for instance, will wear traditional gaucho garb—pants buttoned below the knee, boots, a handkerchief at the neck, and a hat—in which the color red predominates. Gilda's followers choose purple, which is a color identified with the singer. The virgin's *promeseras* wear dresses and shawls similar to those used by the virgin on her statues.

Wearing the same clothes as a saint involves no mimesis or identification. Rather, in dressing like the saint there is an evocation, or acknowledgement and homage, evident in the dedication. A special and sacred status is assigned to such individuals, but the distance between the saint and the devotee is clear.

Because of the special status of promise makers, it is seldom necessary to make an explicit request. Often they need only establish some type of connection with the saint. When Antonia, a 58-year-old school assistant, watched her niece become ill, for instance, she did not make any request or promise. Instead she used her *promesera* shawl to cover the hospital bed where the girl was sleeping. When her niece recovered, she paid homage to the virgin by leaving holy cards with the virgin's image all over the hospital. As we can see in this example, being a *promesera* involves daily involvement, including the presence of the saint on home altars, daily "conversations," and the knowledge that the saint is watching over the *promesera* at all times. The exchange of tokens of appreciation or offerings between the saint and the *promeseras* are, in this case, constant.

Official and Unofficial Sanctuaries

Sanctuaries are pilgrimage destinations. The importance of the sanctuary is not related to its history or aesthetics, so its size is irrelevant, as is whether it is managed by a religious institution or informally built by the saint's followers. Instead, its attraction is based on the people's devotion to the saint that is worshiped there. The quality of a sanctuary is based on the presence of the saint on earth, which gives the place a power of a entirely different nature. It is a place where miracles occur.

There are Catholic sanctuaries throughout Latin America. The most important involve basilicas for the virgin. However, there are also other sanctuaries for many different canonized saints, such as St. Cayetano, St. Expedito, and St. Anthony. The principal image of these sanctuaries is the saint or virgin, and greater power is attributed to them in fulfilling the requests of their followers.

The economy of large Catholic sanctuaries is generally based on religious tourism, either directly or indirectly (see Chapter 30 in Volume 3, on tourism). During the celebrations of their patron saints, municipalities charge taxes for setting up street stands, and the church receives all sorts of donations. Most of the locals also receive extra income on such occasions. Some set up stands at the fair; young people get jobs as cooks or wait staff at street restaurants. Almost everyone rents a room, a garage, or even the patio of their homes where pilgrims can sleep. The locals charge for the use of bathrooms and showers; they sell food and beverages; they wash and iron the clothing of the pilgrims. One elderly resident in the towns of one sanctuary defined it in the following way: "Here we make our living with the virgin. If the virgin leaves, this town will die."[7]

For the locals, the sanctuary is seen as the guarantee of the success of their activity. The prosperity and happiness of a community are owed to the saint. This involves more than an economic interest, because a merchant's interest does not govern a sanctuary-based economy. The possibility of "making a living with the virgin" must be understood within a logic of exchange whose cosmic balance is maintained by a reciprocity, of the worlds of "up there" and "down here," between devotees and saints. Multiple forms of individual offerings are fundamental to legitimately obtaining celestial favors. Some go on a pilgrimage and travel substantial distances by foot, bike, horseback, or even on their knees.

Others light up the image of the saint on their home altars or leave the doors of their homes open for the prayer groups that accompany the procession of the saint's image across the city. Some go to the church every day, and others make donations on the days of their patron saint. All include the image of the patron saint on their home altars. Failure to reciprocate, or meet one's obligations to the virgin or the saint, breaks the cosmic balance. Maintaining the "sacred economy" helps to prevent new internal conflicts within one's own community, so the participation of both residents and saints alike is essential to the happiness and prosperity of the town.

However, there are some members of the sanctuary community who refuse or forget to reciprocate. Visiting merchants, religious authorities, or politicians may take advantage of local festivals for their own personal benefit or prestige without offering the saint anything in return. In these cases, such individuals may downplay their religious identity so local community members will continue to do business with them. Hugo, a fruit seller, says that although it is difficult for him, he does not admit to being a Baptist because "otherwise, no one buys your stuff. . . . The first thing they say to you when you admit to another religion is, how can you not worship the virgin when you owe her your livelihood?!"[8]

Hugo's complaint shows how the economic prosperity of local community members in sanctuary towns depends, either directly or indirectly, on the image that is worshiped there. It is impossible to deny the presence of the saint and outrageous to refuse to establish a relationship with him or her because of different religious beliefs. An economy based on bartering with the sacred means that all material benefits granted by the saint must be morally or materially reciprocated by all inhabitants.

There are also sanctuaries constructed by the devotees themselves to pay homage to the "little souls" (the souls of the deceased) or to "popular saints" — "popular" because the Church had no involvement in their consecration. The practice of constructing monuments or hanging crosses at spots where a tragic death has occurred is an ancient practice and very common across Latin America (and in the United States as well).

Unlike Catholic sanctuaries, which have cities built up around them and boast a tourist infrastructure to welcome pilgrims, popular sanctuaries can be found on isolated roadsides. With a small cross or a monument to the deceased, they do not have the infrastructure to support lengthy visits by throngs of devotees. Exceptional cases include Difunta Correa and Gaucho Gil in Argentina, María Lionza in Venezuela, and Jesús Malverde in Mexico, which have inspired groups of followers to organize to oversee activities, finances, annual commemorations, and offerings at these sanctuaries. The followers also take responsibility for other sources of income, such as the sale of souvenirs and books and charging fees for selling wares within the sanctuary. The funds are then used to improve the infrastructure, fund annual celebrations, and help the poor.

One feature of popular sanctuaries is that they generally do not have one central statue. Instead, there are several icons of the saint to whom the sanctuary is dedicated as well as images of other miraculous figures and piles of offerings that offer multicolored proof of the power of the saint. The sanctuary in honor of the Argentine saint Gilda is one of many examples of this type of sanctuary.

TWO SINGERS WHO BECAME SAINTS: SELENA AND GILDA

Born Selena Quintanilla Pérez in Lake Jackson, Texas, in 1971, *Selena* began performing when she was a child and had a successful career as a singer. She was considered the queen of tejano music (a genre that includes various forms of folk and popular music originating among the Hispanic populations of Central and Southern Texas), won a Grammy, and sold thousands of albums. In March 1995, at the age of 23, Selena was shot and killed by Yolanda Saldivar, the founder of her fan club. A few weeks later, Texas governor George W. Bush declared her birthday, April 16, "Selena Day," in her honor. Today, hundreds of pilgrims travel to Texas and leave offerings in places where Selena lived and performed. Like Elvis in Memphis, her grave is always covered with flowers, candles, and letters from her devotees, who also include her image on their home altars.

Gilda was born Miriam Alejandra Bianchi in 1961 into a middle-class household. She was a kindergarten teacher who married and had two children. During the 1990s she decided to start a career as a singer of "cumbia" music, which was very popular with the working classes. She never became rich or famous, and she died in a car accident on September 7, 1996. At the location of her death, 100 kilometers from Buenos Aires, her devotees erected a sanctuary. In the following years, the presence of Gilda increased. She received extensive media coverage, books were written about her life, and TV programs and documentaries were made about her. Gilda's assistance is sought for a wide range of affairs, but she specializes in questions related to love.

Gilda's sanctuary is constructed on a large, shady piece of land that was purchased and donated by a devotee in appreciation for her son's return to health. *La capilla* (the chapel) is a square building with a slanted roof. Inside, it presents diverse Gilda iconography as well as the icons of other saints, deceased miracle makers, images of Jesus, and different advocations of the virgin. An elegant picture frame shows a smiling image of Evita. There are smaller sculptures of Gaucho Gil, St. Cayetano, Difunta Correa, and Virgin Mary, and hundreds of holy cards of popular saints. All of the images have been left by visitors to fulfill promises, and they are all welcome at the sanctuary. By being *present* in the sanctuary, the other saints receive the same gestures of devotion as Gilda. Visitors greet them, leave requests written on tiny sheets of paper, light candles to them, and pray to them. Here, to obtain a miracle, the devotees can resort to the aggregate powers, invoking several saints at the same time and even requesting the intercession of one saint into dealings with another. Such mediation, however, does not necessarily coincide with Catholic doctrine. For instance, devotees can ask Gilda "to take" a request to God or Jesus, or to those who are considered mediators by the Church, such as the virgin or another saint.

Hanging from the roof in separate groups are baby clothes, birthday dresses from *quinceañeras* ("Sweet 15" parties), First Communion and wedding dresses, soccer jerseys, and dozens of handkerchiefs. Shelves along the walls hold objects of all sorts: school notebooks, letters, key chains, lighters, toys, and pictures. The offerings are objects delivered to the saint in recognition of a promise made and favor received. Their presence is evidence of the favors granted and of the powers of the saint. Some offerings, following the Spanish tradition, describe the miracle on loose sheets of paper or framed texts, or replicate them by representing the parts of the human body that suffered some type of illness and were cured. Pictures, wedding dresses, and "Sweet 15" party dresses are offered in appreciation for having lived to see the specific moment and celebrate it. Pictures of babies and baby clothes are evidence of a successful birth. Pictures of children in their school uniforms, or school notebooks and exams passed, show that the devotee was successful in his or her studies. A lighter shows that the follower was able to quit smoking thanks to the saint. Keys reveal that the devotee purchased a house or a car.

Leaving pictures in a sanctuary has another purpose as well. Photography is considered a real representation, a sort of prolongation of the individual that involves the presence, in a strong sense, of the person in the picture. By leaving their pictures in the sanctuary, those photographed enter in direct and permanent contact with the saint by placing themselves before the saint so that he or she can watch over them. Images of the happiness of a couple married, or a girl celebrating her fifteenth birthday, or the health of a newborn, or the success of a student who passes, or the pride of a military cadet in uniform are implicit requests for the success displayed in the photograph to continue over time.

A SAINT FOR EVERYONE

Devotion to a particular saint takes on a special meaning in the case of migrants, many of whom take the image of their saint or patron virgin with them to their new city or country. The image will reign over their new home when it is placed on the home altar. This process allows migrants to maintain and renew their ties to their place of origin. Often, this devotion to the patron saint continues indefinitely. In addition, it allows the migrants to preserve their connection with others from the same place and with the generations born in the new land, transmitting their devotion to them and connecting the new generations to the homeland. In some cases, the devotees erect sanctuaries in their new residences as a way of bringing the saint closer and consolidating the bonds among the community.

Nora, a 35-year-old mother and wife who works as housekeeper, has been attending the annual celebration held in honor of the virgin since she was a girl. The event marks a time for coming together with family members and celebrating. Although Nora's mother lives in the same building as Nora and her cousin Nelly and visits them regularly, the festival represents a real *reunion* because an interruption of the secular year renews, redefines, and celebrates family ties. These ties reinforce the devotion to the virgin as a family heritage that she also hopes to pass on to her children.

While the saints, in some sense, also become migrants when they travel with those who move to new lands, there are other saints who specialize in protecting migrants. In Mexico, there are at least four saints who receive offerings from those attempting to cross the border into the United States: Padre Jesús de Chinantla, Juan Soldado, Toribio Romo, and Saint Peter the Apostle.

Padre Jesús de Chinantla is an eighteenth-century wooden statue of Jesus. According to the story, a procession that reached Chinantla in Puebla was welcomed by musicians, and the music moved the saint so deeply that when the missionaries decided to continue their journey, the statue would not budge. Similar tales of a statue's "decision" to stay in a certain place have their origins in Spanish Catholicism and are frequent at many Latin American sanctuaries. The devotees explain that Padre Jesús protects the emigrants because he also "decided to migrate" when he stayed in Chinantla. From that time on, the image was considered Chinantla's patron saint and renamed Padre Jesús. Hundreds of migrants return to Chinantla on January 25 for Padre Jesús's celebration and make good on their promises. In every case, the migrants recount that even those without documents who ask for the saint's protection will have no trouble crossing the border.

Devotions to Juan Soldado increased noticeably toward the end of the twentieth century at his sanctuary in Tijuana, on the border with California. According to his story, Juan Soldado was accused of a crime he did not commit and then executed by a firing squad. His unjust death made him an object of popular devotion among the locals, and he is currently worshiped by migrants and their children, who return year after year to make requests and offer thanks to the saint. Another saint whose protection is sought by those who dare to cross the U.S. border illegally is Padre Toribio Romo, who was killed by the federal army in 1928 during the Cristero War. His appreciative devotees have constructed a sanctuary to him in Tulsa, Oklahoma.

As for canonized saints who help undocumented Mexicans to cross the border, there is Saint Peter the Apostle from San Pedro Zipiajo in Michoacán. To obtain his help, emigrants promise to return the next year to hang a $20 bill on his garments. This saint has proven so successful that his temple, dating back to 1523, was fully renovated in 2007 with the contributions of those who now live in the United States.

These popular and official saints do not necessarily reflect the ideal model of Catholic virtue. On the contrary, they may get offended or even take revenge against their followers when they feel they have not received the respect owed to them. If devotees do not follow the rules of etiquette, or do not keep a promise, the saints may become angry. Since saints do not demand significant sacrifices, their devotees must make good on their promises when requests are granted. Saints do not forgive those who do not keep a promise. Saints who give generously can be cruel when it comes to taking away what has been given, but devotees do not consider this behavior to be "bad." On the contrary, it is a sign of fairness. Not keeping one's word is paid for with blood, sweat, or tears.

To win a saint's favor, rituals may involve flowers, candles, or other gift offerings, including occasional animal sacrifices. When saints take their time to fulfill requests, followers attribute the delay to various reasons: because they didn't make "the best" offering, or the devotee "didn't deserve it," or "the time wasn't right." In some cases, saints do not respond to the devotee's request in the preferred timeframe. On such occasions a devotee may try to pressure the saint by tying up its statue, threatening it, taking something away, covering it up, or hanging it upside down until the request is fulfilled. This practice is not recommended for certain saints because devotees run the risk of falling out of favor with the saint. As further signs of their power, saints may punish devotees who question them, do not respect their interdictions, or do not make good on their promises.

Some saints are considered stricter in terms of ensuring the devotees make good on their promises or respect the interdictions. Santa Rita (who "can take away as easily as she can give"), the Virgin of Luján, Gaucho Gil, Santa Muerte, and Jesús Malverde can take back what they have given—even something as valuable as the life of a child—if they are transgressed. The saint's followers do not condemn such actions by the saint, but see it is a just arrangement of mutual commitment. Thus, what is seen as fair or in their best interests does not necessarily reflect the dominant law or Catholic morality.

On the other hand, not all requests to the saints correspond to predominant morals. Nor is the type of request always within the realm of the legally acceptable or the morally "good." There are saints, for instance, who protect thieves and those that help Latin Americans to cross the U.S. border illegally. There are *orishas* who look out for traffickers. There is even a virgin for paid assassins. One of the most famous saints who protects bandits is Jesús Malverde, who is renowned from Cali, Colombia, to Los Angeles, California, and across Mexico. According to legend, Jesús Malverde was a social bandit who lived on the Sinaloa Sierra during the late nineteenth century; he would hold up wagons and then distribute the takings among the poor. In a confrontation with a bounty hunter (or a policeman, in certain versions), he was shot in the leg but escaped. Knowing he was badly injured, he asked one of his fellow bandits to hand him over to the governor, take the reward money, and use the money to help the poor. He was condemned to death by hanging, and the governor ordered that his body be left unburied. Little by little, however, people began to pile up stones in a gesture that, disguised as aggression, was in fact meant to protect his body. The pile of stones soon became a site for worshipers, and later a chapel was built in honor of the bandit. The day of his death is celebrated every May 3. Starting in the 1970s, he became the patron saint of drug traffickers, after one trafficker claimed that Malverde had saved his life. The donations to the sanctuary by drug traffickers are generous, allowing those who manage the sanctuary to donate significant amounts to the poor.

As expressed by the French writer Georges Bataille, the Catholic Church refers to the sacred as the infinitely good and as God, while negative forces, the impure, the bad, and the demonical are attributed to the absence of God. Here, the saints perform "good" not only in the sense of the dominant morality as they are also called upon by those seeking "justice" and for individual happiness, and this may involve direct or indirect damage to others.

Marian Devotions

The significance of Marian devotions in Latin America is acknowledged by the clergy, politicians, and social scientists alike. Marian devotions are considered a basis for national unity, in which ethnic or class differences are minimized. The devotion to Mary eradicates differences and brings people together. For the Church, there is only one Virgin Mary, and all of her titles have the same value and are interchangeable. "There is but one Virgin Mary; only her dress changes," say priests from different sanctuaries time and again. However, in spite of the fact that the figure is always the same, in each place the Virgin acquires a different appearance and character.

The Virgin can be white, black, Asian, mestiza, indigenous, blonde, or brunette. There are titles that are considered more propitious for certain requests. Our Lady of Good Childbirth helps future mothers or women hoping to get pregnant. Mary Untier of Knots resolves difficult problems, and Lourdes is known for curing illness. Some titles are considered more "serious" or "penitential," such as the Virgin of Luján, and others, such as the Virgin of Chiquinquirá and the Virgin of Caá Cupé, enjoy music and dance. A virgin's features can change. Virgins can represent diverse political interests, and their ethnicities can even transform during conflict. Some incarnations have met during wars while defending opposing armies on the battlefield, as between the Virgin of Guadalupe and the Virgin de Remedios during Mexico's War for Independence.

Unlike many patron saint festivities, which include dancing and fairs and may last for at least two days, the Virgin of Luján does not have a celebration. Instead, there are several pilgrimages to her sanctuary during the year. The most important is held in March, when devotees travel 68 kilometers from Buenos Aires to her sanctuary, where they attend mass and take communion before returning home. The devotees say that the Virgin of Luján does not have a celebration because she is serious, strict, and jealous. Any action that the virgin disapproves of can result in immediate punishment. During pilgrimages, nothing should distract those who make the journey. Followers recommend not going with one's significant other—to avoid arguments along the way. Although many of those who are on the pilgrimage bring music along for the walk, they should take care not to appear to be having too much fun, or the virgin could see to it that the player is lost or stolen.

Unlike the Virgin of Luján, the patron saint of the city of Maracaibo, Venezuela, the Virgen del Rosario de Chiquinquirá, enjoys festivities. The celebrations held in her honor on November 18 bring together crowds who participate in the religious rites as well as the fun. The virgin's celebrations here involve mass, processions, and prayer, and also bull races, dancing, baseball games, parades, and even a beauty contest that is aired on national television.

In Colombia, one of the most worshiped incarnations is María Auxiliadora. Her sanctuary in Sabaneta, near Medellín, is a pilgrimage site for the *sicarios* (paid assassins), who visit her every Tuesday or before going out on a job. Like other devotees, the *sicarios* ask the virgin for protection and success in their tasks. Since these tasks involve murder, it would seem paradoxical to ask the virgin for assistance. For the *sicarios*, however, María Auxiliadora is like a mother, their "old lady," the one who cares for them, understands them, and forgives them even though she knows what they have done.

DEATH AS AN OBJECT OF WORSHIP

In Latin America, the worship of death is a blend of Catholic and Pre-Columbian rites. The Mayas and Aztecs worshiped death and the gods of death in various ways. The depictions of death, including skeletons and rows of human skulls left on display, were used by different religious groups. Meanwhile, martyr worship involving a dramatic death where suffering makes the deceased sacred, as early as Late Antiquity, gave the dead the power to work miracles. Intense or unjust suffering, or a tragic death, is a purifying rite of passage that can grant the deceased miraculous powers and make him or her into a saint.

Saints are commemorated on the day of their death, and not their birth, since it marks the passage from "this world" to "the other." Among the lower classes of Latin America, there is a common belief that all of the dead, whether or not they are sanctified, can act in the world of the living. For this reason, favors are frequently asked of departed relatives, and miracles are requested from popular saints. In spite of having abandoned the earth, the saints and the deceased are both in heaven *and* present on earth, especially at their grave or the spot when they died. On the other hand, heaven is not "another world," but merely a different dimension of this world.

On November 2, the Day of the Dead is celebrated across Latin America, though the Mexican celebration of this holiday is doubtless the most colorful and well-known. Starting at dawn, relatives visit the graves of dead family members and decorate the tombs with flowers. In some cases, they mount sophisticated altars on the gravestone to help the dead in the afterlife. The cemeteries are brightened by lights, voices, and colors in a grand celebration, during which time the border that separates the living from the dead is temporarily blurred. This strengthens the ties between those who have departed and those who remain in this world. Visitors stay at the graves and picnic there. They touch the gravestones and kiss them to show their affection for the deceased and also to "stay in touch," or in contact.

The deceased's body is more than mere "remains," because the individual is present even after death, with the same likes and dislikes, with the same sense of humor, and with the same quirks as during life. The dead family member's character remains intact and is still capable of action. In fact, those who celebrate the Day of the Dead believe that on November 2 the dead return to their homes to visit. Households are prepared in different ways to welcome visitors. Mirrors are covered up, oil lamps and candles are lit, and a special altar is mounted in the house and adorned with flowers, religious images, pictures, and some of the deceased's favorite objects. The dead relative's favorite food and beverages are prepared, and cigarettes and candies (especially skeletons and bone candies made of sugar and chocolate) are left out. Finally, the sweet *pan de muerto* (dead man's bread) is prepared on this special day. In this celebration, death is not considered an end to life. Instead, it is merely a transition to another phase. The dead are no longer in the physical world, but they nevertheless remain present.

Saint Death: La Santa Muerte *and* San La Muerte

The cult of the female Saint Death in Mexico (*La Santa Muerte*), and a male version of the same saint in South America (*San La Muerte*), has become more widespread and visible over the past few decades. It is difficult to trace the origins of these saints, and some researchers believe that their roots are found in pre-Hispanic cultures and that traditional Catholic features were incor·porated later. However, little can be said of the history of Saint Death. The image is anthropomorphized by followers, though this is obviously not someone who lived in this world before becoming a saint.

In Mexico, *La Santa Muerte* is portrayed as a girl or bride. The South American version of the saint is a masculine figure who is often referred to as the "little saint" (*santito*), either out of the fear of pronouncing his full name or as a pet name. He is worshiped in Paraguay, northeastern Argentina, and southern Brazil. Starting in Argentina in the 1960s, migrants brought *San La Muerte* with them to major urban centers. Worship of this figure is especially common in the poor neighborhoods of Greater Buenos Aires.

In Mexico, people began worshiping Saint Death in Hidalgo in the mid-1960s. The celebration of *La Santa Muerte* is held on August 15 and on the Day of the Dead, as in South America. In spite of the fact that the church expressly prohibits worshiping *La Santa Muerte*, the rituals around the figure of death take on aspects of Catholicism. For example, the statues of *La Santa Muerte* are dressed with special garments on the day before the celebration, which is a practice also common for celebrations of the Virgin Mary. Other Catholic elements include reciting a rosary on the saint's day and every Monday (All Souls' Day); seeking a blessing for the statues, medallions, and tattoos with the image of the saint; and prayer, resignation, and pilgrimages to the sanctuary. These are done just as if the object of worship were a canonized saint, Jesus, or the virgin.

Like other saints, *La Santa Muerte* receives requests related to love, family, health, money, and work. As she is a powerful saint—and one whose morals are in some regard "neutral," she is also sought by those seeking justice, power, vengeance, or death. Her staunchest followers claim that they are safe from harm, curses, accidents, and even violent murder by their enemies. These followers carry the saint's image with them wherever they go in the form of an amulet or medallion, and it has also become increasingly common to tattoo *La Santa Muerte*'s image.

The home altars mounted for *La Santa Muerte* may have one image or several. These are made of diverse materials, and their size may vary. *La Santa Muerte* may be flanked by Pancho Villa, Jesús Malverde, flowers, candles, cigarettes, alcoholic beverages, and other gifts to seek her favor. As payback for a promise fulfilled, a statue of *La Santa Muerte* made of metal and resin was constructed in the city of Tultitlan, just a few kilometers from Mexico City. The lot where the statue is located was donated by a follower who had recovered from cancer. According to the media, the funds used to construct the monument were donated by narcotics traffickers. This is not the first time the media have established ties between the worship of *La Santa Muerte* and the world of crime. Members of the Mara Salvatrucha, a gang from El Salvador that has spread throughout Central America and even into the United States, are devoted to *La Santa Muerte*.

The association with the world of crime is common to both the South American version and the Mexican Saint Death. However, criminals are not the only ones who worship the saint. Anyone who runs risks, including police, prostitutes, or bus and taxi drivers, can seek his or her protection. Followers claim that *San La Muerte* can protect them from a violent death such as a bullet or knife wound. For this reason, some insert a tiny image of the saint carved in bone beneath their skin, generally, on an arm or leg. Ideally, the bone should come from a deceased child who was christened before death. It is said that the most powerful representations of this saint are made by prisoners. More recently, tattooing an image of the saint has also become popular. To enhance the protection, these amulets can be blessed by a Catholic priest. In spite of the Church's repudiation of this practice, devotees figure out clever ways to get a priest's blessing. They may hide the figure of *San La Muerte* beneath another more acceptable figure, or take it to mass and secretly bring it out when the congregation receives the father's blessing.

The celebration of *San La Muerte* is held August 15–20 each year. That day, followers thank the saint for fulfilling their requests and make good on their promises. Though the celebration and rituals may vary at different sanctuaries, the festivities of *San La Muerte* always involve prayer, rosary beads, processions, and a party with plenty of food, drink, and dancing.

HEALING

In the living room of Marta's house there is a coffee table covered with white linen. The table has images of the Virgin of San Nicolás and Mary Untier of Knots. They are surrounded by holy cards displaying Saint Expeditus, Saint Cayetano, and Gaucho Gil. There is also a picture of the Argentine singer and folk saint Gilda and a phosphorescent rosary. Candles burn down most of the way, and a bottle of holy water and plastic flowers are all on the altar. Marta, a middle-class, 50-year-old nurse who lives in a small town in Argentina, has put up a more private altar in her bedroom, including pictures of the people who are "in her prayers," flowers, candles, and small folded pieces of paper with her "intentions" or requests for the people for whom she prays.

The presence of images of the saints, the virgin, or deceased miracle workers is strong in households. This way the saints are always available to family members. People can pray to the saint or even talk with them as if the saint were yet another family member. The way in which these images are incorporated into the domestic sphere is similar throughout Latin America, especially in the homes of healers, prayers, and mediums like Marta.

Healing practices are handed down from generation to generation. They are gender-specific and have specific dates for initiation, such as Good Friday, Christmas, or the Day of the Immaculate Conception (December 8). However, healing involves more than simply learning the rituals, because a healer must be born with the gift. The call of a true healer can be identified in body language such as "a compelling look in his [or her] eyes." Since their gift allows them to counter forces that can be used for "good" or "bad" (depending on the will of the person wielding the forces), healers are highly respected, and sometimes feared, within their community. The ailments that healers can cure include toothache, migraine headaches, upset stomach, fear, and *mal de ojo* (the evil eye). In addition, some healers—like the ritual fathers and mothers of Afro-Brazilian religions—can free those possessed by entities; there are also exorcisms to rid people from spiritual possession, as in the case of *Niño Fidencio* in Mexico and *María Lionza–Simón Bolivar* in Venezuela.

At the end of the nineteenth century, *Niño Fidencio* began to cure people using various techniques such as brewing herbal infusions, concocting pastes used to heal wounds, swinging the patient on a hammock, covering the patient in mud and leaving him or her in a puddle, or throwing fruits, eggs, or other large objects at the patient (after being struck by the object, the patient was cured). *Niño*

Fidencio also helped women give birth, removed teeth, and performed surgery with a piece of glass. His fame soon extended beyond the borders of the small town of Espinazo, where he lived, and he was sought after by the rich and powerful. He died in 1938, but not before sharing his gifts by "possessing" hundred of mediums known as "little boxes" (*cajitas*), most of whom were women. Through the *cajitas*, Niño Fidencio has continued to cure the sick ever since. Espinazo has become a pilgrim's destination for thousands of people from across Mexico. The pilgrims generally arrive in the month of October, when the birth and death of *Niño Fidencio* is celebrated. As in all popular religious celebrations, the signs of devotion, prayers, and healing rituals performed by the *cajitas* are mixed with music, dancing, food, and general festivities.

In Venezuelan neighborhoods it is possible to find healers who claim to have inherited the spirit of María Lionza. They are also in contact with the spirit of Simón Bolivar, who was known for curing a wide range of ailments. The origins of María Lionza worship date back to the fifteenth century but grew even stronger in the mid-twentieth century, when Venezuelan president Marcos Pérez Jiménez erected a statue to the saint on the side of a major highway. The followers make the pilgrimage to Sorte Mountain to make their requests during Holy Week and on October 12, the date marking the arrival of the Spaniards to the Americas. Devotees construct small altars there, where her image of is placed next to that of the Indian chief Guaicaipuro (who fought against the Spaniards) and Negro Felipe (the only black official of the Venezuelan army). Offerings include flowers, candles, rum, cigarettes, and tobacco leaves. The presence of the three saints is replicated at home altars across Venezuela, which also include Catholic saints and statuettes of Simón Bolivar, who is asked to perform miracles. Some authors claim that the combination of these characters represents racial harmony in Venezuela, making them a symbol of national integration and patriotism.

As a practice, healing has its roots in rural life and indigenous knowledge. The treatment of certain ailments involves specific techniques and prayers, and it may include the laying on of hands; rituals involving candles, water, or plants that are eaten (generally as an infusion or as a poultice) or kept near the body (placing rue leaves under a child's pillow to keep nightmares away); and prayers that may or may not be of Christian origin.

HEALING BELIEFS

Evil eye produces a wide range of symptoms (headache, fever, nausea, diarrhea) and is the result of staring at someone with desire, envy, or hatred, or while wishing them harm. Wearing a red ribbon around the wrist, or carrying holy cards and rue leaves, may serve to ward off the evil eye. Once struck by the evil eye, however, one must be treated. The cure may combine prayer with techniques involving water, candles, infusions, smoke, or one's own dirty clothing (or a parent's garment in the case of a child) to provide relief.

Upset stomach (*empacho*) involves digestive trouble, generally caused by overeating. It can be cured in two ways: by massaging the lower back or stomach of the person who is ill, or by "measuring the stomach" using a belt, measuring tape, or necktie, which allows the healer to reduce the problem during prayer by marking distances on the patient's stomach using a measuring tape. Purges and herbal infusions are two other possible treatments.

Shingles, or herpes zoster, is a rash that generally appears in a line along the patient's torso. In Spanish, it is referred to as *culebrilla*, or little snake, and it is believed that when the snake's head meets up with its tail, thus surrounding the patient's body like a belt, it can be fatal. Treatments include combining prayer with herbal poultices, applications in Chinese ink (or writing the words *Jesus*, *Maria*, and *Joseph* on the patient's body in ink), and rubbing a toad on the rash.

Fear (*susto*), which can be caused by nightmares, accidents, seeing ghosts, or losing a loved one, causes one's "soul to be lost," leaving a patient very weak. Symptoms include insomnia, lack of appetite, vomiting, and nausea. Treatments include prayers combined with herbal baths, holy water, smoke, and rubbing the body with ointments. In all cases, healers treat illnesses that cannot be cured by a doctor or psychologist, which are ailments that attack the body-mind-spirit as a single entity. Symptoms and treatments are not limited to mere physiology or psychology. This type of illness involves a suffering of a moral or spiritual nature that affects the body. The origin of the suffering can be attributed to gluttony, excessive desire, or sadness, so that the cure involves more than merely treating the symptom. For this reason, all healing practices involve prayer as well as other sacred elements (holy water, crosses, or holy cards), and they also require the healer's spiritual fortitude to beat the illness. Therefore, efficiently treating such ailments involves striking a balance between the body and a world in which nonhuman forces, energies, and powers are constantly at work. The body, mind, and spirit are indissoluble and closely connected to the sacred, thereby transcending any definition of the self that is restricted to the limits of body or consciousness.

DAILY RELIGIOUS PRACTICES AND THE CATHOLIC CHURCH: CONFLICTS AND CHANGES

Over the past five centuries, the historic presence of the Catholic Church in Latin America has become a cultural paradigm of the region. In spite of the drop in their numbers over the past few years, Catholics are still the majority on the continent. In this regard, a distinction between "belief" and "practice" lies beyond the people's concern. The gap between dogma and behavior represents a problem only for those who write the rules (i.e., the Church). In any case, as we have seen, Catholic dogma is ubiquitous in everyday practices.

In spite of the ubiquity of Catholic dogma, many of the daily religious practices of Latin Americans do not directly reflect Catholic doctrine, but mix Catholicism with other traditions or denominations. In popular Latin American experience, religious practices are hierarchically sacred according to specific powers so that different denominations can be incorporated and combined (while respecting the hierarchy and specific mandates) without followers considering this multiple affiliation, ecumenism, or constant conversion. Sacred forces predate all religion and have real power in the world. Catholics are merely "misbehaving" if they visit other churches and suffer no inner conflict, or ask a saint who is forbidden by the Church for favors, or visit a folk healer, or consult astrology, or believe in special energies or the evil eye.

Traditionally, the Church has dealt with different or opposing religious practices in two ways: it either prohibits them or appropriates them. When the Church opts to appropriate a different practice, it adapts them to Catholic doctrine, in effect making them Catholic.

In colonial times, evangelization was based on "cleaning the slate" of indigenous cultures, imposing what is sacred for Catholicism onto what was sacred for the native population. At that time, the clergy believed that the aboriginals needed to be enlightened, so their "diabolical" practices were prohibited. Their statues to the gods were destroyed and their temples replaced by Catholic churches. More recently, as the result of changes to the Church after the Second Vatican Council, practices of inculturation have increased. The post-council inculturation was based on the idea of acknowledging and negotiating with the other, though it does not involve accepting the other as a cultural equal:

> Unlike the anthropological term *acculturation*, which refers to changes that results when two or more different groups come into significant contact productive of changes in all, inculturation refers to encounters whose outcome is a convergence that does not replace either of the cultures from which arose.

Both parties to the inculturative exchange undergo internal transformation, but neither loses its autonomous identity. ... [I]nculturation occurs when a dominant culture attempts to make itself accessible to a subdominant one without losing its own particular character.[9]

Any practices that are foreign to the Catholic canon are considered "superstition" or "folkloric remains" and are viewed as deviations that can provoke unnecessary obligations and unfounded fear among believers. Thus, the Catholic Church tries to "channel" and "purify" the local culture to eliminate what it considers a denaturalized religion.

Sanctuaries clearly reveal the tension inherent to inculturation. The Church's goal of becoming universal can be achieved only by making two major concessions: first, by allowing local churches more room to express their individuality, and second, by transforming a strictly theological message into a living ethics with an international scope. As we have seen, most of the manifestations of popular religion have some sign of institutional religious presence. The Catholic Church has incorporated different kinds of popular practices and symbols, in both the decision to develop policies of inculturation and in the everyday work of some priests. Thus, these relationships are more complex than the dichotomy between dominance and resistance, and they occur within an interstitial sphere of negotiation and conflict where concessions are fundamental for success.

NOTES

1. *Gauchos* are South American cowboys.
2. In Spanish, as in French, the term "popular sectors" refers not necessarily to the working class as such, but to the portion of the population with the least participation in hegemonic categories of power, income, and prestige.
3. Statistics are taken from Aurelio Alonso, ed., *América Latina y el Caribe. Territorios religiosos y desafíos para el diálogo* (Buenos Aires: CLACSO, Consejo Latinoamericano de Ciencias Sociales, 2008), pp. 15–40: "Exclusión y diálogo en la confrontación de hegemonías. Notas sobre la relocalización de influencias en el campo religioso latinoamericano."
4. Allan Kardec Spiritualism combines the belief in the soul's immortality and the possibility to establish a direct communication with spirits of the deceased with Social Evolucionism, August Comte's positivism, Hindu conceptions of reincarnation and karma, and Christian charity. Kardecism practitioners in Brazil have been traditionally from the urban settings and have had medium and high educational levels. Although Kardecism was created in France, Brazil is the country with the largest number of practitioners.
5. Author's fieldwork.

6. Author's fieldwork.
7. Author's fieldwork.
8. Author's fieldwork.
9. Michael Angronsino, "The Culture Concept and the Mission of the Roman Catholic Church," *American Anthropologist* 96.4 (1994), p. 825.

BIBLIOGRAPHY

Alonso, Aurelio. *América Latina y el Caribe. Territorios religiosos y desafíos para el diálogo.* Buenos Aires: CLACSO, Consejo Latinoamericano de Ciencias Sociales, 2008.

Burdick, John. *Looking for God in Brazil: The Progressive Catholic Church in Urban Brazil's Religious Arena.* Berkeley: University of California Press, 1996.

Carozzi, María Julia, and César Ceriani Cernadas, eds. *Ciencias sociales y religión en America Latina. Perspectivas en debate.* Buenos Aires: Biblos, 2007.

Corten, Andre, and Ruth Marshall-Fratani. *Between Babel and Pentecost: Transnational Pentecostalism in Africa and Latin America.* London: Hurst, 2001.

De La Torre, Renée, and Cristina Gutiérrez. *Atlas de la diversidad religiosa en México.* México: Colegio de la Frontera, 2007.

Garma Navarro, Carlos. *Buscando el Espíritu.* México: Plaza y Valdés, 2004.

Fernandes, Rubem César. *Os Cavaleiros do Bom Jesus. Uma introdução às religiões populares.* Brasília, Primeiros voôs 7, Brasiliense, 1982.

Hall, Linda. *Mary, Mother and Warrior: The Virgin in Spain and the Americas.* Austin: University of Texas Press, 2004.

Maríz, Cecilia. *Coping with Poverty: Pentecostals and Christian Base Communities in Brazil.* Philadelphia: Temple University Press, 1994.

O'Hanlon, Michael. *Acts of Faith in Contemporary Brazil.* Oxford: Pitt Rivers Museum/University of Oxford, 2001.

Parker, Cristián. *Popular Religion and Modernization in Latin America: A Different Logic.* Maryknoll, NY: Orbis Books, 1996.

Ruiz, Mario, and Carlos Garma Navarro. *Protestantismo e el Mundo Maya Contemporáneo.* México: Universidad Nacional Autonoma, 2005.

Chapter 14

Montréal

Géraldine Mossière and Deirdre Meintel

INTRODUCTION

Whereas religious revival movements have recently spread throughout the globe, in great part due to migration, public management of new urban religious landscapes is strongly influenced by historically rooted relationships of societies to religion and religious institutions. Comparing the United States with Western European countries, Foner argues that the role of religion as a resource for negotiating immigrant inclusion in host societies is anchored in local factors, such as in the religious backgrounds of immigrants and processes of secularization in the host country. In the United States, most newcomers are Christian; conversely, in Western Europe, many immigrants are Muslim. Moreover, as Foner points out, Western European nation-states are more reluctant to respond to civic claims based on religion, including new religions, since these countries generally consider themselves to be more secular than "the religiously involved United States."[1] These nation-states, and France in particular, have generally emerged out of conflict over the political claims of hegemonic religious institutions. In Canada, the multicultural model is based on the Charter of Rights and Freedoms that was enacted in 1982 as part of the constitution of Canada; it guarantees respect for the ethnocultural identities of Canadian citizens, no matter what their religion or system of beliefs. In the province of Québec, which is part of the Canadian confederation, such recognition is framed as a mutual contract whereby acceptance of cultural pluralism is promoted in exchange for commitment by newcomers to the host society's values and beliefs.[2]

In Canada, as in the United States, migration policies and administrative practices have long encouraged the immigration of Christian Europeans. However, the immigration law reforms of 1968 opened the door to new source countries with non-Christian populations, giving rise to a more ethnically and religiously diverse population. This change occurred just as Québec was experiencing what has come to be known as the "Quiet Revolution." As the political system became liberalized in the 1960s, the once-hegemonic Catholic Church lost control of social institutions (schools, hospitals, social welfare). In consequence, Québec society became thoroughly secularized and far more open to religious diversity.[3] Recent years have seen an ever-increasing number of places of worship in the province, especially in cities.[4]

Census figures show that in 2001, 706,965 residents of Québec reported having been born abroad, accounting for 9.9 percent of the total population. The relative demographic weight of immigrants in the population has been growing steadily: in 1996 immigrants accounted for 9.4 percent of the province's population, whereas in 1951, they represented only 5.6 percent of the province's population.[5] In recent years, the numbers of Muslims among immigrants have increased markedly, such that this population in Québec increased by 140 percent over the 1990s.[6] Most of them come from countries that were part of the French sphere of influence in the past—Lebanon and Morocco and, in recent years, mainly Algeria. Concerns about the integration of this culturally diverse religious group have recently stirred debate over the adjustments to be made by the receiving society, and, indeed, over whether the host society can reasonably be expected to adapt to this new population.

Upon their arrival, newcomers face risks of social isolation, as well as the lack of social networks and knowledge about practical resources in their new home country. A variety of social actors and groups play a part in the settlement trajectory of immigrants, including public institutions, nongovernmental and nonprofit organizations such as the YMCA, ethnic associations, and religious groups.[7] Funded by contributions from various sources, public and private, non-religious groups such as local organizations provide material, psychological, and symbolic resources to newcomers. Montreal counts a large number of religious organizations that are also committed to conducting such activities, although they are not generally accorded public recognition or funding for these purposes.

Annick Germain and her colleagues in urban studies found some 800 places of worship in Montreal, of which 35 percent were occupied mainly by immigrant minorities.[8] Most new places of worship belong to non-Christian religions or to Christian evangelical congregations, the latter attracting mostly immigrants of African, Haitian, Latin American, or Filipino origins. However, though immigrants from a particular country may predominate in these groups, it is unusual to find a religious group whose members are all drawn from a single ethnic category; rather, most include immigrants from more than one national origin and often have at least a few native-born Québécois members. Religious diversity in Québec has not been the source of conflicts that have occurred elsewhere (Paris, Los Angeles). This may be a factor of the cosmopolitan values that have considerable influence in Québec—a question we return to at a later point.

Mossière's study of a Congolese Pentecostal church based in Montreal shows that pastors and other religious leaders act as cultural brokers between immigrants and the host society.[9] Here we examine more generally the question of the role that religious groups play in the adaptation of newcomers to the receiving society. How are these groups organized, and what kind of services do they offer to their members? How do religious groups function, in terms of their belief system, as institutions, and as communities, so as to provide immigrant minorities with social networks, identity, and a sense of belonging? In what ways do these congregations differ from others that have sprung up in the same period (post-1960) but whose members were mostly born in Québec?

Our research in North African mosques, Congolese and Salvadorian Pentecostal congregations, Hindu temples, Tamil Catholic churches, and many other groups shows that individuals and religious institutions are often highly mobile; among immigrants, religious mobility continues well after migration. Not only do individuals often go from one congregation to another, or even one religion to another, but also groups themselves are likely to change location depending on access to space and changing needs. We will explain how, beyond their role in assisting members with the material aspects of settlement, religious groups offer new forms of sociality (that is, social relationships) that shape new identities and replace, at least to a certain extent, the social groups and ties left behind in the home country. We then discuss how religious beliefs and faith shape the way migrants adapt to the receiving society and their relationships with the host population. Finally, we briefly compare religious groups made up mostly of immigrants with those formed by nonimmigrants in recent decades.

TIMELINE

1951:	Immigrants represent 5.6 percent of Québec's population
1968:	Canadian immigration laws are reformed: quotas are increased and immigrants from southern countries may now enter the country
2001:	Census reports 706,965 (9.9 percent) of residents of Québec were born abroad; September 11 attack in New

York City increases negative stereotypes of Muslims and of foreign religiosities

2002:   Québec's Muslim population increases 140 percent since 1990

2003:   Annick Germain identifies 280 immigrant majority places of worship in Montréal out of a total of 800

2006–present: Géraldine Mossière visits Montréal's Congolese Pentecostal church; Pr. Meintel receives funding to coordinate a research study of religious pluralism in Montréal

IMMIGRANT RELIGIOUS COMMUNITIES

Several authors have noted that the Protestant and Catholic churches of early European immigrants to North America often supported new arrivals. Early evangelical churches often found converts among new migrants, such as the Cape Verdeans studied by Meintel.[10] The same can be said of Jewish congregations in regard to the immigrants of their faith who arrived from Russia and Eastern Europe. However, the influence of religious institutions and ideologies on more recent waves of immigrants coming from more southern, non-European countries has only recently been documented. In the United States, two large-scale studies[11] have established the major role played by religious communities in the daily life of immigrant members, and show that they have a decisive impact on the settlement of newcomers, providing them both institutional and social anchoring.[12] According to Warner, migration experiences make religiosity more meaningful for newcomers even though their religious beliefs and practices may change in the process.[13] In some cases, immigrants adapt religious principles or practices to the habits and customs of the new society. For example, although the Muslim day of rest is typically Friday, many mosques organize their activities on Saturdays or Sundays in North America.

Ebaugh and Chafetz argue that in the United States, church-based networks offer the most sustained and reliable support for immigrants helping them become familiar with their new environs more quickly and easily.[14] Not only do religious congregations usually offer material support as well as counsel with legal matters, but also the leader is likely to play a role of counsellor or "spiritual father," this term being widespread in evangelic settings.[15] Hurh and Kim find that among Koreans in the United States, religious practice is more regular than in the homeland, to such a point that for some, religiosity becomes a prominent part of their lifestyle. For such immigrants, religion is as much an identity and a system of meanings as a source of psychological comfort.[16] In

Canada as in the United States, Evangelical congregations are organized through small cells and units that agglomerate and give a role to each member in such a way that all of them interconnect and develop strong collective solidarity.[17]

Sociologists of religion consider immigrants' religious commitment to be a voluntary act based on a personal choice that corresponds to the logic of what Yang and Ebaugh define as "the new voluntarism" that characterizes contemporary religious congregations in North America. Immigrants are often targeted for proselytizing by newer religious groups.[18] At the same time, long-established churches try to attract new arrivals by incorporating ethnic and cultural practices in worship activities.[19] In her comparison of Catholic and Evangelical Salvadoran churches in three American cities (San Francisco, Washington, and Phoenix), Menjivar observes that Catholics organize educative and information programs targeting a large audience of Christian immigrants while Evangelicals are more likely to convert newcomers on a one-to-one basis, and then change their ethics as well as their social and economic behavior. Mossière has found that some congregations are so active in regard to their immigrant members that they develop close links with congregations in the home country of their members.[20]

Bramadat has noted the important role of religious symbolism and discourse in migrant narratives.[21] For example, the Theravada Buddhist temples of Regina introduce a new kind of social setting to North American urban landscapes, such that immigrants originating from non-Western countries frequently move between these familiar cultural and social spaces and the receiving society.[22] In general, the literature on religious communities in the migratory context focuses mainly on the articulation of ethnicity and religion.[23] For example, by continuing to practice their Buddhist faith and practices, Tibetan groups in Ontario have overcome the hardships of adaptation to their host environment, while preserving ethnic and religious cohesion.[24] Dorais shows that in Montreal, Buddhist religious practice is useful for preserving family continuity and ethnic identity among Vietnamese immigrants.[25] Beyond the comfortable cultural and social milieu they provide and the spiritual needs they satisfy, some immigrant evangelical groups also preach to their members the importance of insertion in the receiving society through economic and social mobility.[26]

When immigrants continue to practice the same religion in the new country, the structure of the group is likely to change and sometimes, religious activities are as well. In some cases, immigrants from a given country of origin collectively adopt a new religion, typically, the mainstream tradition of the hosting country. In the United States, Ng contends that "in the process of conversion, immigrants come to learn the American way through a creative development of their own cultural categories, symbols, and practices."[27] The case of Chinese immigrants' conversion to Christianity in the United States is indicative: Christian congregations offer various concrete forms of help, such as picking up arriving students at the airport, inviting new immigrants to dinner, or helping them prepare to pass driving tests, in the hope that they will become members of the church.[28] In Canada, Winland has studied Hmong refugees in Ontario who were assisted in settlement by Mennonites and who adopted the Mennonite religion; our own study includes a Korean Presbyterian church in Montreal, whose members converted after immigrating in many cases.[29] Similarly, in her work on Indonesian Chinese settled in Toronto, Nagata has shown the positive aspect of sharing a religious identity with natives of the host country as it constitutes a "message that the immigrants are willing to express some ideological and normative solidarity with their hosts, and to present an ethnic image acceptable to the latter without necessarily generating an actual forum for strong social relationships or intermarriage."[30]

Not only do migrant religious communities provide essential resources for newcomers in the host society, but also they establish new spaces of socialization where identities and social relationships challenged by the migratory process are recomposed. Certain social roles may be imported from the home country, whereas gender and intergenerational relationships may be redefined under the influence of the norms that prevail in the host society.[31] For instance, women are likely to get new responsibilities for transmitting religious and cultural (mainly linguistic) knowledge to the younger generation of the group.[32] Haddad, who studies Muslim women in the United States, shows that by being more present in public spaces and by gaining access to mosques, they are likely to experience a change of social status. However, the author also finds that some Muslim leaders are still very reluctant to let women participate in the mosque's activities since they never do so in the homeland; also, certain issues such as homosexuality are highly taboo.[33] There is a general consensus that religious groups have a significant impact on the political, economic, social, and cultural experience of immigrants, and that they function as a bridge between the host society and immigrants. In this chapter, we will show how religious behavior can change with migration and give examples of how religious beliefs and practices are adapted to the new context.

THE STUDY AND ITS METHODS

Our analysis is based on a broad ethnographic study[34] of religious diversity in Québec (Canada) as it has developed since the 1960s. Although the study includes religious groups in Québec's outlying regions as well as in Montreal, the present analysis is based on data collected in the metropolis, and focuses mainly on religious groups made up of immigrants. The research, still in progress, aims at documenting the new religious diversity that has appeared in the aftermath of the Quiet Revolution as well as the meaning of religion in the everyday lives of the Québécois today.

Over the past two years, observations have been carried out on religious groups that either represent (1) religions established in Québec since the 1960s (e.g., Baha'i; Neoshamanism, including Druidism and Wicca); (2) new forms of religious practice in long-established religions (the case of some Jewish and Catholic congregations); (3) religions imported by immigrants (Islam, Hinduism, certain forms of Buddhism); or (4) congregations of established religions that include a substantial proportion of immigrants among their members.

Although the project concerns the whole of the province, most of the data has been gathered in Montreal, the province's largest and most multicultural city. Thus far, observations have been carried out on a total of 79 groups; of these, 29 have been studied in-depth with extended participant observation and interviews of members and leaders.

Group Type	Case Studies	Limited Studies
Muslim	5	13
Jewish	2 (1 in progress)	5
Catholic	6 (4 in progress)	8
Non-Evangelical Protestant	1 (in progress)	3 (1 in region)
Evangelical	5 (2 in progress)	18 (in progress)
Hindu	1	10
Buddhist	2	6
Modern religions	–	6
Neoshamanic (networks)	5	7
Personal development and new Age groups drawing on oriental spiritualities	2	3
TOTAL	29	79

Observations have been carried out on religious rituals and other religious activities such as neighborhood prayer groups as well as on social activities, such as communal meals and picnics, funding events, and courses that are sponsored by religious groups. We examine members' personal religious practices as well as the perspectives of religious leaders. Interviews have been conducted with members who have diversified social profiles in regard to sex, age, profession, matrimonial status, and level of commitment to the group. These focus on individuals' personal and religious trajectories, as well as the role of the religious group in their everyday lives, the level of economic, social, and ideological commitment to the community, and when relevant, religious activities pursued outside the group's purview. The results presented here show some of the patterns that have emerged from the research to date. Not surprisingly, our data confirm that a wide range of resources is now available in Québec's religious "market." However, more surprising patterns have also emerged. For example, we find that both individuals and religious traditions are highly mobile and adaptable and that most of our informants have changed groups or religious affiliation at least once in their lives. Some established religions have adjusted to religious transformations brought by immigrants and to the new trends of charismatic religiosity that have become visible in Montreal's religious landscape. For example, there are many Catholic churches where immigrants are able to find religious expression in their own language, musical forms and prayer styles, such as those where Tamil Catholics worship.[35] A number of these offer charismatic services, in part so as not to lose members to Evangelical groups. In fact, Tamils do not have a Catholic parish at present, but rather a "mission" that serves the religious needs from across the city. Charismatic Catholic healing services in Tamil are held in a parish church in another part of the city. On these occasions, Tamil priests visiting from Sri Lanka or Toronto perform the laying on of hands for the throngs of worshipers who line up for healing, the men in dark suits and the women making a rainbow of colourful saris. On some occasions, rather than laying on hands himself, the priest asks worshippers to do so for others in the congregation.

This paper focuses on religious groups whose members are mostly immigrants. We find that these groups are organized in such a way as to give a central place to the experience and needs of newcomers and they have great influence on how their immigrant members adapt to Québec, as well as their relationships to Québécois of other origins, including the native born, and their interactions with the institutions of the host society.

RELIGION: COMMUNITY, IDENTITY, AND ETHNICITY

Most of the immigrant religious groups in our sample are organized as "congregations." According to Yang and Ebaugh, immigrant congregations are characterized by "the increased voluntary participation of members in religious functions, a lay-centered community, and multiple functions of the religious community."[36]

In his research on a Muslim group in our study, Boucher shows that the mosque functions as a community center, becoming a sacred space only for worship and prayers. Solidarity and feelings of belonging are generated on the basis of religious references held in common and the shared experience of migration.[37] His work shows how the religious group helps replace community ties fractured by migration and plays a major role in the settlement process of members in the receiving society: more than simply a place for worship, the mosque is a community space open to all Muslims. Upon arrival in the region, new migrants receive the keys of the building so as to be able to come and go autonomously. According to its leader, the mosque provides a "social space for mutual help. For example, when some of us go to pick up *halal* meat, we all go to the slaughterhouse together. People share . . . The best help is from belonging, when you share the same objective of transcendance, where you are recognized for who you really are. This is the best help. You maybe didn't eat that evening but nonetheless you feel satisfied after being together, because it's worth so much more, it recharges your batteries."

To give another example from our research, Betbeder's work on Hindus in Montreal shows that temples are organized as personalized spaces where members re-create a family atmosphere that helps compensate for ties with families and friends in the home country that have become attenuated by distance.[38] In Sri Lankan temples in Montreal, she observes that, unlike the custom in the home country, religious deities are portrayed as representations of a cosmic family, so that the temple is devoted to Durga as mother goddess, with her husband Shiva, and their two sons Ganesh and Murugan. In the migratory context where family relationships and roles are challenged by underemployment and the cultural norms of the host society, presenting and worshiping these deities as a family acquires new importance and meaning; through devotion centered on family life among the gods, these temples offer a "family" context to migrants whose social ties have been fractured by migration. Somewhat like the mosques that we have observed, Hindu temples provide a space for socializing and, bring the diasporic community together in the new country.

The immigrant religious groups in our study tend to form communities based on common values, symbols, and practices, as well as deep feelings of belonging. Religious rituals often constitute key moments in the life of the group when the community is reinforced. Coexperience of the sacred, by shared verbal practices and habitual gestures, fosters the creation of an effervescent community of feelings and, in many cases, ecstatic experiences. In Pentecostal congregations, ritual techniques using music, hymns, and well-staged sermons, engender deep emotional sharing between members and inspire physical expressions of faith (dancing, jumping, clapping, screaming, embracing). In this kind of atmosphere, individual manifestations of religiosity and personal religious experience are encouraged. Most new members relate their attraction to Pentecostal congregations to this freedom and relative autonomy of expression such that those who were Catholic before converting contrast it with what they see as the more austere liturgy of Catholic churches.[39]

IDENTITY TRANSMISSION

Most immigrant religious groups we have studied organize weekend or evening courses. Some of these are focused on religious themes (ethics; sacred and choral music; study of the Bible, Quran, or other sacred texts). Church-based social activities also gather members sharing common interests as in the Congolese congregation, where meetings are also organized for married couples on how to keep a marriage healthy and how to care for the partner. Religious groups also sponsor classes in French, English, ethnic music, traditional dance, and for Vietnamese Buddhists, martial arts. Whereas some of these activities attract adults, many address the needs of the younger generation. In Hindu temples, for example, leaders organize conferences about cultural diversity in Montreal and they also participate in public events like blood donation campaigns or marches to encourage kidney donations. By promoting multiculturalism and shaping civic behavior, such activities help the second and later generations make sense of

Members of a Congolese evangelical church during Sunday worship, Montréal, Canada (ca. 2007). (Photo by Géraldine Mossière.)

identities and affiliations that are strung between ancestral homelands and the country where they are born and raised.[40] By learning the language of the Holy Scriptures, young Hindus absorb their parents' religious philosophy, while developing a vision of Hinduism that transcends the ethnic frontiers that characterize India (e.g., between Indians from the north of the country versus those from the south).

Identity transmission in many immigrant communities implies religious socialization as much as it does passing on cultural and social practices. In some instances, religious leaders take on symbolic parental authority or act as substitutes for a missing parent. For example, pastors sometimes play the role of a social father by advising teenagers about marriage and family life, and other subjects. In Evangelical churches, the biparental family model is promoted, and single women are encouraged to hope for a responsible breadwinner husband.[41] Congolese pastors also oversee the care given to young refugees who arrive in Montreal as unaccompanied minors; typically the public agency that oversees the reception and protection of unaccompanied minors seeks to place them with families in their own ethnic communities. Congolese Evangelical pastors and Catholic priests play an important role in giving counsel and support to young Congolese who arrive alone in Canada and help find families to take them in.[42]

Sociability among members is encouraged in immigrant religious groups; for example, the Congolese and Central American Pentecostals in our study enjoy a communal meal after Sunday worship.[43] Hindu parents bring their children to Indian classical dance or music classes, and other events where they can practice speaking their parents' mother tongue. Such activities strengthen community ties among members but can also create social differentiation within the group, since they are usually structured by age, gender, and socioeconomic situation. Teenagers, for example, may organize evening gatherings to socialize between the sexes and talk about sexuality in ways that are in line with the religious tenets of their group, whereas men may meet to share meals and exchange about employment or business opportunities.[44]

LOCAL RESOURCES NETWORKS AND MUTUAL AID

The organizational structures of local religious groups rely more on network dynamics and the affinities of individuals, than on geographical logic.[45] Functioning as "community centers,"[46] they support newcomers in the settlement process by providing members with material, social, and emotional resources, along with recreational activities, information, and advice for finding employment and housing usually transmitted by word of mouth. In addition to examples already given, let us mention the "murids," or Senegalese Muslim brotherhoods in our study that offer substantial material assistance to any member who is newly arrived from Africa. This includes providing housing and hospitality, often for months. Members of the mosque studied by Boucher in a city north of Montreal habitually offer newcomers information on housing, jobs, and government services, as well as a welcoming social environment. It is assumed that once established, the new arrivals will give similar help to others.

The beliefs and the ethics that immigrant religious groups foster also provide symbolic resources such as vocabulary and language for immigrant members to reassess the hardships induced by migration. In Pentecostal congregations sermons delivered by the pastor give meaning to the migratory experience and members' everyday life, in the same way as the conversion narratives that figure in weekly services for Central American Evangelicals.[47] Verses from the Bible are cited so as to shed light on members' personal experiences, whereas biographical events are revisited through the prism of biblical teachings in such a way that everyday challenges become divine signals.

A Sunday sermon on the subject of debt observed by Mossière serves as an illustration. On this occasion, the pastor compared credit facilities with traps set by Satan—traps that the believer is meant to overcome by the strength of his or her regular and diligent religious practice. "God doesn't want you to live on social welfare! That is not the place for you, go back to your studies!" In the case of well-educated Muslim immigrants who have settled in Montreal, Maynard has met men who have found value in the experience of deskilling by intensifying their activities in the service of the religious groups. In sum, religious belief reframes the experiences of migration, resettlement, and difficulties experienced in the host society such as discrimination and unemployment and allows immigrants to reinvest them with positive meaning through constant reference to the presence and intervention of God in their lives.[48]

On the other hand, use of such resources by members varies considerably. Whereas most are actively committed to the community, some only join the group for religious activities and worship.[49] Informal resources offered by religious groups to their immigrant members do not substitute for public institutions and government-provided services; rather, they complement the resources provided by the state and often convey information about them to new arrivals.[50] Finally, as in the case of unaccompanied minors taken in by Pentecostal families,[51] religious groups often offer services that the public system is unable to give, for lack of human or financial resources.

RELIGIOUS GROUPS AND ETHNICITY

All the religious leaders interviewed in the study affirm that the ethnic origin of members is not an issue and that their doors are open to all well-intentioned believers. Although some congregations are more pluriethnic than others, virtually none of the groups in our study is composed of members originating from a single country. Rather, like Nagata we find that language is often influential in defining the social boundaries of the religious group.[52] Tamil Catholic services are usually held in the Tamil language, and those of the Vietnamese Catholic congregation now under study are in Vietnamese, though a few Québécois (non-Vietnamese) spouses may be present. In most cases, immigrant religious congregations tend to support ethnic identifications that are somewhat broader than those their members held before migrating. In some cases, members and leaders assert the primacy of religious belonging over ethnic differences. This is the case, for example, of the Muslims who frequent the mosques in our study; similarly, Evangelicals often mention that their fellow church members are from diverse ethnic backgrounds.

At the same time we find that most of these congregations are made up of members who share general cultural similarities, a common language and come from the same general region of the world. For example, there are many Latin American Spanish-speaking congregations in Montreal, including the Central American Spanish-speaking congregation studied by Recalde (2009) whose members come from Guatemala, El Salvador, and Honduras.[53] Similarly, for new immigrants from various regions of the Indian subcontinent, Hindu temples are often a focal point of social participation and offer an arena where common cultural and religious practices are emphasized.[54] In the immigration context, for example, the cults of the gods Shiva and Vishnu that were part of some members' backgrounds have lost ground, and boundaries between members in the city's temples are based on cultural heritage rather than particular cults or beliefs. In fact, most Montreal Hindus identify primarily as Hindus and social divisions are more likely structured according to levels of education rather than by region of origin. In one of Montreal's temples, populations coming from very different areas of India place their respective divinities on the same altar, while each community holds its own rituals. Although different groups may conduct rituals at different times, the divinities of all remain on the same altar. As Betbeder's informants explain, these religious adjustments are compatible with Hindu tradition, which holds that gods and goddesses are merely intelligible representations of the Divine. Betbeder's research, which includes observations in four temples in the Montreal area, shows that this encompassing pan-Hindu vision grows broader as the social status of believers rises and that it continues expanding in the second generation, such that temple environments tend to grow ever more inclusive over time.

Though ethnic boundaries are often blurred in religious groupings, the reverse is not the case for the groups we studied; that is, we did not find much in the way of pan-religious gatherings among immigrant groups. However, the one exception we encountered suggests that the host society context may play a role. The Tamil Catholics studied by Melissa Bouchard typically share pilgrimages and processions with their Hindu neighbors in Sri Lanka; however, when Hindus accompanied their Tamil friends on a pilgrimage to a sanctuary in the Montreal area, local Catholic authorities objected.[55] For the Tamil Catholics, including Hindu friends and in some cases, relatives, to such gatherings is part of what they see as a Tamil way of living their Catholicism. Moreover, Bouchard notes, some Tamil Catholics visit Hindu temples on occasion.

The dynamics of ethnic inclusion and exclusion in religious groups vary, partly depending on whether the religion of the group is closely linked to the culture of the milieu of origin as is the case, for example, with Vietnamese Buddhism and ancestor worship. Though Buddhism finds followers all over the world, for those who frequent the pagoda studied by Détolle,[56] it is linked to cults of the ancestors traditional to Vietnam. In this pagoda, proselytism is nonexistent; at the same time, visitors are welcomed, and are free to participate as they wish, and are even invited for a vegetarian meal at the end of religious celebrations. However, traditional Vietnamese values of inhibition, modesty, respect for elders, and dignity prevail and make for a culturally different religious milieu than that of other Buddhist groups in our study where native-born Québécois predominate.

In such cases as just described, the religious group tends to perpetuate the practices and symbolism of the homeland. Language also makes a difference; Spanish, for example, is the mother tongue of Montrealers of various national origins and is understood by many others, whereas few non-Tamils and non-Vietnamese speak the language of those groups. Finally, as we have seen for certain Pentecostal groups that actively proselytize beyond social boundaries, ethnicity may become a second-order identity, less important than religion.[57]

IMMIGRANT RELIGIOUS GROUPS AND THE HOST SOCIETY

Whereas the role of religious groups in the life trajectories of immigrants is widely documented, the impact of these groups on how members relate to the host society is still being debated. Assimilationist models of the past tended to regard ethnic belonging as an obstacle to full participation in the host society. More recently questions have been raised in the mass media about whether Muslim immigrants can be fully integrated into the host societies where they live. We have found that overt religiosity on the part of immigrants (whatever their religion) may be criticized by counselors, potential employers, and others. For example, we have learned that a counselor in a Montreal social agency complained about an African (Evangelical) client who "talks about God too much." In another case, a well-educated African immigrant was unable to find employment. Eventually one of his employment counselors discovered that this was because he mentioned church activities on his curriculum vitae.

A number of recent studies portray immigrant religious communities as facilitating adaptation to the new society by providing a space where identities can be renegotiated.[58] In this sense, Hurh and Kim's work indicates that religious commitment among immigrants is not determined by the level of participation in the host society, length of residence, age, sex, education, economic status, or sociocultural assimilation.[59] Mossière's study of a Congolese Pentecostal church shows how ethnic, family, religious, and gender identities are reorganized in ways that facilitate in part members' adjustment to the receiving society without preventing them from acquiring other social resources outside the religious group.[60] Maynard has studied a Muslim group mainly comprising Moroccan immigrants where members are encouraged to let go of the "myth of return" (to Morocco) and instead, take part in civic activities in Montreal and contribute to the society where they are living.[61] In some cases, however, we note that religious groups attempt to shield members from what are perceived to be the moral dangers of the wider society (drinking, sexual promiscuity, etc.).[62] We explore this issue further in the following section.

SYMBOLIC CAPITAL AND (DIS)CONTINUITIES BETWEEN RELIGIOUS COMMUNITIES AND HOST SOCIETY

Symbolic capital (for example, educational, cultural, and linguistic resources that are valued by others) is a key factor in negotiating inclusion in a receiving society,[63] as it influences access to economic and social resources. While Muslims have been the object of negative stereotypes in Québec as in Western countries generally since 2001,[64] our research (which includes 11 Muslim groups) shows that such images affect how individuals of the group concerned are included or excluded from participating in public life and the social institutions of the society where they live. Although Muslim believers may also identify by ethnicity, social class, or level of education, they shape their relationships with the dominant group in terms of their religious belonging, which they consider a source of pride and a positive distinction that distinguishes them from others. One man interviewed by Maynard explains that, despite the criticism of Muslim beliefs as regards women' roles he encounters in Québec, he is proud of abiding by Divine Law. Pointing his finger toward the sky, he declares: "At the end of the day, it's He who will judge." Some believers perceive the hostility or suspicion encountered in the host country as challenges to their faith imposed by the Lord, and therefore a means of spiritual advancement.

Muslim immigrants themselves are active in the process of representing their group to the wider society. After interviewing members of a mosque that receives a great deal of media exposure, some of it unfavorable, Maynard concludes that his subjects present Islam as a resource that provides an interpretative grid for believers to frame and give value to such experiences as well as a vocabulary within which they can rework their identity as Others.[65] A collective Muslim "we" emerges out of a dialogue whereby the identity assigned by the dominant group is not only accepted, but also given value. However, asserting Muslim identity in the face of negative stereotypes also means reworking it so as to divest it of invidious qualities ascribed by others. For example, Muslim women refuse the notion that the veil means "oppression" of their gender and assert that wearing it is their personal choice. Maynard finds that religious faith is sometimes used as a way of rehabilitating the standing of the group and its members; it becomes the framework for an alternative moral order to the one where the group is stigmatized.

Similarly, we find that Black (Caribbean- and African-born) Evangelicals engage in a process of self-construction by using Pentecostal idiom to overcome racism. For instance, one Haitian believer who converted to Pentecostalism a few years ago finds in her faith the tools for transcending memories of racism: "Now I don't see this one as Black or this one as White. We are all human beings doing the work of God. I have White friends, we talk on the phone, but they have been baptized . . . You have to differentiate whether or not people are baptized."[66]

We sometimes find that religious doctrines of new groups are presented as converging with dominant values in the host society. For example, Hindu philosophy advocates a vision of the world whereby all life forms take their meaning through interactions between each other. Accordingly, Hindus in Montreal have presented their religion as a holistic philosophy of life, rather than as religious dogma.[67] Similarly, a Muslim scholar in Québec, Khadiyatoulah Fall (2007), has argued that Islam has its own notion of "reasonable accommodation" (the term currently used in Québec to describe how social pluralism should be managed); that is, the concept of

"Arrouhsatou," or "compromise" that allows adaptation of religious practice to the social and physical environment.[68] We should also add that there are groups from proselytizing religions such as Islam, Caodaïsm, and Evangelical Christianity that do not hide their agenda of eventually converting the whole Québécois society; one might say that Québec is in fact a missionary field for them. The Latin Americans studied by Recalde see saving lost souls in Québec as their mission in Québec and obligation toward God.

Issues surrounding the occupation of physical space by immigrant religious groups show the impact of negative stereotypes. At present, the growing needs of religious groups in Montreal for places of worship exceed the existing supply of religious facilities in the city.[69] The majority of the groups in our study, immigrant and nonimmigrant, are of modest financial resources and have difficulty finding affordable, appropriate rental space; this is all the more the case for immigrant groups. When they have sought to purchase property, Tamil Catholics, Congolese Pentecostals, and North African Muslims have all faced objections by owners or neighbours. Traffic difficulties and noise are common objections; however, it is likely that other factors are at work. We note, for example, that several years ago, when Tamil Catholics of the Catholic mission studied by Bouchard sought to buy a Catholic church that was for sale because its congregation had shrunk in recent decades, they were rebuffed by the remaining parishioners.[70] Though difficult to prove, it is likely that this refusal was motivated to some degree by ethnic prejudice.[71]

FAMILY MODELS AND RELIGIOUS DIFFERENCE

For most immigrant groups in Québec, the encounter between different world views seems to show most clearly in differing interpretations of family models.[72] Such models are, of course, bound up with religious beliefs and rituals, as our current research shows. For example, Hindu marriages seal unions not only between two persons, but also above all, between two families, one that is sacralized through religious ritual. The notion of marriage as a religiously sanctioned, nearly unbreakable bond that unites two families, and not only two individuals, is at variance with prevailing notions of couple relationships in Québec, where cohabitation without marriage and divorce are extremely common.

The Tamil Catholics studied by Bouchard distinguish between arranged marriages considered the norm, and "love" marriages seen as risky, especially love marriages with Hindus. In effect, her informants believe, family norms (including arranged, endogamous marriages) support the maintenance of religious traditions and Catholic faith. Some Tamils express regret that

Québec society does not provide better examples for young people; they see a causal relationship between the low levels of religious practice among the Québécois and the breakdown of family structures, as expressed in high rates of divorce, cohabitation without marriage, single-parent families and children born out of wedlock. A priest interviewed by Bouchard points proudly to the low divorce rate among Tamil Catholics.

The Congolese Pentecostal leader in Géraldine Mossière's study also distances himself from the Québec family patterns. His teachings regarding the gender roles are clear. In accordance with the family model conveyed in the Holy Scriptures, he asserts that a man's role is that of breadwinner, whereas a woman's duties are to be discrete and modest, in matters of dress among others. Moreover, he expresses the hope that the "irregular" situation of single mothers in his congregation is only temporary; ideally, such a woman should marry a Pentecostal man as soon as possible.[73]

Similar critiques of the host society's family models are voiced in a Latin American Evangelical group studied by Recalde.[74] In this case, and unlike the group studied by Mossière where efforts are made to convert native-born Québécois, religious activities are designed so as to occupy virtually all the members' free time, reducing the likelihood of interaction with non-Evangelicals. This group also distrusts public institutions, including courts of law, schools, hospitals, and governments, and encourages believers to simply "turn to God" rather than seek recourse for problems in nonreligious institutions.

Overall, immigrants are wary of the family and couple patterns they see in the wider Québec society. Those who practice a religion, we find, are also dismayed by the much-diminished religious practice of the social majority that has given rise to current family patterns. Thus, they are all the more motivated to transmit their religious faith and practices to their children, as they hope to inculcate the family and gender norms of their religion as well.

RELATIONSHIPS WITH THE WIDER SOCIETY

Apart from the somewhat sectarian approach adopted by a few religious groups such as that studied by Recalde,[75] most immigrant religious groups build their identity through the contacts they establish with the dominant society. In one of the mosques studied by Maynard that we will call "Mosque A," he finds that the members base their identity on a clear dichotomy between "us" and "them," with a strict boundary between Muslims and the rest of Québec society.[76] In this case, the aim is not to isolate the Muslim community, but rather to emphasize its distinctness within the host society. With this objective, the imam who used to lead the group (he is no longer in Québec) delivered public conferences on Islam to Québécois-born adults and scholarly groups to represent "the Muslim community" to the general public: "Even though there is a clash between us and the society, we have to do it otherwise, we will be locked in our place." However, in the same mosque, Maynard also met other Muslims who expressed disagreement with this imam's positions while in another Muslim group he studied, he found less emphasis placed on differences between Muslims and others, and more on the contributions that "good Muslims" (i.e., practicing Muslims) can make to the wider society.

Several Montreal Hindu temples also organize activities that contribute to society as a whole and thus make the group known to a wider public, the premise being that mutual understanding and recognition are possible through education.[77] A similar position has been taken by leaders of certain mosques in Montreal, notably those of Sufi Muslims. Yet another mosque in our study situated in a smaller city where there are few immigrants as compared to Montreal, has maintained a very discreet profile until now. However, the group is beginning to move toward becoming somewhat more socially visible.[78] In short, attitudes regarding visibility in the host society vary between religious groups, even within the same tradition.

Apart from the orientation given by leaders as to how the group is positioned in the wider society, within the same group members may vary widely in how they see relationships with the dominant group. Some Muslims in "Mosque A" hold that non-Muslim lifestyles and beliefs are too different from those of Muslims for there to be social mixing and so choose to limit their personal networks to Muslims exclusively. Nonetheless, a minority who go to the same mosque expresses more openness. For example: "I like to adapt, I can be with everybody, I can be with nobody. I have friends from the university, I go out with them, but I am not on their side. I can go to the mosque, but I am not on their side either."

The range of positions individuals take regarding the dominant society is to some extent a factor of subjective attitudes regarding religious identity, and personal beliefs and practices. Maynard identifies two profiles among his Muslim interviewees: whereas the first is deeply anchored in religious performance and follows a dogmatic approach to Islam, the second emphasizes moral values carried by the Qur'anic message without advocating a narrow interpretation of religious precepts.

CONVERGENCE AND ADAPTATION

In recent years, public debate about the place of religion in the public sphere has centered around issues such as how religion is presented in public schools, the Sikh kirpan, Muslim veils, and the Jewish *eruv*.[79] Immigrant religious groups have developed various strategies for dealing with added public attention along with existing challenges of fitting into a secular society. Often these groups choose to emphasize the commonalities between the religious community's vision of the world and the dominant Québécois worldview. Hindus modify rituals such as cremation, which in India, would be performed along a riverbank, to conform with Québec law. Certain Hindu festivals involving sacred fireworks are supervised by police and firemen because of the crowds involved and the danger of fire. Even gurus visiting from the home country interpret Hinduism in ways that are geared to making it more accessible and acceptable in the host environment.

Pentecostal congregations display similar strategies of integration. A Congolese pastor explains that sermons and Pentecostal norms are aimed at making members into "good citizens" and promoting their social and economic participation and mobility in their new country.[80] This perspective is illustrated by his pastoral approach, which he terms "The Church in the City." By this, he means that, "the Church must contribute to the society's development by equipping believers to be more efficient and productive."

In Pentecostalism, the notion of citizenship usually includes active behavior oriented toward economic prosperity, in accordance with Protestant values such as work, discipline, and economic accumulation. All these are values that fit well with prevailing norms in capitalist societies, including Québec. Seen in this light, the religious community can have a positive effect on an immigrant's adaptation into broader society.[81]

As mentioned earlier, family ties and gender roles are often seen differently from the models promoted in the wider society. The same Congolese pastor who preaches that men and women should adopt gender roles prescribed in the Bible also runs seminars to help members adapt to Québécois laws and norms. One typical activity that he organized was entitled, "How to Interpret Marriage as a Christian, in Accordance with Québec Law." Similarly, child-rearing practices are promoted that reinforce parental authority, but in conformity with Québec law, which prohibits the sorts of corporal punishment that is common in African and Caribbean societies. Most religious groups we have encountered espouse a discourse of integration or adaptation, and see their members as social actors who have a positive contribution to make to Québec society. Religious leaders often mention the important role of immigrants for the province's prosperity, cultural enrichment, and social development.

In the church studied by Recalde, religious rhetoric presents proselytizing as a way of improving Québec society. Socioeconomic mobility and educational achievement are presented as a ways of contributing to Québec society and overcoming the image of Latin Americans as members of street gangs and drug traffickers. In their view, Evangelical immigrants are endowed with the mission of saving Christian souls in a province one of them describes as "devastated for decades because of the collapse of Catholicism." Concerned by the urgency of Québec's "spiritual situation," the group works hard to bring in new members.

In a similar vein, Maynard observes that some Muslim groups seek to assert their presence in the public sphere with the intention of transforming it, while others attach less importance to the public status of their religion and only wish to practice it without hindrance. Although the imam mentioned earlier tried to promote a public presence of what he considered to be the "real" Islam, he was often at odds with other Muslim leaders. In other cases, religious leaders emphasize gratitude to the receiving society (e.g., the Vietnamese Buddhists who invite political figures to all their major celebrations, and regularly give thanks to Canadian public servants in their prayers).[82]

TRADITION AND TRANSITION

Religious leaders and believers who follow the same religion that they did before migrating tend to think that their religious practices have not substantially changed since migration. Nonetheless, we find many instances where religious practices have been adapted to conditions in Québec, beyond the cases mentioned earlier where changes were made for legal reasons. For example, Tamil Catholics find new sites for pilgrimage in Québec; in the homeland, pilgrimages are usually performed on mountains also held sacred by Hindus, Buddhists, and Muslims. This expression of devotion may result in miracles and healing, as reported by some of the Tamils interviewed by Bouchard. Tamil believers seek to perpetuate this practice in Québec's Catholic traditional sites of pilgrimage such as Mont Rigaud in the area of Montreal. On one occasion, the rituals involved in the pilgrimage (these include a procession of a statue of the Virgin followed by a celebration of the Eucharist) were followed by a family picnic with food provided by the organizing committee. Bouchard notes that Tamil pilgrimages are an occasion for a social gathering and for strengthening family ties, and that their Hindu friends are usually invited as well. Although this religiously inclusive practice is normal in the homeland, it faces strong opposition from Catholic authorities in Québec, who are dismayed to see Hindus taking communion and by the picnicing and socializing on the pilgrimage site. They argue that the pilgrimage sites are not designed to host such a large population. In fact, the site is equipped to receive a few hundred pilgrims, not the some 5,000 Tamils who came on one recent occasion. Recently, local Catholic authorities have imposed restrictions on admission on the site, something much regretted by Tamil Catholics, who feel that their traditional forms of religiosity are not welcome in Québec.

Another example of religious change after migration is to be found in a Vietnamese pagoda in our study where new chants have been introduced by the Chinese members (a minority in this pagoda), with the help of DVDs imported from Taiwan.[83] Muslims consider the ritual sacrifice of sheep for the annual celebration of Aïd el-Kebir (commemoration of Abraham's total submission to God) as religiously significant, but its performance in Western urban contexts has proven so complicated that many avoid it or send remittances to family back home to have the ritual performed there. Muslims also send charitable donations (that is *zakat*, a religious obligation) home for the family to distribute among the poor; others decide to volunteer in nonprofit, charitable organizations in their host country.

In some cases we find a deliberate effort to not change practices based on religion despite the difficulty of maintaining them in Québec. In one of the mosques Maynard observed, the imam's sermons were aimed at adapting Muslim behavior in a non-Muslim context while adhering to the rules of Islam. Since the prohibition on paying interest makes it nearly impossible for Muslims to acquire a home in Québec, the imam proposed that the mosque develop a real estate project where members could purchase property directly from the mosque without paying interest, and thus adhering to Muslim rules. In another mosque Maynard has studied, members prefer to respect the spirit of the rule rather than the rule itself: they contend that the principle is that wealthy people should not abuse the poor by imposing usurious rates of interest. By their interpretation, as long as the loan is made at a reasonable rate of interest, a Muslim may acquire a house without breaking his religion's rules. Both positions can be found among Muslims in Montreal, the first being more typical of conservative believers.

For the most part, religious traditions imported from countries where immigrants originate do not form the basis of religious ghettos, but rather are renegotiated in ways that provide believers with ideological resources for adjusting to a new social and cultural context. On the individual level, we find considerable religious change over the life course, whether it takes the form of conversion or not. For example, we find changes in how religion is practiced and the intensity of religious practice. Further changes can be expected as religious groups evolve over time and the second generation comes of age; already we find groups introducing French or, more rarely, English, so as to accommodate younger cohorts.

To conclude, let us mention some of the trends that we find across immigrant religious groups that distinguish them from groups mainly composed of members born in Québec. As we have seen, groups formed by immigrants tend to be concerned with (1) giving members the help they need to adapt to the new society; (2) providing symbolic resources that allow migrants to give value to the difficult experiences associated with migration; (3) providing community structures that help compensate for social ties and support that have been attenuated by migration[84]; (4) positioning the group and its members in the new society in ways that are valued in religious terms. The nonimmigrant groups in our study are typically less preoccupied with their place in the wider society, and take their members' status as Québécois and Canadian as a given. At the same time, they are usually less developed on the community level; in many cases, nonimmigrant groups provide religious and spiritual services but little in the way of sociability for their members.

At the same time we note certain convergences: just as immigrant religious groups offer symbolic resources for dealing with the difficulties of migration and settlement, so other groups allow their members to reframe the problems of modern living (family issues, illness, unemployment) in ways that give them value. On the individual level, we have noted that some migrants change religion or the congregation to which they belong over their life trajectories; if anything, such changes are even more evident among nonmigrants. Nonmigrants who practice any kind of religion (often termed "spirituality" by those concerned) tend to frequent groups different from the religion of their primary socialization or to frequent several kinds of groups at the same time. Finally, we note that virtually none of the groups in our study are entirely composed of members of the same ethnic origin; moreover, most immigrant religious groups have at least a few members who were born in Québec.

Our research in Québec confirms Foner's argument that North America provides a relatively favorable environment for immigrant religions and shows how immigrant religious groups themselves take an active role in shaping how their members fit into Québec society. Moreover, there is reason to believe that the vitality of immigrant religious groups and the diversity of religious resources they bring in Québec are likely to have an impact on the social and political dynamics of the province and on the religious behavior and identifications of future generations of Québécois.

NOTES

1. Nancy Foner and Richard Alba, "Immigrant Religion in the U.S. and Western Europe: Bridge or Barrier to Inclusion?" *IMR* 42 (2008), p. 361.

2. Denise Helly, Le traitement de l'islam au Canada. Tendances actuelles, *Revue Européenne des Migrations Internationales* 20 (2004), pp. 47–72. Ministère de l'Immigration et des Communautés Culturelles (MICC). *Tableaux sur l'immigration au Québec 1997–2001*. Gouvernement du Québec (2002).

3. Paul-André Linteau, René Durocher, Jean-Claude Robert, and François Ricard. *Histoire du Québec contemporain, Tome II: Le Québec depuis 1930*, Montréal, Éditions Boréal (1989).

4. Germain A, Gagnon JE, Polo A-L. 2003. *L'aménagement des lieux de culte des minorités ethniques: enjeux et dynamiques locales*, Institut National de la Recherche Scientifique Urbanisation, Culture et Société, Montréal.

5. Immigration et Communautés Culturelles Québec. *Population immigrée recensée au Québec et dans les régions en 2001: caractéristiques générales*. Gouvernement du Québec. (2004).

6. Ministère de l'Immigration et des Communautés Culturelles (MICC). 2002. *Tableaux sur l'immigration au Québec 1997-2001*, Gouvernement du Québec.

7. Yannick Boucher. *L'islam en contexte minoritaire: étude de cas d'une mosquée au Saguenay-Lac-Saint-Jean* Document de Travail Groupe de Recherche Diversité Urbaine. Montréal. (2009). Ana Maria Alonso. *L'immigration et la communauté d'accueil: le cas du Saguenay-Lac-Saint-Jean*. Mémoire présenté à l'Université du Québec à Chicoutimi comme exigence partielle de la maîtrise en études régionales. (1998). Vatz-Laaroussi, Michèle, Myriam Simard, and Nasser Baccouche, dir. *Immigration et dynamiques locales*. Chicoutimi: Université du Québec à Chicoutimi, (1997), p. 247. Michèle Vatz-Laaroussi, Maria Elisa Montejo, Diane Lessard, and Monica Viana. 1995. "Femmes immigrantes en région: une force pour le développement local?" *Collectif de recherche et d'études sur les femmes et le changement (CREFEC)*. Université de Sherbrooke, Nouvelles pratiques sociales, vol. 8, no. 2 automne, Presses de l'Université du Québec, 1995), pp. 123–137.

8. Germain et al., 2003.

9. Géraldine Mossière, "Former un citoyen utile au Québec et qui reçoit de ce pays," Le rôle d'une communauté religieuse montréalaise dans la trajectoire migratoire de ses membres *Cahiers du GRES/Diversité Urbaine* 6 (2006), pp. 45–62.

10. Meintel, Deirdre, Race, Culture and Portuguese Colonialism in Cabo Verde. FACS, Syracuse University, (1984). Timothy L. Smith, "Religion and ethnicity in America," *American Historical Review* 83 (1978), pp. 1155–1185. Raymond A. Mohl, and Neil Betten. "The Immigrant church in Gary, Indiana: Religious adjustment and cultural defense," *Ethnicity* 8 (1981), pp. 1–17. Jay P. Dolan, *The American Catholic Experience: a History from Colonial Times to the Present* (New York: Doubleday: Garden City, 1985).

11. R. Stephen Warner and Judith G. Wittner, *Gatherings in Diaspora: Religious Communities and the New Immigration*. (Philadelphia: Temple of University Press, 1998). Helen Rose Ebaugh and Janet S. Chafetz, *Religion and the New Immigrants*. (Walnut Creek, CA: AltaMira Press, 2000).

12. Cecilia Menjivar, "Religion and Immigration in Comparative Perspective: Catholic and Evangelical Salvadorans in San Francisco, Washington, D.C., and Phoenix." *Sociology of Religion*, 64(1) (2003), pp. 21–45.
13. Stephen R. Warner, "Religion and Migration in the United States." *Social Compass*, 45(1) (1998), pp. 123–134.
14. Ebaugh and Chafetz, 2000.
15. Menjivar, 2003.
16. W. M. Hurh and K. C. Kim, "Religious participation of Korean immigrants in the United States." *Journal for the Scientific Study of Religion* 29 (1990), pp. 19–34.
17. Mossière, 2006; Warner, 1998.
18. Yang, Fenggang, and Helen Rose Ebaugh, "Transformations in New Immigrant Religions and Their Global Implications," *American Sociological Review*, 66 (2001), pp. 269–288.
19. Menjivar, 2003; Warner, 1998.
20. Mossière Géraldine. (Forthcoming). "Mobility and Belonging among Transnational Congolese Pentecostal Congregations: Modernity and the Emergence of Socioeconomic Differences," in *Religion Crossing Boundaries*, éds. Afé Adogamé and Jim Spickard Religion and Social Order series (E. J. Brill, publisher, 2009).
21. Paul Bramadat, *Religion and Ethnicity in Canada* (Toronto: Pearson Longman, 2005).
22. A. Hayford, *Atelier La religion* (Toronto: CERIS, 2000).
23. Paul Bramadat, *Religion and Ethnicity in Canada* (Toronto: Pearson Longman, 2005).
24. Janet McLellan, "Religion and Ethnicity: The Role of Buddhism in Maintaining Ethic Identity Among Tibetans," *Canadian Ethnic Studies*, 19(1) (1987), pp. 63–76.
25. Jean Dorais, "Vie religieuse et adaptation: les Vietnamiens de Montréal," *Culture*, vol. 13, no. 1, (1993), pp. 3–16.
26. Mossière, 2006.
27. Kwai Hang Ng, "Seeking the Christian Tutelage: Agency and Culture in Chinese Immigrants' Conversion to Christianity," *Sociology of Religion*, 63(2) (2002), pp. 195.
28. Andrew Abel, "Favor Fishing and Punch-Bowl Christians: Ritual and Conversion in Chinese Protestant Church." *Sociology of Religion*, 67(2) (2006), pp. 161–178. Yang, Fenggang, and Joseph B. Tamney, "Exploring Mass Conversion to Christianity among the Chinese: an Introduction," *Sociology of Religion*, 67(2) (2006), pp. 125–130.
29. Daphne N. Winland, "Christianity and Community: Conversion and Adaptation Among Hmong Refugee Women," *Canadian Journal of Sociology*, 19(1) (1994), pp. 21–45.
30. Judith Nagata, "Religion, Ethnicity and Language: Indonesian Chinese Immigrants in Toronto," *Southeast Asian Journal of Social Science*, 16(1) (1988), pp. 116–30.
31. Ebaugh and Chafetz, 2000. Pyong Gapmin. "The Structure and Social Functions of Korean Immigrants Churches in the United States," *International Migration Review* 26 (1992), pp. 1370–1395. Warner, 1998.

32. Warner, 1998.
33. Y. Haddad, J. Smith, and K. Moore, *Muslim Women in America: The Challenge of Islamic Identity Today*. (Oxford: Oxford University Press, 2006).
34. The study is funded by the Fonds Québécois de la Recherche sur la Société et la Culture (FQRSC), Québec, and the Social Sciences and Humanities Research Council (SSHRC), Ottawa, and is directed by Deirdre Meintel. Co-researchers include Marie-Nathalie Le Blanc, Josiane Le Gall, John Leavitt, Claude Gélinas and Sylvie Fortin. Géraldine Mossière is coordinator of the project.
35. Bouchard Mélissa, "La Mission catholique tamoule: présentation ethno-graphique et enquête sur la dévotion mariale," *Document de Travail, Groupe de Recherche Diversité* (Urbaine, Montréal: (2009)).
36. Yang and Ebaugh, (2001), p. 273.
37. Boucher, 2009.
38. Anne-Laure Betbeder, "Hétérogénéité et force d'intégration dans les temples Hindous Montréalais," *Document de Travail, Groupe de Recherche Diversité* (Urbaine, Montréal: (2009)).
39. Géraldine Mossière, "Emotional Dimensions of Conversion: An African Evangelical Congregation in Montreal." *Anthropologica* 49 (2007), pp. 113–124.
40. Betbeder, 2009.
41. Mossière, 2006.
42. Marie-Noëlle Fortin, "Les jeunes migrants seuls d'origine congolaise : Le rôle inter-médiaire de la communauté," Université de Montréal, Anthropology, Master's Thesis (2007).
43. A. Recalde, "Being a Good Christian in Montréal: On How Religious Principles Regulate Behavior in the Secular World among a Group of Latin American Evangel-icals, *Document de Travail Groupe de Recherche Diversité* (Urbaine, Montréal: (2009)).
44. Mossière, 2006.
45. Warner, 1998.
46. Ebaugh and Chafetz, 2000.
47. Recalde, 2009.
48. Serge Maynard, "Vivre sa foi sous le regard de 'l'autre.' Étude de cas de la mosquée Zitouna," *Document de Travail, Groupe de Recherche Diversité* (Urbaine, Montréal: 2009). Serge Maynard, "Vivre au Québec selon l'islam. Étude de cas d'une association musulmane montréalaise," *Document de Travail, Groupe de Recherche Diversité* (Urbaine, Montréal: (2009)).
49. Mossière, 2006.
50. Boucher, 2009.
51. Fortin, 2007.
52. Nagata, 1988.
53. Recalde, 2009.
54. Betbeder, 2009.
55. Bouchard, 2009.

56. Détolle Anais, "Étude de cas d'une pagode bouddhiste à Montréal," *Document de Travail, Groupe de Recherche Diversité* (Urbaine, Montréal: 2009).

57. Compare Nagata, 1988, on Chinese Christians in Toronto.

58. Bramadat, 2005; Hayford, 2000.

59. Hurh and Kim, 1990.

60. Mossière, 2006.

61. Maynard, *Vivre sa foi sous le regard de 'l'autre.' Étude de cas de la mosquée Zitouna*, Document de Travail, Groupe de Recherche Diversité Urbaine, Montréal (2009).

62. For instance, the Evangelical Church studied by Recalde, 2009.

63. Sylvie Fortin, *Destins et défis. La migration libanaise à Montréal*. Montréal, Éditions Saint-Martin, collection Pluriethnicité / Santé / Problèmes sociaux, (2000). Sylvie Fortin, "Les Libanais d'immigration récente: insertion ou exclusion?" in Deirdre Meintel, Victor Piché, Danielle Juteau, and Sylvie Fortin, dir. *Le quartier Côte-des-Neiges à Montréal. Les interfaces de la pluriethnicité* (Paris: L'Harmattan, 1997), pp. 263–288.

64. Helly, 2004.

65. Maynard, *Vivre sa foi sous le regard de 'l'autre.' Étude de cas de la mosquée Zitouna*, Document de Travail, Groupe de Recherche Diversité Urbaine, Montréal (2009).

66. Mossière, 2006.

67. Betbeder, 2009.

68. Khadiyatoulah Fall, "Pour un islam du Québec" (Le Devoir, mercredi le 19 septembre 2007). Available at http://www.ledevoir.com/2007/09/19/157463.html (consulted Jan. 17, 2009). Thanks to Yannick Boucher for this reference.

69. Germain et al., 2003.

70. Bouchard, 2009.

71. Such prejudice in Catholic parishes is hardly new. In her earlier work on Cape Verdeans in Rhode Island and Massachusetts, Meintel found that Cape Verdean Catholic immigrants who arrived in New Bedford Providence near the turn of the twentieth century founded their own parish in 1905 because of the prejudice they encountered in a Portuguese parish (http://www.umassd.edu/specialprograms/caboverde/cvchurch98.html). See Deirdre Meintel, Race, Culture and Portuguese Colonialism in Cabo Verde, *FACS*, (Syracuse University, 1984). Deirdre Meintel, "Cape Verdean-Americans," in *Hidden Minorities*, ed. Joan Rollins (Washington, DC: University Press of America, 1981), pp. 233–256.

72. Deirdre Meintel, "Identité ethnique chez de jeunes montréalais d'origine immigrée," *Sociologie et Sociétés*, vol. XXIV, no. 2, (1992), pp. 73–89. Deirdre Meintel, "Les Québécois vus par les jeunes d'origine immigrée," *Revue internationale d'action communautaire* no. 21/61 (1989), pp. 81–94.

73. Mossière, 2006.

74. Recalde, 2009.